THE

HERMETIC MUSEUM

RESTORED AND ENLARGED

Volume's One and Two combined

MOST FAITHFULLY INSTRUCTING ALL DISCIPLES OF THE SOPHO-SPAGYRIC
ART HOW THAT GREATEST AND TRUEST MEDICINE OF

THE PHILOSOPHER'S STONE

MAY BE FOUND AND HELD.

NOW FIRST DONE INTO ENGLISH FROM THE LATIN ORIGINAL PUBLISHED AT
FRANKFORT IN THE YEAR 1678.

Translated by

Arthur Edward Waite

Containing Twenty-two most celebrated Chemical Tracts.

A Yesterday's World Publishing

Published by A Yesterday's World Publishing
Copyright © 2025 A Yesterday's World Publishing
First impression 2025
ISBN - 978-1-916923-13-3

CONTENTS VOLUME ONE

CONTENTS VOLUME TWO

THE

HERMETIC MUSEUM

RESTORED AND ENLARGED

Volume One

MOST FAITHFULLY INSTRUCTING ALL DISCIPLES OF THE SOPHO-SPAGYRIC
ART HOW THAT GREATEST AND TRUEST MEDICINE OF

THE PHILOSOPHER'S STONE

MAY BE FOUND AND HELD.

NOW FIRST DONE INTO ENGLISH FROM THE LATIN ORIGINAL PUBLISHED AT
FRANKFORT IN THE YEAR 1678.

Translated by

Arthur Edward Waite

Containing Twenty-two most celebrated Chemical Tracts.

PREFACE TO THE ENGLISH EDITION.

THE HERMETIC MUSEUM RESTORED AND ENLARGED was published in Latin at Frankfort, in the year 1678, and, as its title implies, it was an enlarged form of an anterior work which, appearing in 1625, is more scarce, but, intrinsically, of less value. Its design was apparently to supply in a compact form a representative collection of the more brief and less ancient alchemical writers; in this respect, it may be regarded as a supplement to those large storehouses of Hermetic learning such as the *Theatrum Chemicum*, and that scarcely less colossal of Mangetus, the *Bibliotheca Chemica Curiosa*, which are largely concerned with the cream of the archaic literature, with the works of Geber and the adepts of the school of Arabia, with the writings attributed to Hermes, with those of Raymond Lully, Arnold de Villa Nova, Bernard Trevisan, and others.

THE HERMETIC MUSEUM would also seem to represent a distinctive school in Alchemy, not altogether committed to certain modes and terminology which derived most of their prestige from the past, and sufficiently enigmatical as it was, still inclined to be less obscure and misleading than was the habit of the older masters. For it belonged to a period which had inherited a bitter experience of the failures, impostures, and misery surrounding the Magnum Opus and its mystical quest, which was weary of unequipped experiment, weary of wandering "multipliers," and pretentious "bellows-blowers," while it was just being awakened to the conviction that if Alchemy were true at all, it was not to be learned from books, or, at least, from any books which had hitherto been written on the subject. Running through all the tracts which are comprised in the following volumes, the reader will recognize traces of a central claim in alchemical initiation—that the secrets, whatever they were, must be understood as the property of a college of adepts, pretending to have subsisted from time almost immemorial, and revealing themselves to the select and the few, while the literature, large as it is, appears chiefly as an instrument of inter-communication between those who knew. At the same time, it may also be regarded as a sign and omen to the likely seeker, an advertisement that there was a mystery, and that he must go further who would unravel it.

While the treatises now translated are for the most part anonymous, as befits veiled masters, the literary reader will remember that the name of John de Meung connects the allegorical "Romance of the Rose" with the parables of Alchemy; Flamel will be familiar to all Hermetic students as the most celebrated of the French adepts; the saintly name of Basil Valentine, investigator of the properties of antimony, will not even now be unhonoured by the chemist; Eirenaeus Philalethes, equally revered and unknown by all devout Spagyrites, is supposed to have been the most lucid of hierophants, and the "Open Entrance" to be the clearest of all his works. Helvetius was an illustrious chemist, and Michael Maier is a person of some repute in the Rosicrucian controversy. Michael Sendivogius was an uninstructed disciple of Alexander Seton, and the "New Chemical Light," which he published and claimed as his own, was really the work of his master, who has been called the chief martyr of Alchemy. It may be added in this connection that some critics have cast doubt upon the genuine nature of the "Testament of John Cremer," and it is true that the annals of Westminster do not include an abbot of that name.

It should be understood that the writer of this brief note must not be accredited

2

with the translation which it seeks to introduce. That is the work of a gentleman who is said to have had a life-long acquaintance with alchemical literature; it has been subjected to a searching revision at the hands of the present editor, who may himself be permitted to claim some experience in Hermetic antiquities; the version as it stands does not uncreditably represent both the spirit and the sense of the original without the original's prolixity. While affording to the modern student of secret doctrines an unique opportunity for acquiring in English a collection of alchemical writers, this edition of THE HERMETIC MUSEUM also claims consideration at the hands of the historian as a contribution of real value to the early history of chemistry.

ARTHUR EDWARD WAITE.

ADDRESSED TO THE CANDID READER.

IT would be unjust to doubt, most gentle reader, that of all the arts invented for the use of life by the reason of man, that of *Alchemy* is the most noble and glorious. For all philosophers exclaim, as it were, with one voice, albeit in many languages, that this art is not only true, but (after the Divine Law by which our souls are saved) the best and most magnificent gift bestowed upon man by God; and that it should therefore be investigated with all zeal and with the greatest pains. But as good wine needs no praise, so neither does this art require a herald; for its truth is undoubted, and its utility in human life universally acknowledged, and shewn forth, not only in the Art of Medicine, in Pharmacy, and many other sciences, but more especially in the Art of Transmuting Metals, is so clearly and perspicuously demonstrated, that it in no way requires to be adorned by the splendour of oratory, or tricked out with the device of language. I will not enlarge upon the blessing which the elaboration of minerals and metals has bestowed upon our race. I merely point it out, but refrain from discussing it at length. Different men devote themselves to the study of this science from different motives. The philosopher is impelled by the love of truth, and the thirst after wisdom. He delights in knowledge for its own sake. He welcomes every elegant and copious treatise on the marvels of Nature, to the glory of Almighty God. This is a sufficiently generous reward for a philosopher. He has at his command the most effectual means of becoming rich, if he would only use them. But he is fired by the love of philosophy, and does not care for the mocking grandeur of fortune. So thought the Sages of the Saracens, Egyptians, Arabs, and Persians; for when they were oppressed by tyrants, and violently driven into exile, they protected and supported themselves by means of their Art, and, through their knowledge of the transmutation of metals, they had at their command, not only sufficient to live upon, but all the comforts and pomp of life, and thus practically demonstrated that they could obtain all that gold and silver could give. Concerning this true transmutation of metals, which is accomplished only by the Elixir or Stone of the Philosophers, we here propose to speak. This art is set forth in a series of treatises by different authors, which appeared several years ago, and, like the present volume, was entitled "A Museum of Hermes." But many writers having discussed this subject, and treated it from various points of view (so that one writes more clearly than another, and each throws light on the other's meaning), some of my friends, who are adepts in this Art, urged me to add to the former collection certain treatises supplementary of those already given. For though that former collection contained the most select writings on the subject, yet it was not as complete as it might have been, nor was it calculated to furnish to the reader in full measure the eagerly expected fruit of his study. To this wish of my friends I have all the more readily submitted, because its fulfilment must redound to the advantage of the student. I have, therefore, enlarged the collection with several most select treatises, and caused it to be adorned with many engravings. I was most strongly impelled to undertake the task by this consideration, viz., that through the fraudulent machinations of greedy impostors many false, so-called chemical treatises have been put forward, in which there is not a single spark of truth, and that very many have been, and are still being deceived by them. These dupes, by reading this book, in which the Magistery of the Stone is most clearly and plainly set forth, and into which no error or forgery has been admitted, will be secured against the imposture of that wicked and mercenary band who delight in fraud For in this book all errors are shewn up and dispelled. For this reason I confidently offer this volume to the sons of knowledge, in order that while they think upon and investigate the secret working of Nature, they may obtain from it nothing but the truth, and gain a clear insight into the very nature of things. In this alone consists the perfection of the entire most Holy Art of Philosophy. Only let them go forward along the Royal Road which Nature prescribes in all her operations. As to the rest, I heartily beg the friends of this Art to give a kindly reception to the present volume, and when, through the Will of God, by constant labour, they have put ashore in the desired haven of philosophy, after the manner of philosophers to exclude all that are unworthy from the knowledge thereof, and, being mindful of charity towards their needy neighbour in the fear of God (without any vain ostentation), to sing eternal praises to the Good and Thrice Great God for this Wonderful and Divine Gift (without any abuse thereof) in a silent and devoutly joyful heart.

Quæ sunt in superis, hæc inferioribus insunt :
  Quod monstrat cœlum, id terra frequenter habet
Ignis, Aqua et fluitans duo sunt contraria : felix,
  Talia si jungis : sit tibi scire satis !

D. M à C. B. P. L. C.

THE GOLDEN TRACT

CONCERNING

THE STONE OF THE PHILOSOPHERS.

BY AN ANONYMOUS GERMAN PHILOSOPHER.

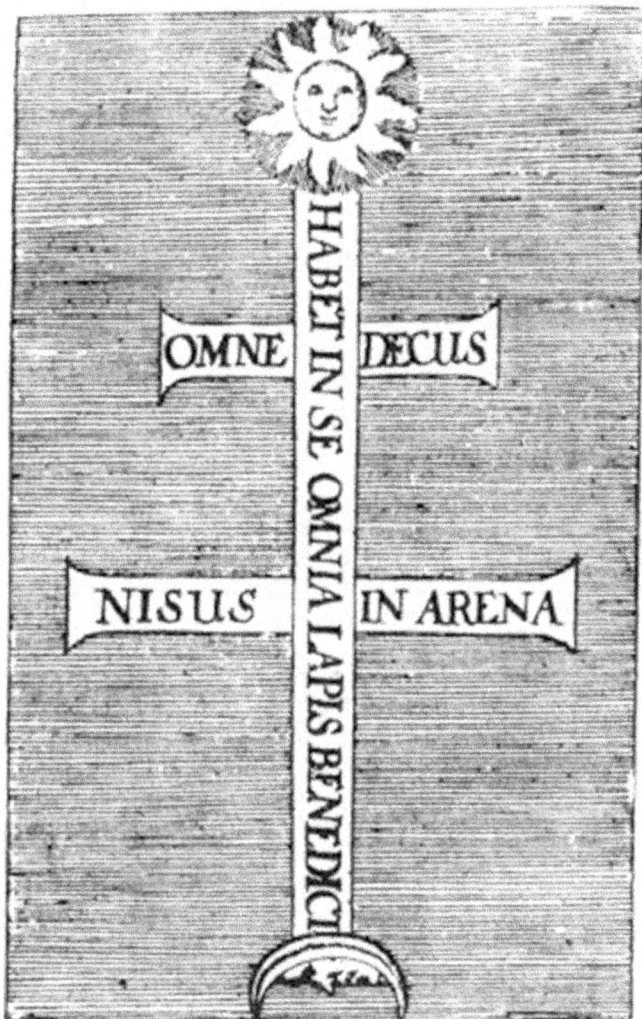

THE GOLDEN TRACT

CONCERNING THE PHILOSOPHER'S STONE.

The Author's Preface to the Art-loving Reader.

WORTHY reader, and true enquirer into the secrets of nature, marvel not that in the old age of this world, when it seems to have one foot already in the grave, I have determined to write this tract, although all libraries are already full of books on this subject—of which, however, the greater part are false, and wear merely the rouge and powder of philosophy. I have written it not for my own pleasure, but for your advantage, that, by pointing to the foundation of truth, I might lead you back from the pathless wilderness into the right way—which is certainly for your own interest. As far as I am concerned, I have long known all that I seek to know in regard to this matter, and have no need of many books, seeing that during the last twenty-two years I have read and re-read all the works that fell into my hands—including numerous manuscripts, as well as many printed volumes.

In this my tract you will find the subject set forth, and the true solution given, not only theoretically, but also from a practical and allegorical point of view, with a clearness and lucidity such as I believe to be almost unparalleled in any previous philosophical treatise. In quoting, I have always been careful to give the exact reference, so that you may look out the passage for yourself, and by diligently considering it, sharpen your understanding. I could more easily have composed this treatise, and made myself known to the Brethren of the Golden Cross, if I had left out those references; but for your sake I decided otherwise. Do not wonder that I conceal my name, and refuse to appear to you face to face. I have come forward, not for the sake of any paltry glory, or of worldly praise, but to do you good. Moreover, my teachers, even the true philosophers, advised me not thus to risk my life for the sake of obtaining a high place in the world's esteem, to expose myself to greedy robbers or to give occasion for many crimes by the prostitution of this profound secret. No doubt the gentle reader has learned by the works of Sendivogius that whenever he sheaved himself openly to the powerful, he went in constant fear of his life. Experience teaches that many philosophers who gave no thought to their personal safety, have been killed and deprived of their tincture by greedy and powerful robbers; and it stands to reason that any one going about with a great treasure in his hand, must fall a prey to brigands. Sendivogius concealed his name by an anagram. Thus also a short time ago another philosopher and Brother of the Golden Cross, whose real name has long been familiar to me, concealed it beneath an anagram, and made himself known to his friends by an enigmatical designation. Why then should I place myself at the mercy of this impure world? Permit me rather, dear friend; to follow the example of the sages, and leave the rest to the thrice good and great God, who will make my true self known to you in good time, if it be for the glory of His name, and for your and my good. Do not be eager to enquire after my name. For even if you should get to know it, or become personally acquainted with me, you would have to rest satisfied with the contents of this tract. For I have solemnly promised two

8

philosophers—Bernard, Count of Trevisan, and Neigens—that I will not betray to any one more than has been revealed in this book. Neither be anxious to ask whether I actually possess this precious treasure. Ask rather whether I have seen how the world was created; whether I am acquainted with the nature of the Egyptian darkness; what is the cause of the rainbow; what will be the appearance of the glorified bodies at the general resurrection; what is the most indelible colour. Of you that rightly understand this little book, I will enquire whether you have seen that great salt sea, without any corrosion, raise a sufficiency of the moisture of all nature to the summits of the highest mountains. Tell me where there is sulphur out of sulphur, and mercury out of mercury—or where sulphur springs from mercury, and again mercury from sulphur. When was there placed before your eyes the idea of most fervent love, the male and the female embracing each other so closely that they could no more be torn asunder, but through unsearchable love became one? If you understand what I am alluding to, and have performed the experiment with your own hands, and seen it with your own eyes, I welcome you as fellow partakers of the mystery, and have no dearer wish than to enjoy your familiar intercourse—for which reason I have also sent forth into the world this little tract.

If any one complain of the difficulty of our Art, let him know that in itself it is perfectly simple, and can present no obstacle to those who love God, and are held worthy by Him of this knowledge. If any one blame me for setting forth the truths of this Art too plainly and clearly, so as to render it possible for any one to gain a knowledge thereof, I answer that I have indeed explained them with sufficient lucidity for those who are worthy and foreordained of God, but that the unworthy can derive no profit from them. To some foolish and shallow persons I have several times expounded this Art in the simplest manner, and even word for word, but they despised it only, and would not believe me that there is exhibited in our work a twofold resurrection of the dead. Our Art, its theory as well as its practice, is altogether a gift of God, Who gives it when and to whom He elects: it is not of him that wills, or of him that runs, but simply through the mercy of God. Though I had diligently studied this Art for 17 or 18 years, yet I had, after all, to wait for God's own time, and accept it as a free gift. No one need doubt the truth or certainty of this Art. It is as true and certain, and as surely ordained by God in nature, as it is that the sun shines at noontide, and the moon shews her soft splendour at night. But I must conclude this preface, and gird myself for writing the tract itself. But ye, beloved Brethren of the Golden Cross, who are about to learn how to enjoy and use this most precious gift of God in secret, do not remain unknown to me, and if ye know me not, be sure that the faithful will be approved and their faith become known through the Cross, while security and pleasure overshadow it. God be with us, Amen!

THE GOLDEN TRACT

CONCERNING THE STONE OF THE PHILOSOPHERS.

ANCIENT as well as modern philosophers, most beloved reader, and devoted seeker after true wisdom, when through the grace of God they had reached the goal of their desires, have endeavoured to make their discovery known to their fellow inquirers in all parts of the world—not only because they wished to inform them that the thrice great and good God had enlightened their minds, blessed the labours of their hands, and shewn to them the greatest and most profound secret of earthly wisdom (for which benefit all praise, honour, and glory are justly due to Him)— but also that they might afford assistance to beginners in the Art, by which, with God's permission, they too might attain to the knowledge of this most holy mystery. Such men there have been in all countries. Amongst the Egyptians Hermes Trismegistus holds the highest place; then come Chaldæans, Greeks, Arabs, Italians, Gauls, Englishmen, Dutchmen, Spaniards, Germans, Poles, Hungarians, Hebrews, and many others. Though the aforementioned Sages wrote at different times, and in different languages, yet their works exhibit so marvellous an agreement, that any true philosopher may easily see that all their hearts had been gladdened by God in the discovery of this stone, and that they all had performed this work with their own hands. Now, as the truth of their views is perceived by their agreement, so the disagreement of certain others marks them as false philosophers. For, not knowing the foundation of this glorious Art, and making up fanciful theories out of their own heads, they exhibit their ignorance to all.

The aforesaid agreement exists in regard to the Matter, its solution, its weight, and the regulation and increase of the fire.

As concerns the Matter, it is *one*, and contains within itself all that is needed. Out of it the artist prepares whatever he wants. Its "Birth is in the sand," as the philosopher Anastratus says in "The Crowd": "Nothing is more precious than the red sand of the sea; it is the distilled moisture of the Moon joined to the light of the Sun, and congealed." That only this one substance is required is attested by Agadmon in the same book. He says: "Know that unless you take my body [sulphur] without the spirit [mercury] ye will not obtain what ye desire. Cease to think of many things. Nature is satisfied with one thing, and he who does not know it is lost."

In the same way Arnold, of Villa Nova, writes in his "Flower of Flowers"; "Our stone is made out of one thing, and with one thing." To the same effect he says to the King of Naples: "All that is in our stone is essential to it, nor does it need any foreign ingredient. Its nature is one, and it is *one* thing." And Rosinus says: "Know that the object of your desire is one thing, out of which all things are made." Lilium: "You have need only of one thing, which at any stage of our experiment can be changed into another nature." So Geber says in his "Summary": "Our stone is one, one medicine, to which we add nothing, from which we take nothing away, only removing that which is superfluous." Again, Scites in "The Crowd" says: "The essence of this Art is in like manner a certain one thing which is stronger and more exalted than all other things, and is called the most powerful acid, because it changes gold into a clear spirit, without which there is neither whiteness, nor blackness, nor redness. When the spirit is joined to the body it becomes one with it; and yet again becomes a spirit, and is saturated with the spiritual and unchangeable tincture, and thus again by combination receives a bodily tincture which cannot be annihilated. If you place the body without the acid over the fire, it will be burnt and destroyed." From these words of Scites the reader might conclude, that not one but two things, namely a body and an acid (as he calls it) are required, and that a liquid must be combined with a dry thing lest the dry thing should be consumed by the fire, in order that by the moist thing it may be preserved from such combustion. To such a conclusion, if rightly accepted, I gladly subscribe. But from the above mentioned philosophical dicta (however obscurely worded they may be) it is clearer than day that the substance of our Blessed Stone is one (although different sages call it by different names), and that Nature has made it ready to the hand of the adept, having willed this one thing, and no other thing in all the world, to be the material of the Stone. This Matter lies before the eyes of all; everybody sees it, touches it, loves it, but knows it not. It is glorious and vile, precious and of small account, and is found everywhere. Theophrastus Paracelsus, in his book concerning "The Tincture of Physical Things," calls it the Red Lion, which is named by many, but known by few. Hermes, in the first chapter of his Treatise, calls it "Quick Silver coagulated in its innermost chambers." In the "Rosary of the Philosophers" it goes by the name of Salt. But, to be brief, our Matter has as many names as there are things in the world; that is why the foolish know it not. Foolish I call those who, without any previous knowledge of Nature and her properties, undertake to learn this Art, and come to it (as Arnold says) like the ass to the crib, not knowing for what they open their mouths. Hence it is well said by Geber, in the "Sum of Perfection": "He who has no elementary knowledge of Nature is far from a proper appreciation of this Art." And Rosarius says: "I advise no one to approach this Art unless he knows the principle and the regimen of Nature: if he be acquainted with these, little is wanting to him except one thing, nor need he put himself to a great expense, since the stone is one, the medicine is one, the vessel one, the rule one, the disposition one." Yet this one substance is so divided by the operation of Nature, and the skill of the Artist, that it is transmuted into our White Eagle, nor does the splendour of the sun illuminate more abundantly the spagyric matter with its beams; or, as Basilius Valentinus hath it, that, "thence is born a spirit white as scow, and another spirit red as blood, which two spirits are contained in a third hidden thing." Hence King Aros well says: "Our medicine is composed out of two things having one essence, namely, through the mercurial union of a solid and a liquid, a spiritual and a corporeal, a cold and a moist, a warm and a dry, and in no other way can it be made." And Richard the Englishman says: "The stone is one, the medicine one, which, however, according to the philosophers, is called Rebis (Two-thing), being composed of two things, namely, a body and spirit [red or white]. But over this many foolish persons have gone astray, explaining it in divers ways." Rebis is two things, and these two things are one thing, namely, water joined to a body, by which the body is dissolved into a spirit, that is, mineral water, out of which it was first made; and this body and spirit make up one mineral water, which is called Elixir, that is to say, ferment; for then water and spirit are one thing, of which is composed a tincture and medicine for purging all bodies. And thus, according to the philosophers, we have the nature of sulphur and mercury above ground, while underground they become gold and silver. Bernard, Count of Trevisan and the March, says: Our work is performed by means of one root, and two crude mercurial substances, drawn and extracted from a mineral, pure and clear, being conjoined by the heat of friendship, as this matter requires, and carefully cooked until the two things become one thing," &c. Basilius Valentinus (*Lib. Nat. et Supernal.*, c. 4) says: "I will make this known to thee in all truth [for the love of God], that the root of philosophic sulphur, which is a heavenly spirit, is united in the same material with the root of the spiritual and supernatural mercury, and the principle of spiritual salt—out of which is made the Stone, and not out of several things. That universal thing, the greatest treasure of earthly wisdom, is one thing, and the principles of three things are found in one, which has power to change all metals into one. The three things are the true spirit of mercury, and the soul of sulphur, united to spiritual salt, and dwelling in one body; they are dragon and eagle, king and lion, spirit and body, etc."

In this way our prepared material is also called male and female, active and passive. So Zimon says, in "The Crowd": "Know that the secret of the work consists in male and female, *i.e.*, an active and a passive principle. In lead is found the male, in orpiment the female. The male rejoices when the female is brought to it, and the female receives from the male a tinging seed, and is coloured thereby." And Diomedes says: "Join the male child of the 'red servant' to the fragrant spouse, and they will produce the object of our Art. But you must not introduce any foreign matter, neither dust, nor any other thing. The conception will then be perfect, and a true son will be born. Oh, how precious is the nature of the 'red servant,' without whom nothing can be effected!" Others call it quicksilver, or mercury, and sulphur, or fire, as Roger Bacon says, in the third chapter of his "Mirror": "Out of sulphur and mercury are all metals, and nothing adheres to them, neither is joined to them, or transmutes them, but what is of them. And thus we must accept mercury and sulphur as the matter of the stone." So also Menabadus says: "He who joins quicksilver to the body of magnesia, and the woman to the man, extracts the secret essence by which bodies are coloured." Lullius in his "Codicil" says: "The property of our mercury is to be coagulated by its sulphur" And, in the Practice of his Testament: "The silver is a flowing moisture, floating above and preserving the whole from combustion."

Others use the names, body, spirit, and soul. Thus Arnold, in his Flower of Flowers, says: "The Sages have affirmed that our Stone is composed of body, soul, and spirit, and they have spoken truly. For the imperfect part they have compared to a body, because it is weak. The water they have called spirit, and truly, because it is spirit. The ferment they have termed soul, because it gives life to the imperfect body (which before was dead), and makes its form more beautiful."

Again, he says: "A spirit is never joined to a body but by the interposition of a soul. For the soul is the medium between body and spirit, joining them together." Morienus says: "The soul quickly enters its own body—but if you tried to join it to a foreign body, you would labour in vain." And Lilium says: "Body, soul, and spirit make up one thing, which has all in itself, and to which nothing is added."

But why should we mention and explain all the names by which our Matter is designated? We will be content with the foregoing, seeing that they are the most common and the most germane to our purpose. In the following pages, after endeavouring to find where our substance lies hid, and where it may be obtained, we will say some words about the mode of its dissolution, that being after all the principal object of our inquiry. And first, as concerns the search after our Matter, we should remember that in the beginning, when there was nothing but Himself, God, who is infinite in wisdom, created two classes of things, namely, those that are in heaven, and those that are under heaven. The heavenly things (about which we need not here speak at length) are the heavens themselves, and the dwellers in heaven The things that are under the heavens were created out of four elements, and are commonly divided into three classes. Those that live and feel hold the first place, and are called animals. The second class are the plants, that grow out of the earth, but do not feel. The third class, that of the minerals, has its origin underground. These three classes include all that (beneath the moon) has been created out of the elements. They can never become more or less, and God has bound each thing to its own genus and species, so that it cannot change from one genus to another. If any one tried to make a man or a tree out of a stone, or a monkey or lead out of a plant, or an animal or a plant out of lead, he would be prevented from doing so by the eternal order of the Great King. If such a thing were possible, all classes of natural objects could be changed into one. But, because such a change would put an end to the world, the Ruler of the Universe does not permit it. Nay, what is more, He not only restricted everything to its own kind, but gave each created thing its own seed, by which it might be propagated after its own manner—always remaining in its own class, and not overstepping the bounds of some other species. If any one wished to change a man into a horse, an apple into a lettuce, a diamond or any other jewel into gold, he would make an enormous mistake. For such an attempt would be against the nature of sublunar things. And as it was in the beginning so it shall be in the end, when the Almighty, who in the beginning said "Let it be," shall say "Let it perish." But among those things which have a common substance, seed, and elementary compositior, it is not difficult to accomplish an amelioration and improvement, by the purification of their matter. So we may see a man of a clear and subtle mind attain to a higher degree of human excellence than others who are less gifted. This difference arises from the superior purity and subtlety of his spiritual substance, which again has its origin in a rectified and well constituted body. Thus also we see one horse excel the strength and speed of another; and it is the same with all kinds of living beings. A like rule holds good to an even greater degree in regard to plants and trees— with trees, by transplanting, grafting, and kindred methods well familiar to gardeners; while as to other vegetable natures, we are taught by daily experience how plants and flowers of the same kind differ from each other in glory, in beauty, in fragrance, and savour. Of this cloves and tulips afford a striking instance. Into how many different species have these flowers been developed; and even these. new developments are being made more beautiful from day to day, and it is universally admitted that never were there such fine and fragrant flowers before. What am I to say about metals which have a common substance, namely, quicksilver, digested and consolidated by the power of sulphur? Concerning this common substance, Richard the Englishman has the following words: "Nature has elaborated all kinds of fusible things by a natural process out of mercury, and the substance of its sulphur, because it is the property of quicksilver to be consolidated by steam, as by the heat of white and red sulphur which does not burn."

The same view is expressed by Arnold (pt. 1., cp. ii.): "Quicksilver is the elementary form of all things fusible; for all things fusible, when melted, are changed into it, and it mingles with them because it is of the same substance with them. Such bodies differ from quicksilver in their composition only so far as itself is or is not free from the foreign matter of impure sulphur." Similarly Rosinus (*Ad Saratantam*) says: "The substance of all metals in the heart of the earth is solidified and imperfect quicksilver; for by the quickening heat of sulphur different metals (according to the different varieties of sulphur) are generated in the earth; their original substance is one and the same, and is modified only by a greater or smaller external influence." Hence we see daily how busily Nature is occupied in bringing them to mortification and perfection. Now the perfection of metals, and the final intention of Nature in regard to them, is gold. For all metals shew that Nature has done something for them towards ultimate perfection; no metal is so base as not to contain a single grain of gold or silver Nature would always change quicksilver that has within itself its own sulphur into gold, if she were not often hindered by some outward impediment, viz., impure, foetid, and combustible sulphur. In most cases gold is dug out pure, clear, free from dross, and unmixed with any other metals. But most frequently a large quantity of foreign sulphur mingles with the quicksilver, and thus prevents its perfect development; and, according to the variety of that sulphur, different kinds of metals are generated, as Aristotle says (4. Meteor.): "If the quicksilver be of a good substance but the sulphur impure and combustible, it changes the quicksilver into brass. If the quicksilver be stony, impure, and earthy, and the sulphur not pure, it becomes iron. Tin seems to have good and pure quicksilver; but the sulphur is bad and not well mixed. Lead has gross, bad, and ill-smelling quicksilver, and is thus not properly coagulated."

That retarding, combustible, and foetid sulphur is not the true fire that fashions metals; but quicksilver has its own sulphur in itself, which is sufficient for the purpose of fashioning it, as Bernard, Count of Trevisan, says: "Some believe that in the generation of metals, a sulphuric substance is introduced from without; but, on the contrary, it is clear that in the working of Nature sulphur is already enclosed in the mercury. Yet it has no power in it except through the moving heat, by which the said sulphur is changed, and with it two other qualities of the mercury. In this way, then, Nature generates by means of this sulphur the different kinds of metals in the veins of the earth, according to the diversity of degrees and alterations." For in metals, according to Arnold (pt. i., cp. iii.), "there is a two-fold superfluity: one that is enclosed in the innermost nature of the quicksilver, and got there at the first mingling of the metal; the other does not belong to the essence of it, is external to it, and corruptible. To remove the former is a difficult task; the latter may be removed without any difficulty. The combustible sulphur is taken away by being subjected to the action of fire, or is destroyed by foreign bodies; but the other, which is in the quicksilver, is preserved by it from combustion." But again, that inward sulphur which fashions the quicksilver belonging to it, and matures it towards perfection, is either pure or impure, combustible or incombustible. Impure sulphur hinders the digestion of the quicksilver, which cannot be transformed into gold until that which does not belong to it has been entirely separated from it; but the pure, incombustible, fixed sulphur remains with it, and then at length it passes either into gold or silver, according as the sulphur is either white or red. This internal sulphur is nothing but mature mercury, and the most advanced part of the quicksilver, and for this reason the quicksilver receives it so kindly, as being of its own essence, while it rejects the other which is foreign to it. So Richard the Englishman says, in his ninth chapter: The more simple the sulphur is, the more readily does it combine with simple and pure mercury, and the more intimately they combine the more precious is the metal which is produced." But such sulphur, says Avicenna, "is not found on earth, except in so far as it exists in metallic bodies through the action of the sun and moon. In the sun it exists in a perfect state, because there it is better digested and decocted." According to Richard, in his twelfth chapter, the red sulphur of the philosophers exists in the sun on account of its greater digestion, and the white sulphur in the moon on account of its inferior digestion."

Since, then, the substance of the metals is one, and common to all, and since this substance is (either at once, or after laying aside in course of time the foreign and evil sulphur of the baser metals by a process of gradual digestion) changed by the virtue of its own indwelling sulphur into GOLD, which is the goal of all the metals, and the true intention of Nature—we are obliged to admit, and freely confess that in the mineral kingdom, as well as in the vegetable and animal kingdoms, Nature seeks and demands a gradual attainment of perfection, and a gradual approximation to the highest standard of purity and excellence.

I thought it would be best, O friendly searcher of Nature, to discuss the matter more in detail, in order that you might the more readily know and make use of the substance of our Stone! For if you attempted to produce our Stone out of an animal substance you would fail, because the two things belong to different natural orders. For the Stone is a mineral, but you would be trying to fashion it out of an animal substance. "But nothing," says our Richard, in his first chapter, "can be got out of a thing which is not in it. Therefore every species, every genus, every natural order, is naturally developed within its own limits, bearing fruit after its own kind, and not within some other essentially different order: everything in which seed is sown must correspond to its own seed." And Basil. Valentinus says: "Consider and know, my friend, that you must not select an animal soul for this your purpose. For flesh and blood were given by the Creator to animals, and are proper to animals, and from them animals are formed and brought forth." For this reason I wonder at those who wish to be regarded as great adepts, and yet look for the substance of the stone in female menstruums, the seminal fluid, eggs, hairs, urine, and similar things, and are not ashamed to fill so many volumes with their vain and worthless recipes, and to deceive the ignorant with such foolish, futile, and useless speculations. Roger, in his "Mirror" (cp. iii.), expresses his amazement at the folly of these men when he exclaims: "How strange that any sane person should look for what he wants in the animal and vegetable worlds, which have nothing whatever to do with the object of his search, while the mineral world is quite as ready to his hand. It is incredible that any philosopher should establish his art on such a remote foundation, except indeed by way of allegory." "For our Stone (says Basil.) is not made of combustible things. Verily that Stone and the matter thereof are safe from all such violence, therefore cease to seek it in the animal kingdom; for Nature herself could not find it there." Again, whoever hopes to find it in the vegetable world, as, for instance, in trees, herbs, flowers, is quite as much mistaken as he who would change an animal into a stone. Plants and trees, with all that they produce, may be consumed by fire, and leave nothing behind but the dust out of which they are made, and the salt which at the first creation of their species they received from Nature. Let no one be misled by the confident assertions of those who pretend that they can produce the Philosopher's Stone out of wheat, or out of wine. These persons fancy they understand the meaning of a certain passage in the writings of Raymond Lullius, but they exhibit the depth of their folly by the assumption of profound wisdom, and thus only deceive themselves and others. I do not deny that some excellent solvents, indispensable both to the physician and to the chemist, are obtained from these sources; but I do most positively deny that the Philosopher's Stone can be prepared, or its seed elicited, from them, since the Creator has ordained that nothing should overstep the bounds of the natural order to which it was originally assigned. Hence every true disciple of wisdom may gather that the substance of the Stone is to be obtained neither in the animal nor in the vegetable world, seeing that both are combustible. We must therefore look for it among incombustible things, that is to say, in the mineral world, and thence only can we prepare it. Since, then, the Stone of the Wise is mineral, and there are different kinds of minerals, as stones (including clay and the different varieties of earth), salts, general minerals, and metals, we must further ask, in which of all these it is contained. We may at once eliminate stones, because they contain no fusible mercury, and cannot be incited, dissolved, or divided into their component parts on account of the large quantity of foreign sulphur and earthly substance which cleave to them.

Nor will the wise investigator of Nature's secrets expect to find the substance of the Blessed Stone in salts, alums, or similar minerals. [n them he meets with a sharp, corroding, destructive spirit, but mercury and sulphur, as understood by philosophers, he would vainly look for. General minerals, like magnesia, bismuth, antimony, etc., can never under any circumstances become metals; how, then, can the substance of this Stone, which is the essential perfection of all metals and minerals, be obtained from them? Moreover, they have nothing in common with metals, but do burn, corrode, and destroy them:—how then can they be the means of their improvement?

Hear what Richard the Englishman has to say on this head (cp. x.): "The lesser minerals cannot become metals—First, because they were not generated out of the elementary substance of metals, which is quicksilver. But seeing that their generation differs from the generation of metals in form, and substance, and composition, they can never become metals, because things belonging to the same species have the same elementary substance, and spring from the same seed. But the lesser minerals are not generated from mercury, as we learn from Aristotle and Avicenna. If they were to become metals, they would have to change into the elementary substance of metals. And, since such a transformation is beyond the power of chemistry, they can never become metals; that is to say, they can never be the substance of the Stone. Second, since the lesser minerals cannot become the elementary substance of metals, which is mercury, they can never reach the middle and the end of the same development, namely, metals and the tincture. But because the properties of the lesser minerals are foreign to those of the metals, although they may have some of the virtues of minerals, yet on the whole they are less excellent and are liable to be injured by fire. Therefore the nature of metals delights not in them, but repels them, while it receives that which is suited to it.

For this reason they are foolish who bring in so many foreign speculations for the purpose of imposing upon their hearers; for the things they put forward are altogether unlike metals and can never receive nor impart their nature."

The student must not suffer himself to be misled by the language occasionally employed with regard to salts by the philosophers whom we have quoted, as, for instance, when it is said, in the mystic language of our Sages, "He who works without salt will never raise dead bodies"; or, again, when he reads in the book of Soliloquies, "He who works without salt draws a bow without a string." For you must know that these sayings refer to a very different kind of salt from the common mineral. This you may see from the following passage of the "Rosary of the Philosophers: "The salt of metals is the Philosopher's Stone; for our Stone is water congealed in gold and silver; it is hostile to fire and may be dissolved into the water of which it is composed after its kind." And that the "congealed water" of the Sages does not mean ordinary water may be gathered from the following words of Geber (lib. Forn., cp. xix.): "Seek to resolve the sun and the moon into their dry water, which the vulgar call mercury." The Sages have also described their earth under the name of salt—e.g., in the "Sounding of the Trumpet," where it is said: "That which is left at the bottom of the distilling vessel is our salt—that is to say, our earth." And in the "Allegories of the Wise" one bursts forth into these words: "Mark well that those bodies which flow forth from our bodies are salts and alums." At times they call the medicine itself "Salt," as in the following passage of the "Scale": "The virtue of the second water is to exalt earth into its own mineral salt, as though assimilating it by its own strength." And Arnold, in his work concerning the "Preservation of Youth," (lib. iii.) says: "This prepared salt has great virtue in preserving youth. The Sages have compared it to the natural heat of healthy youth. The Stone itself has sometimes been called by the wise the Animal Stone, sometimes the Mineral Secret, on account, of this similitude; sometimes the Everlasting Remedy, or the Water of Life. The whole preparation may be reduced to the purest drinking water, like other things that have the same properties." From the aforesaid it clearly appears that we are forbidden both by the teaching of the Sages and by the nature of the thing to suppose that the Stone can be made out of the lesser minerals.

We should next enquire more carefully whether the matter of our Stone may be obtained from the intermediate minerals—like bismuth, antimony, magnesia, and so on. They are certainly often mentioned in this connection by the Sages. Thus Senior says, in a certain passage: "If yellow orpiment has not the power of coagulating mercury our Magistery can never attain its goal." Thomas de Aquinas recommends us to take "our antimony, or black earth," while Parmenides, in "The Crowd," says: "Take quicksilver and coagulate it in the body of magnesia, or corruptible sulphur." But in all such passages these terms are used metaphorically; it is not meant that the Great Stone can ever be made out of such substances. The orpiment and magnesia of the Sages are not the common minerals, but the substance which in other passages is called the Agent, the Lion, the King, Sulphur, and by many other names. They call it orpiment because it gives a deeper and more brilliant colouring to gold; magnesia because of the excellence and greatness of that which is gained from it; antimony, with Thomas Aquinas, on account of the brilliant blackness which it assumes after solution. As a matter of fact, when the Stone has assumed its ebony colour they are in the habit of comparing it to all black things.

But it may be said that some of these intermediate minerals are, as a matter of fact, composed of mercury and sulphur, and may become metals, *e.g.*, magnesia unites with lead and tin, and antimony not only mingles with metals, but also produces a lead not very different from natural lead. Moreover, it is asserted that many persons of high and low degree have actually seen gold made of these minerals. It is further said that as these minerals are composed of mercury and sulphur (and can by chemical means be reduced to them), and are therefore of a common origin with the metals, the substance of the Stone may also be elicited from them. But, in the first place, we must draw a distinction between the various minerals of this class, namely those which contain mercury, and those which hardly ever contain it. Those that are full of mercury are of greater account, since, by means of our Medicine, their mercury may be transformed into gold and silver; and, their nature being partly metallic, they may well be called half metals. But the rest, which have no mercury, are of no use for our purpose. But forasmuch as, on account of the gross and combustible sulphur which is in them, even the first are very far indeed from the metallic goal, so they cannot be taken for the substance of our Stone, which should be pure and perfect mercury combined with pure, subtle, and incombustible sulphur. That they are most impure and deeply infected with the grossness of their sulphur, may be easily seen by the test of a chemical experiment. One of them (zinetum) might, by reason of its weight and brilliance, be taken at first sight for pure mercury by the careless; but when brought to the test of fire it is consumed with a smoke, like that of sulphur. Bismuth, on the other hand, is not even fusible by fire—such is its earthy grossness and impurity. Antimony, again, can be purged by a chemical process, and reduced to a very white and beautiful regulus. As we gaze upon it in this purified state, it seems difficult to believe that it may not be transformed into something glorious. Hence it is natural that some self-conceited people should have supposed that the Stone may be prepared from it. But however much antimony is purged of its blackness, it still retains its grossness, hardness, and sulphuric properties; it can never become malleable (like the metals), and therefore, in spite of its numerous affinities, cannot be regarded as a metal. Moreover, it has gross and impure mercury; and its sulphur is combustible. Ye, then, who would be great philosophers and do deceive many with your voluminous writings, in which you put this mineral forward as the essence of the universal remedy—I ask you again and again to reconsider your opinion, and to mark the saying of Arnold, that "it is foolish to seek in a thing that which it does not contain." He also says, in his Commentary on "The Crowd": "The philosopher's stone is a pure substance." Again, Lullius in his "Last Testament," observes: "Our tincture is nothing but pure fire." There is an expression to the same effect in his "Vade Mecum": "It is a subtle spirit which tinges bodies, and cleanses them of their leprous infirmities." But this mineral (like all the rest, without a single exception) is so gross and impure that it can only be cleansed by the mediation of our tincture. Therefore, the substance of our Great Stone cannot be elicited from it, since (Richard, cp. 1.) nothing can be obtained from a body which does not exist therein. What shall we say of vitriol, which misleads many by its wonderful qualities, especially as some part of it changes into copper, and itself has the power of transforming icon into copper? As a matter of fact, it is the elementary substance of copper, and when this mineral vapour (or aeriform mercury) finds in the mineral veins of the earth a place where its bitter, acid, salt, and venereal sulphur lies hid, it immediately amalgamates with it into a metal. But since the quantity of the aforesaid sulphur greatly exceeds that of the mercury, when the pure is separated from the impure, and the combustible from the incombustible by the segregating office of Nature, the mercury itself is changed into a greenish inferior substance. When common sulphur is added to copper, and the whole brought in contact with fire (for art can do by intense heat in a few moments what it takes the gentle heat of Nature a long time to accomplish) it corrodes the copper, and changes it into vitriol, and, in proportion to the quantity of the sulphur, the vitriol assumes a richer or fainter colour; whence it comes that some vitriol contains more copper and some less. In iron, too, there is gross sulphur; hence it is corroded by vitriol which seeks its mercury (the mercury of iron being very like that of vitriol), and (the mercury being joined to the sulphur) the iron becomes pure copper.

It should be carefully noticed that the acid spirit of vitriol is generated from sulphur; for the smell of sulphur is perceived in the spirit of vitriol, and the spirit of sulphur, like the spirit of vitriol, has power to change into vitriol. Since, then, this corrosive sulphur is hid in vitriol, and since it contains so small a quantity of impure mercury, we may be sure that it cannot be the object of our search. In this we agree with Alphidius, who says: "Take heed, my son, and eschew dead bodies, and stones; in these things there is no true way of procedure, for their life preserves not, but destroys. Such are salts, orpiments, arsenic, magnesia, bismuth, tutty, and the like." And Arnold (Flos Flor.) says: "The reason of these mistakes is that the four spirits, viz., orpiment, salt of ammonia, mercury, and sulphur, are not the seed of perfect or imperfect metals (except, of course, mercury and sulphur by themselves)."

But from these last words of Arnold it might be inferred that common mercury and quicksilver are the substance of the stone, seeing that these are referred to the four spirits, and that sulphur is supposed to consolidate the mercury. But I answer, with Richard the Englishman, in his eleventh chapter, that it does not really do so. For every kind of common sulphur is repugnant to metals, as the Sage says: "Indeed you must know that sulphur comes forth out of the fatness of the earth, and is thickened in the minera by gentle heat; when it becomes hard it is *called* sulphur."

Now there are two kinds of sulphur, the living and the combustible. Quick sulphur is the active principle of metals, and, when purged from all foreign matter, is the Matter of our Stone. But the common combustible variety is not the Matter of metals or of our Stone; rather, it is injurous to them. Common, combustible sulphur—so we are told by Avicenna and Richard the Englishman—has nothing to do with our art. However carefully prepared, it still disintegrates and destroys metals, because it has no affinity with them. When enclosed in metals, it retards their fusion. This is clearly seen in the case of iron, which contains hard, gross, and impure sulphur. When this sulphur is burned it is nothing but a dead, earthy, powdery substance. How then can it impart life to other things? For it has two principles of decay—its inflammability and its earthy impurity. The sulphur of the Sages, on the other hand, is living fire; it is quick, and quickens and matures lifeless substances. Common sulphur, then, cannot be the substance of the Stone.

But what shall we infer concerning common mercury? The Sages tell us that the Matter of our Stone is a mercurial substance, and many of its qualities closely resemble those of vulgar mercury. For it is the elementary substance of all fusible minerals, as Arnold says (Ros., pt. I., cp. ii.): "Since all fusible substances, when melted, are changed into it, and it mingles with them because of its common nature: they can differ from it only in so far as it contains impure foreign sulphur." And, again (cp. iv.): "Living mercury is clearly most perfect, and proved in all its operations, since it saves from combustion and promotes fusion. It is the red tincture, the sum of perfection, and quick as lightning; nor is it severed from that with which it has mingled so long as it exists. The same is full of affinity, cleaving faithfully, and is the medium by which tinctures are united, for it mingles most intimately with them, penetrating naturally into their inmost part, for it is of the same nature. We imitate Nature exactly, who in her minera hath no other matter whereon she works except a pure mercurial form. It is the only thing that overcomes fire, and is nut overcome by it, but delights in its amicable warmth." Again, Bernard says: "In this mercury is enclosed essential sulphur, which the fire cannot touch; and it accomplishes our object without any other substance than that of pure mercury." Seeing, then, that mercury has such excellent properties, it must surely be the substance of our Stone? True; but as there are two kinds of sulphur, so there are two kinds of mercury, the common mercury and the mercury of the Sages. Common mercury is gross and crude; nor does it stand the test of fire like our mercury, but is dissipated in the form of smoke, even by gentle heat. Hence the Sages have laid down this rule: "Our mercury is not the mercury of the vulgar herd." So Lullius says (Clav. cp. I.): "Common quicksilver, however carefully prepared, can never become the quicksilver of the Sages, for common quicksilver can only stand the test of fire by the aid of some other dry and more highly digested quicksilver." But most students of this art have spoken largely about the sublimation of common mercury, and have persisted in seeking the treasure of earthly wisdom where it cannot be found, because Nature has not placed it there. And, truly, the working even of common mercury is so wonderful that it has misled some who supposed themselves to be adepts in this art. The following is a case in point. I knew a man who succeeded in giving to his amalgam an orange colour, but he could not get it any nearer to the colour of gold. At last this clever chemist determined to increase the heat of the furnace, thinking that this would have the desired effect of more intimately combining the various ingredients. But alas! the alembic burst, the gold was hurled into the fire, and almost changed from its nature by the still volatile mercury. Hence it appears that the mercury (which is its body) so strongly affected the gold in its minutest particles as to reduce it to a tincture, although several colours were obtained by the action of the heat on the melted mass. If that good man had taken to heart Arnold's words in the "Flower of Flowers," he would never have made that experiment. For the said Arnold makes reference to those who adopt this method in the following terms: "They knew that mercury is the elementary principle of the metals, and that they are produced through its digestion by the heat of sulphur; they therefore sublimed mercury by itself, then fixed and consolidated it, again melted it and did again coagulate it: but when they came to examine the alembic, they found no gold, etc." Therefore we cannot believe that common quicksilver is the substance of the Stone. At the same time I do not deny that it is indispensable both to the philosophical chymist and to the physician.

We have carefully sought the substance of our stone in the animal and vegetable world, among stones, lesser, intermediate, and greater minerals, but in vain. We must now see whether we can find it in the metals, and if so, whether in all or only in some. It is a well-known fact (to which Roger bears witness, Spec., cp. iii.), that all metals are generated out of sulphur and quicksilver, and that nothing will become one with them, or change them, but what originates in themselves; since a thing can be developed and improved only by that which belongs to its own nature (Richard, cp. i.).

I need not say that the Great Artist has ordained that throughout the whole of Nature things should generate and produce only that which is like them, so that, for instance, a horse can never be the offspring of a man. "As brute animals," says Basil Valentine, "cannot multiply after their kind by way of generation except by virtue of their common nature; so you cannot expect to obtain the Blessed Stone, but out of its own seed, out of which it was made from the beginning. Now to find the seed you should diligently consider for what purpose you require the Store. You will at once see that it can be obtained only from the metallic root from which God has ordained that the metals themselves should be generated. Moreover, there is a great conformity between the generation of the metals and the Stone. For in both sulphur and quicksilver (containing that salt which is their quickening soul) are indispensably required; nor can any useful metal be generated until these three (making up the metallic substance) have been combined; for in the composition of metals there must be nothing which has not been obtained from a metallic source." "No external thing," says Draco, "which is not derived from these two [sulphur and mercury] has power to produce or transmute metals. On this account we must select a metallic substance for the production of the Stone." We must next briefly enquire whether it is to be found in imperfect metals. Many imagine that the substance of the white (tincture) may be elicited from tin or lead, and that of the red out of copper or iron, or both. This idea is doubtless owing to a misconception of the words of the Sages. For Geber (lib. forn. cp., ix.) says: "The mass for fermentation we generally gain from the imperfect [base] bodies." Therefore we lay it down as a general rule that the white paste may be extracted from Jupiter and Saturn, the red from Venus, Saturn, and Mars. And Basil. Valentinus says (Lib. de phys. et hyperphys.), that the tincture is prepared out of a conjunction of Mars and Venus. Again (Triumph. Antimon.), he uses these words: "After this tincture of the Sun and Moon comes the tincture of Venus and Mars, which two make up the tincture of the Sun, when they have been thoroughly perfected and condensed. After these come the tinctures of Jupiter and of Saturn (for the coagulation of mercury), and at last the tincture of mercury itself." But the searcher of Nature must know that there can be no contradiction of opinion between Geber or Basil, for it is impossible that the true philosophers should ever lie, and so these words should be parabolically understood. For no perfection can be obtained from imperfect metals, either by themselves or mixed, nor can that which is itself imperfect bring other things to perfection. For the purest substance of mercury is required for our purpose, as is testified in the "Sounding of the Trumpet," and by Avicenna, Lullius, and almost all the Sages, who unanimously affirm that "the purest substance of mercury is selected by us for our work." Now this highly refined substance of mercury is not found in the base metals, since they are rendered so gross by their impure and unessential sulphur, that, like leprous bodies, they can never be thoroughly purged and cleansed, in which process is the essence of our artifice. Nor do they well stand the test of fire, which is one of the properties required in our Matter. Let us hear what Geber has to tell us (Summa, cp. lxiii.) concerning the impurity of imperfect metals, and the properties of perfect mercury: "Thus," he says, "we happen upon two most wonderful secrets. The one is that there exists a twofold cause for the destruction of every [imperfect] metal by fire: namely, (1), the combustible sulphur enclosed in their interior substance is kindled by fierce heat, and (unimpeded by any excellence in their mercury) annihilates, and converts into smoke their entire substance; (2), the outward flame is fed by them, penetrates into their interior, and dissolves them into smoke, even though they be very solid; (3), their interior is laid bare by calcination. Now when all these conditions of destruction are found together, bodies must needs be destroyed; if they are not found together, they are destroyed somewhat more slowly. The second secret is the excellence which quicksilver imparts to bodies. For quicksilver (no other condition of decay being present) does not permit itself to be separated into its elements, but proves its perfection by preserving its substance intact in the fire. Blessed be God who created it, and gave it such a substance and such properties as are not found in all Nature besides. This is that which overcomes fire, and delights in its amicable heat." Here Geber clearly shews that the substance of our Stone cannot exist in imperfect metals; because things that are impure in themselves do not abide the fire which might purify them, while our mercury (on account of its purity) is not in the slightest degree injured by the fire. Thus we perceive that no one imperfect metal can contain the substance of our Stone. But neither is it to be found in a mixture of impure metals—for by mixing they become less pure than they were before. Moreover we said above that the substance we required was *one*. This fact is clearly set forth by Halys (lib. secret., cp. vi.), when he says: "The Stone is One; nothing else must be added to it: out of one substance the Sages obtain our remedy. Nothing else must mingle with the Stone itself, or with its substance." And Morienus says: "This Magistery grows from one original root, which branches out into several parts, and from which springs one thing."

But if base metals cannot be the substance of the Stone, why do the Sages bid us employ them? I will tell you. When they speak of impure bodies, they do not mean copper, iron, lead, tin, &c., but its own *body*, or its earth—as Arnold (Flos Flor.) says: "Mercury is united to earth, *i.e.*, to an imperfect substance [or body]." "For though this earth" is so perfect and pure that in these respects it would seem to attain the utmost possibility of Nature, yet in regard to the Stone it is still imperfect and impure. In this point art leaves Nature behind, since it accomplishes what Nature could not perform. That this earth before its plenary purgation and regeneration is imperfect, may be seen from the fact that it cannot yet accomplish more in the matter of tinging than Nature has given to it, while after its regeneration it is most powerful. Its grossness is clearly perceived in an actual experiment: for first it is black and looks like lead or antimony; then it is of a whitish colour, and is called Jupiter (or tin, or magnesia), and this also before it has attained true whiteness, but when it has passed the white stage, it is called Mars and Venus; after that it becomes perfect and red. That Basil. Valentinus agrees with me, and did not really hold the opinion which he expressed in some of his writings, is clear from his tract concerning the Great Stone, where (speaking of the Matter of the Stone) he says that in the Sun all three perfections are found together, whence it derives its power of resisting the fire, and that the Moon, on account of its fixed mercury, does not easily yield to the fire, but endures the trial. "That noble paramour Venus," he continues, "is furnished with an abundance of colour, and the greater and richer part of her body is full of tincture. The colour is the same which dwells in the most precious of metals, and on account of its abundance has a reddish appearance. But its body is leprous, for which reason the tincture cannot remain fixed in it, but evaporates when the former is destroyed. For when the body decays the soul cannot remain, but is dissipated and driven off. Its habitation is destroyed and burnt with fire, and its place knows it no more. In a fixed body it would without difficulty remain. The fixed 'salt' gives to brave Mars a hard, strong, and heavy body; whence the strength of his soul is perceived: for this warrior is not easily overcome. For his body is hard and difficult to wound."

But let no one conclude from these words of Basilius that that fixed sulphur of Venus, when united to the spirit of perfect mercury, will become the tincture. We must again repeat that our substance is not collected from many sources; but, as Basilius says, it is one universal thing, and is found in, and obtained from one thing, being the spirit of mercury, the soul of sulphur, and a spiritual salt, united under one heaven and dwelling in one body. Therefore let us turn our backs upon the base metals, and turn our minds to the precious metals, taking to heart those words of Plato (qu. ii.): "Why do you melt and dissolve other bodies with great labour, when in these [the precious metals] you have what you seek? If you wish to use the base metals, you must first change them into the substance of perfect bodies." Therefore, beloved inquirer into the secrets of Nature, leave on one side all things animal and vegetable, all salts, alums, vitriols, bismuths, magnesias, antimonies, and all base and impure metals, and seek thy Stone with Arnold de Vill. nov. (Pt. I., cp. vii.): "in Mercury and the Sun for the Sun, and in Mercury and the Moon for the Moon; since the whole virtue of this art consists in them alone." "For as the source of ignition is fire, so gold is the principle of gold making," says Ripley, in his "First Gate." If, therefore, thou wouldest make gold and silver by the philosopher's art, take for this purpose neither eggs, nor blood, but gold and silver, which, being subjected to the action of fire naturally, prudently, and not manually, generate new substances after their own kind, like all things in Nature. Richard (cp. x.) tells us "to sow gold and silver, that aided by our labour they may bring forth fruit, through the mediation of Nature: for these two have [and are] what you seek and nothing else in all the world." And why should I not fix on them since they contain pure and perfect mercury, with red and white sulphur. (Richard, cp. xvii.) So Avicenna teaches that, "in all silver is white, as in all gold there is red, sulphur. No other sulphur like that which exists in these bodies is found on all the earth. Therefore we cunningly prepare these two bodies, that we may have sulphur and quicksilver of the same substance as that which generates gold and silver under the earth. For they are shining bodies, whose rays tinge other bodies with true whiteness and redness, according to the manner of their own preparation." "For our Magistery," says, Arnold (Rosar., pt. I., cp. v.) "aids perfect bodies, and works upon the imperfect without the admixture of anything else. Gold, then, being the most precious of all the metals, is the red tincture, tinging and transforming every body. Silver is the white tincture, tinging other bodies with its perfect whiteness." Let me tell the gentle reader that the metals, that is to say, gold and silver in their metallic form, are not the Matter of our Stone—being in the middle between them and the base metals, as our Matter is in the middle between the former and our Great Stone. So Bernard says, (pt. ii.): "Let them be silent who affirm that there is any tincture but our own, or any other sulphur than that which lies hid in magnesia; also those who would extract the quicksilver from any but the red slave, and who speak of some other water but our own which is incorruptible and combines with nothing except that which belongs to its own nature, and moistens [tinges] nothing except that which is one with its own nature. There is no acid but our own, no other regimen, no other colours. In the same way, there is no other true solution, sublimation, consolidation, putrefaction. I therefore advise you to have done with alums, vitriols, salts, black bodies, borax, aqua fortis, herbs, animals, beasts, and all that proceeds from them, hairs, blood, urine, human seed, flesh, eggs, and all minerals, and to keep to the metals. But though the quicksilver required for our Stone is found in metals only, and in these is the beginning of the work, they are not therefore our Stone, so long as they retain their metallic form. For one and the same substance cannot have two forms. How can they be the Stone which holds an intermediate form between metals and mercury, unless their present form is first destroyed and removed?" Therefore, also, Raymond Lully says in his "Testament" (cp. vi.): "On this account a good artist takes metals for his media in the work of the magistery, and especially the Sun and Moon, because in them the substance of the Mercury and Sulphur is ripened, pure, and well-digested by Nature's own artifice. The artist would vainly endeavour to produce this exact proportion out of the natural elements, if he did not find it ready to his hand in these bodies." And in the "Codicil" he says: "Without these two, viz., gold and silver, our art would have no existence since the sulphur they contain has been purified by nature with a thoroughness such as art would vainly strive to imitate. From these two bodies, with their prepared sulphur [or prepared arsenic] our Medicine may be elicited, but without them we can never obtain it." In the preface to his "Key" he says: "I advise you, my friends, to operate on nothing but the Sun and Moon; but these you should resolve into their elementary substances, viz., our quicksilver and our sulphur." In like manner Arnoldus assures us that "from these bodies there is extracted an exceedingly white and red sulphur; for in these there is a most pure substance of sulphur, cleansed to the highest degree by Nature's own artifice." Nicarus, in "The Crowd," says: "I bid you take gold, which you desire to multiply and renew, and to divide its water into two parts; for that metal falling into that water will be called the fermenting matter of gold." How can this Sage call his "water" gold? To assist the student in solving this enigma I must tell him that the gold of the Sages is not common gold, as also Senior tells us. In "The Crowd" it is said: "As mercury is the element of all metals, so gold is their ultimate goal; hence in all metals, pure and impure, there are gold, silver, and mercury. But there is one true gold which is the essence of all." Thus you see that there is a gold of the Sages, which, though derived from common gold, is yet very different from it. The following words occur in the "Rising Dawn" (cp. xvi.) "The philosopher's gold resembles common gold neither in colour nor in substance. That which is extracted from it is the red and white tincture." "The philosopher's gold may be bought at a low price" (Aphidius). "All that is bought at a high price is false. With little gold we buy much" (Morienus). Moreover, our gold is living gold, and our silver is living silver, so that they can cause nothing but life and growth. Common gold and silver are dead, They can effect nothing until they are raised from the dead and quickened by the Sage. Then they live, and possess in a high degree the power of propagating and multiplying their race. Concerning the life of our metals that great philosopher, Sendivogius (who is still living), has the following words: "Let me advise you not to receive the gold and silver of the vulgar herd, for they are dead. Take our living metals. Place them in our fire, and there will result a dry liquid. First, earth will be resolved into water [for thus the Mercury of the Sages is called]. That water will solve gold and silver, and consume them until only the tenth part with one part is left. This will be the humid radical of the metals."

It is to be noted that Sages sometimes call their water, as well as their earth, gold. Hereunto we have already heard the words of Nicarus, and after a like manner we are told in the "Rosary of the Philosophers: "Our gold and silver are not the gold and silver of the vulgar. We call gold the water which rises into the air when exposed to fire. Verily, this gold is not the gold of the vulgar. The vulgar would not believe of their gold that it could be volatilised on account of its solid nature."

The philosopher's "earth," then, is sometimes designated their gold, as the same author testifies: "Know that our ore, which is the gold of the philosophers, is their earth." This "earth" is also called ore, ferment, or tincture; just as the "water" is called white and flaky "earth" So we read in the "Sounding of the Trumpet": "Wherefore Hermes says, 'Sow your gold in white, flaky earth which by calcination has been made glowing, subtle, and volatile.' That is to say: Sow gold, *i.e.*, the soul and quickening virtue, into the white earth, which by preparation has been made white and pure and freed from all its grossness. Thus natural gold is not the fermenting matter, but the philosopher's gold is the quickening ferment itself." Again, in the Seventh Step of the "Ladder of the Philosophers": "Their earth is white in which their gold [which is the soul] is sown, and this body is the centre of knowledge, the concentration thereof, and the habitation of tinctures." Once more: "Therefore Hercules says; 'Solve the body of magnesia which has become white and like the leaves of the bramble.' This is the body; the soul is the essence which is called the philosopher's gold." (For with water the spirit ascends into the upper air.) "Mix," says Senior, "gold with gold, that is water [mercury] and ashes." Again, Hermes says: "Sow gold into the white flaky earth." From these expressions, however obscurely worded. it is clear that our gold is not common gold.

But why do the philosophers call their gold now "water," and now "earth"? Do they not contradict themselves, or each other? No; our Sages, in expounding the truth, veil it under obscure and allegorical expressions, but nevertheless agree with each other so marvellously that they all seem to speak, as it were, with one mouth. They do nit confound one thing with another, nor do they wish to lead the earnest enquirer astray. They express themselves in mystic phrases to hide the truth from the unworthy and impious, lest they should seem to be casting pearls before swine, and giving the holy thing to be trodden underfoot by these who think only of indulging their lustful desires. But the noble student of our art has been told more than once, not only from what quarter our Stone may be obtained, but also that its substance must be *one*, which by the artist's skill may be resolved into two, viz., earth and fire, or mercury and sulphur.

The Sages, then, do well to call their gold earth or water; for they have a perfect right to term it whatever they like. So they have frequently called their Stone their gold, their super-perfect gold, their regenerate gold, and by many other names besides. If any one does not perceive their meaning at the first glance, he must blame his own ignorance, not their jealousy.

The reader now knows that the substance of our Stone is neither animal nor vegetable, and that it does not belong to the minerals or the base metals, but that it must be extracted from gold and silver, and that our gold and silver are not the vulgar, dead gold and silver, but the living gold and silver of the Sages. We must now say something about the mode of solution, as the greatest arcanum of all, and the root of the matter. A solution takes place when we transform a dry thing into a liquid, a hard thing into a soft, a hidden thing into one that is manifest, *i.e.*, when a solid is changed into water; not, however, the vulgar water (as Parmenides and Agadmon in "The Crowd" teach us: "When some persons hear of the liquefaction, they think a change takes place into the water of the clouds. But if they had read and understood our books, they would know that our water is permanent), but into the water of the Sages, i e., the elementary substance, as Arnold (Ros. I., cp. ix.) says: "The object of the Sages is to dissolve the Stone into its mercury, or elementary matter" And Avicenna says: "Thou who wouldest attain our object must first endeavour to dissolve and sublime the two luminaries, which is the first stage of the experiment, that they may become quicksilver." Therefore Arnold (Ros. II., cp. ii.) describes the solution as a resolving of bodies, and a preparation of the first Matter or Nature. And Richard the Englishman (cp. xviii.) writes thus: "First the Stone must be resolved into its elementary substance [seeing that it is an union of body and spirit], that the two may become one mercurial water." But even as this first solution is the most vital part of our process, so is it also the most difficult, as Eobold Vogelius testifies when he says: "How hard this achievement is can be affirmed by those who have performed it." Bernard of Trevisan, in his book addressed to Thomas of Bononia, says: "He who knows the secret of the solution is acquainted with the arcanum of the Art, which is, to mingle kinds, and effectually to extract elements from elements which lie hid in them." The solution must not be made with aqua fortis; for aqua fortis corrodes and destroys the body which should be only liquefied and improved. The solution does not take place into any water that wets the hands, but into a dry water, which is called both sulphur and mercury, as Zneumo says (Turba): "Unless by resolving it into its elements you extract from the body its marrow, and make it an impalpable spirit, you labour in vain." And Richard the Englishman, following Avicenna, affirms (cp. xi.): "The Sages have striven to discover how those sulphurs may be extracted from those more perfect bodies, and how their qualities may be so refined by Art, that that which was not manifest before (although it always lay hid in them) may appear by the mediation of the said Art with Nature." And this they confess cannot be done unless the body be resolved into its First Matter, which is quicksilver, out of which it was made in the beginning, without admixture of any outward things; since foreign matter cannot improve the nature of our Stone. "For no water," says Bernard, "dissolves our bodies, but that which is of their kind, and may be inspissated by them." (Ep. to Thom. of Bonon.) And in the same Epistle he writes: "The solution should be permanent, so that from both elements, viz., the male and female seed, a new species may result. Amen, I say unto you that no natural water can dissolve metals, except that which is always in them substantially and formally, and which the metals themselves, being dissolved, may again consolidate." Thus Morfoleus, in "The Crowd" says: "Every body is dissolved with the spirit that is joined to it, and doubtless also becomes spiritual. And every spirit is modified and coloured by bodies, to which spirit is thus added a tinging colour which stands the test of fire."

Hence the student of our art must diligently enquire what that water is. "For the knowledge of the menstruum," says Raymond (Comp. An., p. i.) "is a thing without which nothing can be done in the magistery of this Art. Nothing preserves the metals while it dissolves them, but our menstruum," which, as he further states in his 'Codicil,' is "the water by which the metals are solved, while all their essential properties are conserved." Though this is the Great Arcanum which our Sages have always kept secret, and have forbidden us to reveal, yet, as far as we may, we will put you on the right track by two quotations. The first is found in the abridged Rosary, and runs as follows: "The first preparation and foundation of this Art, is the solution [*i.e.*, reduction] of the body into water, *i.e.*, into quicksilver, and this they call the solution, when they say: Let the gold be dissolved, which is hid in the body of magnesia, that it may be reduced to its First Matter, that thence it may become sulphur and quicksilver, and not be again liquefied into water. The object of our solution is to make it liquid, and resolve it into the substance of quicksilver that the saltness of its sulphur may be diminished, which divine sulphur is prepared by extraction from two sulphurs, when the spirit meets the body." The second quotation is from the "Prœmium of the Twelve Gates," by Ripley: "I will straightway teach thee that thou mayest know that there are three mercuries, which are the keys of knowledge [which Raymond calls his menstrua], without which nothing is properly done. But two of them are superficial. The third is of the essence of the Sun and Moon, the properties of which I will describe to thee. For mercury, the essence of other metals, is the principal substance of our Stone. In Gold and Silver our menstrua are not visible to the eye, and are only perceived by their effect. This is the Stone of which we speak, if anyone understand our books aright. It is the soul and shining substance of the Sun and Moon, that subtile influence from which the earth derives its splendour. For what are gold and silver (says Avicenna) but pure red and white earth? Take away from it the aforesaid splendour, and it will be nothing but worthless earth. The whole compound we call our lead. The quality of splendour comes from the Sun and Moon. And, in brief, these are our solvents. Perfect bodies we naturally calcine with the first, without adding any impure body but *one*, commonly called by philosophers the green lion, and this is the medium for perfectly combining the tinctures of the Sun and Moon. With the second, which is a vegetable liquid, reviving what before was dead, the two principles [both material and formal] must be solved; else they would be of little value. With the third, which is a permanent, incombustible liquid, of unctuous quality, the tree of Hermes is burnt to ashes. This is our natural, most sure fire, our mercury, our sulphur, our pure tincture, our soul, our Stone raised with the wind, born in the earth. These things take to heart. This Stone, I dare to tell thee, is the powerful essence of the metal, and thou must be careful how thou dost obtain it. For this solvent is invisible, although with the secondary philosophic water it may, by the separation of elements, become visible in the form of pure water. Out of this solvent, and with it, thou mayst obtain the sulphur of Nature, if it be naturally turned into a pure spirit. Then thou mayst with it dissolve thy fundamental mass [*i.e.* gold and silver]."

In these two quotations the whole mystery of the solution is revealed. If you will consider the properties and powers of Nature, and compare them with these words, and annihilate all the workings of Nature (*i.e.* reduce them, and unroll them like the thread of a skein), you will find in them all truth plainly and fundamentally. But if you cannot gather from them where are the bolted gates, and do not know the substance and the powers of Nature, you shall be conducted to them, not by contemptuous self-conceit, but by ardent prayer and indefatigable study.

For (by the revelation of the great and good God) I have attained this Art only by persevering application, vigils, and repeated reading of authentic books. I do not speak of the matter—that was made known to me by the revelation of God alone; but I have by study discovered the secret of its solution, which is the same with ancient and modern Sages, and the true arcanum of the Art, in the absence of which neither past nor present Philosophers could have performed anything, whence it is a secret of Art and an arcanum of wisdom which no one but God must reveal, for which benefit I give undying thanks with heart and lips to the Creator of all things, world without end, Amen.

That you may have no cause to complain of me, gentle reader, I will, however, for the love of God, expound to you another mystery. You are to know that, although the solution is *one*, yet in it there may be distinguished a first, and a second, as they say in the schools. The *first* solution is that of which Arnold speaks in the above quotation, *viz.*, the reduction of it to its First Matter; the *second* is that perfect solution of body and spirit at the same time, in which the solvent and the thing solved always abide together, and with this solution of the body there takes place simultaneously a consolidation of the spirit.

Here you may clearly and plainly see with your eyes what you have long desired to see. If you understand it, it is mere child's play; therefore, I will forbear to speak any further about it. If you know the beginning, the end will duly follow by the help of God, from whom alone we may obtain all glory, the corruptible glory of this world, and that eternal glory in which with glorified bodies we shall see God face to face—despising all mundane pleasure that we may behold with our own eyes that eternal, infinite, and unspeakable joy of heaven.

With these words I will conclude my little tract. Everything else that remains to be said I will set forth in the followingparable, where you will find the entire system and practice clearly expounded. If you duly follow it, you will doubtless attain to the true wisdom. May it be shewn to you, and to all good men, by God the Father, God the Son, and God the Holy Spirit, Blessed for evermore!

M.S.

The thing is one in number, and one essence, which Nature strives to transform, but with the help of Art, into two, and twice two: mercury and sulphur impart nourishment to themselves. Spirit, and soul, and body, and four elements: the fifth which they furnish is the Philosopher's Stone. Select your substance without guile, let it be double, and let its splendour be of pure mercury. Take sulphur free from every foreign substance, and consume it in a fiery furnace. But when you put it together again, let it still be of the same weight. Then I will believe that you are upon the road of the mystery. When you have dissolved, quickly sublime it. Pound what you obtain, and ceaselessly distil it. Then endeavour to condense it, and continue to expose it to heat. After this begin to "tinge" largely. You have the panacea of men, and the sum of the metals, and you shall be able to cure whomsoever and whatsoever you please.

Here follows a Parable in which the Mystery of the whole
Matter is Declared.

Once upon a time, when I was walking abroad in a wood, and considering the wretchedness of this life, and deploring that through the lamentable fall of our first parents we had been reduced to this pitiable state, I suddenly found myself upon a rough, untrodden, and impracticable path, which was beset with briars. Then I was afraid, and strove to retrace my steps. But it was not in my power to do so; for so violent a tempest blew upon me from behind that it was easier to take ten steps forward than to take one backward. So I had to hurry forward, and follow the rugged path up and down hill. After a while, I reached a beautiful meadow, surrounded with heavy-laden fruit trees, which the inhabitants of the place called the Meadow of Happiness. There I met a crowd of decrepit men with grey beards, one of whom, an elderly personage, had a long darkish beard, whom also I knew by name, but whose face I had never seen. These men were discussing various subjects, *e.g.*, the goodness and wisdom of God, all natural objects, and especially the great mystery which lies hid in Nature, which—they said—God conceals from the whole world, and makes known only to a few who truly love Him. I listened to them for a long time (for I was pleased with their discourse) till I thought that some were talking rather wildly, not in regard to the substance and the method, but as concerns parables, similitudes, etc., which were the figments of Aristotle, Pliny, and others. When I heard these things, I could no longer contain myself, and, like Saul among the prophets, I began to give my opinion, and to refute those futile assertions by arguments drawn from experience and reason. Some of them agreed with me, and began to test my knowledge with many questions. But I was so well grounded that I stood the test to the admiration of all. They all marvelled at the soundness of my knowledge, and affirmed with one voice that I should be received into their fellowship. These words filled me with great joy. But they said I could not be their Brother until I knew their Lion, and his internal and external properties. They told me I must summon up my whole strength to subdue him. I confidently replied that I would leave no stone unturned to attain this object. For their kindness affected me so that I would not have left them for all the wealth of this world. Therefore they conducted me to the Lion, and were at great pains to declare to me his nature. But no one would tell me how I must treat him at first. Some of them did indeed mutter a few words on this point, but so confusedly and obscurely, that scarce one in a thousand would have understood their meaning. However, they said that when I had bound him without being harmed by his sharp claws and terrible teeth, I should know all the rest. This Lion was old, fierce, great, and terrible to behold with his flowing yellow mane. Then I repented of my temerity, and would gladly have retreated if I had not been held to my purpose by my vow, and the old men that surrounded me. So I carefully descended into the

Lion's den, and strove to pacify him; but he glared upon me with red eyes, and affrighted me so that I could hardly stand upon my feet, and thought that my last hour had come. But calling to mind what one of the old men had said to me when I entered the den, namely, that many had undertaken to tame the Lion, but that only few had accomplished it, I summoned up courage, and tried several artifices, which I had learned by diligent training. Moreover, I had some knowledge of natural magic. I therefore relinquished my blandishments, and seized him so gently, skilfully, and subtly, that almost before he knew what I was about I had drawn all the blood from his body, and from his very heart and bowels. This blood was red indeed, but choleric. Then I proceeded to dissect him, and made a most marvellous discovery:—his bones were as white as snow, and their quantity more considerable than that of the blood. When the old men who stood round the den, and had watched our struggle, saw this, they began to converse with great eagerness, as I could see from their gestures—for, being in the den, I could not hear their words. But anon their dispute began to run high, and I could distinguish these words: "He must bring him to life again if he wishes to be our brother." Therefore, without further delay, I stepped out of the den into a large open space, and then suddenly (I know not how) found myself upon a very high wall, which rose more than 100 yards into the air, but at the top was not more than a foot in width, and along the middle of it ran an iron battlement of great strength. Now as I passed along I thought I saw one walking before me on the right side of the battlement. When I had followed him a short distance I became aware of another person following me on the other side; but, whether it was a man or a woman I cannot undertake to say. This person hailed me, and said that there was more convenient footing on his side than on mine. This I was quite ready to believe; for the battlement, which was on the middle of the wall, made the path so narrow as to render progress extremely difficult at such a great height, indeed, I noticed that some of those who followed me actually fell. Therefore I got over the battlement on to the other side, and proceeded to the end of the wall, which presented a most difficult and dangerous descent. Then I was sorry that I had deserted my own side, as I could neither advance nor retreat. But, remembering that fortune befriends the bold, I attempted the descent, and by using my hands and feet, I got down safely. Now when I had advanced a little further, I put away all thought of danger, and forgot all about the wall and the battlement. Then lighting upon a certain place, I found white and red roses, but the latter were more abundant; so I gathered some of them and stuck them in my cap. In that place were some most beautiful women, and in the neighbouring garden a number of young men were to be seen. But a wall which surrounded the garden prevented the latter from joining the women. They were eager to do so, but were not allowed to go round the garden and find the gate. The sight moved me to pity, and therefore I hastily went back by the smooth path along which I had come, and soon reached some houses, among which I expected to find the gardener's cottage. But I found there many men, of whom each had his own cell (in very few there were two living together). They were all busily at work, each labouring by himself. Their work was of a kind long and familiarly known to me—indeed, far too well known. So I said to myself: "Behold, here are many persons at work upon vain and foolish experiments, which have a certain specious plausibility (according to each man's idiosyncrasy), but no, real foundation in Nature. Surely you, too, will obtain forgiveness." At least, I would not suffer myself to be detained with these barren futilities, but went on my way. When I reached the gate of the garden some looked askance at me, and I was afraid they would prevent me from carrying out my purpose. Others murmured, and said: "Look, this fellow presumes to approach the gate of the garden, and we who have spent so many years in these horticultural labours, have never gained admittance! How we will jeer at him if he meets with a repulse." But I paid no attention to their talk (for I knew the interior of that garden better than they, although I had never been in it), and approached the gate, which was double-locked, and in which there appeared to be no keyhole, but soon I perceived a keyhole which would have escaped any common observer. So I inserted my master key (called by some "the adulteress"), which I had diligently fashioned for the purpose, pushed back the bolt, and entered. After passing this gate, I came upon other bolted gates, which, however, I opened without any difficulty. So I entered the garden, and found in the middle of it a small square garden, which was surrounded with a rose hedge covered with beautiful roses, and as a little rain was falling, and the rays of the sun shone upon it, I beheld a rainbow. But I was hastening past the small garden, to that place where I thought I could aid the young women, when, behold, there came forward the most beautiful of all the maidens, arrayed in silk and satin, with the most beautiful of the youths, dressed in a scarlet robe. They walked arm in arm to the rose garden, and carried many fragrant roses in their hands. I greeted them, and asked how she had got over. "This my beloved bridegroom," she said, "helped me, and now we are leaving this pleasant garden, and hastening to our chamber to satisfy our love." "I am glad," I returned, "that without any trouble on my part your desires have been fulfilled. But you see how much trouble I have taken on your behalf, having traversed so great a distance in so short a time." Then I came to a water-mill, built within of stones, where there were no flour bins or other miller's requisites; yet I saw wheels driven round by the water. I asked the decrepit miller the reason, and he told me the grinding took place somewhere out of view. At the same moment I saw a miller enter that place by a small bridge, and immediately followed him. When I had passed the bridge, which was on the right side of the wheels, I paused and beheld a wonderful sight. In a moment the wheels were above the bridge; I saw very black water, with white drops; the bridge was only about three inches wide; but by clinging to the rails I got safely back, without being wetted at all, and asked the old man how many wheels he had. He answered, "Ten." I was troubled by the marvellous incident, and would gladly have known its meaning, but felt that it was labour lost to ask the old man any questions, and so departed. Before the mill was a raised platform on which some of the aforesaid old men were walking to and fro in the warm sunshine, discussing a letter which they had received from the Faculty of the University. I guessed the tenor of the letter, and, feeling sure that it concerned me, I addressed to them a question to that effect. "It *does* concern you," they said, "the wife whom you married a long time ago, you must keep for ever, or else we must tell our chief." "You need not trouble yourselves about this matter," I said, "for we were born together, and brought up together as children, and now that I have married her, I will never forsake her, but cherish her till her last breath; nay, even death itself shall not sever us." "It is well," they said, "your wife is satisfied, too; you must be joined together." "I am content," I said. "It is well," they repeated. "For thus the Lion will be restored to life, and be more powerful and more active than he was before." Then I remembered my labours, and knew by certain signs that this matter concerned not myself, but a very good friend of mine. As these thoughts crossed my mind, I saw our bridegroom and his beloved bride—both clothed in the aforesaid garments—come forward, eager to be joined together. This sight gladdened me; for I had been afraid that the whole matter concerned me. Now when the bridegroom, in his bright scarlet robe, with his bride, whose silk dress gave out shining rays, reached the old men, they were straightway joined together. And I marvelled that the maiden, who was said to be the mother of her bridegroom, was of so youthful an appearance, that she might have seemed his daughter. But I know not what sin they had committed, except that brother and sister had been drawn to each other by such passionate love that they could no more be separated; and, being charged with incest, they were shut up for ever in a close prison, which, however, was as pellucid and transparent as glass, and arched like the heavenly vault, so that all that they did could be seen from without. Here they were to do penance for their sins with ever-flowing tears, and true sorrow. All their clothes and outward ornaments were taken away. None of their servants and friends were allowed to be with them, but after they had received sufficient meat and drink (the latter taken from the aforesaid water), the door was shut and locked, and the seal of the Faculty was affixed to it. I was entrusted with the charge of heating their chamber in the winter, so that they might be neither. too hot nor too cold, and I was further to see that they did not escape. If any accident of any kind happened, I was to be severely punished. I did not like this charge; and, as I remembered that the matter was most important, and that the College of Sages were not wont to say what they did not mean, I was filled with fear. But since I had to bear that which I could not alter, and since the chamber was situated in a strong tower, and surrounded with battlements and lofty walls, and, moreover, could be easily heated with a gentle and continuous fire, I called upon God for help, and began to heat the chamber. But what happened? As soon as they felt the grateful warmth, they fell to embracing each other so passionately that the husband's heart was melted with the excessive ardour of love, and he fell down broken in many pieces. When she who loved him no less than he loved her, saw this, she wept for him, and, as it were, covered him with overflowing tears, until he was quite flooded and concealed from view. But those complaints and tears did not last long, for being weary with exceeding sorrow, she at length destroyed herself. Alas! what fear and anguish fell upon me, when I saw those who had been so straitly committed to my charge, lying, as it were, melted and dead before me. I felt sure that I should be put to death for it; but the jeers, the derision, and the contempt which I would have to undergo seemed more grievous even than death. In this anxious state of mind I spent several days, until the thought occurred to me that, if Medea had restored a dead body to life, I might perhaps be able to do the same. But I could think of no better plan than to keep up the warmth of the chamber until the water should have evaporated, and the dead bodies of the lovers could again be seen. I doubted not that then I should most honourably escape from all danger. So I kept up the fire forty days, the water diminishing from day to day, and the dead bodies beginning to reappear. Now, however, they looked as black as coals. This effect would have been produced sooner if the chamber had not been so closely shut and sealed so that I could in no wise open it. For I noticed that the water rose to the roof of the chamber, and then came down again like rain; but it could find no exit from the chamber, until the dead bodies had putrefied and began to give out a grievous smell. In the meantime the rays of the sun, shining upon the moisture of the chamber, produced a most beautiful rainbow; and, after all my sorrow, the sight of its gay colours filled me with great delight; and I was particularly pleased to see my lovers lying before me. But as there is no joy without a drop of bitterness, so I was still disturbed by the thought that those who had been committed to my care were still lying lifeless. Nevertheless, I comforted myself with the reflection that the chamber (being so tightly closed) must still contain their souls and spirits. Therefore I continued diligently to perform my office of warming them, being assured that they would not return to their bodies while they could enjoy that moist atmosphere. This conjecture was justified by the event. For towards evening I noticed that many vapours rose from the earth through the heat of the sun, and were lifted up as water is attracted by the sun; afterwards when night fell, they watered the earth as fertilising dew, and washed our bodies, which became more beautiful and white the oftener this sprinkling took place. And the whiter they became, the more the quantity of moisture in the air diminished, until at last the atmosphere was too thin for the spirit and soul to remain therein any longer; so they were at length compelled to return to the clarified body of the Queen, which (to my great joy) was straightway restored to life. My joy was all the greater, because now she was arrayed in a beautiful and magnificent garment such as is rarely seen by mortal eye, and had a glorious crown, all made of diamonds, upon her head. Thus attired, she stood upon her feet and cried: "Know this, ye mortals, and let it enter your hearts, that the most High God is one God, who has power to set up and pull down kings. He makes rich and poor as He, wills. He has killed, and raised again. I was great, and was brought low; but now, having been humbled, I have been made Queen of many more kingdoms. After death life has been restored to me. When I was poor, the treasures of the wise and mighty were committed to me. Therefore I, too, can make the poor rich, give grace to the humble, and restore the health of the sick. But I am not yet able to raise my beloved brother, the most mighty King, from the dead. Nevertheless, when he comes, he will show that my words are true." When she had thus spoken the sun lighted up the world with his glorious rays, and the heat waxed great (for the dog days were approaching). Long before this, garments of rich black silk, of grey or ash-coloured damask, of rare white silk, embroidered with silver, precious pearls, and brilliant diamonds, had been got ready towards the marriage of our Queen; and now garments of many colours, of flesh colour, orange, and saffron, and of red and scarlet silk, richly embroidered with rubies and carbuncles, were being prepared for the adornment of our new King. But there was no one to be seen working at those garments; yet one after another was got ready, insomuch that I greatly marvelled, because I knew that none but the bride and the bridegroom had entered the chamber. My wonder increased when I observed that as each dress was finished, those that had been there before straightway vanished, though I could see no one put them away. Now when that most precious scarlet garment had been finished, the great and mighty King appeared in great splendour and indescribable magnificence, and when he saw that he was shut in, he besought me, in the most persuasive accents, to open the door, as it would be to my advantage to let him out of the chamber. Now, though I had been most strictly enjoined not to open the chamber, I was filled with awe by the majesty and persuasive speech of the King, and acceded to his request. When he left the chamber, he bore himself so kindly, so gently, and so humbly, that I could not help reflecting that these virtues are the most glorious ornaments of the great. As he had passed the dog days in great heat he was extremely thirsty, spent, and weary; wherefore he humbly requested me to bring him some water from the river where it raged and foamed under the wheels. I gladly acceded to his request, and, after slaking his thirst with a deep draught, he returned to the chamber, requesting me to shut the door carefully so that no one might disturb him or rouse him from his sleep. So he slept a few days, and then called me back to open the door again. He looked much more beautiful, ruddier, and more royal, and said that this water was very precious and full of virtue. When at his request I had fetched him some more, he took a deeper draught than before, insomuch that the size of the chamber seemed to become enlarged. After drinking of this water (which is lightly esteemed by the ignorant) as much as he desired, he became so beautiful and glorious that in all my life I do not remember to have seen a more glorious man, or more glorious deeds. For he took me into his kingdom and showed me all the treasures and riches of the whole world, till I was obliged to confess, that so far from exaggerating his power, the Queen had not told me the half of it. Of gold and precious carbuncles there was no end. There was also to be found renewal and restoration of youth, and of the natural faculties, and recovery of lost health, with a never failing panacea for all diseases. What pleased me most of all, was that the people of that kingdom knew, feared, and honoured their Creator, and asked and obtained of him wisdom, understanding, and, after this life, eternal glory and beatitude. May this latter be given to us also by God the Father, God the Son, and God the Holy Spirit, the Blessed Trinity, to Whom belong praise, glory, and honour, world without end, Amen.

THE GOLDEN AGE
RESTORED:

HAVING NOW APPEARED A SECOND TIME, FLOURISHED
BEAUTIFULLY, AND BROUGHT FORTH FRAGRANT AND
GOLDEN SEED. THIS RARE AND PRECIOUS
SEED IS SHEWN AND IMPARTED TO ALL
THE SONS OF TRUE WISDOM AND
THE DOCTRINE,

BY

HENRY MADATHANAS.

"If any of you lack wisdom, let him ask of God, who gives simply, and without upbraiding, and it shall be given to him."—JAMES i., 5.

MOTTO OF THE AUTHOR:

"The Centre of the World—a Grain of Sand."

PREFACE.

To the Worthy and Christian Reader.

BELOVED and pious reader, above all, ye who are Sons of Wisdom and the Doctrine, some years ago Almighty God, in answer to my daily prayers, opened my eyes by the light of His Holy Spirit (Who was sent us through Christ by the Father, and from Whom we receive all wisdom), and enabled me to discover the True Centre in the Centre of the Triangle and the one true Matter of the precious Philosopher's Stone, so that I now hold it in my hands; but it took me five years longer to discover how the blood of the Red Lion and the glue of the White Eagle were to be extracted, and how these were to be mixed in their natural proportions, enclosed, sealed, and committed to the secret fire. Nor did I even then find the arcanum without constant and untiring application. I have, indeed, studied the writings, parables, and various figures of the philosophers with singular industry, and laboured hard to solve their manifold wonderful enigmas, most of which are simply the vain products of their imaginations. It was long before experience taught me that all their obscure verbiage and high pretensions are mere folly and empty phantasms (as is amply testified by our leading Sages). Then I understood that their preparations (of which we read in Geber, Albertus Magnus, and others), their purgations, sublimations, cementations, distillations, rectifications, circulations, putrefactions, conjunctions, solutions, coagulations, calcinations, incinerations, mortifycations, revivifications, &c., as also their tripods, athanors (furnaces), reverberatory alembics, excrements of horses, ashes, sand, stills, pelican-violas, retorts, fixatories, &c., are mere plausible impostures and frauds. This must be apparent to any one who considers the truth of the matter. Nature, who, in her noble simplicity, delights in her ownnproper substance, knows nothing of these futilities. Hence Theophrastus (Sec. Mag. de Phil. Lap.) rightly says of those who seek the substance of the Stone in wine, imperfect bodies, blood, bismuth, mercury, sulphur, wine, dung, orpiment, and in plants, as chelidonia, hyssop, ivy, &c., that they are full of lies and thievery—deceiving the credulous, milking their purses dry, and, as to the rest, following their own foolish fancies, that are quite unable to realise the requirements of Nature. (Tell me now who will help me with the minerals of the earth, distillations of water, &c.?) Some of them take new wine and urine for the purpose of changing them into metals. To hear them talk, you might suppose all that is sold at the apothecaries to be good for metals. Thou foolish man, dost thou not perceive that none of these things have anything to do with them?

You might as well try to sever Nature, as endeavour to make metals out of blood. Make a man out of a horse, or a milch cow out of a mouse: this would be according to the same method of multiplication. Art cannot change or overstep the natural order of the universe. If a woman bring forth a male child, you cannot change him into a little girl. From this rule, which evidently obtains throughout Nature, any sane person may gather where, and how, we must look for, and find, our Blessed Matter. But let no one imagine, or suffer any quack to delude him into the belief, that he has all that he requires when the substance has been made known to him either by God, or by one of the initiated. Let him not suppose that the solution and purification are a very simple matter. He could fall into no more serious mistake. He has scarcely got beyond the most elementary stage of his task. Let me once more tell him that I spent five entire years, after discovering the true Matter of the Stone, in the search after the right method of manipulating it, until at length, in the sixth year, the key of power was entrusted to me by the secret revelation of the most High God. That same key the ancient Patriarchs, Prophets, and Sages have always kept secret. "For if," says Monarcha, in a certain passage, "they had described it in an universally intelligible manner, and placed it within the reach of every labourer and porter, it would have been a great theft, and no true mystery; moreover, many evils would arise from such a profanation of the arcanum, which would also be manifestly contrary to God's will." For these and other reasons (which I have stated in the Epilogue), lest I should seem to be hiding the talent committed to me by God, I have in this my "Golden Age Come Back" (as far as Nature and God allow) revealed the Great Mystery of the Sages, which, through the grace of God, I have seen with these eyes, and handled with these hands. The just and pious reader will regard my undertaking with a kindly eye, and not suffer seeming contradictions to mislead him: the theory of and practice of this Art, and the laws which obtain in the Republic of the Chemists, forbade me to write more openly or plainly. I hope and trust that, nevertheless, all who look upon this book with the eyes of the mind, pore over it by day and by night, and pray to God from the bottom of their hearts, will, together with me, enjoy the wonderful hidden fruits of philosophy. In this way the Brethren of the true Golden Cross, and the elect members of the philosophic communion, are and remain joined together in a great confederation.

In conclusion, that the learned and worthy Christian reader may know my Christian name and my surname, I will remove every cause of complaint by making it known in the following manner. Let all and sundry be certified that the number of my name is 1613: by this number my whole name is written in the book of Nature with two dead ones, and seven living ones. After that, the letter 5 is the fifth part of B, and 15 the fifth part of 12. With this information you must be satisfied. Written at Tannenberg, March 23rd, 1622.

Epigram to the Sons of Wisdom and the Doctrine.

I have sought; I have found; I have often purified; and I have joined together; I have matured it: Then the golden tincture has followed, which is called the Centre of Nature (hence so many opinions, so many books, so many parables). It is the Remedy, I openly declare it, for all metals, and for all sick persons. The solution is of God.

HERMAN DATICHIUS,
The Author's Famulus.

THE GOLDEN AGE RESTORED.

AS I pondered in my mind the marvels of the Most High, and the duty of fervent love to our neighbours, which He laid upon us; I remembered the wheat harvest, when Reuben, the son of Leah, found Dudaim in the field, which Leah gave to Rachel for the love of the Patriarch Jacob. Then I was carried forward, being plunged in profound thought, to the time of Moses, who rendered potable the golden calf (which Aaron had formed) by reducing it to powder in the fire, throwing it into the water, and giving it the children of Israel to drink; and I marvelled greatly at the wonderful and masterly destruction of the metal by the man of God. But when I reflected upon the matter, the truth was borne in upon my mind, and my eyes were opened like those of the disciples at Emmaus, who knew their Master in the breaking of bread; and my heart burned within me. Then I retired to rest, that I might consider the matter further (on the morrow), and fell into a deep slumber; when, behold, Solomon appeared to me in all his power, wealth, and glory, and with him came his whole harem: sixty were queens, eight hundred concubines, and of virgins there was a countless number. One of them was his most beautiful dove, and was dearest to his heart. They formed a procession according to the Catholic rite, in the centre of which was one greatly praised and beloved, whose name was like ointment poured out, and whose fragrance was sweeter than that of spices; the fiery spirit of this person was the Key for the opening of the Temple, for entering the Holy of Holies, and taking hold on the horns of the Altar.

When the procession had been performed in the manner aforesaid, Solomon shewed me the One Centre in the Triangle of the Centre, and opened my understanding. Then I observed that a woman stood behind me, who had bared her breast, from a deep wound in which blood and water gushed forth. Her thighs were like two half-moons, made by the Master; her navel was like a round goblet; her belly like a heap of wheat, set about with roses; her breasts like two young roes that are twins; her neck like a tower of ivory; her eyes like the fish-pools in Heshbon, by the Gate of Bathrabbim; her nose like the Tower of Lebanon, which looketh towards Damascus; her head like Carmel, and the hair of her head like royal purple. Her garments, which were rancid, ill-savoured, and full of venom, lay at her feet, whither she had cast them; and at length she broke forth into these words: "I have put off my coat; how shall I put it on? I have washed my feet; how shall I defile them? The watchmen that went about the city found me, they smote me, they wounded me; they took away my veil from me." Thereupon I fell to the ground with great and ignorant terror. But Solomon bade me rise, and said: "Fear not; for you see Nature bared, and the most secret of all secrets that is found beneath the sky and earth: She is beautiful as Tirzah, comely as Jerusalem, terrible as an army with banners—and nevertheless the pure and chaste virgin of whom Adam was formed and created. The entrance of her tabernacle is sealed. She lives in gardens, sleeps in the double cave of Abraham, in the field of Hebron, and her palace is in the depths of the Red Sea, and in transparent caverns. The air bare her, the fire nourished her: therefore she is the Queen of the earth, and has honey and milk in her breasts; her lips are as a dropping honeycomb; honey and milk are under her tongue; and the smell of her garments is to the wise like the smell of Lebanon—but to the ignorant an abomination." And Solomon said further: "Awake, and see my whole harem, and say what it is like." And straightway his whole harem was stripped naked. Yet could I not find or judge, and my eyes were sealed lest I should know the secret. When Solomon saw my infirmity, he set that naked woman apart from the rest of the harem, and said: "Thy thoughts are vain, and thy mind is sunburnt; thy memory is shrouded in a thick mist, so that thou canst judge nothing rightly. But if thou art on the watch, and makest good use of thy present opportunity, the bloody sweat and snowy tears of this virgin will have power to restore thee, and to strengthen and clarify thy intellect and memory that thy eyes may see the secret wonders of the Most High, the height of the things above, the depth of the things beneath, and that thou mayst clearly understand the powers and operation of all Nature, and of the elements. Thy intellect shall be silver, and thy memory golden. The colour of all precious stones shall appear before thy eyes; thou shalt know their birth, and separate the good from the bad, the sheep from the goats. Thy life shall be peace, but the bells of Aaron shall rouse thee from sleep, and the lyre of David, my father, from drowsiness." These words of Solomon awed and terrified me still more; in part I was adread at such emphatic speech, and in part also at the splendour and glory of the King's harem. But King Solomon seized my right hand, and led me through a wine cellar into a most splendid secret palace, where he refreshed me with flowers and apples. The windows were of transparent crystal, and I gazed through them. And he said: "What do you see?" I said: "I see the former chamber whence we came, and on the left stands thy royal harem, and on the right naked virgins. Their eyes are redder than wine, and their teeth whiter than milk. But the garments that lie at their feet are fouler, blacker, and more unsightly than the river Kidron." "Choose out one of these," said Solomon, "to be your love. I esteem the virgins even as my own harem. And the more their loveliness delights me, the less am I deterred by their foul garments." With this, the King turned himself and spoke most kindly to one of his queens. There was in the chamber a mistress of about a hundred years of age. She was arrayed in a grey robe, and had a black fillet on her head, that was embroidered with many brilliant jewels, and lined within with red, yellow, and blue silk; her mantle was heavily ornamented with all kinds of Turkish and Indian colours and figures. This ancient woman nodded to me, and swore piously that she was the mother of that naked virgin, and that she was a pure, chaste, and sealed virgin, who had never before suffered the eye of man to dwell upon her, nor had any one ever touched her. She was the virgin of whom the Prophet had spoken: "Behold, we have a secret son, who with others has been changed. Behold, a virgin has conceived, the virgin that is called Apdorossa, that is, the sealed one, who suffers not others." Because her daughter was still unmarried, she had concealed her dowry beneath her feet, lest in the present war she should be deprived of her wealth by soldiers. But I was not to be deterred by her foul garments, but to choose her daughter from among all the rest for my beloved one, and the pleasure of my life. If I did so she would give me a lye with which I could cleanse her garments. Moreover, with her hand I should receive the flowing salt, the incombustible oil, and an inestimable treasure. She was about to declare this to me more in detail, when Solomon turned round, looked askance at me, and said: "I am the wisest of men, and my pleasant harem and the glory and the beauty of my queens excel the gold of Ophir. The ornaments of my concubines shame the rays of the sun, and the beauty of my virgins the light of the moon. My virgins are heavenly, my wisdom inscrutable, my mind past finding out."

Then I answered, while I bowed down to the ground with awe: "Behold, if I have found grace in your eyes—for I am lowly—give me that naked virgin whom I have chosen from among all, to preserve my life. Her garments are old, defiled, and foul, but I will purge them, and love her with all my heart. Let her be my sister, my spouse, since one glance of her eyes has stolen away my heart, and I am sick with love for her." On hearing this Solomon straightway gave her to me. With that there arose a tumult in the harem, which roused me from my sleep. Now I knew not what had happened to me; but I took it for some dream, and thereupon until the light dawned I was full of subtle thoughts. But when I had risen, and poured forth my prayers, behold, I saw the garments of the naked virgin lying by my bedside, and when I saw not her, my hair stood on end, and I was covered with a cold perspiration. But I took heart and recalled my dream, and endeavoured to remember whether it had been real or not. But seeing that my pondering could explain nothing, I would by no means look again upon the garments, much less did I dare to touch them. So I changed my chamber, and, out of sheer ignorance, left those garments lying there a long time. For I feared that if I touched them or turned them over, something remarkable would happen to me. Now the poisonous odour of the garments which I had inhaled in my sleep was so sickening that my eyes could not see the time of grace, or my heart understand the great wisdom of Solomon.

After the garments had lain five years in the chamber, I at length determined to throw them into the fire, and change my dwelling. In the night after I had formed this resolution, that ancient woman appeared to me in a dream, and rebuked with the following angry words: "Most ungrateful of mortals, the garments of my daughter, beneath which lie concealed those priceless jewels, have now been committed to thee for more than five years. Yet in all that time thou hast not cleansed or purified them, and now thou thinkest to burn them; is it not enough that thou art the cause of my daughter's death?" Then I answered, wrathfully: "How am I to understand thy words? Wouldst thou make me out to be a robber, though during those five years I have never seen thy daughter, or heard a syllable about her? How can I possibly be the cause of her death?" Here she took me up: "All this is true. Nevertheless thou hast sinned grievously against God, and on that account hast not received from me my daughter, or the lye of the Sages wherewith to cleanse her garments. For since thou wert from the very first horrified at the sight of my daughter's garments, the planet Saturn, her grandfather, was wroth, and changed her into what she was before her birth. Moreover, thou hast offended him by despising her, and being the cause of her death, corruption, and final destruction. She it is of whom Senior thus speaks: 'Woe, woe unto me! Bring me a naked woman, while my body was yet invisible, and I had not yet become a mother, till I should be born a second time; then I brought forth all the strength of the vegetable roots, and carried off the victory in my essence.'" These words sounded strange and mysterious to me, yet I manfully repressed my wrath, and solemnly protested that I knew nothing of her daughter's decease, and certainly had not been the cause of her death, corruption, and destruction; that I had kept her garments five years in my chamber, but had been prevented by my great blindness from understanding their use; and that I felt innocent before God and men. My excuse satisfied the ancient woman; she looked kindly at me, and said: "I see that thy conscience is pure from guilt, and for thy innocence thou shalt receive a great reward. Therefore, I will reveal to thee this matter faithfully, but secretly. My daughter, for the great love she bare thee, has left thee under her garments a grey box wrapped in a thick, black, mouldy cloth." With this she gave me a glass bottle full of lye, and continued: "Purge that box well of the dirt and bad smell with which the garments have infected it, and then thou shalt want no key, but the box will open of its own accord, and in it thou shalt find two things, viz., a white silver casket full of polished diamonds, and a rich robe intertissued with precious solar jasper stones. All these treasures belonged to my dear daughter, and she left them all to thee before she was transformed and perished. If thou wilt skilfully transpose this treasure, carefully purify it, and silently and patiently place it in some warm, moist, vaporous, and transparent chamber, and guard it there from cold, wind, hail, swift lightning, and all outward injury, till the season of the wheat harvest, thou shalt perceive and behold the great glory and beauty of thine heritage."

When she had thus spoken, I awoke, and devoutly prayed that God might grant me wisdom to find the box which had been described to me in my dream. Then I instituted a careful search among the garments, and was soon rewarded with success; but the cloth in which the box was wrapped was so hard and so firmly glued to it that I could not tear it off; moreover, I could not cleanse it with lye, or cut it with iron, steel, or any other metal. So I did not know what in all the world I should do, and began to think that it was a poisoned cloth, and to call to mind the saying of the Prophet: "Though thou wash thee with nitre and take thee much soap, yet thine iniquity is marked before me saith the Lord God."

So another year passed away, and still all my patient toil and thought had met with no success. At last, to drive away melancholy, I took a walk in a certain garden; and, after some time, I sat down upon a stone and fell into a deep sleep. I slept, but my heart waked. Then the ancient woman appeared to me once more, and said: "Have you entered upon the heritage of my daughter?" I sorrowfully replied, "I did indeed find the box, but I cannot remove the cloth, nor will the lye that thou gayest me avail to soften it." Then she laughed at my simplicity, and said: "Dost thou try to eat oysters or crabs in their shells? Must they not first be prepared by the ancient cook of the planets? I told thee to purify the grey box with the lye I gave thee, but not the cloth which is wrapped round it. The latter thou shouldest first have burned with the fire of the Sages." For this purpose she gave me some glowing coals, wrapped in a silk cloth, from which I was to obtain the subtle fire of the Sages, and told me that if with this fire I burned away the cloth I should get at the box. When she had ended, straightway there arose a north and south wind, and blew through the garden. Then I awoke again, shook off sleep, and beheld the glowing coals lying at my feet. I took them up with a grateful heart, and began to work day and night, remembering the saying of the Sages: "Fire and Azoth are sufficient for thee"; and the passage in Esdras (Bk. iv.): "And he gave me a goblet filled with fire, and when I had drunk it wisdom grew in me; and God granted me understanding, and my spirit was preserved, and my mouth opened, but nothing else was added." After forty nights I had finished 204 books, of which seventy were worthy to be read by the most wise, and were written upon box tablets. I thus continued in silence and hope, as that ancient woman had bidden me do, until at last, after a long time, my understanding, in fulfilment of Solomon's prophecy, became silver, and my memory gold.

When, in obedience to the directions of the ancient lady, I had skilfully placed the treasure of her daughter in a chamber by itself, and closed it up, I gazed upon those brilliant lunar diamonds, and solar rubies, and understood the meaning of Solomon when he says: "My Beloved is white and ruddy, the chiefest among ten thousand. His head is as the most fine gold, his locks are bushy, and black as a raven; his eyes are as the eyes of doves by the rivers of waters, washed with milk, and fitly set; his cheeks are as a bed of spices, as sweet flowers; his lips like roses dropping fragrant myrrh; his hands are as gold rings set with the beryl; his belly is as bright ivory overlaid with sapphires; his legs are as pillars of marble set upon sockets of fine gold; his countenance is as Lebanon, excellent as the cedars; his mouth is most sweet; yea, he is altogether lovely. This is my beloved, and this is my friend, O ye daughters of Jerusalem. Hold him, and suffer him not to go, till I have brought him into my mother's house, into my mother's chamber."

To these words of Solomon I could find no answer, and had already determined to take the treasure out of the chamber that I might at length enjoy quietness and peace, when I happened upon this other passage: "I charge you, O ye daughters of Jerusalem, by the roes and by the hinds of the field, that ye stir not up nor awake my love till he please. She is a garden enclosed; a spring shut up; a fountain sealed; a vineyard at Baal-hamon; a vineyard at Engedi; an orchard; a spice garden; a hill of myrrh; a mountain of incense; a bed; a crown; a palm tree; a rose of Sharon; a sapphire; a beryl stone; a wall; a tower, and battlement; a garden of herbs; a fountain in a garden; a spring of living waters; a daughter of princes, and the pleasant love of Solomon; she dearly loves her mother, and is her mother's chosen one; her head is full of dew, and her locks wet with the drops of night."

These words enlightened me, and shewed unto me the aim of the wise: wherefore I patiently left the treasure in the chamber, and waited till through God's mercy all should have been happily perfected by the operation of Nature, and the labour of my hands.

Shortly afterwards, on the day Of the new moon, an eclipse of the sun was seen, which was terrible to behold, for it began with a misty greenness, somewhat shot over with other colours, but it was followed by entire blackness; all heaven and earth were shrouded in thick darkness, and men were full of fear, but I rejoiced. For I remembered God's great mercy, and the Mystery of Regeneration, as Christ Himself told us that unless a grain of wheat was cast into the earth, and decomposed, it could bring forth no fruit. Now it happened that the eclipse was covered by clouds, and the sun began to shine, but as yet three-fourths of it were darkened. And, behold, an arm held out from the clouds a letter sealed at the four corners, on which was written: "I am black, but comely, O daughters of Jerusalem, as the tents of Kedar, as the curtains of Solomon. Look not upon me, because I am black, and burnt by the sun." Then there was seen a rainbow, and I remembered the Covenant of the Most High, and the faithfulness of my Teacher, and, behold, by the help of the planets and the fixed stars, the sun at last overcame the eclipse, and shone out once more in perfect brightness upon the mountains and valleys. Then all fear and terror were at an end, and all that had seen that day rejoiced in the Lord, and said: "Lo, the winter is past, the rain is over and gone; the flowers appear on the earth; the time of the singing of birds is come, and the voice of the turtle is heard in our land; the fig tree putteth forth her green figs, and the vines with the tender grapes give a good smell. Take us the foxes, the little foxes that spoil the vines, that we may gather the ripe grapes and drink wine, and be satisfied in due season with milk and the honeycomb." At the approach of evening the sky changed its aspect, and the Seven Stars rose with a lurid light, till, having completed their natural course, they paled and vanished before the Redness of the Sun. And, behold, the wise that dwelt upon earth awoke from their sleep, and gazed up to heaven, and said: "Who is it that bursts forth like the Dawn, beautiful like the Moon, mighty like the Sun, in whom there appears no spot? his fervour is kindled, and the flame of the Lord: Many waters cannot quench love, neither can the floods drown it. Therefore, we will not forsake her; she is our sister, though she be small, and have no breasts. We will take her back to the house of her mother, into the transparent palace where she was before, that by sucking the breasts of her mother, she may become great like the tower of David, strengthened with battlements, on which hang a thousand shields and all the weapons of the strong. When she went forth the daughters called her blessed, the Queen and the concubines praised her." But I knelt down, and returned thanks to God, and glorified His Holy Name.

EPILOGUE.

And now, my beloved Sons of Wisdom and the Doctrine, herein is the great Mystery of the Sages, in all the power and glory thereof, and the Revelation of the Spirit, concerning Whom the prince and monarch Theophrastus has these words, in his Apocalypse of Hermes: "He is the only God, and holds the whole world together; through Him alone can we be true, and truly vanquish the Elements, and, obtain the Quintessence. No eye has seen, no ear has heard, neither has it entered into the heart of any man to conceive that which is in thy. mind of this Spirit of Truth. In Him alone is truth, and through Him alone Adam and the other patriarchs, Abraham, Isaac, and Jacob, were enabled to secure constant health, and a long life, and to provide for themselves great wealth. Through this Spirit the Seven Sages invented the Arts, and gained riches. With His aid Noah built the Ark, Solomon the Temple, and Moses the Tabernacle; through Him vessels of pure gold were borne into the Temple; through Him Solomon gained his excellent knowledge, and performed mighty deeds. He enabled Ezra to restore the Law; Miriam, sister of Moses, to exercise liberality; and the Prophets of the Old Covenant to predict the future. He is the Sanctification and Healing of all things, the highest knowledge, the ultimate Mystery of Nature, that is to say, the Spirit of the Lord, Who fills the whole universe, and Who brooded over the waters in the beginning—without Whose secret teaching the world cannot be understood, and Whom the whole world desires on account of His power, while the Saints have sought and longed ardently to see Him from the beginning of the world. For He dwells in the seven Planets, raises the clouds, dispels the mist, gives light to all things, changes everything into gold and silver, imparts all health, abundance, and treasure, heals the leper,, cures dropsy and gout, prolongs life, comforts the sorrowful, restores health to the sick, removes all defects, and, in short, is the Mystery of all mysteries, the Arcanum of all arcana, the true healing and Medicine of all things. He gives the desired knowledge, and is the best of all sublunar things, by which Nature is strengthened, and the heart with all the members renewed, the flower of youth kept fresh, old age driven away, diseases destroyed, and the whole earth renewed. His Nature is unsearchable, His power infinite, His excellence and glory unapproachable.

"Moreover, this Spirit presides over all heavenly things, gives health, fortune, joy, peace, love, destroys every evil after its kind, puts an end to poverty and misery, renders men incapable of doing, saying, or thinking any evil, and gives to the godly temporal felicity, but to the wicked who abuse it, eternal punishment."

And thus, in the Name of the Holy Trinity, we will, in these few words, conclude our exposition of the Great Mystery of the Most Precious Philosophical Stone, and of the Arcanum of the Sages. To the Most High and Almighty God, the Creator of this Art, Whom it hath pleased to reveal to me, wretched, sinful man (in answer to my prayer), this most precious knowledge, be eternal praise, glory, honour, and thanksgiving; and to Him be addressed a most humble and fervent prayer that He may so direct my heart and mind, that I may not speak of this Mystery, or make it known to the wicked, lest I be found unmindful of my Vow, a Breaker of the Heavenly Seal, a perjured Brother of the Golden Cross, and guilty of the Sin against the Holy Ghost. From this may God the Father, God the Son, and God the Holy Ghost, the Blessed and Indivisible Trinity, in mercy PRESERVE ME. Amen, Amen, Amen.

THE SOPHIC HYDROLITH

OR,

WATER STONE OF THE WISE,

THAT IS, A CHYMICAL WORK, IN WHICH THE WAY IS SHEWN,
THE MATTER NAMED, AND THE PROCESS DESCRIBED;
NAMELY, THE METHOD OF OBTAINING THE
UNIVERSAL TINCTURE.

NOW PUBLISHED FOR THE FIRST TIME.

PRINTED AT THE PUBLIC COST FOR THE ADVANTAGE OF THE PUBLIC.

A BRIEF EXPOSITION

OF THE

WONDERFUL WATER STONE OF THE WISE,

COMMONLY CALLED

THE PHILOSOPHER'S STONE.

FROM the beginning of the world, there have always been God-enlighted men and experienced philosophers and wise Gentiles who diligently studied the nature and properties of the lower Creation. They laboriously endeavoured and fervently longed to discover whether Nature contained anything that would preserve our earthly body from decay and death, and maintain it in perpetual health and vigour. For by the light of Nature, and Divine revelation, they intuitively perceived that the Almighty, in His love to men, must have concealed in the world some wonderful arcanum by which every imperfect, diseased, and defective thing in the whole world might be renewed, and restored to its former vigour.

By the most diligent and careful search they gradually found out that there was nothing in this world that could procure for our earthly and corruptible body immunity from *death*, since death was laid upon the Protoplasts, Adam and Eve, and their posterity, as a perpetual penalty. But they did discover *one* thing which, being itself incorruptible, has been ordained of God for the good of man, to remove disease, to cure all imperfection, to purge old age, and to prolong our brief life—a boon actually enjoyed by the Patriarchs.

This wonderful remedy was industriously sought by the wise and under-standing, until they discovered it, and its precious virtue. Thus, the Patriarchs used it to restore their bodily vigour, and prolong their lives; and it was no doubt revealed by God to Adam, our thrice great parent, who bequeathed the secret to all the Patriarchs who were his descendants, who thereby procured for themselves length of days and boundless wealth. When the aforesaid Gentiles had received this knowledge, they justly regarded it as a most precious gift of God, and a most holy Art, and forasmuch as they perceived that, by God's providence, it had been revealed only to a few, and concealed from the majority of mankind, they always made it a point of conscience and honour to keep it secret.

But that the secret might not be lost, but rather continued and preserved to posterity, they expounded it most faithfully, both in their writings and in oral teaching to their faithful disciples, for the benefit of posterity; nevertheless, they so clothed and concealed the truth in allegorical language that even now only very few are able to understand their instruction and turn it to practical account. For this practice they had a very good reason; they wished to force those who seek this wisdom to feel their dependence on God (in Whose hand are all things), to obtain it through instant prayer, and, when it has been revealed to them, to give all the glory to Him. Moreover, they did not wish the pearls to be cast before swine. For they knew that if it were made known to the wicked world, men would greedily desire nothing but this one thing, neglect all labour, and give themselves up to a dissolute and degraded life.

But although the said philosophers have treated this subject with so great a variety of method, and used many peculiar and singular expressions, curious parables, and strange and fanciful words, yet they all agree in pointing out the same goal, and one and the same Matter as essential to the right conduct of the Art. Nevertheless, many students of the Art have entirely missed their meaning, and the secret Matter of which they speak. For at the present day there are (as there have always been) a large number not only of low charlatans, but of grave and learned men, who have sought this knowledge with unwearied industry, and yet have not been able to attain to it. Nay, some, angling with a golden hook, have utterly ruined themselves, and have been compelled to abandon their search in despair. Therefore, lest anyone should doubt the existence of this secret Art, or, after the manner of this wicked world, look upon it as a mere figment, I will enumerate some of the true Sages (besides those named in Holy Scripture) who really knew this Art, in the natural order of their succession. They are Hermes Trismegistus, Pythagoras, Alexander the Great, Plato, Theophrastus, Avicenna, Galen, Hippocrates, Lucian, Longanus, Rasis, Archelaus, Rupescissa, the Author of the Great Rosary, Mary the Prophetess, Dionysius, Zachaire, Haly, Morienus, Calid, Constantius, Serapion, Albertus Magnus, Estrod, Arnold de Villa Nova, Geber, Raymond Lully, Roger Bacon, Alan, Thomas Aquinas, Marcellus Palingenius; and, among moderns, Bernard of Trevisa, Frater Basil. Valentinus, Phillip Theophrastus (*i.e.*, Paracelsus), and many others. Nor is there any doubt that, among our own contemporaries, there might be found some, who, through the grace of God, daily enjoy this arcanum, though they keep it a close secret from the world. But, side by side with these great Sages who have written truly and uprightly concerning this Magistery, there are found many charlatans and imposters who falsely pretend to have a knowledge of this Art, and, by tricking out their lies in the phraseology of the Sages, throw dust into men's eyes, make their mouths water, and at length fail to make good their promises. Their dupes should well ponder the following warning: "Trust not him who distills gold out of your money-box. If you are wise you will be on your guard against such. If you would not suffer both loss and mockery, beware of these dishonest charlatans. Follow those who are simple, straightforward, and modest. He who has the good, enjoys it in silence." But where are you to find such? "Seek the good; you may know them by their excelling the rest in weight, matter, and performance." Now, since there are many students of this Art who would fain learn its secret by a true and straight path, and are yet so bewildered by these impostors and charlatans, by their empty talk and their high pretensions, that they do not know which way to turn: therefore I have determined briefly to expound the true principles of this Art. For though I account myself unworthy to speak of so great a Mystery, yet I may say, without any self-glorification, that, through the grace of God, I have made greater progress in this Magistery than most; and I consider it as my duty not to hide the talent which my Lord and Master, the great and good God, has committed to my unworthy keeping. For this reason I am willing to show the right way, by which they may attain a true knowledge of this subject, to all lovers of chemistry, and have put forth this Brief Epitome and Declaration of the Whole Art (so far as it may be committed to writing), in the hope that through my means, God may perchance open the eyes of some, and lead them back from their preconceived notions to the right path, and so manifest to them His mighty works. For the greater convenience of the reader I will divide the work into four parts.

In the First part I will set forth the rudiments of the Art, and the best mode of preparing oneself for its study.

In the Second I will shew and describe the quality and properties of the substance required, as also the method of its preparation and manipulation.

In the Third something will be said concerning the great utility of the Art, and its unspeakable efficacy and virtue.

In the Fourth will follow a Spiritual Allegory, in which this whole Magistery is set forth, being the true form of the Heavenly, Everlasting, and Blessed Corner Stone of the Most High. It will also contain a true, brief, and simple, practical manual of the method of proceeding, for I am no friend of many specious words.

PART I.

PSALM 25.

"Who is he that fears the Lord? He will instruct him in the right path."

In the first place, let every devout and God-fearing chemist and student of this Art consider that this arcanum should be regarded, not only as a truly great, but as a most holy Art (seeing that it typifies and shadows out the highest heavenly good). Therefore, if any man desire to reach this great and unspeakable Mystery, he must remember that it is obtained not by the might of man, but by the grace of God, and that not our will or desire, but only the mercy of the Most High, can bestow it upon us. For this reason you must first of all cleanse your heart, lift it to Him alone, and ask of Him this gift in true, earnest, and undoubting prayer. He alone can give and bestow it.

If the omnipotent God, who is the unerring searcher of all hearts, should find in you uprightness, faithfulness, sincerity, and a desire to know this Art, not for any selfish end, but for His true honour and glory, He will doubtless hear your prayer (according to his promise), and so lead you by His Holy Spirit that you will begin to understand this art, and feel that this knowledge would never have entered your heart if the most gracious Lord had not answered your petition, and revealed to you the understanding even of the most elementary principles.

Then fall upon thy knees, and with a humble and contrite heart render to Him the praise, honour, and glory due for the hearing of thy prayer, and ask Him again and again to continue to thee His grace, and to grant that, after attaining to full and perfect knowledge of this profound Mystery, thou mayest be enabled to use it to the glory and honour of His most Holy Name, and for the good of thy suffering fellow men.

Moreover, as you love your soul, beware of revealing the Mystery to any unworthy or wicked man, even in the smallest particular, or by making him in any sense a partaker thereof. If you in any way abuse the gift of God, or use it for your own glorification, you will most certainly be called to account by the Almighty Giver, and you will think that it would have been better for you if you had never known it.

When you have thus, as it were, devoted yourself to God (who is not mocked), and learned to appreciate justly the aim and scope of this Art, you should, in the first place, strive to realise how Nature, having been set in order by God the Triune, now works invisibly day by day, and moves and dwells in the will of God alone. For no one should set about the study of this Art without a just appreciation of natural processes. Now Nature may truly be described as being one, true, simple, and perfect in her own essence, and as being animated by an invisible spirit. If therefore you would know her, you, too, should be true, single-hearted, patient, constant, pious, forbearing, and, in short, a new and regenerate man.

If you know yourself to be so constituted and your nature adapted to Nature, you will have an intuitive insight into her working, such as it would otherwise be impossible to obtain.

For the study of this Art is such a perfect guide to excellence that a good knowledge of its principles will (as it were, against your will) hurry you on to an understanding of all the wonderful things of God, and teach you to rate all temporal and worldly things at their true value. But let not him who desires this knowledge for the purpose of procuring wealth and pleasure think that he will ever attain to it. Therefore, let your mind and thoughts be turned away from all things earthly, and, as it were, created anew, and consecrated to God alone. For you should observe that these three, body, soul, and spirit, must work together in harmony if you are to bring your study of this Art to a prosperous issue, for unless the mind and heart of a man be governed by the same law which develops the whole work, such an one must indubitably err in the Art.

When you are in inward harmony with God's world, outward conformity will not be wanting. Yet our artist can do nothing but sow, plant, and water: God must give the increase. Therefore, if any one be the enemy of God, all Nature declares war against him; but to one who loves God, heaven and earth and all the elements must lend their assistance. If you bear these things in mind, and know the true First Matter (of which we shall speak later on) you may at once set about the practical part of this study, calling on God for grace, direction, and guidance, so that your work may be carried successfully through all its stages.

ECCLESIAST. XI.

"He that abides in the fear of the Lord, and cleaves to His Word, and waits faithfully on His office, will transform tin and copper into silver and gold, and will do great things with the help of God: yea, with the grace of Jehovah, he will have power to make gold out of common refuse."

PART II.

ISAIAH XXVIII.

"Therefore, thus saith the Lord: Behold I lay in Zion for a foundation a Stone, a tried Stone, a precious corner Stone, a sure foundation. He that has it shall not be confounded."

The numerous writers on our most noble Art have never wearied of singing its praises, and inventing for it new and glorious names. Its most precious object they have called the PHILOSOPHER'S STONE, or the most ancient, secret, natural, incomprehensible, heavenly, blessed, beatified, and triune universal Stone of the Sages. Their reason for naming it a stone, or likening it to a stone, was this: First

51

because its original Matter is really a kind of stone, which, being hard and solid like a stone, may be pounded, reduced to powder, and resolved into its three elements (which Nature herself has joined together), and then again may be re-combined into a solid stone of the fusibility of wax by the skilled hand of the artist adjusting the law of Nature.

The importance of starting with an exact knowledge of the first or otherwise the second Matter of the Philosophical Stone has been largely dwelt upon by all writers on this subject. This Matter is found in one thing, out of which alone our Stone is prepared (although it is called by a thousand names), without any foreign admixture; and its quality, appearance, and properties have been set forth in the following manner. It is composed of three things, yet it is only one. Likewise, having been created and made of one, two, three, four, and five, it is everywhere found in one and two. They also call it the universal Magnesia, or the seed of the world, from which all natural objects take their origin. Its properties are of a singular kind; for, in addition to its marvellous nature and form, it is neither hot and dry like fire, nor cold and wet like water, nor cold and dry like earth, but a perfect preparation of all the elements. Its body is incorruptible, and is not destroyed by any of the four elements, but its properties far exceed those of the four elements, and the four qualities, like heaven and the Quintessence. With respect to its outward appearance, figure, form, and shape, they call it a stone, and not a stone; they liken it to gum and white water, and to the water of the Ocean. It is named the water of life, the purest and most blessed water, yet not the water of the clouds, or of any common spring, but a thick, permanent, salt, and (in a certain sense) dry water, which wets not the hand, a slimy water which springs out of the fatness of the earth. Likewise, it is a double mercury and Azoth which, being supported by the vapour or exudation of the greater and lesser heavenly and the earthly globe, cannot be consumed by fire. For itself is the universal and sparkling flame of the light of Nature, which has the heavenly Spirit in itself, with which it was animated at first by God, Who pervades all things, and is called by Avicenna, the Soul of the world. For as the soul lives and moves in all the members of the body, so that spirit lives and moves in all elementary creatures, and is the indissoluble bond of body and soul, the purest and most noble essence in which lie hid all mysteries in their inexhaustible fulness of marvellous virtue and efficacy. Moreover, they ascribe to it infinite Divine power and virtue when they say that it is the Spirit of the Lord who fills the Universe, and in the beginning moved upon the face of the waters. They also call it the spirit of truth that is hid in the world, and cannot be understood without the inspiration of the Holy Spirit, or the teaching of those who know it. It is found potentially everywhere, and in everything, but in all its perfection and fulness only in one thing. In short, it is a Spiritual Essence which is neither celestial nor infernal, but an aerial, pure, and precious body, in the middle between the highest and lowest, the choicest and noblest thing under heaven. But by the ignorant and the beginner it is thought to be the vilest and meanest of things. It is sought by many Sages, and found by few; suspected by those that are far away, and received by those that are near; seen by all, but known by few, as you may see from the following lines:

"Into three the great good is divided, yet it is one, and highly esteemed by the world. Men have it before their eyes, handle it with their hands, yet know it not, though they constantly tread it under their feet. It is the greatest wealth, and he who knows the Art may rival the richest."

AN ENIGMA OF THE SAGES,

In which the underlying substance of the Art, called the Phœnix of the Sages, is found to be thrice threefold.

"If I tell you three parts of a thing you have no cause to complain. Seek one of three, and of the three one will be there: for where there is body and soul, there is also Spirit, and there shine salt, sulphur, and mercury. Trust my word, seek the grass that is trefoil. Thou knowest the name, and art wise and cunning if thou findest it."

ANOTHER ENIGMA.

(Much easier.)

"There is one thing in this world which is found occasionally. It is bluish-grey and green, and, wonderful to say, there is in this thing a red and white colour. It flows like water, yet it makes not wet; it is of great weight, and of small. I might give it a thousand names, yet the thousand know it not. It is mean to look upon, yet to the Sage it is precious. He who solves it with the second and condenses it with the third, he has our glorious subject."

YET ANOTHER ENIGMA.

Everything contributes to the formation of this Stone. It is conceived below the earth, born in the earth, quickened in heaven, dies in time, obtains eternal glory.

Now when you have the substance indicated (which is in part heavenly, in part earthly, and in its natural state a mere confused chaos without certain name or colour), and know it well (for this knowledge the Sages have always accounted the principal part of this work), then you must give your whole mind to manipulating it in the proper manner. But before doing anything to it with his hands, the student should remember not to begin the preparation of this great and inscrutable arcanum before he knows well the spirit that lurks in it according to its essential qualities and properties. "With this spirit," says a certain philosopher, "you should not meddle until you first have a full and exact knowledge of it. For God is marvellous in His works, and He is not mocked. I could give some instances of men who set about this matter with great levity and were heavily punished by meeting (some of them) with fatal accidents in their laboratories. For this work is no light thing, as many suppose, perhaps, because the Sages have called it child's play. Those to whom God has revealed His secret may indeed find the experiment simple and easy. But do thou carefully beware of exposing thyself to great danger by unseasonable carelessness. Rather begin thy work with reverent fear and awe and with earnest prayer, and then thou wilt be in little danger."

Now when you have exercised yourself with exceeding diligence in the oratory, the matter being ready to your hand, go into the laboratory, take the substance indicated, and set to work in the following manner.

Above all things you must let it be your first object to solve this substance (or first Entity, which the Sages have also called the highest natural good). Then it must be purged of its watery and earthy nature (for at first it appears an earthy, heavy, thick, slimy, and misty body), and all that is thick, nebulous, opaque, and dark in it must be removed, that thus, by a final sublimation, the heart and inner soul contained in it may be separated and reduced to a precious essence.

All this can be accomplished with our Pontic and Catholic water, which in its refluent course irrigates and fertilizes the whole earth, and is sweet, beautiful, clear, limpid, and brighter than gold, silver, carbuncles, or diamonds. This blessed water is enclosed and contained in our Matter.

Then the extracted Heart, Soul, and Spirit must once more be distilled and condensed into *one* by their own proper salt (which in the interior of the substance is first of a blood-red colour, but then becomes of a bright, clear, and transparent white, and is called by the Sages the Salt of Wisdom). You have thus first, by what is called the anterior process, separated the pure from the impure, and first rendered the visible invisible, then, again, the invisible visible or palpable (but yet no longer so gross and shapeless as it was at first), and it is now a bright body with a pleasant, penetrating smell, and withal so subtle and ethereal that if it were not fixed it would evaporate and vanish away. For this reason the Sages call it mercurial water, or water of the sun, or mercury of the sun, or mercury of the wise. But so long as it remains in the aforesaid form it would, if used as a medicine, produce no good effect, but rather act as a poison. If, therefore, you wish to enjoy its glorious virtue, and manifold power, you must subject it to some further chemical processes

For this purpose you must diligently observe the working of Nature (extending over a considerable period of time), and strictly follow her guidance. When you have this knowledge, you should take two parts of the aforesaid prepared aqueous matter, and again three different parts. The first two parts you should keep; but to the three parts add another matter, viz., the most precious and divinely endowed Body of Gold, which is most intimately akin to the First Matter. Of this add one twelfth for the first fermentation; for both, the spiritual and heavenly prepared substance, and this earthly Body of Gold, must be joined together, and coagulated into *one* body.

But it should be noted that common gold is useless for this purpose, being unsuitable and dead. For though it has been declared by God the Omnipotent to be the most precious and beautiful of metals, yet so long as it lay hid in the mine its perfect growth and development was hindered. Daily use, moreover, blunts its indwelling powers, namely, sulphur, or its soul, and it is continually becoming mingled and defiled with other things that are foreign to its nature. Hence it becomes daily more and more unfit to be the subject of art. You must, therefore, seek to obtain gold which has a pure, living spirit, and of which the sulphur is not yet weakened and sophisticated, but is pure and clear (by passing through antimony, or by the heaven and sphere of Saturn, and being purged of all its defilement): otherwise the first substance, being spiritual and ethereal, will not combine with it. For this Magistery deals only with pure bodies, and suffers no unclean thing near, on, or around it.

Now when these unequal parts of the water and gold (differing not only in quality, but also in quantity, for the first is, after its preparation, ethereal, thin, subtle, and soft, while the other is very heavy, firm and hard) have been combined in a solutory alembic, and reduced to a dry liquid or amalgam, they should be left six or seven days exposed to gentle heat of at least a tepid character. Then take one part of the three parts of water, and pour it into a round, oval glass phial, similar to an egg in shape; put the tempered liquid in the midst thereof, and leave it once more for six or seven days; the Body of the Sun will then be gradually dissolved by the water. Thereupon both will begin to combine, and one will mingle with the other as gently and insensibly as ice with warm water. This union the Sages have shadowed out in various ways, and likened it, for instance, to the wedlock of a bride and bridegroom (as in the Song of Solomon). When this is done, add the third part (which you have kept) to the rest, but not all at once, or in one day, but in seven different instalments: otherwise the Body would become too liquid, and entirely corrupted by too much moisture.

For as seed, when cast into the ground, is destroyed and rendered useless by an excess of moisture and rain, so our work cannot prosper unless the water is judiciously administered. All this being done, let the phial be carefully closed and sealed, to prevent the compound from evaporating or losing its odour; and place it in the furnace, there exposing it to a gentle, continuous, airy, vaporous, and well-tempered heat, resembling the degree of warmth with which the hen hatches her eggs. [NOTE.—The Sages have said much about vaporous fire, which they have called the fire of wisdom, which is not elementary or material, but (according to them) essential and preternatural. They also call it the Divine fire, *i.e.*, the water of mercury, roused into action by common fire.] Digest and heat it well, yet take care that none of it is sublimed, or, in the parabolic language of the Sages, that the wife does not rule the husband, and that the husband does not abuse his authority over the wife, &c.,—if you do this, the whole will proceed normally, without any interference on your part (except that, of course, you must keep up the fire). At first the earthly Body of the Sun is totally solved, and decomposed, and robbed of all strength (the Body, which was first of a muddy impurity, changing to a coal-black colour, called by the Sages the Raven's Head, within the space of forty days), and is thus despoiled of its Soul. The Soul is borne upward, and the Body, being severed from the Soul, lies for some time, as if dead, at the bottom of the still, like ashes. But if the fire is increased, and well tempered, the Soul gradually descends again in drops, and saturates and moistens its Body, and so prevents it from being completely burned and consumed. Then, again, it ascends and descends, the process being repeated seven times. The temperature you must keep at the same point from beginning to end. Haste slowly—for it is of the greatest importance that the influence of the fire should be brought to bear gently and gradually. In the meantime you will observe various chemical changes (*e.g.*, of colour) in the distilling vessel, to which you must pay careful attention. For if they appear in due order, it is a sign that your undertaking will be brought to a prosperous issue.

First there appear granular bodies like fishes' eyes, then a circle around the substance, which is first reddish, then turns white, then green and yellow like a peacock's tail, then a dazzling white, and finally a deep red—until at last, under the rarefying influence of the fire, the Soul and Spirit are combined with their Body, that lies at the bottom, into a fixed and indissoluble Essence, which union and conjunction cannot be witnessed without unspeakable admiration and awe. Then you will behold the revivified, quickened, perfected, and glorified Body, which is of a most beautiful purple colour (like cochineal), and its tincture has virtue to change, tinge, and cure every imperfect body, as we shall hereafter show more in detail. When thus, by the grace and help of God, you have happily attained the goal of your labours, and found the Phœnix of the Sages, you should once more return thanks to Him with your whole heart, and use His unspeakable gift solely for His glory, and for the advantage of your suffering brethren. Thus I have most faithfully explained to you the whole process by which this most noble Art, and highest achievement, to wit, the Egg of the Sages, or Philosopher's Stone, may be begun and successfully completed.

If, however, during the operation, any accidental mishap should occur, it must be seen to in time, or else the chemical process will never be brought to perfection. If you (1) observe that before the compound is solved and turns black, anything is sublimed, or evaporated, or something resembling a red oil floats on the surface of the substance (which is a bad sign); or (2) if before or after it has turned white, it turns red too suddenly; or (3) if, towards the end, it does not properly coagulate; or (4) if the substance is so strongly affected by the heat that, being taken out, it does not instantly *melt* on *red hot iron* like *wax*, but tinges and colours the iron, and afterwards will not remain fixed in the fire—you may regard all these indications as symptoms of a false composition and temperature, or of some kind or other of carelessness.

If these defects are not immediately seen to, they will speedily become incorrigible. A cunning adept should be acquainted with the various devices by which they may be remedied; and I will recount them here for the sake of the beginner.

If one or more of the above defects are observed, the whole compound must again be taken out of the phial, and once more solved in the aforesaid water of mercury (also called virgin's milk, or the milk, blood, and sweat of the First Matter, or the never-failing fountain, or the water of life, which nevertheless contains the most malignant poison); with this water it must once more be moistened and saturated, and then subjected to the action of the fire, until there is no longer any sublimation or formation of gaseous vapours; or till the final coagulation has duly taken place, as described above. Of its subsequent fermentation and multiplication, and of its uses, more will be said in the third part.

Of the *time* required for the whole process, it is impossible to say anything very definite; and, indeed, the Sages have put forward the most conflicting opinions on this point—no doubt because some have been occupied with it longer than others. But if any man will carefully observe the working of Nature, and be guided by her teaching, and in all things hold a middle course, he will gain his object sooner than one that trusts too blindly to his own wisdom.

But I tell thee not to go beyond the middle point of the letter X either in the former or latter stage of the operation, but to take one half (V) for the time of the solution and the other half for the composition. Then, again, for the final union, the number XX should be thy guide (unless anything unforeseen should occur). Be satisfied with that space of time. On the other hand, do not try to hurry on the consummation, for one hour's mistake may throw thee back a whole month. If thou strivest unduly to shorten the time thou wilt produce an abortion. Many persons have, through their ignorance, or self-opinionated haste, obtained a Nihilixir instead of the hoped for Elixir.

In view of the importance of this magical science, I have thought it right to lay this before the sons of knowledge, for their careful consideration.

RIDDLE.

There are seven cities, seven metals, seven days, and the number seven; seven letters, seven words in order meet, seven times, and as many places; seven herbs, seven arts, and seven stones. Divide seven by three, and thou shalt be wise. No one will then strive to precipitate the half. In brief, all will proceed favourably in this number."

In the following lines the whole Process is briefly described:—

(I.)—THE FIRST STAGE.

"Dissolve your substance, and then let it be decomposed; then let it be distilled, and once more condensed."

(II.)—THE SECOND STAGE.

"Combine two things, decompose them, let them become black. Digest them and change them to white by your skill; at last let the compound change to a deep red, let it be coagulated, and fix it; and you will be a favoured man. If, afterwards, you cause it to ferment, you will have conducted the whole work prosperously. Then tinge therewith whatsoever you will, and it will multiply to you infinite treasure."

Or, more briefly, thus:—

"Seek three in one, again seek one in three. Dissolve, and condense, and thou shalt be master of the Art."

A Riddle in which also the Process is indicated:—

"A spirit is given for a time to the body, and that spirit is the life of a soul. If the spirit draw the soul to itself, they are both severed from the body. Then are there three abiding in the same place, until the precious body is dissolved, and is decomposed and dies. But after a time the spirit and the soul are brought back by gentle warmth, and hold once more their former seat. Then you have the essence; no perfection is wanting, and the work is glorified by a joyful end."

PROV. XXIII.

"My son, give me thy heart, and let thine eyes observe my ways."

PART III.

Sirach xliii: "Who has seen Him that he should tell of Him? Who can exalt Him according to His greatness? We see but the smallest of His works: those that are much greater are hidden from us. For God has made all, and gives understanding thereof to those that fear Him."

Concerning the end of this great Art, and the excellence, virtue, efficacy, and unspeakable utility of the marvellous Philosopher's Stone, much has been written: yet has no one been able to tell out its thought-surpassing glory or to adequately set forth its fame. All Sages have regarded it as the chief felicity that this earth can afford, without which no one can attain perfection in this world. For Morienus says: "He who has this Stone has all, and needs no other help." For it includes all temporal felicity, bodily health, and solid good fortune.

They have also commended the Stone for that the spirit and efficacy which lie concealed in it are the spirit of the Quintessence of all things beneath the disc of the moon; on this account they say that it upholds the sky, and moves the sea. They also describe it as the most elect, the most subtle, the purest, and noblest of all the heavenly spirits, to which all the rest yield obedience as to their King, that bestows on men all health and prosperity, heals all diseases, gives to the God-fearing temporal honour and a long life, but to the wicked, who abuse it, eternal punishment. It is also extolled by the Sages because it has never been known to fail of effecting its purpose, but is found to be in all proved, perfect, and unerring. Therefore Hermes and Aristotle call it the true, undeceiving, and unfailing arcanum of all arcana, the Divine Virtue which is hidden from the foolish. In brief, they have designated it the chief of all things under heaven, the marvellous conclusion or epilogue of all philosophic works. Hence some devout Sages have affirmed that it was Divinely revealed to Adam, and by him handed down to all the holy Patriarchs.

For by its aid Noah is said to have built the Ark, Moses the Tabernacle with all its golden vessels, and Solomon the Temple, besides accomplishing many other great deeds, fashioning many precious ornaments, and procuring for himself long life and boundless riches.

Moreover, the Sages own that through its means they invented the seven liberal arts, and sought and obtained sustenance for themselves. God gave them this gift that they might not be hindered in their researches by poverty, or driven to flatter the rich for the sake of gain, and thus become contemptible, and as a jest or by-word in His sight.

The Stone enabled them to discern the great mysteries of the Divine wonders, and the inexhaustible riches of the Divine Glory, By it their hearts were roused and stirred up to a more intimate knowledge of God. For they sought not to obtain great wealth, or the honour and pleasures of this world, but all their delight was to search out and contemplate the marvellous secrets of Nature. They regarded the works of God with very different eyes, and in a very different manner than most men in our own times, who, alas, look on them like cows or calves, and pursue the study of our noble Art for the sake of wealth, and temporal advantage and pleasure. But they will never find what they seek. For God gives not this gift to the wicked, who despise His word, but to the godly who strive to live honestly and quietly in this wicked and impure world, and to lend a helping hand to the needy brethren; or, in the words of the poet:—

"God gives this Art to the sincere and good, nor can the world purchase it with all its gold. The vulgar know nothing of this Mystery, for if any man be impious, he seeks the Stone in vain. He who holds it in silence dwells where he would, and fears neither accidents, nor thieves, nor any evil. For this reason this sacred gift is granted to few: it is in the hands of God, and He gives it to whomsoever He will."

Much has been said concerning the operation, virtue, and utility of this Art in a variety of writings which have heretofore seen the light, as, for example, unto what extent the said Stone, prepared and made more than perfect, becomes a medicine which is above every medicine. It has been denominated the universal panacea, to which not only all diseases yield (as, for instance, leprosy and gout), but by the use of which old men may become young again, recover their lost faculties, and their former strength, and by which those who are already half dead may be revivified and quickened. But, as I am no physician, I will forbear to give an opinion on this point. That the Stone has this virtue, every one that possesses it can discover for himself. I prefer to set down a few observations concerning those qualities and uses of the Stone which are known to me by daily experience.

In the first place, the practice of this Art enables us to understand, not merely the marvels of Nature, but the nature of God Himself, in all its unspeakable glory. It shadows forth, in a wonderful manner, how man is the image of the most Holy Trinity, the essence of the Holy Trinity, and the Oneness of Substances in that Trinity, as well as the difference of Persons; the Incarnation of the Second Person of the Holy Trinity, His Nativity, Passion, Death, and Resurrection; His Exaltation and the Eternal Happiness won by Him for us men; also our purification from original sin, in the absence of which purification all good actions of men would be vain and void—and, in brief, all the articles of the Christian faith, and the reason why man must pass through much tribulation and anguish, and fall a prey to death, before he can rise again to a new life. All this we see in our Art as it were in a mirror, as we shall take occasion to set forth in our Fourth Part.

Secondly, its earthly and natural use consists in changing all imperfect metals, by means of its tincture, into pure and solid gold, as I will try to show as briefly as I can.

The Stone or Elixir cannot be used for this purpose in the form in which we left it at the completion of the previous stage of our process; but it should be still further fermented and augmented in the following manner, as otherwise it could not be conveniently applied to imperfect metals and bodies.

Take one part of the Essence, and add to it three parts of purest gold, which has been purged and melted by means of antimony, and reduced to very thin plates. Let them be placed together in the crucible.

Thereupon the whole compound will be transformed into a pure and efficacious Tincture, which, when applied to base metals, in the ratio of 1 :: 1000, will change them into pure gold.

NOTE.—The purer the metals are, and the greater their affinity to our substance, the more easily are they received by the Tincture, and the more perfect and rapid is the process of regeneration. For the transformation consists in all that is impure and unsuitable being purged off, and rejected like dross. In the same manner flawed stones can be transmuted into precious diamonds, and common crystal can be so tinged as to become equal to the most precious stones. Moreover, many other things may be done with the Tincture which must not be revealed to the wicked world. These virtues of the Stone, and others of a like kind, are looked upon as the least important by the Sages, and by all Christians on whom God has bestowed this most precious gift. Such men think them vile indeed when compared with the knowledge of God and of His works which is afforded by the Stone.

For let me tell you that he on whom the Most High has conferred the knowledge of this Mystery esteems mere money and earthly riches as lightly as the dirt of the streets. His heart and all his desires are bent upon seeing and enjoying the heavenly reality of which all these things are but a figure; as Solomon, the wisest of wise Kings, testifies in chapter vii. of the Book of Wisdom, where he says: "I preferred wisdom before sceptres and thrones, and esteemed riches nothing in comparison of her. Neither compared I unto her any precious stone, because all gold in respect of her is as a little sand, and silver shall be counted as clay before her." Those, therefore, that desire this Art as a means of procuring temporal honour, pleasure, and wealth, are the most foolish of men; and they can never obtain that which they seek at so great an expense of money, time, and trouble, and which fills their hearts, their minds, and all their thoughts. For this reason the Sages have expressed a profound contempt for worldly wealth (not as though it were in itself a bad thing, seeing that it is highly commended in Holy Scripture as an excellent gift of God, but because of its vile abuse). They despised it because it seemed to hinder men from following the good and the true, and to introduce a mischievous confusion into their conceptions of right and wrong. These abuses of money the illustrious Marcellus Palingenius Stellatus has graphically described in the poem entitled the "Zodiac of Life," under the sign of Sagittarius, where he draws a vivid picture of the evils of avarice. To this poem I would therefore refer the gentle reader.

From this poem we may gather how lightly this distinguished man, though evidently a possessor of the Stone, as appears out of his "Zodiac of Nature," held gold and silver, and all things temporal, in respect of virtue.

Nor is his case by any means exceptional. All Sages have regarded wisdom, and the knowledge of heavenly things, as far better than the transient things of earth, and have so ordered their lives and actions that at the last they might obtain immortality and eternal glory. This feeling is well expressed by Solomon, in his Book of Proverbs (cp. xvi.), where he says: "How much better is it to get wisdom than gold! and to get understanding rather to be chosen than silver!"—and again in the xxii: chapter: "A good name is rather to be chosen than great riches, and knowledge rather than silver and gold." The same aspiration prompted the following words of the son of Sirach: "See that thou keep a good name, for it is better than a thousand treasures of gold."

By reason of these and other virtues which result from the philosophy of the Stone, the Sages have never wearied of extolling its marvellous excellence; and they have taken great pains to make it known to the worthy, in order that its wisdom might be accepted and practically exhibited by them. But to the foolish everything is obscure and difficult to be understood. This is the gist of the first six chapters of Solomon's Book of Proverbs, where he says that men should strain every nerve to attain to our wisdom. In the Book of Ecclesiastes, too, he uses the following words: "My son, be satisfied with a lowly station: for it is better than all that this world desires. The greater thou art, the more humble thyself, and God will give thee grace. For the Lord is a most High God, and does great things through the lowly."

PART IV.

PSALM LXXVIII. AND MATTH. XIII.

"I will open my mouth in parables, and declare things hidden from the foundation of the world."

When it pleases Almighty God by His Divine Word to make known unto the human race His marvellous, deep, and celestial mysteries, He is wont to do so in parables, and to shadow forth His meaning in things familiar to our eyes which are depicted visibly before us. For instance, when pronouncing upon Adam in Paradise, after the Fall, the sentence of death, He told him that as he was made and formed of dust, he should also return to dust—dust being a thing which in itself has no life. Again, when promising to Abraham an innumerable posterity, He illustrated His meaning by pointing to the stars of the heavens, the sand of the sea shore, and the dust of the earth. In the same manner, God made use of divers precious types in declaring His will to the children of Israel through the Prophets. This practice was also adopted in the New Testament by Christ Himself—the Foundation and Express Image of the Truth—who set forth His teaching in parables in order that it might be better understood. So He compares His Divine and Blessed Gospel—the highest happiness of man—to seed that is sown in a field, amongst which the enemy scatters evil seed; to a hidden treasure; to a pearl of great price; to a grain of wheat; to a mustard seed; to leaven, etc.

[Cp. Luke viii. Matthew xiii. and xxii. Luke xix. Matthew xx.]

The Kingdom of Heaven He describes under the image of a great Wedding Feast. The Christian Church, again, He compares to a Vineyard, and to a King calling upon his servants to render up an account. He also uses the similitude of a noble lord who entrusted his goods to his servants, of a lost sheep, a prodigal son, and others of a similar nature.

[Cp. Matthew xviii. Luke xvi. Matthew xxv. Luke xviii.

Mark xii. Luke xviii. Luke x.]

These types and similitudes were given to us on account of our human infirmity, which prevents us from understanding and picturing to ourselves the things of heaven. And since it is God's wont to reveal His mind in parables and figures, we can but regard it as of a piece with all the other dealings of God, that the Chief Good, His Son, our Lord and Saviour Jesus Christ, who by His obedience saved all mankind from eternal death and restored to us the Kingdom of Heaven, should have expressed His nature in a concrete bodily form. This is the greatest mystery of Almighty God, and the highest and worthiest object of knowledge.

[Ephes. iii. Col. i. Isaiah xlv.: *"Let the heavens drop down from above, and let the skies pour down righteousness. Let the earth open and bring forth the Saviour."*]

And although this great Good had been prefigured to us in the Old Testament by types such as the sacrifice of Isaac, the ladder of Jacob, the betrayal and wonderful exaltation of Joseph the brazen serpent, Samson, David, and Jonah; yet, besides all these, Almighty God deigned to give us a fuller revelation and a corporal, visible, and apprehensible Idea of His heavenly treasures and gifts in the Person of His Son. This earthly and bodily manifestation He plainly foretold in the Prophet Isaiah (cp. xxviii.): "Behold, I lay in Zion for a foundation a corner stone, a tried stone, a sure foundation: he that believeth shall not make haste." To the same effect the Royal Seer David speaks, through the Holy Spirit, in Psalm cxviii.: "The Stone which the builders rejected is become the head stone of the corner. This is the Lord's doing, and it is marvellous in our eyes." This type, the aforesaid Corner Stone, Christ applies to Himself (Matth., cp. xxi.) when He says: "Have ye never read in the Scriptures? The Stone that the builders rejected is become the chief stone of the corner. This is the Lord's doing, and it is marvellous in our eyes. And whosoever shall fall on this Stone shall be broken; but on whomsoever it shall fall it shall grind him to powder." And Peter (Acts, cp. iv.) and Paul in his Epistle to the Romans (cp. ix.) repeat almost the same words.

This tried, blessed, and heavenly Stone Jesus Christ was longingly expected from the beginning of the world by the Fathers and Holy Patriarchs; God-enlightened men prayed that they might be accounted worthy to see the promised Christ in His bodily and visible form. And if they rightly knew Him by the Holy Spirit, they were comforted by His presence in their lives, and had an invisible Friend on whom they could stay themselves, as upon a spiritual fulcrum, in trouble and danger even unto the end of their life.

But although that heavenly Stone was bestowed by God as a free gift on the whole human race, the rich as well as the poor (Matth. xi., 6.); yet to this very day comparatively few have been able to know and apprehend Him. To the majority of mankind He has always been a hidden secret, and a grievous stumbling block, as Isaiah foretold in his eighth chapter: "He shall be for a stone of stumbling and a rock of offence, a gin and a snare, so that many shall stumble and fall, and be broken, and be snared, and be taken." The same was revealed to the aged Simeon, when he spake thus to Mary, the Mother of the Corner Stone: "Behold, He shall be for a fall and rising again of many in Israel, and for a sign that shall be spoken against." To this S. Paul also bears witness (ad. Rom. ix.): "They fell from the Stone of offence, and the rock of stumbling. He that believes in Him shall not be confounded." This Stone is precious to them that believe, but to the unbelieving "a stone of offence and stumbling, seeing that they are broken against the word, and believe not in Him on whom they are founded (Eccl. xliii.)." In all these respects the Precious, Blessed, and Heavenly Stone agrees most wonderfully with our earthly, corporal, and philosophical Stone; and it is, therefore, well worth our while to compare our Stone with its Heavenly prototype. We shall thus understand that the earthly philosophical Stone is the true image of the real, spiritual, and heavenly Stone Jesus Christ.

Thus, then, those who would truly know and prepare the first Matter of the Philosopher's Stone (the chief and principal mystery of this earth) must have a deep insight into the nature of things, just as those who would know the Heavenly Stone (i.e., the indissoluble, triune essence of the true and living God) must have a profound spiritual insight into the things of heaven: hence we said in our first part, that the student of our Art must first have a thorough knowledge of Nature and her properties. If a man would come to know the highest good, he must rightly know, first God, and then himself (Acts xvii.: "For in Him we live," etc.). If anyone learn to know himself and God (i.e. our duty as men, our origin, the end of our being, and our affinity to God), he has the highest scholarship, without which it is impossible to obtain happiness, either in this world, or in the world to come.

If we would find that high and heavenly Stone, we must remember that, as our earthly Philosophical Stone is to be sought in one thing and two things, which are met with everywhere, so we must look for Him nowhere but in the eternal Word of God, and the Holy Scripture (consisting of the Old and New Testaments)—as God the Father testified at His Transfiguration on Mount Tabor (Mark ix., Luke ix.), when He said: "This is My Beloved Son: hear ye Him." In the same way Christ, the essential and eternal Word of God, speaks of Himself: "No one comes to the Father, but by Me"—according to the Scripture, the infallible testimony of the Divine Word (Isaiah xxxiv.). In Isaiah viii. we find the words: "to the Law and the Testimony." And Christ, the aforesaid Corner Stone, bears witness to the necessity of Scripture, when He says: "Search the Scriptures, for in them ye believe that ye have eternal life, and it is they that testify of Me." Therefore, David says in Psalm cxix., long before the coming of Christ: "My delight, O Lord, is in Thy commandments, for they are my counsellors; Thy word is a lamp unto my feet; I rejoice in the way of Thy testimonies more than in great riches. Also, I consider Thy ways, and walk in Thy testimonies."

[Cp. Gen. xiii. Psal. xlv. Isaiah ix., 49. Jerem. xxxii. John x., 14.
Rom. ix. I. Cor. v.]

Moreover, when and where the First Matter of this heavenly Stone was founded ("from the beginning of the world"), is expressly set forth in several passages of Holy Scripture, especially in the fifth chapter of Micah: "Whose goings forth have been from of old, from everlasting." When the Jews asked the Corner Stone Himself who He was, He answered: "I that speak to you was from the beginning," and again: "Before Abraham was, I am." From these passages it follows that He had His being, without a beginning, from all eternity, and that He will abide throughout all eternity.

And although this knowledge is to be found and obtained nowhere but in the Old and New Testaments, nevertheless he who would gain it must proceed with the greatest care (II. Timothy, iii.), for one false step may render all our subsequent labour useless. He who would gain a golden understanding of the word of truth, should have the eyes of his soul opened, and his mind illumined by the inward light (I. John, v.) which God has kindled in our hearts from the beginning; for he who strives to obtain this knowledge without the Divine light, may easily mistake Saul for Paul, and choose a false road instead of the right path. This happens continually in regard to our earthly Stone. Ten persons may read the same description of it, and yet only one may read the words aright. So the majority of mankind daily miss the knowledge of the Heavenly Stone; not because it is not before their eyes, but because they have not eyes to see it. Therefore Christ says: (Luke xi.) "The eye is the light of the body, and if the eye be dark the whole body will be full of darkness." In the seventeenth chapter of the same Gospel He says: "Behold the kingdom of God is within you." From these words it most clearly appears that the knowledge of the light in man must come from within, and not from without.

The external object, as they say, or the letter, is written for the sake of our infirmity, as a further aid to the implanted light of grace (Matth. xxiv.), as also the outward spoken word is used as an auxiliary means for the conveyance and advancement of knowledge. For example, if a white and a black tablet were put before you, and you were asked to say which was white and which black, you would not be able to answer the question if you had no previous knowledge of those colours; your ability to do so, comes, not from looking at the tablets, but from the knowledge that before was in your mind. The object only stirs up your perceptive faculty, and calls out the knowledge that before was in you, but does not of itself afford that knowledge. In the same way, if any one put into your hand a flint, and asked you to bring outward and visible fire out of it for him, you would be unable to do so without the steel that belongs to it, with which you would have to elicit the spark slumbering in the stone. Moreover, you would have to catch and fan it into flame on a piece of tinder—or else the spark would immediately vanish again. If you do this, you will have a bright fire, and so long as you keep it up, you will be able to do with it whatever you like. In the same manner, the heavenly light slumbers in the human soul, and must be struck out by outward contact, namely, by the true faith, through reading and hearing, and through the Holy Spirit whom Christ restored to us, and promised to give us (John xiv.: "No man comes to the Father but by me"), and to put into our dark, but still glowing hearts, as into a kind of tinder, where He may be fanned and kindled into a bright flame, working the will of God in our souls. For He delights to dwell in light unapproachable, and in the hearts of believers. Although no man ever has, or ever can, see God with his outward bodily eyes, yet with the inward eyes of the soul He may well be seen and known. But notwithstanding that inward light casts its bright beams over the whole world, and into the heart of every man without any difference, the world, by reason of its innate corruptness, cannot see it rightly, and refuses to acknowledge it; and on this account so many false and pernicious notions are current concerning it. But we shall do well to consider that God has, not without a good purpose, furnished our heads with two eyes and two ears; for He would thereby teach us that man has a double vision and a double hearing; namely, the outward and the inward. With the inward he is to judge spiritual things, and the outward is also to perform its own proper office. The same distinction we find in the spirit and the letter of Scripture. For this reason I thought fit to explain this matter for the sake of students of the simple sort, who might otherwise be at a loss to apprehend the full significance of the triune Stone.

Again, as the substance of the earthly Stone is nothing accounted of in the world, and rejected by the majority of mankind, so Christ, the eternal Word of the Father, and the Heavenly Triune Stone, is lightly esteemed in this world, and scarcely even looked at; nay, we may say that nothing is so profoundly and utterly despised by mankind, as the Saving Word of God. Hence (Cor. i., 2) it is called foolishness by the wise of this world. Nor is it only contemned and regarded as worthless; it is even proscribed and laid under a ban, like some false heretical doctrine, and it is grievous for a God-fearing man to listen to the blasphemous words that are spoken against it. But the believer must be tried by it, and the world sifted by its appearance. So S. John says (cp. i.): "He came unto His own, and they received Him not;" and again: "He was in the world, and the world knew Him not."

Again, as the physical and earthly water-Stone of the Sages has, on account of its unsearchable excellence, been called by a great variety of names by the multitude of philosophers, so the Heavenly Light, the one Noumen and Illuminant, whose riches and glory are past finding out, is designated in Holy Scripture by a large number of titles. We will go through the most important names of both. The Philosopher's Stone is called the most ancient, secret or unknown, natural, incomprehensible, heavenly, blessed, sacred Stone of the Sages. It is described as being true, more certain than certainty itself, the arcanum of all arcana—the Divine virtue and efficacy, which is hidden from the foolish, the aim and end of all things under heaven, the wonderful epilogue or conclusion of all the labours of the Sages—the perfect essence of all the elements, the indestructible body which no element can injure, the quintessence; the double and living mercury which has in itself the heavenly spirit—the cure for all unsound and imperfect metals—the everlasting light—the panacea for all diseases—the glorious Phœnix—the most precious of treasures—the chief good of Nature—the universal triune Stone, which is naturally composed of three things, and, nevertheless, is but one—nay, is generated and brought forth of one, two, three, four, and five. In the writings of the Sages we may also find it spoken of as the Catholic Magnesia, or the seed of the world, and under many other names and titles of a like nature, which we may best sum up and comprehend in the perfect number of one thousand. And as the earthly Philosopher's Stone and its substance have a thousand names, so an infinite variety of titles is even more justly predicated of the Chief Good of the Universe. For He is God, the Word of God, the Eternal Son, the real, eternal, tried, and precious corner and foundation Stone which the builders refused and rejected. He is true, and more ancient than all things seeing that He was before the foundation of the world, and from everlasting. He is the true, hidden, and unknown God, supernatural, incomprehensible, heavenly, blessed, and highly praised. He is the only Saviour, and the God of Gods (Deut. x.). Sure He is, and true, and cannot lie (Nu. xxiii., Rom. iii.). He is the only Potentate who does what He will, according to His good pleasure. He is secret and eternal, and in Him lie hid all the treasures and mysteries of knowledge (Rom. xvi., Col. ii.). He is the only Divine virtue and omnipotence, which is unknown to the foolish, or the wise of this world. He is the only true essence of all elements, seeing that of Him all things are and were created (Rom. ii., Ja. i.). He is the quintessence, the essence of all essences, and yet Himself not an essence of anything. He has in Himself the Heavenly Spirit which quickens ail things with life itself (Wisd. vii., Isaiah xlii., John xiv.). He is the one perfect Saviour of all imperfect bodies and men, the true heavenly physician of the soul, the eternal light that lights all men (Isaiah lx., John i.), the universal Remedy of all diseases, the true spiritual panacea. He is the glorious Phœnix that quickens and restores with His own blood His little ones whom the old Serpent, the Devil, had wounded and killed. He is the greatest treasure, and the best thing in heaven or upon earth, the triune universal essence, called Jehovah— of one, the Divine essence—of two, God and Man—of three, namely three Persons—of four, namely three Persons, and one Divine Substance—of five, namely of three Persons, one Divine, and one Human Substance. He is also the true Catholic Magnesia, or universal seed of the world, of Whom, through Whom, and to Whom are all things in heaven and upon earth—the Alpha and Omega, the beginning and the end, says the Lord that is, and was, and is to come, the Almighty (Apoc. i.).

But again, as in the case of the philosophical work, it is not enough for anyone to know its substance and its triune essence, with the quality and property thereof, if he does not also know where to obtain it, and how to become a partaker of its benefits—which can only be done, as we said above, by dissolving the substance into its three parts, decomposing it, and so depriving it of its caliginous shadow and hirsute essence, subliming its inner hidden heart and soul by means of the sweet, universal, fiery, marine water (extracted from itself) into a volatile essence--so we cannot know that glorious triune Essence, called Jehovah, unless the image of Him is first dissolved and purified in our own souls, the veil of Moses (*i.e.*, our own desperate sinfulness which prevents us from seeing God as He is) being taken away, and our inner heart and soul being purified, cleansed, and sublimed by the Divine illumination of Him that dwells within, namely, Christ, who washes our hearts like pure water (Isaiah xliv.), and fills them with His sweet and gentle comfort. So you first behold the wrath, but afterwards the love of God.

Once more: As our Matter, in the philosophical work, after being dissolved into its three parts or principles, must again be coagulated and reduced into its own proper salt, and into *one* essence, which is then called the salt of the Sages: so God, and His Son, must be known as One, by means of their essential substance, and must not be regarded as two or three Divinities, possessing more than one essence. When you have thus known God through His Son, and united them by the bond of the Holy Spirit, God is no longer invisible, or full of wrath, but you may feel His love, and, as it were, see Him with your eyes, and handle Him with your hands, in the person of Jesus Christ, His Son and express image. But even this knowledge of the Triune God will avail you little, unless you continue to advance and grow in His grace, for God otherwise will be still terrible, and as it is said of Him (Deut. vii., 18), "a consuming fire." For as the substance of the Sages, after all the changes that it has undergone, will do more harm than good as a medicine applied to the body, without the final preparation, so unless you fully and perfectly apprehend Christ, the mere knowledge of Him will tend to your condemnation rather than to the salvation of your soul (I. John, iv.). Therefore if you wish to become a partaker of Christ, and if you desire to possess and enjoy His heavenly gifts and treasures, you must advance in the personal knowledge of Christ, and look upon Him, not merely as a pure and immaterial Spirit, but as the Saviour who in the fulness of time took upon Himself a human body, and became the Son of Man, as well as the Son of God.

For as in our philosophical work another most noble and cognate metallic body must be united to our first substance (if it is to be rendered effectual for the perfecting of other metals), and joined together with it into one body, so the Divine Nature of the Son of God had to take upon itself, as it were, another kindred "metallic" body, namely our human nature, our human flesh and blood (which, having been created in the image of God, has the greatest affinity with Him), and to be joined with it into one indissoluble whole, in order that He might have the power of bringing imperfect men to perfection.

But again, we said that common gold, on account of its imperfection and impurity, would not combine with our substance, because its manifold defects had rendered it "dead" and useless for our purpose, and that, for this reason, it must first receive a bright and pure body (not adulterated or weakened by the presence of bad internal sulphur). In the same way, the Divine essence of the Son of God could not be joined to common human nature, which is conceived in sin, defiled with hereditary uncleanness, and many actual sins and besetting infirmities (though all these are no integral part of human nature as such), but required a pure, sinless, and perfect humanity.

For if the earthly Adam, before the Fall (though after all only a created being), was holy, perfect, and sinless, how much more must the heavenly Adam, to whom the only begotten Son of God was joined, have a perfect humanity? Therefore the heavenly, eternal, fundamental Corner Stone, Jesus Christ (like the earthly Philosophical Stone), is now One, uniting in Himself, after an inscrutable manner, a dual nature of admirable generation and origin, and the properties both of God and of man. For according to His Divine Nature, He is true God, of the Substance of His heavenly and eternal Father, and the Son of God, whose goings out (as the Scripture says) were from everlasting (Mic. v.). According to His human nature, on the other hand, He was born in the fullness of time as a true and perfect man, without sin, but with a real body and soul (Matth. xxvi.). Therefore He now eternally represents the indissoluble and personal union of the Divine and the human substance, the oneness of the natures of God and man.

It is much to be wished that the eyes of our self-opinionated doctors were opened, or the nebulous film, or sophistical mask, which obscures their vision, taken away, that so they might see more clearly. I am particularly alluding to the Aristotelians, and other blind theological quibblers, who spend their lives in wrangling and disputing about Divine things in a most unchristian manner, and put forth no end of manifold distinctions, divisions, and confusions, thus obscuring the Scriptural doctrine concerning the union of natures and communication of substances in Christ. If they will not believe God and His Holy Word, they might at least be enlightened by a study of our chemical Art, and of the union of two waters (viz., that of mercury and that of the Sun) which our Art so strikingly and palpably exhibits. But the scholastic wisdom of their Ethnic philosophy is entirely based upon pagan philosophy, and has no foundation in Holy Scripture or Christian Theology. Their Aristotelian precepts, their "substances" and "accidents," entirely blind them to the true proportions of things, and they forget Tertullian's saying "that philosophers are the patriarchs of heresy." But we do not think it worth while to pursue this subject any further.

Again, as our chemical compound (in which the two essences have been combined) is subjected to the action of fire, and is decomposed, dissolved, and well digested, and as this process, before its consummation, exhibits various chromatic changes, so this Divine Man, and Human God, Jesus Christ, had, by the will of His heavenly Father, to pass through the furnace of affliction, that is, through many troubles, insults, and sufferings, in the course of which His outward aspect was grievously changed; thus He suffered hunger when, after His Baptism and His entrance upon the ministry of the Word, the Holy Spirit led Him into the wilderness to be tempted of the Devil, and there waged with Him a threefold contest, as an example to all baptized Christian men, who, having declared themselves followers of Christ, are, like Him, tempted, and have to sustain the shock of various grievous assaults. Again, He was subject to weariness, He shed tears, He trembled, He wrestled with death, He shed drops of sweat mingled with blood, He was taken captive and bound, was struck in the face by the high priest's servant, was mocked, derided, spitted upon, scourged, crowned with thorns, condemned to die upon the Cross, which He had to bear Himself; was nailed to it between two malefactors, received vinegar and gall to drink, cried out with a loud voice, commended His spirit into the hands of His Father—and so gave up the ghost and died upon the Cross. These and other tribulations, which are faithfully related by the Evangelists, He had to bear in the course of His earthly life.

And as the Sages say that the above mentioned process of chemical digestion is generally completed within forty days, so the same number seems to have a most peculiar significance in Scripture, more particularly in connection with the life of our Lord. The Israelites remained forty years in the wilderness; Moses was forty days and forty nights on Mount Sinai; Elijah's flight from Ahab occupied the same length of time. Christ fasted forty days and forty nights in the wilderness; He spent forty months in preaching upon earth; He lay forty hours in the grave—appeared to His disciples forty days after His Resurrection. Within forty years from Christ's Ascension Jerusalem was destroyed by the Romans, and made level with the ground.

Then again, the Sages have called our compound, while undergoing the process of decomposition, the Raven's Head, on account of its blackness. In the same way, Christ (Isaiah liii.) had no form nor comeliness—was despised and rejected of mena a man of sorrows and acquainted with grief—so despised, that men hid, as it were, their faces from Him; and in the 22nd Psalm He complains that He "is a worm, and no man," "a scorn and laughing-stock of the people." We may also see an analogy to Christ in the tact that the decomposed body of the sun lies for some time dead and lifeless, like burnt-out ashes, at the bottom of the phial, and that its "soul" gradually descends to it under the influence of greater heat, and once more saturates, as it were, the dead and decaying body, and saves it from total destruction. For when, on the Mount of Olives, and on the Cross, Christ had experienced a feeling of utter dereliction, He was afterwards comforted and strengthened, and nourished (as it were) with Divine nectar from above. And when at length He had given up the ghost, and all the strength forsook His body, so that He went down to the parts below the earth, even there He was preserved, refreshed, and filled with the quickening power of the eternal Deity, and thus, by the reunion of His spirit with His dead body, quickened, raised from the dead, lifted up into heaven, and appointed Lord and King of all—where, sitting at the right hand of His Father, He now rules, governs, preserves, and quickens all things with the power of His Word. This marvellous Union and Divine Exaltation angels and men in heaven, upon earth, and under the earth can scarce think upon without holy fear, and trembling awe—Whose power, strength, and purple Tincture (*i.e.*, Blood) changes us imperfect men and sinners in body and soul, and is a marvellous medicine for all our diseases, as we shall see further on.

We have briefly and simply considered the most obvious analogies that serve to establish the typical connection between Jesus Christ, the heavenly Corner Stone, and our earthly Philosopher's Stone, and to illustrate its figurative resemblance to the Incarnation of the Saviour of men. We will now proceed to shew that the earthly Stone also shadows forth His transmuting, strengthening, healing, and quickening power towards us sinful, wretched, and imperfect human beings.

For though God created man at the beginning in His own image, and made him more glorious and perfect than other creatures, and breathed into him a living and immortal soul, yet by the fall the image of God was defaced, and man was changed into the very reverse of what God had intended that he should be.

But in order that we might be restored to our former glorious state, God in His great mercy devised the following remedy: As the perfect earthly Stone, or Tincture, after its completion extends its quickening efficacy, and the perfecting virtue of its tincture to other imperfect metals, so Christ, that blessed heavenly Stone, extends the quickening influence of His purple Tincture to us, purifying us, and conforming us to the likeness of His perfect and heavenly Body. For, as S. Paul says: (Rom. viii.), He is the first-born among many brethren, as He is also the first-born before all creatures, through whom all things in heaven and earth were created, and reconciled to God. If we who are by Nature impure, imperfect, and mortal, desire to become pure, immortal and perfect, this transmutation can be effected only through the mediation of the Heavenly Corner Stone Jesus Christ, who is the only holy, risen, glorified, heavenly King, both God and man in the unity of one Person.

For as the Philosopher's Stone, which is the Chemical King, has virtue by means of its tincture and its developed perfection to change other imperfect and base metals into pure gold, so our heavenly King and fundamental Corner Stone, Jesus Christ, can alone purify us sinners and imperfect men with His Blessed ruby-coloured Tincture, that is to say, His Blood, from all our natural filth and uncleanness, and perfectly heal the malignant disease of our nature; seeing that there is no salvation but in Him, and that no other name is given under heaven whereby men can obtain happiness and perfection.

The blind and insensate world has, indeed, through the craft and deceit of the Devil, tried many other ways and methods of obtaining everlasting salvation, and has toiled hard to reach the goal; but Christ nevertheless is and remains the only true Saviour and Mediator, who alone can make us appear just in the sight of God, and purify us from our spiritual leprosy—just as, upon earth, there is only one royal, saving, chemical Stone by which all imperfect metals must be brought to perfection and all bodily diseases healed (especially that fearful, and otherwise incurable leprosy). All other spiritual remedies—such as those invented and used by Jews, Turks, heathens, and heretics—may be compared to the devices of false and sophistical alchemists; for by them men are not purified, but defiled—not quickened, but enfeebled, and given over to a state of more helpless spiritual deadness. So the pseudo alchemists, or malchemists, as they may be more appropriately termed, discover many tinctures and colours by which men are not only deceived, but, as daily experience teaches, often ruined in fortune, body, and soul.

Again, if we men would be purified and cleansed of our original sin and the filth of Adam (in whom, through the subtilty of the Cacodæmon, our whole race was corrupted in the very Protoplast), we can obtain perfection and eternal happiness only through the regeneration of water and the Spirit, as the royal chemical substance is regenerated by water and its spirit. In this new and spiritual regeneration, which is performed in baptism through water and the Spirit, we are washed and purified with the Blood of Christ, united to His Body, and clothed with Him as with a garment (Col. iii., Eph. v.). For, as the Philosophical Stone becomes joined to other metals by means of its tincture and enters into an indissoluble union with them, so Christ, our Head, is in constant vital communion with all His members through the ruby tincture of His Blood, and compacts His whole Body into a perfect spiritual building which after God is created in righteousness and true holiness. Now, that regeneration which is wrought in baptism through the operation of the Holy Spirit is really nothing but an inward spiritual renewal of fallen man, by which we become God's friends instead of His enemies, and thus heirs of God and fellow heirs with Christ (i. Cor. ii., Rom. xii., Ephes. ii., Hebr. iii.). For to this end Christ died and rose again, that through this means, namely, through His passion, death, resurrection, and ascension, He might enter the Holy Place made without hands, and prepare for us the way to our everlasting Fatherland. Therefore, we, too, as His brothers and sisters, should follow His passion, and grow like Him in love, humility, and all other virtues, till we are conformed to His glorified body, and until, having lived and died with Him, we also reign with Him, and share His everlasting glory.

But this inward quickening and imitation of Christ, our heavenly King, in our daily lives, is not the outgrowth of our own merit or natural will (for by nature all men are blind, deaf, and dead, as to spiritual things), but is produced solely through the effectual working of the Holy Spirit, who dwells in us through the blessed laver of regeneration. In like manner, the minerals and metals are in themselves gross and dead, and cannot purify or ameliorate themselves, but are purified, renewed, dissolved, and perfected through the agency of the spagyric spirit. Now when we have been incorporated in the Body of our heavenly King, and washed and cleansed of original sin through His purple Tincture, and so rendered capable of bringing forth the first fruits of the Holy Spirit, we are fed up, like little children, and nourished with the pure and health-giving milk of grace, until at length we become living stones, fit for the heavenly building and the highest priesthood, which consists in offering up spiritual sacrifices such as are acceptable to God the Father, through Jesus Christ. For even a Christian, though regenerated through water and the Word, cannot grasp or apprehend all things at once, but must grow gradually, and daily, in the knowledge of God and of Christ.

For as, in our philosophical experiment, the union of the two essences, namely of the earthly gold and the heavenly prepared Matter, which have first been reduced to a kind of dry liquid, or amalgam, in a solutory alembic, does not take place all at once (seeing that the different parts are added gradually and at stated intervals), so we must expect the growth of the quickened spirit to be slow and gradual. For when the spiritual union of a man with Christ in baptism has once taken place, and he is united once for all with His Body, he must gradually advance in the Christian faith, and assimilate in his soul one article after another, until he has obtained perfect knowledge, and is firmly established in all the fullness of conviction.

Now the Christian faith, like the prepared aqueous substance, consists of twelve articles, according to the number of the Apostles, and these again fall into three principal sections, viz. (1) that which treats of our creation, (2) that which deals with our redemption, and (3) that which describes our sanctification. All these articles the Christian must, one by one, and little by little, make his own. He cannot master them all at once; for if too much spiritual nourishment were administered to him at a time, his soul might begin to loathe its food, and he might be entirely estranged from the faith. Therefore, the third article, for instance, should be divided into seven parts, and taught in seven different lessons (just as the matter was not put into the phial all at once). When a man has made the whole faith thoroughly his own, he must carefully preserve it pure from all corruption and falsification.

Moreover, in the chemical process, the Stone cannot bring its influence to bear on imperfect metals, unless it is first combined with three several parts of highly refined and purified gold, not because the tincture of the Stone itself is imperfect, but on account of the grossness of the metals which otherwise could not receive its subtle influence. The Stone itself is perfect; but the base metals are so feeble and dead that they cannot apprehend the angelical and spiritual perfection of the Tincture, except through the more congenial medium of gold, refined and fused through Antimony. In the same way, our heavenly King, Jesus Christ, has, through His obedience to His Father's will, once for all delivered us from sin and impurity, and made us sons and heirs of God; nevertheless, His saving Blood, the true purple Tincture, cannot he received by us, on account of our inborn infirmity and gross sinfulness, except through three media appointed by God for this purpose, namely:

(1), His Holy Word, which is better and purer than earthly gold seven times refined; (2), saving faith, which is a marvellous gift of God, comes through the Word of God, unites the hearts of men, and is tried in the fire of affliction; (3), unfeigned love towards God and our neighbour, which is also a gift of God, the fulfilment of the law, and a perfect imitation of God's nature. If we have and possess in a proper manner these three things, the Word, faith, and love, Christ can operate rightly upon us with his heavenly Tincture, and celestial Unction, make their blessed influence felt throughout our imperfect natures, and thus, by pervading our entire being, cause us to be partakers of His own heavenly nature. But Satan, that grim pseudo-alchymist, ever lies in wait to draw those whom Christ has regenerated, and made sons of God by faith through baptism, and who are warring the good warfare, and keeping faith and a good conscience, away from the right path—and in this attempt he and his faithful servants, our sinful flesh, and the wicked, seductive world, are, alas, very frequently successful (for even the just man falls seven times a day. Prov. xxiv.). For as he lay in wait for Christ, our Lord, Master, and Guide, and soon after His Baptism made a violent assault upon Him; so to the present day he spreads his crafty nets and pernicious snares in the Christian Church. Our Lord he first endeavoured to delude into doubting the Word of God, and questioning His Father's love, by pointing to the want, hunger, and bodily affliction, that God suffered Him to endure in the wilderness. But if Christians do not yield to this temptation, Satan attacks them on another point, and tries to induce them to place a foolhardy confidence (such as is not warranted by God's word) in their heavenly Father, just as he strove to persuade Christ to cast Himself down from the pinnacle of the Temple, seeing that God would surely protect Him. If this device does not succeed, the Evil One is not ashamed to try a third expedient: he promises us all the riches of this world, and the glory thereof, if we will forsake God, become idolators, and worship Satan himself—a proposal which he actually had the hardihood to make to Christ. These Satanic machinations God, in His inscrutable wisdom, permits, in order that men may thereby be exercised in faith, hope, patience, and true prayer, and prepared for the agony of death which the old man will one day have to undergo—that thus they may gain a final victory over their hereditary foe. This victory they will gain if they are taught by the grace of God how to encounter the Devil's deceitful and crafty wiles.

For since, as S. Paul says, we wrestle not with flesh and blood, but with principalities and powers, with the rulers of the darkness of this world, with the spiritual forces of wickedness in the heavenly places; we cannot successfully oppose our own strength to their spiritual assaults, but we must, after the example of our Standard-bearer, Jesus Christ, arm ourselves against our spiritual foes with spiritual weapons, such as the Word of God, and the sword of the Spirit. We must take from the armoury of the Holy Spirit the breast-plate of righteousness, and have our loins girt with truth, our feet shod with the preparedness of the Gospel of peace; and we must cover ourselves with the great shield of faith, with which we shall be able to quench all the fiery darts of the wicked one: for faith in Jesus Christ is a most strong shield which no weapon of the Evil Demon has power to pierce.

Again, we. saw that in our chemical operation the regulation of the fire, and a most patient and careful tempering of its heat, was of the greatest importance for the proper digestion of the substance. We also spoke of the "fire of the Sages" as being one of the chief agents in our chemical process, and said that it was an essential, preternatural, and Divine fire, that it lay hid in our substance, and that it was stirred into action by the influence and aid of the outward material fire. In like manner, the true Word of God, or the Spirit of God, whom Jeremiah compares to a fire, lies hid in our hearts, having been planted in our souls by Nature, and only defaced and obscured by the fall. This spirit must be aided, roused into action, and fanned into a bright flame, by another outward fire, viz., the daily fire of godliness, the exercise of all the Christian virtues in good days and in evil, and the study of the pure Divine Word, if, indeed, the internal light of grace, or the Spirit of God, is to work in us, instead of being extinguished. For as an earthly craftsman polishes iron, which in itself is cold, till it is heated by continual friction, and as a lamp must go out if it is not constantly fed with oil; so the inward fire of man, unless it is assiduously kept up, gradually begins to burn low, and is at length completely extinguished. Therefore it is indispensable for a Christian diligently to hear, carefully to study, and faithfully to practice the Word of God.

Again, what we said of spiritual sight, viz., that it must take place not with the outward eyes of the body, but with the inward eye of the soul, is equally applicable to spiritual hearing. I speak of listening, not to the outward speech of men, or to the Pharisaic leaven of the new Scribes, which nowadays, alas, is substituted for the sincere and unadulterated Word of God, but to the Voice of God Himself. I speak of the thrice refined Word of God (Psalm cxix.), which proceeds out of the mouth of God, and is declared by His Holy Spirit—which is not, as these false teachers presumptuously assert, a vain and empty sound, but the Spirit, the life, and the saving power of God to all that believe. Of it the Royal Seer David speaks as follows: "I will hear what the Lord shall say unto me." Of this inward and Divine hearing of the Word of God, as from a kind of fountainhead, good and living faith, which works by love, takes its source. For it is, as S. Paul says (Rom. x.): "Faith comes by hearing, and hearing by the Word of God."

Now if the Word is pure and undefiled, the hearing, too, may be pure and undefiled, and the faith which comes of such hearing will also be true, and show itself by love and humble obedience to the will of God in prayer, praise, and thanksgiving. It will also find expression in all good works towards our neighbour. To the exercise of this love Christ exhorts us in His long valedictory discourse (John xiii.), and leaves it with us as His farewell saying: "This is my commandment that ye love each other, even as I also loved you." "If any one say, I know God, and love not his brother, he is a liar, and the truth is not in him. But he who keeps the Word of God, in him the love of God is perfected" (I. John, ii.). And again (I. John, iv.): "God is love, and he that abides in love abides in God, and God in him." From these passages we learn that love is the bond of perfection by which we are united to Christ, and by which we are in Him, He in His Father, and His Father in Him. "If any one," says Christ, "will keep my word, this is he that loves me, and I will love him, and we will come to him and take up our abode with him." Again: "If ye keep my commandments, ye shall abide in my love." But this our love to God must also find expression towards our neighbour. For "if any one love not his brother whom he has seen, how can he love God, whom he has not seen? And this commandment we have of Him, that he that loves God love his brother also." The nature of this love is described by S. Paul (i. Cor. xiii.) in the following words: "Love suffereth long, and is kind; love envieth not; love vaunteth not itself, is not puffed up, and never fails." Hence it appears that there is no true love which does not show itself in works of kindness towards our fellow men; and hence also it appears that the good works which are acceptable to God cannot precede faith, but are its outgrowth and precious fruit; works do not make faith good and acceptable, but it is faith that gives their real value to works—for we are justified and obtain eternal life by faith alone. And if a regenerate man bear himself thus lovingly and humbly in all his life, he will never lack fruit in due season. For such a man is placed by God in the furnace of affliction, and (like the hermetic compound) is purged with the fire of suffering until the old Adam is dead, and there arises a new man created after God in righteousness and true holiness, as S. Paul says (Rom. vi.): "We are buried with Christ by baptism into death, that like as Christ was raised up from the dead, even so we also should walk in newness of life." When this has been accomplished, and a man is no longer under the dominion of sin, then there begins in him something analogous to the solution of the gold added to the substance of our chemical process. The old nature is destroyed, dissolved, decomposed, and, in a longer or shorter period of time, transmuted into something else. Such a man is so well digested and melted in the fire of affliction that he despairs of his own strength and looks for help and comfort to the mercy of God alone. In this furnace of the Cross, a man, like earthly gold, attains to the true black Raven's Head, *i.e.*, loses all beauty and reputation in the eyes of the world; and that not only during forty days and nights, or forty years, but often during his whole life, which is thus often more full of sorrow and suffering than of comfort and joy. And, through this spiritual dying, his soul is taken from him, and lifted upon high; while his body is still upon earth, his spirit and heart are already in his eternal Fatherland; and all his actions have a heavenly source, and seem no longer to belong to this earth. For he lives no longer according to the flesh, but according to the Spirit, not in the unfruitful works of darkness, but in the light and in the day—in works that stand the test of fire. This separation of body and soul is brought about by a spiritual dying. For as the dissolution of body and soul is performed in the regenerated gold, where body and soul are separated from one another, and yet remain close together in the same phial, the soul daily refreshing the body from above, and preserving it from final destruction, until a set time: so the decaying and half-dead bodily part of man is not entirely deserted by its soul in the furnace of the Cross, but is refreshed by the spirit from above with heavenly dew, and fed and preserved with Divine nectar. (For our temporal death, which is the wages of sin, is not a real death, but only a natural and gentle severing of body and soul). The indissoluble union and conjunction of the Spirit of God, and the soul of the Christian, are a real and abiding fact. And here again we have an analogy to the (sevenfold) ascending and descending of the soul in the chemical process. For the tribulations and temporal sufferings of God's people have now lasted six thousand years; but during this whole time, men have again and again been refreshed, comforted, and strengthened by the Spirit of God—and so it is now, and ever will be, until the great universal Sabbath and rest-day of the seventh millennium. Then this occasional spiritual refreshing will cease, and everlasting joy will reign, since God will be all in all.

While the digestion of the dead spiritual body in man goes forward, there may be seen (as in the chemical process) many variegated colours and signs, *i.e.*, all manner of sufferings, afflictions, and tribulations, including the ceaseless assaults of the Devil, the world, and the flesh. But all these signs are of good omen, since they show that such a man will at length reach the desired goal. For Scripture tells us that all that are to obtain the eternal beatitude of Christ must be persecuted in this world, and we must enter into the kingdom of heaven through much tribulation and anguish. This truth is well expressed in the following words of S. Augustine: "Marvel not, brother, if after becoming a Christian you are assailed by many troubles. For Christ is our Head, and, as His members, we must follow and imitate, not only Him, but His life and sufferings. The life of Christ was closely beset with all manner of tribulations, poverty, insult, mockery, scorn, sorrow, and acute bodily suffering; and it is clear that if you would obtain the life of Christ, you must, like Him, become perfect through suffering. For without these afflictions and tribulations we cannot come to God. A man who would enter Paradise must go through fire and water, whether he be Peter, to whom the keys of heaven were entrusted, or Paul, a chosen vessel of God, or John, to whom all the secrets of God were revealed. Every brother must enter the kingdom of heaven through much tribulation."

It should further be observed that the Antimony of the Sages with which the gold must be refined before being added to the Elixir, or royal chemical substance (or before undergoing a sudatory bath with ancient grey-headed Saturn) is expressed by the sign ♁. In the same way, a ball with a cross upon it is put into the hands of the Lord of the Holy Roman Empire, whereby it is indicated that he, too, must experience, and be tried by the tribulations of this world, before he can be peacefully seated upon his throne. To all this we may find an analogy in the aforesaid School of the Cross, and the tribulations and persecutions through which all Christians must pass, and the struggle which they must wage with grey-headed Saturn, that is to say, the old Adam and Satan, before they can enter into everlasting joy and rest.

Besides the aforesaid sorrows and afflictions, there are also in this world certain signs and marvels, and great mundane revolutions, which we must diligently consider and perpend. We must first hear of wars, and rumours of wars, various sects, plagues, and famines; for all these things are the true forerunners and heralds of our redemption. Then must come the general resurrection of the dead, by which those who obtain the victory through the Blood of the Lamb (for this second regeneration is begun and rendered possible by their first regeneration in this life) pass into a new and unending life through the final indissoluble union of their bodies, souls, and spirits. For by the power and effectual working of Christ, our almighty heavenly King (to whom we are joined in a supernatural manner by faith), we shall be endued with pure spiritual health, strength, glory, and excellence. This marvellous union of body, soul, and spirit, this Divine glorification and exaltation of the elect, is a consideration fraught with reverential and unspeakable awe (like the sight of the final chemical transformation); it is a sight at which the very angels will stand rapt in inexpressible wonder; and then they will see us pass into the heavens to reign with Christ, and with them, and the ministering spirits, in everlasting glory, and joy unspeakable, world without end.

To conclude—as, in our chemico-philosophical process, it was possible and necessary to correct at once any defect or irregularity, since otherwise the whole compound would be corrupted and rendered useless; so, in the Christian life, every fault must at once be carefully corrected, and put away, lest it afford a loophole for Satan, the world, and the flesh, to creep in again, and to cause in us, so to speak, a pernicious sublimation, or a premature redness (corresponding to the first and second chemical defects), or to make us despair of God's mercy when we consider our many grievous sins, or to stir up in us a spirit of murmuring against the great furnace heat of God's discipline (which two latter failings correspond to the third and fourth chemical defects). If any of these unfortunate accidents happen to our souls, they must be dissolved again (after the analogy of the chemical compound), by repentance, by the solutory key of holy Absolution, and thus, as often as is required, be purged of sin and post-baptismal defilement by Absolution, as well as by the pure heavenly milk of the Lord's Supper, which is the sweat of the heavenly Lamb, and water and blood, the fountain of life—which (like the mercurial water of the chemical process) is, to the unworthy and wicked, the most deadly poison, but food, drink, and a source of strength to the repentant believer. Thus he may still attain to what corresponds to the final coagulation and perfect chemical condensation, namely, to the heavenly perfection of eternal beatitude. These two most wholesome remedies for post-baptismal sin (viz., Absolution and the Lord's Supper), God in his mercy has ordained, and entrusted to the keeping of His most Beloved Church, for the healing of repentant Christian men. Through her, we are either, by absolution, pronounced free from guilt, or, if we remain impenitent, and persist in our wicked course, we are, by excommunication, delivered over to Satan, that by the destruction of the flesh, our souls may be saved in the day of the Lord Jesus.

EPILOGUE.

Thus, gentle and well-wishing reader, I have briefly and simply set forth to you the perfect analogy which exists between our earthly and chemical and the true and heavenly Stone, Jesus Christ, whereby we may attain unto certain beatitude and perfection, not only in earthly but also in eternal life. I might have done so more grandly and copiously; but you must know that I am neither a theologian, nor, according to the modern fashion, an Aristotelico-theologian, but a simple and unsophisticated layman. For the knowledge which God has committed to me, I have obtained, not at any learned academy, but in the universal school of Nature, and by perusing the open book of God. For this reason I have expressed my thoughts simply, and not tricked them out in sesquipedalian words, as is the manner of professional theologians; nor do I pretend to have exhausted the subject; all that I have done is to throw out some hints for the guidance of those who wish to investigate it more carefully. In doing my best, I have also endeavoured to do my duty; for every lover of the truth is bound to praise God by revealing the knowledge entrusted to him. Besides all this, I desired to profess publicly my belief in the true Christian faith; since at the present time many devout and godly Christians are falsely represented and decried by lying slanderers as heretics. Let not the blasphemies and reckless judgment of the wicked world trouble the true Christian, against whom they are directed; for the Devil and his servants have at all times done to the followers of Christ what they did to Christ Himself. Therefore I will say no more on this subject, but I will leave it to be decided by the Judge of all the world.

As to the earthly Stone itself I must ask the reader to study diligently what has gone before in our treatise as to this subject. For as in an excellent poem a verse is sometimes repeated at least once, so on this point we are accustomed to do the same, because the reader ought not to direct his aims and thoughts to the earthly Philosophical Stone until he has attained a right knowledge of the Celestial Stone, and has prepared it, or, at least, has commenced with the utmost zeal the preparations of both together. For the earthly Stone is a gift from God, descending by the clemency of the Celestial Stone. I agree with all the Sages that it would be folly to attempt the study of so profound a mystery without a good previous knowledge of Nature and her properties. But I also say that it is not merely difficult, but quite impossible, to prepare the Philosopher's Stone without a true knowledge of Christ, the heavenly Corner Stone, in whom all Nature lives and moves, and has its being. This warning should be duly considered; and he who would not expose himself to the certainty of ignominious failure, should reflect that the mastery of any art requires persevering exercise, and that, before setting about this search after the Philosopher's Stone, he must prepare himself by careful and patient study. If any neglect this warning, his failure will be the result of his own ignorance and mental immaturity.

But I wonder still more that there are to be found some men, who not only study this Art, but even try to practice it, and yet do not quite know whether it proceeds by natural and legitimate magic, or whether it is not after all a necromantic, or black art, which is exercised by the illegitimate aid of the powers of hell. No, my good friend. The Devil, wicked angels, and wicked men, have no power but that which God suffers them to possess—and with our present glorious Art they positively have nothing whatever to do. It is entirely in the hand of God, who imparts it to whom He will, and takes it away from whom He will; and He does not suffer any votaries of pleasure, or evil spirits, to partake of it. He gives it only to the pure, true, and humble of heart. This excellence is neither known, nor understood, by the majority of the present generation; and when the sound of it strikes upon their ears, and they do not comprehend it, they straightway call it foolishness. On account of this their blindness, that spirit will always be hidden from their minds, and will at length be entirely taken away from them.

Let me, however, be permitted to impress one thing on the minds of my pious and devout readers. In so far as a man orders his life, soul, heart, and actions aright in the sight of God, in so far will he perceive that he is making good progress in the discovery, preparation, and use of the Stone. This assertion is the result of my own personal experience during many years, and it embodies my deliberate conviction. Therefore, the best preparation for this study is, in my judgment, a diligent amendment of heart and life.

I am aware that I here lay myself open to the objection that it is possible to enumerate several men who actually possessed this Stone, or Tincture, and with it transmuted base metals into gold and silver; and who yet were not good men, but vain, profligate, and without knowledge of God. To this objection, I answer that from whencesoever these men may have obtained the Tincture, I certainly never will believe that they prepared it—i.e., the true and right Tincture—themselves. The tragic end of many of these men, and the headlong destruction brought upon them by their Tincture, prove but too clearly the truth of what I say. Moreover, all that call themselves alchemists are not therefore necessarily true possessors of the Stone. For, as in other branches of knowledge, there are found many different schools and sects, so all that are in search of this precious Tincture are called alchemists, without necessarily deserving the name.

In this tract I have spoken of true, natural, and scientific alchemy, which teaches us to distinguish the evil and impure from the good and pure, and thus, to aid the weakness, and correct the corruption, of Nature. We help the metals to arrive at maturity, just as a gardener may assist fruit, which by some accident is prevented from ripening, or as a seed or grain of corn may easily be multiplied by being sown in the ground. Of pseudo-alchemy I neither pretend, nor care, to know anything, because I perceive that the ways of its teachers are crooked, and that they promise mountains of gold, without being able to redeem the least part of their pledge; I also see that those who follow them incur great expense, ceaseless toil, and are often ruined in body and soul. Therefore, if you encounter alchemists of this description, who speak boastfully of their Art, and offer to teach it you for money, I warn you to be on your guard against them. For with such men there is mostly a serpent lurking in the grass (Mic. ii.).

I think I may confidently assert that the cost of preparing the Tincture (apart from your own daily maintenance, and the fuel required) does not exceed three florins. For the Matter, as has already been said, is for most part, very common, and may be everywhere obtained in abundance; and the labour is easy and simple. In brief, the whole design can present no difficulty whatever to those whom God has chosen for this purpose, i.e., to those who love Him; but to the wicked it is beset with insuperable impediments. In conclusion, let me tell you that if God in His gracious mercy should vouchsafe to reveal to you this open secret, it will then become your sacred duty to use it well, and to conceal your knowledge from the unworthy, to put a seal upon your lips, and to preserve unbroken silence about it. If you neglect this well-meant warning, you may bring upon yourself the anger of God, and persecutions of wicked men, and be justly punished with temporal and eternal ruin.

> "If any one seek riches by means of this sacred Art, let him
> be devout, and simple-hearted, silent, and wise. He who
> strives not after these virtues, will receive the opposite of
> that which he desires: he will be poor, needy, naked and
> wretched."

All this, beloved Reader, I desired to enjoin upon you as a farewell admonition. I devoutly hope that God has opened your eyes, and that you have completely apprehended my meaning. To explain the matter more clearly and openly than I have done, I am forbidden by my vow. I can only ask you once more to peruse this treatise carefully, and to ask God to enlighten your understanding.

APPENDIX.

If, after obtaining this knowledge, you give way to pride or avarice (under the pretext of economy and prudence), and thus gradually turn away from God, the secret will most certainly fade out of your mind in a manner which you do not understand. This has actually happened to many who would not be warned.

RECAPITULATORY LINES.

"If you will follow my teaching, and if you are a devout Christian man, you may take the substance which I have before indicated, and, by following the directions I have given, you may possess all the riches of the whole world."

To this end—if you are worthy—may God in His mercy vouchsafe you His blessing. This prayer I offer up for you from the bottom of my heart.

PRAYER.

Almighty, everlasting God, Father of heavenly light, from Whom proceed all good and perfect gifts: we pray Thee, of Thine infinite mercy, to reveal to us Thine eternal wisdom, which is evermore about Thy throne, and by which all things were created and made, and are still governed and preserved: send it down to us from heaven, and from the throne of Thy glory, that it may be with us, and work with us, seeing that it is the teacher of all heavenly and secret arts, and knows and understands all things. Let it accompany us in all our works, that by Thy Spirit we may attain a true understanding and certain knowledge of this Blessed Art, and of the marvellous Stone of the Sages, which Thou art wont to reveal only to Thine elect, and hast concealed from the world. And so further us with Thy wisdom, that we may begin, continue, and complete this work without any error, and enjoy its fruits for ever with great joy—through the Heavenly and Eternal Foundation and Corner Stone, Jesus Christ, Who with Thee and the Holy Spirit liveth and reigneth, ever One God, world without end. Amen.

Joshua xxi., 43-44.

"And the Lord gave unto Israel all the land which He sware to give unto their fathers; and there failed not aught of any good thing which the Lord had spoken unto the house of Israel; all came to pass."

Deuteronomy xxxii., 3.

"Ascribe the Glory unto God Alone!"

AMEN.

EPIGRAM.

"It is an easy matter to prepare gold in the furnace out of metals: at times there is found a man to whom the secret is revealed. Why is not every alchemist rich? The reason is that one thing is wanting which many seek with anxious care. Common gold is not fixed, and, when brought to the test of fire, quickly disappears and perishes. But he who knows the fixed gold, which at all times remains the same, and from which nothing is lost, he is the possessor of the true Art, and may be called a good and practical Sage and Chemist."

ANOTHER EPIGRAM.

"Theology without alchemy is like a noble body without its right hand. This is graphically shewn and exhibited in the picture before us. First look at the helmet and the two wings, which signify the love of the Art. They bear us onward to

Sophia (Wisdom), who is bright like Phœbus. Her body is naked because she is ardently loved. She is loved because she has at her disposal the riches of the whole world. He that gazes upon her beauteous form cannot refrain himself from loving her, goddess as she is. Although this love is, as it were, hidden, yet it is constant; and that is indicated by the mask. Her heart is sincere, her words are modest, righteousness upholds her steps, she is free from malice and guile. Her valiant appearance shews that she is of an open mind. Yet she seems to be falling, too: that is because the base world hates her, and with fierce truculence tries to cast her down to the ground. But evermore she bravely rises on high, though ambition moves her not. She is beloved by God and man. Though mockery is to her for a garment, as is shewn by the noisy cymbals, yet she cares nothing for it, but cleaves all the more faithfully to wisdom; to it she lifts her eyes, to it she directs her steps. For she knows that it is the only true salvation, and therefore she occupies herself with it by day and by night. She is not anxious for worldly praise, nor does she heed the hatred and injustice of men, or care for their opinion too little or too much. Much suffering and tribulation are inflicted upon her by this wicked world, yet she bears it with a valiant heart and holds it in disdain. For she possesses the treasure which gives her all that she desires, and avarice dwells not in her thoughts. That in which the world delights, she accounts as the dirt beneath her feet, since fortune is a wheel, and its revolutions are swift. Therefore she delights to tread the path of thorns, until, leaving the world, she finds rest in the tomb. Then her righteous soul will soar aloft to heaven, and for a just reward there shall be given unto her a diadem of stars. After her death, her praise and glory shall wax bright in the world, like unto the glorious splendour of the sun; nor will it ever pale, but become more intense as the years advance, and her name shall shine like a bright star for evermore."[1]

UNTO GOD ALONE BE THE GLORY.

AMEN.

---

[1] Note.—The Latin original contains no engraving illustrative of this Epigram.

A

DEMONSTRATION

OF

NATURE,

MADE TO THE ERRING ALCHEMISTS, AND COMPLAINING
OF THE SOPHISTS AND OTHER FALSE TEACHERS.

SET FORTH BY

JOHN A. MEHUNG.

NATURE (speaks).

GOOD heavens, how deeply I am often saddened at seeing the human race, which God created perfect, in His own image, and appointed to be the lords of the earth, depart so far away from me! I allude more particularly to you, O stolid philosophaster, who presume to style yourself a practical chemist, a good philosopher, and yet are entirely destitute of all knowledge of me, of the true Matter, and of the whole Art which you profess! For, behold, you break vials, and consume coals, only to soften your brain still more with the vapours. You also digest alum, salt, orpiment, and atrament; you melt metals, build small and large furnaces, and use many vessels: nevertheless, I am sick of your folly, and you suffocate me with your sulphurous smoke. With most intense heat you seek to fix your quicksilver, which is the vulgar volatile substance, and not that out of which I make metals; therefore you effect nothing. For you do not follow my guidance, or strive to imitate my methods, rather mistaking my whole artifice. You would do better to mind your own business, than to dissolve and distil so many absurd substances, and then to pass them through alembics, cucurbitas, stills, and pelicans. By this method you will never succeed in congealing quicksilver. For the revivification you use a reverberatory fire, and make it so hot as to render everything liquid—thus do you finish your work, and in the end ruin yourself and others. You will never discover anything unless you first enter my workshop, where, in the inmost bowels of the earth I ceaselessly forge metals: there you may find the substance which I use, and discover the method of my work.

Do not suppose that I will reveal my secret to you unless you first find the growing seed of all metals (resembling that of the animals and vegetables). I preserve in the bosom of the earth both that which is used for their generation, and that with which they are nourished up.

Metals *Exist*, vegetables *Live and Grow*, and animals *Feel*, which is more than merely to grow. I make metals, stones, and the atramental substances out of certain elements, which I mix and compound in a certain way. These elements you must seek in the heart of the earth, and nowhere else. Vegetables contain their own seed, and image; in like manner, animals are propagated, and by the same means do generate their own likeness. Everything proceeds by the laws laid down for it. Only you, wicked man, who try to usurp my office, have departed further from me than any other creature. Metals have no life, or principle of generation and growth, if they lack their own proper seed. The first is accomplished by the four elements in nine days; the Moon goes through the twelve heavenly signs in twenty-nine and a half days.

By the aforesaid laws, winter and summer relieve each other, the elements are changed, generations take place in the earth—through my working, through the working of God and the heavens, do all things subsist, the perceptible, the visible, and the invisible. Thus all things in heaven which are comprehended under the Moon, do work, and impart their influence to the substance, which, like a woman, longs to conceive seed. Each star influences its own substance, and according to their peculiar nature, they produce different things. They work first in heaven above, then in the earth beneath in the elements, each according to its own peculiar virtue; and hence arise species and individual things.

You are to know that these manifold influences do not pour themselves fruitlessly upon the earthly elements. For though their working is invisible, yet it is a most certain and real thing. The earth is surrounded by heaven, and from it obtains her best influences and substances. Every sphere is ready to communicate its truth, and therewith to pervade her centre. Through this motion and heat, there arise upon earth vapours, which are the first substances. If the vapour is cold and moist, it sinks down again to the earth, and is there preserved; that which is moist and warm ascends to the clouds. That which is shut up in the earth I change, after a long time, into the substance of sulphur, which is the active, and into quicksilver, which is the passive principle. The metals are another mixture of this first composition. The whole is obtained from the four elements, which I form into one mass. This process I repeat so often that you have no excuse for a mistake.

After the putrefaction comes the generation, which is brought about by the internal incombustible warmth heating the coldness of the quicksilver, which gladly submits to this heat because it wishes to be united to its sulphur. All these things, fire, air, and water, I have in one alembic in the earth. There I digest, dissolve, and sublime them, without any hammer, tongs, file, coals, vapour, fire, "bath of S. Mary," or other sophisticated contrivances. For I have my own heavenly fire which excites the elemental according as the matter desires to put on a suitable and comely form. Thus I extract my quicksilver from the four elements, or their substance. This is always accompanied by its sulphur, which is its second self, and warms it gradually, gently, and pleasantly. Thus the cold becomes warm, and the dry moist and oily. But the moist is not without its dry substance, nor is the dry without its moist: one is conserved by the other in its first essence (which is the elementary spirit of the essence, or the quintessence) from which proceeds the generation of our child. The fire brings it forth, and nourishes it in the air, but before that, it is decomposed in virgin earth; then water flows forth (or it flows forth from the water), which we must seek, since it is my first Matter, and the source of my mineral. For contrary resists strenuously to contrary, and doth in such wise fortify itself, lest perchance it be carried away in operating; then does it suffer transmutation, and is stripped of its form by the concupiscence of matter, which incessantly attracts a new form.

By my wisdom I govern the first principle of motion. My hands are the eighth sphere, as my Father ordained; my hammers are the seven planets, with which I forge beautiful things. The substance out of which I fashion all my works, and all things under heaven, I obtain from the four elements alone. Chaos, or Hyle, is the first substance. This is the Mistress that maintains the King, the Queen, and the whole court. A horseman is always ready to do her bidding, and a virgin performs her office in the chambers. The more beautiful she is, the more beautiful do I appear in her. Know also that I have power to give their essence to all essences, that it is I who preserve them, and mould them into shape. Moreover, observe the three parts into which God has divided the first substance. Of the first and purest part He created the Cherubin, Seraphin, Archangels, and all the other angels. Out of the second, which was not so pure, He created the heavens and all that belongs to them; of the third, impure part, the elements and their properties. First and best of these is *Fire*. Fire admits of no corruption, and contains the purest part of the quintessence. After *Fire*, He made the subtle Air, and put into it a part (but not so large a part) of the quintessence. Then came the visible element of Water, which has as much of the quintessence as it needs. Last of all comes the *Earth*. All these (like all the rest of Nature) He created in a moment of time. The earth is gross and dark, and though it is fruitful, yet it contains the smallest part of the quintessence. At first the elements remained as they were in their separate spheres. So Air is really moist, but is properly tempered by Fire. Water is really warm, but obtains its moisture from the air. The Earth is really dry, but it is also cold; its great dryness renders it akin to fire. Fire, however, is the first of elements which causes life and growth by its heat.

Now all these elements influence and qualify each other, so that each in its turn is now active, now passive. For instance, Fire works upon air and earth. Earth is the mother and nurse of all things, and sustains all that is liable to decay under heaven. Now God has given me power to resolve the four elements into their quintessence; this is that first substance which in every element is generically qualified. I resolve them for my own purpose, and thereby bring about all generation. But no one will be able to resolve me into my first substance, as he strives to resolve the elements. For I alone can transmute the elements and their forms, and he who thinks otherwise deceives himself. For you will never be able to assign to each substance its proper influence, or to find the correct proportions of the elements which are required by that substance. I alone, I say, can form created things, and give to them their peculiar properties and substance. By my heavenly mysteries I produce perfect works, which are justly called miracles, as may be seen in the Elixir which has such marvellous virtue, and is of my own forming. No art upon earth can add anything to, or improve upon, my workmanship. Every sane person must see that nothing can be accomplished without a perfect knowledge of the heavenly bodies, or apart from the efficacy which abides in them; without these everything is error and misuse; and yet, whence is a mere man to obtain this influence, and how is he to apply it to the substance? How can he mingle the elements in their right proportions? Even if a man were to spend a long life in the investigation of this secret (says Avicenna, De Vir. Cord., cp. ii.), he would not get any nearer to its solution. It is entrusted to my keeping alone, and can never be known to any man. By my virtue and efficacy I make the imperfect perfect, whether it be a metal or a human body. I mix its ingredients, and temper the four elements. I reconcile opposites, and calm their discord.

This is the golden chain which I have linked together of my heavenly virtues and earthly substances. I accomplish my works with such unerring accuracy that in them all my power is shewn forth, and with so much skill that the wisest of men cannot attain to my perfection. Go forth then, and behold my works, you who think yourself so skilled a workman, and (without any knowledge of me), with your coal fires and your S. Mary's bath, strive to make gold potable in my alembics—and know that I cannot bear the sight of your folly. Are you not ashamed, after considering my works, to attempt to rival them with your malodorous decoctions in your coloured and painted vials, and thus lose both your time and your money? I am at a loss to conceive what you can be thinking. Have pity upon yourself, and consider my teaching. Try to understand rightly what I tell you, for I cannot lie. Consider how that most glorious metal, gold, has received its beautiful form from heaven and its precious substance from the earth. The generation of the precious stones, such as carbuncles, amethysts, and diamonds, takes place in the same manner. The substance itself is composed of the four elements; its form and qualities it receives through heavenly influences, although the capacity of being thus wrought upon slumbers in the element and is only brought out and purified in the course of time. All this is accomplished by my hands alone. I am the architect, and no one else knows the secret of life. For, however wise he may think himself, he does not know how much to take of each element, or where to obtain it, or how to mingle hostile elements so as to allay their discord, or how to bring the heavenly influences to bear on these essences. He cannot even make iron, or lead, or the very basest of metal; how then should he be able to make gold except by stealing my treasure? The object which he desires can be accomplished by my art alone—an art which it is impossible for man to know.

And even though we allow gold to be the most precious of metals, yet gold by itself cannot cure diseases, or heal the imperfections of other metals, or change them into gold. In the same way glass (which might otherwise be the Philosopher's Stone) can never become so soft as to be rendered malleable. Gold alone is the most precious and the most perfect of all the metals. But if you cannot even make lead, or the minutest grain of any metals, or produce the fruit of any herb, how hopeless must your search after the art of making gold appear! Again if you say that you wish to produce some chemical result, even if it do not turn out to be gold, I answer that you thereby only give a fresh proof of your folly. Can you not understand that the secret of my innermost working must always remain a sealed book to you? What Nature does can never be successfully imitated by any created being. Nay, if I made gold out of seven metals, and you do not understand my method, how can you ever hope to prepare the substance which itself changes all metals into the purest gold, and is the most precious treasure that God has given me? You are foolish and ignorant, if you do not know that this precious thing which you seek is, to the created mind, the greatest mystery of Nature, and that it is compounded by heavenly influences—and thus has power to heal and deliver men from all diseases, and to remove the imperfection of the base metals. If, therefore, it is in itself so perfect that it has not its like upon earth, it must surely be the workmanship of the highest Intelligence, since no one else can even make gold, and certainly not produce a thing which has itself the power of making gold. Surely, to maintain that you are able to prepare such a thing, is like saying that you cannot carry ten pounds, but that you are strong enough to carry a hundred pounds. Put to heart, therefore, the true scope and responsibility of your intent.

I, myself, again, receive all my wisdom, virtue, and power from heaven, and my Matter, in its simplest form, is the four elements. This is the first principle and the quintessence of the elements, which I bring forth by reductions, time, and circulations, by which I transmute the inferior into the more perfect, the cold and dry into the moist and warm; and thus I preserve stones and metals in their natural state of moisture. This is brought about by the movements of the celestial bodies, for by them the elements are ruled; by their controlling influence like is brought to like. The purer my substance is, the more excellent are the results produced by the heavenly influence. And do you think that there in your alembic, where you have your earth and water, I will be induced by your fire and heat, and by your white and red colour, to bend my neck to your yoke, and to do your will and pleasure? Do you think that you can move the heavens, and force them to shed their influence upon your work. Do you think that that is an organic instrument which gives forth sweet music only when it is touched by the musician's fingers? You take too much upon yourself, you foolish man. Do you not know that the revolutions of the heavens are governed by a mighty Mind, which, by its influence, imparts power to all things?

I beseech you to remember that all great things proceed from me, and, in the last instance, from God; and not to suppose that the skill of your hands can be as perfect as the operation of Nature. For it is void and vain, and, ape-like, must imitate me in all things. Nor must you suppose that your distilling, dissolving, and condensing of your substance in your vessel, or your eliciting of water out of oil, is the right way of following me. Far from it, my son. All your mixing and dissolving of elements never has produced, and never can produce, any good result. Do you wish to know the reason? Your substance cannot stand the heat of the furnace for a single half-hour, but must evaporate in smoke, or be consumed by the fire. But the substance with which I work, can stand any degree of heat, without being injured. My water is dry, and does not moisten what it touches; it does not evaporate, or become less, neither is its oil consumed. So perfect are my elements; but yours are worse than useless.

In conclusion, let me tell you that your artificial fire will never impart my heavenly warmth, nor will your water, oil, and earth supply you with any substitute for my substance. It is the gift of God, shed upon the elements from heaven, and upon one more than upon another; but how, is known only to me, and to the Great Artist who entrusted me with this knowledge. One thing more let me tell you, my son. If you would imitate me, you must prepare all out of one simple, self-contained Matter, in *one* well-closed vessel, and in *one* alembic. The substance contains all that is needed for its perfect development, and must be prepared with a warmth that is always kept at the same gentle temperature. Let me ask you to consider the birth and development of man, my noblest work. You cannot make a human body out of any substance whatsoever. Of my method in forming so subtle a body neither Aristotle nor Plato had the remotest knowledge. I harden the bones and the teeth, I make the flesh soft, the muscles cold, the brain moist, the heart, into which God has poured the life, warm, and fill all the veins with red blood. And in the same way, I make of one quicksilver, and of one active male sulphur, one maternal vessel, the womb of which is the alembic. It is true that man aids me with his art, by shedding external heat into the matrix; more than this, however, he cannot do. He, then, that knows the true Matter, and prepares it properly in a well-closed vessel, and puts the whole in an alembic, and keeps up the fire at the proper degree of warmth, may safely leave the rest to me. Upon the fire all depends, and much, therefore, does it behove you to see thereto. Consider, therefore, the fire, which they call epesin, pepsin, pepausin, and optesin, or natural, preternatural, and infranatural fire, which burns not. Without the true Matter and the proper fire, no one can attain the end of his labour. I give you the substance; you must provide the mere outward conditions. Take, then, a vessel, and an alembic of the right kind and of the right size. Be wise, and perform the experiment in accordance with my laws. Help me, and I will help you. I will deal with you as you deal with me. To my other sons, who have treated me well, have obeyed their father and mother, and submitted themselves to my precepts, I have given a great reward, as John de Mehung, for instance, will tell you. His testimony is also borne out by Villanova, Raymond, Morienus the Roman, Hermes (whom they call Father, and who has not his like among the Sages), Geber, and others who have written about this Art, and know by experience that it is true.

If you, my son, wish to prepare this precious Stone, you need not put yourself to any great expense. All that you want is leisure, and some place where you can be without any fear of interruption. Reduce the Matter which is *one*), to powder, put it, together with its water, in a well-closed vessel, and expose it to continuous, gentle heat, which will then begin to operate, while the moisture favours the decomposition. The presence of the moisture prevents the dryness of the quicksilver from retarding its assimilation. Meanwhile, you must diligently observe what I do, and remember the words of Aristotle (Meteor iii. and iv.), who says: Study Nature, and carefully peruse the book concerning Generation and Corruption." You must also read the book concerning heaven and the world, in which you will find indicated the beautiful and pure substance. If you neglect this study, you will fail. On this subject consult Albertus Magnus, De Mineralibus. But if your eyes are opened by such studies, you will discover the secret of the growth of minerals, viz., that they are all produced from the elements.

First learn to know *me*, before you call yourself Master. Follow me, that am the mother of all things created, which have one essence, and which can neither grow, nor receive a living soul, without the heavenly and elementary influences. When you have learned by persevering study to understand the virtues of the heavenly bodies, their potent operations, and the passive condition of the elements, and its reason—if you further know the media of transmutation, the cause of generation, nutrition, and decay, and the essence and substance of the elements—you are already acquainted with the Art, notwithstanding that a most subtle mind is still needed for the studying of my operations. But if you do not possess part at least of this knowledge, you will be fortunate indeed if you succeed in discovering my secret. It is a secret that is read not by those that are wise in their own conceits, but by those that humbly and patiently listen to my teaching. Therefore, if you desire to own this treasure, which has been the reward of the truly wise in all ages, you must do as I bid you. For my treasure has such virtue and potency that the like of it is to be found neither in heaven nor upon earth. It holds an intermediate position between Mercury and the Metal which I take for the purpose of extracting from it by your art and my knowledge that most precious essence. It is pure and potable gold, and its radical principle is active humidity. Moreover, it is the universal Medicine described by Solomon (Eccles. xxxviii.); the same also is taken from the earth, and honoured by the wise. God has assigned it a place among my mysteries, and reveals it to the Sages, although many who call themselves learned doctors of Theology and Philosophy, hold it in ignorant contempt—as Alchemy is also despised by the doctors of Medicine, because they do not know me, and are ignorant of that which they profess to teach. They must be insufficiently furnished with brains, or they would not direct their foolish scorn against the panacea which renders all other medicines unnecessary. Happy is the man, even though he be sinking under the weight of years, whose days God prolongs until he has come to the knowledge of this secret! For (as Geber says) many to whom this gift was imparted late in life, have, nevertheless, been refreshed and delighted by it in extreme old age.

He that has this secret possesses all good things and great riches. One ounce of it will ensure to him both wealth and health. It is the only source of strength and recreation, and far excels the golden tincture. It is the elixir and water of life, which includes all other things. In my treasure are concealed quicksilver, sulphur, incombustible oil, white, indestructible, and fusible salt. I tell you, frankly, that you will never be able to accomplish its preparation without me, just as I can do nothing without your help. But if you understand my teaching, and cooperate with me, you can accomplish the whole thing in a short time.

Have done with the charlatans, and their foolish writings; have done with all their various alembics, and phials; have done with their excrements of horses, and all the variety of their coal-fires, since all these things are of no use whatever. Do not perplex yourself with metals, or other things of a like nature: rather change the elements into a mutable form. For this is the most excellent substance of the Sages, and is rejected only by the foolish. Its substance is like, but its essence unlike, that of gold. Transmute the elements and you will have what you seek. Sublime that which is the lowest, and make that which is the highest, the lowest. Take quicksilver which is mixed with its active sulphur; put it into a well-closed vial, and one alembic, plunge one-third of it into the earth, kindle the fire of the Sages, and watch it well so that there may be no smoke. The rest you may leave to me. I ask you to do no more, but only bid you follow my unerring guidance.

THE ANSWER OF THE CHEMIST,

In which he confesses his errors, asks pardon for them, and returns thanks to Nature.

Dearest Mother Nature, who, next to the angels, art the most perfect of all God's creatures, I thank thee for thy kindly instruction. I acknowledge and confess that thou art the Mother and Empress of the great world, made for the little world of man's mind. Thou movest the bodies above, and transmutest the elements below. At the bidding of thy Lord thou dost accomplish both small things and great, and renewest, by ceaseless decay and generation, the face of the earth and of the heavens. I confess that nothing can live without a soul, and that all that exists and is endued with being flows forth from thee by virtue of the power that God has given to thee. All matter is ruled by thee, and the elements are under thy governance. From them thou takest the first substance, and from the heavens thou dost obtain the form. That substance is formless and void until it is modified and individualized by thee. First thou givest it a substantial, and then an individual form. In thy great wisdom thou dost cunningly mould all thy works through the heavenly influences, so that no mortal hand can utterly destroy them. Under thy hands God has put all things that are necessary to man, and through thee, He has divided them into four kingdoms, namely, those that have being and essence, like the metals and stones; those that have essence and growth, like the vegetables; those that have feeling and sensation, like the beasts, birds, and fishes. These are the first three classes; in the fourth it pleased God to place only the noblest and most perfect of His works, namely, man, to whom He also gave a rational and immortal soul. This soul is obscured by the defilement which found its way into the body through the senses, and, but for the grace and mercy of God, would have become involved in its condemnation. Hence the chief perfection of man is not derived from thee, nor dost thou impart to us our humanity. Nevertheless, the material part of man is the work of thy hands alone.

And, surely, our bodies are cunningly and wonderfully made, and, in every part of them, bear witness to the masterly skill of the workman. How marvellous are the uses of our various members! How wonderful that the soul can move them and set them to work at will! But, alas! oftener still the body is master of the soul, and forces it to do many things which pure reason condemns. If we consider the matter from this point of view, it seems as though thou hadst begun well, and yet thy work had, after all, turned out an abortion. Wert thou wanting in wisdom, or knowledge, or couldst thou not do otherwise? Pardon me if I speak too presumptuously about thy wisdom, I only desire to be rightly and truly informed. For, indeed, even now thy stern rebuke has made many things clear to me. I have spent my whole life in attending to thy lessons; and the more closely I have listened, the more clearly have I understood my mistakes and the depth of thy wisdom. Now, whether I lie, or stand, or walk, I can think of nothing but thy great mystery. And yet I am unable to conceive what substance and form I must take for it. Thou didst sternly rebuke me for not following thy way; but thou knowest that, if I do not obey thee, it is only because I do not know what thou wouldst have me do. I shall' never be able to attain any satisfactory result in this Art, unless thou wilt enlighten my blindness. Thou hast rightly said that it is not for man to know the mystery of thy working: how then can I be guided to this knowledge, unless thou wilt take me by the hand? Thou sayest that I must follow thee; and I am willing to do so. But tell me what I must do, and what books I must study for that purpose. Of the books which I have read, one says, "Do this," and the other, "No, do that "; and they are full of unintelligible expressions and of dark parables. At last I see that I cannot learn anything from them. Therefore I take refuge with thee, and instantly beseech thee to advise and to tell me how to set about this difficult task. On my knees I implore thee to show me the way by which I can penetrate into the lower parts of the earth, and by what subtle process I am to obtain the' perfect mercury of the metals. And yet I doubt whether any man, even after obtaining this mercury, can really make gold. That is thy work, and not the work of man; as thy words and my own experience most clearly shew.

We see that the cold and moist mercury needs the assistance of its sulphur, which is its seed after its kind, or its homogeneous sperm, out of which the metal or Stone must be produced. But thou sayest only: Take the proper substance, the proper vessel, the proper mineral, the proper place, and the proper fire; then form, colour, and life will grow and spring forth from thence. Thou art the Architect; thou knowest the glorious properties of the Matter. The active principle can do nothing unless there be a passive principle prepared to receive its influence. Thou knowest how to mix the warm and the cold, the dry and the moist; by reconciling hostile elements, thou canst produce new substances and forms. For I did indeed understand all that thou didst tell me, but am unable to express it so well as thou. This thou hast firmly impressed on my mind, that the Elixir is composed by the reconciling and mutual transmutation of the four elements. But what man is sufficient for such a task? For who knows how earth can have its essence in common with air, or how it can be changed into moisture which is contrary to its nature? For humidity will not leave a cold and humid element, not even under the influence of fire. This, too, is the work of Nature, that it becomes black, and white, and red. These three visible colours correspond to the three elements, earth, water, and fire, and are pervaded by the air.

Then, again, thou sayest that the Stone is prepared of one thing, of one substance, in one vessel, the four (elements) composing one essence in which is one agent which begins and completes the work; man, thou sayest, need do nothing but add a little heat, and leave the rest to thy wisdom. For all that is needed is already contained in the substance, in perfection, beginning, middle, and end, as the whole man, the whole animal, the whole flower is contained each in its proper seed. Now, in the human seed the human specific-substance is also included, as flesh, blood, hair, &c.; and thus every seed contains all the peculiar properties of its species. In the whole world men spring from human seed, plants from plants, animals from animals. Now I know that when once the seed is enclosed in the female vessel, no further trouble or work of any kind is required—everything is brought to perfection by thy gradual and silent working. And the generation of the Stone, thou sayest, is performed in a similar manner. Only one substance is required, which contains within itself air, water, and fire—in short, everything that is needed for the completion of this work. No further handling of any kind is necessary, and a gentle fire is sufficient to rouse the internal warmth, just as an infant in the womb is cherished by natural heat. The only thing in which man must aid thee, is, by preparing the substance, removing all that is superfluous, enclosing this simple earth, which is combined with its water, in a vessel, and subjecting it to the action of gentle heat in a suitable alembic. This, thou sayest, is all that needs to be done by man; when all has been prepared for thee, thou dost begin thy part of the work. Thou dissolvest the substance, and makest the dry watery; then thou sublimest it, and bearest it upward into the air, and thus, without any further aid, bringest that to perfection which can itself impart perfection to all imperfect things. Therefore, thou, Nature, art the first mother, since thou dost cunningly combine the four elements into an essence by a process of which none but thou has any knowledge. Thus far have I understood thee, and do not quite despair, if it be pleasing unto God and to thee, of seeing thy great reward with my own eyes.

But at present I earnestly desire to know but one thing: and that is, how can that substance be obtained, what are its qualities, and what its powers to impart perfection to imperfect things?

I am well aware that gold is the most precious of the metals; but I cannot see that it has any capacity of becoming more potent than it already is. For whatever man may do with it, it will never be able to perfect anything but itself. If any one told me to dissolve it and extract from it its quicksilver, I should regard that as a very foolish direction; for nothing can be got out of gold but what is in it. These philosophasters betray their ignorance by saying that they can reduce gold to its first substance; but thy instruction has made it clear to me that the first substance cannot be obtained, except by destroying the specific properties of a thing, nor can any new species be brought forth by such a destruction, unless the species be first universalized into the genus. Moreover, I make bold to affirm that no man can first resolve gold into its generic substance, and then restore it again; for when it has once lost its specific properties, no mere human skill can change it back into what it was before. Nor can any one really reduce gold to the first form imparted to it by the elements. For gold is not transmuted either by heat or by cold, and is so perfect in its kind that fire only renders it purer. It does not admit of any further development, and therefore no other metal or quicksilver can be obtained from it.

It is true that plants and animals are constantly producing their like by means of their seed, and their capacity of organic nutrition. But I do not see how the same can be said of metals, seeing that at the expiration of any given period they still retain the same size and weight which they had at the beginning. Through thee they receive their being out of the elements without any sowing, planting, or development of any kind. Moreover, I know that no credit is to be attached to the fanciful notions of the old Sages who would prepare our Stone out of a crude metallic substance, and do not understand that the form and substance of a thing are conditioned by its essential nature. Now, I remember a certain juggling charlatan, who was looked upon as a great philosopher, telling me that the only true material was common quicksilver, which must be well mingled with gold, since in such an union the one brought the other to perfection. If I did this, continued that impostor, I should be able to prepare the Elixir. First, however, the four elements must be separated from each other, then, after each had been purified, they must be reunited, the great being combined with the small, and the subtile with the gross. This, he said, was the right way of making the Stone. But I know that all this is sheer nonsense, and that such men are only deceiving themselves and others.

I am also aware that only God can produce anything out of the elements. He alone knows how to mingle and combine them in their due proportions. For He alone is the Creator and Author of all good things, and there is nothing in the world that He has not made. Therefore, let the charlatans cease their vainglorious talk, and remember that they can never hope to gather where they cannot sow; let them make an end of their false calcinations, sublimations, distillations, by which they extract the spirit in a vaporous form, and of their juggling coagulations and congelations, by which they pretend, even among the initiated, to be able rightly to separate the elements of gold and quicksilver. It is certainly true that all things under heaven are composed of the four elements, and mixed of them according to the due proportion of their genus and species; but it is not simply the union of the four elements, but their being combined in a certain way, which constitutes the substance of the Philosophical Stone.

I also understand that in the red quicksilver and perfect body, which is called the Sun, the four elements are combined in a peculiar way, and so inseparably conjoined, that no mere human art can divide them. For all ancient and true Sages say that fire and air are enclosed in earth and water, and contend so violently with each other that none but God and Nature can loosen their grappling embrace. This I can truly affirm and also prove. For we can neither see the fire nor grasp the air; and if any one says that the several elements can be seen he is an imposter, seeing that they are inseparably and inextricably conjoined. For, although the Sophists pretend, and confidently affirm, that they can divide gold and quicksilver into the four elements, yet for all that they speak not the truth. If two elements, fire and air, were thus taken away, all the rest must vanish into nothing. They may say that those two are retained, but they are, nevertheless, densely ignorant as to what becomes of them; for air and fire cannot be seen or perceived. Again, that extract which they call fire and air renders humid, which is not the property either of fire or of air.

Moreover, as thou hast said, even the most learned Doctor cannot know the proportion of each element in any given substance. For God has entrusted this knowledge to thee alone. Nor is any Sage wise enough to be able to mingle and put together the elements so as to produce any natural object. If then he dissolves anything into its elements, how, I pray thee, is he to put them together again into any abiding form, since he is ignorant of their proportionate quantity and quality, and of the method of their composition? Yet it is of no use to separate them, if they cannot be put together again. To thee, O Nature, we must entrust this task, since thou knowest the art of preparing the Philosopher's Stone, and of combining the elements without first separating them. Nevertheless, for the preparation of the true Elixir, thou needest the aid of a wise and truly learned man. Aristotle says: "Where the physicist ends, there the physician begins." Nor can we attain to true alchemy, until we begin to follow Nature, and to be guided by a knowledge of her principles. Where the study of Alchemy is rightly carried on, it is mightily advanced by Nature. But, for all that, we must not suppose that every natural substance must be useful to the alchemist. We must remember that Alchemy has a threefold aim: First, to quicken and perfect the metal, and so to digest its spirit that none of it is lost; secondly, so to digest and heat the substance in a small phial that (without the addition of anything else) the body and spirit are changed into one. The mingling of the elements is performed, not by the artist, but by thee. Thirdly, it (alchemy) proves that the process of preparing the Stone does not include any separation of the four elements (of the quicksilver and the Sun, which is called red and glorious gold). To believe that such a separation must take place is a great mistake, and contradicts the fundamental principles of philosophy.

Again, it is an undoubted fact, that every elementary substance is fed by the elements themselves. If, then, that which now forms one object is dissolved, the object as such is destroyed, the bond which held the elements together being violently broken, and each returning to that from which it was first taken. A father that begets a son must not be destroyed for that purpose; it suffices that the generating spirit shall go forth with the seed, and be conceived by the female seed, and cherished with its warmth. Such a generating spirit has power to beget an infant of the same species, as Avicenna says. Now, it is the same with pure gold, which is the true matter of the Philosophical Stone. For the father is the active principle, and must not be destroyed, or resolved into its elements, but it is sufficient for the paternal Sun (gold) to breathe its virtue and strength through the mother into the son. When the mother (who is of the earth) brings forth, the son is seen to have the father's substance.

Thus, I have learnt from thee, O Nature, that Alchemy is a true science, and that the deep red gold, which is called Sun, is the true father of the Stone or Elixir, from which this great and precious treasure proceeds; which heats, digests, and cunningly tinges (without the least diminution or corruption) the other principle of that gold, and thus brings forth so glorious a son. It is worse than useless, therefore, to meddle with the composition, or to separate the elements, which Nature has so skilfully combined in the quicksilver, and in the perfect body of the gold. All we have to do is to imitate Nature, and use the instruments with which she combines the elements, and which she uses in moulding minerals, and in giving its form to the quicksilver. If we act otherwise, will destroy thy works, and sever the golden chain which thou hast forged. Nevertheless, we must, as Aristotle says, transmute the elements that we may obtain the object of our search.

Thus thou hast wisely led me into thy way, and hast shewn me the utter folly of my own doings. Unto thee I render the most heartfelt thanks for that thou hast delivered me from my own ignorance, and from the disgrace and ruin to which all my endless alembics, quicksilvers, aquæ fortes, dissolutions, excrements of horses, and coal fires, must at length have brought me.

In future, I will read thy book more diligently, and obey thee more implicitly. For this is the surest and safest way that a man can go, because the Art is entirely in thy hands, although, by reason of its gigantic aim, its progress must necessarily be slow. Therefore, I will lose no more time, and first begin to think about the substance, the active principle of which shall yield me most potent quicksilver. That I will enclose in a clean, air-tight phial, and under it I will place an alembic; thereupon thou wilt wait upon thine office. From the bottom of my heart I once more render unto thee the debt of unspeakable gratitude, for that thou hast deigned to visit me, and to bestow upon me so precious an inheritance. in token of my gratitude I will now do thy bidding, and let it be my ceaseless aim to attain to this most glorious Tincture of the Elements, feeling assured that with the help of the thrice great and good God, I shall succeed.

A SHORT TRACT,

OR

PHILOSOPHICAL SUMMARY

By Nicholas Flamell.

HE that would understand the whole subject of metals, and how they are transmuted one into another, ought first to find an answer to the question, from what substance they spring, and how they are formed in their ores. For this purpose he must observe the changes that are continually going forward in the mineral veins of the earth. Hence they may be made subject to transmutation outside of their ores if they are first made spiritual, so that they may be reduced to their sulphur and mercury, which is performed by Nature. Now all metals have been formed out of sulphur and quicksilver, which are the seeds of all metals, the one representing the male, and the other the female principle. These two varieties of seed are, of course, composed of elementary substances; the sulphur, or male seed, being nothing but fire and air (*i.e.*; *good* sulphur, resembling fire, free from the mutable properties of metals, and not that common sulphur which is not a metallic substance at all); while the quicksilver, or female seed, is nothing but earth and water. These two seeds were figuratively represented by the ancient Sages under the forms of two dragons, or serpents, one of which had wings, while the other had none. The wingless dragon is sulphur, because it never flies away from the fire. The winged serpent is quicksilver, which is borne away through the air (the female seed, which is composed of water and earth)—because in a certain degree it flies away or evaporates. Now, if these two seeds, separated one from another, are united spermatically by triumphant Nature, in the book of Mercury, the first mother of metals, the Sages call the substance that results, the flying dragon, because this dragon, being kindled with its fire, in its flight pours abroad into the air fire and a poisonous vapour. The same happens to mercury, which, if placed in a vessel over an ordinary fire, has its internal, hidden fire kindled; and then you may see how the outward vegetable fire kindles the inward natural fire of mercury. You will notice that it exhales into the air a certain poisonous fume or vapour, the stench of which is such as to prove that it is nothing but the head of the dragon which is leaving Babylon in great haste, even the philosophical Babylon which is encompassed by a double or treble vessel.

Other Sages have likened this Mercury to a flying Lion, because the Lion devours other animals, and refreshes and strengthens himself at will with the blood of all animals except those which have power to resist his rage—and because mercury, too, is known to deprive other metals of their specific form, and to absorb and incorporate them. Gold and silver, however, are strong enough to resist its violence; although it is well-known that mercury, when exposed to an exceptional degree of heat, devours and swallows even these two metals. Yet neither of them is changed into the nature of the mercury, howbeit, they are enclosed in its womb; for gold and silver are more permanent and more perfect than crude mercury, this being an imperfect metal, notwithstanding that there is in it the substance of perfection. Common gold, which is a perfect metal, and silver, and all the imperfect metals, are developed out of mercury. For this reason, the ancient Sages have called it the Mother of the Metals, and hence, being itself a metal, it must contain a two-fold metallic substance, namely, the inner substance of the Moon, and that of the Sun (which is unlike the other). Of these two substances mercury is formed, and they are cherished in its body in the form of spiritual essences. Now, as soon as Nature has formed that mercury of these two spirits, she strives to transmute them into a perfect bodily form; and therefore, when those two spirits have grown up, and their two varieties of seed awake, they desire to assume their own proper bodies; and then the Mother, mercury, must die, and having died a natural death, can never be quickened any more into that which it was previously.

Vainglorious and arrogant Alchemists have obscurely hinted that perfect and imperfect bodies must be transmuted into fluid mercury, but this assertion is only a trap for the unwary. It is true that mercury consumes imperfect metals, like lead and tin, and thus increases in quantity; but, by doing so, it loses its perfection, and is no longer the mercury that it was before. If, indeed, it could be so mortified by a chemical process as to shut out all hope of its ever quickening itself again, it would be changed into something else, as happens with cinnabar, or in sublimate. But, when it is coagulated by a chemical process, whether by a swift or a slow method, its two bodies do not assume a permanent form. By the natural process this coagulation is indeed successfully carried out; and thus we never find a vein of lead, for instance, which does not contain a few permanent grains, at least, of gold and silver. The first coagulation of mercury is lead, which is most suitable for fixing it, and bringing it to perfection. For lead is never without some fixed grain of gold and silver, which are imparted to it by Nature for the purpose of multiplication and development, as I myself have experienced, and am able to testify. So long as it is in its mercury, and not separated from its mineral, it can continue to increase its substance from the substance of its mercury. But if this fixed grain is taken away, and severed from its mercury (or the mineral in which it is found), it can no longer gain in size. It is with this grain as with the green fruit that is formed on a tree when the blossom has been shed. If it is plucked off before it is ripe, it can come to nothing. If it is left on the tree, it is nourished and increased by the sap and the juice of the parent stem, and thus gradually attains to its proper size, and to maturity. But, until ripeness has been attained, the fruit continues to attract to itself the sap and juice of the tree, that is to say, so long as the connection with the parent tree is not severed.

Almost the same thing happens with gold. Such a grain attracts to itself the mercury of the lead, and incessantly "fixes" it into its own mercury, whereby it grows and gradually increases in size. The mercury of perfect or imperfect metals is the parent tree, and the grain (of gold) can be nourished with nothing but this mercury. But as soon as you sever the connection with the parent mercury, that growth of the grain must immediately come to an end; it is as though the unripe fruit had been plucked from the tree: you would vainly endeavour to restore the vital connexion. When you have once removed an unripe pear or apple from its native branch, it would be foolish indeed to join it to the tree once more, and expect it to ripen. Instead of growing, it will gradually shrivel up, and become smaller. The same thing may be observed in the case of the metals. For if any one were to take common metallic gold and silver, and tried to resolve those metals into mercury, he would be doing a very foolish thing. It is a result which cannot be brought about by any chemical process, however subtle and ingenious, just as fruit which has once been plucked in an unripe state can never again be vitally joined to the parent tree. It has, indeed, been well said by the Sages that if gold and silver be joined together through their proper mercury, they have power to render all other (imperfect) metals perfect. But these Sages did not speak of common gold and silver, which must always remain what they are, can never become anything else, and certainly cannot aid the development of other metals. It is fruit that has been plucked before the time, and therefore is dead and withered. No, the *living* fruit (the real living gold and silver) we must seek *on the tree*; for only there can it grow, and increase in size, according to the possibilities of its nature. This tree we must transplant, without gathering its fruit, into a better and richer soil, and to a sunnier spot. Then its fruit will receive more nourishment in a single day than it was wont to receive in a hundred years, while it was still in its former sterile soil.

I wish you to understand that Mercury, which is a most excellent tree, and contains silver and gold in an indissoluble form, must be taken and transplanted into a soil that is nearer to the Sun (*i.e.*, in this case, gold), where it may flourish exceedingly, and be abundantly watered. Where it was planted before, it was so shaken and weakened by the wind and the frost, that but little fruit could be expected from it. So there it remained a long time, and bore no fruit.

But in the garden of the Sages, the *Sun* sheds its genial influence both morning and evening, day and night, unceasingly. There our *tree* is watered with the rarest dew, and the fruit which hangs upon the trees swells and ripens and expands, from day to day. It never withers, but makes more progress in one year than it did in a thousand years in its former sterile situation. Or, to drop metaphor, let the mercury be taken, and warmed day and night in an alembic over a gentle fire. Yet it should not be a coal or a wood fire, but a clear and pellucid heat, like that of the *Sun* itself—a gentle and even warmth. Growing fruit must not be exposed to too much heat, or else it is withered, and shrivelled up, and is never brought to perfection. It must have a genial warmth, and be supported by a moderate moisture in the tree, if it is to flourish and expand. For heat and moisture are the food of all earthly things, both animal, vegetable, and mineral. Ordinary coal or wood fires are too violent for our purpose, and give no nourishment like the heat of the Sun which preserves all bodies through its natural influences. For this reason the Sages use none but this natural fire, not because it is made by the Sages, but because it is made by Nature—Nature, that creates all things, whether they be animal, vegetable, or mineral, and warms them, each at its own proper degree.

Therefore, I will not say that man by his art can make natural things; but I do say that human art can impart greater perfection to that which Nature makes. For this purpose the ancient Sages have had but one object in view, namely, to produce from the moon and the true mother mercury, the mercury of the philosophers, which in its operation is much more potent than natural mercury, and is useful for working upon simple, perfect, imperfect, cold, and warm metals. Now, the Philosophical Stone is good for perfect and imperfect metals, and soon restores and brings them to perfection without any diminution, addition, or real change of any kind. For, apart from perfecting them, it leaves them in the state in which they were before. I do not say that the Sages combine common gold, silver, and mercury for this purpose: this is the method only of ignorant charlatans, who thereby hope to prepare the mercury of the Sages; but they never succeed in producing this, the real first substance of the Stone. If they would obtain it they must go to the seventh mountain, where there is no plain, and from its height they must look down upon the sixth, which they will behold at a great distance. On the summit of that mountain they will find the glorious Regal Herb, which some Sages call a mineral, some a vegetable. The bones they must leave, and only extract its pure juice, which will enable them to do the better part of the work. This is the true and subtle mercury of the philosophers which you must take. Now, first it prepares the white tincture, and then the red. For the Sun and Moon are prepared by the same method, and yield the red and white tincture, respectively, and the preparation is so simple that it might be seen to by a woman while she works at her spindle—just as she might set a hen on some eggs, without washing them first, and without any other trouble but that of turning the eggs every day that the chickens may break the shells all the sooner. In like manner, you must not wash your mercury, but only put it with its like (which is fire) into ashes (corresponding to the straw), into one glass vessel (which is the nest), in a suitable alembic (which is the house). If you do this there will come out a chicken, that will deliver you with its blood from all diseases, and feed you with its flesh, and clothe you with its feathers, and shelter you from the cold. Therefore, I pray and beseech the Creator of all things to grant His grace to all faithful Alchemists, that they may find the chicken, which, through God's unspeakable goodness and mercy, has now been vouchsafed to me. I have written this tract for your sakes, to encourage you, and point out to you the right way: I hope and trust that my words will enable you to understand more fully the works of other Sages. Farewell!

THE ONLY TRUE WAY;

OR,

AN USEFUL, GOOD, AND HELPFUL TRACT,

POINTING OUT THE PATH OF TRUTH.

———

1677.

THE ONLY TRUE WAY.

BELOVED friend and brother, under the name of this glorious Art there is to be found much false teaching, which is put forward by pseudo-alchemists, whose writings are nothing but imposture and deceit, and are yet highly esteemed by people of the simpler sort. These charlatans induce their dupes to waste much money and time on that which can profit them nothing; for unless a thing be well begun, it can never be brought to a good end. Yet most men, who, nowadays, have devoted themselves to this exalted art of chemistry, are pursuing a wrong course, and are deceivers or deceived. The deceivers are conscious of their own ignorance, and try to veil it under an obscure and allegorical style. The less they really know, the more pompous and the more unintelligible do their speculations become. But the reader, who is puzzled by their perplexing style, may at least comfort himself with the assurance that he knows as much about the matter as the authors. That assurance must serve for a kind of clue to the endless labyrinth of their false sublimations, calcinations, distillations, solutions, coagulations, putrefactions, and corruptions. Nevertheless, we may almost every day see foolish persons spend their whole substance on those absurd experiments, being induced to do so by the aforesaid pseudo-alchemists, who impose on them with a false process, and fanciful perversions of Nature.

With these useless and unnecessary experiments the true Alchemists will have nothing to do. They follow the method pursued by Nature in the veins of the earth, which is very simple, and includes no solutions, putrefactions, coagulations, or anything of the kind. Can Nature, in the heart of the earth, where the metals do grow and receive increase, have anything corresponding to all those pseudo-alchemistical instruments, alembics, retorts, circulatory and sublimatory phials, fires, and other materials, such as cobbler's wax, salt, arsenic, mercury, sulphur, and so forth? Can all these things really be necessary for the growth and increase of the metals? It is surprising that any one not entirely bereft of his senses can spend many years in the study of alchemy, and yet never get beyond those foolish and frivolous solutions, coagulations, putrefactions, distillations, while Nature is so simple and unsophisticated in her methods. Surely every true Artist must look upon this elaborate tissue of baseless operations as the merest folly, and can only wonder that the eyes of those silly dupes are not at last opened, that they may see something besides such absurd sophisms, and read something besides those stupid and deceitful books. It seems that they are so entangled in their sophisms that they can never attain to the freedom of true philosophy.

But let me tell you that so long as you love lies, and turn away from rational philosophy, you will never find the right way. I can speak from bitter experience. For I, too, toiled for many years in accordance with those sophistic methods, and endeavoured to reach the coveted goal by sublimation, distillation, calcination, circulation, and so forth, and to fashion the Stone out of substances such as urine, salt, atrament, alum, etc. I have tried hard to evolve it out of hairs, wine, eggs, bones, and all manner of herbs; out of arsenic, mercury, and sulphur, and all the minerals and metals. I have striven to elicit it by means of aqua fortis and alkali. I have spent nights and days in dissolving, coagulating, amalgamating, and precipitating. Yet from all these things I derived neither profit nor joy. I had hoped much from the quintessence, but it disappointed me like the rest.

Therefore, beloved brother, let me warn you to have nothing to do with sublimations of sulphur and mercury, or the solution of bodies, or the coagulation of spirits, or with all the innumerable alembics, which bear little profit unto veritable art. So long as you do not seek the true essence of Nature, your labours will be doomed to failure; therefore, if you desire success, you must once for all renounce your allegiance to all those old methods, and enlist under the standards of that method which proceeds in strict obedience to the teaching of Nature—in short, the method which Nature herself pursues in the bowels of the earth. For you see that Nature uses only one substance in her work of developing and perfecting the metals, and that this substance includes everything that is required. Now, this substance appears to call for no special treatment, except that of digestion by gentle heat, which must be continued until it has reached its highest possible degree of development. For this simple heating process the cunning sophists have substituted solutions, coagulations, calcinations, putrefactions, sublimations, and other fantastical operations—which are only different names for the same thing; and thereby they have multiplied a thousand-fold the difficulties of this undertaking, and given rise to the popular notion that it is a most arduous, hazardous, and ruinously expensive enterprise. This they have simply done out of jealousy and malice, to put others off the right track, and to involve them in poverty and ruin. But they will find it difficult to justify their conduct before God, who has commanded us to love our neighbours as ourselves. For out of sheer malice they have rendered the road of truth impassable, and perplexed a simple natural process with such an elaborate tissue of circumstantial nomenclature, as to make the amelioration of the metals appear a hopelessly difficult task.

For while you heat, you also putrefy, or decompose, as you may see by the changes which a grain of wheat undergoes in the, ground under the influence of the rain and of the sun; you know that it must first decay before new life can spring forth. It is this process which they have denominated putrefaction and solution. Again when you heat, you also sublime, and to this coction they have applied the terms sublimation and multiplication, that the simple man might err more easily. In like manner coagulation takes place in heating; for they say that coagulation takes place when humidity is changed into the nature of fire, so as to be able to resist the action of fire, without evaporating, or being consumed. And heating also includes that which they call "circulation," or conjunction, or the union of fire with water to prevent complete combustion.

Thus you see that that which they have called by so many names is really but one simple process. The substance, which is *one*, they have described under a similar variety of appellations, to prevent men from finding that which, by the grace of God, can provide for them so many precious blessings. In the first place they call it "our mercury," by which they mean nothing but moisture, which begins to unite itself with the fire, and therefore may be compared to mercury. Again, they use the expression, "our sulphur," whereby they mean nothing but the fire itself, which lies hid beneath the water, or humidity, and is heated by the water to its highest degree. Then, again, they call it Hyle, or the First Substance, because all things are first generated out of water and fire. Other names, such as Arsenic, Orpiment, Bismuth, are not used by the Sages at all, but only by certain ignorant charlatans, of whom we need not take any further notice. Let *us* follow the guidance of Nature: *she* will not lead us astray.

If you let this be your motto, you will surely be able to call to mind the first substance, out of which all metallic substances are generated. But before we consider this question, it will much behove you to understand why the Sun, Moon, Venus, Mars, Jupiter, and Saturn, are metals, and what is their origin. Besides finding an answer to this question, you must also bear in mind that all created things are divided into three kingdoms, viz., the animal, the vegetable, and the mineral. To the first belong all living things that have flesh and blood; to the second all herbs, plants, and trees; to the third all metals, stones, and everything that cannot be burned.

But, though divided into three classes, yet all things, O my brother, may be traced back to one common Principle, from which they derive their generation, or birth. By different varieties of heat this first substance is transmuted in various ways, and assumes different specific forms. Since, then, Nature is so simple, I advise you once more to have done with all those foolish sublimations, coagulations, and putrefactions, and the ridiculous old wives' fables which are even now believed by many, and simply to follow Nature, and her unsophisticated methods: then she will take you by the hand, and guide you to the true substance. For the only method of correcting or ameliorating Nature, consists in the natural heating of essences. Now, this Essence, my friend, is the principal thing, on which depends the whole matter. This simple truth, the vulgar herd of alchemists seem quite unable to understand, and thus go on toiling day by day with substances which have nothing to do with the matter. They might as well sow horn, or wood, or stones, and expect a golden harvest of corn. The *sun* and *moon* cannot be made out of *all* substances, but only out of the natural Essence out of which all things are formed, being afterwards differentiated into divers substances by different varieties of heat. Thus the special quality of every individual thing is to be referred to the degree of its coction. If, therefore, we wish to exercise the true Art of Alchemy, we must imitate the method by which Nature does her work in the bowels of the earth.

The ancients have named many colours in connexion with this process, such as black, white, citrine, red, green, and so forth. All this is simply intended to lead you astray from the right road, and to keep you in ignorance. Those ancient writers were constantly at the greatest pains to obscure their style with such a perplexing variety of allegorical expressions as to render it impossible for the ordinary reader to understand their meaning.

Therefore, I would again and again exhort you not to believe them when they tell you that you must have or take a black substance, or that the substance turns black, white, and red in the course of the chemical process. The black colour was suggested to them by the fact that the substance or essence at first mingles with a brilliant material fire, by which a liquid is separated from the essence in the form of a certain black fume. This black fume the ancients called the Black Raven, and the essence they denominated the Raven's Head. This separation you should carefully observe. From it the ancients learned that the separation of natural substances is nothing but a natural defect of the heating process. This, again, suggested to them the consideration that those essences that had been imperfectly heated by Nature, might be aided in a natural manner by ordinary fire, and that thus the essences which are still combustible, and their liquids (which the ancients invidiously called mercury), being black when they are separated from the essence, might be perfected by art, and the essences guarded against combustion by their liquid, and the liquid rendered incapable of being separated from the essence. This the ancients called "our sulphur." For after this preparation the essence is no longer vegetable or animal, but by the perfection of its heating it has become a mineral essence, and is therefore called sulphur; the essence is nothing but an *elementary* fire, and its liquid, which is guarded against combustion, is true *elementary* air, and, because air is naturally warm and moist, it is called mercury by those jealous ancients. Air contains in itself the nature of fire, and elementary fire, again, contains within itself the nature of air: thus, by the union of their common elements, a true amalgamation of the two can take place. Such are the material fire and water which we *see*. These material elements are nothing but an aid to the essences of the elements by which they can be naturally reduced to the highest degree (of perfection?). This gradation is the only true Alchemy, and there is none beside. The pseudo-alchemy of our modern charlatans is mere waste of money and time.

It would be a great mistake for you to suppose that you can derive any real knowledge from the writings of the Sages. They show you only the outside, and conceal the internal Essence. To you they offer the husks, but the finest of the wheat they keep for themselves. They show you a way which they do not dream of treading. I advise you, therefore, in future, to give them a wide berth; or you will only enrich the apothecaries while you plunge yourself and your family into the deepest poverty; nay, instead of gaining the universal panacea, you will contract the most dangerous diseases from constantly moving in an atmosphere black with sulphurous and mercurial smoke, and fetid with the stench of bismuth and all manner of salts.

It is truly amazing that none of the seekers after this great treasure, though willing to submit to any amount of labour and hardship for its sake, seem capable of perceiving the lesson which constant failure is striving to impress upon them. What, I pray you, have those thousands of persons, who have tried the solutions, coagulations, putrefactions, amalgamations, and circulations, gained by their agonising toil? What good result have they produced with their waters, solutions of metals, blood, hair, eggs, milk, sugar, and all manner of herbs? Let me beseech you to profit by their heart-breaking experience, and to have done with everything but true Alchemy, which teaches that the substance is brought to perfection, and attains the exaltation of elementary fire, by its own light and liquid—by which also imperfect metals are ameliorated, because their elementary fire was not properly digested by its liquid. And for the same reason the elementary fire cannot remain, for the liquid is separated from that elementary fire by the heat of the ordinary fire, and evaporates in the form of white smoke. The elementary fire, on the other hand, does not evaporate, but abides with its earth, and must be burned with it, because its protecting liquid has vanished in white smoke. This is that whiteness of which the Ancients have said that it comes after the black colour. For this reason, they are in the habit of saying that you must make it black before you make it white. We begin our process with blackness, and transmute the black smoke, but do not take it for our substance, and make it white. The latter would be a foolish supposition and imposture. If you would avoid such misapprehensions, you must not attempt the study of this subject until you have a sound knowledge of the operations of Nature, and more especially of the essential properties of the metals.

I am afraid, my Brother, that my book will cause you heaviness of heart, instead of joy, because I sweep away at one fell stroke all those false sophistical notions which had become so dear to you. Nevertheless, you must once for all relinquish that idea of yours that you are profoundly versed in the mysteries of this Art, and leave these childish absurdities to those who derive wealth and profit from them. Among these persons, Adam de Bodenstein held a very distinguished place; for he wrote all manner of so-called theosophical books, and boasted of his attainments in the alchemistic Art, of which he was really quite ignorant. Yet to the present day many people believe that he (whose expressions are those of a mere charlatan) had a real knowledge of true alchemy. It is true that his nonsense cannot for a moment impose on the initiated; but among the blind (as the proverb says) it is easy to win golden opinions as a good fencer. On this account, and as Bodenstein is no more among the living, I will dismiss the subject, for nothing but what is favourable should be spoken of the dead and of the absent. This I will say, however, that he was a good Sophist and a good physician; but of Alchemy he knew little or nothing. I should not have said this much if I were not really anxious to warn the unwary against being dazzled by the splendour of his name, and to prevent them from being lured on by it to their own ruin.

If, then, you are a lover of the truth, you will bid farewell to these specious absurdities, and henceforth entrust yourself to the guidance of Nature alone; be sure that she will lead you onward without faltering to the desired goal, even that method by which she works towards the essence. Moreover, she will demand of you neither much labour nor any considerable outlay. The whole thing is done by a simple process of heating, which includes the solution and coagulation of the bodies, and also the sublimation and putrefaction. But some writers have substituted for the simple and true essence a certain other essence, with which they have deceived the whole world, and involved many persons in considerable losses. Whether their conduct was upright and loving will one day be decided by the Great Judge. It would be better not to publish such writings, since the false statements and groundless assertions with which they swarm, plunge so many credulous persons into grievous losses. For if there were not so many books put forward by ignorant writers, many thousands of persons who at the present moment are hopelessly floundering about in a sea of specious book-learning, would have been led by the light of their own unaided intellects to the knowledge of this precious secret; they are prevented, these many years, from seeing the plain truth by a vast mass of printed nonsense which commands their reverence, because they do not understand it. The Ancients did indeed know something about the Art; but at the present day we can very well dispense with the cumbrous phraseology under which they (most successfully) attempted to veil their meaning. It can only tend to the bewilderment of honest enquirers, who are thereby thrown off the true scent, unless indeed they should come to be instructed by living Masters.

I myself may not speak out as plainly as I would, for I am silenced by the vow which binds all the masters of the Art, the curse that lights on those who violate the sacred seal of Nature's secrets, and the malediction of all the philosophers. Therefore, I must exhort you again and again to trust your own observations rather than the writings of others, and to let the Book of Nature be the most favoured volume of your library. Observe her methods, not only in the production of metals, but in the procreation of the fruits of the earth, and their constant growth and development, in the winter and summer, in the spring and autumn, by rain and sunshine. If you had a sound knowledge of Nature's methods in producing the bud and the flower, and in ripening the green fruit, you would be able to set your hand to the germs which Nature provides in the bowels of the earth, and to educe from them (or their substance) that which you so much desire.

Forgive me then, my Brother, for so unceremoniously overthrowing all your old settled and dearly cherished convictions. My excuse must be that I have done it for your own good, as you would otherwise never learn the true secret of transmuting metals. You may believe and trust me, for I can have no conceivable motive for filling the world with fresh lies, of which, God knows, it is already full enough, through the agency of the aforesaid deceivers and their willing dupes, who after being lured on by those false books to the loss of all their worldly goods, have not suffered their eyes to be opened by their losses, and seem unable to find their way out of that gigantic labyrinth of falsehood. Nay, they have even taken upon themselves to write books, and to speak as if they were perfect masters of the Art, and had derived great advantage from it, though in reality they have been brought so low as to be able to afford nothing but miserable decoctions. They dissolved until their whole fortune had undergone a process of dissolution; they sublimed until all their gold and silver had evaporated; they putrefied until their clothes decayed upon their bodies; and they calcined until all their wood and coal were consumed to ashes, and they themselves were reduced to wallet and staff.

This is the prize which they have won with all their trouble. Let their ruin be a warning to you, my Brother. For *their* alchemy, instead of imparting health, is followed by penury and disease; instead of transmuting copper into gold, it changes gold into copper and brass. Consider also how many ignorant persons, such as cobblers, tailors, bankrupt merchants, and tavern keepers, pretend to a knowledge of this Art, and, after a few years' unsuccessful experimenting in the laboratory, call themselves great doctors, announce in boastful and sesquipedalian language their power to cure many diseases, and promise mountains of gold. Those promises are empty wind, and their medicines rank poison, with which they fill the churchyards, and for the impudent abuse of which God will one day visit them with heavy punishment. But I will leave the magistrates and the jailers to deal with these swindling charlatans. I speak of them only to put you on your guard. If so many persons write on the subject of Alchemy, who know nothing whatever about the nature and generation of metals, it becomes all the more necessary for you to be careful what books you read, and how much you believe.

For I tell you truly that so long as you have no real and fundamental knowledge of the nature of the metals, you cannot make much progress in the true Art of Alchemy, or understand the natural transmutation of metals. You must grasp the meaning of every direction before you can put it into effect. Always mistrust that which you do not understand (*i.e.*, in studying this art). There are *many* false ways, but there can be only *one* that is true, and indicates a process which does not require many hands, or much labour. For this reason, beloved friend and Brother, you must work hard by day and by night to obtain a thorough knowledge of the metals, and of their essential nature. Then you will be able to understand the requirements of the art. You will know without being told what is the true substance and the true method. You will see the utter uselessness of your former labour, and you will be amazed at your former blindness. Study the nature of metals and the causes of their generation, for they derive their birth from the same source as all other created things.

For as by a heating process the infant is developed in the mother's womb out of the father's seed, and as the chicken is brought forth out of the egg by the natural incubation of the hen, so the metals, too, are developed in a certain way out of a certain substance. Yet I do not say, my Brother, that mercury and sulphur are the first substance of metals. Those juggling deceivers have told you so; but in the veins of the earth, where the metals grow, are found neither mercury nor sulphur. Therefore, when they speak of sulphur, you must understand them to allude to elementary fire, and by mercury you must understand the liquid. In a similar lying spirit they have called fire (elementary) "our Sun," and the liquid "our Moon," or the elementary fire soul, and the elementary liquid spirit, because elementary substances are invisible. The soul is invisible fire, and the spirit invisible moisture: the outward essential fire and water they have called '*bodies*,' because they are visible and palpable. Nay, they try to make you believe that these are metallic bodies, and that you must dissolve them. But do not let them deceive you. Be on your guard against their dishonest tricks, and cunning devices, by which they set you to experiment with metallic bodies, when they really mean the metallic essence.

They point out to you various materials and substances, notwithstanding that there is only *one* true substance, and *one* true method. Be sure that their solutions, coagulations, sublimations, calcinations, and putrefactions, do not represent the method of Nature in the heart of the earth, where the metals grow. For pious Nature only heats the elementary fire which is thereby ameliorated and fixed through its liquid; which latter she also changes, by various degrees of heat, into all the various objects which compose the three natural kingdoms—and although now it is differentiated into bodies so different as vegetables, animals, and minerals, yet they have all originally sprung from one common substance, all have one root, which the Ancients denominated the first Matter or Hyle. But it is really nothing but hidden elementary fire, with its liquid, which the Ancients called the root liquid, radical moisture, or humid radical, because it is the root of all created things.

This liquid, with its fire, is differentiated into the various kinds of natural bodies, by the various degrees of heat, or '*coction*,' which take place in them. One thing is more perfectly heated in its elementary fire through its liquid, than another. The *vegetable* nature is that in which the coction is least perfect. Therefore its essence is easily burned, and its liquid easily separated from its elementary fire, by common fire.

The coction of the *animal* is almost as imperfect as that of the vegetable substance: for its essence is easily burned. The coction of the *mineral* substances is the most perfect of all, because in them the metallic liquid is more closely united (by coction) to its elementary fire. Hence metals are better able to resist common fire than the vegetable and animal substances. When a metal is placed in the fire, it does not burn with a bright flame like wood; for the liquid of wood is not so completely joined (by coction) to its essence, as the liquid of metals is to *its* essence. The union of the liquid with the essence is not metallic, but vegetable, for which reason the latter is consumed with a black smoke, when, by a higher degree of coction, the vegetable has been transmuted into a metallic essence, it no longer gives out a black smoke in common fire, but a white smoke, as you may see when imperfect metals are melted in the fire. That is why the Ancients said that you must first make the substance black before you make it white, *i.e.*, it must first give out a black smoke before it gives out a white. Again they say: You must first make it white before you make it red. To make red is to make perfect, because gold and silver have been rendered perfect by coction, their essence being fully united to their liquid, and changed into pure fire.

Do not then suffer yourself to be thrown off your guard by the obscure phraseology of the Ancients. If you thoroughly study the simple fundamental nature of the metals, you will know what their enigmatic expressions mean, and will not, like some moderns, conclude from their writings that you must take a certain substance and dissolve it until it turns black, then again purify and calcine it till the blackness disappears and it begins to turn white; and after that, once more increase the fire and calcine and toil until the substance turns red. Such an interpretation of the language of the Ancients can only suggest itself to persons entirely ignorant of the nature of metallic substances; indeed, the Ancients wrote as they did solely in order to hide their real meaning from all but the close students of Nature. To this end they were in the constant habit of employing the terms "mercury" and "sulphur." And although the metallic essence is the true substance which, by natural coction, must be raised from the lowest to the highest stage of development, and although the meaning of the Ancients is intelligible enough to the initiated, yet the ignorant can gather from their language no more than the fact that the substance must be taken from the metals. But where are they to obtain it, and how are they to bring it to perfection? The metallic essence can not be separated from the imperfect metals without being injured; for if it be separated with fire the liquid must evaporate, and the essence (with its earth) be consumed. Nor will you be able to separate the essence of the imperfect metals by means of aqua fortis, arsenic, aqua vitæ, or alkali, without injuring the essence and its liquid by the foreign moisture: for the metallic nature can bear no foreign substance, and if any foreign moisture combines with the metallic liquid, it loses its proper quality and is entirely corrupted.

The metallic essence of the perfect metals you cannot obtain in a separate form; for their liquid and elementary fire are welded together by so perfect a process of coction, and so closely united with their earth, that neither fire nor water can avail to separate them, seeing that the fire has no power over them, and no foreign moisture can combine with, or corrupt, the liquid of perfect metals. All your labour will be in vain: the coction has done its work so well that you will never be able to undo it.

Hence, the Ancients said that there was no sulphur in anything but in the metals, and hence also they called the metallic liquid quicksilver. But names do not alter facts: the fact is that the elementary fire must be so united to its elementary liquid by natural coction that they become indivisible. For the liquid protects the fire against combustion, so that both remain fixed and unchanged in common fire. This perfected substance the Ancients have well called Elixir, or fire which has undergone a process of perfect coction: for that which before was crude and raw is "cooked," or digested by the process of coction. That element which, by its imperfection, causes base metals to be broken up and disintegrated by fire, has been digested and perfected by natural heat.

For this reason you must not grudge the labour which the proper performance of this heating process demands, seeing that it includes purification, sublimation, dissolution, and all the other chemical processes enumerated by the ancient alchemists. All these you may safely dismiss from your mind, as they can cause you nothing but trouble, loss, and waste of time. My purpose in writing this faithful admonition is to caution you again and again to beware of those pitfalls with which the contemptuous obscurity of the Ancients has so plentifully beset the path of the ingenuous enquirer. I also desired to suggest to you the true *substance*, and the one true *method*, and have throughout endeavoured to express myself in a style as free from allegorical obscurity as possible. I have recalled you from your wanderings in the pathless wilderness, and put you in the right way. Now you must beseech Almighty God to give you the real philosophical temper, and to open your eyes to the facts of nature. Thus alone you will be able to reach the coveted goal.

THE

GLORY OF THE WORLD;

OR,

TABLE OF PARADISE;

THAT IS TO SAY,

A TRUE ACCOUNT OF THE ANCIENT SCIENCE WHICH ADAM
LEARNED FROM GOD HIMSELF; WHICH NOAH, ABRAHAM, AND
SOLOMONHELD AS ONE OF THE GREATEST GIFTS OF GOD;
WHICHALSO ALL SAGES, AT ALL TIMES, PREFERRED
TO THEWEALTH OF THE WHOLE WORLD,
REGARDED ASTHE CHIEF TREASURE OF
THE WHOLE WORLD, AND
BEQUEATHED ONLY
TO GOOD MEN;

NAMELY,

THE SCIENCE OF THE PHILOSOPHER'S STONE.

----

2 PET. iii., 5:

*"For this they willingly, through their wickedness, are ignorant of, that
through the Word at God the heavens were of old, and the earth standing out of
the water, and in the water."*

THE GLORY OF THE WORLD,

OR,

TABLE OF PARADISE:

A most precious book, containing art, the like of which is not to
be found upon earth; showing the truth concerning the true
Philosophy, and the most noble medicine, and priceless
Tincture, together with divers other valuable Arts,
and the Instruments required for them.

NOW, in the name of God, the Almighty Creator and Preserver of this World, I
venture to show forth the hidden mysteries of Nature, which God has planted
there, and deigns to reveal to men, that they may see how marvellously things are
created, and how wonderfully all classes of natural objects are brought forth: for a
testimony to all believing Christian men, and for a comfort to all afflicted and
troubled hearts—seeing that all things created perish and are decomposed only to
be renewed again, to be multiplied, animated, and perfected after their kind. For
nothing that is created, or born, is at rest, but daily undergoes increase or
multiplication on the part of Nature, until it becomes that which is created and
ordained to be the treasure of all mankind.

Therefore, beseech God to give you such wisdom and understanding as will
enable you to understand this Art, and to bring it, by His blessing, to a good issue
for His own glory, and the good of your neighbour.

If then you would obtain this knowledge at the hand of God, you must confess
yourself a miserable sinner, and implore His blessing, which alone can enable you
to receive His Gift worthily, and to bear in mind that He has bestowed it upon you
out of pure mercy, and that any pride or presumptuous insolence on your part will
most certainly entail its loss, in addition to His wrath, and eternal condemnation.
You must resolve to begin this blessed and divine work in the name of God, for
the service of all good Christians, and the building up of our faith; to be a good
athlete in the war against unbelievers; to shun the company of wicked men; never
to open your mouth against the righteous; but to bestow your bounty upon the
needy in order that after this life you may receive the crown of eternal joy and
beatitude. For this treasure, which is above all other earthly treasures, is granted to
him alone who approves himself humble, honest, gentle, and faithful, as far as the
weakness of human nature allows, and keeps the laws of God through God's
bounty and blessing, and who is not likely to mistake the true nature of the gift, or
to abuse it against his own eternal welfare. It is the gift of the Holy Spirit, the
loving bounty of the great God, which comes down from the Father of light. He
who masters this Art, must have asked and obtained wisdom of God, since he has
not only gold, silver, and all the riches of this world, but also perfect health, length
of days, and, what is better still, the comfort to he derived from a reassuring type
of the bitter passion and death of our Lord and Saviour Jesus Christ, His descent
into hell, His glorious and most holy Resurrection on the third day, and His victory
and triumph over sin, death, Devil, and hell—a victory that must carry joy and

comfort to all that have the breath of life.

Let me now show you how wonderfully the human and divine natures of Jesus Christ were united and joined together in one Person. The soul and body of Christ and His divine nature were so inseparably joined together that they cannot be severed throughout all eternity. Nevertheless Christ had to die, and His soul had to be separated from His body, and once more joined to it on the third day, that His body might be glorified, and rendered as subtle as His soul and spirit. For He had received His body of the substance of the most Blessed Virgin Mary, and therefore it had to be perfected by temporary separation from His soul and spirit. Nevertheless, His divinity remained united in one essence with the body and soul of Christ—it was with the body in the tomb, and with His soul in Paradise.

The body of Christ had to be separated from its soul in order that it might receive the same power and glory. But now, Christ having been dead, and His soul having afterwards been reunited to His body, they are henceforth inseparably conjoined into one subtle essence. His divine omnipotence which He received from His Father, which governs all things in heaven and earth, and is equally perfect from all eternity, is now one Person with the Christ Jesus, who suffered, died, rose again, and ascended into heaven, in endless power, glory, majesty, might, and honour.

Therefore, O sinful man, render thanks to Almighty God for the grace and fatherly loving kindness shewn to you; and rest assured that you may obtain the glorification which was given to Christ. For Christ rose first that he might open up for you a way unto His heavenly Father. Like Him, you too must be crucified to this world by many hardships, tribulations, and anxieties. But that you may understand the glorification of the body, and its renewal to eternal life, you should diligently consider God's fatherly love and mercy towards fallen man. Bear in mind that all things that come down from Him are good and perfect gifts. Take care, therefore, lest you foully abuse the gifts bestowed upon you freely, without any merit of your own, to the destruction of your soul; rather let all your actions show that you love and fear God, and then every labour to which you set your hand will prosper, and from beginning to end you will pursue the work successfully and joyously. Commit your care to God, trust His word, and keep His holy commandments: then God will be with you in all things, will bless your toil, and in His fatherly love forefend all loss and harm. Your art will then afford you true comfort, yield you all you need, refresh you amid all your hardships, supply you with the means of relieving the necessities of others, and constantly keep before your eyes a living type of your own glorious resurrection, and of that of all Christian believers—whereby we must exchange this earthly and mortal life for endless joy and the glory of eternal and incorruptible beatitude.

Let me then tell you, who would be a true lover of this Art, that it was first delivered by God to Adam in Paradise. For it is a true revelation of many secrets and mysteries. It shows you the vanity of your body and of your life in this world; but it also solaces you with the hope of eternal salvation. It suggests to you the reflection that if God has infused such wonderful virtues into mere inanimate natural objects, surely we, who are so much better than they, must be reserved for some high and glorious destiny. I beseech you, therefore, to acquit yourself wisely in all that you do—not to be in haste,—but to reveal this mystery to no mortal man, unless he be a lover of this Art and of a godly, sincere, and merciful temper.

Such was the practice of the ancient Sages to whom this wisdom was revealed by the inspiration of the Holy Spirit. You must also confess that this Art is real, for the sake of those who will not believe that Jesus Christ proceeded from His Almighty Heavenly Father, and was also born of a pure virgin. Moreover, you must ask God to enlighten you by the gift of His Holy Spirit, to sharpen your understanding, to open your eyes, and to grant you a profound insight into that unfathomable wisdom which lies hid in our Art, and which no Sage has ever been able to express in his writings. For there are many secrets in Nature which it is impossible for our unaided human reason to apprehend. If you follow my directions and suffer yourself to be guided by the grace of God, then the work which you undertake for the glory of God, and for the good of your neighbour, will have a joyful issue. Feed the hungry; give drink to the thirsty; clothe the naked; comfort the afflicted; visit the sick and the prisoners: and you shall have what you desire.

ROBERT VALENS RUGL.

A spirit is within, which by deliberate skill you must separate from the body. Simply disjoin the material part from the vapour. You should then add the cold water of the spring. With this you should unweariedly sprinkle both. You will then have the true Elixir of all this Art.

Exhortation and Information

To all the lovers of this Art, in which they can see, as in a mirror, all the fundamental and essential requirements thereof; whether it is possible or not to arrive at the true Art, and concerning the same.

I would warn all and sundry, but especially you, my beloved disciples, in clear and impressive language, to be on your guard against all fantastical teaching, and to listen to the truthful information which I shall now proceed to give you.

In the first place, you must give a wide berth to the false Alchemy of the vulgar herd. I have experienced this so much that I am loath to recommend any to undertake the work, since this Art is so well hidden that no mortal on earth can discover it unless Sol and Luna meet. If you give diligent heed to my warning you may attain to a knowledge thereof, but if you do not, you will never approach any nearer to it. Know also that there is only *one* thing in the whole world that enters into the composition of the Stone, and that, therefore, all coagulation, and admixture, of different ingredients, would shew you to be on a wrong scent altogether. If you could perform all the different operations of our art, yet all your dissolving, coagulating, decomposing, distilling, augmenting, albefying, &c., would be useless, without a true knowledge of our Matter. For our Art is good and precious, nor can any one become a partaker of it, unless it be revealed to him by God, or unless he be taught by a skilled Master. It is a treasure such as the whole world cannot buy. Do not, therefore, my sons, spend your toil until you know what that is on which you are to operate. For even if you knew the right Matter, your information would be useless to you without a knowledge of the method of preparing it. The Stone in its final and effective form is not to be found anywhere

111

in the whole world, either in the heavens above, or in the earth beneath; nor in any metal, nor in anything that grows, nor yet even in gold or silver. It must he prepared, *i.e.*, developed, into its final form; yet for all that, it cannot, strictly speaking, be made better than God created it, nor can the Tincture be prepared out of it: the 'Tincture' must be added to it, and therefore has nothing to do with our main object, since it is a different thing altogether. If it were in. any metal, we should surely have to look for it in the Sun or Moon; yet the Moon cannot contain it, or it would long since have become the Sun. Neither is it in mercury, or in any sulphur, or salt, or in herbs, or anything of that nature, as you shall see hereafter. Now we will conclude our exhortation, and proceed to describe the Art itself.

There follow some Methods of Recognising our Stone.
I.

Know that our Stone is one, and that it is justly called a Stone. For it *is* a Stone, and could bear no name so characteristic, as that of the Stone of the Sages. Yet it is not any one of our existing stones, but only derives its appellation from its similarity to them. For our Stone is so prepared as to be composed of the four elements. On this account it has been called by different names, and assumes different forms, although it is *one* thing, and its like is not found upon earth. It is a Stone, and not a stone in the sense of having the nature of any one stone; it is fire, yet it has not the appearance, or properties, of fire; it is air, yet neither has it the appearance, or properties, of air; it is water, but has no resemblance, or affinity, to the nature of water. It is earth, though it has not the nature, or appearance, of earth, seeing that it is a thing by itself.

Another way of Knowing our Precious Stone.
II.

An ancient philosopher says: Our Stone is called the sacred rock, and is divided, or signified, in four ways. Firstly, into earth; secondly, into its accretion; thirdly, into fire; and fourthly, into the flame of fire. If any one knows the method of dissolving it, of extracting its salt, and of perfectly coagulating it, he is initiated in the mysteries of the Sages. Therefore if the salt turn white, and assume an oily appearance, then it tinges. There are three stages in our Art. Firstly, the transmutation of the whole thing into one salt; secondly, the rendering of three subtle bodies intangible; thirdly, the repetition of the whole solution of the whole thing. If you understand this, set your hand to the work. For the Matter is only one thing, and would remain one thing, though a hundred thousand books had been written about it, because this Art is so great a treasure that the whole world would not be a sufficient compensation for it. It is described in obscure terms, yet openly named by all, and known to all. But if all knew its secret, no one would work, and it would lose its value. On this account it would he impious to describe it in universally intelligible language. He to whom God will reveal it, may understand these dark expressions. But because most men do not understand them, they are inclined to regard our Art as impossible, and the Sages are branded as wicked men and swindlers. Learned doctors, who thus speak of us, have it before their eyes every day, but they do not understand it, because they never attend to it And then, forsooth, they deny the possibility of finding the Stone; nor will any one ever be able to convince them of the reality of our Art, so long as they blindly follow their own bent and inclination In short, they are too wise to discern it, since it transcends the range of the human intellect, and must be humbly received at the hand of God.

Yet Another Way of Knowing our Blessed Stone.

The philosopher, Morienus, calls our Stone, water: and he had good reasons for the name. O water of bitter taste, that preservest the elements! O glorious nature, that overcomest Nature herself! O thou that resemblest Nature, which dissolvest her tractable nature, that exaltest Nature—that art crowned with light, and preservest in thyself the four elements, out of which the quintessence is made! Thou art for the simple, seeing that thou art most simple in thy operation. Having conceived by a natural process, thou bringest forth vapour, and art a good mother. Thou needest no outward help; nature preserves nature, and is not separated from nature by the operation of nature. The thing is easy to find, the knowledge is easy, altogether familiar, yet it is as a miracle to many. Thy solution is great glory, and all thy lovers are named above. Thou art a great arcanum and to the many thou appearest impossible!

Explanation.

Know, my son, that our Stone is such that it cannot adequately be described in writing. For it is a stone, and becomes water through evaporation; yet it is no stone, and it by a chemical process it receives. a watery form it is at first like any other liquid water, being a thin fluid; yet its nature is not like that of any other water upon earth. There is only one spring in all the world from which this water may be obtained. That spring is in Judæa, and is called, the Spring of the Saviour, or of beatitude. By the grace of God its situation was revealed to the Sages. It issues in a secret place, and its waters flow over all the world. It is familiar to all, yet none knows the principle, reason, or way to find the spring, or discover the way to Judæa. But whoever does not know the right spring will never attain to a knowledge of our Art. For this reason, that Sage might well exclaim, "O water of a harsh and bitter taste!" For, in truth, the spring is difficult to find; but he who knows it may reach it easily, without any expense, labour, or trouble. The water is, of its own nature, harsh and bitter, so that no one can partake of it; and, because it is of little use to the majority of mankind, the Sage doth also exclaim, "O water, that art lightly esteemed by the vulgar, who do not perceive thy great virtues, in thee lie, as it were, hid the four elements. Thou hast power to dissolve, and conserve, and join nature, such as is possessed by no other thing upon earth." If you would know the properties and appearance of this Stone, know that its appearance is aqueous, and that the water is first changed into a stone, then the stone into water, and the water at length into the Medicine. If you know the Stone without the method of its preparation, your knowledge can be of no more use to you than if you knew the right method without being acquainted with the true Matter. Therefore our hearts are filled with gratitude to God for both kinds of knowledge.

Concerning the Treasure in the Tincture.

For let me tell you that when you have the red [tincture] you have something that all the treasures of the world will not buy. For it transmutes all metals into true gold, and is therefore much better than the preparation of the Sun. As a medicine it excels all other gold; all diseases may be cured by drinking one drop of the tincture in a glass of wine; and it has power to work many other marvels which we cannot here mention at length. If you wish to prepare the tincture for the Moon, take five half-ounces of the red tincture, and mix it well with five hundred half-ounces of the Moon, which have. been subjected to the action of fire, then melt it, and the whole will be changed into the Tincture and the Medicine. Of this take half an ounce, and inject it into five hundred half-ounces of Venus or any other metal, and it will be transmuted into pure silver. Of the red tincture, which you have diligently prepared, take one part to a thousand parts of gold, and the whole will be changed into the red tincture. Of this, again, you may take one part to a thousand parts of Venus, or any other metal, and it will be changed into pure gold. For this purpose you need not buy any gold or silver. The first injection you can make with about a drachm of both; and then you can transmute with the tincture more ands more.

You should also know that in our Art we distinguish two things—the body and the spirit: the former being constant, or fixed, while the other is volatile. These two must be changed, the one into the other: the body must become water, and the water body. Then again the body becomes water by its own internal operation, and the two, *i.e.*, the dry and the liquid, must once more be joined together in an inseparable union. This conjunction could not take place if the two had not been obtained from *one* thing; for an abiding union is possible only between things of the same nature. Of this kind is the union which takes place in our Art; for the constituent parts of the Matter are joined together by the operation of nature, and not by any human hand. The substance is divided into two parts, as we shall explain further on. For instance, the Eagle is a "water," which being extracted is then a body dead and lifeless: if it is to be restored to life, the spirit must once more be joined to it, and that in a unique fashion, as we see that it devours gradually again the one eagle after the other. Then the body loses all its grossness, and becomes new and pure; nor can this body and soul ever die, seeing that they have entered into an eternal union, such as the union of our bodies and souls shall be at the last day.

Another Description of our Stone.

The Enigma of the wise (the Stone) is the Salt and Root of the whole Art, and, as it were, its Key, without which no one is able either to lock or unlock its secret entrance. No man can understand this Art who does not know the Salt and its preparation, which takes place in a convenient spot that is both moist and warm; there the dissolution of its liquid must be accomplished, while its substance remains unimpaired. These are the words of Geber.

Explanation.

Know that the Salt of which Geber speaks has none of the specific properties of salt, and yet is called a Salt, and is a Salt. It is black and fetid, and when chemically prepared, assumes the appearance of blood, and is at length rendered white, pure, and clear. It is a good and precious Salt which, by its own operation, is first impure and then pure. It dissolves and coagulates itself, or, as the Sage says, it locks and unlocks itself. No Salt has this property but the Salt of the Sages.

Its chemical development it may undergo in a moist and convenient place, where its moisture (as the Sage says) may be dissolved in the Bath of Mary. He means that it must be warm enough for its water to be distilled, yet not warmer than the excrement of horses, which is not fresh.

Another Description of our Stone.

Alexander the Great, King of Macedonia, in his "Philosophy" has the following words: Know that the Salt is fire and dryness. Fire coagulates, and its nature is hot, dry, and penetrating, even unto the inmost part. Its property is to become white even as the Sun and the Moon with the variations in the extremes of fire, to wit, of the natural fire, while the Sun restores redness and the Moon whiteness, and brings bodies to their spiritual condition at the same time that it removes their blackness and bad sulphur. With it bodies are calcined: it is the secret of the red and white tincture, the foundation and root of all things, and the best of all created things after the rational soul of man. For no Stone in the whole world has a greater efficacy, nor can any child of this earth find the Art without this Stone. Blessed be God in heaven, who hath created this Art in Salt for the transmutation of all things, seeing that it is the quintessence which is above all things, and in all things. God Most High has not only from Heaven blessed creatures in this fashion, but praise, excellence, power, and wisdom are to be recognised as existing in this Salt. He who can dissolve and coagulate it, is well acquainted with the arcana of this Art. Our Salt is found in a certain precious Salt, and in all things. On this account the ancient Sages called it the "common moon," because all men need it. If you would become rich, prepare this Salt till it is rendered sweet. No other salt is so permanent, or has such power to fix the "soul," and to resist fire. The Salt of the earth is the soul; it coagulates all things, is in the midst of the earth when the earth is destroyed; nor is there anything on the earth like its tincture. It is called Rebis (Two-thing), is a Stone, Salt, *one* body, and, to the majority of mankind, a vile and a despised thing. Yet it purifies and restores bodies, represents the Key of our whole Art, and all things are summed up in it. Only its entering in is so subtle that few perceive it: yet if it enter a body, it tinges it and brings it to perfection. What then should you desire of God but this Salt and the ingression thereof?

If a man lived a hundred thousand years, he could never sufficiently marvel at the wonderful manner in which this noble treasure is obtained from ashes, and again reduced to ashes. In the ashes is Salt, and the more the ashes are burnt, the more ashes it affords; notice also, that that proceeds from fire, and returns to fire, which proceeds from [the] earth. All must confess that in the Salt there are two salts that kill mercury. This is a most profound saying. For sulphur, and the radical liquid, are generated in earth of a most subtle nature, and thus is prepared the Philosopher's Stone, which causes all things, even as the philosophers set forth, to arise out of *one* thing, and one nature, without the addition of any foreign substance. Our Matter is one of the commonest things upon earth, and contains within itself the four elements. It is, indeed, nothing short of marvellous that so many seek so ordinary a thing, and yet are unable to find it. We might put down many other characteristics of this Salt, but I prefer to leave the further elaboration of this subject to the reader, and to confine myself to a more detailed account of its fruits, entrance, and life, of the mode of opening the garden, and catching a glimpse of the glorious roses, of the way in which they multiply, and bear fruit a thousand-fold; also how you may cause the dead body to re-appear, and to be raised again to immortal life, by the power of which it may be able to enter imperfect bodies, purify them, and bring them to perfection, and to a state of immutable permanence.

I now propose to speak of the Stone under three aspects, viz., as the vegetable, the animal, and the mineral Stone; and among these again, of the one which contains those four elements that impart life to all. Place this one substance in an air-tight alembic, and treat it according to the precepts of our Art, which we shall set forth further on. Then the sowing in the field can take place, and you obtain the Mineral Stone, and the Green Lion that imbibes so much of its own spirit. Then life returns to its spirit through the alembic, and the dead body lies at the bottom of the vessel. In the latter there are still two elements which the fire cannot sever— for sooner [than that] the ashes are burned in the fire itself, and the Salt thereby becomes stronger. The earth must be calcined until it turns white; then the earth is severed of its own accord, and is united .to its own earth. For every thing strives to be joined to its like. Give it the cold and humid element to drink, and leave it standing eight days, that the two may be well mixed. You must see yourself what is best to be done after this: for I cannot give you any further information at present. Sun and Moon must have intercourse, like that of a man and woman: otherwise the object of our Art cannot be attained. All other teaching is false and erroneous. Think upon this Salt as the true foundation of our Art; for its worth outweighs all the treasures of this world. Itself is not developed into the tincture, but the tincture must be added to it. Nor is the substance of our Art found in any metal.

Another Description of the Matter and the Method.
By Senior.

Natural things, according to this Sage, are those which have been generated and produced out of a natural substance by a natural method. Now in its first, or lunar, stage, our Stone is produced from a coagulated white earth, as the Sage says: Behold our Sun in our white earth, and that by which the union in our Art is effected; which is twice transmuted into water, and whose volatile exhalation, representing that which is most precious in our Substance, is the highest consolation of the human body. With this water the inward mercury of the metals must be extracted. Hence it follows that our Stone is obtained from the elements of two luminaries (gold and silver), being called our quicksilver and incombustible oil, the soul and light of bodies—which alone can afford to dead and imperfect bodies eternal light and life. Therefore I pray and beseech you, my son, to crush quicksilver from our Substance with intelligence and great activity.

The Purging the "Earth" of Its Superfluous Earth.

The aforesaid earth, or Matter, you must purify, or calcine, so as to extract its water and spirit. The latter you must enclose in a phial, and pour common aqua vitæ upon it till the substance is covered to the height of three or four fingers; then subject it to the action of fire for an hour, and diligently distil it by the bath. What remains you must again calcine, and extract with its water till you find nothing more in the "earth." The earth keep for the second stage of the process. The water you have extracted distil over a gentle fire. Then you will find at the bottom of the distilling vessel a certain beautiful substance, resembling a crystal stone, which is purged of all earthly grossness, and is called "our earth." This substance you must place in a glass (pumpkin-shaped) distilling vessel, and calcine until it becomes dry and white, and yet liquid withal. Then you have obtained the treasure of this world, which has virtue to purify and perfect all earthly things: it enters into all, it nourishes the fixed salt in all things by means of Mercury or the body.

Another Description of our Stone.

Know, my sons, that the Stone out of which our Art is elaborated, never touches the earth after its generation. If it touch the earth, it is of no use for our purpose, although at its first birth it is generated by the Sun and Moon, and embodies certain earthy elements. It is generated in the earth, then broken, destroyed, and mortified. Out of it arises a vapour which is carried with the wind into the sea, and thence brought back again to the land, where it almost immediately disappears. It must be caught in the air, before it touches the ground; otherwise it evaporates. As soon as it is borne from the sea to the land, you must promptly seize it, and enclose it in your phial, then manipulate it in the manner described. You may know its coming by the wind, rain, and thunder, which accompany it; therefore it should not escape you. Though it is born anew every day, yet it existed from the beginning of the world. But as soon as it falls to the ground, it becomes useless for the purposes of our Art.

> "From our earth wells forth a fertilizing fountain, whence flow two precious stones. The first straight-way hastens to the rising of the Sun; the other makes its way to the setting thereof. From them fly forth two Eagles, plunge into the flames, and fall once more to the earth. Both are furnished with feathers, and Sun and Moon, being placed under their wings, are perfected."

Know also that two waters flow forth from this fountain; the one (which is the *spirit*) towards the rising Sun, and the other, *the body*, towards the setting Sun. The two are really only *one* very limpid water, which is so bitter as to be quite undrinkable. The quantity of this water is so great that it flows over the whole earth, yet leads to nothing but the knowledge of this Art. The same also is misused too often by those who desire it. Take also the "fire," and in it you will find the Stone, and nowhere else in the whole world. It is familiar to all men, both young and old, is found in the country, in the village, in the town, in all things created by God; yet it is despised by all. Rich and poor handle it every day. It is cast into the street by servant maids. Children play with it. Yet no one prizes it, though, next to the human soul, it is the most beautiful and the most precious thing upon earth, and has power to pull down kings and princes. Nevertheless, it is esteemed the vilest and meanest of earthly things. It is cast away and rejected by all. Indeed it is the Stone which the builders of Solomon disallowed. But if it be prepared in the right way, it is a pearl without price, and, indeed, the earthly antitype of Christ, the heavenly Corner Stone. As Christ was despised and rejected in this world by the people of the Jews, and nevertheless was more precious than heaven and earth; so it is with our Stone among earthly things: for the spring where it is found is called the fount of nature. For even as through Nature all growing things are generated by the heat of the Sun, so also through Nature is our Stone born after that it has been generated.

When you have found the water which contains our Stone, you must take nothing away from it, nor add anything to it: for it must be entirely prepared by means of that which it contains within itself. Then extract the water in an alembic, and separate the liquid from the dry. The body will then remain alone on the glass, while the water runs down into the lower part. Thereupon unite the water once more to the body in the manner described above, and your task will be accomplished. Know also that the water in which is our Stone, is composed in well-balanced proportions of the four elements. In the chemical process you will learn to distinguish earth, oil, and water, or body, spirit, and soul: the earth is at the bottom of the glass vessel, the oil, or soul, is with the earth, and the water is the spirit which is distilled from it. In the same way you will come upon two colours, namely, white and red, representing the Moon and the Sun. The oil is the fire, or the Sun, the water is air, or the Moon; and Sun and Moon are silver and gold which must enter into union. But enough, what I have said in this Epistle ought to enable you to find the Stone, and if herein you fail to discover it, rest assured that it will never become known to you. Be thou, therefore, a lover of the Art, and commended unto God the Almighty even unto all eternity. Written in the year 1526 after the birth of our Lord.

Thus do the Sages write concerning the two waters which yet are only *one* water—and in this alone the Stone is to be found. Know also that by so much as the earthly part is wanting, by also so much does the heavenly part abound more fully. Now this Stone renders all dry and arid bodies humid, all cold bodies warm, all impure bodies clear and pure. It contains within itself all healing and transmuting virtue, breathed into it by the art of the Master and the quickening spirit of fire. Thanks be unto God therefore in all time.

The Sun is its Father, the Moon its Mother.

If you have those two spirits, they bring forth the Stone, which is prepared out of one part of Sulphur, or Sun, and four parts of Mercury, or Moon. The Sulphur is warm and dry, the Mercury cold and moist. That must again be dissolved into water, which before was water, and the body, which before was mercury, must again become mercury.

Concerning the First Matter, or Seed of the Metals, including that of the Husband, and that of the Spouse.

Metals have their own seed, like all other created things. Generation and parturition take place in them as in everything else that grows. If this were not the case, we should never have had any metals. Now, the seed is a metallic Matter which is liquefied from earth. The seed must be cast into its earth, and there grow, like that of every other created thing. Therefore, we must prepare the earth, or our first Matter, and cast into it the seed, whereupon it will bring forth fruit after its kind. This motion is required for the generation out of *one* thing, viz., that first Matter; the body must become [a] spirit, and the spirit body: thence arises the medicine which is transmuted from one colour to another. Now, that which is sought in the white produces white, and the red, in like manner, gives red. The first

Matter is *one* thing, and fashioned into its present shape by the hand of God, and not of man—joined together, and transmuted into its [being] essence by Nature alone. This we take, dissolve, and again conjoin, and wash with its own water, until it becomes white, and then again red. Thus our earth, in which we now may easily see our Sun and Moon, is purified. For the Sun is the Father of metals, and the Moon is their Mother: and if generation is to take place, they must be brought together as husband and wife. By itself neither can produce anything, and therefore the red and the white must be brought together. And though a thousand books have been written about it, yet for all that, the first substance is riot more than one. It is the earth into which we cast our grain, that is to say, our Sun and Moon, which then bear fruit after their kind. If itself be cast into metals, it is changed into that which is best, viz., Sun and Moon. This is most true. Thanks be unto God.

A Simple Account of the True Art.

According to the Sages, no body is dissolved without the coagulation of the spirit. For as soon as the spirit is transmuted into the body, [the Stone] receives its power. So long as the spirit is volatile, and liable to evaporate, it cannot produce any effect: when it is fixed, it immediately begins to operate. You must therefore prepare it as the baker prepares the bread. Take a little of the spirit, and add it to the body, as the baker adds leaven to the meal, till the whole substance is leavened. It is the same with our spirit, or leaven. The Substance must be continuously penetrated with the leaven, until it is wholly leavened. Thus the spirit purges and spiritualizes the body, till they are both transmuted into one. Then they transmute all things, into which they are injected, into their own nature. The two must be united by a gentle and continuous fire, affording the same degree of warmth as that with which a hen hatches her eggs. It must then be placed in a St. Mary's Bath, which is neither too warm nor too cold. The humid must be separated from the dry, and again joined to it. When united, they change mercury into pure gold and silver. Thenceforward you will be safe from the pangs of poverty. But take heed that you render thanks unto God for His gracious gift which is hidden from many. He has revealed the secret to you that you may praise His holy name, and succour your needy neighbour. Therefore, take diligent heed, lest you hide the talent committed to your care. Rather put it out at interest for the glory of God, and the good of your neighbour. For every man is bound to help his fellowman, and to be an instrument in the hand of God for relieving his necessities. Of this rule Holy Scripture affords an illustration in the example of Joseph, Habakkuk, Susanna, and others.

Here follows my TESTAMENT which I have drawn up in your favour, my beloved Sons, with all my Heart.

For your sakes, beloved students of this Art, and dear Sons, I have committed to writing this my testament, for the purpose of instructing, admonishing, warning, and informing you as to the substance, the method, the pitfalls to be avoided, and the only way of understanding the writings of the Sages. For as Almighty God has created all things out of the dry and the humid elements, our Art, by divine grace, may be said to pursue a precisely similar course. If therefore any man know the principle and method of creative nature, he should have a good understanding of our Art. If anyone be unacquainted with Natures methods, he will find our Art difficult, although in reality it is as easy as to crush malt, and brew beer. In the beginning when, according to the testimony of Scripture, God made heaven and earth, there was only *one* Matter, neither wet nor dry, neither earth, nor air, nor fire, nor light, nor darkness, but one single substance, resembling vapour or mist, invisible and impalpable. It was called Hyle, or the first Matter. If a thing is once more to be made out of nothing, that "nothing" must be united, and become *one* thing; out of this *one* thing must arise a palpable substance, out of the palpable substance *one* body, to which a living soul must be given—whence through the grace of God, it obtains its specific form. When God made the substance, it was dry, but held together by moisture. If anything was to grow from that moisture, it had to be separated from that which was dry, so as to get the fire by itself, and the earth by itself. Then the earth had to be sprinkled with water, if anything moist was to grow out of it, for without moisture nothing can grow. In the same way, nothing grows in water, except it have earth wherein to strike root. It then the water is to bedew the earth, there must be something to bring the water into contact with the earth; for example, the wind prevents all ordinary water from flowing to the sea, and remaining there. Thus one element without the aid of another can bear no fruit; if there was nothing to set the wind in motion it would never blow—therefore the fire has received the office of impelling and obliging it to do its work. This you may see when you boil water over the fire; for then there arises a steam which is really *air*, *water* being nothing but coagulated air, and air being generated from water by the heat of the Sun. For the Sun shines upon the water, and heats it until steam is seen to issue forth. This vapour becomes wind, and, on account of the large quantity of [the] air, we get moisture and rain: so air is once more changed or coagulated into water, or rain, and causes all things upon earth to grow, and fills the rivers and the seas.

It is the same with our Stone, which is daily generated from [the] air by the Sun and Moon, in the form of a certain vapour, yea, even through the Red Sea; it flows in Judea in the channel of Nature whither it behoves us to bring it. If we catch it, we lop off its hands and feet, tear off its head, and try to bring it to the red [colour]. If we find anything black in it, we throw it away with the entrails and the filth. When it has been purified, we take its limbs, join them together again, whereupon our King revives, never to die again, and is so pure and subtle as to pervade all hard bodies, and render them even more subtle than itself. Know also that when God, the Almighty, had set Adam in Paradise, He shewed him these two things in the following words: "Behold, Adam, here are two things, one fixed and permanent, the other volatile: their secret virtue thou must not make known to *all* thy sons."

Earth, my brother, is constant, and water volatile, as you may see when anything is burnt. For then that which is constant remains, while that which is volatile evaporates. That which remains resembles ashes, and if you pour water on it, it becomes an alkali, the efficacy of the ashes passing into the water. If you clarify the lye, put it into an iron vessel, and let the moisture evaporate over a fire, you will find at the bottom the substance which before was in the lye, that is to say, the salt of the matter from which the ashes were obtained. This salt might very well be called the Philosopher's Stone, from being obtained by a process exactly similar to that which is employed in preparing the *real* Stone, though at the same time it profits nothing in our work. For the substance which contains our Stone is a lye, not indeed prepared by the hand of man from ashes and water, but joined together by Nature, according to the creation and ordination of God, commingled of the four elements, possessed of all that is required for its perfect chemical development. If you take the substance, which contains our Stone, subject it to a S. Mary's Bath in an alembic, and distil it, the water will run down into the antisternium, and the salt, or earth, remain at the bottom, and is so dry as to be without any water, seeing that you have separated the moist from the dry. Pound the body small, put it into the S. Mary's Bath, and expose it to heat till it is quite decomposed. Then give it its water to drink, slowly, and at long intervals, till it is clarified. For it coagulates, dissolves, and purifies itself. The distilled water is the spirit which imparts life to its body, and is the alone soul thereof. Water is wind (air), and wind is life, and the life is [in the] soul. In the chemical process, you find water and oil—but the oil always remains with the body, and is, as it were, burnt blood. Then it is purified with the body by long-continued gentle heat. But you should be careful not to set about this Art before you understand my instructions, which at the end of this first part are bequeathed to you in the form of a Testament. For the Stone is prepared out of nothing in the whole world, except this substance, which is essentially one. He who is unacquainted therewith can never attain the Art. It is that one thing which is not dug up from mines, or from the caverns of the earth, like gold, silver, sulphur, salt, &c., but is found in the form which God originally imparted to it. It is formed and manifested by an excessive thickening of air; as soon as it leaves its body, it is clearly seen, but it vanishes without a trace as soon as it touches the earth, and, as it is never seen again, it must therefore be caught while it is still in the air—as I told you once before. I have called it by various names, but the simplest is perhaps that of "Hyle," or first principle of all things. It is also denominated the One Stone of the Philosophers, composed of hostile elements, the Stone of the Sun, the Stone of the Metals, the runaway slave, the aëriform Stone, the Thirnian Stone, Magnesia, the corporeal Stone, the Stone of the jewel, the Stone of the free, the golden Stone, the fountain of earthly things, Xelis, or Silex (flint), Xidar, or Radix (root), Atrop, or Porta (gate). By these and many other names it is called, yet it is only *one*. If you would be a true Alchemist, give a wide berth to all other substances, turn a deaf ear to all other advisers, and strive to obtain a good knowledge of our Stone, its preparation, and its virtue.

My Son, esteem this my Testament very highly: for in it I have, out of love and compassion towards you, given the reins to the warm-hearted impulse which constrains me to reveal more than I ought to reveal. But I beseech you, by the Passion of our Lord and Saviour Jesus Christ, not to communicate my Testament to ignorant, unworthy, or wicked men, lest God's righteous vengeance light upon you, and hurl you into the yawning gulf of everlasting punishment, from which also may the same merciful God most mercifully preserve us.

It is by no means a light thing to shew the nature of the aforesaid Hyle. Hyle is the first Matter, the Salt of the Sages, Azoth, the seed of all metals, which is extracted from the body of "Magnesia" and the Moon.

Hyle is the first principle of all things—the Matter that was from the beginning. It was neither moist, nor dry, nor earth, nor water, nor light, nor darkness, but a mixture of all these things, and this mixture is HYLE.

In the beginning, when God Almighty had created our first parent Adam, together with all other earthly and heavenly bodies, He set him in Paradise, and forbade him, under penalty of eternal death, to eat of the fruit of the tree of the knowledge of good and evil. So long as Adam obeyed the Divine precept he had immortality, and possessed all that he needed for perfect happiness. But when he had partaken of the forbidden fruit, he was, by the command of God, driven forth into this world, where he and his descendants have since that time suffered nothing but poverty, disease, anxiety, bitter sorrow, and death. If he had been obedient to the Divine injunction, he would have lived a thousand years in Paradise in perfect happiness, and would then have been translated to heaven; and a like happy destiny would have awaited all his descendants. For his disobedience God visited him with all manner of sufferings and diseases; but in His mercy also shewed him a medicine whereby the different defects brought in by sin might be remedied, and the pangs of hunger and disease resisted, as we are, for instance, preserved and strengthened by bodily meat and drink.

It was on account of this original sin that Adam, in spite of his great wisdom and the many arts that God had taught him, could not accomplish his full thousand years. But if he had not known the virtues of herbs, and the Medicine, he would certainly not have lived as long as he did. When, however, at length his Medicine would no longer avail to sustain life, he sent his son Seth to Paradise to fetch the tree of life. This he obtained after a spiritual manner. But Seth did seek also and was given some olives of the Tree of the Oil of Mercy, which he planted on the grave of his father. From them sprang up the blessed Tree of the Holy Cross, which through the atoning death of our Redeemer became to us wretched, sinful men, a most potent tree of life, in gracious fulfilment of the request of our first parent Adam. On the other hand, the suffering, disease, and imperfection brought not only upon men, but also upon plants and animals, by the fall of Adam, found a remedy in that precious gift of Almighty God, which is called the Elixir, and Tincture, and has power to purge away the imperfections not only of human, but even of metallic bodies; which excels all other medicines, as the brightness of the sun shames the moon and the stars. By means of this most noble Medicine many men, from the death of Adam to the fourth monarchy, procured for themselves perfect health and great length of days. Hence those who had a good knowledge of the Medicine, attained to three hundred years, others to four hundred, some to five hundred, like Adam; others again to nine hundred, like Methusalem and Noah; and some of their children to a longer period still, like Bacham, Ilrehur, Kalix, Hermes, Geber, Albanus, Ortulanus, Morienus, Alexander of Macedonia, Anaxagoras, Pythagoras, and many others who possessed the Medicine of the Blessed Stone in silence, and neither used it for evil purposes, nor made it known to the wicked; just as God Himself has in all times hidden this knowledge from the proud, the impure, and the froward. But cease to wonder that God has put such excellent virtue into the Stone, and has imparted to it the power of restoring animal bodies, and of perfecting metals: for I hope to explain to you the whole matter in the three parts of my Book, which I have entitled GLORY of the WORLD. If you will accept my teaching, and follow my directions, you will be able to prove the truth of my assertions by your own happy experience. Now when you have attained this great result, take care that you do not hide your talent. Use it for the solace of the suffering, the building of Christian schools and churches, and the glory of the Holy Trinity. Otherwise God will call you to an eternal account for your criminal neglect of His gift. May God deign to keep us from such a sin, and to establish us in His Holy Word!

To the Reader.

If it should seem unto you a tedious matter, my friendly reader, to read through and digest my book, I advise you to cheer yourself on by bearing in mind the great object you have in view. If you do so you will find the book very pleasant reading, and a joy indeed. Since God—praised in all times be his Holy and Venerable Name!—in His unspeakable mercy has made known to me the magistery of this most true and noble Art, I am moved and constrained by brotherly love to shew you the manner of producing this treasure, in order that you may be able to avoid the ruinous trouble and expense to which I was put in the course of a long and fruitless search. I will endeavour to be as clear and outspoken as possible, in order to vindicate myself from the possible charge of imposture, malice, and avarice. I am most anxious that the gift which God has committed to my trust shall not rust, or rot, or be useless in my hands. For this most precious Medicine is so full of glorious potency as to be most justly styled the Oil of Mercy, for reasons which your own understanding will suggest to you. It is therefore unnecessary for me to go into this preliminary question at any great length. I may at once proceed to give you an account of the Art itself, and to put you on your guard against all seducing deceivers,—in short, to open up to you a true, unerring, and joyful road to the knowledge and possession of the Stone, and to the operations of this Art.

Therefore, I—who possess the Stone, and communicate to you this Book— would faithfully admonish and beseech you to keep this my TABLE of PARADISE and GLORY of the WORLD, from all proud and unjust oppressors of the poor; from all presumptuous, shallow, scornful, calumnious, and wicked persons, so as not to put it into their hands, on pain of God's everlasting punishment. I beseech you to take this warning to heart; but, on the other hand, to communicate and impart this my Table to all true, poor, pious, honest, and benevolent persons, who will gratefully reverence and rightly use the merciful gift of God, and conceal it from the unworthy. Nevertheless, even if my book should find its way into the hands of wicked men, God will so smite them with blindness as to prevent them from apprehending too much of my meaning, and frustrate all their attempts to carry out my directions. For God knows how to confound the wicked, and bring their presumption to nought; as we are also told by David in his psalms: "Thine enemies shalt thou hold in thine hand, and shalt restrain them in the snares of their mind." I beseech you, therefore, my sons, to give diligent heed to my teaching; then you will spend this life in health and happiness, and at length inherit everlasting joy. I pray that God the Father, the Son, and the Holy Ghost, may grant this my petition.

An Account of the True Art.

I make known to all ingenuous students of this Art that the Sages are in the habit of using words which may convey either a true or a false impression; the former to their own disciples and children, the latter to the ignorant, the foolish, and the unworthy. Bear in mind that the philosophers themselves never make a false assertion. The mistake (if any) lies not with them, but with those whose dulness makes them slow to apprehend the meaning. Hence it comes that, instead of the waters of the Sages, these inexperienced persons take pyrites, salts, metals, and divers other substances which, though very expensive, are of no use whatever for our purpose. For no one would dream of buying the true Matter at the apothecary's; nay, that tradesman daily casts it into the street as worthless refuse. Yet the matter of our Stone is found in all those things which are used by ignorant charlatans: for it is our Stone, our Salt, our Mercury, our verdigris, halonitre, salmiac, Mars, sulphur, &c. It is not dug out with pick-axes from ordinary mountains, seeing that our Stone is found in our mountains and springs; our Salt is found in our salt-spring, our metal in our earth, and from the same place we dig up our mercury and sulphur. But what we mean by our mines and springs these charlatans cannot understand. For God has blinded their minds and made gross their senses, and left them to carry on their experiments with all manner of false substances. Nor do they seem able to perceive their error, or to be roused from their idle imaginations by persistent failure. Where they should have distilled with gentle heat they sublime over a fierce fire, and reduce their substance to ashes, instead of developing its inherent principles by vitalizing warmth. Again, when they should have dissolved, they coagulated instead, and so on. By these false methods they could, of course, obtain no good result; but instead of blaming their own ignorance they lay the fault on their teacher, and even deny the genuineness of our Art. As a matter of fact, all their mistakes arise from their misinterpreting the meaning of words which should have put them on the right scent. For instance, when the Sages speak of calcining, these persons understand that word to mean "burning," and consequently render their substance useless by burning it to ashes. When the Sages "dissolve," or transmute into "water," these shallow persons corrode with aqua fortis. They do not understand that the dissolution must be effected with something that is contained within our substance, and not by means of any foreign appliance. These foolish devices bear the same relation to our Art that a dark hole bears to a transparent crystal. It is their own ignorance that prevents them from attaining to a true knowledge; but they put the blame on our writings, and call us charlatans and impostors. They argue that if the Stone could be found at all, they must have discovered it long ago, their eyes being as keen and their minds as acute as they are. "Behold," say they, "how we have toiled day and night, how many books we have read, how many years we have spent in our laboratories: surely if there were anything in this Art, it could not have escaped us." By speaking thus, they only exhibit their own presumption and folly. They themselves have no eyes, and they make that an argument for blaspheming our high and holy Art. Therefore, you should first strive to make yourself acquainted with the secrets of Nature's working, and with the elementary principles of the world, before you set your hand to this task. After acquiring this knowledge, carefully peruse this book from beginning to end; you will then be in a position to judge whether our Art is true or false. You will also know what substance you must take, how you must prepare it, and how your eager search may be brought to a successful issue. Let me enjoin you, therefore, to preserve strict silence, to let nobody know what you are doing, and to keep a good heart: then God will grant you the fulfilment of all your wishes.

Here follows my own Opinion and Philosophical Dictum.

I now propose to put down a brief statement of the view which I take of this matter. He who understands my meaning, may at once pass on to the opinions of the various Sages, which I have placed at the end of my book. He who does not apprehend my meaning, will find it explained in the following treatise.

Since I know the blessed and true Art, with the nature and the matter of the Stone, I have thought it my duty freely to communicate it to you—not in a lawyer's style, nor in pompous language, but in few and simple words. Whoever peruses this book carefully, and with an elementary knowledge of natural relations, cannot miss the secret which I intend to convey. I am afraid that I shall be overwhelmed with reproaches for speaking out with so much plainness, seeing that this Art has never, from the beginning of the world, been so clearly explained as I mean to explain it in this Book. Nevertheless, I am well aware that I am now declaring a secret which must for ever remain hidden from the wise of this world, and from those who are established in their own conceits. But I must now proceed to give you the result of my experience.

My beloved sons and disciples, and all ye that are students of this Art; I herewith, in the fulness of Christian faith and charity, do make known to you that the Philosopher's Stone grows not *only* on "*our*" tree, but is found, as far as its effect and operation are concerned, in the fruit of all other trees, in all created things, in animals, and vegetables, in things that grow, and in things that do not grow. For when it rises, being stirred and distilled by the Sun and the Moon, it imparts their own peculiar form and properties to all living creatures by a divine grace; it gives to flowers their special form and colour, whether it be black, red, yellow, green, or white; in the same way all metals and minerals derive their peculiar qualities from the operation of this Stone. All things, I say, are endowed with their characteristic qualities by the operation of this Stone, *i.e.*, the conjunction of the Sun and Moon. For the Sun is the Father, and the Moon the Mother of this Stone, and the Stone unites in itself the virtues of both its parents. Such are the peculiar properties of our Stone, by which it may be known. If you understand the operation, the form, and the qualities, of this Stone, you will be able to prepare it; but if you do not, I faithfully counsel you to give up all thought of ever accomplishing this task.

Observe, furthermore, how the seeds of all things that grow, as, for instance, grains of wheat or barley, spring forth from the ground, by the operation of the Stone, and the developing influences of Sun and Moon; how they grow up into the air, are gradually matured, and bring forth fruit, which again must be sown in its own proper soil. The field is prepared for the grain, being well ploughed up, and manured with well rotted dung; for the earth consumes and assimilates the manure, as the body assimilates its food, and separates the subtle from the gross Therewith it calls forth the life of the seed, and nourishes it with its own proper milk, as a mother nourishes her infant, and causes it to increase in size, and to grow upward. The earth separates, I say, the good from the bad, and imparts it as nutriment to all growing things; for the destruction of one thing is the generation of another. It is the same in our Art, where the liquid receives its proper nutriment from the earth. Hence the earth is the Mother of all things that grow; and it must be manured, ploughed, harrowed, and well prepared, in order that the corn may grow, and triumph over the tares, and not be choked by them. A grain of wheat is raised from the ground through the distillation of the moisture of the Sun and Moon, if it has been sown in its own proper earth. The Sun and Moon must also impel it to bring forth fruit, if it is to bring forth fruit at all. For the Sun is the Father, and the Moon the Mother, of all things that grow.

In the same way, in our soil, and out of our seed, our Stone grows through the distilling of the Sun and Moon; and as it grows it rises upwards, as it were, into the air, while its root remains in the ground. That which is above is even as that which is below; the same law prevails; there is no error or mistake. Again, as herbs grow upward, put forth glorious flowers and blossoms, and bear fruit, so our grain blossoms, matures its fruit, is threshed, sifted, purged of its chaff, and again put in the earth, which, however, must previously have been well manured, harrowed, and otherwise prepared. When it has been placed in its natural soil, and watered with rain and dew, the moisture of heaven, and roused into life by the warmth of the Sun and Moon, it produces fruit after its own kind. These two sowings are peculiar characteristics of our Art. For the Sun and Moon are our grain, which we put into our soil, as soul and spirit—and such as are the father and the mother will be the children that they generate. Thus, my sons, you know our Stone, our earth, our grain, our meal, our ferment, our manure, our verdigris, our Sun and Moon. You understand our whole magistery, and may joyfully congratulate yourselves that you have at length risen above the level of those blind charlatans of whom I spoke. For this, His unspeakable mercy, let us render thanks and praise to the Creator of all things, through Jesus Christ our Lord. Amen.

Concerning the Origin of Metals.

My son, I will now proceed to explain to you more in detail the generation of the metals, and the way in which they receive their growth and development, with their special form and quality. You will thereby be enabled to understand, even from the very foundation, with marvellous accuracy and clearness, the principle that underlies our whole Art. Permit me, therefore, to inform you that all animals, trees, herbs, stones, metals, and minerals, grow and attain to perfection, without being necessarily touched by any human hand: for the seed is raised up from the ground, puts forth flowers, and bears fruit, simply through the agency of natural influences. As it is with plants, so it is with metals. While they lie in the heart of the earth, in their natural ore, they grow, and are developed, day by day, through the influence of the four elements: their fire is the splendour of the Sun and Moon; the earth conceives in her womb the splendour of the Sun, and by it the seeds of the metals are well and equally warmed, just like the grain in the fields. Through this warmth there is produced in the earth a vapour or spirit, which rises upward and carries with it the most subtle elements. It might well be called a fifth element: for it is a quintessence, and contains the most volatile parts of all the elements. This vapour strives to float upward through the summit of the mountains, but, being covered with great rocks, they prevent it from doing so: for when it strikes against them, it is compelled to descend again. It is drawn up by the Sun, it is forced down again by the rocks, and as it falls the vapour is transmuted into a liquid, *i.e.*, sulphur and mercury. Of each of these a part is left behind—but that which is volatile rises and descends again, more and more of it remaining behind, and becoming fixed after each descent. This "fixed" substance is the metals, which cleave so firmly to the earth and the stones that they must be smelted out in a red-hot furnace. The grosser the stones and the earth of the mountains are, the less pure will the metal be; the more subtle the soil and the stones are, the more subtle will be the vapour, and the sulphur and mercury formed by its condensation—and the purer these latter are, the purer, of course, will the metals themselves be. When the earth and the stones of the mountain are gross, the sulphur and mercury must partake of this grossness, and cannot attain to their proper development. Hence arise the different metals, each after its own kind. For as each tree of the field has its own peculiar shape, appearance, and fruit, so each mountain bears its own particular ore; those stones and that earth being the soil in which the metals grow. The quality of this soil is to a great extent dependent upon planetary influences. The nearer the mountains lie to the planets, the more do metals grow in them; for the qualities of metals are determined by planetary influences. Mountains that are turned towards the sun have subtle stones and earth, and produce nothing but gold. If they are more conveniently situated for being influenced by the moon, their metallic substance is turned into silver. For all metals, when perfectly developed, must ultimately become Moon and Sun, though some need to be operated on by the Sun and Moon longer than others: for the Sun is the Father, and the Moon the Mother, of all things that grow. Thus you see that gold glitters like the Sun, and silver like the Moon. Now, children always resemble their parents; and all metallic bodies contain within themselves the properties of the Sun: to change the baser metals into gold and silver, there is positively nothing wanting but gentle solar warmth. In this respect there exists a close analogy between animal and vegetable growth. When the Sun retires in the winter, the flowers droop and die, the trees shed their leaves, and all vegetable development is temporarily suspended. In the summer again, when the heat of the Sun is too great, not being sufficiently tempered by the cooling influences of the Moon, all vegetation is withered and burnt up. If there is to be perfect growth, the Sun and Moon must work together, the one heating and the other cooling. If the influence of the Moon prevails unduly, it must be corrected by the warmth of the Sun; the excessive heat of the Sun must be tempered by the coldness of the Moon. All development is sustained by solar fire. Imperfect metals are what they are, simply because they have not yet been duly developed by solar influences.

Now, by the special grace of God, it is possible to bring this natural fire to bear on imperfect metals by means of our Art, and to supply the conditions of metallic growth without any of the hindrances which in a natural state prevent perfection. Thus by applying our natural fire, we can do more towards "fixing" imperfect bodies and metals in a moment, than the Sun in a thousand years. For this reason our Stone has also power to cure all things that grow, acting on each one according to its kind. For our Matter represents a perfect and inseparable union of the four elements, which indeed is the sum of our Art, and is consequently able to reconcile and heal all discord in all manner of metals and in all things that grow, and to put to flight all diseases, For disease is discord of the elements, (one unduly lording it over the rest) in animal as well as in metallic bodies. Now as soon as our blessed Medicine is applied, the elements are straightway purified, and joined together in amity; thus metallic bodies are fixed, animal bodies are made whole of all their diseases, gems and precious stones attain to their own proper perfection.

You should also know that all stones are generated by the Sun and Moon out of the sulphur and volatile mercury; if they do not become metals, that is entirely due to their own grossness. In the same way, all plants are generated from sulphur and mercury, and that by the heat of the Sun and Moon. For the Sun and Moon are the mercury in our Matter. The Sun is warm and dry, the Moon warm and moist; for in [the] earth is hid a warm and dry fire, and in that fire dwells warm and moist air—and from these is generated mercury which is both warm and moist. Hence there may be distinguished two chief constituent principles, to wit, moist and dry, that is, earth, wind, and water, unto which mercury is conjoined, and the same is warm and moist. Mercury and sulphur, in our substance, and in all things, spring from the moist and dry, the moist and dry being stirred by the warmth of the Sun, and distilled and sublimed,—in each thing according to its specific nature. Thus our Stone is that mercury which is mixed of the dry and the moist. But the common mercury is useless for our purpose—for it is volatile, while our mercury is fixed and constant. Therefore have nothing to do with the common mercury, but take our mercury which is the principle of growth in all bodies, whether human, vegetable, or metallic; which imparts to all flowers their fragrance and colour. This mercury represents an harmonious mixture of the four elements, hot and dry, Sun and Moon. It is generated in the form of a vapour in the fields and on the mountains, by the warmth of the Sun: that vapour is condensed into a moisture, from which arise sulphur and mercury, and from them again metals The same process takes place in our Art, which represents the union of the warm and moist, by means of warmth. For our substance is generated in the form of a vapour out of warmth and moisture, and changed into sulphur. In this fire and water, and nowhere else, is our Stone to be found. For the vapour carries upward with it most subtle earth, most subtle fire, most subtle water, and most subtle air, and thus presents a close union of the most subtle elements. This is the first Matter, and may be divided into water and earth, which two are again joined together by gentle heat, even as in the woods and mountains mercury is joined with a quick earth and rare water by means of a temperate warmth, and in the long process of time is converted into metal. So is it ordained in our Art, and not otherwise does the process take place. When you, therefore, see that our substance, having been first generated in the form of a vapour, permits itself to be separated into water and earth, you may know that the Stone is composed of the four elements. Know also that the vapour in the mountains is true mercury (which cannot be said of the ordinary mercury); for wherever there is vapour in the mountains, there is true mercury, which by ascending and descending, in the manner described above, becomes fixed, and inseparable from its earth, so that where the one is, there the other must abide.

Thus I have told you plainly enough how the metals are generated, what mercury is, and how it is transmuted into metals. I will therefore conclude this part of my treatise, and tell you in the following section how you may actually perform the chemical process. You see that it is not so incredible, after all, that all metals should be transmuted into gold and silver, and all animal bodies delivered from every kind of disease; and I hope and trust that God will permit you practically to experience the truth of this assertion.

Now I will tell you how you must produce the Fire and
Water, in which is prepared the Mercury required
for the red and white Tincture,

Take fire, or the quicklime of the Sages, which is the vital fire of all trees, and therein doth God Himself burn by divine love. In it purify Mercury, and mortify it for the purposes of our Art; understand, with vulgar Mercury, which you wish to fix in water or fire. But the Mercury which lies hidden in this water, or fire, is therein fixed of itself. The Mercury which is in the fire must be decomposed, clarified, coagulated, and fixed with indelible, living, or Divine fire, of that kind which God has placed in the Sun; and wherein God Himself burns as with Divine love for the consolation of all mankind. Without this fire our Art can not be brought to a successful issue. This is the fire of the Sages which they describe in such obscure terms, as to have been the indirect cause of beguiling many innocent persons to their ruin; so even that they have perished in poverty because they knew not this fire of the Philosophers. It is the most precious fire that God has created in the earth, and has a thousand virtues—nay, it is so precious that men have averred that the Divine Power itself works effectually in it. It has the purifying virtue of Purgatory, and everything is rendered better by it. It is not wonderful, therefore, that a fire should be able to fix and clarify Mercury, and to cleanse it from all grossness and impurity. The Sages call it the living fire, because God has endowed it with His own Divine, and vitalising power.

In the writings of the Sages, this fire goes by different names. Some call it "burnt" wine, others assign to it three names from the analogy of the Three Persons of the Holy Trinity, God the Father, God the Son, and God the Holy Ghost; Body, Soul, and Fire, or Spirit.

The Sages further say: The fire is fire, and also water, containing within itself both cold and heat, moisture, and dryness, nor can anything extinguish it but itself. Hence others say that it is an inextinguishable fire, which is continually burning, purifying, and tinging all metals, consuming all their impurities, and combining Mercury with the Sun in so close an union that they become one and inseparable.

Therefore our great Teachers say that as God the Father, the Son, and the Holy Ghost, are three Persons, and yet but one God; so this fire unites these three things, namely, the Body, Spirit, and Soul, or Sun, Mercury, and Soul. The fire nourishes the Soul which binds together the Body and the Spirit, and thus all three become one, and remain united for ever. Again, as an ordinary fire, on being supplied with fuel, may spread and fill the whole world, so this Tincture may be multiplied, and so this fire may enter into all metals; and one part of it has power to change two, three, or five hundred parts of other metals into gold.

Again, the Sages call this fire the fire of the Holy Spirit, because as the Divinity of Christ took upon itself true flesh and blood without forfeiting anything of its Divine Nature, so the Sun, the Moon, and Mercury, are transmuted into the true Tincture, which remains unaffected by all outward influences, and endures, and will endure, for ever. Once more, as God feeds many wicked sinners with his blood, so this Tincture tinges all gross and impure metals, without being injured by contact with them. So also, therefore, may it be compared with the sacro-saintly Sacrament of the Most Holy Eucharist, from which no sinner is excluded, how impure soever he may have been. You have thus been made acquainted with the all but miraculous virtue of this fire: remember that no student of this Art can possibly do without it. For another Sage says: "In this invisible fire you have the whole mystery of this Art, as the three Persons of the Holy Trinity are truly concluded in one substance." In this fire the true Art is summed up in three palpable things, which yet are invisible and incomprehensible, like the Holy Spirit. Without those three things our Art can never be brought to perfection. One of them is fire; the second, water; the third, earth; and all those three are invisibly present in one essence, and are the instrumental cause of all perfection in Nature.

Now will I also describe the operation of those Three
Things in our Art, and will at once begin
with all Three.

Our wise Teacher Plato says: "Every husbandman who sows good seed, first chooses a fertile field, ploughs and manures it well, and weeds it of all tares; he also takes care that his own grain is free from every foreign admixture. When he has committed the seed to the ground, he needs moisture, or rain, to decompose the grain, and to raise it to new life. He also requires fire, that is, the warmth of the Sun, to bring it to maturity." The needs of our Art are of an analogous nature. First, you must prepare your seed, *i.e.*, cleanse your Matter from all impurity, by a method which you will find set forth at length in the Dicta of the Sages which I subjoin to this Treatise. Then you must have good soil in which to sow your Mercury and Sun; this earth must first be weeded of all foreign elements if it is to yield a good crop. Hence the Sage enjoins us to "sow the seed in a fruitful field, which has been prepared with living fire, and it will produce much fruit."

What is the Urine of Children?

I will now truly inform you concerning the Urine of Children, and of the Sages. The spirit which is extracted from the metals is the urine of children: for it is the seed and the first principle of metals. Without this seed there is no consummation of our Art, and no Tincture, either red or white. For the sulphur and mercury of gold are the red, the sulphur and mercury of silver are the white Tincture: the Mercury of the Sun and Moon fixes all Mercury in imperfect metals, and imparts excellence and durability even to common Mercury. Dioscorides has written an elegant treatise concerning this Urine of Children, which he calls the first Matter of metals.

What is the Mercury of the Sages?

Mercury is nothing but water and salt, which have been subjected for a long space of time to natural heat so as to be united into one. This is Mercury, or dry water, which is not moist, and does not moisten anything; of course, I do not speak of crude common mercury, but of the Mercury of the Sages. The Sages call it the fifth element. It is the vital principle which brings all plants to maturity and perfection. The other quintessence, which is in the earth, and partly material, contains within itself its own seed which grows out of its soil. The heavenly quintessence comes to the aid of the earthly, removes the grossness of its earth, and brings the aforesaid seed to maturity. For Mercury, and the Celestial Quintessence, drain off all harmful moisture from the quintessence of the earth. This Mercury is also called sulphur of the air, sulphur being a hardening of mercury; or we may describe them as husband and wife, from whom issue many children in the earth. You must not think that I desire to hide from you my true meaning: nay, I will further endeavour to illustrate it in the following way. Common sulphur, as you know, coagulates common mercury; for sulphur is poisonous, and mercury deadly. How then can you obtain from either of them anything suitable for perfecting the other, seeing that both require to be assisted by some external agent? On the other hand, I tell you that if, after the conjunction of our fixed sulphur with our sublimed mercury, you sprinkle a mere particle of it upon crude mercury, the latter is at once brought to perfection. Again, you may clearly perceive that the quintessence of the earth has its operation in the winter when the earth is closed up with frost; while the Quintessence of the Stars operates in the summer time, when it removes all that is injurious in the inferior quintessence, and thus quickens everything into vigorous growth. The two quintessences may also be driven off into water, and there conserved. An earthly manifestation you may behold in the colours of the rainbow, when the rays of the Sun shine through the rain. But, indeed, there is not a stone, an animal, or a plant, that does not contain both quintessences. In short, they embody the secret of our whole Magistery, and out of them our Stone is prepared. Hermes, in his Emerald Table, expresses himself as follows: "Our Blessed Stone, which is of good substance, and has a soul, ascends from earth to heaven, and again descends from heaven to earth. Its effectual working is in the air; it is joined to Mercury; hence the Sun is its Father, the Moon its Mother; the wind has borne it in her womb, the earth is its nursing mother, and at length that which is above is also that which is below. The whole represents a natural mixture: for it is a Stone and not a Stone, fixed and volatile, body and soul, husband and wife, King and Queen." Let what I have said suffice, instead of many other words and parables.

Composition.

Albertus expresses himself thus concerning the conjunction of the Stone: "The elements are so subtle that no ordinary method of mingling will avail. They must first be dissolved into water, then mixed, and placed in a warm spot, where they are united after a time by natural warmth. For the Elixir and the two solutions must be conjoined in the proportion of three parts of the Elixir and one part of the crushed body. This must again be coagulated and dissolved, and so also again until the whole has become *one*, without any transmutation. All this is accomplished by the virtue of our mercurial water; for with it the body is dissolved. It is that which purifies, conjoins, dissolves, and makes red and white." Aristotle says of it as follows: This water is the earth in which Hermes bids us sow the seed; the Sun or Moon, as Senior hath it, for extraction of the Divine water of sulphur and mercury, which is fire, warming and fructifying by the igneous virtue thereof. This is the Mercury and that is the water which wets not the hand. It is the Mercury which all Sages have loved and used, and of which they have acknowledged the virtue so long as they lived.

THE THIRD PART OF THIS TREATISE, CONTAINING
THE DICTA OF THE SAGES.

i. I will now proceed to quote the very words of the various Sages in regard to this point, in order that you may the more easily understand our meaning. Know then that Almighty God first delivered this Art to our Father, Adam, in Paradise. For as soon as He had created him, and set him in the Garden of Eden, He imparted it to him in the following words: "Adam, here are two things: that which is above is volatile, that which is below is fixed. These two things contain the whole mystery. Observe it well, and make not the virtue that slumbers therein known to thy children; for these two things shall serve thee, together with all other created things under heaven, and I will lay at thy feet all the excellence and power of this world, seeing that thou thyself art a small world."

ii. ABEL, the son of Adam, wrote thus in his Principles: After God had created our Father, Adam, and set him in Paradise, He subjected to his rule all animals, plants, minerals, and metals. For man is the mountain of mountains, the Stone of all stones, the tree of trees, the root of roots, the earth of earths. All these things he includes within himself, and God has given to him to be the preserver of all things.

iii. SETH, the son of Adam, describes it thus: Know, my children, that in proportion as the acid is subjected to coction, by means of our Art, and is reduced into ashes, the more of the substance is extracted, and becomes a white body. If you cook this well, and free it from all blackness, it is changed into a stone, which is called a white stone until it is crushed. Dissolve it in water of the mouth, which has been well tempered, and its whiteness will soon change to redness. The whole process is performed by means of this sharp acid and the power of God.

iv. ISINDRUS: Our great and precious Matter is air, for air ameliorates the Matter, whether the air be gross or tenuous, warm or moist. For the grossness of the air arises from the setting, the approach, and the rising of the Sun. Thus the air may be hot or cold, or dry and rarefied, and the degrees of this distinguish summer and winter.

v. ANAXAGORAS says: God and His goodness are the first principle of all things. Therefore, the mildness of God reigns even beneath the earth, being the substance of all things, and thus also the substance beneath the earth. For the mildness of God mirrors itself in creating, and His integrity in the solidity that is beneath the earth. Now we cannot see His goodness, except in bodily form.

vi. SENIOR, or PANDOLPHUS, says: I make known to posterity that the thinness, or softness, of air is in water, and is not severed from the other elements. If the earth had not its vital juice, no moisture would remain in it.

vii. ARISTEUS delivers himself thus briefly: Know that the earth is round, and not flat. For if it were perfectly flat, the Sun would shine everywhere at the same moment.

viii. PYTHAGORAS: That which is touched and not seen, also that which is known but not looked upon, these are only heaven and earth; again, that which is not known is in the world and is perceived by sight, hearing, smell, taste, or touch. Sight shews the difference between black and white; hearing, between good and evil; taste, between sweet and bitter; touch, between subtle and gross; smell, between fragrant and fetid.

ix. ARISTEUS, in his Second Table, says: Beat the body which I have made known to you into thin plates; pour thereon our salt water, i.e., water of life, and heat it with a gentle fire until its blackness disappears, and it becomes first white, and then red.

x. PARMENIDES: The Sages have written about many waters, stones, and metals, for the purpose of deceiving you. You that desire a knowledge of our Art, relinquish Sun, Moon, Saturn, and Venus, for our ore, and our earth, and why so? Every thing is of the nature of no thing.

xi. LUCAS: Take the living water of the Moon, and coagulate it, according to our custom. By those last words I mean that it is already coagulated. Take the living water of the Moon, and put it on our earth, till it becomes white: here, then, is our magnesia, and the natures of natures rejoice.

xii. ETHEL: Subject our Stone to coction till it becomes as bright as white marble. Then it is made a great and effectual Stone, sulphur having been added to sulphur, and preserving its property.

xiii. PYTHAGORAS: We exhibit unto you the regimen concerning these things. The substance must drink its water, like the fire of the Moon, which you have prepared. It must continue drinking its own water and moisture, till it turns white.

xiv. PHILETUS: Know, ye sons of philosophy, that the substance, the search after which reduces so many to beggary, is not more than one thing of most effectual properties. It is looked down upon by the ignorant, but held in great esteem by the Sages. Oh, how great is the folly, and how great also is the presumptuous ignorance of the vulgar herd! If you knew the virtue of this substance, kings, princes, and nobles would envy you. We Sages call it the most sharp acid, and without this acid nothing can be obtained, neither blackness, whiteness, nor the Tincture.

xv. METHUSALEM: With air, vapour, and spirit we shall have vulgar mercury changed into as good a silver as the nature of minerals will allow in the absence of heat.

xvi. SIXION: Ye sons of philosophy, if you would make our substance red, you must first make it white. Its three natures are summed up in whiteness and redness. Take, therefore, our Saturn, subject it to coction in aqua vitæ until it turns white, becomes thick, and is coagulated, and then again till it becomes red. Then it is *red lead*, and without this lead of the Sages nothing can be effected.

xvii. MUNDINUS: Learn, O imitators of this Art, that the philosophers have written variously of many gums in their books, but the substance they refer to is nothing but fixed and living water, out of which alone our noble Stone can be prepared. Many seek what they call the essential "gum," and cannot find it. I reveal unto you the knowledge of this gum and the mystery which abides therein. Know that our gum is better than Sun and Moon. Therefore it is highly esteemed by the Sages, though it is very cheap; and they say: Take care that you do not waste any of our "gum." But in their books they do not call it by its common name, and that is the reason why it is hidden from the many, according to the command which God gave to Adam.

xviii. DARDANIUS: Know, my sons, that the Sages take a living and indestructible water. Do not, then, set your hands to this task until you know the power and efficacy of this water. For nothing can be done in our Art without this indestructible water. For the Sages have described its power and efficacy as being that of spiritual blood. Transmute this water into body and spirit, and then, by the grace of God, you will have the spirit firmly fixed in the body.

xix. PYTHAGORAS, in his Second Book, delivers himself as follows: The Sages have used different names for the substance, and have told us to make the indestructible water white and red. They have also apparently indicated various methods, but they really agree with each other in regard to all essentials, and it is only their mystic language that causes a semblance of disagreement. Our Stone is a stone, and not a stone. It has neither the appearance nor the properties of stone, and yet it is a stone. Many have called it after the place where it is found; others after its colour.

xx. NEOPHIDES: I bid you take that mystic substance, white magnesia. And have a care that the Stone be pure and bright. Then place it in its aqueous, vessel, and subject it to gentle heat, until it first becomes black, then again white, and then red. The whole process should be accomplished in forty days. When you have done this, God shows you the first substance of the Stone, which is an eagle-stone, and known to all men.

xxi. THEOPHILUS: Take white Magnesia, *i.e.*, quicksilver, mingled with the Moon. Pound it till it becomes thin water; subject it to coction for forty days; then the flower of the Sun will open with great splendour. Close well the mouth of the phial, and subject it to coction during forty days, when you will obtain a beautiful water, which you must treat in the same way for another forty days, until it is thoroughly purged of its blackness, and becomes white and fragrant.

xxii. BÆLUS says: I bid you take Mercury, which is the Magnesia of the Moon, and subject it and its body to coction till it becomes soft, thin, and like flowing water. Heat it again till all its moisture is coagulated, and it becomes a Stone.

xxiii. BASAN says: Put the yellow Matter into the bath, together with its spouse, and let not the bath be too hot, lest both be deprived of consciousness. Let a gentle temperature be kept up till the husband and the wife become one; sprinkle it with its sweat, and set it in a quiet place. Take care you do not drive off its virtue by too great heat. Honour then the King and his Queen, and do not burn them. If you subject them to gentle heat, they will become, first black, then white, and then red. If you understand this, blessed are ye. But if you do not, blame not Philosophy, but your own gross ignorance.

xxiv. ARISTOTLE: Know, my disciples, the Sages call our Stone sometimes earth, and sometimes water. Be directed in the regulation of your fire by the guidance of Nature. In the liquid there is first water, then a stone, then the earth of philosophers in which they sow their grain, which springs up, and bears fruit after its kind.

xxv. AGODIAS: Subject our earth to coction, till it becomes the first substance. Pound it to an impalpable dust, and again enclose it in its vessel. Sprinkle it with its own moisture till an union is effected. Then look at it carefully, and if the water presents the appearance of) (, continue to pound and heat. For, if you cannot reduce it to water, the water cannot be found. In order to reduce it to water, you must stir up the body with fire. The water I speak of is not rain water, but indestructible water which cannot exist without its body, which, in its turn, cannot exist, or operate, without its own indestructible water.

xxvi. SIRETUS: What is required in our Art is our water and our earth, which must become black, white, and red, with many intermediate colours which shew themselves successively. Everything is generated through our living and indestructible water. True Sages use nothing but this living water which supersedes all other substances and processes. Coction, califaction, distillation, sublimation, desiccation, humectation, albefaction, and rubrefaction, are all included in the natural development of this one substance.

xxvii. MOSINUS: The Sages have described our substance, and the method of its preparation, under many names, and thus have led many astray who did not understand our writing. It is composed of red and white sulphur, and of fixed or indestructible water, called permanent water.

xxviii. PLATO: Let it suffice you to dissolve bodies with this water, lest they be burned. Let the substance be washed with living water till all its blackness disappears, and it becomes a white Tincture.

xxix. ORFULUS: First, subject the Matter to gentle coction, of a temperature such as that with which a hen hatches her eggs, lest the moisture be burnt up, and the spirit of our earth destroyed. Let the phial be tightly closed that the earth may crush our substance, and enable its spirit to be extracted. The Sages say that quicksilver is extracted from the flower of our earth, and the water of our fire extracted from two things, and transmuted into our acid. But though they speak of many things, they mean only *one* thing, namely, that indestructible water which *is* our substance, and our acid.

xxx. BATHON: If you know the Matter of our Stone, and the mode of regulating its coction, and the chromatic changes which it undergoes—as though it wished to warn you that its names are as numerous as the colours which it displays—then you may perform the putrefaction, or first coction, which turns our Stone quite black. By this sign you may know that you have the key to our Art, and you will be able to transmute it into the mystic white and red. The Sages say that the Stone dissolves itself, coagulates itself, mortifies itself, and is quickened by its own inherent power, and that it changes itself to black, white, and red, in Christian charity and fundamental truth.

xxxi. BLODIUS. Take the Stone which is found everywhere, and is called Rebis (Two-thing), and grows in two mountains. Take it while it is still fresh, with its own proper blood. Its growth is in its skin, also in its flesh, and its food is in its blood, its habitation in the air. Take of it as much as you like, and plunge it into the Bath.

xxxii. LEAH, the prophetess, writes briefly thus: Know, Nathan, that the flower of gold is the Stone; therefore subject it to heat during a certain number of days, till it assumes the dazzling appearance of white marble.

xxxiii. ALKIUS: You daily behold the mountains which contain the husband and wife. Hie you therefore to their caves, and dig up their earth, before it perishes.

xxxiv. BONELLUS: All ye lovers of this Art, I say unto you, in faith and love: Relinquish the multiplicity of your methods and substances, for our substance is one thing, and is called living and indestructible water. He that is led astray by many words, will know the persons against whom he should be on his guard.

xxxv. HIERONYMUS: Malignant men have darkened our Art, perverting it with many words; they have called our earth, and our Sun, or gold, by many misleading names. Their salting, dissolving, subliming, growing, pounding, reducing to an acid, and white sulphur, their coction of the fiery vapour, its coagulation, and transmutation into red sulphur, are nothing but different aspects of one and the same thing, which, in its first stage, we may describe as incombustible and indestructible sulphur.

xxxvi. HERMES: Except ye convert the earth of our Matter into fire, our acid will not ascend.

xxxvii. PYTHAGORAS, in his Fourth Table, says: How wonderful is the agreement of Sages in the midst of difference! They all say that they have prepared the Stone out of a substance which by the vulgar is looked upon as the vilest thing on earth. Indeed, if we were to tell the vulgar herd the ordinary name of our substance, they would look upon our assertion as a daring falsehood. But if they were acquainted with its virtue and efficacy, they would not despise that which is, in reality, the most precious thing in the world. God has concealed this mystery from the foolish, the ignorant, the wicked, and the scornful, in order that they may not use it for evil purposes.

xxxviii. HAGIENUS: Our Stone is found in all mountains, all trees, all herbs, and animals, and with all men. It wears many different colours, contains the four elements, and has been designated a microcosm. Can you not see, you ignorant seekers after the Stone, who try, and vainly try, such a multiplicity of substances and methods, that our Stone is one earth, and one sulphur, and that it grows in abundance before your very eyes? I will tell you where you may find it. The first spot is on the summit of two mountains; the second, in all mountains; the third, among the refuse in the street; the fourth, in the trees and metals, the liquid of which is the Sun and Moon, Mercury, Saturn, and Jupiter. There is but one vessel, one method, and one consummation.

xxxix. MORIENUS: Know that our Matter is not in greater agreement with human nature than with anything else, for it is developed by putrefaction and transmutation. If it were not decomposed, nothing could be generated out of it. The goal of our Art is not reached until Sun and Moon are conjoined, and become, as it were, one body.

xl. THE EMERALD TABLE: It is true, without any error, and it is the sum of truth; that which is above is also that which is below, for the performance of the wonders of a certain one thing, and as all things arise from one Stone, so also they were generated from one common Substance, which includes the four elements created by God. And among other miracles the said Stone is born of the First Matter. The Sun is its Father, the Moon its Mother, the wind bears it in its womb, and it is nursed by the earth. Itself is the Father of the whole earth, and the whole potency thereof. If it be transmuted into earth, then the earth separates from the fire that which is most subtle from that which is hard, operating gently and with great artifice. Then the Stone ascends from earth to heaven, and again descends from heaven to earth, and receives the choicest influences of both heaven and earth. If you can perform this you have the glory of the world, and are able to put to flight all diseases, and to transmute all metals. It overcomes Mercury, which is subtle, and penetrates all hard and solid bodies. Hence it is compared with the world. Hence I am called Hermes, having the three parts of the whole world of philosophy.

xli. LEPRINUS says: The Stone must be extracted from a two-fold substance, before you can obtain the Elixir which is fixed in one essence, and derived from the one indispensable Matter, which God has created, and without which no one can attain the Art. Both these parts must be purified before they are joined together afresh. The body must become different, and so must the volatile spirit. Then you have the Medicine, which restores health, and imparts perfection to all things. The fixed and the volatile principle must be joined in an inseparable union, which defies even the destructive force of fire.

xlii. LAMECH: In the Stone of the Philosophers are the first elements, and the final colours of minerals, or Soul, Spirit, and Body, joined unto one. The Stone which contains all these things is called Zibeth, and the working of Nature has left it imperfect.

xliii. SOCRATES: Our Mystery is the life of all things, or the water. For water dissolves the body into spirit, and summons the living spirit from among the dead. My son, despise not my Practical Injunction. For it gives you, in a brief form, everything that you really need.

xliv. ALEXANDER: The good need not remain concealed on account of the bad men that might abuse it. For God rules over all, according to His Divine Will. Observe, therefore, that the salt of the Stone is derived from mercury, and is that Matter, most excellent of all things, of which we are in search. The same also contains in itself all secrets. Mercury is our Stone, which is composed of the dry and the moist elements, which have been joined together by gentle heat in an inseparable union.

xlv. SENIOR teaches us to make the Salt out of ashes, and then, by various processes, to change it into the Mercury of the Sages, because our Magistery is dependent on our water alone, and needs nothing else.

xlvi. ROSARIUS: It is a stone, and not a stone, viz., the eagle-stone. The substance has in its womb a stone, and when it is dissolved, the water that was coagulated in it bursts forth. Thus the Stone is the extracted spirit of our indestructible body. It contains mercury, or liquid water, in its body, or fixed earth, which retains its nature. This explanation is sufficiently plain.

xlvii. PAMPHILUS: The Salt of the Gem is that which is in its own bowels; it ascends with the water to the top of the alembic, and, after separation, is once more united and made one body with it by means of natural warmth. Or we may, with King Alexander, liken the union to that of a soul with its body.

xlviii. DEMOCRITUS: Our Substance is the conjunction of the dry and the moist elements, which are separated by a vapour or heat, and then transmuted into a liquid like water, in which our Stone is found. For the vapour unites to the most subtle earth the most subtle air, and contains all the most subtle elements. This first substance may be separated into water and earth, the latter being perceptible to the eye. The earth of the vapour is volatile when it ascends, but it is found fixed when the separation takes place, and when the elements are joined together again it becomes fixed mercury. For the enjoyment of this, His precious gift, we Sages ceaselessly praise and bless God's Holy Name.

xlix. SIROS: The body of the Sages, being calcined, is called everlasting water, which permanently coagulates our Mercury. And if the Body has been purified and dissolved, the union is so close as to resist all efforts at separation.

l. NOAH, the man of God, writes thus in his Table: My children and brethren, know that no other stone is found in the world that has more virtue than this Stone. No mortal man can find the true Art without this Stone. Blessed be the God of Heaven who has created this property in the Salt, even in the Salt of the Gem!

li. MENALDES: The fire of the Sages may be extracted from all natural things, and is called the quintessence. It is of earth, water, air, and fire. It has no cause of corruption or other contrary quality.

lii. HERMES, in his second Table, writes thus: Dissolve the ashes in the second element, and coagulate this substance into a Stone. Let this be done seven times. For as Naaman the Syrian was purged of his leprosy by washing himself seven times in Jordan, so our substance must undergo a seven-fold cleansing, by calcining and dissolving, and exhibiting a variety of ever deepening colours. In our water are hidden the four elements, and this earth, which swallows its water, is the dragon that swallows its tail, *i.e.*, its strength.

liii. NUNDINUS: The fire which includes all our chemical processes, is three-fold: the fiery element of the air, of water, and of the earth. This is all that our Magistery requires.

liv. ANANIAS: Know, ye Scrutators of Nature, that fire is the soul of everything, and that God Himself is fire and soul. And the body cannot live without fire. For without fire the other elements have no efficacy. It is, therefore, a most holy, awful, and divine fire which abides with God Himself in the Most Holy Trinity, for which also we give eternal thanks to God.

lv. BONIDUS: In the fountain of Nature our Substance is found, and nowhere else upon earth; and our Stone is fire, and has been generated in fire, without, however, being consumed by fire.

lvi. ROSINUS: Two things are hidden in two things, and indicate our Stone: in earth is fire, and air in water, yet there are only two outward things, viz., earth and water. For Mercury is our Stone, consisting as it does both of moist and dry elements. Mercury is dry and moist in its very nature, and all things have their growth from the dry and moist elements.

lvii. GEBER: We cannot find anything permanent, or fixed, in fire, but only a viscous natural moisture which is the root of all metals. For our venerable Stone nothing is required but mercurial substances, if they have been well purified by our Art, and are able to resist the fierce heat of fire. This Substance penetrates to the very roots of metals, overcomes their imperfect nature, and transmutes them, according to the virtue of the Elixir, or Medicine.

lviii. AROS: Our Medicine consists of two things, and one essence. There is one Mercury, of a fixed and a volatile substance, composed of body and spirit, cold and moist, warm and dry.

lix. ARNOLDUS: Let your only care be to regulate the coction of the Mercurial substance. In proportion as it is itself dignified shall it dignify bodies.

lx. ALPHIDIUS: Transmute the nature, and you will find what you want. For in our Magistery we obtain first from the gross the subtle, or the spirit; then from the moist the dry, *i.e.*, earth from water. Thus we transmute the corporeal into the spiritual, and the spiritual into the corporeal, the lowest into the highest, and the highest into the lowest.

lxi. BERNARDUS: The middle substance is nothing but coagulated mercury; and the first Matter is nothing but twofold mercury. For our Medicine is composed of two things, the fixed and the volatile, the corporeal and the spiritual, the cold and the warm, the moist and the dry. Mercury must be subjected to coction in a vessel with three divisions, that the dryness of the active fire may be changed into vaporous moisture of the oil that surrounds the substance. Ordinary fire does not digest our substance, but its heat converted into dryness is the true fire.

lxii. STEPHANUS: Metals are earthly bodies, and are generated in water. The water extracts a vapour from the Stone, and out of the moisture of [the] earth, by the operation of the Sun, God lets gold grow and accumulate. Thus earth and water are united into a metallic body.

lxiii. GUIDO BONATUS writes briefly concerning the quintessence, as being purer than all elements. The quintessence contains the four elements, that is, the first Matter, out of which God has created, and still creates, all things. It is Hyle, containing in a confused mixture the properties of every creature.

lxiv. ALRIDOS: The virtue and efficacy of everything is to be found in its quintessence, whether its nature be warm, cold, moist, or dry. This quintessence gives out the sweetest fragrance that can be imagined. Therefore the highest perfection is needed.

lxv. LONGINUS describes the process in the following terms: Let your vessel be tightly closed and exposed to an even warmth. This water is prepared in dry ashes, and is subjected to coction till the two become one. When one is joined to the other, the body is brought back to its spirit. Then the fire must be strengthened till the fixed body retains that which is not fixed by its own heat. With this you can tinge ten thousand times ten thousand of other substances.

lxvi. HERMES, in his Mysteries, says: Know that our Stone is lightly esteemed by the thankless multitude; but it is very precious to the Sages. If princes knew how much gold can be made out of a particle of Sun, and of our Stone, they would never suffer it to be taken out of their dominions.

> "The Sages rejoice when the bodies are dissolved; for our
> Stone is prepared with two waters. It drives away all sickness
> from the diseased body, whether it be human or metallic."

By means of our Art, we do in one month what Nature cannot accomplish in a thousand years: for we purify the parts, and then join them together in an inseparable and indissoluble union.

lxvii. NERO: Know that our Mercury is dry and moist, and conjoined with the Sun and Moon. Sun and Moon in nature are cold and moist mercury and hot and dry sulphur, and both have their natural propagation by being joined in one thing.

Here follows a True Explanation of some of the Foregoing
Philosophical Dicta, the meaning, word for word
and point for point, being clearly set forth.

I now propose to say something about the meaning of the obscure and allegorical expressions used by some of the Sages whom I have quoted. Be sure that they all were true Sages, and really possessed our Stone. It may have been possessed by more persons since the time of Adam, but the above list includes all of whom I have heard. I need not here review all their sayings; for the words of the least of them are sufficient for imparting to you a knowledge of this Art; and my ambition goes no higher than that. If I have enumerated so large a number of authorities, I have only done so in order that you might the better understand both the theory and practice of this Art, and that you might be saved all unnecessary expense. For this reason I have declared this true philosophy with all the skill that God has given me. I hope the initiated will overlook any verbal inaccuracy into which I have fallen, and that they will be induced by my example to abstain from wilfully misleading anxious enquirers. I may have fallen into some errors of detail, but as to the gist of my work, I know what I have written, and that it is God's own truth.

Explanation of the Saying of Adam.

When God had created our first parent Adam, and set him in Paradise, He showed him two things, namely, earth and water. Earth is fixed and indestructible, water is volatile and vaporous. These two contain the elements of all created things: water contains air, and earth fire—and of these four things the whole of creation is composed. In earth are enclosed fire, stones, minerals, salt, mercury, and all manner of metals; in water, and in air, all manner of living and organic substances, such as beasts, birds, fishes, flesh, blood, bones, wood, trees, flowers, and leaves. To all these things God imparted their efficacy and virtue, and subjected them to the mastery and use of Adam. Hence you may see how all these things are adapted to the human body, and are such as to meet the requirements of his nature. He may incorporate the virtue of outward substances by assimilating them in the form of food. In the same way, his mind is suitably constructed for the purpose of gaining a rational knowledge of the physical world. That this is the case, you may see from the first chapter of Genesis.

On the sixth day of the first year of the world, that is to say, on the 15th day of March, God created the first man, Adam, of red earth, in a field near Damascus, with a beautiful body, and after His own image. When Adam was created, he stood naked before the Lord, and with outstretched hands rendered thanks to Him, saying: O Lord, Thy hands have shaped me: now remember, I pray Thee, the work of Thy hands, which Thou hast clothed with flesh, and strengthened with bones, and grant me life and loving-kindness.

So the Lord endowed Adam with great wisdom, and such marvellous insight that he immediately, without the help of any teacher—simply by virtue of his original righteousness—had a perfect 'knowledge of the seven liberal arts, and of all animals, plants, stones, metals, and minerals. Nay, what is more, he had perfect understanding of the Holy Trinity, and of the coming of Christ in the flesh. Moreover, Adam was the Lord, King, and Ruler of all other creatures which, at the Divine bidding, were brought to him by the angel to receive their names. Thus all creatures acknowledged Adam as their Lord, seeing that it was he to whom the properties and virtues of all things were to be made known. Now the wisdom, and knowledge of all things, which Adam had received, enabled him to observe the properties, the origin, and the end of all things. He noted the division and destruction, the birth and decay of physical substances. He saw that they derive their origin from the dry and the moist elements, and that they are again transmuted into the dry and the moist. Of all these things Adam took notice, and especially of that which is called the first Matter. For he who knows how all things are transmuted into their first Matter, has no need to ask any questions. It was that which existed in the beginning before God created heaven and earth; and out of it may be made one new thing which did not exist before, a new earth, fire, water, air, Sun, Moon, Stars, in short, a new world.

As in the beginning all things were created new, so there is a kind of new creation out of the first substance in our Art. Now although God warned Adam generally not to reveal this first substance—viz., the moist and the dry elements— yet He permitted him to impart the knowledge to his son Seth. Abel discovered the Art for himself, by the wisdom which God had given him, and inscribed an account of it on beechen tablets. He was also the first to discover the art of writing; further, he foretold the destruction of the world by the Flood, and wrote all these things on wooden tablets, and hid them in a pillar of stone, which was found, long afterwards, by the children of Israel Thus you see that our Art was a secret from the beginning, and a secret it will remain to the end of the world. For this reason it is necessary carefully to consider all that is said about it, and especially the words of the Lord to Adam: for they exhibit in a succinct form the secret of the whole Art.

Explanation of the Saying of Abel.

This saying partly explains itself, and is partly explained by what we said about God's words to Adam. Yet I will add a few remarks concerning it. Man hath within him the virtue and efficiency of all things, whence he is called a small world, and is compared to the large world, because the bones which are beneath his skin, and support his body, may be likened to the mountains and stones, his flesh to the earth, his veins to the rivers, and his small veins to the brooks which are discharged into them. The heart is the sea into which the great and small rivers flow; his hair resembles the growing herbs—and so with all other parts of his body. Again, his inward parts, such as the heart, lungs, and liver, are comparable to the metals. The hairs have their head in the earth (i.e., the flesh) and their roots in the air, as the Sages say, that the root of their minerals is in the air, and their head in the earth. That which ascends by distillation is volatile, and is in the air; that which remains at the bottom, and is fixed, is the head, which is in the earth. Therefore, the one must always exist in conjunction with the other if it is to be effectual. Hence man may be compared to an inverted tree: for he has his roots, or his hair, in the air, while other trees have their hairs. or their roots, in the earth.

And of our Stone, too, the Sages have justly said that it has its head in the earth, and its root in the air. This similitude has a two-fold interpretation. First, with regard to the place in which our Matter is found; secondly, with regard to the dissolution and second conjunction of the Stone. For when our Stone rises upward in the alembic, it has its root in the air; but if it would regain its virtue and strength, it must once more return to its earth, and then it has its head and perfect potency in the earth. Hence our Stone, too, is not inaptly denominated a small world; it is called the mountain of mountains, from which our ore is derived, since it is evolved from the first substance in a way analogous to that in which the great world was created. Know that if you bury anything in [the] earth, and it rots, as food is digested in the human body, and the gross is separated from the subtle, and that which is fetid from that which is pure, then that which is pure is the first Matter which has been set free by decay. If you understand this, you know the true Art. But keep it to yourself, and cast not pearls before swine; for the vulgar regard our Art with ignorant contempt.

Explanation of the Saying of Seth, Son of Adam.

By "acid which is to be subjected to coction, and transmuted into ashes," the Sage Seth means distilled water, which we call seed. If this, by diligent coction, is condensed into a body—which he calls ashes—the body loses its blackness by being washed till it becomes white; for, by constant coction, all blackness and gross impurity are removed. If it were not for this earth, the spirit would never be coagulated; for it would have no body into which it could enter—seeing that it cannot be coagulated and fixed anywhere but in its own body. On the other hand, the spirit purifies its body, as Seth says, and makes it white. He says further: "If you diligently heat it, and free it from its blackness, it is changed into a Stone, which is called the white coin of the Stone." That is to say, if it is slowly heated with a gentle fire, it is by degrees changed into a body which resists fire, and is named a Stone. It is fixed, and it has a brilliantly white appearance. A coin it is called, because, as he who has a coin may purchase with it bread or whatever else he needs, so he who has this Stone may purchase for himself health, wisdom, longevity, gold, silver, gems, etc. Hence it is justly called the Coin, since it can buy what all the riches in the world cannot procure. It is struck by the Sages, who, instead of the image of a prince, impress upon it their own image. Therefore it is denominated the COIN of the SAGES, because it is their own money, struck in their own mint.

Again, when the Sage says, "Heat the Stone till it breaks [itself], and dissolve it in the well-tempered water of the Moon," he means that the Stone must be heated by that which is in itself, until it is changed into water, or dissolved. All this is done by its own agency; for the body is called Moon, when it has been changed into water; and the extracted spirit, or distilled water, is called Sun. For the element of [the] air is concealed in it; but the body must be broken in its own water, or dissolved by itself. The "well-tempered water of the Moon" is the gentle inward heat which changes it into water, and yields two waters, viz., the distilled spirit, and the dissolved body. These two waters are again united by slow and gentle coction, the distilled spirit becoming coagulated into a body, the dissolved body becoming a spirit. The fixed becomes volatile, and the volatile fixed, by dissolution and coagulation, and both assume, first a white, and then a red colour. The change to white and red is produced by the same water, and the white is always followed by the red, just as the black is followed by the white. When the Sage says, in conclusion, "that the whole can be accomplished only with the best acid, through the power of God alone," he means that the one thing from which alone our Stone can be procured may be compared to the sharpest acid, and that, by means of our Art, this acid is changed into the best of earthly things, which all the treasures of all kings and princes are not sufficient to buy.

Explanation of the Saying of Isindrus.

Good Heavens! How skilfully the Sages have contrived to conceal this matter. It would surely have been far better if they had abstained from writing altogether. For the extreme obscurity of their style has overwhelmed thousands in ruin, and plunged them into the deepest poverty, especially those who set about this task without even the slightest knowledge of Nature, or of the requirements of our Art. What the Sages write is strictly true; but you cannot understand it unless you are already initiated in the secrets of this Art. Yea, even if you were a Doctor of the Doctors, and a Light of the World, you would be able to see no meaning in their words without this knowledge. They have written, but you are none the wiser. They half wished to communicate the secret to their posterity; but a jealous feeling prevented them from doing so in plain language. To the uninitiated reader these words of Isindrus must appear nothing short of nonsense: "Great is the air, because the air corrects the thing, if it is thin or thick, hot or cold." But the Sage means that when it ascends with the water, it is hot air, for fire and air bear our Stone like secret fire concealed therein, and the water which ascends from the earth, by that

142

ascension becomes air, and thin; and when it descends, it descends into water which contains fire; thus the earth is purified, seeing that the water takes [the] fire with it into the earth. For the fire is the Soul, and the Moon the Spirit. Therefore, the air is great, because it bears with it water and fire, and imparts them to all things, though thereby (by this loss of water) itself becomes cold. Then the air becomes thick, when with its fire it is transmuted into the body, and thus the air corrects the thing by its thickness. For it bears out our Stone as it carries it in, and purifies it both in its ascent and in its descent. In the same way air purifies all things that grow (*i.e.*, plants), gives them their food (*i.e.*, water), and imparts to them its fire, by which they are sustained. Of this you may convince yourself by ocular demonstration. For the air bears the clouds, and sheds them upon earth in the form of rain; which rain contains secret fire derived from the earth, and the rays of the Sun by which it was drawn upward—and this fire it gives to all things as food. And although the rays of the Sun and Moon are immeasurably subtle, swift, and intangible; yet the rays of our Sun and Moon are much swifter and more subtle than those which are received by the plants in their growth. For the earth digests the rays of the Sun and Moon, and they sustain in the most wonderful manner things of vegetable growth; and all the living rays of the Sun and Moon nourish all created things. For by this digestion they obtain their life. For this reason the air may be called great, because through the grace of God it accomplishes great things.

Again, when the Sage says, "If the air becomes thick," *i.e.*, when the Sun turns aside, or is changed, "there is a thickness, till it rises," he means that if the distilled water which is taken for the Sun, or fire, approaches its body, and is changed into it, then the Sun stoops down to the earth. Thereby the air becomes thick, being joined to the earth, and if the Sun is once more elevated the air becomes thin; that is to say, when the water is extracted from the earth by means of the alembic, the fire rises upward, *i.e.*, the Sun is exalted, and the air becomes thin. Again, when he says, "This also is hot and cold, and thickness, and thinness, or softness," the Sage means that the Sun is hot, and the Moon cold; for the earth, when dissolved, is the Moon, and water, in which is fire, is the Sun: these two must be conjoined in an inseparable union. This union enables them to reduce the elements of all metallic and animal bodies, into which they are injected, to perfect purity and health. When the Sage adds that thickness and thinness denote summer and winter, he means that our Art is mingled of thickness and thinness, or two elements which must be united by gentle warmth, like that of winter and summer combined. This temperate warmth, which resembles that of a bath, brings the Sun and Moon together. Thus I have, by the grace of God, interpreted to you the parabolic saying of Isindrus.

Explanation of the Saying of Anaxagoras.

From the beginning of all things God is. He is likened to light and fire, and He may be likened to the latter in His essence, because fire is the first principle of all things that are seen and grow. In the same way, the first principle of our Art is fire. Heat impels Nature to work, and in its working are manifested Body, Spirit, and Soul; that is, earth and water. Earth is the Body, oil the Soul, and water the Spirit; and all this is accomplished through the Divine goodness and lenity, without which Nature can do nothing; or, as the Sage says: "God's lenity rules all things; and beneath the thickness of the earth, after creation, are revealed lenity and integrity." That is to say: If the earth is separated from the water, and itself dissolved into oil and water, the oil is integrity, and the water lenity; for the water imparts the soul to the oil and to the body, and [the body] receives nothing but what is imparted to it by heaven, that is, by the water—and the water is revealed under the oil, the oil under the earth. For the fire is subtle, and floats upward from the earth with subtle waters, and is concealed in the earth. Now oil and air and earth are purified by their own spirit. Therefore the oil is integrity in the body, and the spirit lenity. And the spirit in the first operation descends to the body and restores life to the body; although the oil is pure and remains with the body, yet it cannot succour the body without the help of the spirit; for the body suffers violence and anguish while it is dissolved and purified. Then, again, the "thickness of the earth" is transmuted into a thin substance such as water or oil, and thus the "lenity" is seen in the body. For the body is so mild or soft as to be changed into water, or oil, although before it was quite dry. Therefore oil is seen in the earth, which is the fatness or life of the water, &e., an union of fire, air, and water. Now give the water to the body to drink, and it will be restored to life. And though those three elements have ascended from the earth, yet the virtue remains with the body, as you may see by dissolving it into oil and water. But the oil cannot operate without the spirit, nor can the spirit bear fruit without the oil and the body. Therefore they must be united; and all "lenity" and "integrity" are seen in the body when it is transmuted to white and red.

Explication of the Opinion of Pythagoras.

This Sage asks what that is which is touched, and yet not seen. He means that the substance which is prepared by our Art is one thing, which is tangible and invisible. That is to say, it is felt, but not seen, nor is the mode of its operation known. He who knows it, but knows not its operation, as yet knows nothing as he ought. This one thing, which alone is profitable for the purposes of our Art, proceeds from a certain dark place, where it is not seen, nor are its operation or its virtue known to any but the initiated. A great mystery is also concealed in the Matter itself, namely, air and fire, or the Sun, the Moon, and the Stars. This is concealed in it, and yet is invisible, as the Sage says: What is not seen, or known, is only heaven. That which is felt, and not seen, is earth. Earth, says the Sage, is thickness, or body, which is found at the bottom of the Matter, has accumulated in the Matter, and can be felt and known. By the words, "that is between heaven and earth, which is not known," (*i.e.*, in the world), the Sage means that the Matter of our Stone is found in the small world; not in rocks and mountains, or in the earth, but between heaven and earth, *i.e.*, in the air. Again, when he says that "in it are senses, and entirety, as smell, taste, hearing, touch," he would teach us that in human nature there is entirety of mind and perception; for man can know, feel, and understand. He would also teach us how our Stone is to be found, namely, by sight, hearing, smell, taste, and touch. By sight, because the Matter of the Stone is thick, or thin and clear, and turns black, white, and red. By smell, because, when its impurity is purged away, it emits a most sweet fragrance. By taste, because it is first bitter and disagreeable, but afterwards becomes most pleasant. By touch, because that sense enables us to distinguish between the hard and the soft, the gross and the subtle, between water and earth, and between the different stages of distillation, putrefaction, dissolution, coagulation, fermentation, and injection, which the substance goes through. The different processes of the task are perceived with the senses, and it should be accomplished within forty-six days.

Loosening of the Knot of Aristeus.

"Take the body which I have shewn you, and beat it into thin leaves," *i.e.*, take the earth which cleaves to our substance, and, by having become dry, becomes visible and knowable; for now it is water and earth. The earth is thus shewn, and divided into two parts, earth and water. Let that earth be taken, placed in a phial, and put in a warm bath, by the warmth of which it is dissolved, through its own internal coction, into water; this the Sage calls beating into thin leaves. The body which is thus obtained is variously described as the Philosopher's Stone, or the Stone of leaves. "Add some of our salt water, and this is the water of life." That means: After its dissolution into water, it must receive our salt water to drink—for this water has been previously distilled from it, and is the water of life; for the soul and spirit of the body are hidden in it, and it is called our sea water; the same also is its natural name, because it is obtained from the invisible hidden sea of the Sages, the sea of the smaller world. For our Art is called the smaller world, and thus it is the water of our sea. If this water is added to the body, and heated and purified with it, the body is purged by long coction, and its colour changes from black to a brilliant white, while the water is coagulated, and forms, by indissoluble union with the body, the imperishable Philosopher's Stone, which you must use to the glory of God, and the good of your neighbour.

Exposition of the Saying of Parmenides.

Jealous Sages have named many waters and metals and stones, simply for the purpose of deceiving you; herein the philosophers would warn us that they have used secrecy, lest the whole mystery should be manifested before all the world. Those who follow the letter of their directions are sure to be led astray, and to miss entirely the true foundation of our Art. The fault, however, lies not with the Sages so much with the ignorance of their readers. The Sages name it a *stone*; and so it *is* a stone, which is dug up from our mine. They speak of metals; and there are such things as metals liquefied from our ore. They speak of water; but our water we obtain from our own spring. The red and white sulphur they refer to are obtained from our air. Their salt is obtained from our salt mines. *It* is our Sun, our verdigris, halonitre, alkali, orpiment, arsenic, our poison, our medicine, etc. By whatever name they call it they cannot make it more than one thing. It is rightly described by all the Sages, but not plainly enough for the uninitiated enquirer. For such an one knows neither the substance nor its operation. The Sage says: "Relinquish Sun, Moon, and Venus for our ore," *i.e.*, it is not to be found in any earthly metals, but only in *our* ore. Whoever rightly understands the concluding words of the Sage has received a great blessing at the hand of God.

Explanation of the Saying of Lucas.

By the living water of the Moon this Sage means our water, which is twofold. The distilled water is the Moon; the Sun, or fire, is hidden in it, and is the Father of all things. Hence it is compared to a man, because the Sun is in the water. It is also called living water; for the life of the dead body is hidden in the water. It is the water of the Moon, because the Sun is the Father and the Moon the Mother.

Hence, also, they are regarded as husband and wife. The Body is the Moon, or Mother, and the distilled water, or male principle, rises upward from the earth; and for that reason is sometimes called Moon. For it is the water of the Moon, or Body. It has left the Body, and must enter it again before our Art can be perfected. Hence the Body, or Moon, has well been designated the female principle, and the water, or Sun, the male principle, for reasons which have been set forth at length in this book.

Again, when the Sage says, "Coagulate it after our fashion," those last three words mean that the body must receive its spirit to drink gradually, and little by little, until it recovers its life, and health, and strength, which takes place by means of the same gentle heat which digests food in the stomach, and matures fruit in its place. For it is our custom to eat, drink, and live in gentle warmth. By this regimen our body is preserved, and all that is foul and unprofitable is driven out from our body. According to the same fashion of gentle coction, all that is fetid and black is gradually purged out of our Stone. For when the Sage says "after *our* fashion," he wishes to teach you that the preparation of the Stone bears a strict analogy to the processes of the human body. That the chemical development of our substance is internal, and caused by the operation of Nature and of its four elements, the Sage indicates by the words, "Everything is already coagulated." The substance contains all that is needed; there is nothing to be added or taken away, seeing that it is dissolved and again conjoined by its own inherent properties. When the Sage continues, "I bid you take water of life, which descends from the Moon, and pour it upon our earth till it turns white," he means that if water and earth are separated from each other, then the dry body is our earth, and the extracted water is the water of the Moon, or water of life. This process of adfusion, desiccation, attrition, coagulation, etc., is repeated till the body turns white; and then takes place our conglutination, which is indissoluble. "Then," as the Sage says, "we have our Magnesia, and the Nature of natures rejoices." Its spirit and body become one thing: they were one thing, and after separation have once more become one thing; therefore, one nature rejoices in the restoration of the other.

Exposition of the Saying of Ethelius.

He says: "Heat our Stone until it shines like dazzling marble; then it becomes great, and a mystic Stone; for sulphur added to sulphur preserves it on account of its fitness." That is to say: When the moist and the dry have been separated, the dry which lies at the bottom, and is called our Stone, is as black as a raven. It must be subjected to the coction of our water (separated from it), until it loses its blackness, and becomes as white as dazzling marble. Then it is the mystic Stone which by coction has been transmuted into fixed mercury with the blessing of God. The Stone is mystic, or secret, because it is found in a secret place, in an universally despised substance where no one looks for the greatest treasure of the world. Hence it may well be called The HIDDEN STONE. By the joining of two sulphurs and their mutual preservation, he means that though, after the separation of spirit and body, there seem to be two substances, yet, in reality, there is only one substance; so the body which is below is "sulphur," and the spirit which is above is also "sulphur." Now, when the spirit returns to the body, one sulphur is added to another; and they are bound together by a mutual fitness, since the body cannot be without the spirit, nor the spirit without the body. Hence there are these two sulphurs in the body, the red and the white, and the white sulphur is in the black body, while the red is hid beneath it. If the spirit is gradually added to the body, it is entirely coagulated into the body, sulphur is added to sulphur, and perfection is attained through the fitness which exists between them. The body receives nothing but its own spirit; for it has retained its soul, and what has been extracted from a body can be joined to nothing but that same body. The spirit delights in nothing so much as in its own soul, and its own body. Hence the Sage says: "When the spirit has been restored to the body, the sulphur to the sulphur, and the water to the earth, and all has become white, then the body retains the spirit, and there can be no further separation." Thus you have the well purged earth of the Sages, in which we sow our grain, unto infinity, that it may bring forth much fruit.

Explanation of the Saying of Pythagoras.

You have good cause to wonder at the great variety of ways in which the Sages have expressed the same thing. Nevertheless, their descriptions apply only to one Matter, and their sayings refer only to a single substance. For when our Sage says, "We give you directions concerning these things: We tell you that it is dry water, like the water of the Moon, which you have prepared," he means that we Sages must give directions, according to the best of our ability. If those directions, rightly understood, do not answer the purpose, you may justly charge us with fraud and imposture. But if you fail through not taking our meaning, you must blame your own unspeakable stupidity, which follows the letter, but not the spirit of our directions. When the Sage further says that it must drink its own water, he would teach you that after the separation of the dry from the moist, the water extracted from the body is the right water, and the water of the Moon, prepared by putrefaction and distillation. This extracted water is regarded as the male principle, and the earth, or body, as the female principle. The water of the husband must now be joined in conjugal union to that of the wife; the body must, at intervals, drink of its own prepared water, and become ever purer, the more it drinks, till it turns most wonderfully white. Then it is called "our calx," and you must pour the water of our calx upon the body, until it is coagulated, becoming tinged, and a most bright quality returns to it, and the body itself is saturated with its own moisture. If you wish to obtain the red tincture, you should dissolve and coagulate, and go through the whole process over again. Verily, this is God's own truth, an accurate, simple, and plain statement of the requirements of our Art.

Explanation of the Emerald Table of Hermes.

Hermes is right in saying that our Art is true, and has been rightly handed down by the Sages; all doubts concerning it have arisen through false interpretation of the mystic language of the philosophers. But, since they are loth to confess their own ignorance, their readers prefer to say that the words of the Sages are imposture and falsehood. The fault really lies with the ignorant reader, who does not understand the style of the Philosophers. If, in the interpretation of our books, they would suffer themselves to be guided by the teaching of Nature, rather than by their own foolish notions, they would not miss the mark so hopelessly. By the words which follow: "That which is above is also that which is below," he describes the Matter of our Art, which, though one, is divided into two

147

things, the volatile water which rises upward, and the earth which lies at the bottom, and becomes fixed. But when the reunion takes place, the body becomes spirit, and the spirit becomes body, the earth is changed into water and becomes volatile, the water is transmuted into body, and becomes fixed. When bodies become spirits, and spirits bodies, your work is finished; for then that which rises upward and that which descends downward become *one* body. Therefore the Sage says that that which is above is that which is below, meaning that, after having been separated into two substances (from being one substance), they are again joined together into one substance, *i.e.*, an union which can never be dissolved, and possesses such virtue and efficacy that it can do in one moment what the Sun cannot accomplish in a thousand years. And this miracle is wrought by a thing which is despised and rejected by the multitude. Again, the Sage tells us that all things were created, and are still generated, from one first substance, and consist of the same elementary material; and in this first substance God has appointed the four elements, which represent a common material into which it might perhaps be possible to resolve all things. Its development is brought about by the distillation of the Sun and Moon. For it is operated upon by the natural heat of the Sun-and Moon, which stirs up its internal action, and multiplies each thing after its kind, imparting to the substance a specific form. The soul, or nutritive principle, is the earth which receives the rays of the Sun and Moon, and therewith feeds her children as with mother's milk. Thus the Sun is the father, the Moon is the mother, the earth the nurse—and in this substance is that which we require. He who can take it and prepare it is truly to be envied. It is separated by the Sun and Moon in the form of a vapour, and collected in the place where it is found. When Hermes adds that "the air bears it in its womb, the earth is its nurse, the whole world its Father," he means that when the substance of our Stone is dissolved, then the wind bears it in its womb, *i.e.*, the air bears up the substance in the form of water, in which is hid fire, the soul of the Stone; and fire is the Father of the whole world. Thus, the volatile substance rises upward, while that which remains at the bottom, is the "whole world" (seeing that our Art is compared to a "small world"). Hence Hermes calls fire the father of the whole world, because it is the Sun of our Art, and air, Moon, and water ascend from it; the earth is the nurse of the Stone, *i.e.*, when the earth receives the rays of the Sun and Moon, a new body is born, like a new fœtus in the mother's womb. The earth receives and digests the light of Sun and Moon, and imparts food to its fœtus day by day, till it becomes great and strong, and puts off its blackness and defilement, and is changed to a different colour. This, "child," which is called "our daughter," represents our Stone, which is born anew of the Sun and Moon, as you may easily see, when the spirit, or the water that ascended, is gradually transmuted into the body, and the body is born anew, and grows and increases in size like the fœtus in the mother's womb. Thus the Stone is generated from the first substance, which contains the four elements; it is brought forth by two things, the body and the spirit; the wind bears it in its womb, for it carries the Stone upward from earth to heaven, and down again from heaven to earth. Thus the Stone receives increase from above and from below, and is born a second time, just as every other fœtus is generated in the maternal womb; as all created things bring forth their young, even so does the air, or wind, bring forth our Stone. When Hermes adds, "Its power, or virtue, is entire, when it is transmuted into earth," he means that when the spirit is transmuted into the body, it receives its full strength and virtue. For as yet the spirit is volatile, and not fixed, or permanent. If it is to be fixed, we must proceed as the baker does in baking bread. We must impart only a little of the spirit to the body at a time, just as the baker only puts a little leaven to his meal, and with it leavens the whole lump. The spirit, which is *our* leaven, in like fashion transmutes the whole body into its own substance. Therefore the body must be leavened again and again, until the whole lump is thoroughly pervaded with the power of the leaven. In our Art the body leavens the spirit, and transmutes it into one body, and the spirit leavens the body, and transmutes it into one spirit. And the two, when they have become one, receive power to leaven all things, into which they are injected, with their own virtue.

The Sage continues: "If you gently separate the earth from the water, the subtle from the hard, the Stone ascends from earth to heaven, and again descends from heaven to earth, and receives its virtue from above and from below. By this process you obtain the glory and brightness of the whole world. With it you can put to flight poverty, disease, and weariness; for it overcomes the subtle mercury, and penetrates all hard and firm bodies." He means that all who would accomplish this task must separate the moist from the dry, the water from the earth. The water, or fire, being subtle, ascends, while the body is hard, and remains where it is. The separation must be accomplished by gentle heat, *i.e.*, in the temperate bath of the Sages, which acts slowly, and is neither too hot nor too cold. Then the Stone ascends to heaven, and again descends from heaven to earth. The spirit and body are first separated, then again joined together by gentle coction, of a temperature resembling that with which a hen hatches her eggs. Such is the preparation of the substance, which is worth the whole world, whence it is also called a "little world." The possession of the Stone will yield you the greatest delight, and unspeakably precious comfort. It will also set forth to you in a typical form the creation of the world. It will enable you to cast out all disease from the human body, to drive away poverty, and to have a good understanding of the secrets of Nature. The Stone has virtue to transmute mercury into gold and silver, and to penetrate all hard and firm bodies, such as precious stones and metals. You cannot ask a better gift of God than this gift, which is greater than all other gifts. Hence Hermes may justly call himself by the proud title of "Hermes Trismegistus, who holds the three parts of the whole world of wisdom."

ANOTHER TRACT,

CORRESPONDING TO THE FIRST, WHICH MAY BE READ WITH GREAT PROFIT.

PREFACE.

We may justly wonder that the Sages who have written about this most precious and secret Art, have thought it necessary to invent so many occult and allegorical expressions, by means of which our Art is concealed not only from the unworthy, but from earnest and diligent students of the truth. Foolish persons, indeed, who read their books, and hear of the riches and all the other good things which this Art affords, experience a pleasant tickling sensation in their ears, and straightway behold visions of themselves sitting on golden thrones, and commanding all the treasures of the universe; they fancy that the Art can be learned in the twinkling of an eye, soon come to regard themselves as great Doctors, and are unable to conceive the possibility of their making a mistake, or being led astray by the Sages. Much less are they aware that it has always been the custom of the philosophers to conceal the fundamental facts of this Art, and to reveal them to their own sons and disciples only in sententious allegorical sayings. It is impossible to read through all that the Sages have ever written on this subject; but it is a still more hopeless undertaking to gather from their books a full and sufficient knowledge of our Art, unless, indeed, God opens your understanding, and gives you a real insight into the natural properties of things, and thereby into the sayings of those who speak of them. For it is Nature alone that accomplishes the various processes of our Art, and a right understanding of Nature will furnish you with eyes wherewith to perceive the secrets thereof. Thus Bason says: "Take care not to add anything else; for it is the property of our substance to overcome all other things." And Bondinus tells us that the whole process is accomplished by means of the water which issues from the Stone. Alphidius declares that the Philosopher's Stone contains four different natures, and thereby possesses a virtue and efficacy such as are found in no other stone. Therefore, the question of the Royal Sage Haly, whether there is another stone upon earth which may be compared with our Stone, and possesses the same wonderful properties, is answered by Morienus in the following words: "I am aware of no other stone of equal excellence, potency, and virtue; for it contains the four elements in a visible form, and is singular of its kind among all the created things of the world. If, therefore, any person should take any [other] Stone but the one demanded by this Magistery, his labours must result in failure." Moreover, the ancient Sage Arros says: "Our Stone is useless for our purpose, until it be purged of its gross earth." In like manner we are informed by Morienus that "unless the body be purged of its grossness, it cannot be united to its spirit; but when it has put off its gross nature, the spirit joins itself to it, and delights in it, because both have been freed from all impurity." The truth of his words is attested by Ascanius in "The Crowd," who says: "Spirits cannot join themselves to impure bodies; but when the body has been well purged, and digested by coction, the spirit becomes united to it, amidst a phenomenal exhibition of all the colours in the world, and the imperfect body is tinged with the indestructible colour of the ferment; this ferment is the soul, in and through which the spirit is joined to the body, and transmuted with the body into the colour of the ferment, whereupon all three become one thing." Hence it is well, though somewhat enigmatically said by the Sages, that there takes place a conjugal union of husband and wife, and that of the two a child is born after their likeness, just as men generate men, metals metals, and all other things that which is like them.

Hence all that would exercise this Art must know the properties of the most noble substance thereof, and follow the guidance of Nature. But many enquirers conduct their operations at haphazard, they grope in the dark, and do not know whether their art be an imitation of Nature, or not. Yet they undertake to correct, and intensify, the operation of Nature. Of such persons Arnold says that they approach our Art as the ass goes up to the crib, not knowing for what it opens its mouth. For they do not know what they would do, nor are they aware that they must listen to the teaching of Nature. They seek to do the works of Nature, but they will not watch the hand of her whom they pretend to imitate. Yet our Art has a true foundation in natural fact. For Nature prepares the metals in the earth, some perfect, like gold and silver; others imperfect, like Venus, Mars, Saturn, and Jupiter, according to the labour and influence of the planets. He, then, who would accomplish our Magistery, and desires to participate in this most noble Art, must know the seed from which the metals are naturally generated in the earth, which seed we remove by Nature, and purify and prepare it by Art, making it so glorious, and full of wonderful potency, that with it we can impart instant purity and perfection to the imperfect bodies of men and metals. This seed we must extract from perfect, pure, and mature bodies, if we would attain the desired end. Now, in order that you may the more readily attain this knowledge, I have composed the following Tract concerning the first principle of Nature, and the creation and generation of man—which the student of our Magistery should diligently peruse, consider, and digest. Then he will not so easily miss the right path.

The Fear of the Lord is the Beginning of Wisdom.

All true Sages and philosophers have earnestly sought to obtain a knowledge of Almighty God as He is revealed in His marvellous works; this knowledge they attained, in so far as it can be attained by the human mind, by diligently considering the origin and first principles of all things. For they were enabled to realize the omnipotence of the Creator by the contemplation of the secret powers, and miraculous virtues, which He has infused into natural things. They were led to consider how they might employ their knowledge for the good of the human race, and how they might reveal it to others, and they received wisdom to expound the first principles of natural things, but more especially the birth and death of man, in something like the following way: In the beginning God created all things out of a subtle liquid, or impalpable vapour which was neither moist, nor dry, nor cold, nor hot, nor light, nor dark, but a confused chaos. This subtle vapour God first changed into water, which He then separated into a hard and a liquid part, or into earth and water. Out or elementary water He further evolved air, and out of elementary earth He brought forth fire, that is, elementary fire. And it may still be seen that the two first elements contain the two last; for daily experience teaches us that in water there is air, and that in earth there is fire. Out of these God created the firmament, the Sun, the Moon, and the Stars, and all other natural objects. At last He created a being in His own image, which He formed out of moist earth— i.e., for the most part out of earth (which encloses fire) moistened with water (containing air). Hence it is said that man was created out of the four elements, and he is called a "small world." But man lay like one dead upon the ground, until God breathed into his nostrils the spirit of life, and Adam became a living soul. In like manner God created all other animals, and all plants and minerals, out of the four elements. Then God set Adam in the Garden of Eden, in Paradise, which He had planted with His own hands, and in which flourished all manner of flowers, fruit, roots, herbs, leaves, and grass. Then Adam's heart was filled with joy, and he understood the great power of his Creator, and praised and magnified Him with his lips; at that time he suffered no lack of any thing, having all that his heart desired, and he was appointed lord of all other creatures. Therefore, the eternal Creator bade the holy angels bring every other living being to Adam, that all might acknowledge him as their lord, and that Adam might give to each one its own name, and distinguish one from the other.

Now when God beheld the animals walking about in Paradise, each with its own mate (except Adam, for whom no mate was found); when God saw them approaching him, and yet eager to flee from him, because of the reverence and awe with which he inspired them –God said: "It is not good for man to be alone"; therefore He caused a deep sleep to fall upon Adam, and taking one of his ribs, not far from his heart, He formed it into a beautiful woman. This woman God brought unto the man, calling her Eve, and gave her to him for a wife, that he might protect her, that she might obey him, and that they might be fruitful and multiply.

The Glory and Excellence of Adam.

God had appointed that Adam and Eve should spend a thousand years in Paradise, and then be translated, body and soul, to the Eternal Life of Heaven; the same glorious destiny was in reserve for their posterity. For as yet man was pure, good, and sinless, and not subject or liable to any kind of distemper, or sickness. He was acceptable and perfect in the sight of His Creator, who had made him in His own image, and given him all the produce of Paradise to eat, except the fruit of the Tree of Knowledge, from which he was to abstain on pain of eternal punishment, both bodily and spiritual. But when he gave ear to the seducing words of the Evil One, and ate the forbidden fruit, he straightway became poor and wretched, perceived his own nakedness, and concealed himself amongst the trees of the garden. He had deserved eternal death, and it would have fallen upon him, if the Son of God, our Lord and Saviour Jesus Christ, had not promised to give satisfaction for him. Yet in this world God punished Adam with a heavy yoke of wretchedness, tribulation, poverty, and disease, followed by the bitter agony of death. He also drove him forth from Paradise, and laid a heavy curse upon the ground, that thenceforward it should not bring forth fruit of its own accord, but that it should bear thorns and thistles. Now, when Adam found himself in the midst of a wild and uncultivated earth, compelled to gain his bread by tilling the field in the sweat of his brow, and to endure much suffering, care, and anxiety, he began to think seriously of what he had done to provoke the wrath of God, to experience deep sorrow for his grievous sin, and to implore God's gracious mercy and forgiveness. His prayers appeased the paternal heart of God, and induced Him to ease the grievous yoke laid upon Adam. The central fact of his punishment, however, remained, and death, though deferred, at length overtook him.

But, as I say, God mitigated the punishment of Adam, and took away from his neck the grievous yoke of suffering, by shewing him the means of warding off the strokes of impending calamity. For this purpose the natural properties of things were revealed to Adam by the inspiration of the Holy Spirit; and he was taught to prepare medicines out of herbs, stones, and metals, wherewith he might alleviate his hard lot, ward off disease, and keep his body in good health until the end of his days, which, however, was known to God alone. For, although from the very beginning Adam had a clear insight into the working of the natural world, the greatest of all secrets was still hidden from him, till God one day called him into Paradise, and set forth to him this marvellous mystery—the mystery of our Stone—in the following words:

"Behold, Adam, here are two things, the one fixed and immutable, the other volatile and inconstant. The great virtue and potency that slumber in them you must not reveal to all your sons. For I created them for a special purpose, which I will now no longer conceal from you." Now, when Adam had learned the mystery out of God's own mouth, he kept it a strict secret from all his sons, until at length, towards the close of his life, he obtained leave from God to make the preparation of the Stone known to his son Seth. Unless Adam had possessed the knowledge of this great mystery he would not have been able to prolong his life to the age of 300 (let alone 900) years. For he was never for a moment free from an agonizing sense of his guilt, and of the terrible evils which he had, by his disobedience, brought upon himself and his posterity, who, through his fault, were one and all involved in the condemnation of eternal death. If we consider this, it must appear amazing that Adam could keep alive even so long as a single year after his fall; and we thereby clearly perceive (from the fact that he attained to so great a length of days) that the goodness of God must have furnished him with some life-preserving remedy. If Adam had not possessed our Medicine, or Tincture, he could not have borne up under so much tribulation, anxiety, wretchedness, grief, sorrow, and disease. But against all these ills he used our Medicine, which preserved his limbs and his strength from decay, braced his faculties, comforted his heart, refreshed his spirit, relieved his anxiety, fortified his mortal body against all manner of disease, and, in short, guarded him from all evil until the last hour of his life.

At length, however, Adam found that the Remedy had no longer any power to strengthen him, or to prolong his life. So he began to consider his end, refrained from applying the Medicine any more, threw himself upon the mercy of God, and sent his son Seth (to whom he had confided the secret), to the gate of Paradise, to demand some of the fruit of the Tree of Life. His request was denied him, whereupon he returned, and carried back to his father the answer of the Angel. It was heavy news for Adam, who now felt that his end was approaching, and therefore sent Seth a second time to fetch the oil of mercy. Before he could return, Adam died; but, at the bidding of God, Seth obtained from the Angel some olive-stones from the Tree of the Oil of Mercy, and planted them on his father's grave, where they grew into the tree from which the Cross of our Blessed Redeemer was made. Thus, though in a carnal sense the Oil was denied to Adam, and brought him no surcease from temporal death; yet, in a spiritual sense, it was freely given to him and obtained for him and all his offspring eternal life, and free, gracious, and merciful forgiveness of all their sins, concerning which God promised that He would remember them no more.

Thus, through the Heavenly Tree of Life, God fulfilled the prayer of our first parent Adam, and granted his request in a way which he had not looked for; and he now tastes the joy which is at the right hand of God, and is for ever removed from the hostile power of hunger, thirst, heat, cold, death, and all the other evils which flesh is heir to. Let us then diligently strive to realize that the Mystery of the Redemption is the most precious, the most excellent, and the most awful of the mysteries revealed by God to man, a mystery which no human thought can sound, and which no human lips can ever fully utter. But of this Awful Mystery, or Medicine of the Soul, God has also bestowed upon us an earthly antitype, or Medicine of the Body, by means of which wretched man may, even in this world, secure himself against all bodily distempers, put to. flight anxiety and care, and refresh and comfort his heart in the hour of trouble—namely, the Mystery of the

Sages, or the Medicine of the Philosophers. If, therefore, a man would be perfectly happy in this world, and in the world to come, he should earnestly and devoutly strive to become possessed of these two Remedies; and for this purpose, he should turn to God with his whole heart, and ask for His gracious help, without which neither can be obtained; and, above all, he should be most eager to receive that Remedy by which the soul is healed of the mortal disease of sin.

This is the true fountain of the Sages; and there is nothing like it upon earth, but one eternal thing, by which the mortal body may, in this vale of tears, be fortified against all accidental disease, shielded from the pangs of poverty, and rendered sound, healthy, and strong, being protected against all mischances to the very end; and by which also metallic bodies may be changed into gold through a quickening of the process which Nature uses in the heart of the earth. The preparation and effects of this Stone are not unjustly considered to bear a close analogy to the creation of the world; therefore, I thought well to give an account of it from the very beginning.

I will now proceed briefly to expound my view of this Art, which, as all Sages testify, corresponds most closely to the creation and generation of man. I will attempt to make my meaning as plain as I dare, for the glory of the Holy Trinity, and the good of all Christian believers. When God had created the world, and adorned it with all manner of green things, herbs, roots, leaves, flowers, grass, and also with animals and minerals, he blessed them, and appointed that everything should bring forth fruit and seed after its kind. Only Adam (who is our Matter) was not yet in a position to produce any fruit out of himself. Before he could propagate his species, it was necessary that a part of him should be taken away, and again joined to him, *i.e.*, his wife Eve. Hereunto we must understand that so long as our substance is still gross and undivided, it can produce no fruit. It must first be divided, the subtle from the gross, or the water from the earth. The water is Eve, or the spirit; the earth Adam, or the body. And as the male is useless for purposes of generation until it be united to the female, so our earth is dead till it is quickened by the union with water. This is what that ancient Sage, Hermes, means when he says that the dead must be raised to life, and the feeble made strong.

It is necessary, then, to unite body and soul, and to change that which is below into that which is above, *i.e.*, body into spirit, and spirit into body. By this expression you are to understand not that the spirit by itself is changed into a body, or that the body by itself is changed into a spirit, but that both are united, and that the spirit, or water, dissolves, or resuscitates the body, or earth, while the body attracts the spirit, or water; and that they are thus joined into one substance, the earth being softened by the water, and the water hardened by the earth—as the boys in the street pour water on dry dust, and knead the whole into one mass. For this reason the Sages call our process child's play, in which the death of one is the life of the other, *i.e.*, in which the hardness of the one is softened by the other, and *vice versa*, seeing that the two are nothing but body and spirit originally belonging together. When contemplating this union, the Sage, Hermes, bursts forth into the following exclamation: "Oh, how strong, victorious, and precious is this nature that so unspeakably comforts its supplementary nature!" This nature is water, which stirs up and quickens the nature of the body. Hence it is said that Adam, or the body, would be dead without Eve, the spirit; for when the water has been distilled from our substance, the body lies dead and barren at the bottom of the alembic, and is described by the Sages as being, after the loss of its spirit, black, poisonous, and deadly. If the body is to be resuscitated, it must be rendered fit for generation by being purged of its blackness and fetid smell, and then its sweat or spirit must be restored to it; the spirit cannot conceive unless the body be allowed to embrace its Eve, or spirit. Senior says that the higher vapour must be brought back to the lower vapour; the Divine water is the King that descends from heaven, and leads the soul back to its body which is thereby quickened from the dead. Observe that in the body there is hidden fixed *salt*, which slumbers there just as the male seed slumbered in Adam. This the spirit, or Eve, attracts, and thus becomes pregnant; that is to say: The seed of the body, which we call fixed salt, is extracted from the body by its own water (which has before been separated from it), and is rendered so subtle and volatile that it ascends with the spirit to heaven. Then we say that the fixed has become volatile, that the dead has been revived, and that the body has received life from its spirit. On this account the water is called by some Sages the living water of the man, since it is extracted from the body, or man; and Lucas enjoins us to take it, and heat it after the fashion of Nature. Other Sages call the body the "black soil," because in it the fixed salt is concealed from view, like the seed in the ground. Others, again, call it the "black raven," which has in its maw the "white dove"; and the water which is distilled from the body they call the "virgin's milk," by which the white dove must be brought forth from the black raven. In short, these things are described by the Sages under a great variety of names; but the meaning of those names is the same. In this fashion the water is embraced by the body, and the seed of the body, or the fixed salt, makes the water pregnant. For the water dissolves the body, and bears upward with it some particles of the fixed salt; and the oftener this process is repeated, the thicker does the water become. Hence the repetition of the process is a most important point. Hermes says that when he saw the water gradually grow thicker and harder, he rejoiced, for thereby he knew that he should find what he sought. The water, then, must be poured upon the body, and heated with it, till the body is dissolved, and then again extracted till the body is coagulated. Thus the body must be well broken up, and purified by washing. This process of affusion and extraction must be repeated until all the salt, or potency and efficacy, has been extracted from the body. This is the case when the water becomes white and thick, and, in the cold, hard and solid like ice, while in the heat it melts like butter. Now, when nothing more can be extracted from the body, the residuum must be removed; for it is the superfluous part of the substance. This is what the Sages mean when they say: In the preparation we remove that which is superfluous; but otherwise our whole Magistery is accomplished with one single substance, nothing being added, and nothing taken away, except that which is really superfluous; for it possesses in abundance all that is needed, namely, the water, or "white, flaky earth," which must be injected into "living mercury," that so the transmutation into good and fixed silver may take place. But something much more noble and precious is concealed in this water (fixed salt), which grows and grows like the infant in the mother's womb. For as the embryo in the matrix, which is first a mere seed, grows, and is gradually transmuted into flesh and blood, *i.e.*, into a thicker substance, till at length the limbs are formed; so this water grows from the white colour which distinguishes it at first, till it is changed to another colour. (For the embryo, too, is transmuted from the natural colour of the embryo into flesh and blood.) The substance at length assuming a red colour, may be compared to the forming of the infant's limbs; it is then that we first see what is to become of it. When you perceive this final transmutation—the germ of which lay in the substance all along—you may well rejoice; for you have attained the object of your desire.

Thus I have described the union of the man and woman, that is to say, of the body and spirit, by means of which the child is conceived in the water, and the whiteness extracted from the black body. Nor do we need anything else, except, as Morienus says, time and patience. This coagulated water is the "white, flaky earth," in which the Sage bids us sow our gold and silver that they may bear fruit a hundred-thousand-fold. This is the "clear spring" of the Count of Trevisa, in which the King bathes, though not assisted by any of his ministers, who only watch his clothes until he has dried up the whole spring, when he makes all his ministers lords and kings such as he was at the time of his entering the bath. But now the King's dignity is three times as great as it was before; he wears a three-fold diadem on his head, and is arrayed in garments that shine like carbuncles and amethysts, and beneath them he wears the tunic of purity, and is bound with the girdle of righteousness. He is the most glorious King of life, whose power transcends all human thought. At his side is seated his pure and chaste queen, sprung of his own seed; and of these two are born many royal children. The redness is concealed and preserved in the whiteness, which must not be extracted, but subjected to gentle coction until its full crimson glory flames forth. This whiteness is thus referred to in "The Crowd": "If you see that after the blackness there follows a whiteness, be sure that after the whiteness will come a redness: for the redness slumbers in the whiteness, and should not be extracted, but gently heated, until the whole turns red." Let what I have now said suffice you.

HERMES [says]:

You must have a good knowledge of the True Principle of both Natural and Artificial Substances. For he who knows not the true First Principle will never attain to the end.

THE LOVE OF GOD AND

OF YOUR NEIGHBOUR

IS THE PERFECTION OF ALL WISDOM.

TO LOVE GOD IS THE HIGHEST WISDOM,

AND

TIME IS OUR POSSESSION.

UNTO HIM BE ALL HONOUR, PRAISE, AND

GLORY

A TRACT

OF GREAT PRICE

CONCERNING THE PHILOSOPHICAL

STONE.

PUBLISHED BY A GERMAN SAGE IN THE YEAR

1423,

UNDER THE FOLLOWING TITLE:

THE TRUE TEACHING OF PHILOSOPHY

CONCERNING

THE GENERATION OF METALS

AND

THEIR TRUE ORIGIN.

A TRACT OF GREAT PRICE

CONCERNING THE PHILOSOPHICAL STONE.

CHAPTER I.

ALL temporal things derive their origin, their existence, and their essence from the earth, according to the succession of time. Their specific properties are determined by the outward and inward influences of the stars and planets, (such as the Sun, the Moon, Etc.), and of the four qualities of the elements. From these combined circumstances arise the peculiar forms, and proper substances, of all growing, fixed, and generating things, according to the natural order appointed by the Most High at the beginning of the world. The metals, then, derive their origin from the earth, and are specifically compounded of the four qualities, or the properties of the four elements; their peculiar metallic character is stamped upon them by the influences of the stars and planets. So we are informed by Aristotle, in the fourth book of his Meteor., where he says that quicksilver is the common substance of all metals. The first thing in Nature, as we said before, is the substance which represents a particular conglomeration of the four elements, which the Sages call Mercury, or quicksilver. But this quicksilver is as yet imperfect, on account of its gross and earthy sulphureous nature, which renders it too easily combustible, and on account of its superfluous watery elements, which have all been collected together out of the four elements by the action of the heavenly planets. This substance is composed of a hot sulphureous earth, and a watery essence, in such a way that the Sages have called it imperfect sulphur.

Now, since Nature is always striving to attain perfection, and to reach the goal set before her by the Creator of all things, she is continually at work upon the qualities of the four elements of each substance; and so stirs up and rouses the inward action of the elements by the accidental heat of the Sun, and by natural warmth, that there arises a kind of vapour or steam in the veins of the earth. This vapour cannot make its way out, but is closed in; in penetrating through fat, earthy, oily, and impure sulphureous substances it attracts to itself more or less of these foreign and external impurities. This is the reason that there are seen in it so great a variety of colours before it attains to purity and its own proper colour.

Those mineral and metallic substances which contain the largest proportion of efficacious sulphureous and mercurial vapour are the best; and each quality of the four elements has its own peculiar operation and transmuting influence in such a conglomeration of various substances—their action being roused by the sulphur of the earth and the outward heat of the Sun. Through these agencies the Matter is often dissolved and coagulated, till that which is pure, or impure, is borne upward; and this is the work not of a few years, but of a great length of time. Nature has to purge away the peculiar characteristics of all other metals before she can make gold; as you may see by the fact that different kinds of metal are found in the same metallic vein. This fact may be explained in the following manner. When the sulphureous and mercurial vapours ascend, they are mixed, and united by coction, with the aforesaid substance. If those sulphureous vapours are earthy, thick, and impure, and the heat of the Sun, or their own natural heat, have too sudden and violent an effect, the substance hardens, with all its sulphureous impurities, before it can be purged of its grossness, and it becomes more like metallic sulphur. If the quicksilver is hardened, the whole mass takes the form of some metal, according to the influence of the particular planet with which it is penetrated. For Nature first combines the four elements into some substance or body, which then receives its specific properties through the influence of some planet. Such is the origin of copper, tin, lead, iron, and quicksilver. But it is not essential that I should here describe at length the specific composition and distinctive properties of each of the imperfect metals; they are all mingled in various proportions of impure sulphur and inefficacious quicksilver. Nature, as I said, is ceaselessly at work upon these imperfect metals, purging and separating the pure quicksilver from the impure, and the pure sulphur from the impure, until all their grossness is removed, and they become what God designed that they should be, viz., gold. But if these vapours float upward in their original pure condition, with their inward, pure, and subtle earth, without becoming mixed with gross, earthy, and sulphureous alloy, and if they succeed in breaking forth into the open air, before they become hardened into a sulphureous mass, they remain quicksilver and are not changed into any metal.

If, however, this pure quicksilver floats upward in a pure mineral earth, without any gross alloy, it is hardened into the pure and white sulphur of Nature by being subjected to a very moderate degree of gentle heat, and at length assumes the specific form of silver. Like all the other metals it may still be developed into gold, if it remain under the influence of its natural heat. But if the same pure, unalloyed quicksilver be subjected to a higher degree of natural heat, it is transmuted into the pure *red* sulphur of Nature, and becomes gold without first passing through the stage of silver. In this form it remains, because gold is the highest possible stage of metallic development.

Quicksilver is the mother of all metals, on account of its coldness and moistness; and if it be once purified and cleansed of all foreign matter it cannot be mixed any more with grossness of any kind, neither can it be changed back into an imperfect metal. For Nature does not undo her work, and that which has once become perfectly pure can never become impure again. Sulphur, on the other hand, is the father of all metals, on account of its heat and dryness. In the following chapter we shall refer to this difference, and speak more in detail about quicksilver.

CHAPTER II.

There is, then, in *all* metals true mercury, and good sulphur, in the imperfect as well as in the perfect metals. But in the imperfect metals it is defiled with impure matter, and stands in need of maturing. Hence you see that all metals may be changed into gold and silver, if the golden and silver properties that are in them be freed from all alloy, and reduced by gentle heat to the form of silver or gold. Those metals, indeed, which have been torn up by the roots, that is to say, that have been dug up from their own proper soil in the veins of the earth, can no longer proceed in that course of development which they pursued in their native abode; yet, as much as in them lies, they strive to be perfected.

Now the Spirit of Truth, who imparts all true knowledge, has taught the Sages a Medicine, or Form, by which all the impurities of the imperfect metals may be removed, and the perfect nature, or true mercury, which is in them, transmuted into gold and silver.

CHAPTER III.

But we must now proceed to say a few words about the method of preparing this Medicine, by which the imperfection is removed from imperfect metals through the mediation of perfect mercury, and the mode of gold and silver is developed in them.

I find that the writings of the Sages are all about gold, silver, and quicksilver, which, it is said, must be reduced to the form which they wore before they became metals; that is to say, the form which they wore, perhaps, some thousands of years ago. But the operation of Nature is progressive, not retrogressive. Hence it is a great mistake to suppose that the work of Nature can be reversed by dissolution in aqua fortis, or by the amalgamation of gold or silver and quicksilver. For if the metal be plunged in a solvent, if water be distilled from it, or if quicksilver be sublimed from it, it still remains the same metal that it was before. The specific properties of a metal cannot be destroyed so as to obtain the first substance. Yet Aristotle says that metals cannot be changed unless they are reduced to their original substance.

CHAPTER IV.

What we said in the last chapter shows that Alchemical Art cannot be concerned with the subjecting of gold, silver, or quicksilver to chemical processes. Nevertheless, that which you read in the books of the Sages is most true; and we shall see in the following pages in what sense it is to be understood, that our Art is in gold, silver, and quicksilver. But it is clear that our Art can make no use of quicksilver such as may be obtained from the metals by means of any kind of artificial process, such as dissolution in aqua fortis, or amalgamation, or any other method of chemical purification.

If then, this is not the right substance, or original mercury, it is clear that it is not to be found in the metals. For even if you melt two, three, or four metals together, yet not one of them can give the others any aid towards attaining perfection, seeing that itself stands in need of external aid. And even though you mix some imperfect metal with gold, the gold will not give up its own perfection for the purpose of succouring the other: for it has nothing to spare which it might impart to the imperfect metal. And even if the imperfect metal could assume the virtue and efficacy of the gold, it could only do so at the expense of the gold itself. In vain, then, shall we seek in metals the Medicine which has power to liberate the perfect mercury contained in imperfect metals.

CHAPTER V.

Again, we read in the books of the Sages that quicksilver and mercury are the original substance of all metals. These words are true irk a certain sense. But by many beginners they are supposed to mean ordinary quicksilver. Such an interpretation, however, makes nonsense of the dictum of the Sages. For ordinary quicksilver is an imperfect metal, and itself derived from the original substance of all metals. The Sages, indeed, say little about the *origin* of their mercury; but that is exactly because they use the name of mercury, or sulphur, for the first substance of their perfect metals. If common mercury were not a metal, there would be no metal corresponding to the celestial influence of the planet Mercury, as gold and silver receive their specific properties from the influence of the Sun and Moon.

Now, as it is one of the metals, the other metals cannot be derived from it, much less can their properties be derived from it or from themselves, although the real perfect mercury is quite as abundant in mercury as in any other metal. Nor can common sulphur be the first substance of the metals, for no metal contains so much impurity as common sulphur; and if it be mixed with any metal, that metal becomes even more impure than it was before, and is even partially, or wholly, corroded.

Chapter VI.

Again, the Sages affirm that quicksilver, or mercury, is the spirit of the specific nature of metals, collected out of the four elements by the influence of the Planets, and the operation of Nature in the earth—and that from it is developed either gold, silver, or some other of seven metals, according to the peculiar effects of the predominant planetary influence.

Hence ignorant alchemists have supposed that all this is true of the common quicksilver, because it amalgamates with all metals, and is soft and volatile. But why should its volatile properties prove it to be no metal? According to this definition, we might deny the metallic character of tin, lead, and other metals, because they do not remain fixed in a fierce fire—though one can stand a greater degree of heat than another. If, again, any substance is to be called the first substance of metals because of the facility with which it amalgamates with them, copper would have a better claim to be so regarded, since it enters into a closer union with gold and silver than mercury, and shares both their fusible and malleable nature. But that is no final union, for it admits of separation; and quicksilver may, with the greatest ease, be separated from the metals with which it has amalgamated. A true union of metals can only take place in the original substance which is common to all. We do find amalgams of three, or even more metals; but then this union was consummated in the first substance, which is *one*, and the whole amalgam would have been developed into gold, if its natural growth had not been retarded by gross, sulphureous, arsenical, and earthy impurity, which is found among metals when purified. The metals which we dig up out of the earth are, as it were, torn up by the roots, and, their growth having come to a standstill, they can undergo no further development into gold, but must always retain their present form, unless something is done for them by our Art. Hence we must begin at the point where Nature had to leave off: we must purge away all impurity, and the sulphureous alloy, as Nature herself would have done if her operation had not been accidentally, or violently, disturbed. She would have matured the original substance, and brought it to perfection by gentle heat, and, in a longer or shorter period of time, she would have transmuted it into gold. In this work Nature is ceaselessly occupied while the metals are still in the earth; but she takes away from them nothing save their superfluous water, and the impurity which prevents them from attaining to the nature of gold, as we briefly showed in the second chapter.

Chapter VII.

It is clear, then, that the final union of metals, or their perfection, cannot be attained by the mingling of any specific metals; that the metallic substance becomes useless for our purpose, as soon as it assumes a specific form; but that, at the same time, all metals have a common origin, or Matter, which is one thing, flowing out by the operation of Nature, who ever desires the most perfect form which her own essence and her condition will admit. And this is the form of gold, highest and best of all that belong to the metallic mode. If, then, the purest form of this substance which it is possible for Art to prepare with the help of Nature, be added to the imperfect metals, then it overcomes what is impure in these, for it is not the impure, but the pure matter which is like unto it. But you must not suppose that this power belongs to common gold; common gold has its own specific form, which it is unable to impart to other metals. The power of gold is sufficient only for preserving its own excellence; but our prepared substance is much better and more honourable than gold, and has power to do that which gold cannot do, viz., to change the common matter of all metals into gold.

CHAPTER VIII.

From what I have hitherto said, one ignorant of alchemy might suppose that the teaching of the Sages is altogether false and untrustworthy. Therefore I must now proceed to tell you how it may truly be affirmed that our Art is concerned with quicksilver, silver, and gold, or with quicksilver and sulphur, and in what sense mercury is the spirit of the metals. I will first speak about quicksilver, and at once premise that this word is not here taken to mean that common quicksilver which is one of the metals, but the first substance of all the metals, and itself no specific metal at all. For a metal must have derived its distinctive properties through planetary influences; nor can any one metal be the first substance of all metals. This quicksilver is neither too hot, nor too cold, nor too moist, nor too dry; but it is a well-tempered mingling of all four. When perfectly matured quicksilver is subjected to external heat, operating thereon, it is not burned, but escapes in a volatile essence. Hence it may well be called by the philosophers a spirit, or a swift, and winged, and indestructible soul.

So long as it is palpable and visible it is also called body; when subjected to external cold it is congealed into a fixed body, and then these three, body, soul, and spirit, are one thing, and contain the properties of all the four elements. That outward part which is moist and cold is called *water*, or quicksilver; on account of its inward heat it is called *air*; if without it appear hot and dry it is *fire*, or sulphur; and on account of its internal coldness it is also styled *earth*. In this way quicksilver and sulphur are the original substance of all metals; but, of course, I do not mean that the substance is prepared by mixing common sulphur and quicksilver. The sulphur and quicksilver of the Sages are one and the same thing, which is first of the nature of quicksilver, or moist and watery, and is then, by constant coction, transmuted into the nature of sulphur, which may most justly be described as dry and igneous.

CHAPTER IX.

But I wish to confine my discourse to the quicksilver and sulphur of the philosophers, from which all metals derive their origin; and it is, according to the Sages, a heavy, earthy water, mixed with very subtle white earth, and subjected to natural coction until the moist and the dry elements have become united and coagulated into one body—through the perfect mutual adjustment of all the elementary properties, and by the accidental operation of cold. This is the substance which is used for the purposes of our Art, after it has been perfected and purified by gentle coction, and freed from its earthy and sulphureous grossness, and the combustible wateriness of the quicksilver. It is then one clear, pure, and indestructible substance, proceeding from a duplex substance, exhibiting, in their greatest purity and efficacy, the united properties of quicksilver and of sulphur. In Art the operation is similar to Nature. Hence the Sages have justly affirmed that our Art is concerned with quicksilver, gold, and silver. For in its first stage the substance resembles quicksilver, which is sublimed by gentle natural heat, and purified in the veins of the rocks in the form of a pure vapour, as we explained above. To it we now add silver and gold, and that for the following reason, because we cannot find anywhere else in any one thing the metallic power needed for rousing the sulphur of the quicksilver, and coagulating it, except in gold and silver. For the Sage cannot prepare our quicksilver unless it be first removed from the earth, and separated from the potency of its natural surroundings; and all these natural influences can be artificially supplied only by the addition of gold and silver. Our Art, then, has to find a substitute for those natural forces in the precious metals. By them alone it is able to fix the volatile properties of our quicksilver, for in them alone do we find the powers and influences which are indispensable to our chemical process.

You should also bear in mind that the silver should be applied to our quicksilver before the gold, because the quicksilver is volatile, and cannot with safety be subjected all at once to great heat. Silver has the power of stirring up the inherent sulphur of the quicksilver, whereby it is coagulated into the form of the Remedy for transmuting metals into silver; and this coagulation is brought about by the gentle heat of the silver. Gold requires a much higher degree of heat, and if gold were added to the quicksilver before the silver, the greater degree of heat would at once change the quicksilver into a red sulphur, which, however, would be of no use for the purpose of making gold, because it would have lost its essential moisture; and our Art requires that the quicksilver should be first coagulated by means of silver into white sulphur, before the greater degree of heat is applied which, through gold, changes it into red sulphur. There must be whiteness before there is redness. Redness before whiteness spoils our whole substance.

CHAPTER X.

The quicksilver of the Sages has no power to transmute imperfect metals, until it has absorbed the essential qualities of gold and silver; for in itself it is no metal at all, and if it is to impart the spirit, the colour, and the hardness of gold and silver, it must first receive them itself. It is with the first substance of metals as it is with water. If saffron is dissolved in water, the water is coloured with it, and if mixed with other water, imparts to that water, too, the colour of saffron. Unless the first substance, or quicksilver, is tinged with silver and gold, and coagulated by their efficacy, it cannot impart any colour, or coagulate the (water or) first substance which is latent in the imperfect metals. For it is essentially a spirit, and volatile, and if it be added to imperfect metals, it cannot act upon their water, or undeveloped first-substance, because that is partly fixed by their coagulated sulphur. But if the first-substance has been fixed by means of gold and silver, it has become a fixed and indestructible water; and, if added to imperfect metals, takes up into its own nature their first substance, or water, and mingles with it. By this means all that is combustible and impure in them is driven off by the fire. And herein is the saying true, which was uttered by the Sage Haly: "The spirit (*i.e.*, quicksilver) is not coagulated, unless the body (*i.e.*, gold and silver) be first dissolved." For then gold and silver become spiritual, flowing, capable of being assimilated by the common substance of all metals, and of imparting to it their own metallic strength and potency. And even though this new substance be fusible in the fire, yet, when it cools again, it still remains what it was, nor is it ever again converted into a permanent spiritual substance. It is the quicksilver, then, that constitutes the chief strength and efficacy of our Art; and he that has no quicksilver is without the very seed of gold and silver from which they grow in the earth.

EPILOGUE.

We have sufficiently explained that quicksilver is the first substance of the metals, without which no metal can become perfect, either in Nature or in our Art. But we do not yet know where to look for it, and where to find it. This is the great secret of the Sages, which they are always so careful to veil under dark words that scarcely one in many thousands is thought worthy to find the philosophical Mercury. Many things have been written about it; but I will quote the words of *one* philosopher which I consider as the most helpful: In the beginning, he says, God created the earth plain, simple, rich, and very fertile, without stones, sand, rocks, hills, or valleys; it is the influences of the planets which have now covered it with stones, rocks, and mountains, and filled it with rare things of various colours, *i.e.*, the ores of the seven metals; and by these means the earth has entirely lost its original form, and that through the following causes:—

First, the earth which was created rich, great, deep, wide, and broad, was, through the daily operation of the Sun's rays, penetrated to her very centre with a fervent, bubbling, vaporous heat. For the earth in herself is cold and saturated with the moisture of water. At length the vapours which were formed in this way in the heart of the earth became so strong and powerful as to seek to force a way out into the open air, and thus, instead of effecting their object, threw up hills and hillocks, or, as it were, bubbles on the face of the earth. And since in those places where mountains were formed the heat of the Sun must have been most powerful, and the earthy moisture rich and most plentiful, it is there that we find the most precious metals. Where the earth remained plain, this steam did not succeed in raising up mountains; it escaped, and the earth, being deprived of its moisture, was hardened into rocks. Where the earth was poor, soft, and thin, it is now covered with sand and little stones, because it never had much moisture, and, having been deprived of the little it possessed, has now become sandy and dry, and incapable of retaining moisture. No earth was changed into rocks that was not rich, viscous, and well saturated with moisture. For when the heat of the Sun has sucked up its moisture, the richness of the earth still makes it cohere, although now it has become hard and dry; and earth that is not yet perfectly hard is even at the present time undergoing a change into hard stones, through the diligent working of Nature. But the steam and the vapours that do not succeed in escaping, remain enclosed in the mountains, and are day by day subjected to the maturing and transmuting influences of the Sun and the planets. Now, if this vaporous moisture become mixed with a pure, subtle, and earthy substance, it is the quicksilver of the Sages; if it be reduced to a fiery and earthy hardness, it becomes the sulphur of the Sages. This enquiry opens up the way of finding our quicksilver, or first substance of the metals; but though it be found in great quantities in all mines, it is known only to very few. It is not silver, or gold, or common quicksilver, or any metal, or sulphur. The Sage says: "It is a vaporous substance out of four elements, watery, and pure, and though it is found with all metals, it is not matured in those which are imperfect. Hence it must be sought in the ore, in which we find gold and silver." And when again he says, "If this quicksilver be hardened, it is the sulphur of the Sages," he means that this can only be done by means of gold and silver, which it takes into itself, and by which it is sublimed and coagulated through its own natural gentle coction, under the influence of the Sun's heat, and in its own proper ore.

O heavenly Father, shew this quicksilver
to all whom
Thou biddest walk in Thy paths!

A VERY BRIEF TRACT

CONCERNING THE

PHILOSOPHICAL STONE.

WRITTEN BY AN UNKNOWN GERMAN SAGE, ABOUT 200 YEARS AGO, AND CALLED THE
BOOK OF ALZE, BUT NOW PUBLISHED FOR THE FIRST TIME.

THE BOOK OF ALZE.

Do not, gentle Reader, find fault with me for speaking first about the Moon, then about the Sun, and the other planets, and only in the third place about our most excellent Medicine, ALZE. In this case that which is last is better and more honourable than that which is first. The substance must first become white, and then red; it cannot become red unless it have first become white. Hence Simon the Sage says: "Know that unless you first make the Stone white, you cannot make it red." For by the red are the rest of the planets united, and the Medicine appears unawares unless this order is observed in the matter of the white and red. So is the Moon first taken and makes, with the white, Elixir, that is, the white of the Moon to the white of Mercury out of bodies comes to the red. Whence our Sages say that the red is hidden in the white, which they do not dare to extract, until the whole substance has become red. When the substance has been subjected to the influence of the Moon, it may then, in the second place, be brought under the influence of the Sun, which will bring the Medicine to perfection without any aid from the other planets. By which you may understand why the Medicine comes last, even as from the Father proceeds the Son, and the Holy Spirit from both of these. He that hath ears to hear let him hear, and comprehend the brief statement of our Art, which is given in "The Crowd": "Know that the true Tincture can be prepared only out of our ore." Concerning this ore I therefore propose to give you the only explanation that is required, and I shall be careful to supplement and confirm my own opinion by quotations from other Sages. I shall speak not only about our ore, but also about our union or conjunction of water and mercury. For Eximenus says: "Nothing profitable can arise out of the elements without conjunction and gentle coction." Our ore Lucas calls the white ore, and it goes by many other names on account of the many colours which it exhibits in the various stages of the chemical process. But though the jealousy of the Sages has described it under various names, it is, and remains only one substance. Pythagoras says: "Many names are given to it; nevertheless, it is nothing else but the one and true Matter, and this is by reason of the development of its nature. The envious have described it by the names of all bodies, as, for instance, a coin, lead, copper, etc., according to the variety of its colours." So Lucas tells us that we have no need of many things, but only of one thing. Diamedes and Basan say: "Do not add to it any foreign substance; for the common substance of metals is one thing, and more excellent than all other things." Hence our whole Art is concerned with water, and a twin substance that ameliorates the water. Synon tells us that sulphur and our ore are derived from one thing, and changed into four. Lucas says: "The white ore is subjected to coction till it generates itself. Thus it becomes united in all its four elements, and receives a living soul. It is never more than one thing, but as a man consists of body, soul, and spirit, and yet is no more than one person, so our substance consists of body, soul, and spirit. The ore receives its strength, spirit, and growth from the water." The Sages say: "If the ore be often deadened in its coction, it becomes all the more excellent, and if the body have a soul after the manner of man." The body does not penetrate the soul, but the soul penetrates the body, because it is volatile. The soul, which is hidden in the four parts of the body, is called sulphur. These bodies are male and female, and by their mutual operation our substance becomes water. Aristeus says: "Observe the indestructible water which issues from it." Take the humidity which it gives off. Hence other Sages say: "Take water with its twin substances, and let it be dried up by means of the vapour which is like it, and coagulated in its own water." That water is also called poison; it is the principle of life, because it is a soul, and extracted from many things. All bodies that this Tincture enters are quickened; all bodies from which it is extracted are destroyed. Its potency is spiritual blood, which, if well mixed with bodies, transmutes them into spirits, and combines with them into one substance. The body attracts the spirit, and the spirit tinges the body with a spiritual substance like blood. For the Sages say that whatever has a spirit has blood. If the venom penetrate the body, it imparts to it an indestructible colour, and then the soul cannot be separated from the body any more. If in flying it faces round and meets its pursuer, then is the flight at an end. The two belong together, and Nature always tends to assimilate kindred substances. The final colour is indestructible, because the soul pervades every part of the body, and is inseparably bound up with it. Though the water is naturally cold, yet we must beware of too fierce a degree of heat; for if the moisture of the substance be dried up, our work must come to nought.

That which is called the spirit, is the active, or male principle, and can only be obtained by. the dissolution of the body. Accordingly, we must understand this of the humidity which results, namely, that which is produced, as long as two spouses are conjoined after a lawful manner, even unto the white. Would you know when the body has been rendered liquid by coction? Hear what Bonellus answers: "When you see a black substance floating in the water, you may know that the body has been dissolved."

These two, body and spirit, have a third thing which represents their common substance, and is, in its turn, called their body. It is also called a round cloud, death, blackness, darkness, shadow, ashy lead, or a metallic and subtle ore; or it is described, after that which is obtained from it, as gold that was hidden in the body of Magnesia. Hence it is said: "Extract the shadow thereof from the splendour." This also is the substance of which so many have spoken. Three things constitute the true ore, viz., body, soul, and spirit. Hence it is compared to an egg, because in an egg, too, the chicken is developed out of three things. Thus also Alchemy is produced out of the above-mentioned three things, as many philosophers do testify in "The Crowd." The male principle, or the water, is also called the "nature"; for water is a natural agent which dissolves the elements of bodies, and then again unites them. Concerning this water, it is said by Fictes, that its nature has the wonderful power of transmuting the body into spirit. Where it is found alone it overcomes all other things, and is an excellent, harsh, and bitter acid, which transmutes gold into pure spirit. Without this acid we cannot attain either the red, or the black, or the white. When it is combined with bodies, then the body changes into spirit, by a heavenly fire, and immutable, indestructible tincture. Know also that the union must be brought about by a gentle fire, since the elements cannot stand a fierce fire, until the union has taken place. When the gentle heat is applied, the elements devour and consume each other, and yet again, on the other hand, comfort and strengthen each other, and teach each other to stand the test of fire. Hence the Sages say: "Invert the elements, and you will find what you seek." To invert the elements is to make that which is moist, dry, and that which is volatile, fixed. The husband also enforces conjunction that he may reproduce his own likeness. Many strive to accomplish this separation and conjunction; but few succeed in bringing about an union which can stand the test of fire. The composition which is prepared out of our precious substance is not even in the slightest degree diminished in volume by fire. Rather, it is nourished by fire, as a mother nourishes her child. These are the only things that have the power of making red and white, both inwardly and outwardly. Remember that at first they can only bear a gentle fire. When you see that a whiteness begins to appear it must be your next care to extract it from the black substance; then you should develop the redness which is hidden in it. But the latter object you must attain, not by extraction, but by gentle coction. Do not marvel that the Sages describe our ore under many names, and as consisting of body, soul, and spirit. They are also referred to as brothers, or as husband and wife. But Geber says that sometimes the whole substance is only called body, or spirit; and unless there be a dissolution into water, our work cannot be brought to a successful issue. Of course, we do not mean the water of the clouds, as the foolish say, but a permanent water, which, however, cannot be permanent without its body. Thus Hermogenes says that we are to take the hidden spirit, and not to despise it, because it shares its great power with its brother. For only the union of the two can give us the right Tincture. The water is also called a most sharp acid, with which the body must be washed; this is what Socrates calls "woman's work, and child's play." The secret of our Art is the union of man and woman: the husband receives the tinging spirit from his wife. The union of husband and wife coagulates the female principle; and if the whole be transmuted into red, we have the treasure of the world, of which Synon says: "If the water be changed into the body, the body is changed, first into earth, then into dust and ashes, and you have what you want."

Then the work is over, and the Stone contains within itself the Tincture in the body of Magnesia. Therefore, the Sages say, in conclusion: "My son, extract from the splendour its shadow." Accordingly, we need exertion, and exercise is beneficial to us, seeing that milk is for infants, but that strong men require stronger food. So also is it in this operation of the Stone.

Now, it is laid down by Geber that our Art must do more for the substance than Nature has done for it; otherwise we should never obtain the Medicine which has the power of correcting and perfecting the essences of the seven planets, or metals. For this purpose the Art of Alchemy has been delivered to us by the Sages; but the beginner must be on his guard against being misled by their manner of speaking, and the multiplicity of names which they give to our substance, which has been suggested to them by its great variety of (successive) colouring, and by the fact that it is composed of the four elements. The Stone must be saturated with its water, that it may imbibe it all, and then subjected to the action of fire, until it turns to a kind of dust, like burnt blood, and becomes indestructible by fire. This Stone is sought by Kings, but is found only by those to whom it is given of God. It is publicly sold for money. But if men knew its precious nature, they would cease to think lightly of it. God, however, has hidden it from the world, and he who would accomplish our work should first lay the right foundation, or his building must come to nought. Let me tell you, then, that our Stone requires a gentle fire; and if, after not many days, it die, and lie in the tomb, yet God restores to it its spirit, and removes its disease and its impurity. When it is burnt to ashes, it must be well sprinkled and saturated with its blood, until it becomes like burnt blood. Hermes remarks that both substances rejoice in being united to each other. To the spiritual substance God gives that which Nature could not give it. For Nature has nothing so precious as the true Tincture; and if with its bodies it become liquid, it produces a marvellous effect. For the Tincture changes everything it is mixed with into its own nature, and makes it white both within and without. By one operation and way, by one substance, and by one mixing, the whole work is accomplished, while its purity is also one, and it is perfected in two stages, each consisting of a dissolution and a coction, with the repetition of these.

It must be your first object to elicit the whiteness of the substance by means of gentle and continued coction or heat. I know that the Sages describe this simple process under a great number of misleading names. But this puzzling variety of nomenclature is only intended to veil the fact that nothing is required but simple coction. This process of coction, however, you must patiently keep up, and that with the Divine permission, until the King is crowned, and you receive your great reward. If you ask whether the substance of our Stone be dear, I tell you that the poor possess it as well as the rich.

Many have been reduced to beggary because they foolishly despised that which is highly esteemed by the Sages. If kings and princes knew it, none of us would ever be able to obtain it. Only one vessel is required for the whole process, which should be of stone, and should be capable of resisting fire.

A pound of the body of our ore should be taken, and rendered as pure, refined, and highly rectified, like the virtue of heaven, as the philosophers have it. Then the vessel should be placed in a reverberatory alembic. This should be set over a gentle fire, the vessel being kept tightly closed, in order that it may be able to retain its companion, and permit the same to enkindle the whiteness thereof, as Lucas says. The vessel containing the ore must be placed over the fire, since there can be no perfection without heat and intermixture of elements, seeing that it is produced from blood. When the male and the female principle have been together for a space of forty nights, there is an emission of moist warm seed; and to the same God has liberally given much blood to heat it. This seed develops into an embryo which is supported with a little milk over a moderate fire, and grows stronger day by day. Its growth must be aided by warmth; but the heat of the fire should be temperate, like that of the Sun. This may be effected by placing our vessel over an empty vessel, and that again upon some glowing coals. The process of coction should be continued until the alembic is well dried and the substance begins to assume a liquid aspect; for water alone is sufficient for the coagulation and fixing of the whole, as we are told by Democritus. This water is described under various names, such as sulphur, quicksilver, spirit, and also vapour, for it can scarcely retain its companion. There are in our Art only two substances, and if I speak of two, then I think of four, all which things require one thing, by which Nature, conquering all Nature, is extracted. For Nature, on account of its nature, rejoices in itself, Nature conquers nature, and in itself contains nature. At the same time one is not opposed to the other, but one comprehends the other, whereby it excels the other, and the philosophers call this water the purifying water.

This dissolution first imparts a black appearance to the body. The substance should then turn white, and finally red. The blackness exhibits an intermediate stage between fixedness and volatility. So long as there is blackness, the female principle prevails, till the substance enters into the white stage. This whiteness is called the first power of our Stone, and the water is referred to as that most excellent acid. You must be very careful not to destroy the potency of this water. Avicenna says that natural heat operating in humid bodies, first causes blackness; then removes the blackness; and finally causes whiteness, as may be seen in calx. Hence our substance must become first black, and then white, and be reduced to a kind of powder. Then the soul must be restored to the powder by a powerful fire; and both [be] subjected to coction until they become first black, then white, afterwards red, and finally good venom, the whole being accomplished by the separation of waters. And now, the waters being divided, cook the matter and the vapour till coagulation takes place, and there is made a white stone. Then are the waters divided. Another mortification, or exsiccation, follows, and is called clouds, or smoke. The smoke well coagulated with its feces becomes quick white; roast then the white ore that it may bring forth itself. When the blackness vanishes, the spirit is restored; for the spirit does not die, but rather quickens body and soul. The more perfectly our ore is purged, and subjected to coction, the better it becomes, till it is at length condensed into a Stone. But it must be dissolved again, and subjected to a powerful fire, until it looks like burnt blood. If this Stone be added to any substance, it tinges it into gold. The Sages speak of it as a kind of root. Take, they say, the whole virtue of the Tincture, and concentrate it in the Root. If a body which has no earthy elements receive this Tincture, it receives more benefit than less excellent bodies. The Stone overcomes everything to which it is applied, and tinges foreign bodies with its own colour. The dry fire tinges bodies, the air strengthens them, the white water washes away their blackness, and their earth receives the Tincture. Concerning the coction needed for the development of our substance, the Sages have expressed themselves in a great variety of ways. Observe Hermes, who says that it must be repeated again and again, until the red colour at length is obtained. Herein is the stability of the whole work. Afterwards it assumes many, many colours, not including the red, which appears at the end. For the white must precede it. Set to work by the regimen of fire, and triturate. The above mentioned water volatilizes all bodies; even such as are gross it penetrates until it has assimilated them to its own nature. Know that unless you operate upon bodies until they are destroyed and their soul is extracted, with such you will never tinge any body, for nothing tinges which has not first itself been tinged. If the body be made fluid and burnt, then it bends itself towards its begetter, becoming a subtle Magnesia, and it turns towards the earth, which makes it spiritual and vivifies it. Before the final whiteness of the first stage is attained, the substance turns first of a black, then of an orange, and then of a reddish colour (which, however, is quite different from the final redness of the last stage). These colours, however, need not trouble you, since they are evanescent and merely transitional.

From what I have said you may gather that our substance is found in the gold which is hidden in Magnesia, and that it is *one* thing composed of sulphur from sulphur and mercury from mercury. And as the substance of our Stone is one, so is the method of its preparation. Therefore, do not listen to those ignorant and fraudulent alchemists who speak of many different kinds of sublimation and distillation. Turn a deaf ear to those who say that the substance of our Stone is the powder of the Basilisk. As to the (length of) time required for the preparation, you must begin it in the winter, which is moist, and extract the moisture until the spring, when all things become green, and when our substance, too, should exhibit a variety of colours. In the summer the substance should be reduced to powder by means of a powerful fire. The autumn, the season of ripeness, should witness its maturity, or final redness. About the motions of the stars or planets you need not trouble yourself. Our substance is a body containing the spirit which makes glass malleable, and turns crystals into carbuncles. One drop of our Elixir, as large as a drop of rain, will suffice to tinge and transmute a body a thousand times as large as itself

This most noble Remedy was appointed, like all other things, for the use of man, because he is the most glorious of God's creatures, and the lord of the whole earth. It was given to him for the purpose of preserving his youth, expelling disease, preventing suffering, and providing him with all he requires. Our Elixir is better than all the medicinal preparations of Hippocrates, Avicenna, and others. From it may be prepared a potable antidote which has power to cure leprosy. As fire purges and refines metals, so this Remedy restores to the human body its natural heat, expels from it all health-destroying matter, and fortifies it against every conceivable form of disease. Its virtue is infinitely greater than that of the potable gold dust, which is taken as a preventative among the Gentiles.

Great and wonderful is the potency of the gold that slumbers in Magnesia, both for the purifying of the human system, and for the transmuting of metals. What more shall I say? All the things that I have here faithfully described I have seen with my own eyes, and performed with my own hands.

When I was preparing the substance, after discovering the true method, I was so seriously interfered with by the persons with whom I lived that I was almost on the point of giving up the whole thing in despair. At length I communicated my discovery to a friend, who faithfully executed my instructions, and brought the work to a successful issue. For which Blessed Gift may God be praised, world without end. Amen.

THE BOOK OF

LAMBSPRING,

A Noble Ancient Philosopher,

CONCERNING THE

PHILOSOPHICAL STONE;

RENDERED INTO LATIN VERSE BY

NICHOLAS BARNAUD DELPHINAS,

Doctor of Medicine, a zealous Student of this Art.

PREFACE.

I AM CALLED LAMBSPRING, BORN OF A NOBLE FAMILY, AND THIS CREST I BEAR WITH GLORY AND JUSTICE.

PHILOSOPHY I have read, and thoroughly understood,
The utmost depth of my teachers' knowledge have I sounded.
This God graciously granted to me,
Giving me a heart to understand wisdom.
Thus I became the Author of this Book,
And I have clearly set forth the whole matter,
That Rich and Poor might understand.
There is nothing like it upon earth;
Nor (God be praised) have I therein forgotten my humble self.
I am acquainted with the only true foundation:
Therefore preserve this Book with care,
And take heed that you study it again and again.
Thus shall you receive and learn the truth,
And use this great gift of God for good ends.
O God the Father, which art of all the beginning and end,
We beseech thee for the sake of our Lord Jesus Christ
To enlighten our minds and thoughts,
That we may praise Thee without ceasing,
And accomplish this Book according to Thy will!
Direct Thou everything to a good end,
And preserve us through Thy great mercy.—
With the help of God I will shew you this Art,
And will not hide or veil the truth from you.
After that you understand me aright,
You will soon be free from the bonds of error.
For there is only *one* substance,
In which all the rest is hidden;
Therefore, keep a good heart.
Coction, time, and patience are what you need;
If you would enjoy the precious reward,
You must cheerfully give both time and labour.
For you must subject to gentle coction the seeds and the metals,
Day by day, during several weeks;
Thus in this one vile thing
You will discover and bring to perfection the whole work of Philosophy,
Which to most men appears impossible,
Though it is a convenient and easy task.
If we were to shew it to the outer world
We should be derided by men, women, and children.
Therefore be modest and secret,
And you will be left in peace and security.
Remember your duty towards your neighbour and your God,
Who gives this Art, and would have it concealed.
Now we will conclude the Preface,
That we may begin to describe the very Art,
And truly and plainly set it forth in figures,
Rendering thanks to the Creator of every creature.
Hereunto follows the First Figure,

The Sages will tell you
That two fishes are in our sea
Without any flesh or bones.
Let them be cooked in their own water;
Then they also will become a vast sea,
The vastness of which no man can describe.
Moreover, the Sages say
That the two fishes are only one, not two;
They are two, and nevertheless they are one,
Body, Spirit, and Soul.
Now, I tell you most truly,
Cook these three together,
That there may be a very large sea.
Cook the sulphur well with the sulphur,
And hold your tongue about it:
Conceal your knowledge to your own advantage,
And you shall be free from poverty.
Only let your discovery remain a close secret.

FIGURE I.

BE WARNED AND UNDERSTAND TRULY
THAT TWO FISHES ARE SWIMMING IN OUR SEA.

The Sea as the Body, the two Fishes are Soul and Spirit.

The Sage says
That a wild beast is in the forest,
Whose skin is of blackest dye.
If any man cut off his head,
His blackness will disappear,
And give place to a snowy white.
Understand well the meaning of this head:
The blackness is called the head of the Raven;
As soon as it disappears,
A white colour is straightway manifested;
It is given this name, despoiled of its head.
When the Beast's black hue has vanished in a black smoke,
The Sages rejoice
From the bottom of their hearts;
But they keep it a close secret,
That no foolish man may know it.
Yet unto their Sons, in kindness of heart,
They partly reveal it in their writings;
And therefore let those who receive the gift
Enjoy it also in silence,
Since God would have it concealed.

FIGURE II.

HERE YOU STRAIGHTWAY BEHOLD A BLACK BEAST IN THE FOREST.

Putrefaction.

The Sages say truly
That two animals are in this forest:
One glorious, beautiful, and swift,
A great and strong deer;
The other an unicorn.
They are concealed in the forest,
But happy shall that man be called
Who shall snare and capture them.
The Masters show you here clearly
That in all places
These two animals wander about in forests
(But know that the forest is but one).
If we apply the parable to our Art,
We shall call the forest the Body.
That will be rightly and truly said.
The unicorn will be the Spirit at all times.
The deer desires no other name
But that of the Soul; which name no man shall take away from it.
He that knows how to tame and master them by Art,
To couple them together,
And to lead them in and out of the forest,
May justly be called a Master.
For we rightly judge
That he has attained the golden flesh,
And may triumph everywhere;
Nay, he may bear rule over great Augustus.

FIGURE III.

HEAR WITHOUT TERROR THAT IN THE FOREST ARE HIDDEN A DEER AND AN UNICORN.

In the Body there is Soul and Spirit.

The Sages do faithfully teach us
That two strong lions, to wit, male and female,
Lurk in a dark and rugged valley.
These the Master must catch,
Though they are swift and fierce,
And of terrible and savage aspect.
He who, by wisdom and cunning,
Can snare and bind them,
And lead them into the same forest,
Of him it may be said with justice and truth
That he has merited the meed of praise before all others,
And that his wisdom transcends that of the worldly wise.

FIGURE IV.

HERE YOU BEHOLD A GREAT MARVEL—
TWO LIONS ARE JOINED INTO ONE.

The Spirit and Soul must be united in their Body.

Alexander writes from Persia
That a wolf and a dog are in this field,
Which, as the Sages say,
Are descended from the same stock,
But the wolf comes from the east,
And the dog from the west.
They are full of jealousy,
Fury, rage, and madness:
One kills the other,
And from them comes a great poison.
But when they are restored to life,
They are clearly shown to be
The Great and Precious Medicine,
The most glorious Remedy upon earth,
Which refreshes and restores the Sages,
Who render thanks to God, and do praise Him.

FIGURE V.

A WOLF AND A DOG ARE IN ONE HOUSE, AND ARE AFTERWARDS CHANGED INTO ONE.

The Body is mortified and rendered white, then joined to Soul and Spirit by being saturated with them.

A savage Dragon lives in the forest,
Most venomous he is, yet lacking nothing:
When he sees the rays of the Sun and its bright fire,
He scatters abroad his poison,
And flies upward so fiercely
That no living creature can stand before him,
Nor is even the Basilisk equal to him.
He who hath skill to slay him, wisely
Hath escaped from all dangers.
Yet all venom, and colours, are multiplied
In the hour of his death.
His venom becomes the great Medicine.
He quickly consumes his venom,
For he devours his poisonous tail.
All this is performed on his own body,
From which flows forth glorious Balm,
With all its miraculous virtues.
Here at all the Sages do loudly rejoice.

FIGURE VI.

THIS SURELY IS A GREAT MIRACLE AND WITHOUT ANY DECEPTION—
THAT IN A VENOMOUS DRAGON THERE SHOULD BE THE GREAT MEDI-
CINE:

*The Mercury is precipitated or sublimed, dissolved in its own proper water, and
then once more coagulated.*

A nest is found in the forest,
In which Hermes has his brood;
One fledgling always strives to fly upward,
The other rejoices to sit quietly in the nest;
Yet neither can get away from the other.
The one that is below holds the one that is above,
And will not let it get away from the nest,
As a husband in a house with his wife,
Bound together in closest bonds of wedlock.
So also do we rejoice at all times,
That we hold the female eagle fast in this way,
And we render thanks to God the Father.

FIGURE VII.

WE HEAR OF TWO BIRDS IN THE FOREST,
YET WE MUST UNDERSTAND THEM TO BE ONLY ONE.

*The Mercury having been often sublimed, is at length fixed, and
becomes capable of resisting fire: the sublimation must
be repeated until at length fixation is attained.*

In India there is a most pleasant wood,
In which two birds are bound together.
One is of a snowy white; the other is red.
They bite each other, and one is slain
And devoured by the other.
Then both are changed into white doves,
And of the Dove is born a Phœnix,
Which has left behind blackness and foul death,
And has regained a more glorious life.
This power was given it by God Himself,
That it might live eternally, and never die.
It gives us wealth, it preserves our life,
And with it we may work great miracles,
As also the true Philosophers do plainly inform us.

FIGURE VIII.

HERE ARE TWO BIRDS, GREAT AND STRONG—THE BODY AND SPIRIT; ONE DEVOURS THE OTHER.

Let the Body be placed in horse-dung, or a warm bath, the Spirit
having been extracted from it The Body has become white
by the process, the Spirit red by our Art. All that
exists tends towards perfection, and thus is
the Philosopher's Stone prepared.

Now hear of a wonderful deed,
For I will teach you great things,
How the King rises high above all his race;
And hear also what the noble lord of the forest says:
I have overcome and vanquished my foes,
I have trodden the venomous Dragon under foot,
I am a great and glorious King in the earth.
There is none greater than I,
Child either of the Artist or of Nature,
Among all living creatures.
I do all that man can desire,
I give power and lasting health,
Also gold, silver, gems, and precious stones,
And the panacea for great and small diseases.
Yet at first I was of ignoble birth,
Till I was set in a high place.
To reach this lofty summit
Was given me by God and Nature.
Thence from the meanest I became the highest,
And mounted to the most glorious throne,
And to the state of royal sovereignty:
Therefore Hermes has called me the Lord of the Forests.

FIGURE IX.

THE LORD OF THE FORESTS HAS RECOVERED HIS KINGDOM, AND
MOUNTED FROM THE LOWEST TO THE HIGHEST DEGREE.
IF FORTUNE SMILE, YOU MAY FROM A RHETOR BECOME A CONSUL;
IF FORTUNE FROWN, THE CONSUL MAY BECOME A RHETOR.

Thus you may know that the Tincture has truly attained the first degree.

In all fables we are told
That the Salamander is born in the fire;
In the fire it has that food and life
Which Nature herself has assigned to it.
It dwells in a great mountain
Which is encompassed by many flames,
And one of these is ever smaller than another—
Herein the Salamander bathes.
The third is greater, the fourth brighter than the rest—
In all these the Salamander washes, and is purified.
Then he hies him to his cave,
But on the way is caught and pierced
So that it dies, and yields up its life with its blood.
But this, too, happens for its good:
For from its blood it wins immortal life,
And then death has no more power over it.
Its blood is the most precious Medicine upon earth,
The same has not its like in the world.
For this blood drives away all disease
In the bodies of metals,
Of men, and of beasts.
From it the Sages derive their science,
And through it they attain the Heavenly Gift,
Which is called the Philosopher's Stone,
Possessing the power of the whole world.
This gift the Sages impart to us with loving hearts,
That we may remember them for ever.

FIGURE X.
A SALAMANDER LIVES IN THE FIRE,
WHICH IMPARTS TO IT A MOST GLORIOUS HUE.

This is the reiteration, gradation, and amelioration of the Tincture, or Philosopher's Stone; and the whole is called its Augmentation.

Here is an old father of Israel,
Who has an only Son,
A Son whom he loves with all his heart.
With sorrow he prescribes sorrow to him.
He commits him to a guide,
Who is to conduct him whithersoever he will.
The Guide addresses the Son in these words:
Come hither! I will conduct thee everywhere,
To the summit of the loftiest mountain,
That thou mayest understand all wisdom,
That thou mayest behold the greatness of the earth, and of the sea,
And thence derive true pleasure.
I will bear thee through the air
To the gates of highest heaven.
The Son hearkened to the words of the Guide,
And ascended upward with him;
There saw he the heavenly throne,
That was beyond measure glorious.
When he had beheld these things,
He remembered his Father with sighing,
Pitied the great sorrow of his Father,
And said: I will return to his breast.

FIGURE XI.

THE FATHER AND THE SON HAVE LINKED THEIR HANDS
WITH THOSE OF THE GUIDE:
KNOW THAT THE THREE ARE BODY, SOUL, AND SPIRIT.

Says the Son to the Guide:
I will go down to my Father,
For he cannot live without me.
He sighs and calls aloud for me.
And the Guide makes answer to the Son:
I will not let thee go alone;
From thy Father's bosom I brought thee forth,
I will also take thee back again,
That he may rejoice again and live.
This strength will we give unto him.
So both arose without delay,
And returned to the Father's house.
When the Father saw his Son coming,
He cried aloud, and said:—

Figure XII.

ANOTHER MOUNTAIN OF INDIA LIES IN THE VESSEL, WHICH THE SPI-
RIT AND THE SOUL—
THAT IS, THE SON AND THE GUIDE—HAVE CLIMBED.

My Son, I was dead without thee,
And lived in great danger of my life.
I revive at thy return,
And it fills my breast with joy.
But when the Son entered the Father's house,
The Father took him to his heart,
And swallowed him out of excessive joy,
And that with his own mouth.
The great exertion makes the Father sweat.

FIGURE XIII.

HERE THE FATHER DEVOURS THE SON;
THE SOUL AND SPIRIT FLOW FORTH FROM THE BODY.

Here the Father sweats on account of the Son,
And earnestly beseeches God,
Who has everything in His hands,
Who creates, and has created all things,
To bring forth his Son from his body,
And to restore him to his former life.
God hearkens to his prayers,
And bids the Father lie down and sleep.
Then God sends down rain from heaven
To the earth from the shining stars.
It was a fertilizing, silver rain,
Which bedewed and softened the Father's Body.
Succour us, Lord, at the end,
That we may obtain Thy gracious Gift!

FIGURE XIV.

HERE THE FATHER SWEATS PROFUSELY, WHILE OIL AND THE TRUE
TINCTURE OF THE SAGES FLOW FORTH FROM HIM.

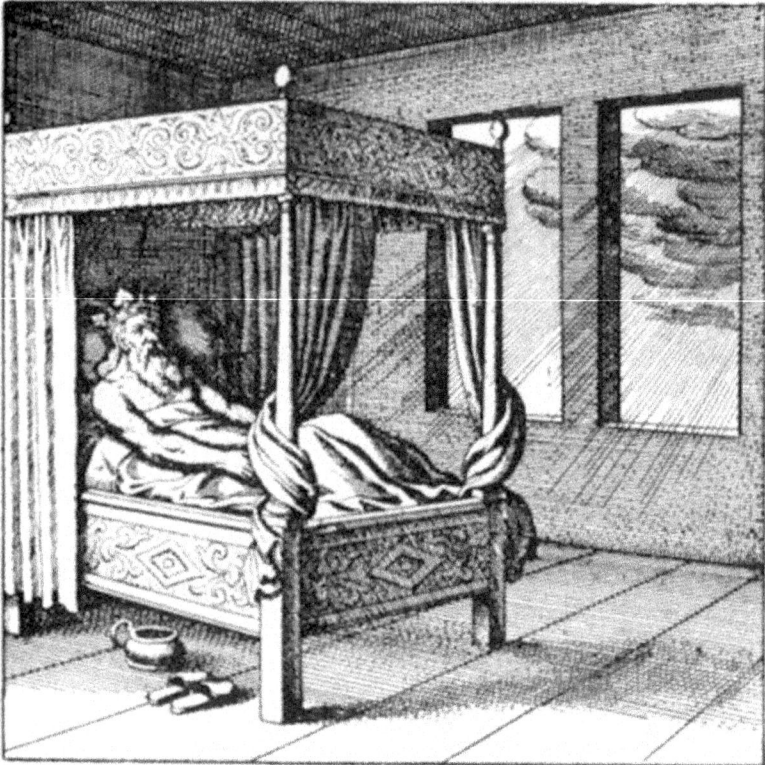

The sleeping Father is here changed
Entirely into limpid water,
And by virtue of this water alone
The good work is accomplished.
There is now a glorified and beautiful Father,
And he brings forth a new Son.
The Son ever remains in the Father,
And the Father in the Son.
Thus in divers things
They produce untold, precious fruit.
They perish never more,
And laugh at death.
By the grace of God they abide for ever,
The Father and the Son, triumphing gloriously
In the splendour of their new Kingdom.
Upon one throne they sit,
And the face of the Ancient Master
Is straightway seen between them:
He is arrayed in a crimson robe.

FIGURE XV.

HERE FATHER AND SON ARE JOINED IN ONE,
SO TO REMAIN FOR EVER.

TO THE INVISIBLE KING

OF

THE WORLD,

TO

THE ONLY TRUE AND IMMORTAL

GOD

BE

PRAISE AND GLORY

NOW

AND

EVERMORE.

AMEN.

THE GOLDEN TRIPOD,

OR,

THREE CHOICE CHEMICAL TRACTS,

NAMELY:

(i.) That of BASILIUS VALENTINUS, a Monk of the Benedictine Order; called PRACTICA, with twelve Keys and an Appendix.

(ii.) The CREDE MIHI, or Ordinal, of THOMAS NORTON, an English Sage.

(iii.) The TESTAMENT of a certain CREMER, Abbot of WESTMINSTER.

EDITED BY

MICHAEL MAIER,

DOCTOR OF MEDICINE.

Being placed in the thick of the struggle between the followers of Dogmatic and Hermetic Medicine, I thought it would throw great and unexpected light on the subject of this controversy, if I published in the Latin tongue the three great classical Tracts bearing upon the matter, viz., that of the Benedictine Monk BASILIUS VALENTINUS, and those of the two great English Sages NORTON and CREMER. This Triad of Tracts I have ventured to call the GOLDEN TRIPOD, and the name suggests to me, as appropriate to our controversy, the answer returned to the enquiring Ionians by the priestess of Delphi:

> "The feud between the Meropes and the Ionians will not
> cease until the Golden Tripod, which Vulcan cast into the sea,
> be brought into the house of the man who knows the things
> that are, that were, and that are to come."

Thus I believe our controversy, too, may be determined, if I dedicate *my* golden Tripod to the most learned of modern physicians. For, as Homer says, "A physician is worth many ordinary men," and if I searched through the whole of Germany, nay, Europe, I could not find a fitter person than him who is set upon the lofty tower of world-wide celebrity, and whose skill is admired and courted far and wide by princes and nobles. Accept, then, this GOLDEN TRIPOD, forged by the hands of the Hermetic Vulcan. Value it as a token of affection and esteem, as well as because of its inward worth. I firmly trust that it will assuage the feud between the adherents of Dogmatic and of Hermetic Medicine, as its namesake of old did that between the Meropes and Ionians; and that it will establish amity and concord among physicians of both schools. In order that its beneficial influence might be as widely spread as possible, I have set it forth in the common language of European scholars. In conclusion, let me pray you to love me, even as I love you—as I also know that you do.

Written at Francfort-on-the-Main in the month of
January, 1618.

THE

"PRACTICA,"

WITH TWELVE KEYS, AND AN APPENDIX THERETO,

CONCERNING

THE GREAT STONE OF THE
ANCIENT SAGES.

BY

BASILIUS VALENTINUS,

A MONK OF THE BENEDICTINE ORDER.

FIRST TRACT.

AN EPIGRAM

UPON

THE PRACTICA OF BASILIUS.

BY

MICHAEL MAIER

"Pactolus contains not such great treasures; nor does gold-bearing Hebrus roll down such precious things in its golden sand, as Valentine scatters abroad in this one book. Here is greater wealth than all the riches of the Inds. For he bore away the golden fruit from the Hesperian garden, and blessed with them fair Germany's fields. He bore away the golden fleece from Colchis, and gave it to us by mighty toil. And when at length he sank into the tomb, he left us his royal Treasure to enjoy. Here is something for you to admire and imitate. Only seek it at the bottom of the vessel, or you will wander astray. All things are one, though they be described under various names. Let this suffice thee; seek not many utensils for thy labour. If thou knowest the substance and the method, it is enough, and thou knowest all."

THE PREFACE

OF

BASILIUS VALENTINUS, THE BENEDICTINE,

CONCERNING

THE GREAT STONE OF THE

ANCIENT SAGES.

WHEN I had emptied to the dregs the cup of human suffering, I was led to consider the wretchedness of this world, and the fearful consequences of our first parents' disobedience. Then I saw that there was no hope of repentance for mankind, that they were getting worse day by day, and that for their impenitence God's everlasting punishment was hanging over them; and I made haste to withdraw myself from the evil world, to bid farewell to it, and to devote myself to the service of God.

When I had spent some years at the monastery, I found that after I had performed my work and my daily devotions I still had some time on my hands. This I did not wish to pass in idleness, lest my evil thoughts should lead me into new sins; and so I determined to use it for the study and investigation of those natural secrets by which God has shadowed out eternal things. So I react a great many books in our monastery written in olden times by philosophers who had pursued the same study, and was thereby stimulated to a more ardent desire of knowing that which they also knew. Though I did not make much progress at first, yet at last God granted my earnest prayer, and opened my eyes that I might see what others had seen before me.

In the convent there was a brother, who was afflicted with a severe disease of the kidneys, and to whom none of the many physicians he had consulted had been able to give even momentary relief. So he had committed himself to the hand of God, and despaired of all human aid.

As I loved him, I gathered all manner of herbs, extracted their salts, and distilled various medicines. But none of them seemed to do him the slightest good, and after six years I found that I had tried every possible vegetable substance, without any beneficial effect.

At last I determined to devote myself to the study of the powers and virtues which God has laid into metals and minerals; and the more I searched the more I found. One discovery led to another, and, after God had permitted unto me many experiments, I understood clearly the nature and properties, and the secret potency, imparted by God to minerals and metals.

Among the mineral substances I found one which exhibited many colours, and proved to be of the greatest efficacy in art. The spiritual essence of this substance I extracted, and therewith restored our sick brother, in a few days, to perfect health. For the strength of this spirit was so great as to quicken the prostrate spirit of my diseased brother, who, from that day to the day of his death, remembered me in his hourly prayers. And his prayers, together with my own diligence, so prevailed with God, that there was revealed to me that great secret which God ever conceals from those who are wise in their own conceits.

Thus have I been wishing to reveal to you in this treatise, as far as may be lawful to me, the Stone of the Ancients, that you, too, might possess the knowledge of this highest of earthly treasures for your health and comfort in this valley of sorrow. I write about it, not for my own good, but for that of posterity; and though my words be few and simple, that which they import is of immeasurable magnitude. Ponder them well, that you also may find the Rock which is the foundation Stone of truth, the temporal blessing, and the eternal reward.

THE TRACT

OF

BASILIUS VALENTINUS, THE BENEDICTINE,

CONCERNING

THE GREAT STONE OF THE

ANCIENT SAGES.

IN the preface, gentle Reader, and zealous Student of this Art, I promised to communicate to you a knowledge of our Corner Stone, or Rock, of the process by which it is prepared, and of the substance from which it was already derived by those ancient Sages, to whom the secret of our Art was first revealed by God for the health and happiness of earthly life. Let me assure you that I fully intend to fulfil my promise, and to be as plain with you as the rules of our Art permit, not misleading you by sophistical deceptions, but opening up to you the spring of all blessings even unto the fountain head. I propose to set forth what I have to say in a few simple, straightforward words, for I am no adept in the art of multiplying words; nor do I think that exuberance of language tends to clearness; on the contrary, I am convinced that it is many words that darken council.

Let me tell you, then, that although many are engaged in the search after this Stone, it is nevertheless found but by very few. For God never intended that it should become generally known. It is rather to be regarded as a gift which He reserves for those favoured few, who love the truth, and hate falsehood, who study our Art earnestly by day and by night, and whose hearts are set upon God with an unfeigned affection.

Hence, if you would prepare our great and ancient Stone, I testify unto you in all truth that you must give diligent heed to my teaching, and before all things implore the gracious blessing of the Creator of all things. You must also truly repent you of all your sins, confessing the same, and firmly resolve to lead a good and holy life. It is also necessary that you should determine to shew your gratitude to God for His unspeakable Gift, by succouring the poor and the distressed, and by opening your hand and your heart to the needy. Then God will bless your labour, and reward your search with success, and yourself with a seat in Heaven as the fruit of your faith.

Do not despise the truthful writings of those who possessed the Stone before us. For, after the enlightening grace of God, it is from them that I received my knowledge. Let your study of them be increased and repeated often, lest you lose the thread of insight, and the lamp of understanding be extinguished.

Give yourself wholly to study, and be not flighty or double-minded. Let your mind be like a firm Rock, in which all the various sayings of the Sages are reduced to the unity of their common meaning. For a man who is easily influenced in different directions is not likely to find the right path.

As our most ancient Stone is not derived from combustible things, you should cease to seek it in substances which cannot stand the test of fire. For this reason it is absurd to suppose that we can make any use of vegetable substances, though the

Stone, too, is endowed 'with a principle of growth.

If our Stone were a vegetable substance, it would, like other vegetables, be consumed by fire, leaving only a certain salt. Ancient writers have, indeed, described our Stone as the *vegetable* Stone. But that name was suggested to them by the fact that it grows and increases in size, like a plant.

Know also that animals only multiply after their kind, and within their own species. Hence our Stone can only be prepared out of its own seed, from which it was taken in the beginning; and hence also you will perceive that the soul of an animal must not be the subject of this investigation. Animals are a class by themselves; nor can anything ever be obtained from them that is not animal in its nature. But our Stone, as it has been bequeathed to me by the Ancients, is derived from two things, and one thing, in which is concealed a third thing. This is the purest truth, and a most faithful saying. For male and female have from of old been regarded as one body, not from any external or visible consideration, but on account of the ardour of that mutual love which naturally draws them together into one; and as the male and female seed jointly represent the principle of propagation, so also the sperm of the matter out of which our Stone is made can be sown and increased. There are in our substance two supplementary kinds of seed, from which our Stone may be prepared and multiplied.

If you are a true lover of our Art, you will carefully weigh and ponder these words, lest, with other sophisticators, you fall into the dangerous pit prepared by the common enemy of man.

But whence are you to obtain this seed? This question you may most easily answer by asking yourself another question. What do you want to develop from this seed, and what use do you wish to make of it? There can be no doubt, then, that it must be the root, or first substance, of metals, from which all metals derive their origin. It is, therefore, necessary that we should now proceed to speak of the generation of the metals.

In the beginning, when the Spirit of God moved upon the face of the waters, and as yet all was involved in darkness, Almighty and Eternal God, Whose beginning and wisdom are from everlasting, by His inscrutable counsel created heaven and earth, and all that in them is, both visible and invisible, out of nothing. How the act of creation was accomplished I will not attempt to explain. This is a matter which is set forth to us in Holy Scripture, and must be apprehended by faith.

To each creature God gave its own seed, wherewith to propagate its kind, that in this way there might always be an increase of men and animals, plants and metals. Man was not to be able to produce *new* seed: he was only permitted to educe new forms of life out of that which already existed. The creating of seed God reserved to Himself. For if man could create seed he would be equal to the Creator.

Know that our seed is produced in the following way. A celestial influence descends from above, by the decree and ordinance of God, and mingles with the astral properties. When this union has taken place, the two bring forth a third, namely, an earth-like substance, which is the principle of our seed, of its first source, so that it can shew an ancestry, and from which three the elements, such as water, air, and earth, take their origin. These elements work underground in the form of fire, and there produce what Hermes, and all who have preceded me, call the three first principles, viz., the internal soul, the impalpable spirit, and visible bodies, beyond which we can find no earlier beginning of our Magistery.

In the course of time these three unite, and are changed through the action of fire into a palpable substance, viz., quicksilver, sulphur, and salt. If these three substances be mixed, they are hardened and coagulated into a perfect body, which represents the seed chosen and appointed by the Creator. This is a most important and certain truth. If the metallic soul, the metallic spirit, and the metallic *form* of body be present, there will also be metallic quicksilver, metallic sulphur, and metallic salt, which together make up the perfect metallic body.

If you cannot perceive what you ought to understand herein, you should not devote yourself to the study of philosophy.

Moreover, I tell you in few words, that you cannot obtain a metallic body except by perfectly joining these three principles into one. Know, also, that all animals are, like man, composed of flesh and blood, and also possess a vitalizing spirit, but are destitute of the rational soul which the Creator gave to man alone. Therefore, when animals die, they perish for ever. But when man yields up his mortal life into the hands of his Creator, his soul does not die. It returns, and is united to the glorified body, in which, after the Resurrection, soul and spirit dwell together once more in eternal glory, never to be separated again throughout all eternity.

Hence the rational soul of man makes him an abiding creature, and, though his body may seem to die, yet we know that he will live for ever. For to him death is only a process of purification, by means of which he is freed from his sins, and translated to another and better place. But there is no resurrection for the brute beasts, because they have no rational soul, for which alone our Lord and Saviour shed His blood.

For though a body may be vitalized by a spirit, yet it need not, therefore, be fixed, unless, indeed, it possess a rational soul, that strong bond between body and spirit, which represents their union, and resists all efforts to separate them. Where there is no soul, there is no hope of redemption. Nothing can be perfect or lasting without a soul. This is a profound and most important truth, which I feel in conscience bound to make known to my readers. Now, the spirits of metals have this property of fixedness in a greater or less degree; they are more or less volatile in proportion to the mutual fitness of their bodies and souls. A metal that has the three conditions of fixedness is not affected by fire or overcome by any other outward agent. But there is only *one* metal that fulfils these conditions, namely, gold. Silver also contains fixed mercury, and is not so quickly volatilised as the imperfect metals, but stands the trial of fire, and yields no food to voracious Saturn.

Amatory Venus is clothed with abundant colour, and her whole body is one pure tincture, not unlike the red colour which is found in the most precious of metals. But though her spirit is of good quality, her body is leprous, and affords no permanent substratum to the fixed tincture. Hence the soul has to share the fate of the imperfect body, and when the body dies the soul has to leave it. For its dwelling has been destroyed by fire, and it is without a house wherein to abide.

Fixed salt has imparted to warlike Mars a hard, firm, and durable body, which is evidence of the generosity of his soul; nor can fire be said to have much power over it. And if its strength be united to the beauty of Venus, I do not say but that a precious and harmonious result may be obtained. For the phlegmatic or humid quality of the Moon may be heated with the ardent blood of Venus, and the blackness of Venus removed with the strong salt of Mars.

You need not look for our metallic seed among the elements. It need not be sought so far back. If you can only rectify the Mercury, Sulphur, and Salt (understand, those of the Sages) until the metallic spirit and body are inseparably joined together by means of the metallic soul, you thereby firmly rivet the chain of love, and prepare the palace for the coronation.

These things represent a liquid key, comparable to the celestial influence, and a dry water joined to the terrestrial substance: all which are *one* thing, derived from three, and two, and one. If you understand this, you have already attained our Magistery. Then you must join the husband and wife together, that each may feed upon the other's flesh and blood, and that so they may propagate their species a thousandfold.

Though I would fain reveal this matter to you more plainly and openly, I am prohibited from doing so by the law of God, and by the fear of His wrath, and of eternal punishment, lest the gift of the Most High should be abused.

If, however, you do not understand the theoretical part of my work, perhaps the practical part will serve to enlighten you more fully. I will therefore proceed to shew how, by the help of God, I was enabled to prepare the Stone of the Ancients, and, for your further instruction, I will add twelve keys, in which I give a figurative account of our Art.

Take a quantity of the best and finest gold, and separate it into its component parts by those media which Nature vouchsafes to those who are lovers of Art, as an anatomist dissects the human body. Thus change your gold back into what it was before it became gold; and thou shalt find the seed, the beginning, the middle, and the end—that from which *our gold* and its female principle are derived, viz., the pure and subtle spirit, the spotless soul, and the astral salt and balsam. When these three are united, we may call them the mercurial liquid: a water which was examined by Mercury, found by him to be pure and spotless, and therefore espoused by him as his wife. Of the two was born an incombustible oil; for Mercury became so proud that he hardly knew himself. He put forth eagle feathers, and devoured the slippery tail of the Dragon, and challenged Mars to battle.

Then Mars summoned his horsemen, and bade them enclose Mercury in prison under the ward of Vulcan, until he should be liberated by one of the female sex.

When this became known, the other Planets assembled and held a deliberation on the question, what would be the best and wisest course to adopt. When they were met together, Saturn first came forward, and delivered himself as follows:

"I, Saturn, the greatest of the planets in the firmament, declare here before you all, that I am the meanest and most unprofitable of all that are here present, that my body is weak, corruptible, and of a swarthy hue, but that, nevertheless, it is I that try you all. For having nothing that is fixed about me, I carry away with me all that is of a kindred nature. My wretchedness is entirely caused by that fickle and inconstant Mercury, by his careless and neglectful conduct. Therefore, I pray you, let us be avenged on him, shut him up in prison, and keep him there till he dies and is decomposed, nay, until not a drop of his blood is to be seen."

Then yellow Jupiter stepped forward, bent his knees, inclined his sceptre, and with great authority bade them carry out the demand of Saturn. He added that he would punish everyone who did not aid the execution of this sentence.

Then Mars presented himself, with sword drawn—a sword that shone with many colours, and gave out a beautiful and unwonted splendour. This sword he gave to the warder Vulcan, and bade him slay Mercury, and burn him, together with his bones, to ashes. This Vulcan consented to do.

While he was executing his office, there appeared a beautiful lady in a long, silver robe, intertissued with many waters, who was immediately recognised as the Moon, the wife of the Sun. She fell on her knees, and with outspread hands, and flowing tears, besought them to liberate her husband—the Sun—from the prison in which, through the crafty wiles of Mercury, he was being detained by the Planets. But Vulcan refused to listen to her request; nor was he softened by the moving prayers of Lady Venus, who appeared in a crimson robe, intertissued with threads of green, and charmed all by the beauty of her countenance and the fragrance of the flowers which she bore in her hand. She interceded with Vulcan, the Judge, in the Chaldee tongue, and reminded him that a woman was to effect the deliverance of the prisoner. But even to her pleading he turned a deaf ear.

While they were still speaking the heaven was opened, and there came forth a mighty animal, with many thousands of young ones, which drove the warder before it, and opening its mouth wide, swallowed Venus, its fair helper, at the same time exclaiming with a loud voice: "I am born of woman, woman has propagated my seed, and therewith filled the earth. Her soul is devoted to mine, and therefore I must be nourished with her blood." When the animal had said these words with a loud voice, it hastened into a certain chamber, and shut the door behind it; whither its voracious brood followed, drinking of the aforesaid incombustible oil, which they digested with the greatest ease, and thereby became even more numerous than they had been before. This they continued to do until they filled the whole world.

Then the learned men of that country were gathered together, and strove to discover the true interpretation of all they had seen. But they were unable to agree until there came forward a man of venerable age, with snowy locks and silvery beard, and arrayed in a flowing purple robe. On his head he wore a crown set with brilliant carbuncles. His loins were girded with the girdle of life. His feet were bare, and his words penetrated to the depth of the human soul. He mounted the tribune, and bade the assembly listen to him in silence, since he was sent from above to explain to them the significance of what they had seen.

When perfect silence prevailed, he delivered himself as follows:

"Awake, O man, and behold the light, lest the darkness deceive thee! The Gods revealed to me this matter in a profound sleep. Happy is the man who knows the great works of the Divine power. Blessed is he whose eyes are opened to behold light where before they saw darkness.

"Two Stars are given by the Gods to man to lead him to great wisdom. Gaze steadily upon them, follow their lights, and you will find in them the secret of knowledge.

"The bird Phœnix, from the south, plucks out the heart of the mighty beast from the east. Give the animal from the east wings, that it may be on an equality with the bird from the south. For the animal from the east must be deprived of its lion's skin, and lose its wings. Then it must plunge in the salt water of the vast ocean, and emerge thence in renovated beauty. Plunge thy volatile spirits in a deep spring whose waters never fail, that they may become like their mother, who is hidden therein, and born of three.

"Hungary is my native land, the sky and the stars are my habitation, the earth is my spouse. Though I must die and be buried, yet Vulcan causes me to be born anew. Therefore, Hungary is my native land, and my mother encloses the whole world."

When all that were present had received these his sayings, he thus continued:

"Cause that which is above to be below; that which is visible, to be invisible; and that which is palpable, to become impalpable. Again, let that which is below become that which is above; let the invisible become visible, and the impalpable, palpable. Here you see the perfection of our Art, without any defect, or diminution. But that in which death and life, destruction and resurrection dwell, is a round sphere, with which the goddess of fortune drives her chariot, and imparts the gift of wisdom to men of God. Its proper name here upon earth, and for the human understanding, is 'All-in-All.'

"Let him who would know what this 'All-in-All' is, give the earth great wings, and make it fly upward through the air to the heavenly regions. Then singe its wings with fierce heat, and make it fall into the Red Sea, and there be drowned. Then dry up the water with fire and air till the earth reappears, and you will have 'All-in-All.'

"If you cannot find it in this way, look around upon the things that are in the world. Then you will find the 'All-in-All,' which is the attracting force of all metals and minerals derived from salt and sulphur, and twice born of Mercury. More I may not say about 'All-in-All,' since all is comprehended in all.

"My friends, blessed are ye if, by listening to the words of the wise, ye can find this great Stone, which has power to cure leprous and imperfect metallic bodies and to regenerate them; to preserve men in health, and procure for them a long life—as it has hitherto kept the vital fire burning within me so long that I am weary of life, and yearn to die.

"For His wisdom and mercy, and for the gracious Gift which He has bestowed upon me so long ago, I am bound to render God thanks, now and evermore. Amen."

When the old man had thus spoken, he vanished from their sight.

But all who had heard him went each man to his house, and meditated on his words by day and by night.

THE TWELVE KEYS

OF

BASILIUS VALENTINUS, THE BENEDICTINE,

WITH WHICH WE MAY OPEN

THE DOORS OF THE KNOWLEDGE OF THE

MOST ANCIENT STONE,

AND UNSEAL

THE MOST SECRET FOUNTAIN OF HEALTH.

FIRST KEY.

Let my friend know that no impure or spotted things are useful for our purpose. For there is nothing in their leprous nature capable of advancing the interests of our Art. There is much more likelihood of that which is in itself good being spoiled by that which is impure. Everything that is obtained from the mines has its value, unless, indeed, it is adulterated. Adulteration, however, spoils its goodness and its efficacy.

As the physician purges and cleanses the inward parts of the body, and removes all unhealthy matter by means of his medicines, so our metallic substances must be purified and refined of all foreign matter, in order to ensure the success of our task. Therefore, our Masters require a pure, immaculate body, that

221

is untainted with any foreign admixture, which admixture is the leprosy of our metals.

Let the diadem of the King be of pure gold, and let the Queen that is united to him in wedlock be chaste and immaculate.

If you would operate by means of our bodies, take a fierce grey wolf, which, though on account of its name it be subject to the sway of warlike Mars, is by birth the offspring of ancient Saturn, and is found in the valleys and mountains of the world, where he roams about savage with hunger. Cast to him the body of the King, and when he has devoured it, burn him entirely to ashes in a great fire. By this process the King will be liberated; and when it has been performed thrice the Lion has overcome the wolf, and will find nothing more to devour in him. Thus our Body has been rendered fit for the first stage of our work.

Know that this is the only right and legitimate way of purifying our substance: for the Lion purifies himself with the blood of the wolf, and the tincture of its blood agrees most wonderfully with the tincture of the Lion, seeing that the two liquids are closely akin to each other. When the Lion's hunger is appeased, his spirit becomes more powerful than before, and his eyes glitter like the Sun. His internal essence is now of inestimable value for the removing of all defects, and the healing of all diseases. He is pursued by the ten lepers, who desire to drink his blood; and all that are tormented with any kind of sickness are refreshed with this blood.

For whoever drinks of this golden fountain, experiences a renovation of his whole nature, a vanishing of all unhealthy matter, a fresh supply of blood, a strengthening of the heart and of all the vitals, and a permanent bracing of every limb. For it opens all the pores, and through them bears away all that prevents the perfect health of the body, but allows all that is beneficial to remain therein unmolested.

But let my friend be scrupulously careful to preserve the fountain of life limpid and clear. If any strange water be mixed with it, it is spoiled, and becomes positively injurious. If it still retain any of the solvent which has been used for its dissolution, you must carefully purge it off. For no corrosive can be of the least use for the prevention of internal diseases.

When a tree is found to bear sour and unwholesome fruit, its branches must be cut off, and scions of better trees grafted upon it. The new branches thereupon become organically united to the trunk; but though nourished with its sap, they thenceforward produce good and pleasant fruit.

The King travels through six regions in the heavenly firmament, and in the seventh he fixes his abode. There the royal palace is adorned with golden tapestry. If you understand my meaning, this Key will open the first lock, and push back the first bolt; but if you do not, no spectacles or natural eyesight will enable you to understand what follows. But Lucius Papirius has instructed me not to say any more about this Key.

SECOND KEY.

In the houses of the great are found various kinds of drink, of which scarcely two are exactly like each other in odour, colour, or taste. For they are prepared in a great variety of different ways. Nevertheless they are all drunk, and each is designed for its own special use.

When the Sun gives out his rays, and sheds them abroad upon the clouds, it is commonly said that he is attracting water, and if he do it frequently, and thereby cause rain, it is called a fruitful year.

If it be intended to build a palace, the services of many different craftsmen must be employed, and a great variety of materials is required. Otherwise the palace would not be worthy the name. It is useless to use wood where stone is necessary.

The daily ebb and flow of the sea, which are caused by the sympathetic influence of heavenly bodies, impart great wealth and blessing to the earth. For whenever the water comes rolling back, it brings a blessing with it.

A bride, when she is to be brought forth to be married, is gloriously adorned in a great variety of precious garments, which, by enhancing her beauty, render her pleasant in the eyes of the bridegroom. But the rites of the bridal night she performs without any clothing but that which she was arrayed withal at the moment of her birth.

In the same way our bridal pair, Apollo and Diana, are arrayed in splendid attire, and their heads and bodies are washed with various kinds of water, some strong, some weak, but not one of them exactly like another, and each designed for its own special purpose. Know that when the moisture of the earth ascends in the form of a vapour, it is condensed in the upper regions, and precipitated to the earth by its own weight. Thus the earth regains the moisture of which it had been deprived, and receives strength to put forth buds and herbs. In the same way you must repeatedly distil the water which you have extracted from the earth, and then again restore it to your earth, as the water in the Strait of Euripus frequently leaves the shore, and then covers it again until it arrives at a certain limit.

When thus the palace has been constructed by the hands of many craftsmen, and the sea of glass has absolved its course, and filled the palace with good things, it is ready for the King to enter, and take his seat upon the throne.

But you should notice that the King and his spouse must be quite naked when they are joined together. They must be stripped of all their glorious apparel, and must lie down together in the same state of nakedness in which they were born, that their seed may not be spoiled by being mixed with any foreign matter.

Let me tell you, in conclusion, that the bath in which the bridegroom is placed, must consist of two hostile kinds of matter, that purge and rectify each other by means of a continued struggle. For it is not good for the Eagle to build her nest on the summit of the Alps, because her young ones are thus in great danger of being frozen to death by the intense cold that prevails there.

But if you add to the Eagle the icy Dragon that has long had its habitation upon the rocks, and has crawled forth from the caverns of the earth, and place both over the fire, it will elicit from the icy Dragon a fiery spirit, which, by means of its great heat, will consume the wings of the Eagle, and prepare a perspiring bath of so extraordinary a degree of heat that the snow will melt upon the summit of the mountains, and become a water, with which the invigorating mineral bath may be prepared, and fortune, health, life, and strength restored to the King.

THIRD KEY.

By means of water fire may be extinguished, and utterly quenched. If much water be poured upon a little fire, the fire is overcome, and compelled to yield up the victory to the water. In the Same way our fiery sulphur must lie overcome by means of our prepared water. But, after the water has vanished, the fiery life of our sulphurous vapour must triumph, and again obtain the victory. But no such triumph can take place unless the King imparts great strength and potency to his water, and tinges it with his own colour, that thereby he may be consumed and become invisible, and then again recover his visible form, with a diminution of his simple essence, and a development of his perfection.

A painter can set yellow upon white, and red or crimson upon yellow; for, though all these colours are present, yet the latter prevails on account of its greater intensity. When you have accomplished the same thing in our Art, you have before your eyes the light of wisdom, which shines in the darkness, although it does not burn. For our sulphur does not burn, but nevertheless its brilliancy is seen far and near. Nor does it colour anything until it has been prepared, and dyed with its own colour, which it then imparts to all weak and imperfect metals. This sulphur, however, cannot impart this colour until it have first by persevering labour been prevailed upon to abjure its original colour. For the weaker does not overcome the stronger, but has to yield the victory to it. The gist of the whole matter lies in the fact that the small and weak cannot aid that which is itself small and weak, and a combustible substance cannot shield another substance from combustion. That which is to protect another substance against combustion must itself be safe from danger. The latter must be stronger than the former, that is to say, it must itself be essentially incombustible. He, then, who would prepare the incombustible sulphur of the Sages, must look for our sulphur in a substance in which it is incombustible—which can only be after its body has been absorbed by the salt sea, and again rejected by it. Then it must be so exalted as to shine more brightly than all the stars of heaven, and in its essence it must have an abundance of blood, like the Pelican, which wounds its own breast, and, without any diminution of its strength, nourishes and rears up many young ones with its blood. This Tincture is the Rose of our Masters, of purple hue, called also the red blood of the Dragon, or the purple cloak many times folded with which the Queen of Salvation is covered, and by which all metals are regenerated in colour.

Carefully preserve this splendid mantle, together with the astral salt which is joined to this sulphur, and screens it from harm. Add to it a sufficient quantity of the volatility of the bird; then the Cock will swallow the Fox, and, having been drowned in the water, and quickened by the fire, will in its turn be swallowed by the Fox.

FOURTH KEY.

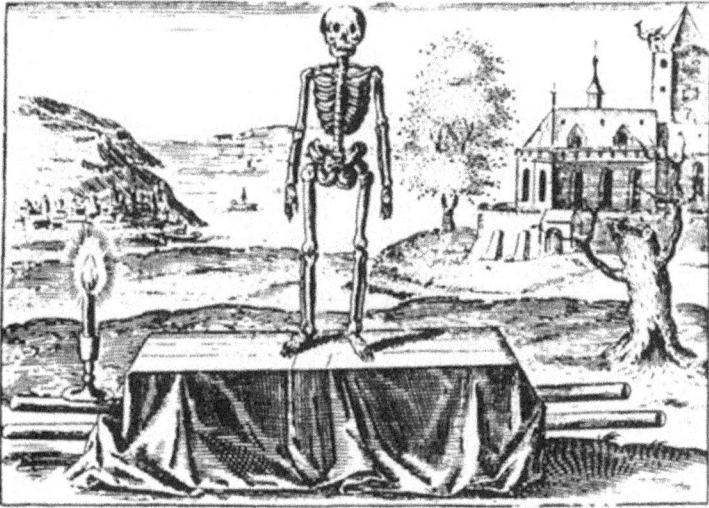

All flesh that is derived from the earth, must be decomposed and again reduced to earth; then the earthy salt produces a new generation by celestial resuscitation. For where there was not first earth, there can be no resurrection in our Magistery. For in earth is the balm of Nature, and the salt of the Sages.

At the end of the world, the world shall be judged by fire, and all those things that God has made of nothing shall by fire be reduced to ashes, from which ashes the Phœnix is to produce her young. For in the ashes slumbers a true and genuine tartaric substance, which, being dissolved, will enable us to open the strongest bolt of the royal chamber.

After the conflagration, there shall be formed a new heaven and a new earth, and the new man will be more noble in his glorified state than he was before.

When the sand and ashes have been well matured and ripened with fire, the glass-blower makes out of it glass, which remains hard and firm in the fire, and in colour resembles a crystal stone. To the uninitiated this is a great mystery, but not to the master whom long experience has familiarized with the process.

Out of stones the master also prepares lime by burning, which is very useful for our work. But before they are prepared with fire, they are mere stones. The stone must be matured and rendered fervent with fire, and then it becomes so potent that few things are to be compared to the fiery spirit of lime.

By burning anything to ashes you may gain its salt. If in this dissolution the sulphur and mercury be kept apart, and restored to its salt, you may once more obtain that form which was destroyed by the process of combustion. This assertion the wise of this world denounce as the greatest folly, and count as a rebellion, saying that such a transformation would amount to a new creation, and that God has denied such creative power to sinful man. But the folly is all on their side. For they do not understand that our Artist does not claim to create anything, but only to evolve new things from the seed made ready to his hand by the Creator.

If you do not possess the ashes, you will be unable to obtain our salt; and without our salt you will not be able to impart to our substance a bodily form; for the coagulation of all things is produced by salt alone.

As salt is the great preserving principle that protects all things from decay, so the Salt of our Magistery preserves metal from decomposition and utter annihilation. If their Balm were to perish, and the Spirit to leave the body, the body would be quite dead, and no longer available for any good purpose. The metallic spirit would have departed, and would have left its habitation empty, bare, and lifeless.

Observe also, thou who art a lover of this Art, that the salt that is gained from ashes has great potency, and possesses many concealed virtues. Nevertheless, the salt is unprofitable, until its inward substance has been extracted. For the spirit alone gives strength and life. The body by itself profits nothing. If you know how to find this spirit, you have the Salt of the Sages, and the incombustible oil, concerning which many things have been written before my time.

> Although many philosophers Have
> sought for me with eagerness, Yet
> very few succeed at length In find-
> ing out my secret virtue.

FIFTH KEY.

The quickening power of the earth produces all things that grow forth from it, and he who says that the earth has no life makes a statement which is flatly contradicted by the most ordinary facts. For what is dead cannot produce life and growth, seeing that it is devoid of the quickening spirit. This spirit is the life and soul that dwell in the earth, and are nourished by heavenly and sidereal influences. For all herbs, trees, and roots, and all metals and minerals, receive their growth and nutriment from the spirit of the earth, which is the spirit of life. This spirit is itself fed by the stars, and is thereby rendered capable of imparting nutriment to all things that grow, and of nursing them as a mother does her child while it is yet in the womb. The minerals are hidden in the womb of the earth, and nourished by her with the spirit which she receives from above.

Thus the power of growth that I speak of is imparted not by the earth, but by the life-giving spirit that is in it. If the earth were deserted by this spirit, it would be dead, and no longer able to afford nourishment to anything. For its sulphur or richness would lack the quickening spirit without which there can be neither life nor growth.

Two contrary spirits can scarcely dwell together, nor do they easily combine. For when a thunderbolt blazes amidst a tempest of rain, the two spirits, out of which it is formed, fly from one another with a great shock and noise, and circle in the air, so that no one can know or say whither they go, unless the same has been ascertained by experience as to the mode in which these spirits manifest

Know then, gentle Reader, that life is the only true spirit, and that that which the ignorant herd look upon as dead may be brought back to permanent, visible, and spiritual life, if but the spirit be restored to the body—the spirit which is supported by heavenly nutriment, and derived from heavenly, elementary, and earthly substances, which are also called formless matter.

Moreover, as iron has its magnet which draws it with the invisible bonds of love, so our gold has its magnet, viz., the first Matter of the great Stone. If you understand these my words, you are richer and more blessed than the whole world.

Let me conclude this chapter with one more remark. When a man looks into a mirror, he sees therein reflected an image of himself. If, however, he try to touch it, he will find that it is not palpable, and that he has laid his hand upon the mirror only. In the same way, the spirit which must be evolved from this Matter is visible, but not palpable. This spirit is the root of the life of our bodies, and the Mercury of the Philosophers, from which is prepared the liquid water of our Art—the water which must once more receive a material form, and be rectified by means of certain purifying agents into the most perfect Medicine. For we begin with a firm and palpable body, which subsequently becomes a volatile spirit, and a golden water, without any conversion, from which our Sages derive their principle of life. Ultimately we obtain the indestructible medicine of human and metallic bodies, which is fitter to be known to angels than to men, except such as seek it at God's hands in heartfelt prayer, and give genuine proofs of their gratitude by service rendered to Him, and to their needy neighbour.

Hereunto I may add, in conclusion, that one work is developed from another. First, our Matter should be carefully purified, then dissolved, destroyed, decomposed, and reduced to dust and ashes. Thereupon prepare from it a volatile spirit, which is white as snow, and another volatile spirit, which is red as blood. These two spirits contain a third, and are yet but one spirit. Now these are the three spirits which preserve and multiply life. Therefore unite them, give them the meat and drink that Nature requires. and keep them in a warm chamber until the perfect birth takes place. Then you will see and experience the virtue of the gift bestowed upon you by God and Nature. Know, also, that hitherto my lips have not revealed this secret to any one, and that God has endowed natural substances with greater powers than most men are ready to believe. Upon my mouth God has set a seal, that there might be scope for others after me to write about the wonderful things of Nature, which by the foolish are looked upon as unnatural. For they do not understand that all things are ultimately traceable to supernatural causes, but nevertheless are, in this present state of the world, subject to natural conditions.

SIXTH KEY.

The male without the female is looked upon as only half a body, nor can the female without the male be regarded as more complete. For neither can bring forth fruit so long as it remains alone. But if the two be conjugally united, there is a perfect body, and their seed is placed in a condition in which it can yield increase.

If too much seed be cast into the field, the plants impede each other's growth, and there can be no ripe fruit. But if, on the other hand, too little be sown, weeds spring up and choke it.

If a merchant would keep a clear conscience, let him give just measure to his neighbour. If his measure and weight be not short, he will receive praise from the poor.

In too much water you may easily be drowned; too little water, on the other hand, soon evaporates in the heat of the sun.

If, then, you would attain the longed-for goal, observe just measure in mixing the liquid substance of the Sages, lest that which is too much overpower that which is too little, and the generation be hindered. For too much rain spoils the fruit, and too much drought stunts its growth. Therefore, when Neptune has prepared his bath, measure out carefully the exact quantity of permanent water needed, and let there be neither too little nor too much.

The twofold fiery male must be fed with a snowy swan, and then they must mutually slay each other and restore each other to life; and the air of the imprisoned fiery male will occupy three of the four quarters of the world, and make up three parts of the imprisoned fiery male, that the death-song of the swans may be distinctly heard; then the swan roasted will become food for the King, and the fiery King will be seized with great love towards the Queen, and will take his fill of delight in embracing her, until they both vanish and coalesce into one body.

It is commonly said that two can overpower one, especially if they have sufficient room for putting forth their strength. Know also that there must come a twofold wind, and a single wind, and that they must furiously blow from the east and from the south. If, when they cease to rage, the air has become water, you may be confident that the spiritual will also be transmuted into a bodily form, and that our number shall prevail through the four seasons in the fourth part of the sky (after the seven planets have exercised power), and that its course will be perfected by the test of fire in the lowest chamber of our palace, when the two shall overpower and consume the third.

For this part of our Magistery skill is needed, in order to divide and compound the substances aright, so that the art may result in riches, and the balance may not be falsified by unequal weights. The sky we speak of is the sky of our Art, and there must be justly proportioned parts of our air and earth, our true water and our palpable fire.

SEVENTH KEY.

Natural heat preserves the life of man. If his body lose its natural heat his life has come to an end.

A moderate degree of natural heat protects against the cold; an excess of it destroys life. It is not necessary that the substance of the Sun should touch the earth. The Sun can heat the earth by shedding thereon its rays, which are intensified by reflection. This intermediate agency is quite sufficient to do the work of the Sun, and to mature everything by coction. The rays of the Sun are tempered with the air by passing through it so as to operate by the medium of the air, as the air operates through the medium of the fire.

Earth without water can produce nothing, nor can water quicken anything into growth without earth; and as earth and water are mutually indispensable in the production of fruit, so fire cannot operate without air, or air without fire. For fire has no life without air; and without fire air possesses neither heat nor dryness.

When its fruit is about to be matured, the vine stands in greater need of the Sun's warmth than in the spring; and if the Sun shine brightly in the autumn, the grapes will be better than if they had not felt his autumnal warmth.

In the winter the multitude suppose everything to be dead, because the earth is bound in the chains of frost, so that nothing is allowed to sprout forth. But as soon as the spring comes, and the cold is vanquished by the power of the Sun, everything is restored to life, the trees and herbs put forth buds, leaves, and blossoms, the hibernating animals creep forth from their hiding places, the plants give out a sweet fragrance, and are adorned with a great variety of many coloured flowers; and the summer carries on the work of the spring, by changing its flowers into fruit.

Thus, year by year, the operations of the universe are performed, until at length it shall be destroyed by its Creator, and all the dwellers upon earth shall be restored by resurrection to a glorified life. Then the operations of earthly nature shall cease, and the heavenly and eternal dispensation shall take its place.

When the Sun in the winter pursues his course far away from us, he cannot melt the deep snow. But in the summer he approaches nearer to us, the quality of the air becomes more fiery, and the snow melts and is transmuted by warmth into water. For that which is weak is always compelled to yield to that which is strong.

The same moderate course must be adopted in the fiery regimen of our Magistery. For it is all important that the liquid should not be dried up too quickly, and that the earth of the Sages should not be melted and dissolved too soon, otherwise your fishes would be changed into scorpions. If you would perform our task rightly, take the spiritual water, in which the spirit was from the beginning, and preserve it in a closely shut chamber. For the heavenly city is about to be besieged by earthly foes. You must, therefore, strongly fortify it with three impassable and well-guarded walls, and let the one entrance be well protected. Then light the lamp of wisdom and seek with it the gross thing that was lost, shewing only such light as is needed. For you must know that the worms and reptiles dwell in the cold and humid earth, while man has his proper habitation upon the face of the earth; the bodies of angels, on the other hand, not being alloyed with sin or impurity, are injured by no extreme either of heat or cold. When man shall have been glorified, his body will become like the angelic body in this respect. If we carefully cultivate the life of our souls, we shall be sons and heirs of God, and shall be able to do that which now seems impossible. But this can be effected only by the drying up of all water, and the purging of heaven and earth and all men with fire.

EIGHTH KEY.

Neither human nor animal bodies can be multiplied or propagated without decomposition; the grain and all vegetable seed, when cast into the ground, must decay before it can spring up again; moreover, putrefaction imparts life to many worms and other animalculæ. The process of augmentation and quickening is mostly performed in [the] earth, while it is caused by spiritual seed through the other elements.

The farmer's wife knows that she cannot hope to obtain chickens except through the decomposition of the egg.

If bread is placed in honey, and suffered to decay, ants are generated; worms are bred in the putrefying bodies of men, horses, and other animals; maggots are also developed by the decay of nuts, apples, and pears.

The same thing may be observed in regard to vegetable life. Nettles and other weeds spring up where no such seed has ever been sown. This occurs only by putrefaction. The reason is that the soil in such places is so disposed, and, as it were, impregnated, that it produces these fruits, which is a result of the properties of sidereal influence; consequently the seed is spiritually produced in the earth, and putrefies in the earth, and by the operation of the elements generates corporeal matter according to the species of Nature. Thus the stars and the elements may generate new spiritual, and, ultimately, new vegetable seed, by means of putrefaction. But man cannot create new seed; for it is not in his power to order the operation of the elements and the essential influences of the stars. By natural conditions, however, new plants are generated simply through putrefaction. This fact is not noticed by the farmer, simply because it is a thing that he has always been used to, and for which he is unable to find an explanation. But you who should know more than the vulgar herd, must search into the causes of things, and endeavour to understand how the process of generation and resuscitation is accomplished by means of decomposition, and how all life is produced out of decay.

Each element is in its turn decomposed and regenerated by that which is contained in it. For you should know that every element contains the three others. In air, for instance, there is fire, water, and earth. This assertion may appear incredible, but it is nevertheless true. In like manner, fire includes air, water, and earth, since otherwise it could generate nothing. Water contains fire, air, and earth; for if it did not, there could be no growth. At the same time, each element is distinct, though each contains the others. All this is found by distillation in the separation of the elements.

In order to rationally prove this to you, who are investigating the separation of Nature, and purpose to understand the division of the elements, lest you should think my words inventions, and not true, I tell you that if you distil earth, you will find that, first of all, there is an escape of air, which, in its turn, always contains fire, as they are both of a spiritual essence, and exercise an irresistible mutual attraction. In the next place, there issues water from the earth, and the earth, in which is the precious salt, remains by itself at the bottom of the vessel.

When water is distilled, air and fire issue from it, and the water and material earth remain at the bottom. Again, when the invisible part of elementary fire is extracted, you get water and earth by themselves. Nor can any of the three other elements exist without air. It is air that gives to earth its power of production, to fire its power of burning, to water its power of generating fruit. Again, air can consume nothing, nor dry up any moisture, without that natural heat which must be imparted to it by fire. For everything that is hot and dry contains fire. From these considerations we conclude that no element can exist without the others, and that in the generation of all things there is a mingling of the four elements. He who states the contrary in no wise understands the secrets of Nature, nor has he investigated the properties of the elements. For if anything is to be generated by putrefaction, the process must be as follows: The earth is first decomposed by the moisture which it contains; for without moisture, or water, there can be no true decay; thereupon the decomposed substance is kindled and quickened by the natural heat of fire: for without natural heat no generation can take place. Again, if that which has received the spark of life, is to be stirred up to motion and growth, it must be acted upon by air. For without air, the quickened substance would be choked and stifled in the germ. Hence it manifestly appears that no one element can work effectually without the aid of the others, and that all must contribute towards the generation of anything. Thus their quickening cooperation takes the form of putrefaction, without which there can be neither generation, life, nor growth. That there can be no perfect generation or resuscitation without the co-operation of the four elements, you may see from the fact that when Adam' had been formed by the Creator out of earth, there was no life in him, until God breathed into him a living spirit. Then the earth was quickened into motion. In the earth was the salt, that is, the Body; the air that was breathed into it was mercury, or the Spirit, and this air imparted to him a genuine and temperate heat, which was sulphur, or fire. Then Adam moved, and by his power of motion, sheaved that there had been infused into him a life-giving spirit. For as there is no fire without air, so neither is there any air without fire. Water was incorporated with the earth. Thus living man is an harmonious mixture of the four elements; and Adam was generated out of earth, water, air, and fire, out of soul, spirit, and body, out of mercury, sulphur, and salt.

In the same way, Eve, our common mother, was created; for her body was built up and formed out of Adam's body—a fact which I wish you particularly to notice.

To return again to putrefaction, O seeker of the Magistery and devotee of philosophy, know that, in like manner, no metallic seed can develop, or multiply, unless the said seed, by itself alone, and without the introduction of any foreign substance, be reduced to a perfect putrefaction.

The putrefaction of metallic seed must, like that of animal and vegetable seed, take place through the co-operation of the four elements. I have already explained that the elements themselves are not the seed. But it ought by this time to be clear to you that the metallic seed which was produced by the combined operation of heavenly, sidereal, and elementary essences, and reduced into bodily form, must, in due course, be corrupted and putrefied by means of the elements.

Observe that this seed contains a living volatile spirit. For when it is distilled, there issues from it first a spirit, and then that which is less volatile. But when by continued gentle heat, it is reduced to an acid, the spirit is not so volatile as it was before. For in the distillation of the acid the water issues first, and then the spirit. And though the substance remains the same, its properties have become very different. It is no longer wine, but has been transmuted by the putrefaction of gentle heat into an acid. That which is extracted with wine or its spirit, has widely different properties and powers from that which is extracted with an acid. For if the crystal of antimony be extracted with wine or the spirit of wine, it causes vomiting and diarrhœa, because it is a poison, and its poisonous quality is not destroyed by the wine. But if it be extracted with a good distilled acid, it furnishes a beautiful extract of a rich colour. If the acid be removed by means of the St. Mary's Bath, and the residuum of yellow powder washed away, you obtain a sweet powder which causes no diarrhœa, but is justly regarded as a marvellously beneficial medicine.

This excellent powder is dissolved in a moist place into a liquid which is profitably employed as a painless agent in surgery.

Let me sum up in few words what I have to say. The substance is of heavenly birth, its life is preserved by the stars, and nourished by the four elements; then it must perish, and be putrefied; again, by the influence of the stars, which works through the elements, it is restored to life, and becomes once more a heavenly thing that has its habitation in the highest region of the firmament. Then you will find that the heavenly has assumed an earthly body, and that the earthly body has been reduced to a heavenly substance.

NINTH KEY.

Saturn, who is called the greatest of the planets, is the least useful in our Magistery. Nevertheless, it is the chief Key of the whole Art, howbeit set in the lowest and meanest place. Although by its swift flight it has risen to the loftiest height, far above all other luminaries, its feathers must be clipped, and itself brought down to the lowest place, from whence it may once more be raised by putrefaction, and the quickening caused by putrefaction, by which the black is changed to white, and the white to red, until the glorious colour of the triumphant King has been attained. Therefore, I say that though Saturn may seem the vilest thing in the world, yet it has such power and efficacy. that if its precious essence, which is excessively cold, be reduced to a metallic body by being deprived of its volatility, it becomes as corporeal as, but far more fixed than, Saturn itself. This transmutation is begun, continued, and completed with Mercury, sulphur, and salt. This will seem unintelligible to many, and it certainly does make an extraordinary demand upon the mental faculties; but that must be so because the substance is within the reach of everyone, and there is no other way of keeping up the divinely ordained difference between rich and poor.

In the preparation of Saturn there appears a great variety of different colours; and you must expect to observe successively black, grey, white, yellow, red, and all the different intermediate shades. In the same way, the Matter of all the Sages passes through the several varieties of colour, and may be said to change its appearance as often as a new gate of entrance is opened to the fire.

The King shares his royal dignity with noble Venus, and appears in splendid state, surrounded by all the dignitaries of his court. Before him is borne a beautiful crimson banner, in which there is an embroidered representation of Charity in green garments. Saturn is the prefect of the royal household, and in front of him Astronomy bears a black standard, with a representation of Faith in yellow and red garments.

Jupiter is the Grand Marshal, and is preceded by a banner of grey colour, borne by Rhetoric, and adorned with a variegated representation of Hope.

Mars is at the head of military affairs, and executes his office with a certain fiery ardour. Geometry carries before him a crimson banner, on which you may behold Courage in a crimson cloak. Mercury holds the office of Chancellor; Arithmetic is his standard bearer, and his standard is of many colours; on it may be observed the figure of Temperance in a many coloured robe.

The Sun is Vice-Regent, and is preceded by Grammar, bearing a yellow banner, on which Justice is represented in a golden robe. Though Venus seems to cast him into the shade by the gorgeous magnificence of her appearance, he really possesses more power in the kingdom than she.

Before the Moon, Dialectic bears a shining silver banner, with the figure of Prudence wrought into it in sky-blue, and because the husband of the Moon is dead, he has transferred to her his task of resisting the domination of Queen Venus. For among all these there is enmity, and they are all striving to supplant each other. Indeed, the tendency of events is to give the highest place to the most excellent and the most deserving. For the present state of things is passing away, and a new world is about to be created, and one Planet is devouring another spiritually, until only the strongest survive.

Let me tell you allegorically that you must put into the heavenly Balance the Ram, Bull, Cancer, Scorpion, and Goat. In the other scale of the Balance you must place the Twins, the Archer, the Water-bearer, and the Virgin. Then let the Lion jump into the Virgin's lap, which will cause the other scale to kick the beam. Thereupon, let the signs of the Zodiac enter into opposition to the Pleiads, and when all the colours of the world have shewn themselves, let there be a conjunction and union between the greatest and the smallest, and the smallest and the greatest.

> If the whole world's nature
> Were seen in one figure,
> And nothing could be evolved by Art,
> Nothing wonderful would be found in the Universe,
> And Nature would have nothing to tell us.
> For which let us laud and praise God.

TENTH KEY.

NATVS SVM EX HERMOGENE.

In our Stone, as composed by me and by those who have long preceded me, are contained all elements, all mineral and metallic forms, and all the qualities and properties of the whole world. In it we find most powerful natural heat, by which the icy body of Saturn is gently transmuted into the best gold. It contains also a high degree of cold, which tempers the fervent heat of Venus, and coagulates the mercury, which is thereby also changed into the finest gold. All these properties slumber in the substance of our Stone, and are developed, perfected, and matured by the gentle coction of natural fire, until they have attained their highest perfection.

If the fruit of a tree be plucked before it is ripe, it is unfit for use; and if the potter fail to harden his vessels in the fire, they cannot be employed for any good purpose.

In the same way you must exercise considerable patience in preparing our Elixir, if it is to become all that you wish it to become. No fruit can grow from a flower that has been plucked before the time. He who is in too great a hurry, can bring nothing to perfection, but is almost sure to spoil that which he has in hand. Remember, then, that if our Stone be not sufficiently matured, it will not be able to bring anything to maturity.

The substance is dissolved in a bath, and its parts reunited by putrefaction. In ashes it blossoms. In the form of sand all its excessive moisture is dried up. Maturity and fixity are obtained by living fire. The work does not actually take place in the Bath of St. Mary, in horse-dung, in ashes, or in sand, but the grades and regimen of the fire proceed after the degrees which are represented by these. The Stone is prepared in an empty furnace, with a threefold line of circumvallation, in a tightly closed chamber. It is subjected to continued coction, till all moisture and clouds are driven off, and the King attains to indestructible fixedness, and is no longer liable to any danger or injury, because he has become unconquerable. Let me express my meaning in a somewhat different manner. When you have dissolved your earth with your water, dry up the water with its own inward fire. Then the air will breathe new life into the body, and you will have that which can only be regarded as that Great Stone which in a spiritual manner pervades human and metallic bodies, and is the universal and immaculate Medicine, since it drives out that which is bad, and preserves that which is good, and is the unfailing corrective of all imperfect or diseased substances. This Tincture is of a colour intermediate between red and purple, with something of a granite hue, and its specific weight is very, considerable.

Whoever gains possession of this Stone, should let his whole life he an expression of his gratitude towards God in practical kindness towards his suffering brethren, that after obtaining God's greatest earthly gift, he may hereafter inherit eternal life.

Praise be unto God everlastingly for this His inestimable gift.

ELEVENTH KEY.

The eleventh Key to the Knowledge of the augmentation of our Stone, I will put before you in the form of a parable.

There lived in the East a gilded knight, named Orpheus, who was possessed of immense wealth, and had everything that heart can wish. He had taken to wife his own sister, Euridice, who did not, however, bear him any children. This he regarded as the punishment of his sin in having wedded his own sister, and was instant in prayer to God both by day and by night, that the curse might be taken from him.

One night, when he was buried in a deep sleep, there came to him a certain winged messenger, named Phœbus, who touched his feet, which were very hot, and said: "Thou noble knight, since thou hast wandered through many cities and kingdoms, and suffered many things at sea, in battle, and in the lists, the heavenly Father has bidden me make known to thee the following means of obtaining thy prayer: Take blood from thy right side, and from the left side of thy spouse. For this blood is the heart's blood of your parents, and though it may seem to be of two kinds, yet, in reality, it is only one. Mix the two kinds of blood, and keep the mixture tightly enclosed in the globe of the seven wise Masters There that which is generated will be nourished with its own flesh and blood, and will complete its course of development when the Moon has changed for the eighth time If thou repeat this process again and again, thou shalt see children's children, and the offspring of thy body shall fill the world."

When Phœbus had thus spoken, he winged his flight heavenward. In the morning the knight arose and did the bidding of the celestial messenger, and God gave to him and to his wife many children, who inherited their father's glory, wealth, and knightly honours from generation to generation.

If you are wise, my son, you will find the interpretation of my parable. If you do not understand it, ascribe the blame not to me, but to your own ignorance. I may not express myself more explicitly; indeed, I have revealed the matter in a more plain and straightforward manner than any of my predecessors. I have concealed nothing; and if you will but remove the veil of ignorance from your eyes, you will behold that which many have sought and few found.

TWELFTH KEY.

If an athlete know not the use of his sword, he might as well be without it; and if another warrior that is skilled in the use of that weapon come against him, the first is like to fare badly. For he that has knowledge and experience on his side, must carry off the victory.

In the same way, he that possesses this tincture, by the grace of Almighty God, and is unacquainted with its uses, might as well not have it at all. Therefore this twelfth and last Key must serve to open up to you the uses of this Stone. In dealing with this part of the subject I will drop my parabolic and figurative style, and plainly set forth all that is to be known.

When the Medicine and Stone of all the Sages has been perfectly prepared out of the true virgin's milk, take one part of it to three parts of the best gold purged and refined with antimony, the gold being previously beaten into plates of the greatest possible thinness. Put the whole into a smelting pot, and subject it to the action of a gentle fire for twelve hours; then let it be melted for three days and three nights more.

For without the ferment of gold no one can compose the Stone or develop the tinging virtue. For the same is very subtle and penetrating if it be fermented and joined with a ferment like unto itself; then the prepared tincture has the power of entering into other bodies, and operating therein. Take then one part of the prepared ferment for the tinging of a thousand parts of molten metal, and then you will learn in all faith and truth that it shall be changed into the only good and fixed gold. For one body takes possession of the other; even if it be unlike to it, nevertheless, through the strength and potency added to it, it is compelled to be assimilated to the same, since like derives origin from like.

Whoever uses this as a medium shall find whither the vestibules of the palace lead, and there is nothing comparable to the subtlety thereof. He shall possess all in all, performing all things whatsoever which are possible under the sun.

O principle of the prime principle, consider the end! O end of the final end, consider the beginning! And be this medium commended unto your faithful care, wherein also God the Father, Son, and Holy Ghost, shall give unto you whatsoever you need both in soul and body.

Concerning the First Matter of the Philosophical Stone.

Seek for that Stone which has no fleshly nature, but out of which a volatile fire is extracted, whence also this stone is made, being composed of white and red. It is a stone, and no stone; therein Nature alone operates. A fountain flows from it. The fixed part submerges its father, absorbing it, body and life, until the soul is returned to it. And the volatile mother like to him, is produced in her own kingdom; and he by his virtue and power receives greater strength. The volatile mother when prepared surpasses the sun in summer. Thus the father by means of Vulcan was produced from the spirit. Body, soul, and spirit exist in both, whence the whole matter proceeds. It proceeds from one, and is one matter. Bind together the fixed and the volatile; they are two, and three, and yet one only. If you do not understand you will attain nothing. Adam was in a bath—wherein Venus found her like, which bath the aged Dragon had prepared when his strength was deserting him. There is nothing, says the Philosopher, save a double mercury; I say that no other matter has been named; blessed is he who understands it. Seek therein, and be not weary; the result justifies the labour.

A short Appendix and clear Resumption of the foregoing
Tract concerning the Great Stone of the
Ancient Sages.

I, Basil Valentine, brother of the Benedictine Order, do testify that I have written this little book, wherein, after the manner of the Ancients, I have philosophically indicated how this most rare treasure may be acquired, whereby the true Sages did prolong life unto its furthest limit.

But, notwithstanding that my conscience doth bear me witness in the sight of the Most High, before whom all concealed matters are laid bare, that I have written no falsehood, but have so exposed the truth that understanding men can require no further light (that which is laid down in the theoretical part being borne out and confirmed by the practice of the Twelve Keys), yet have I been impelled by various considerations to demonstrate by a shorter way what I have written in the said treatise, and thus cast further light thereon, whereby also the lover of the desired wisdom may obtain an increased illumination for the fulfilment of his desire. There are many who will consider that I am speaking too openly, and will hold me answerable for the wickedness that they think will follow, but let them rest assured that it will be sufficiently difficult, notwithstanding, for any thick-headed persons to find what they seek herein. At the same time the matter shall be made clear to the elect. Hearken then, thou follower of truth, to these my words, and so shalt thou find the true way!

Behold, I write nothing more than I am willing to hold by after my death and resurrection! Do thou faithfully and simply lay to heart this shorter way, as hereinafter exhibited, for my words are grounded in simplicity, and my teaching is not confused by a labyrinth of language.

I have already indicated that all things are constituted of three essences—namely, mercury, sulphur, and salt—and herein I have taught what is true. But know that the Stone is composed out of one, two, three, four, and five. Out of five—that is, the quintessence of its own substance. Out of four, by which we must understand the four elements. Out of three, and these are the three principles of all things. Out of two, for the mercurial substance is twofold. Out of one, and this is the first essence of everything which emanated from the primal fiat of creation.

But many may by all these discourses be rendered doubtful in mind as to what they must start with, and as to the consequent theory. So I will, in the first place, speak very briefly concerning Mercury, secondly concerning Sulphur, thirdly concerning Salt; for these are the essence of the Matter of our Stone.

In the first place, you must know that no ordinary quicksilver is useful, but our quicksilver is produced from the best metal by the spagyric art, pure, subtle, clear, and glistening, like a spring, pellucid even as crystal, free from all dross. Hence make water or combustible oil. For Mercury was in the beginning water, and herein all the Sages agree with my dictum and teaching In this oil of Mercury dissolve its own Mercury, from which the water in question was made, and precipitate the Mercury with its own oil. Then we have a twofold mercurial substance; but you must know that gold must first be dissolved in a certain water, as explained in my second Key, after the purification described in the first Key, and must be reduced into a subtle calx, as is mentioned in the fourth Key. Next, this calx must be sublimated by the spirit of salt, again precipitated, and by reverberation reduced into a subtle powder. Then its own sulphur can more easily enter into its substance, and have great friendship with the same, for they have a wondrous love towards each other. Thus you have two substances in one, and it is called Mercury of the Sages, but is yet a single substance, which is the first ferment.

Now follows concerning Sulphur.

Seek your Mercury in a similar metal. Then when you know how to extract the metal from its body by purification, the destruction of the first Mars, and reverberation, without the use of any corrosive (the method of doing which I have indicated in my third Key)—you must dissolve that Mercury in its own blood, out of which it was made before it became fixed (as indicated in the sixth Key); and you have then nourished and dissolved the true lion with the blood of the green lion. For the fixed blood of the Red Lion has been made out of the volatile blood of the Green Lion; hence, they are of one nature, and the unfixed blood again renders that which is volatile fixed, and the fixed blood in its turn fixes that which is volatile, as it was before its solution. Then foster it in gentle heat, until the whole of the mercury is dissolved, and you obtain the *second ferment* (by nourishing the fixed sulphur with that which is not fixed), as all Sages unite with me in testifying. Afterwards this becomes, by sublimation with spirit of wine, of a blood-red colour, and is called *potable gold.*

Now I will also give my Opinion respecting the Salt of the Sages.

The effect of "salt" is to fix or volatilize, according as it is prepared and used. For the spirit of the salt of tartar, if extracted by itself without any addition, has power to render all metals volatile by dissolution and putrefaction, and to dissolve quick or liquid silver into the true mercury, as my practical directions show.

Salt of tartar by itself is a powerful fixative, particularly if the heat of quicklime be incorporated with it. For these two substances are singularly efficacious in producing fixation.

In the same way, the vegetable salt of wine fixes and volatilizes according to the manner of its preparation. Its use is one of the arcana of Nature, and a miracle of the philosopher's art.

When a man drinks wine, there may be gained from his urine a clear salt, which is volatile, and renders other fixed substances volatile, causing them to rise with it in the alembic. But the same does not fix. If a man drank nothing but wine, yet for all that the salt obtained from his urine would have a different property from that gained out of the lees of wine. For it has undergone a chemical change in the human body, having become transmuted from a vegetable into an animal salt—just as horses that feed on oats, straw, etc., change those vegetable substances into flesh and fat, while the bee prepares honey out of the precious juices of flowers and herbs.

The great change which takes place in these and other substances is due to *putrefaction*, which separates and transmutes the constituent elements.

The common spirit of salt, which is extracted according to the direction given in my last declaration, if there be added to it a small quantity of the "spirit of the dragon," dissolves, volatilizes, and raises together with itself in the alembic, gold and silver; just as the "eagle," together with the spirit of the dragon (which is found in stony places), before the spirit is separated from its body, is much more powerful in producing fixation than volatility.

This I also say, that if the spirit of common salt be joined to the spirit of wine, and distilled together with it, it becomes sweet, and loses its acidity. This prepared spirit does not dissolve gold bodily, but if it be poured on prepared calx of gold, it extracts the essence of its colour and redness. If this be rightly done, it reduces the white and pure moon to the colour of that body from which it was itself extracted. The old body may also receive back its former colour through the love of alluring Venus, from whose blood it, in the first instance, derived its origin.

But observe, likewise, that the spirit of salt also destroys the moon, and reduces it to a spiritual essence, according to my teaching, out of which the "potable moon" may be prepared. This spirit of the moon belongs to the spirit of the sun, as the female answers to the male, by the copulation or conjunction of the spirit of mercury or its oil.

The spirit lies hid in mercury, the colour you must seek in sulphur, and their coagulation in salt; then you have three things which together are capable of once more generating a perfect thing. The spirit is fermented in the gold with its own proper oil; the sulphur is found in abundance in the property of precious Venus. This kindles the fixed blood which is sprung from it, the spirit of the salt of the Sages imparts strength and firmness, though the spirit of tartar and the spirit of urine, together with true vinegar, have great virtue. For the spirit of vinegar is cold, and the spirit of lime is intensely hot, and thus the two spirits are found to be of opposite natures. I do not here speak according to the customary manner of the Sages. But I must not say too openly how the inner gates are to be unlocked.

In bidding farewell, let me impart to you a faithful word. Seek your material in a metallic substance. Thence prepare mercury. This ferment with the mercury of its own proper sulphur, and coagulate them with salt. Distil them together; mix all according to weight. Then you will obtain *one thing*, consisting of elements sprung from *one thing*. Coagulate and fix it by means of continuous warmth. Thereupon augment and ferment it a third time, according to the teaching of my two last Keys, and you will find the object and goal of your desire. The uses of the Tincture are set forth plainly in my twelfth Key.

THANKS BE TO GOD.

As a parting kindness to you, I am constrained to add that the spirit may also be extracted from black Saturn and benevolent Jupiter. When it has been reduced to a sweet oil, we have a means of robbing the common liquid quicksilver of its vivacity, or rendering it firm and solid, as is also set forth in my book.

Postscript.

When you have thus obtained the material, the regimen of the fire is the only thing on which you need bestow much attention. This is the sum and the goal of our search. For our fire is a common fire, and our furnace a common furnace. And though some of my predecessors have left it in writing that our fire is not common fire, I may tell you that it was only one of their devices for hiding the mysteries of our Art. For the material is common, and its treatment consists chiefly in the proper adjustment of the heat to which it is exposed.

The fire of a spirit lamp is useless for our purpose. Nor is there any profit in "horse-dung," nor in the other kinds of heat in the providing of which so much expense is incurred.

Neither do we want many kinds of furnaces. Only our threefold furnace affords facilities for properly regulating the heat of the fire. Therefore do not let any babbling sophist induce you to set up a great variety of expensive furnaces. Our furnace is cheap, our fire is cheap, and our material is cheap—and he who has the material will also find a furnace in which to prepare it, just as he who has flour will not be at a loss for an oven in which it may be baked. It is unnecessary to write a special book concerning this part of the subject. You cannot go wrong, so long as you observe the proper degree of heat, which holds a middle place between hot and cold. If you discover this, you are in possession of the secret, and can practise the Art, for which the CREATOR of all nature be praised world without end. AMEN.

END OF VOLUME I.

THE

HERMETIC MUSEUM

RESTORED AND ENLARGED:

Volume Two

MOST FAITHFULLY INSTRUCTING ALL DISCIPLES OF THE SOPHO-SPAGYRIC
ART HOW THAT GREATEST AND TRUEST MEDICINE OF

THE PHILOSOPHER'S STONE

MAY BE FOUND AND HELD.

NOW FIRST DONE INTO ENGLISH FROM THE LATIN ORIGINAL PUBLISHED AT
FRANKFORT IN THE YEAR 1678.

Translated by

Arthur Edward Waite

Containing Twenty-two most celebrated Chemical Tracts.

THE GOLDEN TRIPOD.

SECOND TRACT.

THE

CHEMICAL TREATISE

OF

THOMAS NORTON,

THE ENGLISHMAN,

CALLED

BELIEVE-ME,

OR

THE ORDINAL OF ALCHEMY.

AN EPIGRAM

WRITTEN BY M. M., ON NORTON'S CHEMICAL

TREATISE.

As the Nile with its overflowing waters floods the surrounding country, and covers it with fertilizing slime, bearing in it the promise of a rich and laughing harvest, so the genius of Norton overflows its banks far and wide, while he makes known to us the glorious works of Nature. He spreads himself abroad over an immensity of space, that he may fertilize the fields of Alchemy, and rejoice the hearts of its husband men. If you are fortunate you will catch beneath this wide expanse of waters a fish which will satisfy the longing of your heart. And if you fail of success, yet your mind will be stored with the precious treasures of knowledge, and you will in any case be richly rewarded for your labour. The treasures of Hermes are not laid open in one book: perhaps one writer may render clear to you what another fails to explain.

THE TREATISE, CREDE-MIHI, OR ORDINAL,

OF THOMAS NORTON.

PREFACE FIRST.

(*By the Author himself*)

THIS Book shows to the initiated knowledge, but intensifies the ignorance of the vulgar. It is the book of honouring, increasing riches, and the book of the needy, putting to flight poverty. It is the book of confidence and truth, full of counsel for kings and of teaching for prelates, a book useful for sainted men, who wish to live unspotted of sin; a secret book, the Book of the Gift of God, to chosen men a pathway of true hope, a strength to those constant in firm faith, and who unwaveringly believe in my words. Alchemy is sought by the false and the true— by false seekers without number, but they are rejected. Many are aflame with the desire of gain, but amongst a thousand thousand scarce three are chosen. There are many called to knowledge, noble and poor, learned and ignorant, but they will not submit to toil, or await the time; they do not attain to the goal because they are ungrateful. The Book of our Art is clear as light to the sons of knowledge, to whom God has freely given to understand this matter. Only let them believe this prophetical saying; to the thankful all flows forth from the fount of Divine love.

This noble science is bestowed only on those who love justice with a devout mind, but to the deceitful, the treacherous, and the violent it is denied, because their sin's hinder the coming of God's gifts.

This knowledge would often have been the glory of England's Kings, if their hope had been firmly placed upon God. One who shall have obtained his honours by means of this Art, will mend old manners, and change them for the better. When he comes, he will reform the kingdom, and by his goodness and virtue he will set an everlasting example to rulers. In his time the common people will rejoice, and render praise to God in mutual neighbourly love. O King, who art to accomplish all this, pray to God the King, and implore His aid in the matter! So the glory of thy mind will be crowned with the glory of a golden age, which shall not then be hoped for as future.

PREFACE SECOND.

To the honour of the One God, who is Three Persons in One, this book has been written, in order that, after my death, learned and unlearned men might see how every one who will follow my good counsel, and ponder it well before he begins the work, may obtain great treasure through the Art of Alchemy. But the book is also a storehouse of mighty secrets for the learned. Let me warn the unlearned that they must study this Art with fear and trembling, lest they be led astray by the false delusions of those who counsel many costly experiments, and use high sounding words. For my part, I desire none of that fame which the world can give, but only your prayers to God for me, though you need not utter my name. Let no one trouble himself about the author, but rather let him diligently consider the contents of the Book. If you enquire into the motives of men, you will find many who are induced to give their minds to the study of Alchemy, only by the desire of gain and riches; and such men are found even among Cardinals of highest rank, Archbishops, and Bishops of lofty order, Abbots and religious Priors, also among hermits, monks, and common priests, and among Kings, princes, and lords of high degree.

For men of all classes desire to partake of our good things: merchants, and those who exercise their craft in the forge, are led captive by a longing to know this Art; nor are common mechanics content to be excluded from a share in it: they love the Art as dearly as great lords. The goldsmiths are consumed with the desire of knowing—though them we may excuse since they have daily before their eyes that which they long to possess. But we may wonder that weavers, freemasons, tailors, cobblers, and needy priests join in the general search after the Philosopher's Stone, and that even painters and glaziers cannot restrain themselves from it. Nay, tinkers presumptuously aspire to exalt themselves by its means, though they should be content with the colour with which glass is stained. Many of these workmen, however, have been deceived by giving credulous heed to impostors, who helped them to convert their gold into smoke, and though they are grieved and disappointed at the loss, they yet buoy themselves up with sanguine thoughts, and hope that they will after all reach the goal; alas, too many have I known, who, after amusing themselves with delusive hopes through a long life, have at last died in squalid poverty! For them it would have been better if they had stayed their hands at once, seeing that they met with nothing but disappointment and vexation of spirit. For, surely, he who is not very learned will do well to think twice before he meddles with this Art. Believe me, it is by no means a light matter to know all the secrets connected with the science. Nay, it is a profound philosophy, a subtle science, a sacred alchemy. Concerning which I here intend to write in a style manly, but not curious. For he who desires to instruct the common people should speak to them in a language they understand. But though I must express myself in a plain and unassuming style, no candid reader should therefore contemn me. For all that before me have written on this matter have rendered their books obscure and unintelligible by an exaggerated use of poetical imagery, parables, and metaphors which grievously obstruct the path of those who first enter on this field of knowledge. This is the reason that a beginner, who strives to put their precepts into practice, only loses his trouble and his money, as is daily seen. Hermes, Rhasis, Geber, Avicenna, Merlin, Hortulanus, Democritus, Morienus, Bacon, Raymond, Aristotle, and many others, have concealed their meaning under a veil of obscurity. Hence their books, which they have handed down to us, have been a source of endless error and delusion to the vulgar and the learned, and, in spite of the beautiful conceits which abound in their writings, no one has been able to find a path through the wilderness of their words; yea, many have been reduced to despair. Anaxagoras indeed acquitted himself better than the rest, in his book "Concerning Natural Changes." Of all the ancient Sages whose writings I have read, he lays open most plainly the foundation of our knowledge. For this very reason Aristotle is wroth against him, and attacks him most virulently in many passages, as I can show, his purpose being to keep men from following him. For he (Anaxagoras) was full of wisdom and love: may God above reward him for his goodness, and pardon the evil deeds of those who sow the seeds of enmity and hatred. To the latter class belonged that monk who set forth a pretentious book of A Thousand Receipts, from malice and the love of mischief—

which was copied in many places, and deceived and deluded numerous enquirers, and reduced them to beggary; moreover, he represented true and approved men as forgers and impostors. For this reason I am impelled by pity to set forth the truth in a few simple words, in order to warn you against false and deceitful teaching, if, indeed, you will pay attention to me and to my words. Throw away your volumes of "Recipes," for they are full of falsehood and fraud. Do not believe them, but give diligent heed to the maxim, that nothing is wrought without its own proper cause. This is the mistake into which those self-styled "Practical Sages" fall. They do not place knowledge on a firm foundation by enquiring into the cause of things. You should therefore constantly bear this momentous rule in mind: never to set about an experiment until you fully comprehend the why and the how. He who would make good progress in this Art should also diligently eschew all falsehood. For God is Truth, and it is He who shows this Art to men: therefore keep yourself above all things unspotted from the slightest taint of falsehood. Let it be fixed in your mind as an abiding principle, under no circumstances to procure for yourselves "adulterated" metals, like those who seek to accomplish albifications and citrinations, which cannot abide a searching test, and by which they produce false silver and false coin for the purpose of duping the credulous. But God has provided that no one should succeed in attaining to this Blessed Art, who loves that which is false rather than that which is true. If any man would obtain grace of God to discover the secrets of this Art, he should be a lover of justice and truth; nor let him be too eager in his own mind to follow this Art on account of its outward advantages. He who would enjoy the fruit of his labour, should be satisfied with such wealth as is sufficient. Let him not waste time and trouble on divers methods of procedure, but let him follow the directions of this Book, which is called the "Ordinal of Alchemy," the *Crede-mihi*, an everlasting standard. For as the Ordinal instructs the presbyters concerning the ministry of the days which they must observe, so all the true and useful teaching of ill-digested books on Alchemy is here set forth in proper order. Wherefore, this Book is of inestimable value for the acquisition of the precious science, nor can its truth ever be denied, though it be composed in an unassuming style. As I have received this Art by Divine Grace, so I set it forth to you in seven chapters as fully as my fealty will permit. For I remember what is said about the judgment of God at the last day.

The first chapter will shew what persons from among the common people can attain to this knowledge, and why the science of Alchemy was by the Ancients called blessed and sacred.

In the second chapter will be set forth the wise joy and the long labours of those who follow this Art.

The third chapter will, for the sake of my fellow-men, contain a faithful description of the substance of that Stone which the Arabians call the Elixir. There you will learn whence it is obtained.

The fourth chapter will treat of the gross part of the work, which is foul and little suited to delicate persons.

The fifth chapter is concerned with the subtle part of the process which God has ordained for the learned only, but which few of the learned ever comprehend; so that the secret is really possessed by very few.

The sixth chapter deals with the question of proportion, and with the agreement of this world below with the sphere of heaven above, of which a right understanding greatly helps many learners, and proves of great assistance to them in our wonderful Art.

The seventh chapter will truly set forth to you the principles in accordance with which your fire should be regulated.

Now, O Lord, do Thou guide and assist me, for I desire to gird myself to my task! Everyone that shall happen to read this Book, I implore to offer up prayers for my soul, and not to alter that which I have written, for the better or for the worse, on the pain of my most grevious anathema. For where the sense is obscure this is for the purpose of secrecy; but if a single syllable be altered in a critical passage, it may destroy the value of the whole book. Therefore, see that which I have written be preserved intact, for though the language be humble, yet it conveys truths of most momentous importance, and it should be read not once or twice, but twenty times. Your best plan will be to read many books on Alchemy, and this one last of all.

THOMAS NORTON'S
CHEMICAL TREATISE.

CHAPTER I.

A MOST wonderful Magistery and Archimagistery is the Tincture of sacred
Alchemy, the marvellous science of the secret Philosophy, the singular gift
bestowed upon men through the grace of Almighty God—which men have never
discovered by the labour of their hands, but only by revelation, and the teaching of
others. It was never bought or sold for a price to any of those who sought after it;
but it' has always been granted through the grace of God alone to worthy men, and
perfected by long labour and the lapse of time. It was given to relieve the estate of
man; it puts an end to vainglory, hope, and fear, and removes ambition, violence,
and excess. It mitigates adversity, and saves men from being overwhelmed by it.
Whoever has perfect knowledge of it, eschews extremes, and is content with the
middle way. Some disdain to call this Art sacred, because they say that Paynims
sometimes acquire a knowledge of it, though God cannot be desirous of conferring
any good thing upon them, seeing that their wilful and stubborn unbelief renders
them incapable of possessing that which is the cause of all good. Moreover, it is
affirmed that our Art produces nothing but gold and silver, which are coined into
money, or fashioned into cups and rings, but are approved and accounted by wise
men the least valuable and precious of all things which are upon the earth; and
hence men of this school conclude that this science, if judged by its effects, cannot
claim to be regarded as sacred.

To this objection, we answer what we know to be true, that the science of this
Art has never been fully revealed to anyone who has not approved himself worthy
by a good and noble life, and who has not shown himself to be deserving of this
gracious gift by his love of truth, virtue, and knowledge. From those who are
otherwise minded this knowledge must ever remain concealed.

Nor can anyone attain to this Art, unless there be some person sent by God to
instruct him in it. For the matter is so glorious and wonderful that it cannot be fully
delivered to any one but by word of mouth. Moreover, if any man would receive it,
he must take a great and sacred oath, that as we his teachers refuse high rank and
fame, so he will not be too eager for these frivolous distinctions, and that he will
not be so presumptuous as to make the secret known to his own son; for
propinquity of blood, or affinity, should be held of no account in this our
Magistery. Nearness of blood, as such, does not entitle anyone to be let into the
secret, but only virtue, whether in those near to us or in strangers. Therefore you
should carefully test and examine the life, character, and mental aptitude of any
person who would be initiated in this Art, and then you should bind him, by a
sacred oath, not to let our Magistery be commonly or vulgarly known. Only when
he begins to grow old and feeble, he may reveal it to one person, but not to more—
and that one man must be virtuous, and generally approved by his fellows. For this
Magistery must always remain a secret science, and the reason that compels us to
be so careful is obvious. If any wicked man should learn to practise this Art, the
event would be fraught with great danger to Christendom. For such a man would

overstep all bounds of moderation, and would remove from their hereditary thrones those legitimate princes who rule over the peoples of Christendom. And the punishment of this wickedness would fall upon him who had instructed that unworthy person in our Art. In order, then, to avoid such an outbreak of overweening pride, he who possesses the knowledge of this Art, should be scrupulously careful how he delivers it to another, and should regard it as the peculiar privilege of those who excel in virtue.

But even if this Art could, on account of its effects, be justly denied a claim to sanctity, it would still be sacred on account of its nature and essence. For as, on the one hand, no one can discover it except by the grace of God, so it is also holy, because it is a divine labour and work to change vile copper into the finest silver and gold. For no one could discover a method of producing such effects by his own thought, seeing that the substances are divers, and man cannot separate that which God has joined together. Nor could the course of Nature be quickened, unless God Himself had granted the aid of this mighty science to those whom He loves. Therefore, the ancient Sages have well called Alchemy a sacred science; and no one should be so presumptuous as to cast away the blessed gift of God. For let us only consider that God has hidden this knowledge from great and learned doctors, and out of His mercy has revealed it to men of low degree, who are faithful lovers of truth, and lowly of heart; and as there are only seven planets among the vast multitude of the stars of heaven, so amongst millions of millions of men hardly seven attain to this knowledge. As we watch men's lives, we see and learn that many scholars of profound erudition, with countless other enquirers, have striven to acquire our science, and yet that all their labour has produced as a net result—nothing. Though they have spent all their substance in the search, it has nevertheless turned out a failure. They have again and again missed the mark at which they aimed; and at last they have given up the quest in despair, and have arrived at the bitter conclusion that the Art is nothing but rank fiction and imposture. As the outcome of their fruitless enquiries they have begun to denounce our Magistery for a vain and empty thing. Let me tell such men that they take too much upon themselves in thinking that that must be nought which their wisdom is not sufficient to compass. But we are not greatly troubled by their calumnies and injurious words; for those who are wise in their own conceits, while in reality they understand nothing, are not the guests for whom our feast is prepared. Though these men cannot understand our Magistery, yet, for all that, it must remain true; and though its truth be denied by some who are lifted up by the vain pride of empty wisdom, all wise men will admit that those who have confessedly never looked upon a thing cannot be allowed to give an authoritative opinion about it. It would be foolish indeed to attach any value to a blind man's opinion about a painting; and though these men are so proud of their profundity and wisdom, I very much doubt whether they could build the tower of St. Paul's (London), or remove it from its foundations. But it is more difficult still to believe that they are keen enough to penetrate the most profound secret which this world contains. Well, now, we will say no more about them, but deliver them over to the wretchedness of their own ignorance.

Now, you who seek this wisdom, learn to distinguish the false from the true. All true enquirers into the Art of Alchemy should be well versed in the primary philosophy. Otherwise all their labour will be vain. The true seeker undertakes the search on his own account; for while he eagerly hopes to find our Delectable Stone, he does not wish to see others involved in any loss he may incur. He therefore conducts all the experiments at his own cost, nor does he grudge the expense which their labour requires. He consumes his substance and empties his coffers, and advances step by step with great patience, basing his hope on God's assistance alone. Impostors, on the other hand, wander in ragged gown from city to city, and set traps for the unwary whom they may dupe with their pretended knowledge, and outwit by vain talk and perjury. They, say that they can augment silver, and affirm with a false oath that they can multiply both gold and silver, and thus they ingratiate themselves with the covetous, producing the excellent conjunction of Fraud and Avarice. But in no long time the multiplier of gold is found to have deceived his credulous victim with his magnificent promises and his perjured assertions—and the covetous man is reduced to beggary. This must be the result if one is not from the very first on his guard against the deceitful language of the multiplier. Of these persons I might speak at great length, but am afraid of encouraging men who are of themselves disposed to evil. I fear that by saying any more I might possibly do as much harm as good, and therefore I will only add one word to the wise: If these persons really possessed the knowledge to which they pretend, they would take good care not to make it known to others, nor would they have any need to go about boasting of their knowledge, and cheating the credulous out of their money. If these impostors were punished according to their deserts in all places where they drive their fraudulent trade, there would not be so many of them. Now these fellows put forward lying assertions about Nature when they speak of the multiplication of metals. For of this one thing you may rest assured: Metals are never multiplied. Such a thing would be contrary to Nature's methods. Nature never multiplies anything, except in either one or the other of these two ways: either by decay, which we call putrefaction, or in the case of animate creatures, by propagation. In the case of metals, there can be no propagation, though our Stone exhibits something like it. Putrefaction destroys and corrupts, but in order to be fruitful, it must go forward in some convenient place. Metals are generated in the earth; for above ground they are subject to rust: hence above ground is the place of the corruption of metals and of their gradual destruction. The cause which we assign for this fact is that above ground they are not in their proper element, and an unnatural position is destructive to natural objects, as we see, for instance, that fishes die when they are taken out of the water; and as it is natural for men, beasts, and birds to live in the air, so stones and metals are naturally generated under the earth. Physicians and apothecaries do not look for aquatic flowers on arid hills. God in His wisdom has ordained that everything should grow in its own proper place. I know that some deny this principle, and assert that metals are multiplied. For, they say, the veins of silver, lead, tin, and iron which we find in the earth, are sometimes rich and sometimes poor; and such diversity would be totally inexplicable if the metals did not multiply or grow. This fact then is thought to prove that metals grow underground—and if they grow underground, why, it is asked, should they not grow above ground, in a vessel which protects them from the influences of fire, water, and air? Our answer to this argument is that it proves nothing, because the conditions are not the same in the two cases. For the only efficient cause of metals is the mineral virtue, which is not found in every kind of earth, but only in certain places and chosen mines, into which the celestial sphere pours its rays in a straight direction year by year, and according to the arrangement of the metallic substance in these places, this or that metal is gradually formed. Only few parts of the earth are suitable for such generation—how, then, can they be multiplied above the earth? Every person of average intelligence knows that in the case of congealed water, or ice, the water, before it becomes hardened, is more plentiful in some places than in others. Before its congelation, it exists in small quantities in brooks and ditches, while more considerable veins of it are found in lakes and rivers. Afterwards, large quantities of ice are seen where there was much water; but it would manifestly be absurd to say that the ice must have grown or multiplied in the lakes and rivers, because they contain greater masses of it than ditches or brooks. In the same way, the metals do not necessarily grow in the mountains, because in some places they exist in larger quantities than in others. A certain portion of any metal can never be increased in quantity by the action of an inherent principle; and herein minerals differ from vegetables and animals. A vegetable seed, such as an acorn, virtually contains within itself the trunk and the leaves of a tree, though they cannot at a given moment be discerned with the eye. But metals always remain exactly the same in their composition, though they be dissolved with strong waters. An ounce of silver can never become more or less than an, ounce of silver. For nothing can be multiplied by inward action unless it belong to the vegetable kingdom, or the family of sensitive creatures. But the metals are elementary objects, and possess neither seed nor sensation. Hence we conclude that all multipliers of metals should be forbidden to exercise their fraudulent trade. For when a metal has once been generated, it is never added to by growth. Nevertheless, we have known one metal to be transmuted into another of a different kind by means of the cognate nature of their substances; so, for instance, iron has been changed into bronze. But nothing can produce real silver or gold except the Medicine of the Philosophers. Hence the falsehoods affected by the multipliers are eschewed and shunned by all true Sages. But all honour and reverence is due to the genuine Art of sacred Alchemy, which is concerned with the precious Medicine that has virtue to produce pure gold and silver. Of this an example exists in a certain city of Catalonia, which Raymond Lullius is supposed to have drawn up. It consists of a series of seven images, and is designed to shadow out the way of truth. Three of these pictures represent matronly figures of solid silver, and four of them represent men .of gold in flowing garb. On the hems of their garments appear certain letters, the meaning of which I will proceed to expound.

"I was once an old iron horse-shoe"—such is the inscription on the garment of one woman—"but now I am the purest silver." "I," says another woman, "was iron smelted from the ore, but now I am become pure and solid gold." "I," says a third, "was once a battered piece of copper: now I am all silver." The fourth figure says: "I was once copper, generated in a vile place, but at the bidding of God I have now become perfect gold." "I," says the fifth figure, "who was once fine and pure silver, am now more excellent gold." The sixth figure proclaims that it was during 200 years a leaden pipe, but is now known by all for honest silver. The seventh says: "A wondrous thing has happened to me—I have become lead out of gold. But certainly my sisters are nearer than I."

This science derives its name from a certain King Alchymus of illustrious memory, who, being a generous and noble-hearted prince, first set himself to study

262

this Art. He ceased not to question Nature by day and by night, and at last extorted from her a blessed answer. King Hermes also did a like thing, being deeply versed in every kind of learning. His "Quadripartite" deals with the four great branches of natural science: astrology, medicine, alchemy, and natural magic; and therein he expresses himself as follows: "Blessed is the man who knows things truly as they are, and blessed is the man who duly proves that which appertains to knowledge." It was his opinion that many are deceived in thinking that they understand that of which they do not know the cause. It is an old proverb that in a bushel of imagination there is often not even a grain of true knowledge. It is also true that by the habit of proving everything, and by wise discernment, learned men are even now adding to their stock of information. By knowledge men understand themselves and all things; without knowledge men are beasts, and worse than beasts. Lack of knowledge renders men fierce and wild, but instruction makes them mild and gentle. It is now the custom for nobles to despise those who desire to understand the secrets of Nature; but in olden times even Kings ordained that no one should be instructed in the seven liberal sciences except those who were nobly born, and brilliantly endowed, and that he who had once devoted himself to knowledge should be bound to spend his life in its pursuit. Hence the Ancients called these sciences the seven liberal sciences, because those who wished to become perfect adepts in them should delight in them in a spirit of liberty. Freedom from all mundane cares is necessary for him who would apply himself thoroughly to the study of human law, and he who wishes to become a ripe scholar in many sciences, has much more solid reasons for turning his back on the world's toils and pleasures. This fact sufficiently shows the ground on which learned men are despised. Yet the glorious memory of the man who increases day by day in the knowledge of truth, can never perish. The man who loves wisdom, justice, and grace, may be rejected in many places, but time will circle his brow with a crown of gold. In the meantime, we must expect that those who love knowledge for its own sake shall be scorned by the ignorant multitude. Nevertheless, it should be borne in mind that though many devote themselves to this study for the sake of mere gain, yet avarice and science are incompatible yoke-fellows; he whose affections are set on mere lucre, will never discover the secrets of this Art. But he who delights in knowledge for its own sake approaches the study of our Art in the right spirit, and such a man is bound to succeed. There is no need to lengthen out this chapter any further, since we have already set forth who they are that may, with reasonable hope of success, apply themselves to the study of sacred Alchemy. Let me repeat that any such person should be a faithful Christian, and a man who is not easily moved from his purpose. He should be free from ambition, free from the necessity of borrowing from others, full of patience and endurance, and of unwavering confidence in God. He should be prepared to follow knowledge through good and evil report. His life should be free from guilt, falsehood, and sin. Such men alone possess mental aptitude for becoming proficients in this science. The next chapter deals with joy and sorrow.

CHAPTER II.

In Normandy there once lived a monk, who deceived many persons of different ranks in life. When his mind had become filled with the vain conceit that he had a perfect knowledge of this Art, he gave himself up to such violent joy that he almost went out of his senses. Whose preposterous zeal I will attempt to excuse by adding the following brief narrative for the sake of illustration:—

This monk had led a vagrant life in France, in forgetfulness of his vow, and in the indulgence of his low desires. At last he came to this kingdom, and attempted to persuade all men that he had a perfect understanding of the Art of Alchemy, which he said he had obtained from a certain "Book of Recipes." He was desirous of achieving a mighty deed, which should hand down the glory of his name to posterity, and for ever establish his reputation in this island. He was always thinking how he should spend the vast wealth which (he thought) he would soon be able to procure. At last he said to himself: "Behold, I know where I shall find a faithful man, who can aid me in this matter, and help me to the fulfilment of my wish: which is, to erect in a glorious manner on Salisbury Plain, fifteen magnificent Abbeys in a short space of time, and each within a mile of the other." In pursuance of this design, the monk came to me, and laid open his whole plan, at the same time requesting me to assist him with my counsel. I have promised before the shrine of Saint James not to divulge his name; but yet I may without prejudice to my vow speak about his foolish undertaking. After telling me of his proficiency in this glorious Art, he said that he wanted nothing but an opportunity of labouring for the King's good, and permission from the Council to buy land for the aforesaid Abbeys. As to the expense, he said it would be easy for him to make it good. But he was in great doubt, where, from whom, and how he was to purchase the land. After listening to the exposition of hip lofty design, I desired to test his learning and his knowledge of scholastic science; and I found that in these branches of attainment he was sadly to seek. Yet I contained myself, and kept my own counsel, in order that I might learn more about his designs. So I told him that the matter was not of sufficient importance to be laid before the King, for everyone would look upon the same as an idle tale, if no proof of his pretensions was forthcoming. The monk answered that he had in the fire a substance which would supply him with all that he needed, and that within forty days he could triumphantly demonstrate to me the truth of his words. I replied that I would not now press him any further, but that I would wait the allotted time. But when the date which he had fixed arrived, the monk's science evaporated, and all his Abbeys and lofty designs vanished into thin air; as the impostor had come, so he departed, not without great shame and confusion. But shortly afterwards I heard that he had deceived many kind-hearted people, and had then again returned to France. It seemed a great pity that fifteen abbeys, seats of religion, sanctity, and learning, should so unceremoniously have vanished with him! It was also wonderful that such a man could have deluded himself into the belief that he could erect fifteen abbeys, while he himself could not live true to his vow of obedience, and must needs wander about as an apostate vagabond, for the purpose of obtaining a knowledge of this sacred Art. But I have already repeatedly said that just because it is sacred, no false or deceitful person can attain to it. In order to illustrate my meaning, I will now add another example. There was a man who thought that he was as deeply versed in this Art as Raymond Lullius or Friar Bacon, for which reason he was so presumptuous as to call himself peerless. He was the priest of a small town, not far from the city of London, and was thought by others to have little skill in preaching. This man felt sure that he had discovered the secret of our Art, and so, in order to advance his fame, he formed the design of throwing a bridge over the Thames for the benefit of travellers, and for the convenience of the whole neighbourhood. But nothing would serve him but he must set up a grand and lofty structure which should compel the admiration of all beholders. It was to have towers covered with flaming gold, and its pillars were to be such as had never been seen before. He frequently spoke of the new thing which he was going to accomplish, for his bridge was to be seen far and wide by night, and was to endure for ever; its glory was never to grow dim. Then he revolved different plans in his mind concerning the best manner of carrying out his design. At first he thought that flaming torches would answer his purpose, and elaborated a plan of setting them up in sufficient numbers. But soon he was seized with a fear that after his death the trustees of his benefaction might neglect the torches, and apply the money allotted to that purpose in some other way, Thus he at length arrived at the conclusion that it would be best to light up his bridge by night with great flaming gems and carbuncles, such as should be visible far and wide, and radiate their splendour in all directions. But here again he was troubled with new misgivings, where such carbuncles could be found, and where he should meet with wise and reliable men, who would travel through all the countries of the world, and procure for him a sufficient number of these jewels. These thoughts caused him so much anxiety, that he wasted away to a mere shadow. All this time, of course, he was firmly persuaded that he had found the true secret of our Art. But when the year came to an end, his Art and all his substance vanished with it; for he had opened his glass vessel and found that it contained neither gold nor silver. Then he flew into a great passion, and cursed himself in the bitterness of his heart. For he had spent all his wealth, and passed the rest of his life in poverty. What more shall I say about him? His case speaks for itself.

When learned scholars and those who frequent the schools hear of the melancholy fate of these foolish persons, they ought to take warning, and remember that the same things may happen to themselves, if they are not constantly on their guard. For many of them are but too ready lightly to receive all conclusions, however false, if they only find them boldly asserted in books. This easy and unquestioning confidence may bring in its train poverty and vexation of spirit. The hope afforded by such teaching is an empty delight and a veritable fools' paradise, But the true sons of our Art stay their hope on God alone, since they know that without Him everything is a delusion and a failure, for they know that a man who has not the Beginning of all Knowledge cannot conduct his enquiry to a successful end. No man, O God, can comprehend without Thee, and though the exposition of the Art be uttered in his ears, without Thee it is but idle breath to him! Of Thee, O God, comes all blessed and successful effort! Thou art of all good things both the beginning and the end. Now I have told you something of the joy which is caused by the vain hopes of foolish enquirers; hear now also about the sorrow, of which this Art has been a source to many whose hopes have been grievously disappointed.

The first cause of sorrow is to see and realize that among the many who seek this Art only few ever find it, and that no one can attain this knowledge unless he be taught before he begins; and he is truly learned, and finely endowed, who can apprehend it by the teaching of another. The subtle shades of natural differences must be well known to the man who desires to be initiated in the most profound secret of the universe; and no form of words can be so accurate as to safeguard the learner against error. For many who have now departed this life have gone widely astray before they finally succeeded in their search after our Stone. Either at the very outset, or at a later stage of the work, all are liable to error, until they are enlightened by the teaching of experience, and hit upon the proper regulation of heat and cold. Nobody is more liable to error in respect to this matter than your bold and overconfident enquirer. Nobody sooner mars our work, than he who is in too great a hurry to complete it. The man who would bring this matter to perfection, should set about it cautiously and heedfully. The most grievous circumstance connected with our Art, is that it you make a mistake in any part of it, you have to do it all over again from the very beginning. Anyone who gives himself up to this search must therefore expect to meet with much vexation of spirit. He will frequently have to change his course in consequence of new discoveries which he makes. His experiments will often turn out failures, his mind will often be in a state of doubt and perplexity; and thus he will continue to be vexed by conflicting results, until at length he reaches the goal of his desire. Again, let me tell you a little more about the sorrows and troubles of the Alchemist, which may considerably moderate your desire to acquire the practice of this Art. At first it is most difficult, as the Sages say, to find out among so many impostors, the man who has a perfect understanding of our science. And when you have found a truly learned master, you have not yet by any means left all your trouble far behind you. If your mind is devoted to virtue, the Devil will do his utmost to frustrate your search by one or the other of three stumbling blocks, namely, haste, despair, or deception. For he is afraid of the good works which you may do if you succeed in mastering this secret. The first danger lies in undue haste, which destroys and mars the work of many. All authors who have written about this Art, agree in saying, like the author of the little book of "The Philosopher's Feast," that undue haste is of the Devil. Hence he will the soonest make an end who tarries a little at the beginning; and those who act otherwise will discover to their cost the truth of the proverb which says that: "The greater haste we make, the less will be our speed." For he who is in a hurry will complete his work neither in a month, nor yet in a year; and in this Art it will always be true that the man who is in a hurry will never be without matter of complaint. Rest assured also that haste will precipitate you from the pinnacle of truth. It is the Devil's subtlest device to ensnare us; for this haste is an *ignis-fatuus* by which he causes us to wander from the right path. The man who has found grace stoutly sets his face against hurry; he does so as a matter of habit, for in a moment of time haste may mar your whole work. Therefore be on your guard against hurry, accounting it as a device of the Devil. Time will not allow me to caution you with sufficient vehemence of feeling against habits of hurried work. Many pierce themselves through with sharp sorrows, because they are always in a hurry, and full of impatience to reach the goal, which comes about through the temptation of Satan. I will say no more about hurry, but blessed is he who possesses patience. If the enemy does not prevail against you by hurry, he will assault you with despondency, and will be constantly putting into your minds discouraging thoughts, how those who seek this Art are many, while they are few that find it, and how those who fail are often wiser men than yourself. He will then ask you what hope there can be of your attaining the grand arcanum; moreover, he will vex you with doubts, whether your master is himself possessed of the secret which he professes to impart to you; or whether he is not concealing from you the best part of that which he knows. The Evil One will endeavour to fill your mind with these doubts, in order to turn you from your purpose by diffidence and despondency. Nor will anything avail against his assaults, except the calm confidence inspired by virtue, and the sound conclusions of reason. Your fears will be scattered to the winds if you quietly consider the high character of your master and teacher; nor need you despair if you can call to mind that he was induced to instruct you by love, and by no selfish motive. It is difficult indeed to trust a man who offers you his services; for such a person stands more in need of you than you of him. But if your master be such a man as I have directed you to seek, and if he has waited for you to come to him, you ought to be strongly armed against the shafts of distrust. If your master be at all such a man as mine was, you can have no excuse for doubting him, for mine was noble and true, a lover of justice, and an enemy to deceit. Moreover, he was a good keeper of his secret, and when others ostentatiously displayed their knowledge, he held his peace as if he knew nothing. When others talked in his presence about the colours of the rose, he would listen in grave and impenetrable silence. Him I attended during many years; but he would not impart to me anything of moment, until he had made me submit to many tests for the purpose of proving my disposition; and when he had found me faithful and true, and had seen the great hope which I had conceived in my mind, I obtained favour in his eyes through the will of God, and his heart inclined to me. When at length he thought that I should not be put off any longer—since my scholarly attainments and the generous aspiration of my soul had moved his heart, and made it go out to me—he took up his pen, and wrote to the as follows: "My faithful friend and beloved brother, I am constrained to accede to your request, as no other person like you will ever come to me. The time has arrived for you to receive this favour of me on account of your manly character and firm faith, your approved virtue and wisdom, your truthfulness, love, and perseverance, your constancy, and the generous aspiration of your soul. This your excellent mental condition I will now reward, to your lasting solace and comfort, by divulging to you the mighty secret. For this purpose it is necessary to converse with you by word of mouth; if I laid open to you the secret in writing, I should be violating my oath. Hence it is necessary that we should meet; and when you come, I will make you the heir of my Art, and depart from this land. You shall be my brother and my heir in respect of this grand secret, which is the despair of the learned. For this reason give thanks to God for this message: it is better than to become heir-apparent to a crown. For only those whom God has chosen next to His own heavenly saints, ever receive this Art by which He is so highly honoured. I will write no more to you at the present time: mount on horseback, and come to me without delay." When I had perused these lines, I set out at the very same hour, and at once hastened to my master, though the distance exceeded a hundred miles. I continued with him forty days, and learned all the secrets of Alchemy (although before I had understood philosophy as well as any other person in the kingdom). Yet it would be foolish to suppose that the work itself can be completed within forty days: I say that I was fully instructed within that time, but the work itself requires a longer period. Then all that had been dark became as clear as the light, when I beheld the secret gates of Nature unbarred; I saw so plainly the causes and the rationale of everything, that it was no longer possible for me to doubt or despair. If you are as fortunate in your master as I, you will never be assailed by despondency.

The third enemy against whom you must guard is deceit, and this one is perhaps more dangerous than the other two. The servants whom you must employ to feed your furnaces are frequently most untrustworthy. Some are careless, and go to sleep when they should be attending to the fire; others are depraved, and do you all the harm they can; others, again, are either stupid or conceited and over-confident, and disobey instructions; some have fingers retentive of other people's property, or they are drunken, negligent, and absent-minded. Be on your guard against all these, if you wish to be spared some great loss. If servants are faithful, they are generally stupid; those who are quick-witted, are generally also false; and it is difficult to say whether the deceitful or the stupid are the greater evil of the two. For when I had all my experiments in proper train, some thievish servants ran away with my materials and utensils, and left me nothing but the empty laboratory; and when I calculated the cost, time, and labour of beginning the work all over again, I had almost in the bitterness of my heart resolved to bid an everlasting farewell to this Art of Alchemy. For it will hardly be believed how completely I had been stripped of all that I possessed, although ten trustworthy persons still survive to attest the fact. Indeed the blow was so great that it could hardly have been inflicted on me by human agency alone, without the instigation and co-operation of the Devil. I also made an Elixir of Life, of which a merchant's wife bereft me, and I procured a quintessence, with many other precious preparations, but of all these things I was robbed by wicked men, and thus found, to my smart, that in the sweetest cup of this world's joy, there is a liberal infusion of bitterness. Let me tell you a little more of what has fallen under my observation, concerning the perplexities of this work. The calamity of which I am thinking happened to a good and godly man; and I am the only person that can give a true account of it.

Thomas Dalton, a devout and religious servant of God, possessed a larger quantity of the Red Medicine than has ever been obtained by any other Englishman. Now a certain knight of King Edward's household, named Thomas Herbert, dragged this Dalton forth by violence from an abbey in Gloucestershire, and brought him before the King, where he was confronted with Delvis. For Dalton had been scribe (secretary) to this William Delvis, and Delvis had told the King about Dalton's skill in this Art. Delvis was a faithful servant, who always stood in the presence of King Edward, and he deposed that within an hour Dalton had made for himself one thousand pounds sterling of gold, fully equal to that of the royal coin: and he confirmed his testimony by a most sacred oath upon the Bible. Then Dalton looked full upon Delvis, and said: "O Delvis, thou hast perjured thyself! Thou hast foully broken the pledge thou gayest me, and hast betrayed me even as Judas betrayed his Master." "I did, indeed," rejoined Delvis, "once swear to thee that I would not betray thy secret; yet I do not consider myself as guilty of perjury, since the service of my King and country release me from my oath." Then Dalton soberly answered him thus: "This subterfuge does not excuse thy perjury; for if it did, how could the King himself trust thee, who hast confessed thy perjury in his presence? And," he continued, turning to His Majesty, "I do admit that I possessed this Medicine for a long time; but at length it was only a source of grief and anxiety to me—and therefore after retiring to that abbey from which I was brought hither, I threw it into a tidal river which is daily renewed by the ebb and flow of the sea. Thus as much wealth has been lost as would have sufficed for the outfit and support of twenty thousand knights, who might have been willing to go forth and recover the Holy Sepulchre. For the love of God, I kept this Medicine many years, in order that through its means I might succour a King who should undertake this expedition. But as this sacred duty was forgotten, the Medicine is now irrecoverably lost." The King replied that it was a foolish act to destroy so wonderful a treasure, and demanded that Dalton should prepare some more of the Medicine. "No," said Dalton, "that can never be." "Why not?" enquired the King. "How did you obtain it?" Dalton replied that he had received it from a learned Canon of Lichfield, whose works he had diligently attended to during many years, until at length the Canon had bequeathed to him as much of the Medicine as he had ever possessed. Then the King gave Dalton four marks, with liberty to depart withersoever he desired; and, at parting, he expressed his grief and concern that he had not known Dalton before. But as it often happens that the worst tyrants are found in the retinues of kings, so Herbert now caused Dalton to be seized, robbed of the money which the King had given him, and carried off to Stepney, where he detained him a long time. Thence Dalton was conveyed by Herbert to a castle in Gloucestershire, cast into the dungeon thereof, and kept close prisoner for four years, during which period he was tormented by Herbert in every conceivable manner. At length he was led forth to execution, and when he saw the ministers of death, he said: "O blessed Lord Jesus, I have been separated from Thee too long: Thou didst give me this knowledge, and I have used it without overweening pride. I have not been able to find a fit person to whom I might have bequeathed my wisdom. Therefore, dearest Lord, I now resign Thy gift into Thy own hands." Then he poured forth a devout prayer, and thereupon turned to the executioner and said, with a smile, "Now thou mayest work thy will."

When Herbert heard these words, his eyes filled with tears, because neither deceit, imprisonment, nor death could induce his victim to yield up the precious secret; and he bade his servants let the old man go, as his obstinacy was not to be overcome. Then Dalton arose, looked about him with sadness and disappointment depicted in his countenance, and departed with a heavy heart; for he had no desire to live even another year. This injury happened to him through the greed and cruelty of godless men. Herbert died not long after, and Delvis lost his life at Tewkesbury. Such are the sufferings which they who aspire to a knowledge of this Art, must lay their account with having to bear. Yet we also see how the greed of wicked men over-reaches itself. For if Herbert had treated Dalton with kindness and gentleness, instead of with cruelty, insolence, and violence, much advantage might have been reaped not, only by the King, but also by the entire commonwealth. Yet we need not wonder that gracious means were not used, for sin reigns everywhere in this kingdom. Otherwise, the people might have obtained great relief from rates and taxes, and much money might have been bestowed in charity among knights, priests, and the common people. Hence we may learn that profligate violence is incapable of acquiring wisdom; for virtue and vice are contrary the one to the other, and men abandoned to the one cannot receive the reward of the other. If vicious persons could gain a full knowledge of this Art, their overbearing insolence would grow unendurable, and their ambition would overleap all bounds; they would by its means become worse men than they were before. Now this chapter respecting the delights and sufferings of our Art is finished. The next will declare the Matter of our Stone.

CHAPTER III.

Tonsilus had been engaged in the momentous search during more than sixty years. Bryan, too, and Halton, in the western parts, had been employed day and night in practical experiments; yet they did not find this noble science, because they did not know the Matter and root of the Art, but sought it by a mistaken method, until they had wasted their lives and goods. They were put to great expense, loss, and suffering, by the recipes according to which they worked. Then Tonsil complained to me with tears that he was in great bitterness of soul, because he had spent the better part of his life on false receipts, vile substances, herbs, gums, roots, and grasses, of which he enumerated many species, as, for instance, crowfoot, celandine, mezerion, lunaria, and mortagon—also upon hair, eggs vervein, excrements, and urine—upon antimony, arsenic, honey, wax, and wine— on quicklime, vitriol, marchasita, and all kinds of minerals—on amalgams, albifications, and citrinations. All had been reduced to nothing by his operations; for he had not well considered his purpose, and the due proportions of natural truth. After he had failed with all these substances he thought nothing could be better than to operate on human blood, until I told him that by a fierce fire blood was destroyed, and converted into smoke. Then he besought me by the love of Christ to declare to him the true substance of the Stone. "Tonsil," I replied, "what good would it do an old man like you? Renounce this pursuit and give yourself up to prayer; for that is what your time of life requires. If you did know the substance of our Stone, you would fall a victim to old age before you could prepare it." But he bade me not to trouble myself about what might be the result to himself. "It would be a comfort to me at least to know the substance of the Stone which I have sought so long." "Tonsil," I said, "your request is more easily made than granted. For all the authors who deal with this subject write about it in obscure language, and not one of them declares it plainly; nay, they beseech God to remove them suddenly out of this world, if they ever write books about the grand secret. For many of them have been fearful of committing to paper more than was right about this science; and not one of them has given more than one or two plain hints respecting it. They did not write with the object of divulging their secret to the world, but in an obscurely allusive style, in order that they might be able to recognize those who understood their meaning as brothers and fellow adepts. Hence you must not be content with reading only one book, but you should study a variety of authors; because, according to the learned Arnold, one book opens up the understanding of another. The same thought is expressed by the learned Anaxagoras, who testifies that if a man will not take the trouble of reading many books, he can never attain to a practical knowledge of our Art. But though I may not reveal to you for the sake of charity what has never yet been plainly set forth by the brethren of our Art, I may at least give you some comfort by answering as straightforwardly as I can, any questions which you may like to put to me." "Good Master," he replied, "tell me truly whether the substance be Sun (gold) and Mercury, or Sun and Moon (silver), or whether these three must be taken together; or whether it be Gold by itself, or Mercury by itself, or whether Sulphur with these two be the substance of the Stone? Or, is salt of ammonia nearer the truth, or is some other mineral the right thing to use in our Art?" The questions you have put, Tonsil, are wisely and astutely conceived; neverthelesss, you have not named the substance, except generically. For you must take a part of these, and of other things at various times, according to the requirements of the Art. Divers things are used in the preparation of our Stone, but there are two materials, and only one Stone. Between the two there is the same difference as that between a mother and her offspring; or, looking at the matter from another point of view, the difference resembles that which exists between male and female. These two substances will furnish you with all that you need. As for the white Tincture, if you are wise, one of these you shall find to be a Stone, which is rightly named, because, like a stone, it is indestructible by fire. Yet it is not like a stone to the touch or the sight, but is a fine earthy powder, of a dull red. In its separate form we call it our ground litharge; at first it is brown and ruddy, and then of a whitish colour. It is called our chosen Marcasite, and one ounce of it is worth more than fifty pounds. Yet is it not sold in the cities of Christendom, but he who desires it, must either get it made by someone else, or prepare it himself. There is this advantage concerning it, that to make it once well dispenses with all need of repeating the task. Ancient writers call it a thing of small price, because it is lightly esteemed by the merchants, and no one that finds it cares to pick it up, any more than if it were an ounce of dirt. Few will believe that it is a pearl of great price, for it is known to none but the wise. Thus have I laid bare to you a great secret, more plainly than any of the dead masters. Then, Tonsilus, you must also have another Stone, or else you want your principal material. This Stone is most glorious, fair, and bright. It is sold as a stone, and looks like a stone of singular transparency and brilliance. One ounce of it may, in most places, be obtained for about twenty shillings. Its name is Magnesia, but its real nature is known to few. It is found on the tops of the highest mountains, and in the lowest depths of the earth Plato knew its properties and called it by its name. Chaucer says, in the Canon's Tale, that it is called Dytanos, thus defining an obscure term in language still more hopelessly obscure; but it is impossible to understand a thing if for one unintelligible term another still less intelligible is substituted. Nevertheless, my Tonsilus, I will endeavour to explain to you the meaning of Magnesia in our own tongue. *Magos* is Greek, and is equivalent to the Latin *mirabile*; *aes* is money, *ycos*, science; *A* is God; that is to say, it is a matter in which much divine knowledge is involved. Now you know what Magnesia is—it is *res aeris*, and in it lies hidden a wonderful and divine secret. These two stones, my Tonsilus, you must take as your materials for the preparation of the Elixir. Although at first no further materials are needed, yet, as I have already hinted, divers other things are of great use in our Art. The great secret was never before so plainly expounded. But take my explanation in all its fullness; and I will pray God, lest my excess of frankness be reckoned to me for a crime— for I fear that I have suffered my pen to run riot. Though few may understand what I have said, yet there are some students of this Art so subtle, cunning, and keen-witted, that still fewer data would suffice to them for the discovery of all that we know. Nevertheless, God shall provide that none shall find it except the man of a pure and virtuous life. It was with this end in view that the ancient writers concealed with so much solicitude the matters of our Stone, which I have here declared. You need no other substances but these two for the preparation of the white Stone, except salt of ammonia, and that kind of sulphur which is extracted from metals. These two substances suffice for the fulfilment of your desire; none but these two finally abide the test of the fire. Sulphur is burned, and loses its colour. Rut our Litharge is indestructible. Do not set about with any metal or quicksilver. If you destroy its whole composition, some of its component parts will be of use to you. But the principal substances are the two which I have mentioned, namely, Magnesia and Litharge, its brother."

CHAPTER IV.

I will not attempt to escape from the task which I have undertaken to expound the great work: I will instruct you as fully as possible in this secret, and all my endeavour shall be to make known to you the truth. As far as I may do so without prejudice to my vow, f will be your guide, and shew you the way to the goal of your desire. If you consider into what a state of obscurity and confusion the different parts of this work have been wilfully thrown by the old writers, you will understand the difficulty of my task. None of them has declared more than one point of our experiment; and for this reason their writings, even if you understand them, will not enable you to practise the Art yourself. Arnold testifies in his books that the central secret of our Art is to know the substance on which it is based; and in his work "Multifary," where he shews how pure and simple essences are to be recognised, he says that our fundamental matter is of two kinds; but he does not tell us how they are to be found. Their names you have already learned in the last chapter. Friar Bacon dwells more fully on this point, where he says: "Divide all parts into their cognate elements. For the unlearned do not proceed in this way; but they continue pertinaciously and senselessly to add more and more to a divisible substance—and while they fancy that they are on the point of bringing to perfection the flower of our Art, all that they really effect is the multiplication of error." In this passage Bacon, like his predecessors, appears fearful of saying too much. Perhaps you also remember what Avicenna says, in his "Gate": "You must go forward to perfection by true teaching in accordance with the facts of Nature: you must eat to drink, and drink to eat, and in the mean season be covered with perspiration." Rhasis expresses himself to the same effect, but warns us against suffering the matter to consume its food too quickly: "Let it assimilate its aliment little by little." Of this rule the Prophet also makes mention, if you rightly comprehend his meaning: "Thou hast visited the earth," he says, "and watered it: Thou hast multiplied its wealth: the fruitful land hast Thou turned into a dry place, and the arid land into a river of water." When it has plenty of meat and drink, it is needful to watch at a time when the body craves sleep. For our labour demands constant vigils and great diligence, and it must be nourished and fed with precious substances. "Therefore let all poor men eschew this experiment," says Arnold, "as this Art is for the rich of this world"—and I myself can attest to ail poor men the truth of these words. "Moreover," he continues, "let the enquirer be patient and of an even temper, for those who are in a hurry will never reach the goal." The length of time required for the purification of the substance, is a stone of stumbling to many who will not believe in it. I advise you, therefore, ye poor, not to attempt the solution of this mystery, but to stay your hands before it is too late. One fourth of an ounce too much or too little may in a single hour mar and destroy the labour of weeks. The substance you must prepare with gentle heat, and so long as there is no violent effervescence, you may keep it over the fire: you should gradually consume it by gentle coction, but it must not be suffered to throw up great bubbles, as such a course would be indicative of haste. Gentleness and patience will mark out to you the safest method, and enable you to avoid the manifold dangers which beset the enquirer's path. One of the most difficult experiments in the gross work, is the classification of our intermediate minerals. The different media that are used must all be in a highly purified state, if the work is to be brought to a successful conclusion. For the pure and impure, the mature and immature, are by nature violently opposed to each other; that which is fixed naturally adheres to fixed substances, and volatile substances are sympathetically attracted by that which is volatile. Everywhere Nature strives to produce harmony by drawing like to like. Now you will find our gross work to be generically impure; and it is a matter of great difficulty and danger, requiring the utmost wisdom of the wise, and confounding the folly of the ignorant, to purge our Substance from all foreign matter. The learned as well as the simple are often led astray at this point, and prove the truth of the saying of Anaxagoras, that all men need to be taught discretion by bitter experience. Once I heard a wise man say that, at the present time, magnesia (in a pure state) is sold in Catalonia, together with the other intermediate minerals, so that the hands of a fastidious man need now no longer be defiled with this dirty work; and if this were really true, both the commencement and the consummation of your work would be a much easier matter than it is under ordinary conditions. For if you are compelled to do all that I have had to accomplish, you will be wearied out before you reach the work proper. The work of the Sages does not begin until all substances are pure, both without and within. Let us remember that as we are seeking a tincture which imparts perfection to all things else, we must remove from it all that is foul 'and vile. Of the different media, each has its own properties, and its own function to perform, according to its essential nature; of those media by which our experiment is advanced, some are of their own nature helpful, and others are harmful. Our Apothecaries do not understand the secret of their preparation, and we refuse to instruct them, because we know that they would adulterate them (for the purpose of deceiving their customers) rather than take diligent and conscientious pains to let their drugs be genuine and pure. It is their practice (as I know by bitter experience) to ask a high price, and to furnish an untrustworthy article. If a man would have materials on which he may rely, he must not be afraid of soiling his own hands, nor must he shun expense, though it may swallow up all his hoarded wealth. In the gross work that man is furthest from the goal who is in too great a hurry to reach it. If our great work, with all that belongs to it, could be accomplished in three years, artists might account themselves fortunate; for when it has once been brought to a satisfactory conclusion, there is no need to undertake it a second time, if indeed one is skilled in the art of augmenting his medicine; and the attainment of this skill is one of the great objects of our Magistery. There is no need for me to name in this place the different minerals which are required, seeing that Albertus has most fully discussed this point. I might say much about the properties of minerals; but the discussion would prove barren of results in the advancement of our Art. One of the most important conditions of success is the mechanical skill in the manipulation of experiments; in regard to these it is possible to go astray in a thousand ways, the path being beset with all but insurmountable difficulties at every step. Therefore, believe that which the ancient writers tell us—that nothing can be rightly done without experience. Consider all circumstances, and take care to secure uniformity in all that is required. Use one vessel which is simple both in material and in shape; beware of one made of mixed material, lest some accident happen at a critical moment. This general admonition will save me the trouble of laying down, and you the trouble of remembering, a hundred special cautions; and this instruction may suffice for him who is wisely intent on the practice of our Art. If your servants are faithful and true, you will be able to carry out your experiments without constant vexation. Therefore, if you would be free from all fear, over the gross work, follow my counsel, and never engage married men; for they soon give in and pretend that they are tired out, as I can assure you from my own experience. Hire your workmen for certain stipulated wages, and not for longer periods than twenty-four hours at a time. Give them higher wages than they would receive elsewhere, and be prompt and ready in your payments. For your kindness will stir up in their hearts love and reverence, and a spirit of zeal in the conduct of the work committed to them; for they know withal that they are liable to be discharged at once if they are negligent in your service. Married men will not agree to be engaged for such short periods; therefore, give them a wide berth. If I had known and acted on this principle before, I might have been spared much loss and vexation. In the pursuit of our Art, you must preserve at all times your liberty of action; and you should also take care, from time to time, to unbend your mind from its sterner employments with some convenient recreation; otherwise your spirits might be weighed down with melancholy and despair, and you might lose heart for the continuation of your work. There is no need to add much to this chapter, for the ancient writers have already fully set forth all that I have not yet touched upon. But that which they have omitted is most plainly expounded in this Book. Hence it is called the Ordinal of Alchemy, the supplement of all other works on the subject. The following chapter is for the initiated, and shows all the rules to be observed in the subtle part of the work.

CHAPTER V.

When Briseus was a money-changer, he caused loss to many persons, but to others his dealings were a source of delight and joy; and as this fact seemed at the time a wonder and marvel to all who heard of it, so in our own time—not so very long ago—an almost miraculous event was observed to take place: within the short space of ten days the same bed in a house near Leadenhall was successively occupied by three Masters of this Art, every one of whom possessed both the white and the red Tincture; though hardly one person amongst a million of men ever becomes possessed of the glorious prize. One of them, as I was told, was from the Duchy of Lorraine, the second hailed from the Midland Counties of England, the third was the youngest, and was born near a Cross, which stands at the boundary of three shires. Wise men had foretold from the conjunction of planets that prevailed at his birth, that he would be an ornament to England. Anyone might travel through the length and breadth of Europe without meeting with three such Masters. Two of them are about to depart, but the third will remain and do much good in this part of the world. Nevertheless, the sins of our rulers will delay the good which otherwise he might confer upon our country at once. The oldest of the three Masters prophesied concerning this young adept, that he would have to endure much suffering at the hands of those who owed him the greatest debt of gratitude He also uttered many other prophecies, some of which were verified by the event, while the rest remain to be fulfilled. "One thing is most certain," he said, "after great sorrow there will be great joy in all parts of this country—joy which will be experienced by all good men." The youth enquired when this thing should be, and the old man's answer was that it should come to pass when the Cross was honoured by night and by day in the land of God, and the land of Light: which thing will happen in due time, but is delayed by the grievous wickedness of men. But when the blessed hour arrives, this Art will be revealed to a King; and more glorious things will then be brought to pass than it is possible for us to enumerate in this place, when he shall have reformed our manners and abolished all abuses. He will investigate this science in secret, and will be instructed in it by hermits, or monks. So King Calid, in his time of need, sought this knowledge of many, until it was imparted to him by Morienus, who succoured the King with his counsel, being removed thereto by his nobleness and virtue. But now we will speak of this subject no longer, but proceed to give an account of the subtle work. He that would understand it must be deeply learned. He should know elementary philosophy if he wishes to study Alchemy.

Now, let me tell you who are intent upon this Art, that when materials have by preparation been rendered fit for generation, they must by division be separated into four elements. If you cannot do this, go and learn of Hortulanus, who has written a special treatise on the subject—in which treatise he shows how to divide wine into its elements. Moreover, you should know the effects of the four qualities—heat, cold, moisture, and dryness—of which all things are composed; and because in this Art you are specially desirous of obtaining a colour which abides the fire, you ought also to know, before you set about its production, how colours are generated. For every colour that can be named is seen in our work, before the white colour appears. Moreover, you must be able to melt your substance easily, like wax or gum. Otherwise, according to the Masters, it could not enter or penetrate metals. The substance should be both fixed and fluxible, and have abundance of colour. To conjoin these three contraries in one substance, is the great secret of our Art. Nevertheless, an apt learner may find it expounded in this chapter. And first—to speak as briefly and concisely as possible concerning the aforesaid four primary qualities: heat and cold are active qualities; moisture and dryness, on .the other hand, are qualities of a passive kind. For the latter are always passively subject to the former, as, for instance, stones when they become lime, and water when it is changed to ice. Whence you may easily see that nothing is fully wrought except by heat and cold. Yet the passive qualities have some power, as we find every day in mechanical operations, in the baking of bread, the brewing of beer, and other processes brought about by the operation of moisture and dryness. Aristotle, in his physical treatise, and many others, say that from action proceeds knowledge; thus they call practice the source and root of speculation and of all science. For the properties of all things are perceived by watching their operations, as, from the colour of urine we hear physicians draw conclusions in regard to the excess or lack of animal heat in the body. By means of those four primary qualities, we study the colours in the due order of their succession. But we can have no real assurance respecting the white colour, except in a very pure substance. You will be materially assisted in your task by a knowledge of the way in which colours are daily generated. Colour is the extremity of every transparent body; a clear substance is here beautifully consummated. If dryness dominates in a dry substance, its colour will most certainly be white. Of this fact you may convince yourself by ocular proof in the case of burned bones, or of quicklime made of stones. Where cold prevails in a moist and clear substance, a white colour will be the result, as is seen in the case of ice, or water indurated by frost. The cause has already before been declared in our philosophy; but here I do not speak of common philosophy, but only adduce these facts in illustration of alchemistic principles. And indeed one fact explains another, as the offspring may be known by looking at its mother. If heat operates on a thick and moist substance, a black colour will be the result.

If you desire an illustration of this principle, you need only put some green wood on the fire. When cold is brought to bear on a thick and dry substance, the colour which is produced will be black. The reason is that the substance is compact and very thick, and under the influence of cold which is destructive of life, the thickness causes obscurity and absence of light; and negation of colour is blackness. Thus you may accept it for an universal fact that a clear substance is a white substance. The efficient cause is not always the same; it is sometimes heat, and sometimes it is cold. But blackness and whiteness (as everyone knows) are the two extremes of colour. Hence your work must begin with blackness, if whiteness is its final perfection. Red—as the Sages say—is an intermediate colour between black and white. Nevertheless you may believe what I say: Red is the final colour in Alchemy. The Sages also tell us that pink and orange are colours intermediate between white and red; and that green and grey are intermediate colours between red and black. Flesh colour is seen in very pure substances. Physicians have discovered nineteen colours intermediate between white and black in urine; of these colours one is whitish, like that of the onyx stone. Magnesia appears to partake of this colour—though Magnesia throws out a mild, pure splendour in the subtle stage of our Art; and here we behold all colours that ever were seen by mortal eye—a hundred colours, and certainly a good many more than have been observed in urine; and in all those colours our Stone must be found in all its successive stages. In the ordering of your practical experiments, and in conceiving the different parts of the work in your own mind, you must have as many phases, or stages, as there are colours. If you do not know the different stages of this Art, you will find them in Raymond's "General Exposition of Alchemy." Gilbert Kymer has indeed left us a fanciful book, in which he describes seventeen proportions. But they do not suffice for this science, of which he was never able to discover the true secret, though he was profoundly learned in Medicine.

Such, however, is the strength of the human constitution, that it often overcomes disease in spite of the doctor's physic: and the physician's art is praised in many cases where his remedies had nothing to do with the cure, or even retarded it. But the case is different with respect to our mineral medicine; for our Art is raised far above all generations, and exists only in the wisdom of the Artist, as any wise man may discover by experience. Thus, the true foundation of Alchemy consists in the proper graduation of the work, and in the correct adjustment of heat and cold, moisture and dryness; also in the knowledge that through these qualities others are generated, such as hardness and softness, heaviness and lightness, roughness and smoothness—according to the addition of these primary qualities in certain proportions of weight, number, and measure. Under these three categories we may range everything that God has made. For God has created and ordered all things in accordance with certain proportions of number, weight, and measure; and if you depart from these proportions, you destroy the harmony of Nature. It is therefore a wise caution which is given by Anaxagoras, that we should not proceed to join together our elements, until we have discovered the exact proportion of weight in which all the elements are found in the substances with which we have to deal. Bacon says that the Ancients have concealed nothing except these proportions, respecting which they give us no information. For when they speak of proportions, they bewilder the student with the most contradictory assertions. If you wish to know the truth about these proportions, you may obtain it by studying the works of Albertus, Raymond, Bacon, and Anaxagoras the Elder. You must collect your knowledge from the pages of these four writers, as one of them by himself will not afford it. Though you understand the secret of joining the four qualities together into one cohesive whole, yet the more difficult task of combining the different elements still remains to be accomplished. A proper union has to be effected between earth and water on the one hand, and air and fire on the other. Though the third and the second are the most noble of all, yet the first and the fourth cannot be excluded. Earth is the most useful element, and that of which we have the greatest need. Here lies latent the possibility of growth and the power of generation; it is the earthy litharge of our Stone. Without it there can be no generation and no fixation thereof. For there is nothing fixed save earth alone; all the other elements are volatile. Daily experience teaches you that this is true of fire, water, and air. Fire is the cause of expansion, and renders the substance capable of permixtion; but the transparent splendour and beautiful colour are produced through the influence of air. Moreover, when air is condensed, it produces substances which are easily melted, such as wax, butter, and gum; these are liquefied by a very slight degree of heat. Water purifies by ablution, and causes mortifying things to revive. There is nothing wonderful in the multiplication of fire, and it is greatly inferior to the power of multiplication inherent in earth. For earth daily produces fresh herbs, while one spark of fire is miraculously enlarged only when it is fed with plenty of combustible matter. Fire and earth are the only elements that are capable of multiplication, and they cause the power of multiplication inherent in our Stone. Of this earth Albertus the Great says, that among all mineral substances lithargyrium (which he describes at some length) is the most suitable for our white Elixir. We will now proceed to discuss the conjunction of the elements; and, on this point, we may lay down the following rules: (1) Combine your elements grammatically, in accordance with their own proper rules. These rules are the principal instruments for aiding the learned in this work: for the two greatest contraries upon earth are fixedness and volatility. All the grammarians of England and France cannot skill to teach you this concord. But this Ordinal can show you where you may learn it, namely, in the book called *De Arbore*. (2) Join them together also after the manner of the rhetorician, with purified and ornate essences. Inasmuch as your tincture must be pure and fair, take pure earth, water, fire, and air. (3) In accordance with logical methods, combine such things as admit of a true and natural union. Many learned men, by neglecting this precept, have lost all their labour and pains. (4) Combine them also arithmetically, in accordance with those subtle natural proportions, of which little was known when Boëthius wrote: "Bind together the elements by numbers." (5) Combine your elements musically, for two reasons: first, on account of melody, which is based on its own proper harmonies. Join them according to the rules which obtain in music in the proportions which produce musical consonance; for these musical proportions closely resemble the true proportions of Alchemy, at least, as far as the more general aspects of our Art are concerned. Its more subtle proportions you must learn from the writings of Raymond and Bacon. Bacon discusses them allusively in his three Epistles. Raymond expounds them more fully in his General Treatise. Many who read his words think that they understand them, but they are deceived. (6) Combine your elements also by means of Astrology, that all their operations may prosper, and that the simple, rude, and unformed substance may, in due course of time, and in the proper order of its development, be brought to perfection through the blessed influences of the Stars. (7) The science of perspective (optics) also affords much help to those who labour in our noble Art; and it is materially advanced by many other sciences, (8) as, for instance, that science which deals with the plenum and the vacuum. But, as far as this Art is concerned, we must regard as the mistress of all sciences, (9) the science of Natural Magic. Now, when the four elements have been wisely combined, and each thing ordered in its own proper degree, then we shall behold in the various stages of coction, a constantly shifting succession of colours, until perfection is attained. For the substance is wrought upon from within by the natural warmth, which is found to exist intellectually in our substance, though it can be neither seen, nor felt, nor handled. Its operation is known only to few. When this inward natural heat is stirred up by the influence of outward artificial heat, Nature, having once been roused into activity, will go on to operate, and produce the various changes which the substance has to undergo; and this is one cause, as the Sages will tell you, why so many colours are seen in our work. Many mistakes arise in the study of this Art through ignorance of the difference between outward and inward heat. In order that you may know how these two kinds of heat ought to aid and stimulate each other, and which of the two ought to predominate in our work, you should be guided by the analogy of animate creation, and more especially by the analogy of the coction which goes on in the human body. It was well said by Morienus, that the generation of our Stone exhibits a wonderful analogy to the creation of man, in whom, says Raymond, the four degrees of the four complexions are found together. On account of the close analogy which exists between the generation of man and that of our Stone, it has been said that there are in this world only two microcosms—man and our Stone.

Now, we have described the conjunction or digestion of the elements, and we proceed to give an account of the nutrition of our substance. There is a solid humour rendered firm by dryness, well mixed in all its degrees; and the passive qualities are generated in due mixture by inward and outward heat. Hence our digestion is nothing but perfection produced out of a substantial humour. You must pardon my using these expressions, which to the unlearned must appear obscure and meaningless; but this Art of Alchemy, like all other arts and sciences, has its own proper terminology, from which it is not safe for me to depart. Digestion is sometimes quickened by outward cold, as you may see from the fact that in winter men take a larger quantity of food than in summer, when their heat is more intense For cold drives heat inward and increases its action, giving it greater virtue and power of digestion than it had before. The digestive quality in our Art is the virtual heat of a digestive organism. Nevertheless, the warmth of a digestible substance is also instrumental in aiding digestion. Fever heat digests nothing. Baths may both aid and cause destruction. Digested (fermented) wine has more natural heat than must. Coagulation is not a substantial form, but only a passive state of some material substance. Moreover, you should know when the colours appear, that the principal agent in the substance is either heat, or cold, or moisture, or dryness. To recognise the principal agent at any given stage requires the practised eye of the Master, and a quick observation of the manner in which the colours arise. The principal agent obtains royal power over the four qualities, and during its temporary predominance assimilates them to its own nature. This change is discussed by Anaxagoras in his book entitled "Natural Conversion," and its *rationale* is also given by Raymond. The discernment of your principal agent is not by any means such a simple matter as you may suppose; I will attempt to teach it you by means of four signs or symptoms, viz., colour, taste, smell, and fluxibility. The colour of your substance may guide you in recognising its principal agent, because that colour which a glance at your vessel exhibits as predominant is caused by that quality which, for the time being, is the principal agent. Of course, you will be able to moderate any excessive action of this principal agent, if you are aware of its nature; and its nature I will now enable you to tell, by giving you an account of the causes whereby the different colours which appear in our Art are produced. Whiteness is the effect of transparency in any object. Blackness arises when the clearness of a dense body is obscured by the thickness of its constituent parts: it is produced out of an earthy substance by combustion, particularly when the heat causes a greater hardness of the atoms. By the mixture of the dense and obscure with the clear and pure, we obtain all the intermediate colours. Any clear and transparent body arises out of the substance of air and water condensed in purified earth which does not destroy their transparency. If in such clear and transparent bodies you do not perceive any special shades of colour, you may confidently conclude that they are the effect of intense cold, as is the case with the crystal, beryl, and other formations which you may thus distinguish from each other: Crystal is aeriform water, and is clear, transparent, and fair; but where the aqueous element predominates, it is more obscure, as in the case of beryl, or ice. Where the substance is essentially dry, it is dense, hard, and obscure, as may be seen in the diamond, and other substances of a like nature. In a clear substance light causes a brilliancy such as we behold in Magnesia; and a watery vapour produced by heat is instrumental in the formation of such bodies. Such are the causes of transparency, and of the extreme colours. As to the intermediate colours, that of the ruby is caused by a thin smoke in a clear body, which happens when much light and brilliancy prevail in such a body; and it is more or less brilliant in proportion to the quantity of light. The amethyst comes next in glory after the ruby, its obscurity being greater, and its transparency less; the shining substance of the chalcedony stands next to beryl. Green, or the colour of the emerald, is formed of pure water, mixed with a burned earthy substance, and the greater the transparency of the earth, the more marked is also the brilliant green of the emerald. Yellow is generated out of water and earth, and has the clearness of air dimmed by the obscurity of black vapour. Grey, or lead colour, is the result of and union of watery and earthy elements, and where these atoms are cold and dense, the grey colour is more intense, as is seen in very old lead; or in persons at the point of death. This colour is called livid, and is frequent in men of an envious disposition. It concentrates the natural colour and the blood in the heart, for the purpose of comforting it, and leaves the face cold and dry, as it has been forsaken by its warmth and blood. In the same way, when fevers have reached an extreme point, the finger nails are of a livid hue. The colour of the sapphire is an orient blue, not unlike that of the celestial firmament, and fairer to behold than the colour of lead, because it contains more air, water, and light. Moreover, the colour of the sapphire is esteemed more precious than other shades of light blue, which are more obscure because they contain more earth and less air. Silver may easily be converted into the colour of the lazulite, because the transparency of the silver, produced by air, has a tendency to become assimilated to the colour of the sky; and the abundance of quicksilver which it contains, causes the brilliancy of the silver, while the splendour of the quicksilver, in its turn, is produced by subtle earth, pure water, and clear air. The orange colour, the shade of yellow which appears in gold, is a pleasing colour, and by many is even considered charming; it is generated by a strong and vigorous digestion, as its aqueous elements are exposed to a high degree of heat, which is seen in honey, urine, gall, and lye. The yellow colour of gold is the product of a pure and subtle water perspicuously condensed. For the more pure water is condensed, the more brilliant it becomes. The cause of a mirror is fixed humidity; and for this reason it is also smooth, because air receives no impressions, and is incapable of confining itself. It is the water which produces its clearness. If pure white and pure red be well mixed, the result is a beautiful orange colour. Thus all the different ways in which the elements may be combined, produce different colours in our substance, according to the different degrees of digestion. Observe well the proper colours of elements, that you may be the better able to judge of colours. Physicians say of certain herbs that they are cold without, and warm within at the root. If you wish for an illustration of this saying, observe the nature of fragrant violets. Common philosophy teaches us that the rose is cold within and red without. Anaxagoras says in his "Natural Changes," that the outward and the inward in all things are of a nature directly opposite to each other; and the rule holds true, except in the case of such things as are very plain and simple in their composition, as, for instance, the scammony and laurel, that do not nourish like vegetables. Bear in mind that in every mixture, one of the elements will strive to obtain the mastery. This insolent and greedy disposition is found in man, as in all things beside. But all sorts and conditions of men are placed on a footing of equality by death, which is God's means of laying low men of high degree, and of showing the vanity of all ambitious thoughts and desires. Kings and beggars find their common level in the grave. It is thus that you must treat your principal agent, if it overleaps the proper bounds of equality. In this sense Aristotle says: "Let there be perfect equality in the composition of your Stone, in order that unprofitable strife may be avoided." Let there be all the colours which we have enumerated, in their proper order, and then suffer Nature to bring about the process of generation in her own way, till among this great variety of colours one is found to predominate, which resembles the colour you are seeking to discover. In this way you may make use of the colours for the purpose of guiding you in this work. I might say much more about colours; but what has been said constitutes a satisfactory fulfilment of my promise, and will teach you how far the various colours may be made to serve your purpose in recognising your principal agent. Many learned men indeed will justly wonder that so great a variety of colours should appear in our Stone before the final stage of permanent and immutable whiteness is reached, seeing that the ingredients seem to be so few and simple. But I will explain the mystery in a few words: Those colours are due to the properties of magnesia, the nature of which is capable of change into any proportion and degree, just as crystal, for instance, exhibits the colour of any substance which is placed under it. Hence it is well and generously said by Hermes that "for performing the miracles of one thing, God has so ordained it that out of one thing all these marvels should spring forth." For this reason common philosophers cannot find this virtuous Stone, because it transcends their comprehension.

The sense of smell will also furnish you with indications whereby you may recognise the predominant element; and, in conjunction with the indications afforded by colour, it will teach you where to look for the principal agent. Now as white and black are the two extremes of colour, so stench and fragrance are the extremes of odour. But as fishes are incapable of distinguishing intermediate colours, because their eyes are without eye-lids and cannot be closed, so we cannot become aware of intermediate odours by the sense of smell, because our nostrils are incapable of being shut, like the eyes of fishes. On this account intermediate odours are not perceived by the nostrils as distinctly as intermediate colours are perceived by the eye. An unpleasant smell is not, in the opinion of the Sages, an intermediate smell, but only one less fetid. Yet they have noted it down in their books as the result of their experience—though I have no experimental knowledge of the fact—that if you mix a sweet and fragrant odour with one of a penetratingly fetid character, the fragrant odour alone is smelt, while the fetid one is imperceptible; and the reason which they allege is that all fragrant things are more pure and spiritual than those which are fetid, and therefore penetrate the air more easily, and, being more grateful to the living organisms and more agreeable to nature, are more readily received than fetid smells. An odour is a vaporous steam dissolved by heat, of a substance resembling an exudation, which penetrates the air freely, and affects it and your sense of smell, as your palate is affected by food, your sense of hearing by sound, and your sense of sight by colour. Four things are required for the perfect apprehension of odours. First, it is necessary that a subtle substance should be affected by the operation of heat, and give out a vaporous similitude of itself, which evaporation must then be dispersed through thin, clear air, and act on the sense of smell. But this odorous vapour is not so readily given out by dense and hard substances which, like our Stone, are not easily affected by heat. Heat quickens odours, cold hinders them; manure is more fetid in summer than in winter. Grateful odours are generated out of a pure and vaporous substance, as in the case of ambergris, nard, and myrrh, which are specially pleasing to women. A pure substance under the influence of gentle heat, gives out moderate odours, such as the fragrance of violets; but when moderate heat acts on an impure substance, the result is a disagreeable odour, such as that of aloes and sulphur. When the natural heat of the substance is diminished, the fact is signalized by a most fetid smell, such as that of decomposed fish. Where a stench is produced by the putrefaction of natural heat, it is a vapour or steam issuing from decaying matter. If the juices only are corrupted, while the substance itself is not destroyed, the stench will be extremely disagreeable, yet not so fetid as in the former case. A putrid smell is caused only by the corruption of the substance itself. When an evil substance is decomposed, it gives out a horrible smell; and putrefying carcases of human beings may often cause a pestilence. The smell of extinguished coals is destructive of health, and may occasion even a mare to miscarry. When the qualities of a substance harmonize with your nature, the odour will be pleasant; but if the substance be of a kind that does not sympathise with your nature, you will be disagreeably affected by the odour. Fishes love sweet smells, as is seen from the fact that they are more easily attracted by a fresh than by a stale bait. All fragrant matters have a corresponding degree of natural heat; and though camphor, roses, and other cold substances emit a pleasant fragrance, yet ancient writers tell us that the purity of their substance is equivalent to, and virtually represents, natural heat. You may take for granted the truth of the old saying, that one pleasant smell does not neutralize another. It is different, however, with fetid odours; for the smell of garlic overpowers that of dung. But now we have said enough for our present purpose about smells, and you will be easily able to tell when putrefaction begins to set in. The sense of smell will also enable you to distinguish between a subtle and a gross substance. You will also have knowledge of an intermediate substance which exhibits the corruption of natural heat, and of the difference between corrupted humour and corrupted substance. But our substance has been highly purified, and is conserved by the mean virtue; wherefore, you must not expect a fetid smell to arise from it, though it putrefies after its own proper kind.

The third sign and test by which you may know your principal agent is called taste, which always causes the diminution of the substance tasted. The test of the palate would be more certain than that of the eye or the nose, if it were not dangerous to taste our Stone, seeing that it is destructive of health and life, so penetrating is its quality; hence it is inexpedient and even dangerous to taste of it too often. It strengthens metals, as we know, but it is hurtful to human beings until the perfect red colour appears, which abides the test of fire. A common labouring man, who had devoted himself to the study of this Art, tasted a small piece of the white Stone in the hope that thereby he would be delivered from all pain and disease, instead of which he was suddenly struck down with the palsy. Him my master speedily cured with mineral Bezoar. Therefore, though the palate be the best judge of the progress which has been made in our Art, yet it is of little practical use, because the taste of our substance is both horrible and hurtful. Nevertheless, certain parts may, without any risk, be tasted before they are joined together, for the purpose of discovering whether the operation has been rightly performed or not. At the same time the skilled artist will be able to discover all he wants to know by the colour and odour. Thus many judge of the quality of good wine, but new wine is best tested by the palate. For the sense of smell has only one organ, and is capable of distinguishing nothing but vaporous steam. The sense of taste, on the other hand, undoubtedly possesses six organs for the perception of material qualities. These organs Nature has ordained for the security and protection of living creatures. The ape tests the wholesomeness of his food by the sense of smell, men and parrots rely upon the verdict of the palate. For many things, though fragrant, touch the palate adversely, and repel by their acidity, bitterness, or sickly and nauseating sweetness; or they are poisonous, corrosive, or too highly seasoned. In all these cases it is unadvisable to appeal for a decision to the sense of taste. The ancient writers have distinguished nine different varieties of taste, viz., acrid, oily, and vinegary (indicative of a subtle substance), biting, salt, watery (characteristic of intermediate substances), bitter, acid, and sweet (inherent in substances of great thickness and density). These nine varieties of taste are of common occurrence: five of them are the product of heat—the oily, the acrid, the salt, the bitter, and the sweet; the remaining four are produced by cold—the sour, the acid, the watery or insipid, and the biting. Taste is determined by two things, viz., by diversities of substance, and diversities of quality. A thick substance is generally found to have a sweet taste; a substance which is moist, thick, and warm, produces an oily taste; while a substance of an intermediate quality, which is both hot and dry, is characterised by a salt or pungent taste. A thick substance, that is both hot and dry, is intensely bitter. A subtle substance, on the other hand, which is also hot and dry, is marked by a harsh and acrid flavour. In this way heat is the source of five different varieties of taste, but not of more. That which is cold and dry in the second degree, and at the same time exhibits a subtle substance, is sour—as you may see by the face which a man makes who has tasted unripe apples. The same qualities in the same degree, united to an intermediate substance, produce, as you may easily suppose, a biting effect upon the palate, as, for instance, the rose. But the acid, less acid, and slightly acid flavours are the results of cold and dryness in different degrees. Cold and humidity in the first degree always produce a watery flavour, as is seen in the whites of eggs and in oysters; for these substances are both cold and humid, and have much superfluous moisture—for which reason they are not greatly relished by the human palate. Isaac says that there are only seven varieties of taste, because the acid and the slightly acid, though different in degree, are yet in reality one and the same flavour, and because the watery or insipid variety simply represents negation of taste. We may also speak of compound flavours, such as bitter-sweet, and others of a like kind. Thus, by means of the palate, men may distinguish substances, qualities, and degrees. But if you do not care to subject our matter to the test of the palate, you may be guided by another class of symptoms, just as in medicine we do not rely upon the signs exhibited by the urine alone, but take them in conjunction with the state of the pulse, and the general condition of the body. He would be an ignorant physician indeed who should compete his diagnosis without availing himself of everything which may help him to a knowledge of the exact nature of the disease. Thus, if you would pursue the study of our Art, you should avail yourself of the indications afforded by the four methods of observation for the purpose of forming a correct judgment. Of three of these methods we have already spoken, the fourth is the fluxibility of the liquid. The liquid is the strength of our substance, and its condition affords the most striking evidence of the progress of the work; moreover, by its means the elements are both combined and dissolved. The liquid joins together the male and the female, and causes the dead to be restored to life. The liquid purges by ablution, and is the principal nutriment of our Stone. Without liquid there is no good food; the liquid carries the aliment to all the different parts of the human living body, and it performs the same function in Alchemy. But you should well consider the purity and the quantity of all your liquids, and also their consistency or thinness: otherwise you will make little progress. Now, because our Elixir needs a twofold preparation, it exhibits more natural marvels than any other substance. Physicians say that the denser and more consistent urine is, the more humidity does it indicate; but with us the thickness betokens dryness, and that which is subtle humidity. Many liquids are needed for our Stone in accordance with its requirements. In the book entitled "The Crowd," Aristeus says: that air is invisibly enclosed in water, which lifts up the earth by its aerial potency. Pythagoras remarks that if the matter were so, it would be a most fortunate circumstance. Plato expresses himself most circumspectly when he calls it (the liquid) "the gentle dropping of dew"; and the words are thoroughly applicable to Alchemy. But in the commonplaces of the primary philosophy it is said that condensed air is changed back into rain, and rarefied water into air. Some say that the month of May is the beginning of the year, when air is condensed into water. Others say that such water descends from the sky till the Sun enters the sign of Scorpio. Others, again, tell us that no liquids should be used that are affected by the cold, because, as the ancient writers state, their activity is chained up by the cold. Some Sages affirm that the liquid which you should employ in preparing the Elixir is milk; another expresses himself in the following mystical words: "No liquid is sufficient for the great work but the water of Litharge, which together with the water of Azoch produces virgin's milk." Democritus, on the other hand, states that the best liquid for the preparation of our Stone is permanent water, which is naturally capable of resisting the action of fire, and of enduring its heat. Rupescissa says that aqua vitæ is the liquid required, because it is spiritual and revivifying in its nature, and because it is the quintessence which restores dead things to life (concerning this quintessence Aristotle writes in his "Book of Secrets" that all perfection is in the fifth part). Rupescissa further calls this aqua vitæ the best of all liquids, for that it renders thick and dense substances spiritual. In the works of Pythagoras you will find our aqua vitæ spoken of in different language. He himself calls it the vivifying principle, and bids us volatilize that which is fixed, and fix that which is volatile, as by this strong method of compulsion the fixed materials will become easy to melt. Others say that the best of all liquids is that which stirs up most desire and love. These are best found near islands, and in places that are washed by the ocean. Certain Sages tell us of yet another liquid which is colder than spring water, and has an icy taste; its quantity, however, is never diminished, nor is its substance consumed, though it is in a state of constant activity in the preparation of our Stone. This water is called by Democritus the "shadowless light," or "the water of the rising Sun." Hermes says that no water is of such paramount importance as the water of crude mercury; "for," he says, "this water holds the high place of being the proper water of Alchemy." Thus, ye who pursue the study of this Art, may know by means of all these liquids our Stone must be perfected. A liquid is a shifting substance, of a watery and unstable nature; and all such things are more subject to lunar influences than those of a firmer structure. Of this every initiated Artist may behold a proof in the preparation of the white Tincture. Liquids wash and purify both extreme and intermediate substances. God created liquids for the use of man and for the cleansing of all impurities. Liquids doubtless possess the power of bringing hidden impurities to the surface of a body, as those will tell you who use this simple means for the purpose of cleansing soiled clothing. Liquids comfort and refresh the parched roots of grass and trees; for all natural liquids have the power of restoring any vital juices which have been lost. Liquids are also useful for the dividing and separating of qualities, and for the resolving of substances into their smallest parts. Liquids further cause the generation of our Stone by the conjunction of many things into one. They assist the fluxibility and motion of many things. Again, you should observe how liquids are to be gained from the different substances which exist on earth. Some are derived through incision, as, for instance, the juice of the terebinth; others, by crushing, as the juice of the grape and of the olive; others again, by distillation, like water; some, by combustion, like colophony; some by dissolution, according to the manner in which women prepare lye; others are produced in other ways; while some owe their origin to natural processes, as, for instance, urine, blood, milk, and sweat. Coagulatory substances, again, are of great use and profit in the making of cheese. In these and many other ways we seek and discover liquids which may be useful to us in the preparation of our glorious Elixir, the most precious Philosopher's Stone, for which we daily bless God's name.

All the liquids that we have enumerated are of a more or less adhesive nature, with the solitary exception of quicksilver, which, though fluxible, will not adhere to any other matters but those in which it finds a sister or brother mixed of the same subtle substance; but with any other liquid it will not mingle, though they, too, are composed of the four elements, as milk contains whey, butter, and cheese. These four elements may be separated and put together again, to the great advancement of your experiment; but the manner in which cheese, butter, and whey are obtained is a simpler subject of investigation than are the liquids which exist in our Stone. Not one of them is simple and uncompounded except water alone. Of the several liquids of our Stone you should understand also the qualities and degrees; for thus you will be able to check the various superfluous activities of the principal agent, if this agent itself be permanent and durable. If the predominant quality be dryness, you may correct it by adding, according to your requirements, a greater or less quantity of humid moisture; and in the same way you may proceed with regard to the other qualities, thus compelling the principal agent to submit to the rule of your will. By the knowledge of the diversity, contrariety, and agreement of qualities, you may judge which quality ought to predominate. You will need great wisdom in so adding and diminishing your liquids that all the ingredients are placed on an equal footing. But do not believe that there is anything which has the qualities of heat and moisture in the same degree; for all that maintain the existence of two qualities of this kind, are deceived in their opinion, whoever they be. The commonplaces of philosophy, which set forth this proposition, are not true. Have done with this idea, and let a new one take its place in your mind. For all the ancient writers who have asserted that these two qualities could exist in the same degree, have been mistaken, or they have done so simply for the purpose of preventing enquirers from discovering the secret method of tempering the elements. Hence he who does not know graduations cannot be perfect in our work, seeing that God has allotted to each thing its own proper measure. Without due measurement of time no one can sing correctly; he who errs in the measurement of time, errs in the very essence of the singer's Art—and all that err inflict a wrong on Nature. Consider also that the purer your medium is, the greater will be the perfection which arises out of it. The media embrace the most important part of the virtue and potent essences of our Art. For the solid cannot become fluxible, nor the liquid firm, in the gradual process of preparing our substance, without the help of intermediate substances which partake of the nature of both the extremes. It is thus that, by means of a treble spirit, the soul is joined to the human body; of these three spirits one is called the vital spirit, the other the natural spirit, and the third the animal spirit. Let me also tell you where these spirits dwell. The vital spirit has his habitation in the heart; the natural spirit, according to the ancient writers, abides in the liver, while the animal spirit sojourns in the brain. Now, so long as these three spirits maintain a sound state of health in the human body, the soul dwells in the body without any jarring disagreements, and life is sustained. But when these spirits are unable to abide in man, the soul is also compelled to forsake the body. For the subtle, pure, and immortal soul can never dwell with the gross body, except the spirits act as media between them. In our work we ought also to distinguish between body, soul, and spirit; and our intermediate substances are the spirit which joins the body and soul together by. partaking of the nature of both. Nature has no other way of binding extremes together except by intermediate substances, and these intermediate substances (media) are of different kinds. After all these things you should also know the seven circulations of each element, which agree with the number of the seven planets, and they are known to none except by grace Divine. Certain Sages of great learning tell us that these circulations are nine in number; and perhaps it is safer for us to follow their teaching. Nevertheless, the newest inventions made by modern philosophers, whose assertions are exalted beyond the possibility of doubt, enable us to dispense with two. Some learned men think that they may avoid every risk of a mistake if they go on in due order from fire to air, from air to water, and from water to earth, thus moving downward from that which is most exalted to that which is lowest; and they adduce in support of their assertion the alleged fact that air is the food of fire. But, believe me, this kind of circulation is nothing but one method of rectification, which tends more to separation and correction than to transmutation. Moreover, the favourite food of fire, its own proper nutriment and fuel, is not air but earth, as both fire and earth are dry, and heat depends for its very existence on dryness, while the nature of air, on the other hand, is more humid. Yet it is also true that fire cannot operate without air, since the hand of God has linked together the elements in a bond of mutual dependence, which will not suffer them to be disunited by any human contrivance or device. Of this fact you may find an illustration in trumpets, where, after the ascent of air, you may often observe a deposit of water, the occurrence of which can only be explained on the supposition of the mutually inclusive nature of the elements. But our circulation begins with fire, the most exalted of all elements, and ends with water, which of all elements is the most unlike to fire. Another circulation begins with air and ends with earth. From earth to fire, thence to pure water, thence again to fire, and after this to a 'mean, passing to earth, finally once more recurring to fire—by such circulations, the Red Tincture is perfected. Other circulations are more suitable for the production of the White Tincture. Now every circulation has its own proper time, according to the facility or difficulty of its execution. For as one planet is heavier and slower than another, so some circulations that are performed by the Sages take up a space of thirty weeks, while other circulations require a much shorter period of time; just as some planets are lighter and swifter than others. Thus, after all the gross and crude operations have been performed, our work may often still require twenty-six weeks. Ignorance of this fact has deceived many, and caused them to give up their labour at a point where the Sages are wont to begin. Other inexperienced students of this Art have imagined that it can be accomplished in forty day's. They do not know that in Art as well as in Nature everything has its own time, and its own proper method. The elephant, for instance, being a huge and unwieldy animal, extends its period of gestation over two years, and is fifty years old before it can bring forth young. Anaxagoras says, in his "Considerations," that the generation of the metals requires a thousand years, and that, in comparison to that period of time, our work occupies only a single day. You must therefore conduct your operation in a very subtle manner when you see the earth rise above the water; for as the earth which we tread with our feet supports the water, so, in our Art, you should frequently cause a gentle spring of water to well forth, in order that the same may flow softly, seeing that a violent outpour is positively hurtful. Moreover, the student of Alchemy should be aware of the effects of the seven waters, concerning which you must seek instruction in the books of others; for you cannot expect me to expound our whole system in this brief treatise.

Some think that by means of these waters they can correct all metallic imperfections, and can find the effects of the four elements; for they are confident that all requisite properties are discovered in these waters, not only for the purpose of softening hard metals, but also for hardening those which are too soft, purifying them, and rendering them malleable. For the attainment of each one of these objects, the knowledge of these waters is said to be indispensable. Otherwise our Stone would not receive its proper nourishment. The ancient writers call our Stone a microcosm; and there can be no doubt that its composition greatly resembles that of the world in which we live, consisting as it does of elements, hot, cold, moist, and dry, hard, soft, light, and heavy, rough, smooth, fixed, volatile, and fluxible; and also because, in spite of the manifold variety of its component parts, it is not many things, but one thing. The transmutation of metals implies a change, not only of colour, but also of substance. The elements of the substance which undergoes a change must become the elements of the substance into which it is to be changed, and impress upon it their own character. All transmuted parts must be proportionately impressed in the transmuting elements, so that the thin elemented matter may permanently possess the substance of the one and the virtue of the other. As soon as a child is born, it can feed and cry; and so our Stone, when first prepared, has abundant power of imparting its colour to other substances. Again, as after three years the child walks and talks, so after a certain lapse of time, our Stone receives a still more intense power of colouring, so that it can pervade with its own glorious nature a substance of a thousand times its own size. To this fact I myself can bear witness: for many a time have I seen well-purged metals transmuted into the finest silver and gold. Thus, our Stone may go on growing in quantity, and becoming more excellent in quality, during an infinite period of time; and in this respect it bears a marvellous analogy to the birth and growth of human beings. I must, however, take this occasion to state a truth which may be displeasing to some readers. The time when you first succeed in preparing your Stone should be well and wisely used, or you may even then lose all your pains, and miss your recompense for all the heavy outlay you have undergone.

For the purpose, then, of augmenting your Stone, you should at once divide it into two equal parts, carefully testing the correctness of your division by means of the balance. One-half is for the Red Tincture, and the other moiety for the White. Then, and not till then, will you begin to reap the profits of your labours. But it will be unadvisable to stop even here, seeing that you may go on augmenting your Tincture indefinitely. Miriam, the sister of Aaron, rightly says that life is short, and knowledge long; nevertheless, our Tincture, when it has once attained to the highest perfection of its excellence, has the virtue of greatly retarding old age. Some of our Sages have been so foolish as to give up the further improvement of our Stone at a point when they might have reached the final goal with little trouble and great advantage to themselves. This supine carelessness can only be explained by assuming that they were not aware of the full virtue of that Stone; and I see that I must point out to all its fortunate owners the full extent of their possession. For when I shall have departed out of this world, this testimony will remain behind as a witness, and on this account I am not slow to reveal the secrets of the Art, so far as I may do it without prejudice to my vow. I have instructed you with sufficient clearness how to prepare the White Tincture. But when my master had declared all these things to me, he said that many students have by patient and unwearied diligence independently discovered this our White Stone and Tincture, as if they had derived their knowledge from the wisest of masters; but that scarce one in fifteen kingdoms possesses our Red Stone. With these words, he fixed upon me a steady and unfaltering gaze, and he saw that his speech had clouded my countenance with sorrow. I answered: "Alas, what shall I do? for I love knowledge far beyond all earthly wealth; moreover, the Red Tincture is said to be a most precious substance, which has the virtue of prolonging life. I should account the Red Stone a more glorious acquisition than all the gold of the whole world." He replied that I was still a young man, and that youth was prone to insolence and excess. Could I expect to be enrolled among the Sages at the immature age of twenty-eight? I must be a much older man before I could expect to have this secret unfolded to me. "Alas, good master," I said, "though my body is still young and my years are few, I beseech you to prove me, and you will see that my mind has already attained the ripeness of mellow age." My master said no more at the time, but I soon found that he was trying and testing my character by a course of probationary training, after the manner of the Sages—of which it would be both tedious and indiscreet to publish a lengthy account. Finally, however, by the grace of God, he accounted me worthy of this wonderful proof of his love and esteem, and imparted to me the true secret of preparing the Red Tincture. To inquire into the manner of its preparation would be an aimless quest before the White Tincture has been prepared. Both Medicines are composed from the same substance, in the same vessel; and by the same methods, until the living matters have been mortified. Then the material and shape of the vessel, and the degree of chemical treatment, must be changed. But my heart beats violently, and my hands tremble, when I speak of this glorious thing. Hermes said a true word when he exclaimed: "Fire and Azoth are sufficient." The expositor of Hermes and Aristotle, in the treatise appended to their works, makes a most startling assertion, when he says that Albertus Magnus, and Bacon, the Minorite friar, had no knowledge of the manner in which the Red Stone is multiplied by augmentation. This writer was well aware what he was saying, as my master proved to me by incontrovertible arguments. I myself have never actually prepared the Red Tincture as yet, because I was disheartened by being robbed of my whole wealth of chemical materials and implements—as I set forth at length in a preceding chapter. But I understand the method of its preparation perfectly, and am able to explain it to others. Those who have ventured to unfold this grand arcanum to their disciples say that the redness of this delectable Stone is contained in its whiteness, and may be brought out, and made to appear to the Artist's ravished gaze by the gently compelling heat of fire. Pandophilus, in "The Crowd" tells us that the white Tincture is the type and shadow of the red; and Miriam confirms his words by saying that the redness is concealed in the whiteness. An admirable book entitled *Laudabile Sanctum*, ascribed to Hermes, uses the following expression of the Red Tincture: "There lies the snowy wife wedded to her red spouse." That is to say, in the white Tincture you have a beautiful woman of snowy whiteness espoused to a red husband. If your white Stone is exposed to the heat, and through the action of the fire becomes red as blood, then the marriage is valid and perfect—as in the act of copulation, if it be fruitful, the male seed obtains the ascendancy, and assimilates the female seed to its own nature. That this fact is so, those who have observed the nature of the embryo have been taught by experience. When this has been brought about, our Stone is perfected. The Sages say that it should be nourished with its own poison till it has had enough. When this has been done, you may go wherever you like, for it will defray all your expenses. Thus, then, I have expounded to you the subtle part of the work with all its appurtenances, and more I need not, cannot, and will not, reveal.

CHAPTER VI.

With respect to concords, let me say that there should be no serious difference between those things which ought to agree For difference produces discord, and discord would make all your labour of none effect. Whoever wishes to practise our Art, should be guided by five rules or concords. The first rule to be observed is, that the student's mind should be in perfect harmony with his work. The desire of knowing this Art should hold a dominant place in his mind; else all his labours will come to nothing. The second concord is, that he should know the difference between this Art and those who profess it. The third kind of harmony is that which should exist between the work and the instruments. The fourth concord assigns to the work the place which is most suited to its execution. The fifth concord is the sympathy which should exist between your work and the celestial sphere. I will say something about each one of these five rules, and begin with the first. Few students possess the gift of perseverance. They are in a great hurry and the work seems too long. They wish you to do violence to Nature, and the zeal of some is so much like a straw fire that at the end of six months it has quite burned down. Many change their minds after a week, some after twenty-four hours. Some believe in our Art most fervently for a month; but at the end of the month they will have nothing more to do with it. For such persons it would be better to stay their hands at once than to waste their time with the study of our Art Let these butterflies flutter whither they will. But let us, before we put our hands to this work, learn with our hearts the truth of the saying; "Let us do everything from beginning to end strenuously, and yet softly and gently." All foolish and double-minded people must necessarily be fickle and unstable; and it is natural that simple folk, who have been stripped of all their savings by heartless impostors, should conceive a deep-seated aversion to our Art. But only men of constant and persevering minds are fitted to be students thereof. If any such man undertakes the study of this science, whether he be a layman or a priest, a merchant, a knight, an abbot, or a gentleman, he is not likely to fail of success: for his mind is in harmony with his work. The second concord to which attention must be paid in the pursuit of this Art, is the securing of fit and suitable assistants. No assistant should be chosen that is not sober, discreet, and diligent, faithful, vigilant, a keeper of secrets, and a pure liver; a man of clean hands and of a delicate touch, obedient and humbly content to carry out your orders. Such ministers alone will give close heed to your work, and secure you against all avoidable accidents. Do not imagine, however, that two or three of these will be sufficient for the completion of your experiment. If the quantity of your substance be moderate, eight such servants will be required, but if the quantity be small, the work may be done by four. Of this number, one half should be on duty, while the other half sleep, or are at church; for this experiment cannot be brought to a successful termination, unless it is continually attended to, by night as well as by day; and with the exception of the Sabbath, your men should relieve each other in the morning and in the evening. While they are on duty, they should carefully eschew every wicked word and deed; otherwise your work will most certainly be marred. For this reason your assistants ought either to be all men or all women, and persons of both sexes ought not to be set to work together. If your assistants are members of your own family, you should seek to inspire them with love for the work, and interest in its success; for nothing is more important than that the hearts of your workers should be in their work. Our third rule was, that the instruments should be of a kind suited to the labour to be performed. This rule is not fully apprehended by many students of our science. It means that the different parts of the experiment require their own proper utensils, of a substance and shape closely adapted to the particular purpose which they are intended to serve. The divisions and separations of our substance are best carried out in small vessels; a broad vessel is required for humectation, while the process of circulation demands a vessel of still larger capacity. Those used for precipitation should be long; those which you employ for the purpose of sublimation may be both short and long, while narrow vessels, four inches high, are more appropriate in the process of correction. Some vessels are made of lead, and some of dead clay. Dead clay is that which has been carefully hardened, and having been mixed with sand and gravel, is capable of sustaining a high degree of fierce heat. Other kinds of clay burst when exposed to the fire, and you should reject vessels made of them. Other vessels, again, are made of stone, and endure the test of heat admirably; but vessels of this kind, which are both impervious to water and proof against fire, are now very rarely to be obtained in England; but where they can be had, they are invaluable for our purpose. All other vessels are made of glass, and are admirably adapted to prevent the volatile substance from escaping. In our country they are made of ashes and siliceous material, but elsewhere of little stones. The best kind of glass for our purpose is that made of cinders which have been left to glow in the hearth all night; a still harder and more durable kind is prepared out of smelted glass sherds. What has been said will guide you in selecting the most suitable kind of vessel; as to its form or shape you must consult your own common sense: it is. however, clear that you should, in this case, as in all others, strive to follow as closely as possible in the footsteps of Nature. Moreover, the size and shape of your vessel should be in proportion to the quantity of your substance, and to all the other conditions of the experiment. The general principles which should determine your choice are well laid down by Albertus Magnus in his book on "Minerals." The whole secret was disclosed in a few words by my master, when he said: "If God had not given us a vessel, His other gifts would have been nothing worth—and that vessel is glass." Some other instruments are also needed, such, for instance, as suitable furnaces. The ancients describe a special furnace for use in every stage of our Art, devised differently according to the bent of their minds. Many of these, however, are quite unsuitable, some being too broad, others too high, and others out of harmony with the requirements of Nature. Some of the furnaces described in these books may be used, but by far the greater number ought to be rejected, seeing that they' are the inventions of men who only appeared to be, but were not really, Sages. Of the furnace which can be most highly recommended, you will find a pictorial representation in this volume. One which was unknown to the Ancients, I am proud to call my own invention. I set it up, in the first instance, at a very considerable outlay. But its advantages more than make good its cost. It is so constructed that sixty different chemical operations, for which divers kinds of heat are required, may be carried on in it at the same time, and a very small fire of only a foot square supplies a sufficient degree of heat for all these processes. As all may not be sure of this instrument, it has not been represented in a picture. Another furnace will serve for sixty or more glasses, each of them standing in the same degree of heat, as you may see by the picture. I have also invented another furnace, which is of great use in the work of separation, exaltation, and disjunction or division, and is most 'admirably adapted for the processes of ablution or purging, desiccation, and preparation. These six operations may with great ease be performed in it at the same time, and one fire suffices for them all. But it is a new invention, and I cannot afford to describe it more minutely. might also set down a description of another furnace, which is more dangerous than all the rest. It was constructed by the Ancients for the preparation of our Magnesia; and they said that while it could not with impunity be touched for fear of the flame which rose from the wood, yet a linen rag might be placed on it without being scorched. This ingeniously constructed furnace I was fortunate enough to re-invent, and with its aid I was enabled to perform many wonderful experiments. This furnace and its structure must remain a secret for some years longer; but let me warn you, in conclusion, to be very careful in the selection and structure of your furnace. It must be so arranged as to enable you to regulate the supply of heat, and to abate the fierceness of the flame at any moment. If a man does not understand and know the use of his tools and instruments, all his work will be done in a casual, haphazard manner, and it will be impossible for him to anticipate success with any degree of certainty. Therefore, let me once more repeat my warning: See to your instruments, and test their quality before you set about your work. The fourth rule is also most important. The experiment cannot succeed unless it be performed in a suitable place. Some places must be always dry, free from air and excess of light such as is caused by the bright rays of the sun. Others cannot be too much illuminated. The places more fitted for other parts of the work, are humid and cold. But violent draughts should be carefully avoided throughout. Hence a spot must be wisely chosen to fulfil all the requirements of the different parts of the work. The Sages tell us, in their enigmatic style, that our substance should be prepared within nine bars. Astrologers say that it is a singular mark of Divine grace if a man can find the right place for our work. For many things produce wonderful effects in some places, but are entirely barren of results in others; and opposite consequences are often produced by the same thing in different places. The explanation of these facts is to be found in the knowledge that different places are differently influenced by the celestial bodies, just as a magnet, for instance, affects a needle differently in different latitudes. For this reason the Sages have declared that some places are well, and others ill, suited to our work. But the very worst of all possible places are those which have been defiled by lechery.

The fifth rule is well known to the learned. There should exist a certain harmony between the celestial spheres and our work. Nothing on earth is so simple or so easily influenced as the elements of our Stone; and when they are being prepared they obey their own proper constellations, as the needle yields to the influence of the magnet. Let this amicable concord prevail, then, in a direct and fiery ascendent, and let your happy and favourable ascendent be in fortunate aspect with his Lord. The work should be sheltered from all adverse and evil influences; if these cannot beset aside, let them have a trine aspect. When you prepare the White Tincture, let the Moon be fortunate, as also the Lord of the Fourth House, which is the Treasure of Hidden Things, according to the old Sages. The Sixth House must be favourable for the servants. Preserve your work from all great impediments, and see that it be not affected by the adverse constellation of your Nativity. The virtue of the mover of the orb is the formal influence; the virtue of the eighth sphere is instrumental to it; the virtue of the planet is proper and special; and that of the elements is material, and embodies the working of the other agents. The first resembles the genius of the operator; the second is analogous to his hands; the third corresponds to his instruments; and the fourth answers to the substance which is prepared. Let the things on earth correspond to things in heaven, and you will obtain the Elixir, and become a great Master. Do not trust to Geomancy, which is a superstitious Art; nor to all Astrologers, because this science is secret; like that of Alchemy. Necromancy God forbids, and the Church condemns; therefore, if you wish for success, let your hands be pure from all superstitious practices. Necromancy is of the Devil, and a lying Art. God will bless you if you give yourself wholly to the study of our own Blessed Art. In the next chapter I will speak about the regulation of the fire.

CHAPTER VII.

Would you know the perfect Master? It is he who understands the regulation of the fire, and its degrees. Nothing will prove to you so formidable an impediment as ignorance of the regimen of heat and fire; for our whole Art may be looked upon as being concentrated in this one thing, seeing it is all important for the proper development of our substance that the degree of heat which is brought to bear on it should be neither too great nor too small. In regard to this point many learned men have gone grievously astray. (1) The degree of heat which is employed for the scalding of pigs and geese, is that which we require for our decoction of intermediate minerals, and for the purpose of covering the Litharge with sweat. (2) The degree of heat which is sufficient for drying thin linen is good for our air in thirty operations; for the purpose of division you may employ the degree of heat used by cooks in roasting meat. (3) A similar degree of heat with a circular fire will be found useful for the separation of the dividents. (4) But for the circulation of the elements you will require white heat, which must be maintained at an even temperature, without either increase or diminution, until the whole operation is accomplished. Moreover, there ought not to be in this fire any moisture that can be perceived by the touch, or seen with the eye. (5) There also is such a thing as a moist fire, though the expression sounds like a contradiction in terms. This fire should be used at a certain stage of the work, in order to remove the substances which adhere to the sides of the vessel. The same degree of heat is also employed to dilute thick substances. The Sages declare that, in its highest degree, it causes and generates an even dryness, and that its effect here coincides with that of dry heat in the first degree. (6) There is also another fire which is employed for the purpose of drying substances steeped in moisture. (7) Another variety of fire is that of conservation, because by its operation all things are parched up. (8) In the preparation of Magnesia we use the effusion of fire, which is full of danger, not only to the work, but also to the Master, who may even lose his life by its noxious effects. For this reason you should carefully protect your mouth, ears, eyes, and nose, as the smoke of this fire is ten times more baneful than poison. By neglecting this caution many students have sustained considerable injuries. (9) A corrosive fire answers the purpose of judiciously separating kindred elements. One moment of excess, one moment of premature diminution, may mar the labour of months. He that regulates the fire aright is worthy of being hailed as a great Master of the Fire. It is exceedingly difficult to tell the exact degree of heat which any given fire will produce; and here the sense of sight is the only reliable test. No sound or intelligible directions can be given in writing: the only schoolmistress that can impart to you a thorough knowledge of this branch of our Art is experience. It is in regard to this variety of heat that Anaxagoras says: "Nobody is all at once an accomplished Sage." (10) The next kind of heat is of a consuming fierceness. It is employed to smelt very hard minerals. It cannot be too fierce or powerful, even though it may occasionally be necessary to keep it up for some length of time. (11) The next variety of heat is that of calcination, and is used for the purging of impure metals, the essential qualities of which would be impaired by smelting. (12) The kind of heat used for sublimation comes next, and by its means volatile minerals may be sublimed. (13) The last variety of heat is the most important of all. It should be employed at the time of the projection of our Stone. But experience is a good teacher, and I will say no more, except that he who makes a mistake at this point, must begin the work over again.

I have now told you all things as plainly as if I had been describing to you the way to this or that town. I have, as it were, named every county, river, bridge, and village that has to be passed, and, with this my guide-book in his hand, a judicious traveller may easily find his way. A wise and intelligent man may, by means of this Book, discover the secret of our science; for the foolish and dull-witted it was not intended, and it will not teach them anything. Our Science is the height of earthly knowledge, and is to be attained by neither Pope nor Emperor through their rank, influence, or power, but only by virtue, and by Divine grace. Our Stone cannot be discovered or perfected unless it be sought with intense devotion. In the works of the Ancients, understood in the light of this my Ordinal, the truth of the matter is fully set forth; the present Book, in particular, was written for the purpose of resolving all your doubts; here everything is in its proper place, and nothing is wanting. Time was when I would cheerfully have paid down a thousand pounds for the contents of this volume; and this last chapter I would not have missed for three hundred pounds.

Do not wonder, Masters and Friends, that our Science is here so plainly expounded: I set pen to paper with the requirements of the common people in view. For just because the vulgar are not instructed in this knowledge, infinite wealth is annually wasted in this country, as all Sages know, and many others of all ranks are daily reduced to beggary. Study our Art, then, ye uninstructed, and scorn to abide in fatuous ignorance. It is better for you to take to this study late than never.

Let all that are benefitted by the reading of this Ordinal offer up prayers for my soul, and for the living and the dead.

In the year of our Lord 1477 this Book was begun.

Glory be to God!

THE TESTAMENT

OF

CREMER,

<small>ABBOT OF WESTMINSTER. AND BROTHER OF THE
BENEDICTINE ORDER.</small>

A TETRASTICH ON THIS WORK.

By M. M.

"Either the meaning of the Author or the letter of his writings is deceitful. Be on your guard, therefore. Everywhere a serpent lurks among the flowers. Yet scorn not a friend who spoke as plainly as he might. Beneath the shadowy foliage of words is concealed the golden fruit"

"OF"

"TRUTH."

THE TESTAMENT

OF

CREMER, THE ENGLISHMAN,

ABBOT OF WESTMINSTER, AND FRIAR OF THE BENEDICTINE ORDER.

I HAVE attempted to give a full and accurate account of Alchemy without using any of those obscure technical terms, which have proved so serious a stumbling-block in the way of many students of this Art. I am here describing my own experience during the thirty years which I spent and wasted in perusing the writings of authors whose whole ingenuity seemed to have been concentrated upon the Art of expressing thought in unintelligible language. The more I read the more hopelessly I went astray, until Divine Providence at length prompted me to undertake a journey to Italy, and caused me to be accepted as a disciple by that noble and marvellously learned Master Raymond, with whom I remained for a long time. In his eyes I found such favour that he not only unfolded to me a partial knowledge of this Great Mystery, but at my most earnest entreaty, accompanied me to this island of England, and lived with me here two years. During his stay he thoroughly instructed me in the whole secret of the work. Subsequently, I introduced my noble master to his most gracious Majesty King Edward, who received him kindly and honourably, and obtained from him a promise of inexhaustible wealth, on condition that he (the King) should in person conduct a Crusade against the Turks, the enemies of God, and that he should thenceforward refrain from making war on other Christian nations. But, alas, this promise was never fulfilled, because the King grossly violated his part of the contract, and compelled my dear master to fly beyond the seas, with sorrow and grief in his soul. My heart still burns within me when I think of the unjust treatment which he received, and I have no more earnest longing than once more to behold his bodily presence. For the model of his daily life, and the purity and integrity of his mind, would move the most inveterate sinner to repentance.

In the meantime, rest assured, most blessed Raymond, that I and my brethren day by day pour out our prayers before God on your behalf. All wisdom is derived from God, and ever ends in Him. Any one who desires knowledge should ask it of Him, for he gives liberally, and without upbraiding. The height and the depth of all knowledge, and the whole treasure of wisdom are given unto men of God, because in Him, and to Him, and through Him are all things, and nothing can happen without His will. In beginning my discourse I invoke the help of Him Who is the source and origin of all good things. May the bright light of His Spirit shine in my heart, and guide me into all truth; also enabling me to point out to others the true path of Knowledge! May this prayer be granted by Him who is enthroned on High, and rules and governs all things, world without end! Amen.

"In the Beginning was the Word. . . . . .full of grace and truth."

Prayer.

Holy Lord, Almighty Father, Eternal God, deign to bless and sanctify the fire which we unworthy men, by invocation of Thy only-begotten Son our Lord Jesus Christ, presume to bless. Hallow it, most gracious God, with Thy benediction, and let it tend to the good of the human race, through our Lord Jesus Christ.

Good Lord, Creator of the Red Light,
Who dividest the times by certain seasons,
When the Sun vanishes, fearful Chaos comes again:
Oh Christ, restore the light to Thy faithful people!

Though Thou hast studded heaven's floor with stars,
And inlaid it with the bright lamp of the Moon,
Yet Thou dost teach us also to strike light out of flints,
And to fan it into life out of the stone-born spark.

Thou art the true light of the eyes, and the light of the senses;
A mirror Thou art of things without and of things within.
Accept this light which I bear, ministering,
Tinged with the unction issued from the peace-bearing virgin.

To Thee we come, great Father, thro' Thine only Son,
In whom Thy glory visibly shines forth,
And through Him, the Blessed Comforter,
Whom Thou didst send forth from Thy great heart.

In whom Thy Brightness, Honour, Light, and Wisdom,
Majesty, Goodness, and Mercy
Dwell with us throughout the Ages,
And draw us up to the Fountain of Light. Amen.

CHAPTER I.

How to prepare the living water which constitutes the life of our Art.

Take three oz. of tartar of good claret, strong and pure. Add to it five oz. of Petroleum, two oz. of living sulphur, two oz. of orange-coloured Arsenic, three oz. of Rabusenum, two oz. of willow charcoal. Mix and distil all these ingredients in the "Bath of Neptune," in a well-stoppered glass jar. Let this jar be about one cubit high, and carefully closed to prevent any of the spirits or smoke from evaporating. When you see it turn of a pale colour, take it out of the furnace, and let it cool. You ought to be able to prepare it in about four days. Be careful not to inhale its smell, for it is deadly poison. This water should be kept in a stout well-stoppered glass jar, and used according to the directions given in the following chapters.

The *other water* should be twice distilled out of the urine of an unpolluted youth of eighteen; if he be polluted, the water will have no vitality.

CHAPTER II.

Take the water of an unpolluted youth after his first sleep for three or four nights, until you have three pints. Put it each night into a well-stoppered stone jar; remove the sediment. Strain out one pint of the thinnest and purest part of the liquid. Add two glasses of very strong vinegar, two oz. of quicklime, half-an-ounce of the "living water," of which the preparation has been described above. Put the mixture into an earthen pot, and place over it an alembic or distilling vessel, rendered airtight with clay. Let it stand one day and one night before you put it on the fire. Then expose it to gentle heat, and let it distil continually for five or six days and nights. Thus let it flow by drops; carefully lute your glass receptacle so that neither spirit nor smoke may escape, and when the liquor distilling assumes a blue or pallid colour, then abstract nothing further.

CHAPTER III.

Smelt eight oz. of clear, hard iron ore, having no blemishes, in three or four parts, over a fierce charcoal fire; extinguish it with so much of the Virgin water described in the second chapter as may be necessary for the purpose. Then take three oz. of tin, heat it for a short time in the fire, and steep it in the Virgin water. Pound the iron ore and the tin very small on a marble tablet, and when it begins to cool feed it with some of the water aforesaid. Pour the whole into a narrow-necked glass bottle, and seal it up with lead. Put it in a safe place, and in October you should fill a water-tight box (about one yard in height) with fresh horse dung, and thrust your glass vessel into it. Next to the bottle let there be a layer of unslaked quick-lime. Shut the lid of the box closely, and never look at the mixture but at the time of the full moon. Its colours will continue to change until it becomes fixed and hardened. Then it is precipitated towards the bottom of the vessel. When it has been in the box twelve weeks, it should be quite black. You may then take it out, and keep it till the twentieth day of March, when it should be once more pounded small, according to the directions given below.

CHAPTER IV.

About the fifteenth day of March take three oz. of quicksilver, and add to it half-an-oz. of "living water." Pass the quicksilver five times through a strainer purged with lye and well dried. Melt two pounds of lead, and pour it into a pot. When it becomes liquid, thrust into it a thin round skewer, and when the lead is still warm, but already fixed, remove the skewer, and pour in the quicksilver instead. When the whole mass has cooled turn it out on a slab of marble, pour some oil over it, pound it small, divide it into three parts, mix each with small pilules of soot. Leave them in a closely sealed vessel for eight days, stamp them to powder, and nourish this powder with a liquid compounded in equal proportions of vinegar and "Virgin water." Put the soft paste which must thus be formed into a high glass distilling vessel. Close up the upper part of the vessel with clay, and tie it up with a piece of leather or parchment. Then plunge it into a wooden box, containing glowing coals of juniper wood and oak, and a twentieth part of iron filings. To test the degree of the fire before inserting the vessel put in it a piece of dry paper. If it catches alight the fire is not too hot, but if the thin shreds which remain of the paper after burning are also consumed, then the heat is excessive, and the door must be opened till the temperature lowers; when it has become properly warm, carefully add to it a spoonful of "living water" (described in the first chapter). But take care that the still is only three-quarters covered with the coals, in order that you may, whenever the moon is full, be able quickly to remove the cover, and see how the work is progressing. Whenever you perform this, add a spoonful of "living water." At first the colour of the mixture should be black; afterwards it will become white, and will pass through various changes of colour. When the mixture turns solid or fixed, its colour should be red of a somewhat dark tinge, and it should also be saline and heavy, no longer flowing or bubbling up towards the top of the vessel. It ought to be treated in the manner suggested for forty weeks, beginning on the twenty-fifth of March. By the end of this period the mixture will have become so hard as to burst the vessel. When this happy event takes place, the whole house will be filled with a most wonderfully sweet fragrance; then will be the day of the Nativity of this most blessed Preparation. Remember, that the iron box with the coals ought to be enclosed in another wooden box, of which the object is to preserve the compound from the noxious influences of the air.

CHAPTER V.

Take two pounds of pure and soft lead, two pounds of pure tin, and melt them in the above-mentioned well-covered clay jar. Place the whole on a wood fire, and keep it in a moderate blaze for three hours. Remove the "foam" of the metallic ore, till the whole mixture is pure and transparent, then add to it a fourth part of an ounce of the Red Stone powdered. Stir it gently with an iron spoon until the whole mass turns red. Leave the jar for seventy-two hours, and during the last three hours expose it once more to the gentle heat of a blazing wood fire. While it is still liquid you can mould it into any shape you please; when it hardens you have before your eyes the Consummation of the whole work. Mind you lift up your hands in grateful prayer to the Giver of all good gifts. So be it.

CHAPTER VI.

How to prepare a fire proof clay jar in which to melt the metal.

Take well-tempered potter's clay, or the white earth which is called Taxonium; mix it with a tenth part of horse dung. When the jar has been formed, and is half dried, cover it with thin filings of red or caldarium copper and fine powder of red arsenic. When it is quite dry, smear all its lower part with saltpetre dissolved for twelve hours in the "living water" of our first chapter.

How to prepare the Clay.

Make the "clay" which you are to use for stopping up your vessel and keeping it air-tight, of bitumen, or quicklime mastic, and the white of eggs, well mixed with a little white Armenian bolus. Let your petroleum be clear, pure, and yellow. Your Rabusenum should be clear, and of a bright vermilion.

It is my wish that Brother Alexander, and Richard, of this our Monastery, should copy this Testament in the name of the Most Blessed Trinity, and preserve it carefully.

In the first place, let them diligently keep the secret from all greedy and nefarious persons, and reveal it to none but the Abbot and Prior, for the time being, of our Monastery. Nor should it be made known to them until they have sworn on the four Gospels that they will not reveal it to any men in power, or to any of the inferior brethren of our Monastery.

Moreover, it is my wish that the Art be not actually exercised in this our Monastery, except to save it from penury and ruin—a contingency which is not likely to happen, seeing that I leave to it so great a treasure of precious metals. I also enjoin upon you who are in authority in this house, to wit, the Abbot and Prior, to have this my last will and testament copied once in every sixty years, in order that it may not become illegible, either through the ravages of time, or through a change in the form of those written characters which render man's thought permanent.

Furthermore, I command you not to betray the secret of the preparation of the Red Dragon's Blood, or the quantities of substances required, or the manner of their treatment, or the time when the work should be taken in hand, to any human soul, except to the persons named above; and I adjure you to keep and preserve intact, inviolate, and unbroken the trust committed to you, in the Name of the Father, the Son, and the Holy Spirit, as you will one day have to answer me before the judgment seat of Christ. Whoever does not observe this my mandate, let his name be blotted out from the Book of Life.

Magnesia is the smelted ore of iron. When the mixture is still black it is called the Black Raven. As it turns white, it is named the Virgin's Milk, or the Bone of the Whale. In its red stage, it is the Red Lion. When it is blue, it is called the Blue Lion. When it is all colours, the Sages name it Rainbow. But the number of such names is legion: and I can only mention these few. Moreover, they were only invented for the purpose of confounding the vulgar, and hiding this mystery from the simple. Whenever you meet with a book full of these strange and outlandish terms and names, throw it aside at once: it will not teach you anything.

Rabusenum is a certain red substance and earth coming forth with water, which flows out of minerals, and is brought to perfection in the month of July in a glass jar exposed to the heat of the sun for 26 days.

THE NEW

CHEMICAL LIGHT

DRAWN FROM THE FOUNTAIN OF NATURE AND OF MANUAL EXPERIENCE.

TO WHICH IS ADDED

A TREATISE

CONCERNING

SULPHUR.

[THE AUTHOR'S ANAGRAM]:

"Divi Leschi genus anno."

In this sentence: "I love the Divine Race of Leschi," all the letters of the Author's name are found transposed,—

TO WIT: MICHAEL SENDIVOGIUS.

PREFACE.

Upon all genuine Seekers of the great Chemical Art,
or Sons of Hermes, the Author implores
the Divine Blessing and Salvation.

WHEN I considered in my mind the great number of deceitful books and forged Alchemistic "receipts," which have been put in circulation by heartless impostors, though they do not contain even a spark of truth—and how many persons have been and are still daily led astray by them?—it occurred to me that I could not do better than communicate the Talent committed to me by the Father of Lights to the Sons and Heirs of Knowledge. I also wish to let posterity see that in our own age, as well as in ancient times, this singularly gracious philosophical Blessing has not been denied to a few favoured men. For certain reasons I do not think it advisable to publish my name; chiefly, because I do not seek for praise for myself, but am only anxious to assist the lovers of philosophy. The vainglorious desire for fame I leave to those who are content to seem what they, in reality, are not. The facts and deductions which I have here briefly set down are transcribed from that manual—experience, graciously bestowed upon me by the Most High; and my object is to enable those who have laid a sound foundation in the elementary part of this most noble Art, to advance to a more satisfying fullness of knowledge, and to put them on their guard against those depraved "vendors of smoke," who delight in fraud and imposition. Our science is not a dream, as the vulgar crowd imagines, or the empty invention of idle men, as the foolish suppose. It is the very truth of philosophy itself, which the voice of conscience and of love bid me conceal no longer. In these wicked days, indeed, when virtue and vice are accounted alike, the ingratitude and unbelief of men keep our Art from appearing openly before the public gaze. Yet this glorious truth is even now capable of being apprehended by learned and unlearned persons of virtuous lives, and there are many persons of all nations now living who have beheld Diana unveiled. But as many, either from ignorance or from a desire to conceal their knowledge, are daily teaching and inducing others to believe that the soul of gold can be extracted, and then imparted to other substances; and thereby entice numbers to incur great waste of time, labour, and money: let the sons of Hermes know for certain that the extracting of the essence of gold is a mere fond delusion, as those who persist in it will be taught to their cost by experience, the only arbitress from whose judgment seat there is no appeal. If, on the other hand, a person is able to transmute the smallest piece of metal (with or without gain) into genuine gold or silver which abides all the usual tests, he may justly be said to have opened the gates of Nature, and cleared the way for profounder and more advanced study. It is with this object that I dedicate the following pages, which embody the results of my experience, to the sons of knowledge, that by a careful study of the working of Nature they may be enabled to lift the veil, and enter her inmost sanctuary. To this final goal of our sacred philosophy they must travel by the royal road which Nature herself has marked out for them. Let me therefore admonish the gentle reader that my meaning is to be apprehended not so much from the outward husk of my words, as from the inward spirit of Nature. If this warning is neglected, he may spend his time, labour, and money in vain. Let him consider that this mystery is for wise men, and not for fools. The inward meaning of our philosophy will be unintelligible to vainglorious boasters, to conceited mockers, and to men who smother the clamorous voice of conscience with the insolence of a wicked life; as also to those ignorant persons who have fondly staked their happiness on albefactions and rubrefactions and other equally senseless methods. The right understanding of our Art is by the gift of God, or by the ocular demonstration of a teacher, and can be attained only by diligent, humble search, and prayerful dependence on the Giver of all good things; now, God rejects those who hate Him, and scorn knowledge. In conclusion, I would earnestly ask the sons of knowledge to accept this Book in the spirit in which it was written; and when the HIDDEN has become MANIFEST to them, and the inner gates of secret knowledge are flung open, not to reveal this mystery to any unworthy person; also to remember their duty towards their suffering and distressed neighbours, to avoid any ostentatious display of their power; and above all, to render to God, the Three in One, sincere and grateful thanks with their lips, in the silence of their hearts, and by refraining from any abuse of the Gift

----

SIMPLICITY

IS

THE SEAL OF TRUTH

As after the completion of the Preface, it was found that it did not cover the whole of the space allotted to it, I have, at the publisher's request, there set down the "last will and testament of Arnold Villanovanus," which I once turned into Latin verse. I am conscious that the style of my versification is wanting in neatness and elegance; but this defect was partly caused by the necessity of adhering strictly and faithfully to the Author's meaning.

Testament of Arnold de Villanova.

It is said that Arnold de Villanova, a man who was a credit to his race, signified his last will in the following words: "It has its birth in the earth, its strength it doth acquire in the fire, and there becomes the true Stone of the ancient Sages. Let it be nourished for twice six hours with a clear liquid until its limbs begin to expand and grow apace. Then let it be placed in a dry and moderately warm spot for another period of twelve hours, until it has purged itself by giving out a thick steam or vapour, and becomes solid and hard within. The 'virgin's milk' that is expressed from the better part of the Stone is then preserved in a carefully closed oval-shaped distil ling vessel of glass, and is day by day wondrously changed by the quickening fire, until all the different colours resolve themselves into a fixed gentle splendour of a white radiance, which soon, under the continued genial influence of the fire, changes to a glorious purple, the outward and visible sign of the final perfection of your work."

THE FIRST TREATISE.

*Of Nature, what she is, and what manner of men her
Disciples ought to be.*

MANY Sages, Scholars, and learned men have in all ages, and (according to Hermes) even so early as the days before the Flood, written much concerning the preparation of the Philosopher's Stone; and if their books could be understood without a knowledge of the living processes of Nature, one might almost say that they are calculated to supersede the study of the real world around us. But though they never departed from the simple ways of Nature, they have something to teach us, which we, in these more sophisticated times, still need to learn, because we have applied ourselves to what are regarded as the more advanced branches of knowledge, and despise the study of so "simple" a thing as natural Generation. Hence we pay more heed to impossible things than to those objects which are broadly exhibited before our very eyes; we excel more in subtle speculations than in a sober study of Nature, and of the meaning of the Sages. It is one of the most remarkable features of human nature that we neglect those things which seem familiar, and are eager for new and strange information. The workman who has attained the highest degree of excellence in his Art, neglects it, and applies himself to something else, or else abuses his knowledge. Our longing for an increase of knowledge urges us ever onward towards some final goal, in which we imagine that we shall find full rest and satisfaction, like the ant which is not endowed with wings till the last days of its life. In our time, the Philosophical Art has become a very subtle matter; it is the craft of the goldsmith compared with that of the humble workman who exercises his calling at the forge. We have made such mighty strides in advance that if the ancient Masters of our science, Hermes and Geber and Raymond Lullius, were to rise from the dead, they would be treated by our modern Alchemists, not as Sages, but as only humble learners. They would seem very poor scholars in our modern lore of futile distillations, circulations, calcinations, and in all the other countless operations wherewith modern research has so famously enriched our Art, though without understanding the sense of the ancient writings. In all these respects, our learning is vastly superior to theirs. Only one thing is unfortunately wanting to us which they possessed, namely, the knack they had of actually preparing the Philosopher's Stone. Perhaps, then, their simple methods were after all the best; and it is on this supposition that I desire, in this volume, to teach you to understand Nature, so that our vain imaginations may not misdirect us in the true and simple way. Nature, then, is one, true, simple, self-contained, created by God and informed with a certain universal spirit. Its end and origin are God. Its unity is also found in God, because God made all things. Nature is the one source of all things: nor is anything in the world outside Nature, or contrary to Nature. Nature is divided into four "places" in which she brings forth all things that appear and that are in the shade; and according to the good or bad quality of the "place" she brings forth good or bad things. There are only four qualities which are in all things and yet do not agree among themselves, as one is always striving to obtain the mastery over the rest. Nature is not visible, though she acts visibly; she is a volatile spirit who manifests herself in material shapes, and her existence is in the Will of God. It is most important for us to know her "places," and those which are most in harmony, and most closely allied, in order that we may join things together according to Nature, and not attempt to confound vegetables with animals, or animals with metals. Everything should be made to act on that which is like to it—and then Nature will perform her duty.

Students of Nature should be such as is Nature herself—true, simple, patient, constant, and so on; above all, they should fear God, and love their neighbours. They should always be ready to learn from Nature, and to be guided by her methods, ascertaining by visible and sensible examples whether that which they propose to perform is in accordance with her possibilities. If we would reproduce something already accomplished by Nature, we must follow her, but if we would improve on her performance, we must know in and by what it is ameliorated. For instance, it we desire to impart to a metal greater excellence than Nature has given to it, we must take the metallic substance both in its male and its female varieties, else all our efforts will be in vain. It is as impossible to produce a metal out of a plant, as to make a tree out of a dog or any other animal.

SECOND TREATISE.

Concerning the operation of Nature in our
Substance, and its Seed.

I have already said that Nature is one, true, and consistent, and that she is known by her products, such as trees, herbs, &c. I have also described the qualifications of a student of Nature. Now I will say a few words about the operation of Nature. As Nature has her being in the Will of God, so her will, or seed, is in the Elements. She is one, and produces different things, but only through the mediate instrumentality of seed. For Nature performs whatsoever the sperm requires of her, and is, as it were, only the instrument of some artisan. The seed, if anything, is more useful to the artist than Nature herself; for Nature without seed, is what a goldsmith is without silver and gold, or a husbandman without seed corn. Wherever there is seed, Nature will work through it, whether it be good or bad. Nature works on "seed" as God works on the free will of man. Truly it is a great marvel to behold Nature obeying the seed, not because she is forced to do so, but of her own will. In like manner, God permits man to do what he pleases, not because He is constrained, but of His good and free bounty. The seed, then, is the elixir of anything, or its quintessence, or its most perfect digestion and decoction, or, again, the Balm of Sulphur, which is the same as the radical moisture in metals. We might say much more about this seed, but can only mention those facts which are of importance in our Art. The four elements produce seed, through the will of God and the imagination of Nature; and as the seed of the male animal has its centre or storing place in the kidneys, so the four elements by their continual action project a constant supply of seed to the centre of the earth, where it is digested, and whence it proceeds again in generative motions. Now the centre of the earth is a certain void place wherein nothing is at rest; and upon the margin or circumference of this centre the four elements project their qualities. As the male seed is emitted into the womb of the female, where only so much as is needed is retained while the rest is driven out again, so the magnetic force of our earth-centre attracts to itself as much as is needed of the cognate seminal substance, while that which cannot be used for vital generation is thrust forth in the shape of stones and other rubbish. This is the fountain-head of all things terrestrial. Let us illustrate the matter by supposing a glass of water to be set in the middle of a table, round the margin of which are placed little heaps of salt, and of powders of different colours. If the water be poured out, it will run all over the table in divergent rivulets, and will become salt where it touches the salt, red where it dissolves the red powder, and soon. The water does not change the "places," but the several places differentiate the water. In the same way, the seed which is the product of the four elements is projected in all directions from the earth-centre, and produces different things, according to the quality of the different places. Thus, while the seed of all things is one, it is made to generate a great variety of things, just as the seed of a man might produce a man if projected into the womb of a female of his own species, or a monstrous variety of abortions, if projected into the wombs of different female animals. So long as Nature's seed remains in the centre it can indifferently produce a tree or a metal, a herb or a stone, and in like manner, according to the purity of the place, it will produce what is less or more pure. But how do the elements generate the sperm or seed? There are four elements, two heavy and two light, two dry and two moist, but one driest and one moistest of all; and these are male and female. By God's Will each of these is constantly striving to produce things like to itself in its own sphere. Moreover, they are constantly acting on one another, and the subtle essences of all are combined in the centre, where they are well mixed and sent forth again by Archeus, the servant of Nature, as is more fully set forth in the Epilogue of these twelve Treatises.

THIRD TREATISE.

Concerning the true and first Matter of Metals.

The first matter of metals is twofold, and one without the other cannot create a metal. The first and principal substance is the moisture of air mingled with warmth. This substance the Sages have called Mercury, and in the philosophical sea it is governed by the rays of the Sun and the Moon. The second substance is the dry heat of the earth, which is called Sulphur. But as this substance has always been kept a great mystery, let us declare it more fully, and especially its weight, ignorance of which mars the whole work. The right substance, if the quantity of it which is taken be wrong, can produce nothing but an abortion. There are some who take the entire body for their matter, that is, for their seed or sperm; others take only a part of it: both are on the wrong track. If anyone, for instance, were to attempt the creation of a man out of a man's hand and a woman's foot, he would fail. For there is in everybody a central atom, or vital point of the seed (its 1/8200 part), even in a grain of wheat. Neither the body nor the grain is *all* seed, but everybody has a small seminal spark, which the other parts protect from all excess of heat and cold. If you have ears and eyes treasure up this fact, and be on your guard against those who would use the whole grain as seed, and those who strive to produce a highly rarefied metallic substance by the vain solution and mixture of different metals. For even the purest metals contain a certain element of impurity, while in the inferior the proportion is greater. You will have all you want if you find the point of Nature, which you must not, however, look for in the vulgar metals; it is not to be found therein, for all these, and common gold more especially, are dead. But the metals which we advise you to take are living and have vital spirits. Fire is the lifeof metals while they are still in their ore, and the fire of smelting is their death. But the first matter of metals is a certain moisture mixed with warm air. Its appearance is that of oily water adhering to all pure and impure things; yet in some places it is found more abundantly than in others, because the earth is more open and porous in one place than in another, and has a greater magnetic force. When it becomes manifest, it is clothed in a certain vesture, especially in places where it has nothing to cling to. It is known by the fact that it is composed of three principles; but, as a metallic substance, it is only one without any visible sign of conjunction, except that which may be called its vesture or shadow, namely, sulphur, &c.

FOURTH TREATISE.

How metals are produced in the Bowels of the Earth.

The metals are produced in this way: after the four elements have projected their power and virtues to the centre of the earth, they are, in the hands of the Archeus of Nature, distilled and sublimed by the heat of perpetual motion towards the surface of the earth. For the earth is porous, and the air by distillation through the pores of the earth is resolved into a water, out of which all things are generated. You should know that the seed of metals is the same, in the first instance, as the sperm of all other things, viz., a vaporous moisture. Hence it is foolish to seek the dissolution of metals in the first matter, which is nothing but a vapour, and in so doing philosophers have not comprehended the first matter, but only the second, as Bernard Trevisan well argues, though in a somewhat obscure manner, for he addressed himself to the Sons of the Doctrine. For my part, before openly explaining this theory, I would warn all men not to seek that which exists everywhere by itself in a soft volatile form by so many circulations, calcinations, and reiterations of hard gold and silver, which can never be changed back into their original substance. Let us follow the real meaning of the writers of Alchemy whose works we read, and remember that if Art would produce any solid and permanent effect, it must follow in the footsteps of Nature, and be guided by her methods. It must trust itself to the guidance of Nature as far as Nature will lead, and go beyond her by still adhering to her rules. Now I said that all things are produced of a liquid air or a vapour, which the elements distil into the centre of the earth by a continual motion, and that as soon as the Archeus has received it, his wisdom sublimes it through the pores, and distributes it to each place, producing different things according to the diverse places in which it is deposited. Some think that each metal has its own seed. But this is a great mistake, for there is only one seed. The sperm which appears in Saturn is the same as that which is found in gold, silver, copper, &c.; their difference is caused by the place, and by the time during which Nature was at work upon them, the procreation of silver being achieved sooner than that of gold, and so with the other metals. The vapour which is sublimed by heat from the centre of the earth, passes either through cold or warm places. If the place be warm and pure, and contain adhering to it a certain fatness of sulphur, the vapour (or Mercury of the Sages) joins itself to its fatness, and sublimes it together with itself. If in the course of its further sublimation this unctuous vapour reaches other places where the earth has already been subtilized, purified, and rendered moist by previous ascending vapours, it fills the pores of

308

this earth, and with it becomes gold. But if this unctuous moisture be carried to impure and cold places, it becomes lead; if the earth be pure and mingled with sulphur, it becomes copper. For the purer the place is, the more beautiful and perfect will the metal be. We must also note that the vapour is constantly ascending, and in its ascent from the earth's centre to its superficies, it purifies the places through which it passes. Hence precious metals are found now where none existed a thousand years ago, for this vapour, by its continual progress, ever subtilizes the crude and impure, and as continually carries away the pure with itself. This is the circulation and reiteration of Nature. All places are being more and more purified: and the purer they become, the nobler are their products. In the winter this unctuous vapour is congealed by the frost. At the return of spring it is set free, and is the *Magnesia* which attracts to itself the kindred Mercury of the air, and gives life to all things through the rays of the Sun, the Moon, and the Stars, thus bringing forth grass, flowers, and the like, for Nature is never idle even during a single moment. This, then, is the only true account of the generation of Metals. The earth is purged by a long distillation, and when the unctuous or fatty vapour approaches, the same are procreated, nor are they ever otherwise begotten, notwithstanding the imaginations of those who misinterpret on this point the writings of the philosophers.

FIFTH TREATISE.
On the generation of all kinds of Stones.

The substance of stones is the same as that of all other things; and their quality is determined by the purity of the places in which they arise. When the four elements distil their vapour to the centre of the earth, the Archeus of Nature expels and sublimes it in such a manner that it carries with it in its passage through the pores of the earth, all the impurities of these places up to the surface, where they are congealed by the air, all that pure air engenders being congealed by crude air, their ingression being mutual, so that they join one with another, since Nature rejoices in Nature. Thus rocks and stones are gradually built up and generated. Now the larger the pores of the earth, the greater is the quantity of impurities carried upward; and thus the earth is most completely purified under those places where there is a great accumulation of stones or rocks at the surface, and in this manner the procreation of metals becomes easier in these places. This explains the fact that metals are scarcely ever found in plains, but nearly always in the bowels of rocky hills. The plains are often moist with elemental water which attracts to itself the rising vapour, and with it is digested by the rays of the Sun into the rich clay which potters use. In places where the soil' is gross, and the vapour contains neither unctuousness nor sulphur, it produces herbs and grass in the meadows. The precious stones, such as diamonds, rubies, and emeralds, chrysopras, onyx, and carbuncle, are all generated in the same manner as ordinary stones. When the natural vapour is sublimed by itself without sulphur or the unctuosity of which we have spoken, and reaches a place where there is pure salt water (*i.e.*, in very cold places, where our sulphur cannot exist, for could it exist, this effect would be hindered), diamonds are formed. The unctuous sulphur which rises with the vapour cannot move without warmth, and is instantly congealed, when it reaches a slightly cold place, leaving the vapour to continue its upward movement without it. Colours are imparted to precious stones in this way. When the unctuous sulphur is congealed by the perpetual motion, the spirit of the water digests it in passing and purifies it by the water of the salt, until it assumes a red or white colour. This colour is volatilized by so many repeated distillations, and at length is borne upward with the purifying vapour, which by its aid is able to enter imperfect bodies, and thus to pervade them with colour; the colour is united to the partly congealed water, and fills all its pores so that the two are absolutely one. For water which has no spirit is congealed by heat, and water which has a spirit is congealed by cold; but he who knows how to congeal water by means of heat, and to join to it a spirit, is like to discover something a thousand times more precious than gold, or anything which is in the world. Let him separate the spirit from the water, in order that it may putrefy, and that the grain may appear. Then let him purge off the dross, and reduce the spirit to water. This union will produce a branch which bears little resemblance to the parent stem.

SIXTH TREATISE.

Concerning the Second Matter and Putrefaction.

We have spoken of the first matter of all things, and after what manner they are born by Nature without seed, that is, after what manner Nature receives the matter from the elements whereof she engenders seed. We will now consider this seed and the things evolved from it. Everything that has seed is multiplied thereby, but not without the aid of Nature: for seed is nothing but congealed air, or a vaporous humour enclosed in a body; and unless it be dissolved by a warm vapour, it cannot work. Now, the nature of this seed which is produced out of the four elements, is threefold: it is either *Mineral*, or *Vegetable*, or *Animal*. Mineral seed is known only to the Sages. Vegetable seed is common and vulgar, as we see in fruits. Animal seed is known by imagination. But vegetable seed exhibits most clearly the process by which Nature evolves natural objects out of the four elements. Winter is the cause of putrefaction: it congeals the vital spirit in trees; and when the heat of the Sun, which magnetically attracts moisture, sets it free, the natural heat (of the tree) which is thereby stirred up, drives a subtle vapour of water towards the surface, and makes the sap to flow, always separating the pure from the impure, though the impure may sometimes precede the pure. That which is pure is congealed into flowers, the impure becomes leaves, the gross and thick hardens into bark. The bark of the tree remains fixed; the leaves fall when the pores are obstructed by heat or cold; the flowers receive a colour according to the quality of the natural heat, and bear fruit or seed. We may instance the apple, wherein is the sperm, whence the tree does not spring; but in this sperm is the seed or grain interiorly, whence the tree is born even without sperm, for multiplication is not of the sperm but of the seed. Thus we see how Nature, without our help, creates vegetable seed out of the four elements. But how about Minerals? Nature brings forth Mineral or Metallic seed in the bowels of the earth. This is the reason why so many will not believe in its existence—because it is invisible. And on this account the vulgar unbelief is not so greatly to be wondered at: for if they hardly understand that which is openly before their eyes, how should they know anything about that which they cannot see. Yet, whether they believe it or not, the fact remains the same, and it is most true that that which is above is as that which is below, and that which is born above has origin from the same source which is at work down below, even in the bowels of the earth. What prerogative have vegetables above metals that God should give seed to the one and withhold it from the other? Are not metals as much in His sight as trees? It is certain that nothing can grow without seed; for that which has no seed, is dead. The four elements must either bring forth metallic seed, or produce metals without seed. In the latter case, they cannot be perfect: for nothing is complete without seed. He who can bring himself to believe that metals are destitute of seed, is unworthy to understand the mysteries of our Art. The metals then really contain their own proper seed; and it is generated in the following way. The vapour which (in the manner repeatedly described) rises from the earth's centre, and is called Mercury not on account of its essence but on account of its fluidity, and the facility with which it adheres to anything, is assimilated to the sulphur on account of ifs internal heat; and, after congelation, is the radical humour. Thus metals are indeed generated out of mercury; but those ignorant persons who say that this first substance of metals is ordinary mercury, confound the whole body with the seed that is in it, seeing that common mercury, too, contains metallic seed, as well as the other metals. Let us illustrate the matter by the analogy of the human body. Therein it is certain that there is a seed whereby the species of mankind is propagated. That body (which may be likened to common mercury) *contains* seed, which is not seen, and of which the quantity is very small in proportion to the size of the whole body: the process of generation is performed not by the whole body, but by this seminal "congealed watery vapour." But as no vital generation could take place if the body were dissected in order to get at the seed, as the murdering of the body would kill the seed—so ignorant Alchemists may be said to murder the body and kill the seed of metals, when they dissolve their bodies, whether of gold, silver, or lead, and corrode them with aqua fortis, in order to obtain the metallic seed. All multiplication is performed by means of male and female seed; and the two (which by themselves are barren) must be conjoined in order to bring forth fruit, *i.e.*, a new form. Whosoever, therefore, would bring forth any good thing must take the sperm or the seed, and not the entire body.

Take, then, the living male and the living, female, and join them in order that they may project a sperm for the procreation of a fruit according to their kind, for let no one presume to suppose that he can make the first matter. The first matter of man is earth, and there is no one so bold as to dream that he can create a man. God alone can perform this artifice. But if the second substance (or seed) which is already created, be put in the proper place, Nature will produce a new form of the same species. The Artist only separates what is subtle from its grosser elements, and puts it into the proper "vessel." Nature does the rest. As a thing begins, so it ends. Out of one arise two, and out of two one—as of God the Father there was begotten God the Son, and from the two proceeded God the Holy Ghost. Thus was the world made, and so also shall it end. Consider carefully these few points, and you will find, firstly, the Father, then the Father and the Son, lastly, the Holy Spirit. You will find the four elements, the four luminaries, the two celestials, the two centrics. In a word, there is nothing, has been, and shall be nothing in the world which is otherwise than it appears in this symbol, and a volume might be filled with its mysteries. I say, therefore, it is the attribute of God alone to make one out of one; you must produce one thing out of two by natural generation.

Know, then, that the multiplying sperm is the second substance, and not the first. For the first substance of things is not seen, but is hidden in Nature or the elements: the second substance is occasionally seen by the children of knowledge.

SEVENTH TREATISE.

Concerning the Virtue of the Second Matter.

But in order that you may the better know this second matter, I will describe to you its virtues. Nature is divided into three kingdoms, the mineral, the vegetable, and the animal. It is manifest that the mineral kingdom could subsist of itself were there no vegetables or animals in the world; the vegetable, in like manner, is independent of the animal and mineral. These two kingdoms were created in independence. The animal kingdom alone depends for its subsistence on the two others, and is the most noble and excellent of all; and seeing that it is the last of the three, it governs the two others, because virtue expends itself at the third, even as it is multiplied in the second. In the vegetable kingdom the first substance is the herb or the tree, which you cannot create, but which is produced by Nature alone. The second substance is the seed which you see, by which herbs and trees are propagated. In the animal kingdom the first substance is the beast or man, whom you cannot create; but the seed, or second substance, by which they are propagated, you know. In the mineral kingdom, too, you are unable to create a metal, and if you boast that you can do so, Nature will laugh at your pretensions; given even the possession of that first matter which is vaunted by the philosophers, namely, the centric salt, you cannot multiply it without gold; but the vegetable seed of metals is known only to the Sons of Science. In the case of plants, the seed is seen outwardly, and is digested by warm air. In animals the seed appears inwardly and outwardly, and is prepared in the kidneys of the male Water is the seed of minerals, in the very centre of their heart and life; and the "kidneys of its digestion" are fire. The receptacle of vegetable seed is the earth; the receptacle of animal seed the womb of the female; and air is the receptacle of water—the mineral seed. The receptacles of seed are the same as congelations of bodies; digestion is the same as solution, and putrefaction the same as destruction. The specific property of seed is to enter into union with other substances belonging to the same kingdom, because it is subtle, and, in fact, air congealed by fatness into water. It is recognisable by the fact that it does not become naturally united to anything outside the kingdom to which it belongs. It is not dissolved, but only congealed, as it does not need solution but only congelation. Hence it is necessary that the pores of bodies be opened to admit the sperm, in the centre of which lies the seed (which is air). When it enters its proper womb it is congealed, and congeals the pure or mixed substance which it finds. So long as there is any seed in the body the body lives; when it is all consumed the body dies; and any emission of seed weakens the body, as may be seen in the case of dissolute persons, and of trees which have been too richly laden with fruit. The seed, then, is invisible, but the sperm can be seen, and is even as a living soul, which is not found in dead things. It is extracted after two manners, of which the first is gentle and the second violent. Nothing is produced without seed, but everything comes into being by means of seed. Let all sons of knowledge remember that seed is vainly sought in dry trees, and that it is found only in those which are green.

EIGHTH TREATISE.

How Nature operates through our Art in the Seed.

Seed in itself produces no fruit, if it be not placed by Nature or Art in its own proper womb. Though seed in itself is the most glorious of all-created things, yet the womb is its life, which causes the putrefaction of the enclosing grain or sperm, brings about the congelation of the vital atom, nourishing and stimulating its growth by the warmth of its own body. All this is constantly and regularly being enacted (by months, years, and seasons) in the above said three natural kingdoms. The process can be hastened artificially in the vegetable and mineral, but not in the animal world. In the mineral kingdom, Art can do something which Nature is unable to perform, by removing the crude air which stops up the outward pores of minerals, not in the bowels of the earth but in the circumference. The elements vie in projecting their seed into the centre of the earth in order that it may there be digested. The centre, by a caloric movement, emits it into the womb; of these wombs there are an untold number—as many as there are places, and one place always purer than another. Know that a pure womb will bring forth a pure form of its own species. For instance, as among animals there are wombs of women, cows, mares, bitches, so in the mineral world there are metals, stones, and salts. Now salts principally demand consideration, with their localities, according as they are less or more important.

NINTH TREATISE.

On the Commixtion of Metals, and the Eliciting of the Metallic Seed.

We have spoken hitherto of Nature, of Art, of bodies, sperm, and seed. Let us now proceed to the practical enquiry, how metals should be mixed, and how they are mutually related. For, as a woman is generated in the same womb, and out of the same seed as a man, and the only difference is in the degree of digestion, and the purity of the blood and salts, so silver is produced from the same seed, and in the same womb as gold; but the womb of the silver had more water, and, as it were, less digested blood than that of gold, according to the times of the celestial moon. But if you would understand the sexual union of the metals, and their manner of emitting and receiving seed, look at the celestial bodies of the planets. You will see that Saturn is higher than all the rest, to whom Jupiter succeeds, then Mars, the Sun, Venus, Mercury, while the last place is occupied by the Moon. The virtues of the planets descend, but do not ascend; and so as experiences teaches us, Mars is easily converted into Venus, but not Venus into Mars, which has an inferior sphere. Also Jupiter may be quickly transmuted into Mercury, because Jupiter has a higher place; the one is second after the firmament, the other second after the earth. Saturn is the highest, the Moon lowest; the Sun combines with all, but is never ameliorated by its inferiors. There is a great correspondence between Saturn and the Moon, the Sun being medial between them; as also between Mercury and Jupiter, Mars and Venus, which all have the Sun as their centre. Most operators know how to transmute iron into copper, or Venus, without using gold; they also know how to change Jupiter into Mercury; some can prepare the Moon (silver) out of Saturn; but if they could prepare gold by these changes, their secret would be worth knowing indeed. For this reason I repeat that it is important to know the mutual correspondence of metals, and their possibilities of union. There is *one* metal which has power to consume all others, for it is, so to speak, their water, and almost their mother, and is resisted only by the radical humour of gold and silver, and ameliorated by it. This metal is called Chalybs (steel). If gold is united to it eleven times, and emits its seed, it is weakened even unto death; but the Chalybs (steel) conceives and brings forth a son much nobler than the father; and when the seed of the son is placed in her womb, it purifies it, and renders it a thousand times better fitted to produce excellent fruit. There is another Chalybs (steel) which is like this one, and created as a thing by itself by Nature; this steel is able, with its wonderful virtue, to elicit from the rays of the "sun" that which so many have sought, and which is the chief principle of our Art.

TENTH TREATISE.

On the Supernatural Generation of the Son of the Sun.

We have treated of those things which are produced by Nature and have been created by God, so that those who are searchers of this science may comprehend more easily the possibility of Nature, and the utmost limit of her powers.

I now go on to speak about the method of preparing the Philosopher's Stone. The Stone or Tincture is nothing other than gold digested to the highest degree. Common gold resembles a plant without seed; but when such a plant is matured, it produces seed—and so, when gold is ripened, it produces its seed, or the Tincture. If anyone asks why gold and other metals do not commonly produce seed, I answer: because the crudity of the ore, which has not sufficient heat, prevents it from being matured. In some places pure gold is found which Nature has been striving to mature, but which has not attained to ripeness on account of the crudity of the air. An analogous case is that of the orange tree, which bears no fruit in northern latitudes, because it has not sufficient warmth, while in warmer countries it ripens the most delicious fruit, and a like result it is possible to produce in colder countries, by means of artificial heat. The same thing happens with metallic natures, and so gold may be made to produce seed, by a wise and judicious Artist who knows how to assist Nature. Should he act independently of Nature, he would err, for in this science, as in all others, we can do nothing but supplement Nature, nor can we otherwise aid her than through the agency of heat or fire. Now, in order that Nature may be enabled to work upon a congealed metallic substance, wherein the spirit does not appear, the body must be dissolved and its pores opened. Now, there are two kinds of solution, the violent and the natural; and under the former head come all those methods of solution which are in vogue among the vulgar herd of modern Alchemists, and the same are cold and useless. *Natural* solution takes place when the pores of the body are gently opened in our water, so that the digested seed can be emitted and placed in its womb. Our water is a water which does not wet the hands; it is a heavenly water, and yet not rain water. The "Body" is gold, which gives out the seed. Our silver (not common silver) is that which conceives the seed of the gold. There it is digested by our continual fire, for seven or even ten months, until our water consumes three, and leaves one; and this is something twofold. Then it is nourished with the milk of earth, or the fatness of that which is formed in the breasts of the earth, and is regulated and conserved by the putrefaction of the surrounding substance. In this way that infant of the second generation is born. Now let us advance from theory to practice.

ELEVENTH TREATISE.

Concerning the practical preparation of our Stone or Tincture by means of our Art.

Our discourse in preceding chapters has been enlarged by appropriate examples which will facilitate the understanding of the practice, which, in accordance with natural procedure, must be performed as follows: take eleven grains of our earth, by as many doses, one grain of our gold, and two grains of our silver. Here you should carefully bear in mind that common gold and silver are of no use for our purpose, as they are dead. Those which I ask you to take are the living metals. Expose them to the heat of our fire, and there will come out of them a dry liquid. The earth will first be dissolved into a water, which is called Mercury of the Sages, and this water will dissolve the bodies of the gold and silver, and consume them, till only the tenth part with one part remains, which is the radical metallic humour. Then take the water of saltpetre from our earth, in which is a living river and a flowing wave. Let this water be clear, and pour on it the radical humour: expose the whole to the fire of putrefaction and generation, which is not the same as that of the first operation. Regulate the heat judiciously, until there appear colours like those of the Peacock's Tail; and then continue to apply this well-regulated heat until the colours resolve themselves into a pronounced green. Be not weary, but continue till the rest of the colours have manifested. When you observe at the bottom ashes of a brown colour, while the water is almost red, you should open the vessel and dip a feather into it. With this feather smear a morsel of iron, and if it becomes tinged, pour into the vessel as much of a certain water (which we will describe hereafter) as there is of crude air which has entered in, and then again subject it to coction over the same fire, until it colours the feather again. Further than this my experience does not go. The water I have mentioned is the menstruum of the world, from the sphere of the Moon, and so carefully rectified that it has power to calcine the Sun. Herein have I desired to discourse everything to your understanding, and if sometimes you will take my meaning rather than my words, you will find that I have revealed all, more especially as regards the first and second work. It remains for me to say a few words about the fire. In the first operation the fire should be of one degree and continuous, and should pervade the whole substance with an even warmth. In the second operation we need a natural fire, which digests and fixes the substance. Behold, I say unto you the truth! I have unfolded the regimen of the fire, if only you understand Nature. But it is needful also to speak a few words concerning the vessel, which ought to be such as is indicated by Nature; and two of these vessels suffice. In the first operation, the vessel should be round; in the second it should he somewhat smaller; it should also be of glass, in the form of a vial or egg. But know, above all things, that the fire employed by Nature is *one*, and its differences are determined by differences of distance. The vessel of Nature is also one, but we use two in order to accelerate the development of our substance; its material is one, but consists of two substances. If you would produce anything, look at the things that are produced. If you cannot understand those which are continually before your eyes, it will go hardly with you when you seek to produce those which are as yet unseen. Remember that God alone can create; but He has permitted the Sage to make manifest things that are hidden and concealed, according to the ministry of Nature. Consider, I pray you, the simple water of the clouds. Who would believe that it contains in itself all mundane objects, hard stones, salts, air, earth, and fire? What shall I say of the earth, which seems simple enough, and yet contains water, fire, salts, air, and much besides? O, admirable Nature, who knowest by the means of water how to produce the wonderful fruits of earth, who dost give life to them and nourish them by means of air! Everything depends upon the faculty of seeing which we bring to the study of Nature. Common eyes, for instance, discern that the sun is hot; the eyes of the Sage see that the sun itself is cold, and that it is only its movements which produce heat; for its effect is felt at so great a distance in space. The heat of the sun is the same as our natural fire: for as the sun is the centre of the planets, and thence scatters its heat downward in all directions, so in the centre of the earth there is a sun of the earth, which by its perpetual motion drives heat or rays upward towards the surface of the earth. This inward heat is much more powerful than elemental fire, but it is tempered and cooled by the water which pervades and refreshes the pores of the earth; otherwise all things would be consumed by its fierceness. In the same way, the fierce rays of the sun are tempered and assuaged by the air of the intermediate atmosphere, without which everything would be consumed, and no generation would be possible.

But I must now proceed to explain after what manner the elements act upon each other. In the centre of the earth, then, there is a central sun, of which the heat pervades the whole earth to its surface by reason of the movement thereof, or by the motion of the firmament thereof. This heat changes the water of the earth into air (or vapour), which being much more subtle than water, is violently driven upward through the pores of the earth. But when it reaches the colder atmosphere it is once more condensed into water; and in some places we do indeed see this water, or condensed air, driven high up into the air by the force of the central fire: just as a kettle of water when exposed to gentle heat sends upward a gentle stream of vapour and air, while the steam thickens and the upward movement becomes more intense when the fire is kindled into a blaze. By this action of the "central sun" the elements are distributed over the earth, and each finds the place where it can grow. This upward current of air is not always noticeable, because in many places there is not enough water to make it perceptible: an empty kettle gives out no steam. I say, then, that fire or heat is the cause of the motion of the air, and the life of all things; and the earth is their nurse, or receptacle. If our earth and air were not cooled by water, the earth would be parched up, as it is even now in some places where the pores of the earth are closed up, and by obstructing the movement of the water would be placed at the mercy of the two kinds of solar heat. In this way the destruction of the world will one day be brought about. Now in our Art you should closely imitate these natural processes. There should be the Central Heat, the change of the water into air, the driving upward of the air, its diffusion through the pores of the earth, its reappearance as condensed but volatilized water. Then you must give our Ancient One gold and silver to swallow and consume, till he himself is burnt to death, and his ashes are scattered into the water, which you must then subject to coction for a sufficient space of time. The result will be the Medicine which is a cure for leprosy. But be careful not to take heat for cold, or cold for heat. Mix only things which are like each other, and separate contrary elements by means of heat. If you do not follow the guidance of Nature all your efforts will be in vain. I swear by God that I have spoken to you as a father should to his son. He that bath ears, let him hear, and he that bath sense, let him understand.

TWELFTH TREATISE.

Concerning the Stone and its Virtue.

We have spoken sufficiently in preceding chapters concerning the production of natural things, the elements, the first and second matters, bodies and seeds, as also of their use and virtue. I have written also of the Philosophical Stone, and shall now speak of its virtue, in so far as experience has discovered it to me. Before, however, I proceed to describe the virtues of the Stone, I will, for the better understanding of our Art, once more recapitulate what has already been said. If any one doubts the *reality* of our Art, he should read the books of those ancient Sages whose good faith no one ever yet called in question, and whose right to speak on this subject cannot be challenged. If you will not believe *them*, I am not so foolish as to enter into a controversy with one who denies first principles: the deaf and dumb cannot speak. Why minerals alone should be excluded from God's primal benediction, when He bade all things increase and multiply after their kind, I am unable to see; and if minerals have seed they have it for the purpose of generic propagation. The Art of Alchemy is true in its nature. Nature is true also, but a true Artist is rarely found. Nature is *one*, our Art is *one*, but the workmen are many. Nature, then, generates things through the Will of God out of the first Matter (the product of the elements) which is known to God alone. Nature produces things, and multiplies them out of the *second substance*, which is known to the Sages. All elements are mutually dependent, though they do not agree when joined, but the queen of all is water, because it is the mother of all things and over it broods the spirit of fire. When fire acts on water, and strives with it, the first matter is evolved. Thus arise vapours of sufficient denseness to combine with earth, by means of that crude air which from the very beginning was separated from it. This process is going on ceaselessly, by means of perpetual motion. For motion causes heat, as you may know by continued friction of any substance. Motion causes heat, heat moves the water; the motion of water produces air, which is the life of all living things. Thus all things grow out of water; out of its more subtle vapours are produced light and subtle things; out of its "oil," things of greater weight; out of its salt things far more beautiful and precious than the rest. But as Nature is often hindered by the impurity of this vapour, fatness, and salt, from producing perfection, experience has taught us to separate the pure from the impure. Therefore, if you would ameliorate Nature, and produce a more perfect and elaborated subject, purge the body by dissolution of all that is heterogeneous, arid unite the pure to the pure, the well-digested to the well-digested, and the crude to the crude, according to the natural and not the material weight. For you must know that the central saltpetre never contains more earth than is required, whether it be otherwise pure or impure. But it is different with the fatness of the water, which is never found pure. Art purges it by the action of twofold heat, and then again combines its elements.

EPILOGUE,

OR

CONCLUSION OF THESE TWELVE TREATISES.

I have composed, O friendly reader, the preceding twelve Treatises for the benefit of the students of this Art; in order that they might understand the operations of Nature, and after what manner she produces all things which are in the world, before they put their hands to any experiment. Otherwise, they might be trying to open the gate without a key, or to draw water with a sieve. For in regard to our Holy and Blessed Art he for whom the sun shines not, walks in thick darkness, and he who does not see the light of the moon, is involved in the shades of night. Nature has her own light, which is not visible to the outward eye. The shadow of Nature upon our eyes is the body. But where the light of Nature irradiates the mind, this mist is cleared away from the eyes, all difficulties are overcome, and things are seen in their very essence, namely, the inmost heart of our Magnesia, which corresponds to the respective centres of the Sun and Earth. The bodily nature of things is a concealing outward vesture. If you dressed a boy and a girl of twelve years of age in exactly the same way, you would be puzzled to tell which was the boy and which the girl, but when the clothes are removed they may easily be distinguished. In the same way, our understanding makes a shadow to the shadow of Nature, for our human nature is concealed by the body in the same way as the body by the clothes. I might in this place discourse fully and philosophically of the dignity of man, of his creation and generation, but I will pass over these themes and touch briefly on his life alone. Man is made of earth, and lives through air; for air contains the hidden food of life, of which the invisible spirit, when congealed, is better than the whole world. Truly wonderful and admirable are the ways of Nature, who shows to us day by day the light of truth. I have set down in these twelve Treatises that which she has revealed to me in order that the God-fearing reader may more easily understand that which I have seen with my eyes, that which my hands have performed, without any fraud or sophistication. For without the light and knowledge of Nature it is impossible to attain to the perfection of this Art, unless it be revealed to a man by the Spirit, or secretly by a loving friend. The substance is vile and yet most precious. Take ten parts of our air; one part of living gold or living silver; put all this into your vessel; subject the air to coction, until it becomes first water, and then something which is not water. If you do not know how to do this, and how to cook air, you will go wrong, for herein is the true Matter of the Philosophers. You must take that which is, but is not seen until the operator pleases. This is the water of our dew, which is extracted from the saltpetre of the Sages, by which all things grow, exist, and are nourished, whose womb is the centre of the celestial and terrestrial sun and moon. To speak more openly, it is our Magnet, which I have already called our Chalybs, or steel. Air generates this magnet, the magnet engenders or manifests our air.

Thus Hermes says that its father is the Sun, its mother the Moon, and that the winds have fostered it in their womb, that is to say, the salt Alkali (called by the Sages salt of Ammonia, or vegetable salt) is hidden in the womb of Magnesia. The operation thereof is as follows:—You dissolve condensed air, and in it a tenth part of gold; seal it up, and expose it to our fire, until the air is changed into powder, and there will be seen, given the salt of the world, a great variety of colours. The rest of this process and the method of multiplication you will find fully set forth in the writings of Lullius, and other of the ancient Sages, so therefore I do not dwell on them, being content to treat only of the first and second matters. This I have done frankly, and with open heart. Think not that any man in this world has spoken more fully and clearly than I have. I have not learnt what I tell you from books, but by the experiment of my own hands. If you do not understand it at first, or are unable to accept the truth, accuse not my work, but blame rather yourself, believing that God will not reveal this secret unto you. Take it, then, in all earnestness, read and again read it, especially the Epilogue of these twelve Treatises, and diligently consider the possibilities of Nature, the action of the elements, and which is chief among them, especially in the rarefaction of air or water, by which the heavens and the whole world were created. This I admonish you to do, as a father admonishes a son. Do not wonder that I have written so many Treatises. I am not in need of books for myself, but was impelled to record my experience by pity towards those who are wandering astray in the darkness of their own conceits; and though I might have set forth this secret in few words, I have written at great length in order to equip you with that knowledge of Nature, without which you could not hope to succeed in this Art. Do not be put out by the seeming contradictions with which, in accordance with the custom of the Sages, I have had to conceal my real meaning a little. There is no rose found without thorns. Revolve diligently in your mind all that I have said about the way in which the elements distil the Radical Moisture to the centre of the earth, and how the terrestrial and centric sun again raises and sublimes them, by its continual motion, to the surface of the earth. Note also the correspondence which has been affirmed between the celestial and the centric sun; for the celestial Sun and Moon have a special power and a wonderful virtue in distilling upon earth by their rays. For heat is easily united to heat, and salt to salt. As the central sun has its sea and crude perceptible water, so the celestial sun has its sea of subtle and imperceptible water (the atmosphere). On the surface of the earth the two kinds of rays meet and produce flowers and all things. Then rain receives its vital force out of the air, and unites it to that of the saltpetre of the earth. For the saltpetre of the earth is like calcined *Tartar*, and by its dryness, attracts air to itself—which air it dissolves into water. For this saltpetre itself was once air, and has become joined to the fatness of the earth. The more abundantly the rays of the sun descend, the greater is the quantity of saltpetre generated, and so also is the harvest on earth increased. All this does experience daily teach.

I have willed thus to set forth solely for the benefit of the ignorant the correspondences which exist between all things, and the efficacious virtue of the Sun, Moon, and Stars. The wise have no need of such instruction. Our substance is openly displayed before the eyes of all, and yet is not known. Oh, how marvellous is our heaven, and our water, and our mercury, and our saltpetre which are in the world sea, and our vegetable, and our fixed and volatile sulphur, and our dead head, or dregs of our sea, and our water that does not wet the hands, and without which no mortal can live—without which nothing is born or generated in the whole world! It is lightly esteemed by men, yet no one can do without it: for it is more precious than all the world beside, and, in short, it is nothing but our pontic-water which is congealed in the sun and moon and extracted from the sun and moon, by means of our chalybs (steel) through the skill of the Sages by a philosophical artifice and in a surprising manner . . . . I did not really intend to publish this book, for reasons that are named in the preface; but my love for earnest students of this Art got the better of my caution. So have I sought to make known my good-will to those who know me, and manifest unto the initiated that I am their companion and equal, and that I desire their acquaintance. I doubt not that there are many persons of good conduct and clear conscience who possess this great gift of God in secret. I pray and conjure them that they should preserve even the silence of Harpocrates. Let them be made wise by my example, and take warning from my dangers. Whenever I have revealed myself to the great, it has always been to my peril and loss. But by this work I now show myself to the Sons of Hermes, while at the same time I instruct the ignorant, and direct lost seekers into the right path. Let them know that the secret is here as plainly expounded as it ever will be. I have kept nothing back except the secret of extracting our "salt of Ammonia," or "Mercury of the Sages" out of our "sea water," and the great use to which it is put. If I have not expressed myself very plainly on these points, it is only because I may not do so. The secret can only be revealed by God, who knows men's hearts and minds, and He will vouchsafe this knowledge, in answer to earnest and importunate prayer, after a repeated careful perusal of this Book. The vessel, as I have said, is one, or two at most will suffice; and if you have knowledge of Nature, a continuous fire, and the right substance, you ought to succeed. Let me caution you, in conclusion, not to be led astray by those who waste their time and money on herbs, animals, stones, and all kinds of minerals but the right ones. Farewell, good reader, and may you long enjoy the results of my labours, to the glory of God, the salvation of your soul, and the good of your neighbour.

A PREFACE

TO THE RIDDLE OF THE SAGES.

Addressed to the Sons of Truth.

Though I have already given unto you, O Children of Science, a full and exhaustive account of our Art, and of the source of the universal fountain, so that there seems no further call to say anything, having, in the preceding Treatises, illustrated the mode of Nature by examples, and declared both the theory and the practice, so far as it is permitted me to do, yet there may be some of my readers who think that I have expressed myself here and there in too laconical a fashion. I will therefore once more make known, from beginning to end, the entire process, but in the form of a philosophical enigma, so that you may judge how far I have been permitted to attain by God. There is an infinite number of books which treat of this Art, but you will scarce find any which contain a more clear explication of the truth than is here set down. I have, in the course of my life, met with a good many who fancied that they had a perfect understanding of the writings of the Sages; but their subtle style of interpretation was in glaring contrast with the simplicity of Nature, and they laughed at what they were pleased to call the rustic crudeness of my remarks. I have also frequently attempted to explain our Art to others by word of mouth; but though they called themselves Sages, they would not Believe that there is such water in our sea, and attributed my remarks to temporary insanity. For this reason I am not afraid that my writings will reveal anything to unworthy persons, as I am persuaded that it is only by the gift of God that this Art can be understood. If, indeed, subtlety and mental acuteness were all that is necessary for its apprehension, I have met with many strong minds, well fitted for the investigation of such subjects. But I tell you: Be simple, and not overwise, until you have found the secret. Then you will be obliged to be prudent, and you will easily be able to compose any number of books, which is doubtless more simple for him who is in the centre and beholds the thing itself, than one who is on the circumference only, and can only go by hearsay. You have a clear description of the matter of all things, but I warn you that if you would attain to this knowledge you should continue in earnest prayer to God, and love your neighbour. In the second place, you should not be ready to imagine all manner of subtleties and refinements of which Nature knows nothing. Remain rather in the way of her simplicity, for therein you are far more likely to put your finger on the subject than if you abide in the midst of subtleties.

In reading my book, do not stick too closely to the letter of my words, but read them side by side with the natural facts which they describe. You should also from the first fix your eyes steadily on the object of your search, and the scope and aim of our work. It is much wiser to learn with your mind and your brain first than by bitter experience afterwards. The object of your search should be to find a hidden thing from which, by a marvellous artifice, there is obtained a liquid by whose means gold is dissolved as gently and naturally as ice is melted in warm water. If you can find this substance, you have that out of which Nature produced gold, and though all metals and all things are derived from it, yet it takes most kindly to gold. For all other things are clogged with impurity, except gold wherein there is no uncleanness, whence in a special manner this matter is, as it were, the mother of gold. If you will not follow my instructions, and be warned by my cautions, you can derive no benefit from my book. I have spoken as plainly as my conscience would permit. If you ask who I am: I am a Cosmopolitan. If you know me, and wish to be good and honourable men, keep my name a secret. If you do not know me, forbear to enquire after my name, for I shall make public nothing more than appears in this writing. Believe me, if my rank and station were not what they are, I should enjoy nothing so much as a solitary life, or to have joined Diogenes in his tub. For I behold this world full of vanity, greed, cruelty, venality, and iniquity; and I rejoice in the prospect of the glorious life to come. I no longer wonder, as once I did, that the true Sage, though he owns the Stone, does not care to prolong his life; for he daily sees heaven before his eyes, as you see your face in a glass. When God gives you what you desire, you will believe me, and not make yourself known to the world.

A PARABLE,

OR

ENIGMA OF THE SAGES.

Added by way of an Appendix.

Once upon a time, when I had been for many years of my life sailing from the Arctic to the Antarctic Pole, I was cast ashore by the Will of God, on the coast of a certain great ocean; and though I was well acquainted with the properties of that sea, I did not know whether there was generated near those shores that little fish Edieneis, which is so anxiously sought, even unto this present, by men of high and low degree. But as I watched the Naiads and Nymphs disporting themselves in the water, being fatigued with my previous toils, and overwhelmed by the multitude of my thoughts, I was lulled asleep by the soft murmur of the waves; and as I slept sweetly and gently, I beheld a marvellous vision. I saw ancient Neptune, with a trident in his hand, rise, with venerable aspect, from our sea, who after a friendly salutation, carried me to a most beautiful island. This island was situated in the southern hemisphere, and contained all that is required for man's use and delight. It appeared a more pleasant and delightful abode than Virgil's Elysian fields. The shores thereof were fringed with verdant myrtles and cypresses. The meadows were studded with a large variety of beautiful and fragrant flowers. The slopes of the hills were clad with vines, olives, and cedars. The roads were overhung by the intertwining branches of laurels and pomegranate trees, which afforded grateful shade to the wayfarer. The plains were covered with groves of orange and lemon trees. In short, the island was an epitome of earthly beauty. Concealed under a rock, Neptune showed me two minerals of that island, gold and chalybs (steel). Then I was conducted to an orchard in the middle of a meadow, which was at no great distance, the same being planted with a great variety of beautiful trees. Among these he showed me seven enriched by particular names; and two of them towered above the rest. One bore fruit which shone like the sun, and its leaves resembled gold; the fruit of the other was whiter than lilies, and its leaves were like fine silver. Neptune called the first the Solar, and the second the Lunar tree. The only thing which it was difficult to obtain in the island, was water. The inhabitants had tried to get it from a spring by means of a conduit, and to elicit it from many things. But the result was a poisonous water, and the only water that could be drunk was that condensed out of the rays of the sun and moon. The worst of it was, that no one could attract more than ten parts of this water. It was wonderful water, I can tell you; for I saw with my eyes, and touched with my hands its dazzling whiteness, which surpassed all the splendour of the snow. While I stood wrapt in admiration, Neptune vanished from my sight, and there stood before me a tall man, on whose forehead the name of Saturn was inscribed. He took a vessel, and scooped up ten parts of the water, in which he placed fruit from the Solar tree; and the fruit was consumed like ice in warm water. So I said unto him:—"Lord, I behold here a marvellous thing. This water is small in quantity; nevertheless, the fruit of this tree is consumed therein by a gentle heat. To what purpose is all this?" He graciously replied: "My son, it is true that this thing is wonderful. But this water is the water of life, and has such power to exalt the qualities of this fruit, that it shall afterwards, without sowing or planting—only by its fragrance—transmute the six trees which remain into its own nature. Moreover, this water is as a woman to the fruit: the fruits of this tree can putrefy nowhere but in this water; and though the fruit by itself be wonderful and precious—yet when it putrefies in this water, it brings forth out of this putrefaction a Salamander that endures the fire; its blood is more precious than all treasures, and has power to render fertile six trees such as you see here, and to make their fruit sweeter than honey." Then I said unto him:—"Lord, how is this thing done?" He replied: "I have already told thee that the fruits of the Solar tree are living, and they are

322

sweet; but whereas the fruit while it is cooked in this water can inform but one part, after its coction has been completed it can inform a thousand." I then enquired whether the fruit was boiled in this water over a fierce fire, and how long? He answered "this water has an inward fire, and when this is assisted by continuous outward warmth, it burns up three parts of its own body with this body of the fruit, until nothing but an incredibly small part remains, which, however, possesses the most marvellous virtue. This is cooked by the wise Master first for seven months, and then for ten. But in the meantime, on each fiftieth day, a variety of phenomena is witnessed." Again I besought him whether this fruit was cooked in several waters, and whether anything was added to it. He made answer: "There is no water, either in this island or in the whole country, but only this kind alone that can properly penetrate the pores of this fruit; and you should know the Solar tree also grew out of this water, which is collected by magnetic attraction out of the rays of the Sun and Moon. Hence the fruit and the water exhibit a wonderful sympathy and correspondence. If any foreign substance were added to the water, its virtue would only be impaired. Hence nothing should be put into the water but this fruit. After its decoction the fruit has life and blood, and its blood causes all barren trees to bring forth the same precious fruit." I asked whether the water was obtained by any secret process, or whether it was to be obtained everywhere? He said: "It is found everywhere, and no one can live without it, but it is best when extracted by means of our Chalybs (steel), which is found in the belly of the Ram. If you ask what is its use, I answer that before the due amount of coction has been performed, it is deadly poison, but afterwards it is the Great Medicine, and yields 29 grains of blood, each one of which produces 864 of the fruits of the Solar tree." I asked whether it could be still further improved. "The Sages say," he returned, "that it can be increased first to ten, then to a hundred, then to a thousand, then to ten thousand times its own quantity, and so on." I asked whether that water was known by any particular name. He cried aloud, saying: "Few know it, but all have seen it, and see and love it; it has many names, but we call it the water of our sea: the water that does not wet the hands." "Do they use it for any other purpose?" I enquired; "and is anything born in it?" "Every created thing," he replied, "uses it, but invisibly. All things owe their birth to it, and live in it. Nothing is, properly speaking, in it, though itself mingles with all things. It can be improved by nothing but the fruit of the Solar tree, without which it is of no use in this work." I was going to ask him to speak more plainly, when he began to cry out in such a loud voice that I awoke out of my sleep, and Saturn and the hope of getting my questions answered vanished together. Be contented, nevertheless, with what I have told you, and be sure that it is impossible to speak more clearly. If you do not understand what I have said, you will never grasp the writings of other philosophers. After a while, I fell into another deep sleep, in which I saw Neptune standing over me, congratulating me on our happy meeting in the Garden of the Hesperides. He held up to me a mirror, in which I saw the whole of Nature unveiled. After we had exchanged a few remarks, I thanked him for conducting me to this beautiful garden, and introducing me to the company of Saturn; and I heartily besought him to resolve for me the difficulties and doubts which Saturn had left uncleared. "For instance," I said, "I have read and believe that for every act of generation a male and a female are required; and yet Saturn spoke of generation by placing the Solar fruit in the water, or Mercury of the Sages. What did he mean? As the lord of the sea, I know that you are acquainted with these things, and I entreat of you to answer me." He said, "What you say about the act of generation is true; and yet you know that worms are produced in a different way from quadrupeds, namely by putrefaction, and the place or earth in which this putrefaction occurs is feminine. In our substance the Mother is the water of which so much has been said, and its offspring is produced by putrefaction, after the manner of worms. Hence the Sages call it the Phœnix and Salamander. Its generation is a resurrection rather than a birth, and for this reason it is immortal or indestructible. Now, whatsoever is conceived of two bodies is subject to the law of death; but the life of this fruit is a separation from all that is corruptible about it. It is the same with the Phœnix, which separates of itself from its corruptible body." I enquired whether the substance was compound in its nature. "No," he said, "there is only the Solar fruit that is put into the water, which must be to the fruit in the proportion of ten to one. Believe that what was here revealed to you in a dream by Saturn, after the manner of our island, is not a dream, but a bright reality which will stand the test of broad daylight." With these words he abruptly left me, without listening to my further questions; and I awoke and found myself at home in Europe. May God show to you, gentle reader, the full interpretation of my dreams! Farewell!

To the Triune God be Praise and Glory!

A DIALOGUE

BETWEEN

MERCURY, THE ALCHEMIST, AND NATURE.

On a certain bright morning a number of Alchemists met together in a meadow, and consulted as to the best way of preparing the Philosopher's Stone. It was arranged that they should speak in order, and each after the manner that seemed best to him. Most of them agreed that Mercury was the first substance. Others said, no, it was sulphur, or something else. These Alchemists had read the books of the Sages, and hence there was a decided majority in favour of Mercury, not only as the true first matter, but in particular as the first matter of metals, since all the philosophers seemed to cry with one voice:—"O our Mercury, our Mercury," &c., whatever that word might mean. Just as the dispute began to run high, there arose a violent wind, which dispersed the Alchemists into all the different countries of the world—and as they had arrived at no conclusion, each one went on seeking the Philosopher's Stone in his own old way, this one expecting to find it in one substance, and that in another, so that the search has continued without intermission even unto this day. One of them, however, had at least got the idea into his head that Mercury was the substance of the Stone, and determined to concentrate all his efforts on the chemical preparation of Mercury, saying to himself, for this kind of discourse is very common among Alchemists, that the assembly had determined nothing, and that the dispute would end only with the confection of the Stone. So he began reading the works of the philosophers, and among others that of Alanus on Mercury, whereby he became a philosopher indeed, but not one who had reached any practical conclusion. Then he took (common) Mercury, and began to work with it. He placed it in a glass vessel over the fire, where it, of course, evaporated. So in his ignorance he struck his wife and said: "No one but you has entered my laboratory; you must have taken my Mercury out of the vessel." The woman, with tears, protested her innocence. The Alchemist put some more Mercury into the vessel, and kept close and jealous watch over it, expecting that his wife would once more make away with it. The Mercury rose to the top of the vessel in vaporous steam. Then the Alchemist was full of joy, because he remembered that the first substance of the Stone is described by the Sages as volatile; and he thought that now at last he must be on the right track. He now began to subject the Mercury to all sorts of chemical processes, to sublime it, and to calcine it with all manner of things, with salts, sulphur, metals, minerals, blood, hair, aqua fortis, herbs, urine, and vinegar. All these substances were tried in succession; everything that he could think of was tried; but without producing the desired effect. Seeing that he had still accomplished nothing, the poor man once more began to take thought with himself. At last he remembered reading in some authors that the matter was so contemptible that it is found on the dung hill; and then he began to operate on his Mercury with various kinds of dung. When all these experiments turned out failures, he fell into a deep sleep, and there appeared to him an old man, who elicited from him the cause of his sadness, and bade him use the pure Mercury of the Sages. When the Alchemist awoke he pondered over the words of the old man, and wondered what he could mean by "the Mercury of the Sages." But he could think of no other Mercury but that known to the common herd, and went on with his efforts to purge it; for which purpose he used, first, the excrements of animals, then those of children, and at last his own. He also went every day to the place where the old man had appeared to him, in the hope that he might be able to ask him for a more detailed explanation of his meaning. At times, he would pretend to be asleep; and because he thought that the old man might be afraid to come to him in his waking hours, he would swear to him, and say: "Be not afraid to come, old man I am most certainly asleep. See, my eyes are tightly shut." At length, from always thinking about that old man, he fell into a fever, and in his delirious visions he at last saw a phantom in the guise of that ancient standing at his bedside, and heard him say: "Do not despair, my friend. Your mercury is good, and your substance is good, but it will not obey you. Why do you not charm the mercury, as serpents are charmed?" With this, the old man vanished. But the Alchemist arose, with these words still ringing in his ears: "Serpents are charmed"—and recollecting that apothecaries ornament their mercury bottles with images of serpents, he took up the vessel with the mercury, and repeated the formula of conjuration: "ux, ux, ostas," etc, substituting the word mercury for the name of the serpent: "And thou mercury, most nefarious beast." At these words, the Mercury began to laugh, and said to the Alchemist: "Why dost thou trouble me, my Lord Alchemist?" *Alchemist:* Oho, do you call me your lord? Now I have touched you home. I have found a bit to bridle you with; wait a little, and you shall soon sing the tune that I bid you. (Then as his courage increased, he cried angrily):—I conjure you by the living God—are you not that Mercury of the Sages? *Mercury* (pretending to speak in a whimpering and frightened tone of voice): Master, I *am* Mercury. *Alchemist:* Why would you not obey me then? Why could I not fix you? *Mercury:* Oh, most high and mighty Master, I implore you to spare your miserable slave! I did not know that you were such a potent philosopher. *Alchemist:* Oh, could you not guess as much from the philosophical way in which I operated on you? *Mercury:* I did so, most high and mighty Master, but I wished to hide myself, though now I see that I cannot hide myself from my most potent Lord. *Alchemist:* Then you know a philosopher when you see him, as you now do, my gallant? *Mercury:* My most high Lord, I see, and to my own great cost, that your Worship is a high and mighty and most potent philosopher. *Alchemist* (with a smile of satisfaction): Now at last I have found what I sought. (To the Mercury, in awful tones of thunder): Now mind that you obey me, else it will be the worse for you. *Mercury:* Gladly, Master, if I can: for I am very weak. *Alchemist:* Oho, do you begin to make excuses already? *Mercury:* No, but I am very languid. *Alchemist:* What is the matter with you? *Mercury:* An Alchemist is the matter with me. *Alchemist:* Are you laughing at me, you false rogue? *Mercury:* Oh, no, no, Master, as God shall spare me, I spoke of an Alchemist—you are a philosopher. *Alchemist:* Of course, of course, that is quite true. But what did the Alchemist do? *Mercury:* Oh Master, he has done me a thousand wrongs; he belaboured and mixed me up with all manner of disagreeable and contradictory things, which have stripped me of all my powers, and so I am sick, even to death. *Alchemist:* You deserved such treatment, because you would not obey. *Mercury:* I never yet disobeyed a philosopher, but I cannot help laughing at fools. *Alchemist:* And what is your opinion of me? *Mercury:* Oh Master, your Worship is a great man, and mighty philosopher, greater by far than Hermes, both in doctrine and wisdom. *Alchemist:* Well, I won't praise myself, but I certainly am a learned man. My wife says so too. She always calls me a profoundly learned philosopher. *Mercury:* I quite believe you. For philosophers are men whom too much learning and thought have made mad. *Alchemist:* Tell me, what am I to do with you? How am I to make you into the Philosopher's Stone? *Mercury:* Oh, my master philosopher, that I cannot tell. You are a philosopher, I am the philosopher's humble slave. Whatever he wishes to make me, I become, as far as my nature will allow. *Alchemist:* This is all very fine, but I repeat that you must tell me how to treat you, and whether you can become the Philosopher's Stone. *Mercury:* Mr. Philosopher, if you know, you can make it, and if you don't you can't. From me you cannot learn anything with which you have been unacquainted beforehand. *Alchemist:* You talk to me as to a simple person. Perhaps you do not know that I have lived at the courts of great princes, and have always been regarded as a very profound philosopher. *Mercury:* I readily believe you, my Master, for the filth of your brilliant experiments still cleaves to me. *Alchemist:* Tell me, then, are you the Mercury of the Sages? *Mercury:* I am Mercury, but you should know best, whether I am the Mercury of you philosophers. *Alchemist:* Tell me only whether you are the true Mercury, or whether there is another? *Mercury:* I am Mercury, but there is also another. With these words, the Mercury vanished. The Alchemist shouts and calls aloud, but there is no answer. At last he is fain to derive some little comfort from the thought that he has had speech of Mercury, and therefore must be very dear to it. With this thought he once more sets himself to sublime, distil, calcine, precipitate, and dissolve the Mercury in the most awful manner, and with different sorts of waters. But his efforts turned out failures, and mere waste of time. Then he began to curse Mercury, and to blaspheme Nature for creating it. When Nature heard this, she called Mercury to her, and asked him what he had done to the Alchemist, and why he would not obey him. Mercury humbly protested his innocence. Nature admonished him to obey the Sons of Knowledge who sought to know her. Mercury promised that he would do so, but added: "Mother Nature, who can satisfy fools?" Nature smiled, and departed. Mercury, indignant with our Alchemist, returned also to his own place. The philosopher presently appeared with some excrements of swine, and was proceeding to ply Mercury therewith, when the latter thus wrathfully accosted him: "What do you want of me, you fool? Why did you accuse me?" *Alchemist:* Are you he whom I so much desire to see? *Mercury:* I am; but blind people cannot behold me. *Alchemist:* I am not blind. *Mercury:* You are as blind as a new-born puppy. You cannot see yourself: how then should you be able to see me? *Alchemist:* Oh, now you are proud and despise me because I speak humbly. Perhaps you do not know that I have lived at the courts of princes, and have always been called a philosopher? *Mercury:* The gates of princes stand wide for fools; and it is they that fare sumptuously in the palaces of the great. I quite believe that you have been at court. *Alchemist:* You are, undoubtedly, the Devil, and not a good Mercury, if you speak like that to philosophers. *Mercury:* Now, in confidence, tell me whether you are acquainted with any philosophers. *Alchemist:* Do you ask this of me, when you are aware that I am myself a philosopher? *Mercury* (smiling): Behold the Philosopher! Well, my philosopher, what do you seek, and what would you have? *Alchemist:* The Philosopher's Stone. *Mercury:* Of what substance would you make it? *Alchemist:* Of our Mercury. *Mercury:* Oh, my philosopher, then I had better go: for I am not yours! *Alchemist:* You are none but the Devil, and wish to lead me astray. *Mercury:* Well, my philosopher, I think I may return the compliment: you have played the very devil with me. *Alchemist:* Oh, what do I hear? This is most certainly the Devil. For I have done everything most scientifically, according to the writings of the Sages. *Mercury:* Truly, you are a wonderful operator; your performances exceed your knowledge by as much as they defy the authorities which you have in your books. For they say that substances should be mixed only with substances of a kindred nature. But you have mixed me, against Nature, with dung and other foul things, and are indifferent about defiling yourself so long as you can torture me. *Alchemist:* I do nothing against Nature: I only sow the seed in its own proper earth, according to the teaching of the Sages. *Mercury:* You sow me in dung; at the time of the harvest I vanish, and you reap dung. Verily, you are a good husbandman! *Alchemist:* Yet the Sages say that their substance is found on the dunghill. *Mercury:* What they say is true, but you understand only the letter, and not the spirit of their injunctions. *Alchemist:* Now I see that you are perhaps Mercury. But as you will not obey me, I must once more repeat the words of conjuration: Ux, ux, ostas—*Mercury* (laughing): It is of no use, my friend; your words are as profitable as your works. *Alchemist:* They say true when they call you a wonderful and inconstant and volatile substance. *Mercury:* You call me inconstant. But to the constant I am also constant, and to the man of fixed resolve, I am fixed. But you, and the likes of you, are continually abandoning one substance for another, and are ever vagabonds in experiment. *Alchemist:* Tell me truly, are you the Mercury which, side by side with sulphur and salt, the philosophers describe as the first principle of all things, or must I look for some other substance? *Mercury:* The fruit, when it falls, lies near the tree that bore it. I am the same that I was, except in the matter of age. In the beginning I was young, and I remained so as long as I was alone. Now, I am old, and yet I am the same as ever. I am only older than I was. *Alchemist:* I am glad that you are old. For it is a constant and fixed substance that I require, and this also have I invariably sought. *Mercury:* It is in vain that you come to the old man whom you did not know as a youth. *Alchemist:* What is this you say? Did I not know you when you were young? Have I not subjected you to all manner of chemical processes, and shall I not continue to do so till I have prepared the Philosopher's Stone? *Mercury:* Woe is me! What shall I do? I already scent the foul odour of dung. Woe is me! I beseech you, Master Philosopher, not to ply me with excrements of swine—or the foul smell will drive me hence. And what more do you want of me? Am I not obedient? Do I not mingle with all things that you ask me to amalgamate with? Do I not suffer myself to be sublimated, precipitated, amalgamated, calcined? What more can I do? I have submitted to be scourged and spat upon till my miserable plight might move a heart of stone. I have given you milk, blood, flesh, butter, oil, and water. I have done all that any metal or mineral can do. And yet you have no pity on me! Woe is me! *Alchemist:* Oho, it does you no harm, you rascal; you deserve it all richly, for not changing your form, or for resuming the old form after a mere temporary change! *Mercury:* I do whatsoever you make me do. If you make me a body, I am a body. If you make me powder, I am powder. How can I be more obedient than I am? *Alchemist:* Tell me, then, what you are in your centre, and I will not torment you any more. *Mercury:* I see there is no escape from speaking fundamentally to you. If you will, you may now understand me. With my form which you see you have nothing to do. My centre is the fixed heart of all things, immortal and all-pervading. I am a faithful servant to my master, and a faithful friend to my companions, whom I do not desert, and with whom I perish. I am an immortal body. I die when I am slain, but rise to stand before the judgment seat of a discriminating judge. *Alchemist:* Are you then the Philosopher's Stone? *Mercury:* My mother is such, and bf her is born artificially some one thing—but my brother who lives in the citadel has in his gift that which the Sage desires. *Alchemist:* Tell me, is your age great? *Mercury:* My mother bore me, yet I am older than my mother. *Alchemist:* How in all the world am I to understand you, if you answer my questions in dark parables? Tell me in one word, are you that fountain concerning which Bernard, Count of Trevisan, has written? *Mercury:* I am no fountain, but I am water, and the fountain surrounds me. *Alchemist:* Since you are water, is gold dissolved in you? *Mercury:* Whatever is with me, I love; and to that which is born with me, I impart nourishment. That which is naked I cover with my wings. *Alchemist:* I see plainly that it is impossible to talk to you. Whatever I ask you, your reply is foreign to the point. If you do not answer my questions better, I will torment you again. *Mercury:* Have pity on me, Master, I will gladly tell you all I know. *Alchemist:* Tell me, are you afraid of the fire? *Mercury:* I myself am fire. *Alchemist:* Why then do you seek to escape from the fire? *Mercury:* Because my spirit loves the spirit of the fire, and accompanies it wherever it goes. *Alchemist:* Where do you go when you ascend with the fire? *Mercury:* Every pilgrim looks anxiously towards his country and his home. When he has returned unto these he reposes, and he always comes back wiser than he left. *Alchemist:* Do you return, then? *Mercury:* Yes, but in another form. *Alchemist:* I do not understand what you mean, nor yet about the fire. *Mercury:* If any one knows the fire of my heart, he has seen that fire (proper heat) is my food;

and the longer the spirit of my heart feeds on fire, the fatter will it be: its death is afterwards the life of all things belonging to my kingdom. *Alchemist:* Are you great? *Mercury:* My body, as you must know, can become one drop out of a thousand drops, and, though I am always one, you can divide my body as often as you like. But my spirit, or heart, always produces many thousands of parts out of one part. *Alchemist:* How is this to be brought about? After what manner should my operation be performed on you? *Mercury:* I am fire within; fire is my food and my life; but the life of fire is air, for without air fire is extinguished. Fire is stronger than air; hence I know not any repose, and crude air can neither coagulate nor restrain me. Add air to air, so that both become one in even balance; combine them with fire, and leave the whole to time. *Alchemist:* What will happen then? *Mercury:* Everything superfluous will be removed. The residue you burn in fire, place in water, "cook," and when it is cooked you give as a medicine, and have no fear. *Alchemist:* You do not answer my questions. Wife, bring the excrements of swine, and we will see whether we can get the better of his stubbornness.

In his utmost extremity, Mercury called in the help of Nature, amidst much lamentation and mourning over these threats of our admirable Alchemist. He impeaches the thankless operator; Nature trusts her son, Mercury, whom she knows to be true and faithful, and comes full of wrath to the Alchemist, calling him imperiously before her. *Alchemist:* Who calls me? *Nature:* What are you doing to my son, arch-fool that you are? Why do you torment him? He is willing to give you every blessing, if you can understand him. *Alchemist:* Who dares to rebuke so great a philosopher, and a man withal so excellent as I am? *Nature:* O fool, and of all men most insensate, I know and love all philosophers, and am loved of them. I take pleasure in aiding their efforts, and they help me to do that which I am unable to accomplish. But you so-called Alchemists are constantly offending me, and systematically doing despite to me; and this is the reason why all your efforts are doomed to failure. *Alchemist:* It is not true. I, too, am a philosopher, and understand scientific methods of procedure. I have lived with several princes, and with more than one philosopher, as my wife can testify. Moreover, I possess at this very moment a manuscript which has lain hidden for some centuries in a certain wall. I know very well that I am almost at the end of my labours, and am on the point of composing the Philosopher's Stone; for it was revealed to me a few days ago in a dream. I have had a great many dreams, nor do I ever dream anything untrue; my wife knows it. *Nature:* It is with you as with a great many of your fellows: at first they know everything, but in the end their knowledge turns to ignorance. *Alchemist:* If you are truly Nature, it is you who serve for the operation of the work. *Nature* That is true; but it is performed only by those who know me, and such do riot torment my children, nor do they hinder my working. Rather they clear away the impediments, that I may the sooner reach the goal. *Alchemist:* That is exactly what I do. *Nature:* No; you do nothing but cross me, and deal with my children against my will. Where you should revive, you kill; where you should fix, you sublime; where you should calcine, you distil; and thus my obedient son Mercury you torment in the most fearful manner. *Alchemist:* Then I will in future deal with him gently, and subject him only to gradual coction. *Nature:* That is well, if you possess understanding; otherwise, you will ruin only yourself and your possessions. If you act in opposition to my commands, you hurt yourself more than him. *Alchemist:* But how am I to make the Philosopher's

Stone? *Nature:* That question does not justify your ill-treatment of my son. Know that I have many sons and daughters, and that I am swift to succour those who seek me, provided they are worthy. *Alchemist:* But who is that Mercury? *Nature:* Know that I have only one such son; he is one of seven, and the first among them; and though he is now all things, he was at first only one. In him are the four elements, yet he is not an element. He is a spirit, yet he has a body; a man, yet he performs a woman's part; a boy, yet he bears a man's weapons; a beast, and yet he has the wings of a bird. He is poison, yet he cures leprosy; life, yet he kills all things; a King, but another occupies his throne; he flees from the fire, yet fire is taken from him; he is water, but does not wet the hands; he is earth, and yet he is sown; he is air, and lives by water. *Alchemist:* Now I see that I know nothing; only I must not say so. For I should lose the good opinion of my neighbours, and they would no longer entrust me with money for my experiments. I must therefore go on saying that I know everything; for there are many that expect me to do great things for them. *Nature:* But if you go on in that way, your neighbours will at last find you out, and demand their money back. *Alchemist:* I must amuse them with promises, as long as I can. *Nature:* And what then? *Alchemist:* I will try different experiments; and if they fail, I will go to some other country, and live the same life there. *Nature:* And then? *Alchemist:* Ha, ha, ha! There are many countries, and many greedy persons who will suffer themselves to be gulled by my promises of mountains of gold. Thus day will follow day, and in the meantime the King or the donkey will die, or I myself. *Nature:* Such philosophers are only fit for the gallows. Be off, and take with you my most grievous curse. The best thing that you can do, is to give yourself up to the King's officers, who will quickly put an end to you and your philosophy!

THE NEW CHEMICAL LIGHT

SECOND PART.

CONCERNING SULPHUR.

THE AUTHOR'S ANAGRAM:
Angelus Doce Mihi Jus.
(Angel, Teach me Right.)

PREFACE.

As I am not at liberty to write more plainly than the Ancient Sages, gentle Reader, you may possibly be dissatisfied with my Book, particularly as you have so many other philosophical treatises ready to your hand. But you may be sure that no necessity is laid upon me to write at all, and that if I have come forward it is only out of love to you, having no expectation of personal profit, and no desire for empty glory, for which reason I here refrain, as I have before done, from revealing my identity to the public. I was under the impression that in the first part of this work I had already given a lucid account of our whole Art. But my friends tell me that there is one point with which I have not yet fully dealt, and vehemently urge me to write this second treatise about Sulphur. The question is, whether even this Book will convey any information to one before whom the writings of the Sages and the Open Book of Nature are exhibited in vain. For if you could incline your ear to the teaching of Nature, you would at once be able to emancipate yourself from the tutelage of printed volumes; in my opinion it is better to learn from the master himself than from one of the disciples. In the preface to my twelve Treatises, and again in the twelfth chapter, I have already hinted at the reason why there is snow so great a multitude of books on this subject, that they confound and hinder the student instead of helping him. The confusion is rendered worse confounded by the ill-will of the Sages, who seem to have set pen to paper for the express purpose of concealing their meaning; and by the carelessness with which some of the more important volumes are copied and printed; the sense of a whole passage is often hopelessly obscured by the addition or omission of one little word (*e.g.*, the addition of the word "not" in the wrong place). Yet the student may get information even from these books (as the bee obtains honey even from poisonous flowers), if he reads them by the light of natural fact, and with constant reference to the utterances of other Sages. One writer explains another. Yet some of them are so closely beset with the difficulties of an obscure phraseology, that it is almost impossible to understand them, except by reading them side by side with the facts of Nature; for their interpreters and commentators are more hopelessly unintelligible even than the writers whom they take upon themselves to explain; the exposition is more difficult than the text. If you would succeed in this study, keep your eyes fixed on the possibilities of Nature, and on the properties of the natural substance. It is universally described as common and easy of access and apprehension, and it is so, but only to those who know it. He who knows it can discover it in the dunghill; he who does not will fail to find it even in gold. I have no desire to praise myself, but this one thing I will say, that the reading of my Books, in combination with a careful study of Nature, and of the writings of other genuine possessors of this Stone, must in the end open up to you the understanding of this secret. If I have planted another tree in the dense forest of Alchemistic literature, I have done so, not in order to obstruct the path of students, but in order to aid and refresh them by the way. Let not the diligent and God-fearing enquirer despair. If he seek the inspiration of God he will most surely find it. This knowledge is more easily obtained of God than of men. For His mercy is infinite, and He never forsakes those who put their trust in Him; with Him there is no respect of persons, nor does He despise the humble and contrite heart. He has showered the fullness of His mercy even on me, the unworthiest of all His creatures, in sh0wing to me His wonderful power and ineffable goodness, which I am utterly unable to declare. The only way in which I can, in a small degree, at least prove my gratitude, is by succouring my struggling brother students with friendly counsel and assistance. Rest assured, then, gentle Reader, that He will grant this boon to you, if you wait upon Him day by day with earnest prayer, and in the power of a holy and loving life. He will throw open to you the portals of Nature; and you will be amazed at the simplicity of her operations. Know for certain that Nature is wonderfully simple; and that the characteristic mark of a childlike simplicity is stamped upon all that is true and noble in Nature. If you would imitate Nature, you should take her simplicity for your model in all the operations of Art. If my Book does not please you, throw it away, and take up some other author; it is short, so that you need not spend much time in reading it through. Only persevere: to the importunate knocker the door will at length be opened. The times are at hand when many secrets of Nature will be revealed to men. The Fourth or Northern Monarchy is about to be established; the Mother of Knowledge will soon come; and many things will be brought to light that were hidden under the three preceding monarchies. This fourth kingdom God will found by the hand of a prince who will be enriched with all virtues, and endowed with wisdom greater than that of Solomon. In his time (to adopt the words of the Psalmist) mercy and truth will meet together; peace and justice will kiss each other; truth will spring up from the ground, and righteousness will look down from heaven. There will be one Shepherd and one fold; and knowledge will be the common property of all. For those days I, too, am waiting with longing. Pray to God that it may come soon, gentle Reader. Fear Him, love Him, and read carefully the books of His chosen Sages—and you will soon see, and behold with your own eyes, that I have spoken truly.

CONCERNING SULPHUR.

The Second Principle.

SULPHUR is by no means the least important of the great principles, since it is a part of the metal, and even a principal part of the Philosopher's Stone. Many Sages have left us weighty sayings about this substance: for instance, Geber himself ("Sum of Perfection," bk. i, chap.28), who says: "It illumines all bodies, since it is the light of the light, and their tincture." But seeing that the ancients regarded it as the noblest principle, before we proceed to speak about it, we must first explain the origin of the three principles. The origin of the principles is a subject which has hitherto been but scantily discussed in the works of the Sages; and the student who knows nothing about it, is as much in the dark in regard to this matter, as is a blind man in respect to colour. I therefore propose to make this point which my predecessors have neglected, the subject of my treatise.

Now, according to the ancient Sages there are two principles of things, and more particularly of metals, namely, Sulphur and Mercury; according to the Moderns there are three: Salt, Sulphur, and Mercury, and the source of these principles are the elements; of which it therefore behoves us to speak first. Be it known to the students of this Art that there are four elements, and that each has at its centre another element which makes it what it is. These are the four pillars of the world. They were in the beginning evolved and moulded out of chaos by the hand of the Creator; and it is their contrary action which keeps up the harmony and equilibrium of the mundane machinery; it is they which, through the virtue of celestial influences, produce all things above and beneath the earth. We will say a few words about each of them in due order of succession; and first of all about the nearest element, Earth.

Concerning Elementary Earth.

Earth is an element of considerable quality and dignity. In this element the other three, especially fire, are latent. It is admirably adapted both to the concealment and to the manifestation of things committed to it. It is gross and porous, specifically heavy, but naturally light. It is also the Centre of the World and of the other elements; through its centre passes the axis of the earth to both poles. It is porous, as we have said, like a sponge, and produces nothing of itself; but it receives all that the other three project into it, conscientiously conceals what it should hide, and brings to light that which it should manifest. Whatsoever is committed to it putrefies in it through the action of motive heat, and is multiplied by the separation of the pure from the impure. Heavy substances are hidden in it. Light substances are driven by heat to its surface. It is the nurse and womb of all seed and commixtion; and these seeds and compounds it faithfully preserves and fosters till the season of maturity. It is cold and dry, but its dryness is tempered with water; outwardly it is visible and fixed; inwardly it is invisible and volatile. It is a virgin substance, and dead residue of the creative distillation of the world, which God will one day calcine, and after extracting the humour, create out of it a new crystalline earth. In its present state it consists of a pure and an impure element. The first is used by water for producing natural forms; the latter remains where it is. It is also the storehouse of all treasures, and in its centre is the Gehennal fire, conserving the machine of the world, and this by the expression of water, which it converts into air. This fire is produced by perpetual motion, and the influences of the Stars; it is aided by the Solar heat, which is tempered by the atmosphere, and the two together mature the growth of all things. For this reason the element of earth has fire intrinsically, and the earth is purified by this inward fire, as every element is purified by that which is in it. The inmost part, or centre of the earth, is then the highest purity mixed with fire, in which there is ceaseless motion, and we have shewn at some length in the twelve Treatises that it is, as it were, an empty space, into which the other elements project their products. It is enough for us to remember that this elementary earth is like a sponge, and the receptacle of all other elements.

Concerning Elementary Water.

Water is an element of great specific gravity, full of unctuous moisture. Outwardly it is volatile, inwardly it is fixed, cold, and humid It is tempered by air, and is the sperm of the world, in which the seed of all things is conserved. There is a great difference between sperm and seed. Earth is the receptacle of sperm, water the receptacle of seed. Whatever the air, under the influence of fire, distils into the water, is imparted by the water to the earth. There is always an abundance of sperm awaiting seed, in order that it may carry it into the matrix, which is performed by the movement of the air, excited by the imagination of fire. Sometimes sperm has not a sufficient quantity of seed, for want of heat to digest it. Sometimes, when there is no seed, the sperm enters the womb alone, but is ejected again without producing any fruit. At other times conception does not take place, even when there is plenty of seed in the sperm, because the womb is rendered barren by a superfluity of bad sulphur and malignant phlegm. Water is capable of commixtion with all things, by means of its volatile surface; it purifies and dissolves earth; air is congealed in it, and thus intimately united to it. It is the Solvent of the World, because by the action of heat, it penetrates the air, and carries with it a warm vapour which causes the natural generation of those things with which the earth is like a womb impregnated. When the womb has once received a due portion of seed, Nature never rests until the natural form (whatever it may be) has been produced. The humid residue, or sperm, is putrefied in the earth by means of warmth, and out of it worms and other things are generated. An intelligent Artist will readily understand how great a variety of wonders is performed by Nature through this element, as a sperm, but the said sperm must be operated upon, having already within it an imagined astral seed of a certain weight. For Nature produces pure things by means of the first putrefaction, but things far purer by means of the second, as you see in the case of wood, where vegetable fibre is produced as the result of the first putrefaction, while the putrefaction of wood engenders worms and insects—natural forms endowed with sentient life; and it is clear that animate creatures endowed with sense and motion belong to a higher creative level, and are moulded of a purer substance than plants.

Water is the menstruum (solvent) of the world, and exists in three degrees of excellence: the pure, the purer, and the purest. Of its purest substance the heavens were created; of that which is less pure the atmospheric air was formed; that which is simply pure remains in its proper sphere, where, by the Will of God, and the co-operation of Nature, it is guardian of all subtle substances here below. It has its centre in the heart of the sea; its polar axis coincides with that of the earth, whence flow forth all springs and fountains of water, which are presently swollen into great rivers. This constant movement of water preserves the earth from combustion, and distributes the seeds of things throughout its length and breadth. Yet all water courses return to the heart of the sea. As to the ultimate fate of this water opinions are divided. Some say that all water is generated in the stars, and the sea does not overflow its shores because the water is consumed by fire as it reaches the heart of the sea. But this hypothesis is contrary to Nature's methods of working: Nature produces like out of like—and how can the stars, which are air and fire, produce water? Moreover, the safety of this earth depends on the equilibrium of the four elements; if at any time the total quantity of one element exceeded that of the others, the universe would relapse into chaos. Hence, if the stars generated water, they must manifestly produce an equal quantity not only of air and fire, but also of earth—which is manifestly absurd. It is much more reasonable to suppose that the waters are chained down, as it were, to the foundation of the earth by the circumambient air, and that they are constrained by it to continue in a ceaseless movement towards the Arctic pole—because no vacuum is possible in Nature; which is also the reason why there is a Gehennal fire in the centre of the earth, which is presided over by the Archeus (the first principle) of Nature.

For in the creation of the world, God first of all separated the quintessence of the elements from the weltering mass of chaos; and out of it He evolved fire, the purest of all substances, giving to it the most exalted place in the universe, and making it, in a special manner, the dwelling-place of His Sacred Majesty. In the centre of chaos was kindled that fire which afterwards distilled and carried upward the purest substance of water. But. because this most pure fire now occupies the firmament, and surrounds the throne of God, the waters have been condensed into a body beneath it; and thus the sky is formed, while the water which now forms the atmospheric air and the lower firmament is due to the action of a lower and grosser fire. As the water of the firmament cannot pass the bounds of that highest and celestial fire, so the lower fire cannot pass through the atmospheric air to the earth; nor can the air pass the bounds of this lower fire. The water and the earth were formed together into one organic mass. Only one part of this water was volatilized into air, in order to protect the earth from the fierce and consuming heat of the sun. If there had been a vacuum in the air, all the water would have evaporated; but as the space below the firmament is already filled up with air, the great bulk of the water is kept below, near the centre of the earth, by the pressure of the air. These natural conditions continue to operate day by day, and through their normal action the world will be preserved from destruction during the good pleasure of the Creator. The central fire is kindled day by day by the universal motion and influence of the celestial bodies. This fire heats the water, and a certain quantity of the water is dissolved into air; the air day by day keeps down by its weight the residue of the water, and causes it to form one mass with the earth. And as the equilibrium of the world is thus naturally preserved by the Creator, so every natural generative process in the world must repeat the same conditions on a small scale. Thus the elements below act in perfect unison with the elements above, which God created of a far greater purity and excellence; and the example of obedience to their influences, which is set by the whole universe, is imitated on a small scale by the constituent parts of the world below.

But let us now proceed to explain the flux and reflux of water. There are two Poles—the Arctic Pole in the north, and the Antarctic Pole, or the southernmost point of the earth. The Arctic Pole possesses the property of magnetic attraction; the Antarctic Pole that of magnetic repulsion. Thus the Arctic Pole attracts the waters along its axis, and then they are again repelled by the Antarctic Pole along its axis; and, as the air does not permit inequality, they are once more forced back to their centre, the Arctic Pole. In this their continual course from the Arctic to the Antarctic Pole, they pass through the middle (*i.e.*, along the axis) of the earth, are diffused through its pores, and break out here and there as springs and fountains, which are swollen into rivers, and return to the point whence they first flowed forth. This universal motion is incessantly proceeding. The waters, then, are not generated by the stars and consumed in the heart of the sea; but they flow forth from the centre of the sea into the whole earth, and are diffused through all its pores. On this principle the Sages have constructed conduits and aqueducts, since it is well known that water cannot rise higher than the level of its spring or fount. If this were not an actual fact, art would vainly found its practical conclusions upon it; and the natural principle involved is illustrated in the process by means of which wine is drawn out of a cask.

It may be objected to our view that if the water of our springs were derived from the sea, it would be salt, and not sweet, as we actually find it to be. The answer to this objection lies in the fact that the sea water, in its passage through the pores of the earth, gradually deposits all the salt which it contains, and thus wells forth from the ground in a sweet and fresh condition. It should, however, be remembered that some of our springs—called mineral or saline springs—actually do exhibit all the original saltness of the sea water which has not passed through earth calculated to retain its mineral element. In some places we also meet with hot springs, which are caused by the passage of the water through certain spots where large deposits of sulphur have been set afire by the central heat of the earth; every one who has tasted this water must have observed its sulphureous flavour. Something closely analogous happens when the water passes through large deposits of iron, or alum, or copper, and acquires their taste. Thus the earth is a great distilling vessel, formed by the hand of an all wise Creator, on the model of which all Sages have constructed their small distilling vessels; and if it pleased God to extinguish the central fire, or to destroy the cunning machinery, this universal frame would relapse into chaos. At the end of time, He will kindle the Central Fire into a brighter flame, will cause all the water to evaporate, will calcine the earth—and thus the earth and the water will be rendered more subtle and pure, and will form a new and more glorious earth.

The operations of the earth and the water are always performed in combination, and are mutually dependent, since they are the two tangible elements, in which the other two work invisibly. Fire keeps the earth from being submerged, or dissolved; air keeps the fire from being extinguished; water preserves the earth from combustion. This is what the Sages call the equilibrium of the elements, and it illustrates the aid which they render to each other. Fire is closely associated with earth, and air with water. It will suffice if we remember that elementary water is the sperm and menstruum of the world, and the receptacle of seed.

Concerning Elementary Air.

The most noble element of air is inwardly heavy, visible, and fixed, outwardly light, volatile, and invisible. It is hot and moist, is tempered by fire, and is nobler than earth or water. Air is volatile, but may be fixed, and when fixed, renders all bodies penetrable. Its purest substance has been formed into the vital spirits of animals, that which is less pure into the circumambient atmosphere, and the grosser residue has remained in the water, and associates with it as fire with its kindred earth. In the air the seed of all things is formed, as it were, in the body of the male, and is projected by its circulative motion into its sperm, which is water. It contains the vital spirit of all creatures, is the life of all, and penetrates and forces its seed upon all, as the man does upon the woman. It nourishes, impregnates, conserves the other elements; and we are taught by daily experience that it is the life not only of minerals, animals, and vegetables, but also of the other elements. We see that water becomes foul and unwholesome without a supply of fresh air; without it fire is extinguished—as is well known to Alchemists who regulate the temperature of their fire by the supply of air. Air is also that which conserves the pores of the earth. In short, the whole universe is kept fresh and sweet by air, and it is the vital element of man, beast, plant, and stone. It contains the seed of all things which is forced up, into vegetables for instance, through the pores of the earth by the action of fire, and thus the tree is built up atom by atom out of the vital element of congealed air. This vital force has remained in it ever since the time when the Spirit of Life brooded over the waters in the air. The magnetic power of life which air undoubtedly possesses, was put into it by God at the Creation. As the magnet attracts to itself hard steel, and as the Arctic Pole attracts to itself the water, so the air, by means of the vegetable magnet which is in the seed, draws to itself the nutriment of the menstruum of the world (which is water). This power of attracting water is in a certain part (*viz.*, the 280th part) of all seed. If, then, any one would be a cunning planter of trees, he should take care to turn the point of attraction towards the North; for as the Arctic Pole attracts water, so the vertical point draws to itself the seminal substance. If you would know what the point of attraction in a tree is, submerge it entirely in water; that point which always appears first, will be the point of attraction. In the air, then, is the seed and the vital spirit, or abode of the soul of every creature.

Concerning Elementary Fire.

Fire is the purest and noblest of all elements, full of adhesive unctuous corrosiveness, penetrant, digestive, inwardly invisible, fixed, hot and dry, outwardly visible, and tempered by the earth. Of its purest substance was created the Throne of the Almighty; of that which is less pure, the Angels; out of fire of an inferior purity were created the stars and the heavenly luminaries; that which was less pure still was used to bear up the heavens; that which is impure and unctuous—that, namely, which we have termed the fire of Gehenna—is in the centre of the earth, and was there inclosed and shut up to set this lower world in motion. Though these different fires are separate, yet they are also joined together by natural sympathy.

This element is the most passive of all, and resembles a chariot: when it is drawn it moves; when it is not drawn, it stands still. It exists imperceptibly in all things; and of it is fashioned the vital rational soul, which distinguishes man from all other animals, and makes him like God. This rational soul was divinely infused into his vital spirit by God, and entitles him to be regarded as a microcosm, or small world by himself. But the fire which surrounds the Throne of God is of an infinitely pure and simple essence, and this is the reason that no impure soul can know God, and that no human eye can penetrate this essential fire, for fire is the death and destruction of everything composite—and all material substances are of this nature What I said about the restful passivity of fire, applies in a certain sense to the eternal calm and unchangeableness of the Divine Nature. For as the fire sleeps in the flint, until it is roused and stirred up from without, so the power of God, which is a consuming fire, is only roused to action by the kindling breath of His Almighty Will. How calmly and solemnly does not even an earthly monarch sit enthroned in the pomp and state of his royalty! His courtiers hardly venture to move, and all around is calm and still. But when he rises what a stir of motion and activity does he not cause! All that are about him arise with him, and presently you see him sweeping along in grand and stately majesty. Yet the pomp of an earthly prince is but a faint reflex of the glory of the King of Kings. When He utters the voice of His Will, all heaven is roused, the world trembles, and thousands of angels speed forth on His errand. But it may be asked hew I come to have this knowledge about heavenly things which are removed far beyond human ken. My answer is that the Sages have been taught of God that this natural world is only an image and material copy of a heavenly and spiritual pattern; that the very existence of this world is based upon the reality of its celestial archetype; and that God has created it in imitation of the spiritual and invisible universe, in order that men might be the better enabled to comprehend His heavenly teaching, and the wonders of His absolute and ineffable power and wisdom. Thus the Sage sees heaven reflected in Nature as in a mirror; and he pursues this Art, not for the sake of gold or silver, but for the love of the knowledge which it reveals; he jealously conceals it from the sinner and the scornful, lest the mysteries of heaven should be laid bare to the vulgar gaze. I f you will but rightly consider it, you yourself are an image of God, and a little picture of the great world. For a firmament you have the quintessence of the four elements attracted to the formative womb out of the chaos of seed, and bounded by your skin; your blood is fire in which lives your soul, the king of your little universe, acting through the medium of the vital spirit; your heart is the earth, where the Central Fire is always at work; your mouth is your Arctic, and your stomach your Antarctic Pole, and all your members correspond to some part of the greater world, as I have set forth at some length in my work on the Harmony of the Universe, and in the Chapter on Astronomy. In the microcosm of man's nature the soul is the deputy or Viceroy of the Creator. It governs the mind, and the mind governs the body: the mind is conscious of all that is conceived in the soul, and all the members understand the mind, obey it, and wait eagerly to carry out its behests, The body knows nothing of itself; all its motions and desires are caused by the mind; it is to the mind what the tool is to the craftsman. But though the rational soul operates in the body, a more important part of its activity is exerted on things outside the body: it rules absolutely outside the body, and therein differs from the vital spirits of brute beasts. In the same way, the Creator of the world partly acts in and through things belonging to this world, and is thereby, in a sense, included in this world. But He absolutely transcends this world by that infinite part of His activity which lies beyond the bounds of the universe, and which is too high and glorious for the body of the world. The great difference between the soul's extracorporal, and God's extramundane, activity, is that man's rational activity is purely imaginative and mental, whereas God's thoughts are immediately translated into real existences. I might be mentally in the streets of Rome, but my journey would be purely imaginative; God's conceptions are at once objective essences. God, then, is included in the world, only as the soul is enclosed in the body, while it has power to do things which far transcend the capacity of the body. By material relations such as these you may know God, and learn to distinguish Him from the material manifestations of His power. When once the gates of knowledge have been flung wide for you, your understanding will be enlarged.

We said that fire was the quietest of all elements, and that it is stirred by a kind of motion well known to the Sages. The Sage should be perfectly acquainted with the generation and destruction of all things; he is familiar with the creation of the heavens, and the composition and commixtion of things terrestrial; yet, though he knows everything, he cannot make everything. He knows the anatomy and composition of the human body—yet he cannot make a man. This is a mystery which the Creator has kept in His own hand. Nature cannot work till it has been supplied with a material: the first matter is furnished by God, the second matter by the Sage. But in the philosophical work Nature must excite the fire which God has enclosed in the centre of each thing. The excitation of this fire is performed by the will of Nature, and sometimes also by the will of a skilful Artist who can dispose Nature, for fire naturally purifies every species of impurity.

All composite substances are purified by fire, as all substances that are not fixed owe their purification to water. It is the property of fire to separate and divide composite substances; and this separation means a purging away of the impure from the pure. This element also acts secretly, by marvellous means, not only in opposition to the rest of the elements, but also to all other things For as the reasonable soul was made of this most pure fire, so the vegetable soul was made of the elementary fire which Nature governs The fire which is contained in the centre of any given thing acts in the following way: Nature provides the motive power, which stirs up the air; the air stirs up and rouses the fire, which separates, purges, digests, colours, and brings every seed to maturity, and expels the matured seed through the sperm into places or wombs, either pure or impure, more or less hot, dry, or humid; and according to the nature of the place or womb, different things are produced (cp. the Twelve Treatises). So the Most High God has ordained that, in the economy of the universe, one thing should be at enmity with another, and that the death of one thing should be the life of the other; that one thing should consume what another produces, and evolve out of it some higher and nobler form of life. The elementary separation of all living things is death; and hence it is necessary for man to die, as his body is compounded of the four elements, which cannot hold together forever. In spite of this fact, our science furnishes an incontestible proof of man's original immortality. It is certainly true that all composite substances are liable to decomposition; that this decomposition, when it takes place in the animal world, is called death; and that the human body is a substance compounded of the four elements. But it is also true that the elements of Paradise, where man was created, are not subject to this law, seeing that they are most pure and incorruptible heavenly essences; and if man had remained in this pure and celestial region, his body would have been incapable of natural decay. Adam, however, in an evil day for our race, disobeyed his Creator, and straightway was driven forth to the beasts, into the world of corruptible elements which God had created for the beasts only. From that day forward his food was derived from perishable substances, and death began to work in his members. The pure elements of his creation were gradually mingled and infected with the corruptible elements of the outer world, and thus his body became more and more gross, and liable, through its grossness, to natural decay and death. The process of degeneration was, of course, slow in the case of Adam and his first descendants; but, as time went on, the seed out of which men were generated became more and more infected with perishable elements. The continued use of corruptible food rendered their bodies more and more gross—and human life was soon shortened to a very brief span indeed. In some favoured climes, where men eat and drink moderately, they still sometimes live to a green old age; but in our latitudes men abridge the term of their natural existence by grossly filling themselves with an excess of elementary corruptible food, and thus, before their time, become like "the beasts that perish." When the pure and essential elements are joined together in loving equilibrium, as they are in our Stone, they are inseparable and immortal, like the human body in Paradise; whence also our philosophical treasure has been compared to the creation of man, an analogy which modern wise men, who take all things literally, have understood as referring to the corrupted generation of this present order, which is produced from corruptible elements.

It was the recollection of man's immortality in Paradise, that first set Sages thinking whether those pure and essential elements might not be obtained in this world, and united in one body. At length a merciful Creator made known to them that the desired conjunction of such elements existed in gold. It could not be found among the animals who are sustained by corruptible food, nor in vegetables, because they exhibit the elements in a state of inequality and contention. When corruptible elements are united in a certain subject, their strife must sooner or later bring about its decomposition, which is, of course, followed by putrefaction; in putrefaction, the impure is separated from the pure: and if the pure elements are then once more joined together by the action of natural heat, a much nobler and higher form of life is produced. In the strife of the elements, which follows when a body has been broken up by the victory of water, earth and air unite with fire, and together they overcome the water, digest, cook, and ultimately congeal it—which is the beginning of a new life. For if the hidden central fire, which during life was in a state of passivity, obtain the mastery, it attracts to itself all the pure elements, which are thus separated from the impure, and form the nucleus of a far purer form of life. It is thus that our Sages are able to produce immortal things, particularly by decomposition of minerals; and you see that the whole process, from beginning to end, is the work of fire.

Thus, then, we have briefly set forth as much as will serve our purpose concerning the four elements. Truly the description of each might be extended into a large volume, but we postpone all amplification for our Treatise on Harmony, which, God helping, if our life be spared, will be opportune to a more large discourse upon natural things.

Concerning the Three Principles of All Things.

The three Principles of things are produced out of the four elements in the following manner: Nature, whose power is in her obedience to the Will of God, ordained from the very beginning, that the four elements should incessantly act on one another, so, in obedience to her behest, fire began to act on air, and produced Sulphur; air acted on water and produced Mercury; water, by its action on earth, produced Salt. Earth, alone, having nothing to act upon, did not produce anything, but became the nurse, or womb, of these three Principles. We designedly speak of three Principles; for though the Ancients mention only two, it is clear that they omitted the third (Salt), not from ignorance, but from a desire to lead the uninitiated astray.

Whoever would be a student of this sacred science must know the marks whereby these three Principles are to be recognised, and also the process by which they are developed. For as the three Principles are produced out of four, so they, in their turn, must produce two, a male and a female; and these two must produce an incorruptible one, in which are exhibited the four (elements) in a highly purified and digested condition, and with their mutual strife hushed in unending peace and goodwill. In every natural composition these three represent the body, the spirit, and the hidden soul; and if, after purging them well, you join them together, they must, by a natural process, result in a most pure substance. For though the soul is most noble, yet it cannot reach the goal without the spirit which is its place and abode; and if it is your desire to bring it back to a given place, both the soul and the place must be purged and washed from all impurity, so that the soul may dwell in glory, and nevermore depart. Without these three Principles, the Artist can do nothing, since even Nature is powerless without them. They are in all things, and without them there is nothing in the world, neither, indeed, can be. Their origin being such as we have described, it is from these, by an imitation of Nature, that you must produce the Mercury of the Philosophers, and their first matter, bearing in mind the laws which govern natural things, and especially metals. Do not think that Salt is unimportant because it is omitted by the Ancients; they could not do without it, even if they did not name it, seeing that it is the Key which opens the infernal prison house, where sulphur lies in bonds. The three Principles are necessary because they are the immediate substance of metals. The remoter substance of metals is the four elements, but no one can produce anything out of them but God; and even God makes nothing of them but these three Principles. Why, then, should the Sage lose time and labour over the four elements, when he has the substance made ready to his hand by Nature? It is surely less troublesome to go three miles than four, and as these three Principles exist in all things, and, according to their proportions, etc., produce either metals, or plants, or animals, it is best to use them as our first substance. The body is earth, the spirit water, the soul fire or sulphur of gold. The Spirit augments the quantity of the body, the soul the virtue. But because in the matter of weight there is more of spirit than of fire, the spirit is uplifted, oppresses the fire, and attracts it to itself in such a way that both augment in virtue, and the earth, which is mediate between them, augments in weight. The Artist should determine which of the three Principles he is seeking, and should assist it so that it may overcome its contrary. Afterwards he must seek by his skill to supplement what has been wanting in Nature, and thus his chosen Principle will obtain the necessary victory. The element of earth is nothing but a receptacle, in which fire and air carry on their strife through the mediation of air. If water predominate, temporal and corruptible things are produced; if fire obtains the victory, it produces lasting and incorruptible things. So you know which of the elements ought to receive your aid. Moreover, though fire and water are in all things, they can produce nothing without air and earth. Their activity is aroused by external heat (in Nature, the Central Fire of the earth), and in their struggle they are assisted each by that which is like to it. By this strife they are subtilized in the pores of the earth, and when they ascend to the surface they produce flowers and fruit, in which they closely associate together as friends; and the more they are subtilized and purified in their ascent, the more excellent are the fruits which they produce.

When the purification has thus been performed, let water and fire become friends, which they will readily do in their earth which ascends with them; and the process will be the more speedily and perfectly accomplished, if you combine the two in their proper proportions—thus improving upon Nature. In all natural compounds fire is always the smallest part; but it is aided and stirred up by the action of outward fire; and according as fire is overcome or obtains the mastery. imperfect or perfect things are the result. The outward fire does not enter into the composition as an essential part of it, but only by the effect which it helps to produce. The inward fire is sufficient, if it only receive nutriment from the outward fire, which feeds it as wood feeds elemental fire; in proportion to the quantity of nutriment the inward fire grows and multiplies. Care should be taken, therefore, that the outward fire is not so fierce as to devour, instead of feeding, the inward fire. Gentle coction will be the best means of attaining perfection, and of adding excellence to weight. But as it is difficult to add to a compound substance, I would advise rather to produce the same effect by removing that which is present in an excessive quantity. Remove that which is too much, and let the compound develop itself naturally. But many artists sow straw instead of grain; others sow both; many throw away that which the Sages love; others begin and do not persevere to the end; they look for short and easy labour in a difficult Art. But we say that this Art consists in an even mingling of the virtues of the elements—in the natural equilibrium of the hot, the dry, the cold, and the moist—in the conjunction of the male and female, the female having engendered the male, *i.e.*, of fire and the radical humour of the metals. If you understand that the Mercury of the Sages contains within itself its own good Sulphur, digested and matured by Nature, you can accomplish the whole process by means of Mercury alone; but if you know how to add the supplement which our Art requires to the natural proportions of substances, to double the Mercury, and to triple the Sulphur, you will all the more quickly produce, first the good, then the better, and finally the best—though only one sulphur appears, and two mercuries (which, are, however, of the same stock); they should not be crude nor too much digested, yet well purged and dissolved (if you understand me).

It is really unnecessary to describe the matter of the Mercury and the Sulphur of the Sages, as it has already been as plainly delineated by the Ancients as is consistent with our vow. We do not altogether say that the Mercury of the Philosophers is a common thing, or that they have openly called it by its name, and that the matter from which Mercury and Sulphur are philosophically extracted has been plainly pointed out. For the Mercury itself is not found above ground, but is extracted by an artifice from Sulphur and Mercury conjoined. in short, Sulphur and Mercury are the ore of our quicksilver, and this quicksilver has power to dissolve, mortify, and revive metals, which power it has received from the sulphur (which has some of the properties of an acid). In order to put you on the right track, I will also tell you the difference between our quicksilver and common mercury. Common mercury does not dissolve gold and silver so as to amalgamate with them; but when our quicksilver dissolves gold and silver, it amalgamates with them in inseparable union, as water is mixed with water. Common mercury has bad combustible sulphur, which turns it black; our quicksilver contains incombustible, fixed, good, snow-white and red sulphur. Common mercury is cold and humid; our quicksilver is hot and humid. Common mercury blackens other bodies; our quicksilver renders them white and pure as crystal. Common mercury is changed by precipitation into a yellow powder and bad sulphur; our quicksilver is converted by heat into snow-white, good, fixed, and fusible sulphur. Common mercury becomes more fusible, our quicksilver more fixed, the more it is subjected to coction. Our quicksilver possesses such marvellous virtue that it would by itself be sufficient for our purpose, if subjected to gentle coction; but in order to accelerate its congelation, the Sages add to it its well digested and matured sulphur.

We might well have cited philosophers in confirmation of the points of our discourse, but as our writings are more clear than are theirs, we have no need of their support. Whosoever understands them will understand us better. If you would practise our Art, learn first to hold your tongue, and study the nature of minerals, metals, and vegetables. Our Mercury may be obtained from all things, as everything has it; only from some substances it is more easily procured than from others. Our Art is not a matter of luck or accident, but is founded on a real knowledge, and there is only one matter in the world by which, and of which, the Stone of the Philosophers is prepared. The substance is indeed to be found everywhere, but the method of its extraction out of some matters would take a lifetime, and if you begin your search without a due knowledge of natural things, more especially in minerals, you will be working in the dark and in blindness. It is, indeed, possible to set about our Art in a casual manner; and some who actually operate on our quicksilver, begin at the wrong end, and thus fail in bringing it to perfection, because they are quite in the dark about its real nature. Yet, after all, we must confess that a right knowledge of our Art is the gift of God alone, and is granted to diligent students in answer to earnest and importunate prayer. To the Master it may appear easy enough; but to the beginner it must seem at first very hard and uphill work. He should not, however, despair, for in due time he will receive the reward of his diligence and aspiration; even in the dangers which the knowledge may bring upon him, he will be kept from harm by the loving hand of Providence, as I can testify from personal experience. We have with us God's Ark of the Covenant, which contains the most precious of earthly things, and is guarded by the holy Angel of the Lord. We heard that our enemies had fallen into the snare which they had laid for us; that those who sought our lives had been enclosed in the meshes of death; that those who attempted to rob us of our goods had lost all that they possessed; and that those who strove to blacken our reputation, died in shame and dishonour. Such is the care which God has of us, Who, from our childhood, has kept us safe under the shadow of His wings. And the feeling uppermost in our minds is the humbling consciousness of our utter unworthiness: we do not deserve the very least of His great mercies. But one thing we do and will do: our hope and trust always have been, are, and will be, in Him alone. We will not put our confidence in men or in princes: we will place ourselves in the hands of One who remains unchanged when all earthly power and greatness have passed away. The fear of the Lord is the beginning of wisdom: never did Sage utter truer word than this; and if we would attain to the knowledge of this glorious science, if we would be able to use it well when we possess it, we must wait on God continually, and importune Him with earnest prayer. But to proceed with our description of the Matter. We said that it was quicksilver, and quicksilver only: whatever is added, is gained from this same substance. We have repeatedly affirmed that all things earthly are evolved out of three principles. But for our purpose they must be purged of their impurities, and then recombined; that which is wanting is added—and thus imitating and assisting Nature, we arrive at a degree of perfection such as Nature is unable to attain, on account of the impurities with which her operations are clogged. Do not suffer yourself to be confounded by the apparent contradictions which the Sages have introduced into their writings for the purpose of keeping their secret. Select only those sayings which are agreeable to Nature; take the roses, leave the thorns. If you wish to produce a metal, your fundamental substance should be metallic; only a dog can beget a dog; without wheat you will vainly plough your field; and all your endeavours in this Art will be in vain, unless you take your radical humour from a metal. There is one substance, one Art, one operation It is as erroneous to suppose that any of the particular benefits of our Stone can be enjoyed before the Stone itself has been prepared, as it would be absurd to imagine that you can have a branch without a root or tree. If you have water you can cook in it various kinds of meat, and thus obtain broth of different flavours; but there will be no broth unless you have both the water and the meat. . . . . In metals, then, as in all other things, there is only one first substance, but the universal substance is modified in a vast variety of ways, according to the course of its subsequent development. Thus one thing is the mother of all things. This great fact ought always to be borne in mind in studying the works of the Sages; for nothing but mistakes and disappointment can result from a slavishly literal interpretation of their books. It is a pity that, instead of humbly studying and following Nature, our Alchemists are so ready to adopt any fancy or notion that happens to pass through their minds. They seek to attain the end not only without a middle part, but without so much as a beginning. But how can anyone who sets about our Art in so casual and haphazard a manner expect anything but disappointments? Let our Alchemists have done, then, once for all, with their sophistical methods, to which they ascribe so great an importance—with their dealbations, rubrefactions, fixations of the Moon, extractions of the soul of gold,—and let them place themselves under the unerring guidance of Nature. For though the soul of the metal has to be extracted, it must not be killed in the operation; and the extraction of the living soul, which has to be reunited to the glorified body, must be carried on in a way very different from the violent method commonly prevailing among Alchemists. We do not propose to multiply wheat without seed corn. But let us, in concluding this part of the subject, earnestly inculcate on the student's mind the necessity of having seed that will germinate and grow, and to avoid the use of seed which has been killed by an excess of fiery heat.

Concerning Sulphur.

Among the three principles the Sages have justly assigned the first place to Sulphur, as the whole Art is concerned with the manner of its preparation. Sulphur is of three chief kinds: that which tinges or colours; that which congeals mercury; and essential sulphur, which matures it. The properties and preparation of this Sulphur we propose to describe, not in a set treatise, but in a dialogue like that which brought out the essential properties of Mercury. We will only say, by way of preface, that Sulphur is more mature than the other principles, and that Mercury cannot be coagulated without it. The aim and object of our Art is to elicit from metals that Sulphur by means of which the Mercury of the Sages is, in the veins of the earth, congealed into silver and gold; in this operation the Sulphur acts the part of the male, and our Mercury that of the female. Of the composition and action of these two are engendered the Mercuries of the Philosophers.

In our former dialogue we gave an account of the meeting of Alchemists, which a sudden tempest brought to so abrupt a close Among those who took a prominent part in the proceedings, was a good friend of the first Alchemist; he was not a bad man, or an impostor, but, as they say, nobody's enemy except his own; yet he was foolish withal, and though really very ignorant, had no small opinion of his own wisdom and learning. He had at the meeting been the foremost champion of the claims of Sulphur to be regarded as the first substance of the Stone, and was satisfied that he would have been able to make good that claim, if the meeting had not been prematurely broken up. So when he got home he resumed his operations on Sulphur in a very confident spirit. He subjected it to distillation, sublimation, calcination, fixation, and to countless other chemical processes, in which he spent much time and money, without arriving at any result whatsoever. His failures at length began to prey on his health and spirits, and in order to recruit the former, and raise the latter, he fell into the habit of taking long walks in the neighbourhood of the town where he lived. But wherever he went he could think of nothing but Sulphur. One day, with his mind full of this besetting idea, and being wrought almost to an ecstacy, he entered a certain verdant grove, in which there was abundance not only of trees, herbs, and fruits, but also of animals, birds, minerals, and metals. Of water there was indeed a great scarcity; it was carried to the place by means of aqueducts, and among these was a conduit flowing with water extracted from the rays of the moon;—but this water was reserved for the use of the Nymph of the grove. In the grove there were two young men tending oxen and rams, and from them he learned that the grove belonged to the Nymph Venus. The Alchemist was gratified enough, but all his thoughts were absorbed by the subject of Sulphur, and when he remembered the words of the Sages, who say that the substance is vile and common, and its treatment easy, when he recollected the vast amount of time, labour, and money which he had vainly spent upon it, he lifted up his voice, and in the bitterness of his heart, cursed Sulphur. Now Sulphur was in that grove, though the Alchemist did not know it. But suddenly he heard a voice which said: "My friend, why do you curse Sulphur?" He looked up in bewilderment: nobody was to be seen. "My friend, why are you so sad?" continued the voice. *Alchemist:* Master, I seek the Philosopher's Stone as one that hungers after bread. *Voice:* And why thus do you curse Sulphur? *Alchemist:* My Lord, the Sages call it the substance of the Stone; yet I have spent all my time and labour in vain upon it, and am well nigh reduced to despair. *Voice:* It is true that

Sulphur is the true and chief substance of the Stone. Yet you curse it unjustly. For it lies heavily chained in a dark prison and cannot do as it would. Its hands and feet have been bound, and the doors of the dungeon closed upon it, at the bidding of its mother, Nature, who was angry with it for too readily obeying the summons of every Alchemist. It is now confined in such a perfect labyrinth of a prison, that it can be set free only by those Sages to whom Nature herself has entrusted the secret. *Alchemist:* Ah! miserable that I am, this is why he was unable to come to me! Flow very hard and unkind of the mother '! When is he to be set at large again? *Voice:* That can only be by means of hard and persevering labour. *Alchemist:* Who are his gaolers? *Voice:* They are of his own kindred, but grievous tyrants. *Alchemist:* And who are you? *Voice:* I am the judge and the chief gaoler, and my name is Saturn. Alchemist Then Sulphur is detained in your prison? Voice . Yes; but I am not his keeper. *Alchemist:* What does he do in prison? *Voice:* Whatever his gaolers command. *Alchemist:* And what can he do? *Voice:* He can perform a thousand things, and is the heart of all. He can perfect metals and minerals, impart understanding to animals, produce flowers in herbs and trees, corrupt and perfect air; in short, he produces all the odours and paints all the colours in the world. *Alchemist:* Of what substance does he make the flowers? *Voice:* His guards furnish him with vessels and matter; Sulphur digests it; and according to the diversity of the digestion, and the weight of the matter, he produces choice flowers, having their special odours. *Alchemist:* Master, is he old? *Voice:* Know, friend, that Sulphur is the virtue of the world, and though Nature's second-born—yet the oldest of all things. To those who know him, however, he is as obedient as a little child. He is most easily recognised by the vital spirit in animals, the colour in metals, the odour in plants. Without his help his mother can do nothing. *Alchemist:* Is he the sole heir, or has he any brothers? *Voice:* He has some brothers who are quite unworthy of him; and a sister that he loves, and who is to him as a mother. *Alchemist:* Is he always the same? Voice; As to his nature, it is always the same. But in person his heart only is pure: his garments are spotted. *Alchemist:* Master, was he ever quite free? *Voice:* Yes; in the days of the great Masters and Sages, whom Nature loved, and to whom she gave the keys of the prison. *Alchemist:* Who were these wise adepts? *Voice:* There have been very many, and among them Hermes, who was one and the same with the mother of Sulphur. After him there were kings, princes, a long line of Sages, including Aristotle and Avicenna. All these delivered Sulphur from his bonds. *Alchemist:* What does he give to them for delivering him? *Voice:* When he is set free, he binds his gaolers, and gives their three kingdoms to his deliverer. He also gives to him a magic mirror, in which the three parts of the wisdom of the whole world may be seen and known at a glance: and this mirror clearly exhibits the creation of the world, the influences of the celestial virtues on earthly things, and the way in which Nature composes substances by the regulation of heat. With its aid, men may at once understand the motion of the Sun and Moon, and that universal movement by which Nature herself is governed—also the various degrees of heat, cold, moisture, and dryness, and the virtues of herbs and of all other things. By its means the physician may at once, without consulting an herbarium, tell the exact composition of any given plant or medicinal herb. But now-a-days men are content to trust to the authority of great writers, and no longer attempt to use their own eyes. They quote Aristotle and Galen, as if there was not much more to be learned from the great Book of Nature which is spread open before them. Know that all things on the earth and under the earth are engendered and produced by the three principles, but sometimes by two, unto which the third, nevertheless, adheres. He who knows these three principles, and their proportions as conjoined by Nature, can tell easily by their greater or less coction, the degrees of heat in each subject, and whether they have been well, badly, or passably cooked. For those who know the three principles know also all vegetables—by sight, taste, and odour, for these senses determine the three principles, and the degree of their decoction. *Alchemist:* Master, they say that Sulphur is a Medicine. *Voice:* Nay, you might rather call him a physician, and to him who delivers him out of prison, he gives his blood as a Medicine. *Alchemist:* How long can a man ward off death by means of this universal Medicine? *Voice:* Until the time originally appointed. But many Sages who did not take ft with proper caution, have died before that time. *Alchemist:* Do you call it a poison then? *Voice:* Have you not observed that a great flame swallows up a small one? Men, who had received the Art by the teachings of others, thought that the more powerful the dose they took of our Medicine, the more beneficial would be the effect. They did not consider that one grain of it has strength to penetrate many thousand pounds of metals. *Alchemist:* How then should they have used it? *Voice:* They ought to have taken only so much as would have strengthened and nourished, without overwhelming, their natural heat. *Alchemist:* Master, I know how to make that Medicine. *Voice:* Blessed are you if you do! For the blood of Sulphur is that inward virtue and dryness which congeals quicksilver into gold and imparts health and perfection to all bodies. But the blood of Sulphur is obtained only by those who can deliver him from prison; and therefore he is so closely imprisoned that he can hardly breathe, lest he should come to the Palace of the King. *Alchemist:* Is he so closely imprisoned in all metals? *Voice:* In some his imprisonment is less strict than in others. *Alchemist:* Why, Lord, is he imprisoned in the metals so tyrannously? *Voice:* Because if he once came unto his royal palace, he would no longer fear his guards. He could look from the windows with freedom, and appear before the whole world, for he would be in his own kingdom, though not in that state of highest power whereto he desires to arrive. *Alchemist:* What is his food? *Voice:* His food is air, in a digested state, when he is free; but in prison he is compelled to consume it in a crude state. *Alchemist:* Master, cannot those quarrels between him and his gaolers be composed? *Voice:* Yes, by a wise and cunning craftsman. *Alchemist:* Why does he not offer them terms of peace? *Voice:* He cannot do so by himself: his indignation gets the better of his discretion. *Alchemist:* Why does he not do so through some commissary? *Voice:* He who could put an end to their strife would be a wise man, and worthy of undying honour. For if they were friends, they would help, instead of hindering each other, and bring forth immortal things. *Alchemist:* I will gladly undertake the duty of reconciling them. For I am a very learned man, and they could not resist my practical skill. I am a great Sage, and my Alchemistic treatment would quickly bring about the desired end. But tell me, is this the true Sulphur of the Sages? *Voice:* He is Sulphur; you ought to know whether he is the Sulphur of the Sages *Alchemist:* If I find his prison, shall I be able to deliver him? *Voice:* Yes, if you are wise enough to do so. It is easier to deliver him than to find his prison. *Alchemist:* When I do find him, shall I be able to make him into the Philosopher's Stone? *Voice:* I am no prophet. But if you follow his mother's advice, and dissolve the Sulphur, you will have the Stone. *Alchemist:* In what substance is this Sulphur to be found? *Voice:* In all substances. All things in the world—metals, herbs, trees, animals, stones, are its ore. *Alchemist:* But out of what substances do the Sages procure it? *Voice:* My friend, you press me somewhat too closely. But I may say that though it is everywhere, yet it has certain places where the Sages can most conveniently find it; and they worship it when it swims in its sea and sports with Vulcan (god of fire), though there it is disguised in a most poor garb. Now is it in a dark prison, hidden from sight. But it is one only subject, and if you cannot find it at home you will scarcely do so in the forest. Yet, to give you some heart in your research, I will solemnly assure you that it is most perfect in gold and silver—most easily obtained in quicksilver.

With these words Saturn departed, and the Alchemist, being weary with walking, fell into a deep sleep, in which he saw the following vision: He beheld in that grove a spring of water, near which Salt and Sulphur were walking and quarrelling, until at last they began to fight. Salt dealt Sulphur a grievous wound, out of which there flowed, instead of blood, pure, milk-white water, that swelled into a great river. In this river the virgin goddess, Diana, came to bathe; and a certain bold prince, who was passing by, was inflamed with great love towards her; which she, perceiving and returning, pretended to be sinking under water. The prince bade his attendants assist her; but they excused themselves, saying that the river, though it looked small and all but dried up, was most dangerous. "And," said they, "many of those who have passed here before have perished in it." Then that prince threw off his thick cloak, plunged into the river, and stretched out his arm to save the beautiful Diana; but she grasped it so convulsively that they both sank under water together. Soon afterwards their souls were seen rising upward above the water, and they said, "We have done well, for in no other way could we be delivered from our stained and spotted bodies." *Alchemist* (speaking): Will you ever return into those bodies? *Souls:* Not while they are so polluted—but when they are cleansed, and the river is dried up by the heat of the sun. *Alchemist:* What do you do in the meantime? Souls: We soar above the water till the storm and the mists cease. . . . Then the Alchemist thought that he saw a great number of his fellows come to the spot where the body of the Sulphur lay slain by the Salt; and they divided it among themselves, and gave a piece to him also. Then they went home, and began to operate on their (dead) Sulphur, and are at it to this day. Presently Saturn returned, and the Alchemist said: Master, come quickly, I have found Sulphur—help me to make the Stone. *Saturn:* Gladly, my friend. Prepare the quicksilver, and the sulphur, and give me the vessel. *Alchemist:* Oh, I do not want Mercury. It is a delusion and a snare, as my friend the other Alchemist discovered to his smart. *Saturn:* I can do nothing without quicksilver. *Alchemist:* Oh no, we will make it of Sulphur only. So they set to work on that piece of dead Sulphur, and sublimed, calcined, and subjected it to all manner of chemical operations. But they produced nothing save little bits of sulphurous tow, such as they use for lighting fires. Then the Alchemist confessed the fruitlessness of his endeavours, and bade Saturn set about the work in his own way. Then Saturn took two kinds of quicksilver, of different substance but one root, washed them with his urine, and called them the sulphurs of sulphurs; then he mixed the fixed with the volatile, after which he placed them in a proper vessel, and set a watch to prevent the sulphur from escaping; afterwards he placed them in a bath of very gentle heat—and thus they made the Philosopher's Stone, which must always follow as the outcome of the right substance. Then the Alchemist took it in his hand, admired its beautiful purple colour, and danced about with it, shouting aloud with joy and delight. Suddenly the glass slipped out of his hand and broke into a thousand pieces; the stone vanished; and the Alchemist awoke with nothing in his hand but some pieces of sulphurous tow.

There are a good many Alchemists who, having an extremely favourable opinion of themselves, and fancying that they can hear the grass grow, rail against this Art, because they think that if the Stone were not a mere delusion, they could not have failed to find it. We, for our part, are not over anxious to rob these people of their comfortable conviction. But to men who were worthy (men both of high and low degree) we have repeatedly proved the reality of our Art by incontestable ocular evidence. Let me warn those who wish to follow the true method in studying our Art, always to read with constant reference to natural facts, and never, under any circumstances, to do anything contrary to Nature. If the Sages say that fire does not burn, they must not believe it; for Nature is greater than the Sages; but if they say that it is the property of fire to dry and heat things, they will accept this statement, because it is in accordance with the truth of Nature—and the facts of Nature are always simple and plain. If any one came and taught you to make this Stone, as though he were giving you a receipt for making cheese out of milk, he might speak more plainly than I have done; but I am compelled to veil and conceal my meaning, because of the vow which my Master exacted of me.

My last words shall be addressed to you who have already made some progress in this. Art. Have you been where the bridegroom has been married to the bride, and the nuptials were celebrated in the house of Nature? Have you heard how the vulgar have seen this Sulphur, as much as have you who have taken such pains to seek it? If you wish that even old women should practise your philosophy, show the dealbation of these sulphurs, and say openly to the common people: Behold, the water is divided, and the Sulphur has gone forth; when it returns it will be whiter than snow, and will congeal the water. Burn the Sulphur with incombustible sulphur, wash it, and make it white and purple until the Sulphur becomes Mercury, and the Mercury Sulphur, and you can proceed to quicken it with the soul of gold. Our Mercury must be corrected by means of Sulphur— otherwise it is unprofitable. A prince without a people is a wretched sight—and so is an Alchemist without Sulphur and Mercury. If you .understand me, I have spoken.

The Alchemist went home, bewailed the broken Stone, and his folly in not asking Saturn about the Salt of the Sages, and the way of distinguishing between it and ordinary salt. The rest he related to his wife.

Conclusion.

Every student of this Art should first carefully read what is said—in this and other Treatises—about the creation, operation, properties, and effects of the four elements; otherwise he cannot apprehend the nature of the three principles, or find the substance of the Stone, or understand its development. God has created the elements out of chaos; Nature has evolved the three principles out of the elements; and out of these principles she makes all things, and gives power to her beloved disciples to produce marvellous preparations. If Nature produces metals out of the principles, Art must follow her example. It is one of the rules of Nature to act through intermediate substances; and this book should enable the student to judge what substances are intermediate between the elements and metals, and between metals and the Stone. The difference between gold and water is great, that between water and mercury not so great, and that between gold and mercury very small, for mercury is the habitation of gold, water the habitation of mercury, and sulphur is that which coagulates mercury. The whole arcanum lies hidden in the Sulphur of the Sages, which is also contained iii the inmost part of their Mercury, which has to be prepared in a certain way that shall be described on another occasion.

I have not written this Treatise with the object of refuting the ancient Sages, but only for the purpose of correcting, explaining, and supplementing their statements. After all, they were only men, and they sometimes did make assertions which can now no longer be maintained. For instance, when Albertus Magnus says that gold was once found to have developed in the teeth of a dead man, he is out of harmony with the possibilities of Nature; for an animal substance can never develop into a mineral. It is true that animals and vegetables contain sulphur and mercury, as well as minerals; but these principles are animal and vegetable, not mineral. If there were no animal sulphur in man, the mercury of his blood could not be congealed into flesh and bones; and if plants contained no vegetable sulphur, their mercury or water (sap) would not be congealed into leaves and flowers. The three kinds of sulphur are essentially the same, but, like the three mercuries, they are differentiated according to the three kingdoms, and cannot act outside their own kingdoms. Each kind of mercury can be coagulated by none but its own sulphur, and if gold was found in the teeth of a dead man, it must have been introduced in an artificial manner—either as gold, or in the shape of some other metal which by the gradual action of its own metallic sulphur on its metallic mercury, was afterwards transmuted into gold. It is mistaken impressions and superstitious notions, like this one of Albertus Magnus, that we have set ourselves to correct in this Treatise, by stating once for all the true facts of animal, vegetable, and mineral development.

Let the painstaking student be satisfied to have received a true account of the origin of the Three Principles. There is no greater help towards a successful end than a good beginning. I have in this Treatise started the student on the right road, and given him clear and practical directions. With God's blessing, and by dint of diligent and persevering study, he may now fairly hope to reach the glorious goal. But I, having told out all that is lawful for me to utter, now commit myself to the mercy of a loving Creator, who will receive me to Himself; and I commend the gentle and pious Reader to the same great Father of All, to whom be praise and glory, through the endless succession of the ages.

THE END.

AN

OPEN ENTRANCE

TO THE

CLOSED PALACE

OF THE

KING.

BY

AN ANONYMOUS SAGE AND

LOVER OF TRUTH.

TABLE OF CONTENTS.

THE AUTHOR'S PREFACE.

I, BEING an anonymous adept, a lover of learning, and a philosopher, have decreed to write this little treatise of medicinal, chemical, and physical arcana, in the year 1645 after the Birth of Christ, and in the 23rd year of my age, to assist in conducting my straying brethren out of the labyrinth of error, and with the further object of making myself known to other Sages, holding aloft a torch which may be visible far and wide to those who are groping in the darkness of ignorance. The contents of this Book are not fables, but real experiments which I have seen, touched, and handled, as an adept will easily conclude from these lines. I have written more plainly about this Art than any of my predecessors; sometimes I have found myself on the very verge of breaking my vow, and once or twice had to lay down my pen for a season; but I could not resist the inward prompting of God, which impelled me to persevere in the most loving course, who alone knows the heart, and to whom only be glory for ever. Hence, I undoubtedly gather that in this last age of the world, many will become blessed by this arcanum, through what I have thus faithfully written, for I have not willingly left anything doubtful to the young beginner. I know many who with me do enjoy this secret, and am persuaded that many more will also rejoice in its possession. Let the holy Will of God perform what it pleases, though I confess myself an unworthy instrument through whom such great things should be effected.

CHAPTER I.

Of the need of Sulphur for producing the Elixir.

WHOEVER wishes to possess this secret Golden Fleece, which has virtue to transmute metals into gold, should know that our Stone is nothing but gold digested to the highest degree of purity and subtle fixation to which it can be brought by Nature and the highest effort of Art; and this gold thus perfected is called "our gold," no longer vulgar, and is the ultimate goal of Nature. These words, though they may be surprising to some of my readers, are true, as I, an adept, bear witness; and though overwise persons entertain chimerical dreams, Nature herself is most wonderfully simple. Gold, then, is the one true principle of purification. But our gold is twofold; one kind is mature and fixed, the yellow Latten, and its heart or centre is pure fire, whereby it is kept from destruction, and only purged in the fire. This gold is our male, and it is sexually joined to a more crude white gold—the female seed: the two together being indissolubly united, constitute our fruitful Hermaphrodite. We are told by the Sages that corporal gold is dead, until it be conjoined with its bride, with whom the coagulating sulphur, which in gold is outwards, must be turned inwards. Hence it follows that the substance which we require is Mercury. Concerning this substance, Geber uses the following words: "Blessed be the Most High God who created Mercury, and made it an all-prevailing substance." And it is true that unless we had Mercury, Alchemists might still boast themselves, but all their boasting would be vain. Hence it is clear that our Mercury is not common mercury; for all common mercury is a male that is corporal, specific, and dead, while our Mercury is spiritual, female, living, and life-giving. Attend closely to what I say about our Mercury, which is the salt of the wise men. The Alchemist who works without it is like a man who draws a bow without a string. Yet it is found nowhere in a pure state above ground, but has to be extracted by a cunning process out of the substance in which it exists.

CHAPTER II.

Of the Component Principles of the Mercury of the Sages.

Let those who aim to purify Mercury by means of salts, fæces, and other foreign bodies, and by strange chemical processes, understand that though our water is variously composed, it is yet only one thing, formed by the concretion of divers substances of the same essence. The components of our water are fire, the vegetable "Saturnian liquid," and the bond of Mercury. The fire is that of mineral Sulphur, which yet can be called neither mineral nor metallic, but partakes of both characters: it is a chaos or spirit, because our fiery Dragon, that overcomes all things, is yet penetrated by the odour of the Saturnian liquid, its blood growing together with the Saturnian sap into one body which is yet neither a body (since it is all volatile) nor a spirit (since in fire it resembles melted metal). It may thus be very properly described as chaos, or the mother of all metals. From this chaos I can extract everything—even the Sun and Moon—without the transmutatory Elixir. It is called our Arsenic, our Air, our Moon, our Magnet, and our Chalybs: these names representing the different stages of its development, even unto the manifestation of the kingly diadem, which is cast out of the menstruum of our harlot. Learn, then, who are the friends of Cadmus; who is the serpent that devoured them; what the hollow oak to which Cadmus spitted the serpent. Learn who are the doves of Diana, that overcome the green lion by gentleness: even the Babylonian dragon, which kills everything with its venom. Learn, also, what are the winged shoes of Mercury, and who are those nymphs whom he charms by means of his incantations.

CHAPTER III.

Concerning the Chalybs of the Sages.

Our Chalybs is the true key of our Art, without which the Torch could in no wise be kindled, and as the true magi have delivered many things concerning it, so among vulgar alchemists there is great contention as to its nature. It is the ore of gold, the purest of all spirits; a secret, infernal, and yet most volatile fire, the wonder of the world, the result of heavenly virtues in the lower world—for which reason the Almighty has assigned to it a most glorious and rare heavenly conjunction, even that notable sign whose nativity is declared in the East. This star was seen by the wise men of old, and straightway they knew that a Great King was born in the world. When you sec its constellation, follow it to the cradle, and there you will behold a beautiful Infant. Remove the impurities, look upon the face of the King's Son; open your treasury, give to him gold, and after his death he will bestow on you his flesh and blood, the highest Medicine in the three monarchies of the earth.

CHAPTER IV.

Of the Magnet of the Sages.

As steel is attracted towards the magnet, and the magnet turns towards the steel, so also our Magnet attracts our Chalybs. Thus, as Chalybs is the ore of gold, so our Magnet is the true ore of our Chalybs. The hidden centre of our Magnet abounds in Salt, which Salt is the menstruum in the Sphere of the Moon, and can calcine gold. This centre turns towards the Pole with an archetic appetite, in which the virtue of the Chalybs is exalted into degrees. In the Pole is the heart of Mercury, the true fire (in which is the rest of its Master), sailing through this great sea that it may arrive at both the Indies, and direct its course by the aspect of the North Star, which our Magnet will manifest.

CHAPTER V.

Of the Chaos of the Sages.

Let the student incline his ear to the united verdict of the Sages, who describe this work as analogous to the Creation of the World. In the Beginning God created Heaven and Earth; and the Earth was without form and void, and the Spirit of God moved upon the face of the waters. And God said, "Let there be light," and there was light. These words are sufficient for the student of our Art. The Heaven must be united to the Earth on the couch of friendship; so shall he reign in glory forever. The Earth is the heavy body, the womb of the minerals, which it cherishes in itself, although it brings to light trees and animals. The Heaven is the place where the great Lights revolve, and through the air transmit their influences to the lower world. But in the beginning all was one confused chaos. *Our* Chaos is, as it were, a mineral earth (by virtue of its coagulation), and yet also volatile air—in the *centre* of which is the Heaven of the Sages, the Astral Centre, which with its light irradiates the earth to its surface. What man is wise enough to evolve out of this world a new King, who shall redeem his brothers from their natural weaknesses, by dying, being lifted on high, and giving his flesh and blood for the life of the world? I thank Thee, O God, that Thou hast concealed these things from the wise and prudent, and hast revealed them unto babes!

CHAPTER VI.

Of the Air of the Sages.

Our air, like the air of the firmament, divides the waters; and as the waters under the firmament are visible to us mortals, while we are unable to see the waters above the firmament, so in "our work" we see the extracentral mineral waters, but are unable to see those which, though hidden within, nevertheless have a real existence. They exist but do not appear until it please the Artist, as the author of the *New Light* has testified. Our air keeps the extracentral waters from mingling with those at the centre. If through the removal of this impediment, they were enabled to mingle, their union would be indissoluble. Therefore the external vapours and burning sulphur do stiffly adhere to our chaos, and unable to resist its tyranny, the pure flies away from the fire in the form of a dry powder. This then should be your great object. The arid earth must he irrigated, and its pores softened with water of its own kind; then this thief with all the workers of iniquity will be cast out, the water will be purged of its leprous stain by the addition of true Sulphur, and you will have the Spring whose waters are sacred to the maiden Queen Diana. This thief is armed with all the malignity of arsenic, and is feared and eschewed by the winged youth. Though the Central Water be his Spouse, yet the youth cannot come to her, until Diana with the wings of her doves purges the poisonous air, and opens a passage to the bridal chamber. Then the youth enters easily through the pores, presently shaking the waters above, and stirring up a rude and ruddy cloud. Do thou, O Diana, bring in the water over him, even unto the brightness of the Moon! So the darkness on the face of the abyss will be dispersed by the spirit moving in the waters. Thus, at the bidding of God, light will appear on the Seventh Day, and then this sophic creating of Mercury shall be completed, from which time, until the revolution of the year, you may wait for the birth of the marvellous Child of the Sun, who will come to deliver his brethren from every stain.

CHAPTER VII.

Of the First Operation—Preparation of Mercury by means of the Flying Eagles.

Know, my brother, that the exact preparation of the Eagles of the Sages, is the highest effort of our Art. In this first section of our work, nothing is to be done without hard and persevering toil; though it is quite true that afterwards the substance develops under the influence of gentle heat without any imposition of hands. The Sages tell us that their Eagles must be taken to devour the Lion, and that they gain the victory all the sooner if they are very numerous; also that the number of the work varies between 7 and 9. The Mercury of the Sages is the Bird of Hermes (now called a goose, now a pheasant). But the Eagles are always mentioned in the plural, and number from 3 to 10. Yet this is not to be understood as if there should be so many weights or parts of the water to one of the earth, but the water must be taken so oftentimes acuated or sharpened as there are Eagles numbered. This acuation is made by sublimation. There is, then, one sublimation of the Mercury of the Sages, when one Eagle is mentioned, and the seventh sublimation will so strengthen your Mercury, that the Bath of your King will be ready. . . . Let me tell you now how this part of the work is performed. Take 4 parts of our fiery Dragon, in whose belly is hidden the magic Chalybs, and 9 parts of our Magnet; mingle them by means of a fierce fire, in the form of a mineral water, the foam of which must be taken away. Remove the shell, and take the kernel. Purge what remains once more by means of fire and the Sun, which may be done easily if Saturn shall have seen himself in the mirror of Mars. Then you will obtain our Chameleon, or Chaos, in which all the virtues of our Art are potentially present. This is the infant Hermaphrodite, who, through the bite of a mad dog, has been rendered so fearful of water, that though of a kindred nature, it always eschews and avoids it. But in the grove of Diana are two doves that soothe its rabid madness if applied by the art of the nymph Mercury. Take it and plunge it under water till it perish therein; then the rabid and black dog will appear panting and half suffocated—drive him down with vigorous blows, and the darkness will be dispelled. Give it wings when the Moon is full, and it will fly away as an Eagle, leaving the doves of Diana dead (though, when first taken they should be living). Repeat this seven times, and your work is done; the gentle coction which follows is child's play and a woman's work.

CHAPTER VIII.

Of the Difficulty and Length of the First Operation.

Some Alchemists fancy that the work from beginning to end is a mere idle entertainment; but those who make it so will reap what they have sown—viz., nothing. We know that next to the Divine Blessing, and the discovery of the proper foundation, nothing is so important as unwearied industry and perseverance in this First Operation. It is no wonder, then, that so many students of this Art are reduced to beggary; they are afraid of work, and look upon our Art as mere sport for their leisure moments. For no labour is more tedious than that which the preparatory part of our enterprise demands. Morienus earnestly entreats the King to consider this fact, and says that many Sages have complained of the tedium of our work. "To render a chaotic mass orderly," says the Poet, "is matter of much time and labour"—and the noble author of the Hermetical Arcanum describes it as an Herculean task. There are so many impurities clinging to our first substance, and a most powerful intermediate agent is required for the purpose of eliciting from our polluted menstruum the Royal Diadem. But when you have once prepared your Mercury, the most formidable part of your task is accomplished, and you may indulge in that rest which is sweeter than any work, as the Sage says.

CHAPTER IX.

On the Superiority of our Mercury over All Metals.

Our Mercury is that Serpent which devoured the companions of Cadmus, after having first swallowed Cadmus himself, though he was far stronger than they. Yet Cadmus will one day transfix this Serpent, when he has coagulated it with his Sulphur. Know that this, our Mercury, is a King among metals, and dissolves them by changing their Sulphur into a kindred mercurial substance. The Mercury of one, two, or three eagles bears rule over Saturn, Jupiter, and Venus. The Mercury of from three to seven eagles sways the Moon; that of ten eagles has power over the Sun; our Mercury is nearer than any other unto the first *ens* of metals; it has power to enter metallic bodies, and to manifest their hidden depths.

CHAPTER X.

On the Sulphur which is in the Mercury of the Sages.

It is a marvellous fact that our Mercury contains active Sulphur, and yet preserves the form and all the properties of Mercury. Hence it is necessary that a form be introduced therein by our preparation, which form is a metallic sulphur. This Sulphur is the inward fire which causes the putrefaction of the composite Sun This sulphureous fire is the spiritual seed which our Virgin (still remaining immaculate) has conceived. For an uncorrupted virginity admits of a spiritual love, as experience and authority affirm. The two (the passive and the active principle) combined we call our Hermaphrodite. When joined to the Sun, it softens, liquefies, and dissolves it with gentle heat. By means of the same fire it coagulates itself; and by its coagulation produces the Sun. Our pure and homogeneous Mercury, having conceived inward Sulphur (through our Art), coagulates itself under the influence of gentle outward heat, like the cream of milk—a subtle earth floating on the water. When it is united to the Sun, it is not only not coagulated, but the composite substance becomes softer day by day; the bodies are almost dissolved; and the spirits begin to be coagulated, with a black colour and a most fetid smell. Hence it appears that this spiritual metallic Sulphur is in truth the *moving principle in our Art*; it is really volatile or unmatured gold, and by proper digestion is changed into that metal. If joined to perfect gold, it is not coagulated, but dissolves the corporal gold, and remains with it, being dissolved, under one form, although before the perfect union death must precede, that so they may he united after death, not simply in a perfect unity, but in a thousand times more than perfect perfection.

CHAPTER XI.

Concerning the Discovery of the Perfect Magistery.

There are those who think that this Art was first discovered by Solomon, or rather imparted to him by Divine Revelation. But though there is no reason for doubting that so wise and profoundly learned a sovereign was acquainted with our Art, yet we happen to know that he was not the first to acquire the knowledge. It was possessed by Hermes, the Egyptian, and some other Sages before him; and we may suppose that they first sought a simple exaltation of imperfect metals into regal perfection, and that it was at first their endeavour to develop Mercury, which is most like to gold in its weight and properties, into perfect gold. This, however, no degree of ingenuity could effect by any fire, and the truth gradually broke on their minds that an internal heat was required as well as an external one. So they rejected aqua fortis and all corrosive solvents, after long experiments with the same—also all salts, except that kind which is the first substance of all salts, which dissolves all metals and coagulates Mercury, but not without violence, whence that kind of agent is again separated entire, both in weight and virtue, from the things it is applied to. They saw that the digestion of Mercury was prevented by certain aqueous crudities and earthy dross; and that the *radical* nature of these impurities rendered their elimination impossible, except by the complete inversion of the whole compound. They knew that Mercury would become fixed if it could be freed from their defiling presence—as it contains fermenting sulphur, which is only hindered by these impurities from coagulating the whole mercurial body. At length they discovered that Mercury, in the bowels of the earth, was intended to become a metal, and that the process of development was only stopped by the impurities with which it had become tainted. They found that that which should be active in the Mercury was passive; and that its infirmity could not be remedied by any means, except the introduction of some kindred principle from without. Such a principle they discovered in metallic sulphur, which stirred up the passive sulphur in the Mercury, and by allying itself with it, expelled the aforesaid impurities. But in seeking to accomplish this practically, they were met by another great difficulty. In order that this sulphur might be effectual in purifying the Mercury, it was indispensable that it should itself be pure. All their efforts to purify it, however, were doomed to failure. At length they bethought them that it might possibly be found somewhere in Nature in a purified condition—and their search was crowned with success. They sought active sulphur in a pure state, and found it cunningly concealed in the House of the Ram. This sulphur mingled most eagerly with the offspring of Saturn, and the desired effect was speedily produced—after the malignant venom of the "air" of Mercury had been tempered (as already set forth at some length) by the Doves of Venus. Then life was joined to life by means of the liquid; the dry was moistened; the passive was stirred into action by the active; the dead was revived by the living. The heavens were indeed temporarily clouded over, but after a copious downpour of rain, serenity was restored. Mercury emerged in a hermaphroditic state. Then they placed it in the fire; in no long time they succeeded in coagulating it, and in its coagulation they found the Sun and the Moon in a most pure state. Then they considered that, before its coagulation, this Mercury was not a metal, since, on being volatilised, it left no residue at the bottom of the distilling vessel; hence they called it unmatured gold and their living (or quick) silver. It also occurred to them that if gold were sown, as it were, in the soil of its own first substance, its excellence would probably be enhanced; and when they placed gold therein, the fixed was volatilised, the hard softened, the coagulated dissolved, to the amazement of Nature herself. For this reason they wedded these two to each other, put them in a still over the fire, and for many days regulated the heat in accordance with the requirements of Nature. Thus the dead was revived, the body decayed, and a glorified spirit rose from the grave; the soul was exalted into the Quintessence,—the Universal Medicine for animals, vegetables, and minerals.

CHAPTER XII.

The Generic Method of Making the Perfect Magistery.

The greatest secret of our operation is no other than a cohobation of the nature of one thing above the other, until the most digested virtue be extracted out of the digested body of the crude one. But there are hereto requisite: Firstly, an exact measurement and preparation of the ingredients required; secondly, an exact fulfilment of all external conditions; thirdly a proper regulation of the fire; fourthly, a good knowledge of the natural properties of the substances; and fifthly, patience, in order that the work may not be marred by overgreat haste. Of all these points we will now speak in their proper order.

CHAPTER XIII.

Of the Use of Mature Sulphur in the Work of the Elixir.

We have spoken of the need of Mercury, and have described its properties more plainly and straightforwardly than has ever been done before. God knows that we do not grudge the knowledge of this Art to our brother men; and we are not afraid that it can ever become the property of any unworthy person. So long as the secret is possessed by a comparatively small number of philosophers, their lot is anything but a bright and happy one; surrounded as we are on every side by the cruel greed and the prying suspicion of the multitude, we are doomed, like Cain, to wander over the earth homeless and friendless. Not for us are the soothing influences of domestic happiness; not for us the delightful confidences of friendship. Men who covet our golden secret pursue us from place to place, and fear closes our lips, when love tempts us to open ourselves freely to a brother. Thus we feel prompted at times to burst forth into the desolate exclamation of Cain: "Whoever finds me will slay me." Yet we are not the murderers of our brethren; we are anxious only to do good to our fellow-men. But even our kindness and charitable compassion are rewarded with black ingratitude— ingratitude that cries to heaven for vengeance. It was only a short time ago that, after visiting the plague-stricken haunts of a certain city, and restoring the sick to perfect health by means of my miraculous medicine, I found myself surrounded by a yelling mob, who demanded that I should give to them my Elixir of the Sages; and it was only by changing my dress and my name, by shaving off my beard and putting on a wig, that I was enabled to save my life, and escape from the hands of those wicked men. And even when our lives are not threatened, it is not pleasant to find ourselves, wherever we go, the central objects of human greed. . . . I know of several persons who were found strangled in their beds, simply because they were suspected of possessing this secret, though, in reality, they knew no more about it than their murderers; it was enough for some desperate ruffians, that a mere whisper of suspicion had been breathed against their victims. Men are so eager to have this Medicine that your very caution will arouse their suspicions, and endanger your safety. Again, if you desire to sell any large quantity of your gold and silver, you will be unable to do so without imminent risk of discovery. The very fact that anyone has a great mass of bullion for sale would in most places excite suspicion. This feeling will be strengthened when people test the quality of our gold; for it is much finer and purer than any of the gold which is brought from Barbary, or from the Guinea Coast; and our silver is better even than that which is conveyed home by the Spanish silver fleet. If, in order to baffle discovery, you mix these precious metals with alloy, you render yourself liable, in England and Holland at least, to capital punishment; for in those countries no one is permitted to tamper with the precious metals, except the officers of the mint, and the licensed goldsmiths. I remember once going, in the disguise of a foreign merchant, to a goldsmith's shop, and offering him 600 pounds worth of our pure silver for sale. He subjected it to the usual tests, and then said: "This silver is artificially prepared." When I asked him why he thought so, his answer was: "I am not a novice in my profession, and know very well the exact quality of the silver which is brought from the different mines." When I heard these words I took myself away with great secrecy and dispatch, leaving the silver in the hands of the goldsmith. On this account, and by reason of the many and great difficulties which beset us, the possessors of this Stone, on every side, we do elect to remain hidden, and will communicate the Art to those who are worthily covetous of our secrets, and then mark what public good will befall. Without Sulphur, our Mercury would never be properly coagulated for our supernatural work; it is the male substance, while Mercury may be called the female; and all Sages say that no tincture can be made without its latten, which latten is gold, without any double speaking. Wise men, notwithstanding, can find this substance even on the dunghill; but the ignorant are unable to discern it even in gold. The tincture of gold is concealed in the gold of the Sages, which is the most highly matured of bodies; but as a raw material it exists only in our Mercury; and it (gold) receives from Mercury the multiplication of its seed, but in virtue rather than in weight. The Sages say that common gold is dead, while their's is living; and common gold is dead in the same sense in which a grain of wheat is dead, while it is surrounded by dry air; and comes to life, swells, softens, and germinates only when it is put into moist earth. In this sense gold, too, is dead, so long as it is surrounded by the corporeal husk, always allowing, of course, for the great difference between a vegetable grain and metallic gold. *Our* grain is quickened in *water* only; and as wheat, while it remains in the barn is called grain, and is not destined to be quickened, because it is to be used for bread making—but changes its name, when it is sown in the field, and is then called seedcorn; *so* our gold, while it is in the form of rings, plate, and coins, is called *common* gold, because in that state it is likely to remain unchanged to the end of the world; but *potentially* it is even then the gold of the Sages, because if sown in its own proper element, it would in a few days become the Chaos of the Sages. Hence the Sages bid you revive the dead (*i.e.*, the gold which already appeared doomed to a living death) and mortify the living, *i.e.*, the Mercury which, imparting life to the gold, is itself deprived of the vital principle. Their gold is taken in a dead, their water in a living, state, and by their composition and brief coction, the dead gold revives and the living Mercury dies, *i.e.*, the spirit is coagulated, the body is dissolved, and thus both putrefy together, until all the members of the compound are torn into atoms. The mystery of our Art, which we conceal with so great care, is the preparation of the Mercury, which above ground is not to be found made ready to our hand. But when it is prepared, it is "our water" in which gold is dissolved, whereby the latent life of the gold is set free, and receives the life of the dissolving Mercury, which is to gold what good earth is to the grain of wheat. When the gold has putrefied in the Mercury, there arises out of the decomposition of death a new body, of the same essence, but of a glorified substance. Here you have the whole of our Philosophy in a nutshell. There is no secret about it, except the preparation of Mercury, its mingling with the gold in the right proportions, and the regulation of the fire in accordance with its requirements. Gold by itself does not fear the fire; hence the great point is, to temper the heat to the capacity of the Mercury. If the Mercury is not properly prepared, the gold remains common gold, being joined with an improper agent; it continues unchanged, and no degree of heat will help it to put off its corporeal nature. Without our Mercury the seed (*i.e.*, gold) cannot be sown; and if gold is not sown in its proper element, it cannot be quickened any more than the corn which the West Indians keep underground, in air-tight stone jars, can germinate. I know that some self-constituted "Sages" will take exception to this teaching, and say that common gold and running Mercury are not the substance of our Stone. But one question will suffice to silence their objections: Have they ever actually prepared our Tincture? I have prepared it more than once, and daily have it in my power; hence I may perhaps be permitted to speak as one having authority. Go on babbling about your rain water collected in May, your Salts, your sperm "which is more potent than the foul fiend himself," ye self-styled philosophers; rail at me, if you like; all you say is conclusively refuted by this one fact—you cannot make the Stone. When I say that gold and Mercury are the only substances of our Stone, I know what I am writing about; and the Searcher of all hearts knows also that I say true. The time has arrived when we may speak more freely about this Art. For Elias the artist is at hand, and glorious things are already spoken of the City of God. I possess wealth sufficient to buy the whole world—but as yet I may not use it on account of the craft and cruelty of wicked men. It is not from jealousy that I conceal as much as I do: God knows that I am weary of this lonely, wandering life, shut out from the bonds of friendship, and almost from the face of God. I do not worship the golden calf, before which our Israelites bow low to the ground; let it be ground to powder like the brazen serpent. I hope that in a few years gold (not as given by God, but as abused by man) will be so common that those who are now so mad after it, shall contemptuously spurn aside this bulwark of Antichrist. Then will the day of our deliverance be at hand when the streets of the new Jerusalem are paved with gold, and its gates are made of great diamonds. The day is at hand when, by means of this my Book, gold will have become as common as dirt; when we Sages shall find rest for the soles of our feet, and render fervent thanks to God. My heart conceives unspeakable things, and is enlarged for the good of the Israel of God. These words I utter forth with a herald's clarion tones. My Book is the precursor of Elias, designed to prepare the Royal way of the Master; and would to God that by its means all men might become adepts in our Art—for then gold, the great idol of mankind, would lose its value, and we should prize it only for its scientific teaching. Virtue would be loved for its own sake. I am familiar with many possessors of this Art who regard silence as the great point of honour. But I have been enabled by God to take a different view of the matter; and I firmly believe that I can best serve the Israel of God, and put my talent out at usury, by making this secret knowledge the common property of the whole world. Hence I have not conferred with flesh and blood, nor attempted to obtain the consent of my Brother Sages. If the matter succeeds according to my desire and prayer, they will all rejoice that I have published this Book.

CHAPTER XIV.

Of the Circumstantial and Accidental Requisites of our Art.

We have weeded out all vulgar errors concerning our Art, and have shown that gold and Mercury are the only substances required. We have shown that this gold is to be understood, not metaphorically, but in a truly philosophical sense. We have also declared our Mercury to be true quicksilver, without any ambiguity of acceptation. The latter, we have told you, must be made by art, and be a key to the former. We have made everything as clear as noonday; and our teaching is based, not on hearsay, or on the writings of others, but on our own personal and oft repeated experience. The things we faithfully declare are what we have both seen and known. We have made and do possess the Stone—the great Elixir. Moreover, we do not grudge you this knowledge, but wish you to attain it out of this Book. We have spoken out more plainly than any of our predecessors; and our Receipt, apart from the fact that we have not called things by their proper names, is perfectly trustworthy. It remains for us to give you some practical tests by which the goodness or unsuitableness of your Mercury may be known, and some directions for amending its defects. When you have living Mercury and gold, there remains to be accomplished, first, the purging of the Mercury and the gold, then their espousal, and finally the regulation of the fire

CHAPTER XV.

Of the Incidental Purging of Mercury and Gold.

Perfect gold is found in the bowels of the earth in little pieces, or in sand. If you can meet with this unmixed gold, it is pure enough; if not, purge it with antimony or royal cement, or boil it with aqua fortis, the gold being first granulated. Then smelt it, remove the impure sediment, and it is ready. But Mercury needs inward and essential purging, which radical cleansing is brought about by the addition of true Sulphur, little by little, according to the number of the

Eagles. Then it also needs an incidental purgation for the purpose of removing from its surface the impurities which have, by the essential purgation, been ejected from the centre. This process is not absolutely necessary, but it is useful, as it accelerates the work. Therefore, take your Mercury, which you have purified with a suitable number of Eagles, sublime it three times with common salt and iron filings, and wash it with vinegar and a moderate quantity of salts of ammonia, then dry and distil in a glass retort, over a gradually increasing fire, until the whole of the Mercury has ascended. Repeat this four times, then boil the Mercury in spirits of vinegar for an hour, stirring it constantly. Then pour off the vinegar, and wash off its acidity by a plentiful effusion of spring water. Dry the Mercury, and its splendour will be wonderful. You may wash it with wine, or vinegar and salt, and so spare the sublimation; but then distil it at least four times without addition, after you have perfected all the eagles, or washings, washing the chalybeat retort every time with ashes and water; then boil it in distilled vinegar for half a day, stirring it strongly at times. Pour off the blackish vinegar, add new, then wash with warm water. This process is designed to purge away the internal impurities from the surface. These impurities you may perceive if, on mixing Mercury with purest gold, you place the amalgam on a white sheet of paper. The sooty blackness which is then seen on the paper is purged away by this process.

CHAPTER XVI.

Of the Amalgam of Mercury and Gold, and of their respective Proportions.

When you have done all this, take one part of pure and laminated gold, or fine gold filings, and two parts of Mercury; put them in a heated (marble) jar, *i.e.*, heated with boiling water, being taken out of which it dries quickly, and holds the heat a long time. Grind with an ivory, or glass, or stone, or iron, or boxwood pestle (the iron pestle is not so good; I use a pestle of crystal): pound them, I say, as small as the painters grind their colours; then add water so as to make the mass as consistent as half melted butter. The mixture should be fixable and soft, and permit itself to be moulded into little globules—like moderately soft butter; it should be of such a consistency as to yield to the gentlest touch. Moreover, it should be of the same temperature throughout, and one part should not be more liquid than another. The mixture will be more or less soft, according to the proportion of Mercury which it contains; but it must be capable of forming into those little globules, and the Mercury should not be more lively at the bottom than at the top. If the amalgam be left undisturbed, it will at once harden; you must therefore judge of the merits of the mixture, while you are stirring it; if it fulfils the above conditions, it is good. Then take spirit of vinegar, and dissolve in it a third part of salt of ammonia, put the amalgam into this liquid, let the whole boil for a quarter-of-an-hour in a long necked glass vessel; then take the mixture out of the glass vessel, pour off the liquid, heat the mortar, and pound the amalgam (as above) vigorously, and wash away all blackness with hot water. Put it again into the liquid, let it boil up once more in the glass vessel, pound it as before, and wash it. Repeat this process until the blackness is entirely purged out. The amalgam will then be as brilliant and white as the purest silver. Once more regulate the temperature of the amalgam according to the rules given above; your labour will be richly rewarded. If the amalgam be not quite soft enough, add a little Mercury. Then boil it in pure water, and free it from all saltness and acidity. Pour off the water, and dry the amalgam. Make quite sure that it is thoroughly dried, by waving it to and fro on the point of a knife over a sheet of white paper.

CHAPTER XVII.

Concerning the Size, Form, Material, and Mode of Securing the Vessel.

Let your glass distilling vessel be round or oval; large enough to hold neither more nor much less than an ounce of distilled water in the body thereof. Let the height of the vessel's neck be about one palm, hand-breath, or span, and let the glass be clear and thick (the thicker the better, so long as it is clear and clean, and permits you to distinguish what is going on within)—but the thickness should be uniform. The substance which will go into this vessel consists of ½ oz. of gold, and one oz. of mercury; and if you have to add ⅓ oz. of mercury, the whole compound will still be less than 2 oz. The glass should be strong in order to prevent the vapours which arise from our embryo bursting the vessel. Let the mouth of the vessel be *very* carefully and effectually secured by means of a thick layer of sealing-wax. The utensils and the materials required are not then very expensive—and if you use my thick distilling-vessel you will avoid loss by breakage. The other instruments that are requisite are not dear. I know that many will take exception to this statement; they will say that the pursuit of our Art is a matter of all but ruinous expense. But my answer consists in a simple question: What is the object of our Art? Is it not to make the Philosopher's Stone—to find the liquid in which gold melts like ice in tepid water? And do those good people who are so eager in their search after "Mercury of the Sun," and "Mercury of the Moon," and who pay so high a price for their materials, ever succeed in this object? They cannot answer this question in the affirmative. One florin will buy enough of the substance of our water to quicken two pounds of mercury, and make it the true Mercury of the Sages. But, of course, glass vessels, coals, earthen vessels, a furnace, iron vessels, and other instruments, cannot be bought for nothing. Without a perfect body, our ore, viz., gold, there can be no Tincture; and our Stone is at first vile, immature, and volatile, but when complete it is perfect, precious, and fixed. These two aspects of our Stone are the body, gold, and the spirit, or quicksilver.

CHAPTER XVIII.

Of the Furnace, or Athanor of the Sages.

I have spoken about Mercury, Sulphur, the vessel, their treatment, etc, etc.; and, of course, all these things are to be understood with a grain of salt. You must understand that in the preceding chapters I have spoken metaphorically; if you take my words in a literal sense, you will reap no harvest except your outlay. For instance, when I name the principal substances Mercury and gold—I do not mean common gold in the state in which it is sold at the goldsmiths—but it must be prepared by means of our Art. You *may* find our gold in common gold and silver; but it is easier to make the Stone than to get its first-substance out of common gold. "Our gold" is the Chaos whose soul has not been taken away by fire. The soul of common gold has retired before the fiery tyranny of Vulcan into the inmost citadel. If you seek our gold in a substance intermediate between perfection and imperfection, you will find it; but otherwise, you must unbar the gates of common gold by the first preparatory process (ch. xv.), by which the charm of its body is broken, and the husband enabled to do his work. If you choose the former course, you shall use only gentle heat; in the latter case, you will require a fierce fire. But here you will be hopelessly lost in a labyrinth, if you do not know your way out' of it. But whether you choose our gold, or common gold, you will in either case need an even and continual fire. If you take our gold, you will finish the work a few months sooner, and the Elixir will be ten times more precious than that prepared from common gold. If you work with "our gold," you will be assisted in its calcination, putrefaction, and dealbation by its gentle inward (natural) heat. But in the case of common gold, this heat has to be applied externally by foreign substances, so as to render it fit for union with the Virgin's Milk. In neither case, however, can anything be effected without the aid of fire. It was not, then, in vain that Hermes counts fire next to the Sun and Moon as the governor of the work. But this is to be understood of the truly secret furnace, which a vulgar eye never saw. There is also another furnace, which is called our common furnace, made of potter's earth, or of iron and brass plates, well compacted with clay. This furnace we call Athanor, and the shape which I like best is that of a tower with a "nest" at the top. The "tower" should be about three feet high, and nine fingers wide within the plates. A little above the ground, let there be a little opening of about three or four fingers wide, for removing the cinders; over that, there should be a fire-place built with stones. Above this, we place the furnace itself, which should be such as to exclude all draughts and currents of air. The coals are put in from above, and the aperture should then be carefully closed. But it is not necessary that your furnace should exactly correspond to the description which I have given, so long as it fulfils the following conditions: firstly, it must be free from draughts; secondly, it must enable you to vary the temperature, without removing your vessel; thirdly, you must be able to keep up in it a fire for ten or twelve hours, without looking to it. Then the door of our Art will be opened to you; and when you have prepared the Stone, you may procure a small portable stove, for the purpose of multiplying it.

CHAPTER XIX.

Of the Progress of the Work during the first Forty Days.

When you have prepared our gold and Mercury in the manner described, put it into our vessel, and subject it to the action of our fire; within 40 days you will see the whole substance converted into atoms, without any visible motion, or perceptible heat (except that it is just warm). If you do not yet rightly know the meaning of "our gold," take one part of common gold (well purified), and three parts of our Mercury (thoroughly purged), put them together as directed (cap. xvi), place them over the fire, and there keep them at the boiling point, till they sweat, and their sweat circulates. At the end of go days you will find that the Mercury has separated and reunited all the elements of the common gold. Boil the mixture 50 days longer, and you will discover that our Mercury has changed the common gold into "our gold," which is the Medicine of the first order. It is already our Sulphur, but it has not yet the power of tinging. This method has been followed by many Sages, but it is exceedingly slow and tedious, and is only for the rich of the earth.

Moreover, when you have got this Sulphur do not think that you possess the Stone, but only its true Matter, which you may seek in an imperfect thing, and find it within a week, by our easy yet rare way, reserved of God for His poor, contemned, and abject saints. Hereof I have now determined to write much, although in the beginning of this Book I decreed to bury it in silence. This is the one great sophism of all adepts; some speak of this common gold and silver, and say the truth, and others say that we cannot use it, and they too, say the truth. But in the presence of God. I will call all our adepts to account, and charge them with jealous surliness. I, too, had determined to tread the same path, but God's hand confounded my scheme. I say then, that both ways are true, and come to the same thing in the end—but there is a vast difference at the beginning. Our whole Art consists in the right preparation of our Mercury and our gold Our Mercury is our way, and without it nothing is effected. Our gold is not common gold, but it may be found in it; and if you operate on our Mercury with common gold (regulating the fire in the right way), you will after 150 days have our gold, since our gold is obtained from our Mercury. Hence if common gold have all its atoms thoroughly severed by means of our Mercury, and then reunited by the same agency, the whole mixture will, under the influence of fire, become our gold. But, if, without this preparatory purging, you were to use common gold with our Mercury for the purpose of preparing the Stone, you would be sadly mistaken; and this is the great Labyrinth in which most beginners go astray, because the Sages in writing of these ways as two ways, purposely obscure the fact that they are only *one* way (though of course the one is more direct than the other). The gold of the Sages may then be prepared out of our common gold and our Mercury, from which there may afterwards be obtained by repeated liquefactions, Sulphur and Quicksilver which is incombustible, and tinges all things else. In this sense, our Stone is to be found in all metals and minerals, since our gold may be got from them all—but most easily, of course, from gold and silver. Some have found it in tin, some in lead, but most of those who have pursued the more tedious method, have found it in gold. Of course, if our gold be prepared in the way I have described, out of common gold (in the course of 150 days), instead of being found readymade, it will not be so effectual, and the preparation of the Stone will take 1½ years instead of 7 months. I know both ways, and prefer the shorter one; but I have described the longer one as well in order that I may not draw down upon myself the scathing wrath of the "Sages." The great difficulty which discourages all beginners is not of Nature's making: the Sages have created it by speaking of the longer operation when they mean the shorter one, and *vice versâ*. If you choose common gold, you should espouse it to Venus (copper), lay them together on the bridal bed, and, on bringing a fierce fire to bear on them, you will see an emblem of the Great Work in the following succession of colours: black, the peacock's tail, white, orange, and red. Then repeat the same operation with Mercury (called Virgin's Milk), using the "fire of the Bath of Dew," and (towards the end) sand mixed with ashes. The substance will first turn a much deeper black, and then a completer white and red. Hence if you know our Art, extract our gold from our Mercury (this is the shorter way), and thus perform the whole operation with one substance (viz., Mercury); if you can do this, you will have attained to the perfection of philosophy. In this method, there is no superfluous trouble: the whole work, from beginning to end, is based upon one broad foundation—whereas if you take common gold, you must operate on *two* substances, and *both* will have to be purified by an elaborate process. If you diligently consider what I have said, you have in your hand a means of unravelling all the apparent contradictions of the Sages. They speak of three operations: the first, by which the inward natural heat expels all cold through the aid of external fire; the second, wherein gold is purged with our Mercury, through the mediation of Venus, and under the influence of a fierce fire; the third, in which common gold is mixed with our Mercury, and the ferment of Sulphur added. But if you will receive my advice, you will not be put out by any wilful obscurity on the part of the Sages. Our sulphur you should indeed strive to discover; and if God enlightens you, you will find it in our Mercury. Before the living God I swear that my teaching is true. If you operate on Mercury and pure common gold, you may find "our gold" in 7 to 9 months, and "our silver" in 5 months. But when you have these, you have not yet prepared our Stone: *that* glorious sight will not gladden your eyes until you have been at work for a year-and-a-half. By that time you may obtain the elixir by subjecting the substance to very gentle continuous heat.

CHAPTER XX.

Of the Appearance of Blackness in the Work of the Sun and Moon.

If you operate on gold and silver, for the purpose of finding our Sulphur, let your substance first become like a thin paste, or boiling water, or liquid pitch; for the operation of our gold and Mercury is prefigured by that which happens in the preparation of common gold with our Mercury. Take your substance and place it in the furnace, regulate the fire properly for the space of twenty days, in which time you will observe various colours, and about the end of the fourth week, if the fire be continuous, you will see a most amiable greenness, which will last for about ten days. Then rejoice, for in a short time it will be as a black coal, and your whole compound shall be reduced to atoms. The operation is a resolution of the fixed into the not fixed that both afterwards, being conjoined, may make one matter, partly spiritual and partly corporal. Once more, I assure you, the regulation of the fire is the only thing that I have hidden from you. Given the proper regimen, take the Stone, govern it as you know how, and then these wonderful phenomena will follow: The fire will at once dissolve the Mercury and the Sulphur like wax; the Sulphur will be burnt, and change its colours from day to day; the Mercury will prove incombustible, and only be gradually tinged (and purified, without being infected) with the colours of the Sulphur. Let the heaven stoop to the earth, till the latter has conceived heavenly seed. When you see the substances mingle in your distilling vessel, and assume the appearance of clotted and burnt blood, be sure that the female has received the seed of the male. About seventeen days afterwards your substance will begin to wear a yellow, thick, misty, or foamy appearance. At this time, you must take care not to let the embryo escape from your vessel; for it will give out a greenish, yellow, black, and bluish vapour and strive to burst the vessel. If you allow these vapours (which are continuous when the Embryo is formed) to escape, your work will be hopelessly marred. Nor should you allow any of the odour to make its way through any little hole or outlet; for the evaporation would considerably weaken the strength of the Stone. Hence the true Sage seals up the mouth of his vessel most carefully. Let me advise you, moreover, not to neglect your fire, or move or open the vessel, or slacken the process of decoction, until you find that the quantity of the liquid begins to diminish; if this happens after thirty days, rejoice, and know that you are on the right road. Then be doubly careful, and you will, at the end of another fortnight, find that the earth has become quite dry and of a deep black. This is the death of the compound; the winds have ceased, and there is a great calm. This is that great simultaneous eclipse of the Sun and Moon, when the Sea also has disappeared. Our Chaos is then ready, from which, at the bidding of God, all the wonders of the world may successively emerge.

CHAPTER XXI.

Of the Caution required to avoid Burning the Flowers.

The burning of the flowers is fatal, yet soon committed: it is chiefly to be guarded against after the lapse of the third week. In the beginning there is so much moisture that if the fire be too fierce it will dry up the liquid too quickly, and you will prematurely obtain a dry red powder, from which the principle of life has flown; if the fire be not strong enough the substance will not be properly matured. Too powerful a fire prevents the true union of the substances. True union only takes place in water. Bodies collide, but do not unite; only liquids (and spirits) can truly mingle their substance. Hence our homogeneous metallic water must be allowed to do its work properly, and should not be dried up, until this perfect mutual absorption has taken place in a natural manner. Premature drying only destroys the germ of life, strikes the active principle on the head as with a hammer, and renders it passive. A red powder is indeed produced, but long before the time: for redness should be preceded by blackness. It is true that, in the beginning of our work, when heaven is wedded to earth, and earth conceives the fire of nature, a red colour does appear. But the substance is then sufficiently moist; and the redness soon gives way to a green colour, which in its turn gradually yields to blackness. Do not be in a hurry; let your fire be just powerful enough, but not too powerful; steer a straight course between Scylla and Charybdis: you will behold in your vessel a variety of colours and grotesque transformations—until the substance settles down into a powder of intense blackness. This should happen within the first fifty days. If it does not, either your Mercury, or the regulation of your fire, or the composition of your substance is at fault—if, indeed, you have not moved or shaken your glass vessel.

CHAPTER XXII.

Of the Regimen of Saturn.

All the Sages who have written on our Art, have spoken of the work and regimen of Saturn; and their remarks have led many to choose common lead as the substance of the Stone. But you should know that *our* Saturn, or lead, is a much nobler substance than gold. It is the living earth in which the soul of gold is joined to Mercury, that they may bring forth Adam and his wife Eve. Wherefore, since the highest has so lowered itself as to become the lowest, we may expect that its blood may be the means of redeeming all its brethren. The Tomb in which our King is buried, is that which we call Saturn, and it is the key of the work of transmutation; happy is he who can salute this planet, and call it by its right name. It is a boon which is obtained by the blessing of God alone; it is not of him that willeth, or of him that runneth; but God bestoweth it on whom He will.

CHAPTER XXIII.

Of the different Regimens of this Work.

Let me assure you that in our whole work there is nothing hidden but the regimen, of which it was truly said by the Sage that whoever knows it perfectly will be honoured by princes and potentates. I tell you plainly that if this one point were clearly set forth, our Art would become mere women's work and child's play: there would be nothing in it but a simple process of "cooking." Hence it has always been most carefully concealed by the Sages. But I have determined to write in a more sympathetic and kindly spirit: know then that our regimen throughout consists in coction and digestion, but that it implies a good many other processes, which those jealous Sages have made to appear different by describing them under different names. But we intend to speak more openly in regard to this subject.

CHAPTER XXIV.

Of the First Regimen, which is that of Mercury.

This first regimen has been studiously kept secret by all the Sages. They have spoken of the second regimen, or that of Saturn, as if it were the first, and have thus left the student without guidance in those operations which precede the appearance of that intense blackness. Count Bernard, of Trevisa, says, in his Parable, that when the King has come to the Fountain, he takes off the golden garment, gives it to Saturn, and enters the bath alone, afterwards receiving from Saturn a robe of black silk But he does not tell us how long it takes to put off that golden robe; and thus, like all his brethren, leaves the poor beginner to grope in the dark during 40 or 50 days. From the point where the stage of blackness is reached to the end of the work their directions are more full and intelligible. It is in regard to these first 40 days that the student requires additional light. This period represents the regimen of Mercury (of the Sages), which is alone active during the whole time, the *other* substance being temporarily dead. You should not suffer yourself to be deluded into the belief that when your matters are joined, namely, our Sun and Mercury, the "setting of the Sun" can be brought about in a few days. We ourselves waited a tedious time before a reconciliation was made between the fire and the water. As a matter of fact, the Sages have called the substance, throughout this first period, Rebis, or Two-thing: to show that the union is not effected till the operation is complete. You should know, then, that though our Mercury consumes the Sun, yet a year after you shall separate them, unless they are connected together by a suitable degree of fire. It is not able to do anything at all without *fire*. We must not suppose that when our gold is placed in our Mercury it is swallowed up by it in the twinkling of an eye. This conception rests on a misunderstanding of Count Bernard's teaching about the King's plunge in the fountain. But the solution of gold is a more difficult matter than these gentry appear to have any idea of. It requires the highest skill so to regulate the fire in the first stage of the work as to solve the bodies without injuring the tincture. Attend to my teaching therefore. Take the body which I have shewed you, put it into the water of our sea, and bring to bear on the compound the proper degree of heat, till dews and mists begin to ascend, and the moisture is diminished night and day without intermission. Know that at first the two do not affect each other at all, and that only in course of time the body absorbs some of the water, and thus causes each to partake of the other's nature. Only part of the water is sublimed; the rest gradually penetrates the pores of the body, which are thereby more and more softened, till the soul of the gold is enabled gently to pass out. Through the mediation of the soul the body is reconciled and united to the spirit, and their union is signalized by the appearance of the black colour. The whole operation lasts about 40-50 days, and is called the Regimen of Mercury, because the body is passive throughout, and the spirit, or Mercury, brings about all the changes of colour, which begin to appear about the loth day, and gradually intensify till all be at last completed in black of the deepest dye, which the 50th day will manifest.

CHAPTER XXV.

The Regimen of the Second Part, which is that of Saturn.

The Regimen of Mercury, the operation whereof despoils the King of his golden garments, is followed by the Regimen of Saturn. When the Lion dies the Crow is born. The substance has now become of a uniform colour, namely, as black as pitch, and neither vapours, or winds, or any other signs of life are seen; the whole is dry as dust, with the exception of some pitch-like substance, which now and then bubbles up; all presents an image of eternal death. Nevertheless, it is a sight which gladdens the heart of the Sage. For the black colour which is seen is bright and brilliant; and if you behold something like a thin paste bubbling up here and there, you may rejoice. For it is the work of the quickening spirit, which will soon restore the dead bodies to life. The regulation of the fire is a matter of great importance at this juncture; if you make it too fierce, and thus cause sublimation at this stage, everything will be irrecoverably spoilt. Be content, therefore, to remain, as it were, in prison for forty days and nights, even as was the good Trevisan, and employ only gentle heat. Let your delicate substance remain at the bottom, which is the womb of conception, in the sure hope that after the time appointed by the Creator for this Operation, the spirit will arise in a glorified state, and glorify its body—that it will ascend and be gently circulated from the centre to the heavens, then descend to the centre from the heavens, and take to itself the power of things above and things below.

CHAPTER XXVI.

Of the Regimen of Jupiter.

Black Saturn is succeeded by Jupiter, who exhibits divers colours. For after the putrefaction and conception, which has taken place at the bottom of the vessel, there is once more a change of colours and a circulating sublimation. This *Reign*, or Regimen, lasts only three weeks. During this period you see all conceivable colours concerning which no definite account can be given. The "showers" that fall will become more numerous as the close of this reign approaches, and its termination is signalized by the appearance of a snowy white streaky deposit on the sides of the vessel. Rejoice, then, for you have successfully accomplished the regimen of Jupiter. What you must be particularly careful about in this operation, is to prevent the young ones of the Crow from going back to the nest when they have once left it; secondly, to let your earth get neither too dry by an immoderate sublimation of the moisture, nor yet to swamp and smother it with the moisture. These ends will be attained by the proper regulation of the outward heat.

CHAPTER XXVII.

Of the Regimen of the Moon.

When the Reign of Jupiter comes to an end (towards the close of the fourth month) you will see the sign of the waxing moon (Crescent), and know that the whole Reign of Jupiter was devoted to the purification of the Laton. The mundifying spirit is very pure and brilliant, but the body that has to be cleansed is intensely black. While it passes from blackness to whiteness, a great variety of colours are observed; nor is it at once perfectly white; at first it is simply white— afterwards it is of a dazzling, snowy splendour. Under this Reign the whole mass presents the appearance of liquid quicksilver. This is called the sealing of the mother in the belly of the infant whom she bears; and its intermediate colours are more white than black, just as in the Reign of Jupiter they were more black than white. The Reign of the Moon lasts just three weeks; but before its close, the substance exhibits a great variety of forms; it will become liquid, and again coagulate a hundred times a day; sometimes it will present the appearance of fishes' eyes, and then again of tiny silver trees, with twigs and leaves. Whenever you look at it you will have cause for astonishment, particularly when you see it all divided into beautiful but very minute grains of silver, like the rays of the Sun. This is the White Tincture, glorious to behold, but nothing in respect of what it may become.

CHAPTER XXVIII.

Of the Regimen of Venus.

The substance, if left in the same vessel, will once more become volatile and (though already perfect in its way) will undergo another change. But if you take it out of the vessel, and after allowing it to cool, put it into another, you will not be able to make anything of it. In this Reign you should also give careful attention to your fire. For the perfect Stone is fusible; and if the fire be too powerful the substance will become glazed, and unsusceptible of any further change. This "vitrification" of the substance may happen at any time from the middle of the Reign of the Moon to the tenth day of the Reign of Venus, and should be carefully guarded against. The heat should he gentle, so as to melt the compound very slowly and gradually; it will then raise bubbles, and receive a spirit that will rise upward, carrying the Stone with it, and imparting to it new colours, especially a copper-green colour, which endures for some time, and does not quite disappear till the twentieth day; the next change is to blue and livid, and at the close of this Reign the colour is a pale purple. Do not irritate the spirit too much—it is more corporeal than before, and if you sublime it to the *top* of the vessel, it will hardly return. The same caution should be observed in the Reign of the Moon, when the substance begins to thicken. The law is one of mildness, and not of violence, lest everything should rise to the top of the vessel, and be consumed or vitrified to the ruin of the whole work. When you see the *green* colour, know that the substance now contains the germ of its highest life. Do not turn the greenness into blackness by immoderate heat. This Reign is maintained for forty days.

Chapter XXIX.

Of the Regimen of Mars.

When the Regimen of Venus is over, and therein has appeared the philosophical tree, with all its branches and leaves, the Reign of Mars begins with a light yellow, or dirty brown colour, but at last exhibits the transitory hues of the Rainbow, and the Peacock's Tail. At this stage the compound is drier, and often shows like a hyacinth with a tinge of gold. The mother being now sealed in her infant's belly, swells and is purified, but because of the present great purity of the compound, no putridness can have place in this regimen, but some obscure colours are chief actors, while some middle colours come and go, and they are pleasant to look on. Our Virgin Earth is now undergoing the last degree of its cultivation, and is getting ready to receive and mature the fruit of the Sun. Hence you should keep up a moderate temperature; then there will be seen, about the thirtieth day of this Reign, an orange colour, which, within two weeks from its first appearance, will tinge the whole substance with its own hue.

Chapter XXX.

Of the Regimen of the Sun.

As you are now approaching the end of the work, the substance receives a golden tinge, and the Virgin's Milk which you give your substance to drink has assumed a deep orange colour. Pray to God to keep you from haste and impatience at this stage of the work; consider that you have now waited for seven months, and that it would be foolish to let one hour rob you of the fruits of all your labour. Therefore be more and more careful the nearer you approach perfection. Then you will first observe an orange-coloured sweat breaking out on the body; next there will be vapour of an orange hue. Soon the body below becomes tinged with violet and a darkish purple. At the end of fourteen or fifteen days, the substance will be, for the most part, humid and ponderous, and yet the wind still bears it in its womb. Towards the 26th day of the Reign it will begin to get dry, and to become liquid and solid in turn (about a hundred times a day); then it becomes granulated; then again it is welded together into one mass, and so it goes on changing for about a fortnight. At length, however, an unexpectedly glorious light will burst from your substance, and the end will arrive three days afterwards. The substance will be granulated, like atoms of gold (or motes in the Sun), and turn a deep red—a red the intensity of which makes it seem black like very pure blood in a clotted state. This is the Great Wonder of Wonders, which has not its like on earth.

Chapter XXXI.

Of the Fermentation of the Stone.

I forgot to warn you in the last chapter to be on your guard against the danger of vitrification; too fierce a fire would render your substance insoluble and prevent its granulation. . . . You now possess the incombustible red Sulphur which can no longer be affected in any way by fire. In order to obtain the Elixir from this Sulphur by reiterate solution and coagulation, take three parts of purest gold, and one part of this fiery Sulphur. Melt the gold in a clean crucible, and then cast your Sulphur into it (protecting it well from the smoke of the coals) Make them liquid together, when you will obtain a beautiful mass of a deep red, though hardly transparent. This you should permit to cool, and pound into a small powder. Of this powder take one part, and two parts of our Mercury; mix them well, and put them in a glass vessel, well sealed. They should be exposed to gentle heat for two months. This is the true fermentation, which may be repeated if needful.

CHAPTER XXXII.

The Imbibition of the Stone.

Many authors take fermentation in this work for the invisible external agent, which they call ferment; by its virtue the fugitive and subtle spirits, without laying on of hands, are of their own accord thickened, and our before-mentioned fermentation they call cibation with bread and milk. But I follow my own judgment. There is another operation, called Imbibition of the Stone, by which its quantity rather than its quality is increased. It is this: Add to three parts of your perfect Sulphur (either white or red) one part of water, and after six or seven days' coction the water will become thick like the Sulphur Add again as much water as you did before; and when this is dried up, with a convenient fire, add three distinct times so much water as shall be equal to one-third of the original quantity of Sulphur. Then add (for the 7th imbibition) five parts of water (the parts being equal to the original parts of the Sulphur). Seal up the vessel; subject it to gentle coction, and let the compound pass through all the different Reigns of the original Substance, which will be accomplished in a month. Then you have the true Stone of the third order, one part of which will perfectly tinge 1,000 parts of any other metal.

CHAPTER XXXIII.

The Multiplication of the Stone.

Take the perfect Stone; add one part of it to three or four parts of purified Mercury of our first work, subject it to gentle coction for seven days (the vessel being carefully sealed up), and let it pass through all the Reigns, which it will do very quickly and smoothly. The tinging power of the substance will thus be exalted a thousandfold; and if you go through the whole process a second time (which you can do with ease in three days) the Medicine will be much more precious still. This you may repeat as often as you like; the third time the substance will run through all the Reigns in a day, the fourth time in a single hour, and so on—and the improvement in its quality will be most marvellous. Then kneel down and render thanks to God for this precious treasure.

CHAPTER XXXIV.

Of Projection.

Take four parts of your perfect Stone, either red or white (of *both*, for the Medicine); melt them in a clean crucible. Take one part of this pulverisable mixture to ten parts of purified Mercury; heat the Mercury till it begins to crackle, then throw in your mixture, which will pierce it in the twinkling of an eye; increase your fire till it be melted, and you will have a Medicine of an inferior order. Take one part of this, and add it to a large quantity of well purged and melted metal, which will thereby be transmuted into the purest silver or gold (according as you have taken white or red Sulphur). Note that it is better to use a gradual projection, for otherwise there may be a notable loss of the Medicine. The better the metals are purged and refined, the quicker and more complete will the transmutation be.

CHAPTER XXXV.

Of the Manifold uses of this Art.

He that has once found this Art, can have nothing else in all the world to wish for, than that he may be allowed to serve his God in peace and safety. He will not care for pomp or dazzling outward show. But if he lived a thousand years, and daily entertained a million people, he could never come to want, since he has at hand the means of indefinitely multiplying the Stone both in weight and virtue, and thus of changing all imperfect metals in the world into gold.

In the second place, he has it in his power to make stones and diamonds far more precious than any that are naturally procured.

In the third place, he has an Universal Medicine, with which he can cure every conceivable disease, and, indeed, as to the quantity of his Medicine, he might heal all sick people in the world.

Now to the King Eternal, Immortal, and sole Almighty, be everlasting praise for these His unspeakable gifts and invaluable treasures.

I exhort all that possess this Treasure, to use it to the praise of God, and the good of their neighbours, in order that they may not at the last day be eternally doomed for their ingratitude to their Creator.

TO

GOD ALONE

BE

THE GLORY.

A

SUBTLE ALLEGORY

CONCERNING THE

SECRETS OF ALCHEMY

VERY USEFUL TO POSSESS

AND

PLEASANT TO READ.

BY

MICHAEL MAIER.

THE SECRETS OF ALCHEMY.

AFTER spending the best part of my life in the study of the liberal arts and sciences, and in the company of wise men and judicious scholars, I was compelled, as the result of my observation of mankind, to arrive at the melancholy conclusion that the hearts of most persons are set either on ambitious and vainglorious projects, on sensual pleasures, or on the accumulation of wealth by all and any means; and that few care either for God or for virtue At first I did not quite know whether to become a disciple of the laughing or of the weeping philosopher, or whether to join in the exclamation of the wise Prince of Israel: "All things are vanity." But at length the Bible and experience taught me to take refuge in the study of the hidden secrets of Nature, whether pursued at home, by means of books, or abroad, in the Great Volume of the World. Now, the more I drank of the mighty fount of knowledge, the more painfully my thirst, like that of Tantalus, seemed to increase. I had heard that there was a bird called Phœnix, the only one of its kind in the whole world, whose feathers and flesh constitute the great and glorious medicine for all passion, pain, and sorrow; which also Helena, after her return from Troy, had presented in the form of a draught to Telemachus, who thereupon had forgotten all his sorrows and troubles. This bird I could not indeed hope to obtain entire; but I was seized with an irresistible longing to become possessed of at least one of its smallest feathers; and for this unspeakable privilege I was prepared to spend all my substance, to travel far and wide, and to endure every hardship. There was, of course, much to discourage me. Some people denied the very existence of this bird; others laughed at my faith in its wonder-working properties. I was thus brought for a time to regard all that Tacitus, Pliny, and all other writers have said as fabulous, and to doubt whether, after all, the different narcotics and opiates were not a better remedy for anger and sorrow than the supposed virtues of the Phœnix. Moreover, I had heard of the simple method of curing these mental ailments suggested by a certain wise man to Augustus, whom he bade run through the twenty-four letters before saying anything whenever he was angry; and this suggestion appeared to supersede all other remedies. I had also read the books of those moral philosophers who undertake to prescribe an effective remedy for every disease of the mind. But after giving all these boasted specifics a fair trial, I found, to my dismay, that they were of little practical use. In many cases, the causes of mental maladies appeared to be material, and to consist in an excess or defect of the bile, or of some other bodily substance; in all these cases a medical treatment seemed to be indicated; whence Galen, that prince among physicians, was led to believe that character depends on temperaments of the body. As a soldier may lose all his bravery and strength by being starved and confined in a close prison, so even a good person may yield to anger, simply through some vicious habit of body. This opinion is most reasonable in itself, and is borne out, amongst other things, by the testimony which is given by Arnold of Villanova, in that book of his where he sets forth the virtues of all medicines by means of tables of the four qualities: "The medicines that conduce to intellectual excellence are those which strengthen the digestion, and nourish the brain and the principal vitals, purging out all superfluities, purifying the blood, and preventing the ascent of vapours to the brain; hence you will find that many medical writers speak of their medicines as productive of a direct effect upon the mind, when it is only through the medium of the stomach, the brain, the blood, the liver, etc., that they tend to brighten the intellectual faculties, by improving the general health of the brain, and quickening all processes of the body, that you may say they are productive of joy, because they tend to strengthen the chief limbs, purify the blood, and produce good animal spirits. Other medicines "lead to Paradise," as they dispose the heart to charity and to every good work. by their action upon the blood. Some medicinal herbs have the power of exciting love, by increasing and clarifying the blood, and thus quickening the sexual instinct; while others make men chaste and religious, by inducing poverty and frigidity of blood, and taking away the edge of all sensual appetite. In the same way, it is possible, by means of certain drugs, to make men stupid and insane, as men are rendered dull and stolid by drinking too much wine. You may also notice, sometimes, that after eating a certain kind of food, men become light-hearted, joyous, and inclined to dance and sing—though they are ordinarily staid and grave persons—while other kinds of food have a contrary effect upon them. Thus, a physician has power to make a miser liberal, a chaste person lascivious, a timid person bold, simply by changing the complexion of his vital juices. Such are the wonderful secrets of the medical Art, though, of course, they are hidden from the foolish and the ignorant. There are a great many infatuated persons who will not believe that medicine can do anything but cure a headache; but such people know little of the resources of this science. Hippocrates forbad the physicians whom he taught to reveal these secrets; and it was a wise prohibition." A little further on the same writer says: "What medicine can produce greater heat than anger? or chill the body more than fear? or invigorate the nerves more thoroughly than joy? or nourish and comfort more gently than hope? And what more certain cause of death is there than despair?" These are the words of the philosopher, and they show that medicine may, through the body, cure the mind, and thus supply a remedy for anger as well as other mental disturbances. It is true that if there is a remedy for anger, it would, in the present state of the world, hardly be very highly esteemed. Still it would calm the passions of individuals, although other persons might not recognise its value. But that which men do not care to have just now, may one day be in great demand. Such is the vicissitude of all things human. Galen once said that the savages of England and Germany were as hostile to the science of Medicine as they were ignorant of it. But now the descendants of Galen's countrymen are sunk in barbarism, while the English and Germans are the most skilful physicians in the world. Thus it seems very likely that this Remedy may be one day in great request, especially when we consider its vast utility, and the innumerable evils which anger brings upon men.

What has been said about anger applies with equal force to grief; for while the symptoms of anger are more or less mental, those of grief produce a more perceptible and lasting effect on the body. This great Remedy for anger and grief, then, it. would be most desirable to have, if we could only find the Phœnix which affords it, Where shall I look for it? Where shall I enquire after it? Whom shall I ask? I determined to go abroad, and to search for it till I should have found it. Fortune assists the brave: to the indolent and idle knowledge never comes. I would leave my native country—dearly as I love it, and sadly as I should miss my friends—and wander from land to land until I should be able to return with the eagerly coveted Medicine. All beginnings are difficult: he who has never been sad, cannot rejoice; he who has never erred, cannot be brought back to the right way; and as the Chemists say: "There is in Alchemy a certain noble body, which is moved from master to master, whose beginning is misery and sourness, whose end is sweetness and joy." So I expected to endure hardships, and go through bitter experiences, but I also expected them to be crowned with the delights of success. Of the existence of the Phœnix I had no doubt, or I could not have looked for it. It is enough for me to see thé Sun and its rays, even though I cannot touch it; and perhaps it is as well for us that we cannot get so very close to the Sun. But as to this Medicine which I seek; how can I have a perfect knowledge of it before I see and touch it? How can I become a Master before I have been a scholar? The products of all countries are not the same; and perhaps I may learn in one part of the world what I cannot get to know in another. Moreover, I asked myself the question: Can a pilgrim's life hurt any one? Are we not all pilgrims here below to that land whither our Saviour Christ has gone before? And is not the example of peregrination set us by the swallow, the herald of spring; by the crane, the stork, and other birds of passage? Does not the whole world lie open before man as the air is everywhere accessible to birds? Great Phoebus himself, the god of the Sun, journeys day by day over the wide expanse of the sky. The heart of man beats and pulsates in his bosom from the first to the last hour of his life; and being surrounded by all these models and examples, it is natural for man to lead the life of a pilgrim, particularly if that pilgrimage be directed towards a certain goal. The merchant travels over land and sea to buy the produce of distant climes; but a nobler merchandise by far are science and knowledge, which are the wares of the mind. He who stays at home will there bury his talents, and get to know little about the secrets of the universe Moreover, it is both pleasant to travel and honourable to be always several hours' journey in advance of the Sun. That which is most spiritual is most swift in its movements, while the lifeless earth alone is immovable. The other three elements are in perpetual motion: the air sweeps over the earth in the shape of winds, hurricanes, and gales; fire devours everything before it as it rushes onward in the conflagration of a great city; water runs along in rivers and mighty streams, and hastes to reach the sea. Let us also look up and behold the heavens as they move in their glory. The stars, the sun, and the moon know the times and seasons of their rising and setting. A cannon ball, if projected from one of our most powerful guns, would be more than eight days in making the compass of the world (which is more than 25,000 miles); but the Sun, notwithstanding its vast size, accomplishes the same distance in 24 hours. It would make our thoughts reel if we strove to realise the velocity with which Saturn moves round the Sun, and with which the heavens revolve round their own axis. But greater still, and far more wonderful, is the speed of human thought, which, in a moment of time, travels from one end of the heavens to the other. We may believe that the angels, as spiritual beings, move with the quickness of that which is spiritual in man, viz., thought. God alone does not move; for He is everywhere. For all these reasons, I conceived that it would be both interesting, pleasant, honourable, and eminently profitable for me to follow the example of the whole world, and to undertake a pilgrimage for the purpose of discovering this wonderful bird Phœnix. I therefore braced myself for a long journey, determining to travel. first, through all the countries of Europe, then, if necessary, to America, thence to Asia, and at last to pass on to Africa. If, after carefully searching for the Phœnix in all these parts of the world, I did not succeed in finding it or hearing of it, I might reasonably give up all hopes of ever setting eyes thereon. The plan of my journey was determined by the relative quality of the elements which the different parts of the world represent, *i.e.*, Europe stands for earth, America for water, Asia for air, and Africa for fire; and earth cannot become air except through the medium of water; nor can water become fire except through the medium of air. I determined, then, to go first to Europe, which represents the grossest, and last to Africa, which represents the most subtle element. But my reasons will be set forth more clearly as I come to speak of the different parts of the world.

EUROPE: EARTH.

I left my native town on the day of the vernal equinox, when the Moon and Sun were both in the sign of Aries, with the intention of first travelling through Europe, and to enquire everywhere after the Phœnix. I took Europe to represent the element Earth, because earth forms the foundation of all the other elements, and stands out above the water, so Europe is the mother of the whole world, and though smaller than other continents, is vastly superior to them through the courage, energy, and mental strength of its inhabitants. Some say that one handful of earth gives ten handfuls of water, a hundred handfuls of air, and a thousand handfuls of fire; and this is the relative importance of the different continents, if Europe answers to earth. Europe has produced the bravest warriors, and the most distinguished conquerors; and though she has subdued other continents, she has herself never been subjugated by them. Of the four great world empires, only one was founded by an Asiatic prince; the Macedonian, the Roman, and the Teutonic Empires, have all had their centres in Europe. Alexander the Great and Julius Cæsar were among her sons. If we look at a map of Europe we may easily perceive that in shape this part of the world resembles a virgin; but her heart is that of a lion. For these reasons, I determined to travel first through this Virgin Lion, because it clearly corresponds to the fundamental element: earth.

Europe is a Virgin because of her beauty and spotless purity; a Lion because she has conquered others, but has never herself been conquered. Among the heavenly bodies the Sun answers to Europe, and among the metals, gold. For though she produces little gold, and the sun shines upon her with less fierceness than on Africa, yet she is worthy of being compared to the Sun and gold because of the excellence of her people, though a few years ago even some real lions were born in Germany, yet we call her a Lioness only on account of her stoutness of heart. Europe is the Mother of the World, and Germany is her heart.

Nor is Europe without her marvels. In Pannonia, it is reported, men live in compact stone houses under water. The hot springs of Carlsbad, it is said, are hardened into stones. On the coasts of Prussia, a transparent and pellucid stone (amber), formed out of subterraneous vegetable juices, is cast ashore in large quantities. I do not mention the coral of the Sicilian sea, which, originally a plant, hardens outside water into a white or red tree of stone; or the sealed earth of Germany and Silesia. . . . Europe, then, is the *Lion Earth*. This expression is for those who hear not with their ears only, but also with their brains; it is earth which resists the fire, like gold, and is not resolved into air. Like the boundary pillar of the gods of old, it "yields to none." Hence Europe (the gold of the universe) seemed the very place in which I should be most likely to hear of the Phœnix and its Medicine. But most of those whom I met laughed at my quest, and said that, like Narcissus, I had fallen in love with the shadow of my own mind, the echo of my vain and ambitious thoughts, which had no substantial existence apart from my own folly. "The words of the Alchemists," said they, "are like clouds: they may mean and represent anything, according to the fancy of him who hears them. And even if there were such a medicine, human life is too brief for the search; all that makes life worth living will have to be neglected and thrust aside while you are engaged in hunting after it. If we can pick up a knowledge of this secret casually, and whilst devoting ourselves to other pursuits, well; but if not, we can very ill spare the time for a closer search." These objections (at least the latter half of them) I met as follows: "The quest of this Medicine demands the whole powers of a man's body and mind. He who engages in it only casually, cannot hope to penetrate even the outward rind of knowledge. The object of our search is a profound secret, and a man who is not prepared to give himself wholly to this enquiry had much better abstain from it altogether. I readily acknowledge that the powers of my mind are not such as to justify me in anticipating success. But the spirit within me impels me to undertake this search; and I am confident that God will at the last reward my patience, and my humble waiting upon Him. As every King loves his Queen, as every bridegroom is devoted to his bride, so I regard this science as more beautiful and lovely than anything else in the world besides. Now, beautiful things are hard to win, and hard toil is the way to all that is great and glorious." This was the gist of my answer. Now I had already travelled through a great part of Europe, when it occurred to me that Italy and Spain are constantly mentioned by the Ancients as the great seats of secret knowledge, and I therefore directed my steps thitherward. In Spain I heard that some Arabs (Geber, Avicenna, and others) had lived there a long time ago, and these had possessed the wonderful Medicine; I was also told a great deal about Hercules and his achievement in securing the golden apples of the Hesperides, and also the golden cup, wherein he received the medicine for anger and sorrow. Now all prudent men have decided that it contained a small portion of the feathers of the Phœnix. I saw that Geryon with the three bodies was the theme of the philosopher's writings, that Hercules was a laborious artist, seeker of the Medicine. But nobody was able to give me any definite information. I did not, however, wish to leave Europe without visiting the Canary Islands, which are seven in number and are named: Lancerotta, Bonaventura, Great Canaria, Teneriffe, Gomera, Ferro, and Palma. Three of them, Lancerotta, Gomera, and Ferro, are governed each by its own King. Ferro is naturally destitute of good drinking water, but the inhabitants get a supply of it out of certain broad-leaved trees, which distil sweet water in such quantities as to suffice for the whose island. Strangers and pirates who land in the island, being ignorant of this fact, are prevented by want of water from staying in Ferro very long. Now, it happened about this time that the King of Gomera had died without leaving a male heir, and his subjects refused to acknowledge the authority of his beautiful daughter Blanche, unless she accepted the hand of some royal wooer, because they said that it was unworthy of men to be ruled by a woman, and calculated to injure the manliness of the national character—as was shown by the experience of those peoples over whom women have borne sway for any length of time. For there women had assumed the place of men, while men were degraded to the position of women; and, as a consequence, there followed the wildest excesses of profligacy and lewdness. So the royal maiden was prevailed upon to think of bestowing her hand in marriage. Now, there was in the island a royal youth, named Brumazar (with beautiful dark locks and a splendid golden robe),who was passionately enamoured of the royal maiden Blanche, and was loved by her in return. He wooed and won her, and the wedding was celebrated on condition that she should bring to him as her dower a diamond of great value and magnitude, while he should present to her a splendid ruby of incalculable worth (*i.e.*, worth a million ducats); he, as her King and Lord, should protect her from all dangers and from the robbers with whom that country swarms, while she, on the other hand, promised humbly to obey him without either subterfuge or tergiversation. After these preliminaries, they were linked together in close and indissoluble marriage, in which they lived long and happily; and it was predicted that a son should be born to them, who would be a mighty conqueror, and would carry his victorious arms as far as the Pillars of Dionysus in India. . . . So you see that I was unable to get any information whatsoever about the Phœnix in the course of my wanderings through Europe; I therefore determined to set sail for America, in the hope that I might be more fortunate among the savages of that Continent. For I remembered the words of the poet:—

"Accident is a mighty helper; let your hook always be baited; in the least likely river you may catch your fish."

AMERICA: WATER.

In these days, when commerce has opened up, as it were, a highroad across the seas to America (or India in the West), there is no very great difficulty in reaching that continent; but far different were the circumstances under which it was first discovered. After leaving the "Islands of the Blessed," I became a passenger on board of a ship which had an eagle for its figurehead; and, after weathering many severe gales and hurricanes, we at length landed in Brazil, a great province of America, entirely covered with forests. The surface of the country is only dotted here and there with the homestead of a settler; there are few towns, and the inhabitants are sunk in ignorance, and unskilled in the arts of civilisation. How, then, could I hope to hear anything about the Phœnix among people who could hardly read or write? Yet there are in this country many rare and beautiful birds which are not found elsewhere, though, of course, the Phœnix, being a miraculous bird, must not be sought among common fowls. The trees of the land are of a rich colour and sweet fragrance; and one day when I was enjoying the wild beauty of the forest, and listening to the natural music of the birds, I happened to find an apple of unusual and exquisite beauty, which on a closer view exhibited the following inscription:—

"Within is that which, if you deliver it to its grandmother, there will thence arise a son who may cling to his mother in loving embrace. From this union will arise in a short time a noble tree which will render to the husbandman a golden harvest."

After much thinking, it occurred to me that the seed which was in the fruit must be placed in the earth (its grandmother,, since the parent tree was its mother). So I took it as a gift of God, sowed the seed, and when there had sprung up a little tree, I grafted it into the parent tree (first having sawn off that tree close to the ground) and when the two had grown together, they became a much more glorious tree than either of them had been before; and the fruit was that of the scion which had been inserted into the parent tree. . . . It is said that before the Spaniards reached Brazil, there were no horses in that country, so that the natives regarded a horse soldier as a monster half man and half beast; but when both horses and asses had been introduced by the strangers, it was thought most desirable to obtain also some mules which are the common offspring of these two animals. Now, there was a certain chief who possessed a large number both of asses and horses, and he took particular interest in this matter. He knew very well how to breed horses from horses, and asses from asses, but he was not acquainted with the proper method of breeding mules from both; while he was aware that all experiments which are made in the dark, *i.e.*, without the light of previous experience, are both dangerous and uncertain. The consequence was that all his efforts to produce a mule out of a stallion and a she ass were doomed to failure, no doubt because their seeds were not mixed in the right proportion. At last a Sage who was passing that way, and whose insight into the secret working of Nature was infinitely keener and more complete than that of those ignorant people, gave our chief the following advice:

"If you would obtain a mule resembling the paternal ass in length of ear and slowness of gait, you should feed each of the parents with just as large a quantity of food as their nature requires. Would you know what this proportion is? Give to the male twice as much as to the female, then a mare will conceive a mule from an ass."

This advice was taken by the chief, and, after several failures, his perseverance was crowned with complete success. Nor does it appear contrary to Nature's general plan that two different parents should produce offspring which differs from them both. Look at the leopard, which is said to be the offspring of the pard and the lioness; in the same way the wolf and bitch beget the lynx; a scion inserted into a good tree produces fruit different from those of the parent stock; new varieties of flowers are obtained by a judicious mingling of the pollen; and the red powder called "our Tincture," being mixed with quicksilver over the fire, produces gold which is utterly unlike either the one or the other. Now, these Americans are able to perform a most singular experiment with metals, and particularly with gold. They have a kind of water in which gold becomes soft like wax, and capable of being moulded with the hand into any shape they please. This water is not a corrosive, since it does not burn the fingers of those who take up the gold. But we need not doubt that it is some chemical discovery, and that it is obtained by a distilling process . . . . As I could gain no further information in America, I began to think of taking the first opportunity of crossing to Asia: I took with me a very heavy and valuable piece of a certain kind of wood, the most precious I saw here in Brazil, and which is remarkable for its brilliant ebony colour, for this black colour seems proper to America by reason of the blackish poplars and the soil dyed with various hues. The colour of this wood seems to arise from the heat of the sun, and the wonderful peculiarity of the American soil, of which Monandez, that learned physician of Seville, writes as follows: "The variety of colour exhibited by the soil of Peru is most remarkable. If you look at it from a distance, it has the appearance of a patchwork quilt spread out to air in the sun: one part of it is green, another blue, others again are yellow, white, black, and red. Now all these are different kinds of mineral earth: the black earth, if mixed with water or wine, makes an excellent ink; the red soil is said to be the ore of quicksilver, and the Indians paint themselves with it."—Well, I took my wood, went aboard a ship, with a white unicorn for its figure head, and setting sail for Asia, soon arrived in the Persian Gulf.

ASIA: AIR.

Asia is the third continent of the world, the continent which answers to the element of Air, and its climate is more temperate than that of the other continents, as it is equally remote from the intense cold of Europe, and the intense heat of Africa. Being both warm and moist, it most admirably corresponds to the element of air; its heat is almost everywhere tempered by the vapours which ascend from the sea. Moist, warm air has fire for its father, and water for its mother, and retains the most active qualities of both its parents. Thus air is a mediator between the two hostile elements, and in its own composition reconciles their strife. In the same way Asia binds Europe (earth) and Africa (fire) together, the grossest and the most subtle of the elements; but without Asia (air) there would be no union between them. By means of air, fire clings gladly to earth, and fosters it; but without air, the fire soon goes out. It is the prerogative and distinctive mark of Asia to be the centre of the world, and to bring forth such fruits as require a warm, soft air, as, for instance, dates, balsam, spices of all kinds, and gold itself. Asia is the cradle of our race, the seat of the first Monarchy, the birthplace of our Redeemer. From the Persian gulf I travelled straight through the continent, till I reached those parts of Asia Minor where Jason is said to have obtained the golden fleece. So, being greatly interested in these old world occurrences, I walked out one day to a place said to be the field of Mars, and the site of the Palace of Aëtes, the descendant of the Sun; there I met an old man of venerable aspect and authoritative port, who saluted me graciously, and to whom, after returning his salutation, I addressed the following words: "Master, if I am not troubling you too much, kindly enlighten my ignorance, as I can doubt neither your ability nor your willingness to help a stranger." He having signified his willingness to do for me all that lay in his power, I asked him whether those things which were related in history and poetry concerning Jason and his golden fleece, were real facts or mere poetical fictions. He smiled, and made the following reply to my question: "I myself am Jason, and better able than anyone else to give you information concerning those things which have happened to myself. You need not be afraid, for during my lifetime I was no man's enemy, but succoured all, like a good physician; and now that I no longer belong to this world, I am still as kindly disposed towards my mortal brethren. On this spot stood the royal seat of my father-in-law, Aëtes, whose father was the Sun—not, indeed, that heavenly luminary (which would be incredible), but one likest to him in name, and face, and dignity. The golden fleece of the ram, which Mercury had transmuted, and which Aëtes had hung in the grove of Mars, I obtained in the following manner: Medea was my chief adviser, and she enabled me by her wise counsel to contend successfully against the fierce and venomous monsters. The watchful Dragon I stupefied with a narcotic, which I cast into his maw; and while he was in that helpless state, I hastened to extract his teeth. These had to be buried in earth first prepared and ploughed up by means of bulls vomiting fire, which fire was extinguished by water poured into their mouths. Then Medea gave me the images of the Sun and Moon, without which, she said, nothing could be done." I asked where I should find all these things. His answer was that he obtained them Medea, but he could not tell me where she was to be found. "When she left me in her madness," he said, "she was wedded to old Aegeus, to whom she bore Medus; Medus afterwards went to Asia, and became the founder of the Median race." I wished to ask Jason many more questions, but he excused himself from answering them, and vanished before my eyes. Then I saw that he had been speaking of the Medicine of which I was in search, which also he had shadowed out under the figure of the golden fleece. For the crest of the Phœnix and its feathers are described by the learned as exhibiting a golden splendour. I did not indeed meet with many learned men in Asia; but I was well satisfied to have explored that blessed "aerial earth," especially as Syria and the Holy Land (with their rivers of Adonis and Jordan, in which the leper Naaman was cleansed) form part of it. In Syria, it is related that Adonis was killed by a boar, hounded on by Mars, and that from his wounds there flowed forth that balm by means of which human bodies are preserved from decomposition. On this continent stood the Holy of Holies, into which our Most High Priest entered when He had made atonement for the sins of the whole race on the Cross of Calvary; to Him. let us now utter forth the most ardent desires of our hearts in the following prayer:

O great and merciful Saviour of the world, Jesus Christ, who being God from all eternity, next madest man in time, in order that, as our Mediator, Thou mightest unite God and man, by satisfying the eternal and infinite power of God which human sin had provoked to wrath, that is to say, Thyself, the Father, and the Holy Spirit. For this purpose Thou was born into this world and didst go about doing good among men, and didst sanctify this earth by Thy miracles, Passion, Resurrection, and Ascension. To Thee I pray from the very bottom of my heart that as Thou hast given this Medicine for the use of men by ordinary means, and meanwhile hast Thyself cured incurable diseases by Thy Divine power, Who art the Great Physician: so Thou wouldst bestow the gift of this most precious Medicine upon me, the very humblest of thy servants, who for the sake of this most blessed knowledge have taken upon myself so weary a pilgrimage, and so many toils and hardships, as Thou well knowest—in order that I may use it to the glory of Thy Name, and for the relief of my suffering brethren. Thou who art a searcher of hearts, knowest that I despise all worldly pomp, and desire to consecrate my life to Thee, if Thou wilt but work in me both the will and the power of performance: Grant to me the power of exercising boundless charity, of relieving all sufferings, both bodily and mental: Bless me with the gracious gift of Thy Medicine, which comes next in value after the peace of mind and eternal happiness which Thou hast gained for us, in order that its virtue may be effectual in the cure of human sorrow, disease, and pain; to the everlasting praise of the everblessed Trinity, world without end, Amen.

When I had poured forth this prayer to the Giver of all good things, I remembered that besides the land which once flowed with milk and honey, but now, under Turkish rule, has become utterly barren and sterile, there was also in Asia, Paradise, which was created for man while he was still perfect. Knowing that this blessed garden was situated near Babylon, I journeyed to the spot, but found nothing except a confluence of certain rivers. Thence I travelled to the maritime parts of India, and found a city, called Ormuz, of which there ran a proverb, that if the world was a ring, Ormuz would be its gem. In this city there was a great concourse of eager visitors from the whole neighbourhood; and when I asked one of them whither he was hastening, he said: "To the terrestrial paradise." "What," said I, "was I unable to find the ancient garden of Eden, and do these people speak of a new Paradise!" But the man left me standing there, and pursued his journey as fast as he could. While I was considering whether I should follow him, it occurred to me that I should do well to adopt the plan of Columbus, the discoverer of America. So I went to the different gates of the city, and determined to leave it by that one where the sweetest and most fragrant odours were borne towards me on the air. This I did, and I soon found myself on a road where the air was such as might well come from an earthly Paradise, yet was frequented by very few travellers. Ormuz being situated on an island, we soon had to cross a sea, where I saw men fishing up pearls of the purest whiteness. Having obtained some of these for love and money, I had no doubt that I had come into possession of one of the most important substances of the Medicine, for the whiteness of these pearls was such as to defy exaggeration. After pursuing my journey on the mainland, along a very narrow by-path, for some time, I reached a point where two roads met, and there was a statue of Mercury, of which the body was silver while the head was overlaid with gold. The right hand of this statue pointed towards the Earthly Paradise; and when I had followed for some time the road which it indicated, I came to a very broad and deep river, which it was impossible to cross without a boat, though far and wide there was no boat to be seen; but the beauty of the other shore convinced me that it must be the Earthly Paradise. The trees which grew there were covered with golden, orange, citron-coloured, purple, and intensely red flowers. There were evergreen laurels, junipers, box-trees, and great store of blossoms of all colours and of the sweetest fragrance: sunflowers, amaranths, lilies, roses, hyacinths, &c. The ear was charmed with the songs and cries of nightingales, cuckoos, parrots, larks, thrushes, and hundreds of other known and unknown birds; nor was there wanting the sweet music of instruments and sweet-toned organs; the taste was gratified, as it seemed, with all manner of delicious fruits, and the fragrance which streamed out on the breeze was such as charmed while it rendered insensible the olfactory nerves of all the people who lived round about, just as the noise of the Nile cataracts becomes inaudible to those who are used to it. But what did the sight of all these glories profit me, who, for want of one little boat, was unable to get at them? So I turned away, with the firm resolution of coming back, as soon as I could do so with a better chance of success; in the meantime, I should be most likely to find the Phœnix that I was in search of, if I crossed over to Africa without further delay. So I directed my course towards the Red Sea, and there landed in Africa.

AFRICA: FIRE.

When I reached Africa, more than a year had elapsed from my first setting out; the Sun had once more entered the sign of the Lion, the Moon was at her height in the house of Cancer. All these were circumstances which inspired me with hope. The intense heat of the African climate renders the whole continent torrid, sterile, and dry. It has few rivers, but many wild beasts, which meet together at the riverside, and bring forth among themselves many new and strange shapes, for which Africa is so well known. Satyrs, cynocephali, and semi-human beings are said to live there. There are the Mountains of the Moon, and Atlas that bears up the heavens on its shoulders: all these abound in minerals and in serpents. There also is collected the blood of the Dragon which the Dragon has sucked from the Elephant; but when the Elephant falls dead, the Dragon is crushed, and the blood which it has drunk is pressed out of it. Again, in the neighbourhood of the Red Sea, an animal named *Ortus* has been observed, the colour of whose head is red, with gold lines up to the neck, while its eyes are deep black and its feet white, to wit, the fore feet, but the hind feet are black, the face up to the eyes white—a description which tallies exactly with that which Avicenna gives of our Medicine. . . . Now I heard that not far from the Red Sea there lived a prophetess, named the Erythræan Sibyl, in a rocky cave; and I thought well first of all to enquire of her concerning this Phœnix. It is she that prophesied and predicted the coming of the Son of God in the flesh This assertion has indeed been questioned by many writers, but it is borne out by Eusebius, the great historian of the Early Church, and by Cicero, the great orator, who, as is well known, translated this prophecy into the Latin tongue. Abundant evidence to the same effect may also be collected from the works of Virgil, the prince of Roman poets. The passage of Cicero which is referred to by Eusebius, will be found in the second book of his treatise, *De Divinatione* (On Divination). . . . When I came to her, I found her sitting in her cave, which was beautifully overgrown with the spreading boughs of a green tree, and covered with green sod. I saluted her with the lowliest and most deferential humility. At first she seemed somewhat startled at my sudden appearance, and hastily retreated to the interior of the cave. But she was soon won over by my earnest entreaties, and prevailed upon to show herself at the entrance of her habitation. "Who art thou, stranger?" she enquired, "and what wouldest thou of me? Dost thou not know that a man may not approach a virgin that dwells in solitude?" "It is not forward boldness that has brought me hither," I replied; "but I have come after mature deliberation, because I feel that it is you, and you alone, that can resolve certain doubts which lie heavy on my mind. If you will show me this great kindness, I, on my part. promise to do you suit and service, and to fulfil all your commands, as far as lies in my power." When she heard these words, her countenance cleared, and she asked me in a more kindly tone what my business was. "I cannot," she continued, "deny anything to men like you who are anxious to learn." "There are two things," I returned, "concerning which I would crave plain and straightforward instruction from you. namely, whether there was and is in these countries of Arabia and Egypt a wonderful bird named Phœnix; whether its flesh and feathers are really an effectual medicine for anger and grief; and, if so, where the bird is to be found?" "The object of your search," she rejoined, "is a great and glorious one; doubt is the first stage of knowledge, and you have also come to the right place and the right person. For the country in which you now find yourself is Araby the Blest, and nowhere else has the Phœnix ever been found; moreover, I am the only person who could possibly give you any definite information about it. I will teach you, and this land will exhibit to you, the glad sight of which I speak. Therefore, listen to my words Araby the Blest and Egypt have from of old rejoiced in the sole possession of the Phœnix, whose neck is of a golden hue, while the rest of its body is purple, and its head is crowned with a beautiful crest. It is sacred to the Sun, lives 660 years, and when the last hour of its life approaches, it builds a nest of cassia and frankincense, fills it with fragrant spices, kindles it by flapping its wings towards the Sun, and is burnt to ashes with it. From these ashes there is generated a worm, and out of the worm a young bird which takes the nest, with the remains of its parent, and carries it to Heliopolis (or Thebes), the sacred city of the Sun, in Egypt. Now, this whole tale which you find in the books of the Ancients is addressed to the mind rather than to the ear; it is a mystical narrative, and like the hieroglyphics of the Egyptians, should be mystically (not historically understood. An ancient Egyptian writer tells us that the Phœnix rejoices in the Sun, and that this predilection is its chief reason for coming to Egypt. He also relates that his Countrymen were in the habit of embalming the Phœnix if it died before its time. If you therefore regard this tale as an allegory, you will not be far wrong; and you know that the flesh and feathers of this bird were of old used in Heliopolis as a remedy for anger and grief." When I heard her say this, I was full of joy, and asked her whether she could tell me how to become possessed of this Blessed Bird and Medicine. She promised not to forsake me, and to do all in her power to help me nut of my difficulty. "Nevertheless," she continued, "the most important part of the enterprise must be performed by the toil of your own hands. I cannot describe to you in exact and unmistakable terms the place where the Phœnix lives, yet I will endeavour to make it as plain to you as I may. Egypt, you know, owes all her fertility to the Nile, whose sources are unknown and undiscoverable; but the mouths by which it is discharged into the sea, are sufficiently patent to all. The fourth Son of the Nile is Mercury, and to him his father has given authority to show you this bird, and its Medicine. This Mercury you may expect to find somewhere near the seven mouths of the Nile; for he has no fixed habitation, but is to be found now in one of these mouths, and now in another." I thanked the Virgin Prophetess most cordially for her gracious information, and at once set my face towards the mouths of the Nile, which are seven:—the Canopic, the Bolbitic, the Sebennitic, the Pelusian, the Tenitic, the Phœnetic, and the Mendesic. The way to the Canopic mouth led me through an ancient Christian burial ground, where a most miraculous occurrence is witnessed every year on a certain day in May. From dawn to noon on that day the dead bodies gradually rise from their graves until they are completely visible to the passers by; and from noon to sunset they gradually sink back again into their tombs. If this be true, as eye-witnesses testify, it is a most certain proof of the resurrection of the human body, and exhibits a close analogy to the resuscitation of the dead Phœnix. . . . When I reached the island of Canopus, I enquired where Mercury was to be found. But the people were only hopelessly puzzled by my questions. Some said that, according to Hermes, Egypt exhibits an image of the heavens, and the seven mouths of the Nile (of which the Canopic is the most considerable) correspond to the seven planets; the Canopic mouth they called the habitation of Saturn, the grandfather of Mercury; Mercury was to be found domiciled in some other mouth of the river. At the Bolbitic mouth none of those persons of whom I enquired knew anything about Mercury. Near the third or Sebennitic mouth stood the city of Sebennis, of which the inhabitants were so savage and cruel towards strangers, and so utterly destitute of all the arts and graces of civilisation, that I could not conceive of Mercury, the god of culture and science, living in their midst. Moreover, a certain peasant whom I asked whether Mercury's house was there, told me that he had a house in the town but that he never lived there. So I at once went on to the fourth or Pelusian mouth of the Nile. The famous city of Pelusium is said to have been founded by Peleus, the father of Achilles. It separates Asia and Arabia from Egypt, and was at one time a most wealthy town. When I heard of its greatness in commerce and industry, and of the large quantities of Arabian gold which are imported in this city, one of the wealthiest marts of Egypt, I felt assured that I should find the dwelling of Mercury here; but I was told by the inhabitants that he did not come there very often, though he was received as a most welcome guest whenever he did visit it. This answer filled me with dismay, which was in proportion to the hopes which I had conceived, but I determined not to abandon my search till I should have visited the three remaining mouths of the river.

At the Tenitic mouth of the Nile, I learned quite as much as I had learned everywhere else, namely—nothing. When the people who lived there told me that Mercury never came to them at all, I began to bewail my hapless fate, and the many fruitless journeys I had undertaken; and I now saw that perhaps it would have been wiser to have begun at the other end. There, however, I was; only two mouths of the river were left; and in one of these Mercury would be found, if indeed the Prophetess had spoken true.

At the Phœnetic mouth another disappointment awaited me. Mercury had once lived there, but had long since migrated somewhere else. At the seventh, or Mendesian mouth, nothing whatever was known about him.

It may easily be imagined that, after this long series of disappointments, I began to suspect the Sibyl very strongly of having sent me on a fool's errand; for I had now visited every one of the mouths of the Nile, and yet had not found even a trace of Mercury in any of them. Or if the words of the prophetess had been true, it seemed as if the various people of whom I had enquired must have deceived me with false information. But after more mature consideration of the answers which had been returned to my questions in the different places, I arrived at the conclusion that I had merely misapprehended their meaning. So I retraced my steps, and at length succeeded in finding Mercury in one of the mouths, where the people had at first appeared to know nothing about him. He sheaved me at great length, where I must look for the Phœnix and where I could obtain possession of it. When I reached the place to which he directed me, I found that the Phœnix had temporarily deserted it, having chanced to be chosen umpire between the owl and other birds which pursue it, of which battle we have treated otherwise. It was expected back in a few weeks; but, as I could not afford to wait so long just then, I thought I might be content with the information I had gained, and determined to consummate my search at some future time. So, having returned to my native land, I composed the following epigrams in honour of the Sibyl, Mercury, the Phœnix, and the Medicine.

EPIGRAM

In Honour of the Erythræan Sibyl, named Herophyle.

"I thank thee, great prophetess, whose inspiration is not of the fiend, but of the Spirit of God, that thou didst direct me on my way to the Son of Nilus, who should show unto me the bird Phœnix. Full of sacred knowledge, thou didst utter forth thy oracles when thou didst sing of God who should come in the fashion of a man. Thou dost love Him who, bearing the sentences of highest justice, will be the omnipotent judge of the whole world, though thou wert called a Gentile Maiden, and though men said that thou couldst know nothing of Him. The cave near the Red Sea cannot hold thy. greatness, when Christ shall claim thee for His own in Heaven."

EPIGRAM

Dedicated to Mercury of the Sages.

"The Latins call thee Mercury, the Messenger of the Gods; among the Greeks thy name is that of great Hermes. Thou art called Tenthius on the soil of Egypt; thy father is Nilus, who enriches that soil, and has bequeathed unto thee untold wealth. Thou hast duly conveyed to the peoples of Egypt the laws which Vulcan, being in the secret with thee, has given. All nations of the world behold thee with delight, yet thou desirest to be known to very few. Of how many secrets of Nature have the keys been entrusted to thy keeping! Thy face is red, thy neck is yellow, thy bosom is whiter than purest snow. Thy feet are shod with black sandals, a wand with a double snake in no wise hurts thy hand. This is thine apparel whereby thou art known to all, O Hermes! Thy complexion is fittingly of four hues. Thou didst show to me the glorious bird Phœnix by the mouth of an interpreter, and I thank thee for thy love with all my heart; though the words be light, they are weighty with gratitude."

AN EPIGRAM

In Praise of the Phœnix.

"O Marvel of the World, prodigy without a blot, unique Phœnix who givest thyself to the great Sages! Thy feathers are red, and golden the hues of thy neck; thy nest is built of cassia and Sabœan frankincense. When thy life is drawing to a close, thou knowest the secret way of Nature by which thou art restored to a new existence. Hence thou gladly placest thyself on the altar of Thebes, in order that Vulcan may give thee a new body. The golden glory of thy " "feathers is called the Medicine of health, and the cure of human woe. Thou has power to cast out disease and to make the old young again. Thee. Blessed Bird, I would rather have than all the wealth of the world, and the knowledge of thee was a delight which I sought for many years. Thou art hidden in the retreat of thine own nest, and if Pliny writes that he saw thee in Rome, he does greatly err. Thou art safe in thy home, unless some foolish boy disturb thee: if thou dost give thy feathers to anyone, I pray thee let him be a Sage."

On the Hermetic Medicine of the Phœnix.

"If all the mountains were of silver and gold, what would they profit a man who lives in constant fear of death? Hence there cannot be in the whole world anything better than our Medicine, which has power to heal all the diseases of the flesh. Wealth, and riches, and gold, all yield the prize to this glorious possession: and whoever does not think so, is not a man, but a beast."

"If anyone will not acknowledge the force of reason, he must needs have recourse to authority."

THE

THREE TREATISES

OF

PHILALETHES.

I.

THE METAMORPHOSIS OF METALS.

II.

A SHORT VADE MECUM TO THE CELESTIAL RUBY.

III.

THE FOUNT OF CHEMICAL TRUTH.

CHAPTER I.

Of the Claims of our Art, its Students, and its Method.

ALL men who devote their lives to the study of any art, or to any kind of occupation, have before their eyes, as the aim of their efforts, perfection in the thing which they pursue. But only few attain to the goal of their wishes: there are many architects, but few masters of the art of architecture; many students of medicine, but few men like Hippocrates or Galen; many mathematicians, but few proficients like Archimedes; many poets, but few worthy to rank with Homer. Yet, even men who have nothing more than a respectable knowledge of their calling, are capable of being useful to society.

Among those who devote themselves to the transmutation of metals, however, there can be no such thing as mediocrity of attainment. A man who studies this Art, must have either everything or nothing. An Alchemist who knows only half his craft, reaps nothing but disappointment and waste of time and money; moreover, he lays himself open to the mockery of those who despise our Art. Those, indeed, who succeed in reaching the goal of the Magistery, have not only infinite riches, but the means of continued life and health. Hence it is the most popular of all human pursuits. Anyone who has read a few "Receipts" claims the title of a Sage, and conceives the most extravagant hopes; and, in order to give themselves the appearance of very wise men indeed, such persons immediately set themselves to construct furnaces, fill their laboratories with stills and alembics, and approach the work with a wonderful appearance of profundity. They adopt an obscure jargon, speak of the first matter of the metals, and discuss with a learned air the rotation of the elements, and the marriage of Gabritius with Bega. In the meantime, however, they do not succeed in bringing about any metamorphosis of the metals, except that of their gold and silver into copper and bronze.

When captious despisers of our Art see this, they draw from such constant failures the conclusion that our Art is a combination of fiction and imposture; whilst those who have ruined themselves by their folly confirm this suspicion by preying on the credulity of others, pretending to have gained some skill by the loss of their money. In this way the path of the beginner is beset with difficulties and pestilent delusions of every kind; and, through the fault of these swindlers, who give themselves such wonderful airs of profundity and learning, our Art itself has fallen into utter disrepute, though these persons, of course, know nothing whatever about it. The beginner finds it extremely difficult to distinguish between the false and the true in this vast Labyrinth of Alchemy. Bernard of Trevisa warns him to eschew like the plague these persons who hold out so many vain and empty promises; while I have written this Treatise for the guidance of the blind, and the instruction of the erring. I wish, in the first place, to clear our Art from the slanders which have been cast upon it, then to describe the qualifications of its students and its methods of procedure. After these prefatory explanations, I will gird myself to a description of the Art itself.

Before I say anything else, I would record my most earnest protest against that method of reasoning by which the deceptions of certain wretched sophists are laid to the charge of this science. The wickedness of some of its lying professors can prove nothing either for or against its genuineness. Such a position could be made good only by arguments based on natural relations; but such arguments it is impossible to find. The light of Nature is too bright to be darkened by these obscurists. I hope my Book will show that the Transmutation of Metals, from an imperfect to a perfect state, is a real and true achievement, and that by the co-operation of Nature and Art. The only thing that distinguishes one metal from another, is its degree of maturity, which is, of course, greatest in the most precious metals; the difference between gold and lead is not one of substance, but of digestion; in the baser metal the coction has not been such as to purge out its metallic impurities. If by any means this superfluous impure matter could be organically removed from the baser metals, they would become gold and silver. So miners tell us that lead has in many cases developed into silver in the bowels of the earth; and we contend that the same effect is produced in a much shorter time by means of our Art. It is a fact that the Mercury which is generated in the bowels of the earth, is the common substance of all metals—since this Mercury will enter into combination with every kind of metal—which could not be the case if it were not naturally akin to them all. Mercury is a water that will mix with nothing that is not of the same nature. By Art, the handmaid of Nature, Mercury can be so successively concocted with all metals, that one and the same under the same colour and flux, may subalternately show and express the true temperature and properties of them all. Moreover, all metals are capable of being resolved into running Mercury—and surely this could not be if it were not their common substance. Again, the Mercury of lead may become that of iron, the Mercury of iron that of copper; while the Mercury of tin may even be transmuted into that of silver and gold—a fact which triumphantly demonstrates the substantial affinity of all the metals. From antimony, too, a good Mercury is obtained, which some of our Artists are able to change into metallic mercury. It is also a well-established fact that the Mercury gained from any metallic or mineral body possesses the properties of assimilating common Mercury to its own nature; thus common Mercury may become that of all metals in turn. Do not these arguments clearly show that there is one Mercury, and that in the various metals it is only differentiated according to their different degrees of digestion or purity? I do not see how these arguments can be answered. It is possible indeed that some dull person may allege in refutation of our reasoning his inability to accomplish those chemical transformations on which it is based; but such operators would be vindicating too great an honour for their ignorance if they claimed to advance it as an argument against the truth of our Art. They must not make their own little understandings the standard or measure of the possibilities of Nature. At any rate, my word is as good as theirs (and better, since they can never prove a negative), and I do most positively and solemnly assert that I have with my own hands performed every one of the experiments which I have described; and I know many others whose experience has shown these things to be true. How can our opponents hope to prevail against eye-witnesses by bare negation? My testimony is borne out by the experience of such men as Albertus, Raymund, Riplæus, Flamellus, Morienus, and a host of others. I confess that the transformations of which I have spoken are not easy to accomplish; but whoever has the Key of our Art can unlock all gates, and has power over all the secrets of Nature. But this Key is possessed only by those who have both a theoretical and a practical knowledge of natural processes. I could here reckon up divers mutations of metals, as, for instance, Mars into Venus, by the acid stalagma of vitriol, Mercury into Saturn, Saturn into Jupiter, Jupiter into Lune, which operations, indeed, many vulgar chemists (far enough from the top of the art) know how to perform. I might also add, what is known only to a few philosophers, that there is a secret substance intermediate between metals and minerals, the mixed heavenly virtues of which produce a certain metal without a name, which is, strictly speaking, not a metal at all, but a Chaos, or Spirit, for it is all volatile: from this all metals can be educed without transmutatory Elixir, even gold, silver, and mercury. It is called Chalybs by the author of the "New Light," and it is the true key and first principle of our Art. What though the Sages have hidden all these things, and set them forth parabolically for the true sons of knowledge? Are they any the less true for that reason? . . . All that is wanted for the perfect development of an imperfect substance, is the gentle, digestive action of a homogeneous agent. This agent is gold, as highly matured as natural and artificial digestion can make it, and a thousand times more perfect than the common metal of that name. Gold, thus exalted, radically penetrates, tinges, and fixes metals. This scientific fact we may illustrate in the following manner. If you take six pounds of silver, and gild it with a single ounce of gold, you may afterwards draw out the silver into threads of the greatest fineness, and still distinctly perceive in each thread the brilliancy of gold. If then this dead, bodily, and earthy metal (which, as a body, of course, has no power to enter another body) can produce so wonderful an effect, does it seem incredible that the spirit of this gold, which can enter and animate the bodies of other metals, should transform them into its own nature? If we had this spiritual tincture, is it not clear that it would do inwardly what the body of the gold is seen to do outwardly? Remember that our Tincture is the Quintessence of gold, and infinitely more perfect than the mere body of gold can ever be; and that it has, therefore, an infinitely greater power of diffusing its essential quality. If gold thus spiritually enters another metal, it will clearly assimilate it to its own nature. The method of this spiritual ingestion we shall describe further on. Let us only add in this place, where we are discussing the *rationale* of metallic transmutation, that seed is the perfection of any seed-bearing substance; that which has no seed is altogether imperfect. It is, then, as the poet sings: "Gold contains the seeds of gold, though they be deeply hidden." Gold is not only perfect, but the most perfect thing of its kind (*i.e.*, of metals). If gold has seed, it must be contained in water, which is the habitation of all spirits, seed being a certain spiritual means of conserving any species. If gold is to be dissolved for the purpose of educing its seed, the dissolution will have to take place by means of this same metallic water. When this dissolution takes place, the gold puts off its earthly form, and assumes a watery form. Now, gold being both the starting point and the goal in the whole of this generative process, it is clear that all intermediate operations must be of a homogeneous character, *i.e.*, they must consist in gradual modifications of this seed of gold. The processes of our Art must begin with the dissolution of gold; they must terminate in a restoration of the essential quality of gold. But as the negative can never become the positive, the final form of our gold must be essentially different from its initial one. The final form is so much more noble than the initial one as fire is more subtle and spiritual than earth. What I have written is enough for the faithful student of our Art; and to its hostile and carping critics this book is not addressed. Therefore, I will now go on to add a word or two about the qualifications of those who should study this noble science. Our Art has fallen into disrepute, as I have said, through the stupidity and dishonesty of many of its professors. They are ignorant mechanics who, not having skill and brains enough for an honest trade, must needs meddle with our Art, and, of course, soon lose all they possess. Others, again, are only just less ignorant than these persons; they are in too great a hurry to make gold before they have mastered even the rudiments of natural science; of course they fail, spend all they have, borrow money from their friends, amuse themselves and others with hopes of infinite wealth, learn to talk a barbarous semi-philosophical jargon, and afford a capital handle to those who have an interest in abusing our Art. Again, there are others who really have a true knowledge of the secret, but who grudge others the light which has irradiated their own path; and who therefore write about it in hopelessly puzzling language, which the perplexed beginner cannot possibly understand. To this class belong Geber, Arnold, and Lullius, who would have done much better service to the student, if they had never dipped pen in ink. The consequence is that everyone who takes up this study at once finds himself lost in a most perplexing labyrinth of falsehood and uncertainty, in which he has no clue. I will therefore try to give him some sound advice as to the best way of accomplishing his object.

In the first place, let him carry on his operations with great secrecy in order that no scornful or scurrilous person may know of them; for nothing discourages the beginner so much as the mockery, taunts, and well-meant advice of foolish outsiders. Moreover, if he does not succeed, secrecy will save him from derision; if he does succeed, it will safeguard him against the persecution of greedy and cruel tyrants. In the second place, he who would succeed in the study of this Art, should be persevering, industrious, learned, gentle, good-tempered, a close student, and neither easily discouraged nor slothful; he may work in co-operation with one friend, not more, but should be able to keep his own counsel; it is also necessary that he should have a little capital to procure the necessary implements, etc., and to provide himself with food and clothing while he follows this study, so that his mind may be undistracted by care and anxiety. Above all, let him be honest, God-fearing, prayerful, and holy. Being thus equipped, he should study Nature, read the books of genuine Sages, who are neither impostors nor jealous churls, and study them day and night; let him not be too eager to carry out every idea practically before he has thoroughly tested it, and found it to be in harmony not only with the teaching of all the Sages, but also of Nature herself. Not until then let him gird himself for the practical part of the work, and let him constantly modify his operations until he sees the signs which are described by the Sages. Nor let him despair though he take many false steps; for the greatest philosophers have learned most by their mistakes. For his guidance in these operations he will find all the light he requires in the following treatises.

CHAPTER II.

Of the Origin of this Art and its Writers; its Fundamental Metallic Principles, and the Gradual Production of Metals and Minerals.

Hermes, surnamed Trismegistus, is generally regarded as the father of this Art; but there are different opinions with regard to his identity. Some say he was Moses; all agree that he was a very clear-sighted philosopher, the first extant author on the subject, and was also of Egyptian extraction. Others say that Enoch invented the Art, and, before the coming of the Flood, described it on the so-called emerald tables, which were afterwards found by Hermes in the valley of Hebron. Many assert that it was known to Adam, who revealed it to Seth; that Noah carried the secret with him into the Ark, and that God revealed it to Solomon. But I do not agree with those who claim for our Art a mystical origin, and thus only make it ridiculous in the eyes of a scornful world. If it is founded on the eternal verities of Nature, why need I trouble my head with the problem whether this or that antediluvian personage had a knowledge of it? Enough for me to know that it is now true and possible, that it has been exercised by the initiated for many centuries, and under the most distant latitudes; it may also be observed that though most of these write in an obscure, figurative, allegorical, and altogether perplexing style, and though some of them have actually mixed falsehood with truth, in order to confound the ignorant, yet they, though existing in many series of ages, differing in tongue and nation, have not diversely handled one operation, but do all exhibit a most marvellous and striking agreement in regard to the main features of their teaching—an agreement which is absolutely inexplicable, except on the supposition that our Art is something more than a mere labyrinth of perplexing words. Our Art is most plainly and straightforwardly expounded by Bernard of Trevisa, Ripley the Englishman, Flamellus the Frenchman, Sendivogius, the author of the "New Light," the anonymous author of the "Arcanum of Hermes," who also wrote *Enchiridion Physicæ Restitutæ*, and "The Ladder of Philosophers," the great "Rosary," the "Child's Play," the Tract of Dionysius Zachary, the works of Morienus, the works of Egidius de Vadis, Augurellus' poem entitled "Goldmaking," the works of Peter Bonus of Ferrara, and the "Abridged Rosary." Let the student procure one or more of these, and similar genuine works on Alchemy, and let him study the secrets of Nature by the light which they throw upon it. He will find a knowledge of natural science, and more particularly of mineralogy, indispensable for his purpose.

All philosophers tell us that there are four elements, which compose all things, and, by means of their diverse combination, produce various forms. But the truth is that there are only three elements, *i.e.*, those which of their own nature are cold—air, water, and earth. The defect of heat which we perceive in them is in proportion to their distance from the sun. Fire I do not acknowledge as an element. There is no fire, except the common fire which burns on the hearth; and its heat is essentially destructive. The heat there is in things is the product either of light, or motion, or life, or alterative processes. Fire is not an element, but a robber that preys on the products of the four elements; it is a violent corruptive motion caused by the clashing of two active principles. Thus, we see that it is an operation of two other substances, not a substance in itself—a result of the active co-operation of a comburent and a combustible. The nature and characteristic quality of the three elements is cold, and they possess heat only as an accident. . . . Nor is it true that objects are formed by a mixture of these three elements; for dissimilar things can never really unite, seeing that union is a complete mixture and concretion of the smallest atoms or molecules of two substances. But such a mixture is impossible in the case of two dissimilar matters, as, for instance, between water and earth (or water and wine); they admit of being separated at any time on account of the disproportion of their smallest particles. It may be said that for the sake of union the grosser element becomes as subtle as the other; but if this were the case, if for the purpose of union water became as subtle as air, that would simply mean that water became air, an assumption which would thus fail to prove the possibility of an amalgamation of water and air. Is it not a simpler and more credible supposition that only water or air, as the case may be, enters into the composition of any given object? But if anyone still persists in maintaining this permutation of the elements (which, after all, would only mean that all things consist of air)—let me ask the humble question—by the activity of what agent they are so transmuted? Moreover, one would also be glad to enquire what is the use of this permutation of earth into water, and of water into air? What can earth converted into water, or water converted into air, perform, that could not be just as well accomplished by simple unchanged water or air? Surely, Nature does nothing in vain; but here would be a difficult and wasteful process of transmutation constantly going on, which is not calculated to serve any useful purpose whatsoever. If it be said that earth rarefied into water is like water, yet not exactly water, my answer is that this is a mere quibble about words, and that if the rarefied earth is only like water, and not really water, it cannot possibly combine with it in its smallest particles; so nothing is gained by this hypothesis. Hence we may conclude that all things derive their origin from one element, which can be neither earth nor air. This I could prove at great length if I were not cramped for space. It follows, then, that water must be the first principle of all things, *i.e.*, of all concrete bodies in this world; earth is the fundamental element in which all bodies grow and are preserved; air is the medium into which they grow, and by means of which the celestial virtues are communicated to them. The seed of all things has been placed by God in water. This seed some exhibit openly, like vegetables, some keep in their kidneys, like animals; some conceal in the depths of their essential being, like metals. The seed is stirred into action by its form (*i.e.*, a certain appropriate celestial influence), coagulates the material water, and passes through a series of fermentative processes (fermentation being the principle of all transmutation), until it has produced that for the production of which it was specially suited. If the seed is metallic, there is generated from it first a dry liquid, which does not wet the hand, *viz.*, Mercury, the mother of all metals. Mercury may be described as the true first matter of metals; for not until the elemental water has become Mercury can it be affirmed with any degree of certainty that a metal or mineral must result from it. Water is, in itself, potentially the seed of either an animal, vegetable, or mineral; but Mercury is metallically differentiated water, *i.e.*, it is water passed into that stage of development, in which it can no longer produce anything but mineral substances. Mercury, then, is the common seed of gold, silver, copper, tin, iron, lead, etc.; their difference is only to be sought in the degree of their digestion. The digestive is not any fat sulphur which is brought to bear on them from without; but Mercury contains within itself the active principle of its development, *viz.*, the inward heat due to celestial influences, causing vitality, and dependent on the fitness of the womb. These heavenly influences are at work throughout the world; but their exact mode of action is determined by the potential nature of the seed; if the inward life be metallic, the coupe of its development by means of outward agents will also be metallic. Still Mercury develops only where these outward influences (celestial and terrestrial) can be brought to bear. In every other place it will appear a cold, dead, and lifeless substance. But in the centre of its nativity it is quickened by the action of celestial influences, conveyed to it through the medium of air, whence results heat, wherewith life is necessarily associated. Now, the womb in which this Mercury is placed, is either more, less, or not at all suited to it; and according to the different degrees of this fitness, the substance either remains altogether stationary, or is more or less perfectly developed; imperfection of development yields the imperfect metals, while by means of perfect development are produced silver and gold; but all metals, though differentiated by the degree of their digestion or maturity, have the same first substance, *viz.*, Mercury. The dross and impurities which are so largely found in the base metals, form no part of the original Mercury, but are added afterwards through some flaw in the process of coagulation, or through the impurity of the place or womb in which their metallic generation (fermentation) takes place But I will now go on to deal with the special subject of this Treatise, *viz.*, the renovation or multiplication of gold and silver.

CHAPTER III.

Of the Generation of Gold and Silver from the Mercurial Substance, and the Possibility of bringing Imperfect Metals to the same State of Perfection.

To the aforesaid source (Mercury) we trace the birth of gold, and of its sister, silver; they represent this substance brought to perfection by means of digestion. Perfection is of two kinds, inchaotive or complete, partial or entire. Complete perfection (the complete digestion of all crudities and elimination of all impurities) is the ultimate aim of Nature; and she has reached it in our gold, which with its brilliancy lights up the whole earth. Inchaotive perfection may be so named, not absolutely, but relatively, when compared with essentially imperfect bodies. Those bodies are formally or essentially imperfect in the composition of which the impure predominates over the pure, so that they could never of themselves (by natural development) attain perfection; this is the case with all metals except gold and silver. But whenever the pure is freed from the corruptive tyranny of the impure, and obtains the mastery over it, we have inchaotive perfection, though the development of the body may be still incomplete. These crudities and impurities do not originally belong to the metallic substance, and are very well capable of being separated from it; if they are so purged off before coagulation, we get a perfect metal. But even if they are coagulated together with the Mercury, it is still possible to separate them from it, and thus to perfect the Mercury. It is on this possibility that our Art is based; and its business is to perform this separation. The base metals contain the same Mercury as gold; if we can free this Mercury from the impurities which hinder its development, it must also go on to perfection, *i.e.*, become gold. If we could find some separating agent which would perform this office for the impure minerals, it would also be a digestive, *i.e.*, it would quicken the inward metallic digestion of the long-entombed Mercury. Such a separant is our divine Arcanum, which is the heavenly spirit of water with fiery penetrative power. Compared with common gold, it is what the soul is in comparison of the body; and having attained the highest degree of corporeal fixity, it takes up the Mercury of the base metals into its own nature, and protects it from the fire while the impurities are being burnt up. The Mercury of the base metals (unlike the Mercury of gold), if exposed to the fire without such protection, would not be able to encounter the searching ordeal, but (having no cohesion with its impure body, and possessing no fixity in itself) would simply evaporate, and leave the impurities to be burned. But our Arcanum, being both a spiritual and a homogeneous substance, is capable of entering into a perfect atomic union with the imperfect metals, of taking up into its own nature that which is like to it, and of imparting to this Mercury its own fixity, and protecting it from the fire; so when the fire has burnt up all the impurities, that which is left is, of course, pure gold or silver, according to the quality of the Medicine—which from that time forward is (like all other gold and silver) capable of resisting the most searching ordeal. So you see we do not, as is sometimes said, profess to create gold and silver, but only to find an agent which—on account of its homogeneity and spirituality—is capable of entering into an intimate (atomic) and maturing union with the Mercury of the base metals. And we contend that our Elixir is calculated, by the intense degree of its fixity and colour, to impart these qualities to any homogeneous substance which does not possess them.

CHAPTER IV.

Of the Seed of Gold; and whether other Metals have Seed.

Seed is the means of generic propagation given to all perfect things here below; it is the perfection of each body; and anybody that has no seed must be regarded as imperfect. Hence there can be no doubt that there is such a thing as metallic seed. If metals have seed, they certainly do not lose it in coagulation, which is the effect of perfection (or rather of perfect conditions). Now, in all seed-bearing things maturity means the perfect development of the seeds, and it stands to reason that metallic seed is therefore most certainly not destroyed by coagulation (the maturing process). If it be asked whether all metals have seed, my answer is, that the seed of all metals is the same; but that in some it is found nearer to, and in some further from the surface. All metallic seed is the seed of gold; for gold is the intention of Nature in regard to all metals. If the base metals are not gold, it is only through some accidental hindrance; they are all potentially gold. But, of course, this seed of gold is most easily obtainable from well-matured gold itself. Hence it would be lost labour to endeavour to obtain it from tin or lead by some laborious process, when it may be more readily obtained from gold itself. Remember that I am now speaking of metallic seed, and not of Mercury. Lead is to be multiplied, not in lead, but only in gold; for only when it attains its maturity as gold can its seed become fruitful. It may be admitted that silver has its own seed, as there is a white (as well as a red) multiplicative Tincture. Still, the White Tincture is really contained in the Red; and the seed of silver is nothing but a modification of that of gold. The whiteness of silver is the first degree of perfection, the yellowness of gold is the second, or highest degree. For the mother of our Stone (the silver of the Sages) is white, and imparts its whiteness to our gold, whence the offspring of these two parents first becomes white, like its mother, and then red with the royal blood of its father.

CHAPTER V.

Of the Virtue of Golden Seed, and where it is most readily found.

In order that we may obtain this means of perfecting imperfect metals, we must remember that our Arcanum is gold exalted to the highest degree of perfection to which the combined action of Nature and Art can develop it. In gold, Nature has reached the term of her efforts; but the seed of gold is something more perfect still, and in cultivating it we must, therefore, call in the aid of Art. The seed of metals is hidden out of sight still more completely than that of animals; nevertheless, it is within the compass of our Art to extract it. The seed of animals and vegetables is something separate, and may be cut out, or otherwise separately exhibited; but metallic seed is diffused throughout the metal, and contained in all its smallest parts; neither can it be discerned from its body: its extraction is therefore a task which may well tax the ingenuity of the most experienced philosopher; the virtues of the whole metal have to be intensified, so as to convert it into the sperm of our seed, which, by circulation, receives the virtues of superiors and inferiors, then next becomes wholly form, or heavenly virtue, which can communicate this to others related to it by homogeneity of matter. In respect of the Stone, the whole of gold is its substance. The place in which the seed resides is—approximately speaking—water; for, to speak properly and exactly, the seed is the smallest part of the metal, and is invisible; but as this invisible presence is diffused throughout the water of its kind, and exerts its virtue therein, nothing being visible to the eye but water, we are left to conclude from rational induction that this inward agent (which is, properly speaking, the seed) is really there. Hence we call the whole of the water seed, just as we call the whole of the grain seed, though the germ of life is only a smallest particle of the grain. But the seminal life is not distinct from the remaining substance of metals; rather, it is inseparably mingled with the smallest parts of the body. Roughly speaking, however, we describe the whole of our golden water as the seed of gold, because this seminal virtue pervades it in a most subtle manner. This seminal virtue the ancient Sages called the hidden ferment, the poison, or the invisible fire; again, they said that it was fire, or that fire resided in the water; they distinguished between soul and spirit, of which the former is the medium, the latter the active virtue. If anyone wonders that we describe water as the seat of the seed, or the seminal spirit, let him remember that in the beginning the Spirit of God moved on the face of the waters, *i.e.*, penetrated them with His heavenly quickening power. Thus, from the very first day of Creation, water has been the source and element of all things. For water alone contains the seeds of all things; yet in vegetables they are put forth in crude air; in animals they are preserved in the kidneys; while in minerals they are diffused throughout the whole substance; nevertheless, seed can never leave its original seat (*i.e.*, water). Things are preserved by that from which they derive their origin; for the cause of their origin being removed, the things which are the effect must also cease to exist; hence the multiplication and nutrition of all things is in water and through water. Vegetables are generated and nourished by the aqueous Teffas of the earth; animals by the liquid chyle; metals by the mercurial liquid. Animals preserve their seed in their kidneys, and in due time project it into the proper womb, where it is first moulded into a tender and very watery fœtus; this fœtus is nourished by the liquid female menstruum, and thus grows until the time comes for it to be born. Then it is nourished with milk until it can bear stronger food; but this solid food does not become real nutriment until the stomach has converted it into a liquid chyle (as, for instance, bones in the stomach of the dog). In the same way the metals keep their perfect seed where it cannot be seen; but even there it is preserved in water. Thence the Artist extracts it, puts it into its own proper womb, where it is cherished and grows, until (by means of corruption) it attains to its glorification. This is a most difficult operation, because the metals, in which the seed is hidden, are so firmly and tightly compacted, and will not yield to violence, but only to a gentle and exquisitely subtle chemical process. Then I say to you, that there is a womb into which the gold (if placed therein) will, of its own accord, emit its seed, until it is debilitated and dies, and by its death is renewed into a most glorious King, who thenceforward receives power to deliver all his brethren from the fear of death.

CHAPTER VI.
Of the Mode and Means of Extracting this Seed.

That the most beautiful things are the most difficult to produce, is the experience of all mankind; and it is not to be wondered at, therefore, that the most glorious of sublunary operations is attended with a very great amount of difficulty. If any student of this Art is afraid of hard work, let him stop with his foot upon the threshold. When, indeed, the Father of Lights has entrusted the Key of the Art to any man, that which remains to be done is mere child's play; his eyes are ravished with the sight of the most glorious signs, until the time of harvest arrives. Without this, error and vexation will be the result. Therefore the wise man, before commencing the work, will be chiefly solicitous of knowing it by its marks. Let the sons of knowledge learn that the great object of our Art is the manifestation of the hidden seed of gold, which can be effected only by full and perfect volatilisation of that which is fixed, and the subsequent corruption of its particular form. To break up gold in this way is the most profound secret in the world. It is not brought about by corrosive depravation of the metal, nor by the usual method of dissolution, but by our philosophical solution of the metal into mercurial water, by means of a previous mercurial calcination (made by means of the agent ♀), which is produced through the subtle rotation and conversion of the elements; this calcination, again, is a mortification of our homogeneous liquid with the dry element belonging to it; afterwards the dry is so far revived by means of this same liquid, that the perfectly matured virtue, extracted from the substance by the solvent, is the cause of this calcination and solution. Here, then, there is no room for the action of a corrosive. Gold, which is the most solid, strong, fire-proof, and fixed of all substances, is to be volatilised, and no mere corrosive will accomplish such a perfect change of nature. The mighty agent required for this purpose must be homogeneous, amicable, and spiritual, *i.e.*, it must be akin to the body (of gold), and yet strong enough to overcome it; and penetrate to its very core, still leaving each smallest part of the gold true gold. Gold does not easily give up its nature, and will fight for its life, but our agent is strong enough to overcome and kill it, and then it also has power to restore it to life, and to change the lifeless remains into a new pure body.

CHAPTER VII.
Of the First Agent or Womb, into which our Seed should be emitted, and where it is matured.

There remains to be found an Agent, by means of which the aforesaid operation may be performed. For this purpose we require a homogeneous water. For we have seen that the seed of gold is concealed, and can remain effectual only in water, and this water must be homogeneous with the body, or else it could not penetrate all the thick integuments by means of which this seed is secured. For like generates like, that is to say, every agent that exercises a generative action upon anything, transmutes it (as far as possible) into its own nature. The Agent then must be akin to the body which is to be dissolved, and, moreover, perfectly pure from all dross or alloy. Again, whereas gold is fixed and solid, the Agent must be highly volatile and spiritual; gold is thick and gross, our Agent is subtle; gold is dead, our Agent is living and life-giving: in short, our Agent should have all those qualities which gold has not, and which it is to impart to the gold. Hence we conclude that Mercury alone is the true Key of our Art; for it is in truth the dry water described by the Sages, which, though liquid, does not wet the hands, nor anything else that does not belong to the unity of its substance. Mercury is our doorkeeper, our balm, our honey, oil, urine, may-dew, mother, egg, secret furnace, oven, true fire, venomous Dragon, Theriac, ardent wine, Green Lion, Bird of Hermes, Goose of Hermogenes, two-edged sword in the hand of the Cherub that guards the Tree of Life, &c., &c.; it is our true, secret vessel, and the Garden of the Sages, in which our Sun rises and sets. It is our Royal Mineral, our triumphant vegetable Saturnia, and the magic rod of Hermes, by means of which he assumes any shape he likes. It is of this water that the Sage uses the words: "Let Alchemists boast as much as they like, but without this water the transmutation of metals is impossible. In Nature it is not such as we use it in our Art; it is a most common thing, and yet the most precious treasure of all the world. . . . . . Therefore, Son of Knowledge, pay diligent heed to my words: Take that which in itself is most impure, the strumpet woman, purge it radically of all its uncleanness, and extract from it that which is most pure, namely, our menstruum (solvent), the Royal Diadem." Behold, I have told you in a few words that which ennobles the Sage, delivers him from error, and leads him to the most beautiful meadow of delights. . . . The Arcanum which we seek is nothing but gold exalted to its highest degree of perfection, through the operation of Nature assisted by our Art. When the sperm hidden in the body of gold is brought out by means of our Art, it appears under the form of Mercury, whence it is exalted into the quintessence which is first white, and then, by means of continuous coction, becomes red. All this is the work of our homogeneous Agent, our Mercurial Ponticum, which is pure crystalline without transparency, liquid without humectation, and, in short, the true Divine water, which is not found above-ground, but is prepared by the hand of the Sage, with the co-operation of Nature, which we know, have seen, have made, and still possess; which also we desire to make known to the true students of our Art, while it is our wish to hide it only from the unworthy.

CHAPTER VIII.

Concerning the Genealogy of the Mercury of the Sages,
its Origin, Birth, and the Signs which precede
and accompany it.

Some boastful and arrogant sophists, who have read in books that our Mercury is not common Mercury, and who know that it is called by different names, do not blush to come forward as pretenders to a knowledge of this Art, and take upon themselves to describe this solvent as diaphanous and limpid, or as a metallic gum which is permiscible with metals, though they do not in reality know anything whatsoever about it. The same may be said of those who would extract our

Mercury from herbs or other still more fantastic substances. These gentry know not why the Sages do not use Mercury such as is sold by apothecaries as their substance. They are aware of the fact, but are unacquainted with its causes; and the consequence is the idea which they have that anything which changes the nature of common Mercury, will convert it into that of the Sages. But in regard to these foolish persons, I have already expressed our opinion. . . . All metals, as I demonstrated in the second chapter, have the same substantial principle, *viz.*, Mercury. From this proposition it follows that the substance of common Mercury is homogeneous with that of all the other metals; and if the Mercury of the Sages be the homogeneous metallic water, it can differ from common Mercury only in respect of its purity and heat. The first substance of common Mercury is that of all other metals, *viz.*, our Mercury. So long as it remains in the veins of the earth, in a place perfectly adapted to its generation, and is sheltered from crude air, it retains its inward movement and heat, which are the cause of all metallic development. But if it be marred by any accident, or if the place become unfit for it, the inward movement is stopped, and the germinal life chilled like that of an egg which a hen has left after sitting on it for some time. This is the reason why those who have attempted to digest common Mercury by means of artificial heat have failed as ludicrously as any one who should endeavour to incubate artificially an addled egg. The difference between the egg and the metal is that our Art is capable of making good the damage, but not by artificial means. We have a crude, undigested, frigid, unmatured metallic mass, which wants the form of our Mercury, for which it must exchange its own, if it is to become that which we seek. With this end in view, its deficiencies are twofold; its nature is clogged with superfluous foreign matter, and it does not possess the requisite spiritual virtue. Its superfluities consist of earthy leprosy, and aqueous dropsy. Its deficiency is one of true sulphureous heat, by means of which it would be enabled to purge off these superfluities. Water, indeed, is the womb, but no womb can receive a vital germ without warmth. Supplement your (common) Mercury, therefore, with the inward fire which it needs, and it will soon get rid of all superfluous dross. If you can do this, you have accomplished the great feat of the Sages. Jupiter has recovered his empire; the black clouds of Saturn are dispersed, and the sparkling fountain wells forth clear and pure. This substance will dissolve gold by means of a true philosophical solution, which is as different as can be from that foolish use of corrosives which only destroy the metallic nature. This Mercury (with) gold and silver naturally produces the Arcanum, or potable gold, as all adepts know and can testify.

Here I conclude this Tract, as all that remains to be said is set forth in a special (the next) Treatise.

A

BRIEF GUIDE TO

THE

CELESTIAL RUBY.

Concerning the Philosopher's Stone and its Grand Arcanum.

THE Philosopher's Stone is a certain heavenly, spiritual, penetrative, and fixed substance, which brings all metals to the perfection of gold or silver (according to the quality of the Medicine), and that by natural methods, which yet in their effects transcend Nature.

It is prepared from one substance, with which the art of chemistry is conversant, to which nothing is added, from which nothing is taken away, except that its superfluities are removed. No one will question the utility of our Art, if he believes that it enables us to transmute base metals into gold. That base metals are capable of such transmutation is clear; Nature has destined them all to become gold, but they have not been perfectly matured. If, then, that which hinders their perfect digestion be removed, they will all become gold; for crude, cold, and moist Mercury is the common first substance of gold as well as of the other metals. Hence all other metals may be perfected into gold, by the aid of our Divine Magistery, which, being projected upon imperfect metals, has power to quicken the maturing process by as much as itself exceeds the standard maturity of gold. How patent, then, must the spiritual nature of our Stone be, which can effect more in one hour by a bare projection than Nature in the course of ages. If that substance which Nature supplies be taken in hand by Art, dissolved, coagulated, and digested, its perfection is increased from a monadic to a denary virtue; by repeating the same process, it is increased a hundred-fold, and then a thousand-fold, etc. This wonderful Medicine penetrates each smallest part of the base metals (in the proportion of 1 :: 1,000) and tinges them through and through with its own noble nature: your arithmetic will fail sooner than its all-prevailing power. Each smallest part that is pervaded with the vitalizing power of the-Elixir in its turn tinges that part which is nearest to it until the whole mass is leavened with its marvellous influence, and brought to the perfection of gold. This is done in a very short time, on account of the spiritual nature of the agent; it is the true metallic fire, and as a common fire warms even those parts of any object which are not in immediate contact with the fire, so this Elixir penetrates dissolved and melted metals in a moment of time—just in the same way as the virtue of leaven or yeast is brought to bear even upon those parts of the meal which it never reaches. A reproach is sometimes levelled at our Art, as though it claimed the power of creating gold; every attentive reader of our former tract will know that it only arrogates to itself the power of developing, through the removal of all defects and superfluities, the golden nature, which the baser metals possess in common with that highly-digested metallic substance.

Listen, then, while I make known to you the Grand Arcanum of this wonder-working Stone, which at the same time is not a stone, which exists in every man, and may be found in its own place at all times. The knowledge which I declare is not intended for the unworthy, and will not be understood by them. But to you who are earnest students of Nature, God will, at His own time, reveal this glorious secret.

I have shown that the transmutation of metals is not a chimerical dream, but a sober possibility of Nature, who is perfectly capable of accomplishing it without the aid of magic; and that this possibility of metallic transmutation is founded upon the fact that all metals derive their origin from the same source as gold, and have only been hindered from attaining the same degree of maturity by certain impurities, which our Magistery is able to remove.

Let me tell you, then, what is the nature of this grand arcanum, which the Sages have called the Philosopher's Stone, but which is in every man, in everything, at every season of the year, if it be sought in the right place.

It must consist of the elements, for they are the universal substance of all things, and as it is of a nature homogeneous with that of gold, it must be that which contains the qualities of all elements in such a combination as to render it incapable of being destroyed by fire.

It follows, then, that you must look for the substance of our Stone in the precious metals, since the required combination of elements is not found anywhere else. Those foolish sophists who seek it outside the domain of metals will never arrive at any satisfactory conclusion. For there is only one true principle, and nothing heterogeneous must be introduced into our Magistery.

For as a lion is always born of a lion, and a man of a man, so all things owe their birth to that which they are like; that which is combustible is derived from that which is combustible, that which is indestructible from that which is indestructible. Nor must we expect to find the principle which imparts the qualities of gold anywhere but in gold itself. If, indeed, we were able to create the sperm of things, we might hope to evolve this metallic principle from plants or animals which do not contain it; but that is the privilege of God alone. We must be content to dispose and develop the sperm which is made ready to our hands—new things we are unable to produce, and even if we could, our artificial seed would be no better than that which Nature has provided. If any one calling himself a Sage cannot use the things which are already created, it does not seem likely that he will be able to create new things out of heterogeneous substances—the seeds of metals out of herbs or animals.

Thus, you see that the Stone which is to be the transformer of metals into gold must be sought in the precious metals, in which it is enclosed and contained.

But why is it called a Stone, though it is not a stone; and how is it to be found? The Sages describe it as being a stone and not a stone; and the vulgar, who cannot imagine how so wonderful a thing should be produced except by art-magic, decry our science as impious, wicked, and diabolical. Some silly persons clamour for an Act making the profession or practice of this Art punishable by statute law. Now, one can hardly be angry with the illiterate and ignorant persons who raise this cry; but when it is taken up by men of exalted station and profound learning, one hardly knows what to say. These men I also reckon among the rude multitude, because they are deplorably ignorant of everything pertaining to our Art, and yet, forgetful of their dignity, they join in the hue and cry against it, like so many cowardly village curs. It is neither religious nor wise to judge that of which you know nothing; and yet that is exactly what these people do, who claim to be both Christians and scholars.

But let us return to the point from which we strayed. Some Alchemists who are in search of our Arcanum seek to prepare something of a solid nature, because they have heard the object of their search described as a Stone.

Know, then, that it is called a stone, not because it is like a stone, but only because, by virtue of its fixed nature, it resists the action of fire as successfully as any stone. In species it is gold, more pure than the purest; it is fixed and incombustible like a stone, but its appearance is that of very fine powder, impalpable to the touch, sweet to the taste, fragrant to the smell, in potency a most penetrative spirit, apparently dry and yet unctuous, and easily capable of tinging a plate of metal. It is justly called the Father of all miracles, containing as it does all the elements in such a way that none predominates, but all form a certain fifth essence; it is thus well called our gentle metallic fire. It has no name of its own; yet there is nothing in the whole world whose name it might not with perfect propriety bear. If we say that its nature is spiritual, it would be no more than the truth; if we described it is as corporeal, the expression would be equally correct; for it is subtle, penetrative, glorified, spiritual gold. It is the noblest of all created things after the rational soul, and has virtue to repair all defects both in animal and metallic bodies, by restoring them to the most exact and perfect temper; wherefore is it a spirit or quintessence.

But I must proceed to answer the second and more important part of my question. How is this Stone to be obtained? It does not exist in Nature, but has to be prepared by Art, in obedience to Nature's law. Its substance is in metals; but in form it differs widely from them, and in this sense the metals are not our Stone. For if we would elicit our Medicine from the precious metals, we must destroy the particular metallic form, without impairing its specific properties. The specific properties of the metal have their abode in its spiritual part, which resides in homogeneous water. Thus we must destroy the particular form of gold, and change it into its generic homogeneous water, in which the spirit of gold is preserved; this spirit afterwards restores the consistency of its water, and brings forth a new form (after the necessary putrefaction), a thousand times more perfect than the form of gold which it lost by being reincrudated.

It is necessary, then, to reduce metallic bodies to their homogeneous water which does not wet the hands, that from this water there may be generated a new metallic species which is nobler by far than any existing metal, viz., our Celestial Ruby.

The whole process which we employ closely resembles that followed by Nature in the bowels of the earth, except that it is much shorter. Nature produces the metals out of cold and humid Mercury by assiduous digestion; our Art takes the same crude, cold, and humid Mercury, and conjoins with it mature gold, by a secret artifice; the mixture represents a new and far more potent Mercury, which, by digestion, becomes not common gold, but one far more noble, which can transmute imperfect metals into true gold.

Thus, you see that though our Stone is made of gold alone, yet it is not common gold. In order to elicit our gold from common gold, the latter must be dissolved in our mineral water which does not wet the hands; this water is Mercury extracted from the red servant, and it is capable of accomplishing our work without any further trouble to the Artist. It is that one true, natural, first-substance, to which nothing is added, from which nothing is subtracted, except certain superfluities, which, however, it will cast off without any aid by its own inherent vital action. The chief object of your perseverant efforts should be the discovery of this Mercury, or the albefaction of our red Laton; all the rest is mere child's play, as the Artist has only to look on while Nature gradually matures his substance.

But remember that our albification is by no means an easy task. Gold which has been thus whitened can never resume its old form, for, instead of being corporeal and fixed, it is now spiritual and volatile. Concentrate your whole mind, therefore, on the whitening of the Laton. It is easier to make gold than thus to destroy its form; he who so dissolves it may be said rather to coagulate it—for dissolution of the body and coagulation of the spirit are coincident in it.

Consider these signs, ye sons of knowledge. That which dissolves is spirit; that which coagulates is body. A body cannot enter a body so as to cause dissolution; but a spirit can enter it, attenuate and rarefy it; and as you seek water, you need water to bring it to light; for every Agent has a tendency to assimilate to itself that which it acts upon, and every natural effect is conformed to the nature of the efficient; hence water is necessary if you would extract water from earth.

When I speak of water, I do not mean aquafortis, royal water, or any other corrosive whatsoever, for these waters, instead of dissolving metals, only corrode, mar, and corrupt them, without destroying their old form, to which task they are insufficient, as they are not of a metallic nature. No, our water is the water Mercury, which dissolves homogeneous metallic bodies, and mingles with them in indissoluble union, abides with them, is digested with them, and together with them becomes that spiritual whole which we seek. For everything that dissolves a substance naturally (still preserving the specific properties of the thing dissolved) becomes one with it both materially and formally, coalesces with it, and is thickened by it, thus nourishing it; as we see in the case of a grain of wheat, which, when dissolved by the humid earthy vapour, thereby takes up that vapour as its radical moisture, and grows together with it into a plant. We may also observe that, every natural dissolution being a quickening of that which was dead, this quickening can take place only through some vital agent which is of the same essence with the dead thing; if we wish to quicken the (dead) grain of wheat, we can do this only by means of an earthy vapour, which, like the grain itself, is a product of the earth. For this reason common Mercury can have no quickening effect on gold, because it is not of the same essence with it. A grain of wheat sown in marshy soil, so far from being quickened into life, is, on the contrary, destroyed, because the aqueous humour of the soil is not of the same nature. In like manner, gold, if mixed with common Mercury, or with anything except its own essential humour, is not dissolved, because such waters are too cold, crude, and impure; for which reason, being utterly unlike gold, they cannot amalgamate with it, or attain with it to a far nobler degree of development. Our Mercury, indeed, is cold and unmatured in comparison with gold; but it is pure, hot, and well-digested in respect of common Mercury, which resembles it only in whiteness and fluxibility. Our Mercury is, in fact, a pure water, clean, clear, bright, and resplendent, worthy of all admiration.

If you wish for a more particular description of our water, I am impelled by motives of charity to tell you that it is living, fluxible, clear, nitid, as white as snow, hot, humid, airy, vaporous, and digestive, and that gold melts in it like ice in warm water; moreover, that in it is contained the whole regimen of fire, and the sulphur which exists but does not predominate in it. This water is the true Keeper of our Gates, the Bath of the King and of his Queen, which warms them incessantly, but is not taken of their substance, and is distinct from the whitening substance of the water, though the two are united and appear under the same flowing form and colour. It is our vessel, our fire, the abode of our furnace, by whose continuous and gentle warmth the whole substance is digested. If you know this water, it will be seen to contain all our fires, all our proportions of weight, all our regimens. It is Bernard of Trevisa's clear pellucid Fountain, in which our King is cleansed and strengthened to overcome all his foes. All you have to do is to find this water and to put into it the purified body; out of the two Nature will then produce our Stone.

This mineral water can be extracted only from those things which contain it; and that thing from which it is most easily obtained is difficult to discover, as is also the mode of its extraction. It dissolves gold without violence, is friendly to it washes away its impurities, and is white, warm, and clear Without our Mercury, Alchemy could not be a science, but only a vain and empty pretence. If you can obtain it, you have the key of the whole work, with which you can open the most secret chambers of knowledge. Its nature is the same as that of gold, but its substance is different, and the preparation of it causes a great stench. Weigh well the possibilities of Nature; refrain from introducing any heterogeneous element into our Magistery, and do not blame me if you fail to understand my words. . . . Our Stone is produced from one thing, and four mercurial substances, of which one is mature; the others pure, but crude, two of them being extracted in a wonderful manner from their ore by means of the third. The four are amalgamated by the intervention of a gentle fire, and there subjected to coction day by day, until they all become one by natural (not manual) conjunction.

Afterwards, the fire being changed, these volatile substances should be fixed and digested by means of heat which becomes a little more powerful every day (*i.e.*, by means of fixed and incombustible Sulphur of the same genus) until the whole compound attains the same essence, fixity, and colour.

There are twelve degrees or phases of this our process, which I may briefly enumerate and describe as follows. The first is Calcination.

Calcination is the first purgation of the Stone, the drying up of its humours, through its natural heat, which is stirred into vital action by the external heat of water—whereby the compound is converted into a black powder, which is yet unctuous, and retains its radical humour.

This calcination is performed for the purpose of rendering the substance viscous, spongy, and more easily penetrable; for gold in itself is highly fixed, and difficult of solution even in our water; but through this calcination it becomes soft and white, and we observe in it two natures, the fixed and the volatile, which we liken to two serpents. In order that a full dissolution may be made, there is need of contrition, that calcination may afterwards produce a viscous state, when it will be fit for dissolution.

When the substances are first mixed, they are at enmity with each other, by reason of their contrary qualities, for there is the heat and dryness of the Sulphur fiercely contending with the cold and moisture of the Mercury. They can only be reconciled in a medium which partakes of both natures, and the medium in which heat and cold are reconciled is dryness which can co-exist with both. Thus cold and heat are brought to dwell peaceably together in the dryness of the earth, and dryness and moisture in the coldness of the water. This reconciliation of contrary qualities is the second great object of our calcination.

Its sufficient cause is the action of the inward heat upon the moisture, whereby everything that resists it is converted into a very fine powder; the moving and instrumental cause is the fire contrary to Nature, which, being hidden in our solvent water, battles with its moisture and digests it into a viscous or unctuous powder.

This operation takes place before our dissolution, because whenever bodies are dissolved, the spirits in their turn are congealed. Again, the woman must reign, before she is overcome by the man. The dominion of the woman is in the water, and if the man overcome her in the element in which both her qualities of coldness and moisture inhere, he will easily conquer her where she has only one quality.

Calcination, then, is the beginning of the work, and without it there can be neither peaceable commixtion nor proper union. The first dealbation reduces the substance to its two principles, sulphur and quicksilver, the first of which is fixed, while the other is volatile. They are compared to two serpents, the fixed substance to a serpent without, and the volatile substance to a serpent with, wings. One serpent holds in his mouth the tail of the other, to show that they are indissolubly conjoined by community of birth and destiny, and that our Art is accomplished through the joint working of this Mercurial Sulphur, and sulphureous Mercury. Hence the whole compound is at this stage called Rebis, because there are two substances but only one essence. They are not really two, but one and the same thing; the Sulphur is matured and well digested Mercury, the Mercury is crude and undigested Sulphur. It has already been said that in our Art we imitate Nature's method of producing metals in the bowels of the earth, except that our method is shorter and more subtle. In metallic veins only crude and frigid Mercury is found, in which the inward heat or dryness (*i.e.*, Sulphur) can scarce make its influence felt. No digestive heat is found there, but in the course of ages an imperceptible motion changes this metallic principle. In the course of centuries, however, this imperceptible digestive heat changes the Mercury into what is then called fixed Sulphur, though before it was denominated Mercury.

But in our Art, we have something besides crude and frigid Mercury, *viz.*, mature gold, with its manifold active qualities. These are united to the passive qualities of our Mercury; and so one aids and perfects the other, and as we have two fires, instead of the one slow inward fire of Mercury, the operation is more expeditious, and something far nobler than common gold is produced.

Thus you see that in our Art we have two Sulphurs and two Mercuries (*i.e.*, Sulphur, and Mercury of Mercury, and Sulphur and Mercury of gold), but their only difference consists in degrees of perfection and maturity. Now, the perfect body of gold is reduced to its (two) first principles by means of our Divine water which does not wet the hands (*viz.*, Mercury and Sulphur). This operation for a time gives the ascendancy to the female agent; but this being unnatural, the male agent soon reasserts itself, and by means of its heat dries up the moisture of the female agent, and—through calcination—converts it all into a most subtle and viscous powder, which powder is then changed by dissolution into a water, in which the spirits of the solvent and the thing dissolved, the male and the female principles, are mingled. But the inward heat, which has once been roused into action, still continues to work, separating the subtle (which floats on the surface) from the gross (which sinks to the bottom), until the man has gained the upper hand, the inseparable union takes place, and the male impregnates the female; the female brings forth a nebulous vapour, in which they are putrefied and decay, and from which both arise with a glorious body, no longer two, but only one by inseparable conjunction. This new birth is then coagulated, sublimed, nourished, and exalted to the highest degree of perfection, and may afterwards be indefinitely multiplied by fermentation, and used both for projection and as an Universal Medicine.

We see, then, that these black and fetid ashes are not to be despised, since they contain the Diadem of our King; your substance will never be white, if it has not first been black. It is by means of putrefaction and decay that it attains the glorified body of its resurrection. Therefore, you should honour the tomb of our King, for unless you do so, you will never behold him coming in his glory.

A great many students make a mistake at the very outset, by performing this calcination on a wrong substance—borax, or alum, or ink, or vitriol, or arsenic, or seeds, or plants, or wine, vinegar, urine, hair, blood, gum, resin, etc.; or they choose a false method, and corrode instead of calcining the metallic bodies on which they operate. Calcination can take place only by means of the inward heat of the body, assisted by friendly outward warmth; but calcination by means of a heterogeneous agent can only destroy the metallic nature, in so far as it has any effect at all. Every calcination of gold, which is not succeeded by a spontaneous dissolution, without laying on of hands, is also fallacious.

The true calcination is by means of Mercury, which (being added to gold in due proportions) softens and dissolves the gold, and, by its inward heat, united to outward heat, stirs into action the native heat of the gold, and thus causes it to dry up its humidity into that fine, viscous, black powder. And this is the true key of the work—to incrudate the mature by the conjunction of an immature—being incrudated to calcine it—being calcined to dissolve it—and all this philosophically, not vulgarly.

The outward signs of the calcination are as follows:—When the gold has become saturated with water, and the fire of the Mercury has called into play the heat of the bath, the water which was so brilliant begins to grow dim, then visibly swells and bubbles, until the whole becomes a fatty and viscous powder, which, however, still retains its radical humour. For when the heat first begins to operate, the cold and the moist seek refuge by rising to the top; thence they descend in liquid form and assimilate as much of the substance as they can to themselves; thus the powder is converted into a glutinous water. For between the different processes of our Art, there exists such a concatenation that not one can be produced or understood without the rest. In order to hide our meaning from the unworthy, we speak of several operations; but all these—the whole progress of the substance from black to white and red—should be philosophically understood as one operation, one thing, one successive disposition to black, white, and red.

The following rules should be observed if you wish to bring about true calcination:—

In the first place, you must procure our Mercury; common Mercury will produce no effect if you operate on it till doomsday.

Secondly, the external fire of the furnace should be neither too violent (in order that the equilibrium of chemical forces in the substance may not be disturbed), nor yet too gentle, so that the action of the inward fire may not languish for want of outward heat. It should be just such as to keep up an equable vital warmth.

In the third place, the Laton should receive neither too much nor too little to drink. If it receive too much, it will not be able to give it out, and a nebulous tempest will arise; if too little, it will be burnt to cinders. The activity of the Sulphur must dry up the superfluous humour of the Mercury; therefore, the active (sulphur) must not be swamped with too much sperm; nor must the moisture be choked with too much earth. The proportions should be between two or three parts of water to one of gold; but the larger the quantities of both substances, the more perfect will the calcination and dissolution be. The chief mistake against which you must guard is the swamping of your earth with water. For the earth contains the fire, which is the principal digestive in our Art.

In the fourth place, you should take care to seal up your vessel properly, to prevent the spirit from evaporating. Consider how carefully Nature has closed up the female womb to prevent anything from escaping or entering that might prove hurtful to the young life; and quite as much (if not more) care is required in our Magistery. For when the embryo is being formed, great winds arise, which must not be allowed to escape—or else our labour will have been all in vain.

The fifth requisite in our work is patience. You must not yield to despondency, or attempt to hasten the chemical process of dissolution. For if you do so by means of violent heat, the substance will be prematurely parched up into a red powder, and the active vital principle in it will become passive, being knocked on the head, as it were, with a hammer. But our true calcination preserves the radical humour in the body dissolved, and converts it into an unctuous black powder. Patience is, therefore, the great cardinal virtue in Alchemy. It must not be supposed that the signs and colours which I describe appear on the first day, or even within the first week: Bernard of Trevisa tells us that he waited in an anguish of expectation for forty days, and then returned and saw clouds and mists. You need the patience of the husbandman, who, after committing the seed to the earth, does not disturb the soil every day to see whether it is growing. . . . As soon as you have prepared your substance, *i.e.*, mixed mature yellow sulphur with its crude white sulphur, put them in a vessel and let them stand undisturbed; at the end of twenty-four hours, the Mercury, which is attempting to rouse the latent fire of the sulphur, will begin to effervesce and send up bubbles. But little variation of colour shall appear until the object of the Mercury has been accomplished, and the Royal Bath prepared; at first it is the Mercury alone that is at work. When, however, the Bath has been made hot (*i.e.*, the inward warmth of the gold roused) the greater part of our work is over, and we shall be easily able to distinguish the various operations. The first colour which appears after the silver colour of the amalgamated body, is not perfect blackness, but only a darkish white; the blackness becomes more pronounced day by day, until the substance assumes a brilliant black colour. This black is a sign that the dissolution is accomplished, which does not come about in one hour, but gradually, by a continuous process; for the Tincture which comes out of the Sun and Moon appears black to the eyes, but is insensibly and imperceptibly extracted. When the whole of the Tincture has been extracted from the body that is to be dissolved, the blackness is complete. The more you digest the substance at first, the more you subtilize the gross, and blacken the compound. There are four principal colours, the first of which is blackness; and it is of all colours the most tardy in making its appearance. But as soon as the highest degree of intense blackness has been reached (there being no idle intervals in our work), that colour begins little by little to yield to another. The time during which this blackness is developed is very long, and so is the time during which it disappears; but it is only for one moment that the blackness neither increases nor decreases: for things find rest only in that which is the end of their being, but blackness is not the end of our substance.

The advent of the blackness is like the coming of the night, which is preceded by a long twilight—when the last ray of light has faded away, the blackness of night has come; only our work is more tedious, and the change is, therefore, still less perceptible.

It may be objected that the black tincture begins to be extracted as soon as the inward heat is roused, and that, therefore, the colour which appears must be, from the very first, an intense black. My answer is that the Tincture which is extracted is, as a matter of fact, not black, but of a dazzling white; and that the blackness is produced gradually, through the action of the water on the body, out of which it draws the soul (the tincture), thus giving the body up to decomposition. It is this putrefaction (the result of the mutual action of the Sulphur and Mercury) which imparts to the Tincture its black colour; in itself the Tincture is brilliantly white. How long, then, will you have to wait till perfect blackness appears? Flamellus tells us that this intense blackness comes at the end of about forty days. Ripley advises us to let the mingled substances remain together for six weeks, until the conception has taken place, during which time the fire must be very gentle. And Bernard (of Trevisa) suggests the same thing, when he says in his parable: "The King doffs his glorious robes, and gives them to Saturn, who clothes him in a garment of black silk, which he retains for forty days." Of course, the blackness which is here spoken of is not equally intense all the time, as you will understand from what has been said above.

In the course of this change from white to black, the substance naturally passes through a variety of intermediate colours; but these colours (being more or less accidental) are not invariably the same, and depend very much on the original proportion in which the two substances are combined. In the second stage, during which the substance changes from black to white, it is already far purer, the colours are more lucid, and more to be depended upon. In the two phases there are intermediate colours; but in the first they are more dingy and obscure than in the second, and very much less numerous. In the progress of the substance from blackness to whiteness (*i.e.*, the second phase of our Magistery), the most beautiful colours are seen in a variety such as eclipses the glory of the rainbow; before the perfection of blackness is reached, there are also some transition colours, such as black, azure, and yellow—and the meaning of these colours is that your substance is not yet completely decayed; while the body is dying, the colours are seen, until black night shrouds the whole horizon in pitchy gloom. But when the process of resurrection begins (in the second phase), the hues are more numerous and splendid, because the body is now beginning to be glorified, and has become pure and spiritual.

But in what order do the colours of which we speak appear? To this question no definite answer can be given, because in this first phase there are so much uncertainty and variation. But the colours will be the clearer and more distinct, the purer your water of life is. The four principal colours (white, black, white, red), always follow in the same order; but the order of the intermediate colours cannot be so certainly determined, and you ought to be content if within the first 40 days you get the black colour. There is only one caution you should bear in mind, in regard to this point: if a reddish colour appears before the black (especially if the substance begins to look dry and powdery at the same time), you may be almost sure that you have marred your substance by too violent a fire. You should be very careful, then, about the regulation of your fire; if the fire be just hot enough, but not too hot, the inward chemical action of our water will do the rest.

Our Solution, then, is the reducing of our Stone to its first matter, the manifestation of its essential liquid, and the extraction of natures from their profundity, which is finished by bringing them into a mineral water; nor is this operation easy: those who have tried can bear out the truth of my words.

OF

CHEMICAL TRUTH.

OUR Magistery consists of three parts: the first deals with the essential and substantial composition of our Stone; the second describes their manner of combination; the third the mode of chemical procedure. Our substances are "red ore," or matured Sulphur, and water, undigested Mercury, or "white ore." To these a vessel is added, a furnace, and a triple fire. In discussing their manner of combination, we have to consider their weight and the regimen. The weight is twofold, and so is the regimen: between them they produce the following processes—Calcination, Dissolution, Separation, Conjunction, Putrefaction, Distillation, Coagulation, Sublimation, Fixation, and Exaltation. The first two produce the black, viscous powder, by means of the "unnatural fire," a temperate, incomburent, and altering ignition. There is then a further change into a mineral water. The three operations Which follow are the result of the first and third fires, namely, natural and contra-natural, and "circulate" the substance, until the gross is separated from the subtle, and the whole is evenly tempered, the separated elements being then recombined, impregnated, and putrefied.

The five last operations are the result of natural fire which increases and gets stronger from day to day, purifying the putrefied substance of its dross, by continual ascensions and descents. This process is therefore called distillation, volatilization, ablution, imbibition, humectation of the earth, and is continued until the dryness gradually thickens the substances, and, finally, under the influence of coction or continued sublimation, induces fixation, the terminal point of which is exaltation, an exaltation which is not local, from the bottom to the surface, but qualitative, from vileness to the highest excellence.

These operations are sometimes called regimens; but there. are only two kinds of fire, the natural and the non-natural, the latter being employed to call out the activity of the former. Putrefaction precedes regeneration, and is caused by the strife of the two fires. That part of the work which is subsequent to putrefaction and conjunction, when the Sulphur and the water have become one, and also receive congelation, is effected by the natural fire alone.

The substances are our body (commonly styled Lemnian earth) and our water (our true rain water). Our water is the life of all things, and if you can by much toil obtain it, you will have both silver and gold. It is the water of Saltpetre, and outwardly resembles Mercury, while inwardly at its heart there burns purest infernal fire. Do not be deceived with common quicksilver, but gather that Mercury which the returning Sun, in the month of March, diffuses everywhere, till the month of October, when it is ripe.

Know that our Mercury is before the eyes of all men, though it is known to few. When it is prepared, its splendour is most admirable; but the sight is vouchsafed to none, save the sons of knowledge. Do not despise it, therefore, when you see it in sordid guise; for if you do, you will never accomplish our Magistery—and if you can change its countenance, the transformation will be glorious. For our water is a most pure virgin, and is loved of many, but meets all her wooers in foul garments, in order that she may be able to distinguish the

414

worthy from the unworthy. Our beautiful maiden abounds in inward hidden graces; unlike the immodest woman who meets her lovers in splendid garments. To those who do not despise her foul exterior, she then appears in all her beauty, and brings them an infinite dower of riches and health. Our Queen is pure above measure, and her splendour like that of a celestial being—and so indeed she is called by the Sages, who also style her their quintessence. Her brilliancy is such as baffles imagination, and, if you would have any idea of it, you must see it with your own eyes. Our water is serene, crystalline, pure, and beautiful—though it can assume its true form only through the aid of our Art. In that form it is our sea, our hidden fountain, from which gold derives its birth by natural descent; yet it is also stronger than geld, and overcomes it, wherefore gold is united to it, and is washed in it, and the two together grow up into a strong hero, whom neither Pope nor Emperor can buy for a price. Hence you should, above all things, seek this water, by means of which (with the solitary addition of a clean and perfect body) the Stone may be prepared.

But it requires profound study to become acquainted with all the secrets of our sea, and with its ebb and flow. It took me 18 months, after I had discovered the spring of our water, to find the method of making it well forth, because I did not know the meaning of the fiery furnace of the Sages. When I discovered it, indeed, the sight which I beheld richly rewarded me for all my pains. I was then suddenly, as by a flash of inspiration, enabled to understand all the secret words and enigmas of the Sages. Our water is the fire which causes both death, and, through death, a more glorious life. Whoever discovers it has reached the autumn of his Magistery, as Nature will then (when the pure body has been put into it) perform all the other processes, and carry the substance onward to perfection through all the different regimens. This water, though one, is not simple, but compounded of two things: the vessel and the fire of the Sages, and the bond which holds the two together. So when we speak of our vessel, and our fire, we mean by both expressions, our water; nor is our furnace anything diverse or distinct from our water. There is then one vessel, one furnace, one fire, and all these make up one water. The fire digests, the vessel whitens and penetrates, the furnace is the bond which comprises and encloses all, and all these three are our Mercury. There are many kinds of fire (and of water) in our Magistery, but all these only represent different aspects of our Mercury.

There is only one thing in the whole world from which our Mercury can be obtained. It is like gold in essence, but different in substance, and if you change its elements you will have what you seek. Join heaven to earth in the fire of love, and you will see in the middle of the firmament the bird of Hermes. Do not confound the natures, but separate and re-combine them, and you will reign in honour all your life.

In the South-west there is a high mountain (very near the Sun), one of seven, and the second in height. This mountain is of a very hot temperature (because it is not far from the Sun), and in this mountain is enclosed a vapour or spirit, whose services are indispensable for our work. But it does not ascend, unless it is quickened, nor is it quickened unless you dig knee deep on the summit of the mountain. If you do this, a subtle exhalation (or spirit) ascends, and is congealed by the air into drops of beautifully limpid water—which is our water, our fire, our vessel, and our furnace; not common Mercury, but the hot and moist liquid of most pure Salt, which we call Mercury, because in comparison with the Sun, it is immature and cold. If the Almighty had not created this Mercury, the transmutation of metals would be impossible, because gold does not tinge unless it be first tinged itself. Our Mercury is the beloved spouse of gold, and changes its body into a purely spiritual substance; gold loves it so, that for very love he dies, and is revived by his spouse, and she is impregnated by him, and conceives, and bears a most beautiful royal son. The whole knowledge of our Art consists in the discovery of this our sea; any Alchemist who is ignorant of it, is simply wasting his money. Our sea is derived from the mountain of which I told you above. The exhalation or white smoke which ascends there, will accomplish our whole Magistery. There is another secret which you should know if you wish to see your hope fulfilled, viz., how you are to dig a hole in the mountain, as its surface is impenetrable to ordinary tools, its dryness being such that it has become harder than a flint. But in the places of Saturn a small herb is found, called Saturnia, whose twigs appear dry, but in whose roots there is abundance of juice. This herb you should carefully take up with the roots, and carry with you to the foot of the mountain, and, with the help of fire, bury it beneath the mountain; its virtue will at once penetrate the whole mountain, and soften its earth. Then you may ascend to the summit, easily dig a hole knee deep, and pour in so much dry and viscous water, that it penetrates to where the herb lies buried, and makes it ascend as a fume, which carries upward with it the spirit of the mountain. This spirit is the strength of fire mingling with water, and dwelling in it. The spirit of Saturnia is the whitening fume, the vapour of the mountain is fire, and all these things are fire. Thus you obtain Saturnia, the royal plant and mineral herb, which together with fat flesh makes such a soup as to eclipse the richest banquets in the world.

Here is an enigmatic description of our water, which should in course of time and study, become plain to the diligent enquirer. There is the King (gold), and the water which is the King's Bath; our water is the vessel, inasmuch as our King is enclosed in it, and the furnace, inasmuch as our fire is enclosed in it, and our fire, inasmuch as the virtue or spirit of the mountain dwells in it, and the woman, inasmuch as it receives the vapour of the plant Saturnia; and as the dear friend of the Sun penetrates, whitens, and softens it, and causes it to emit its sperm. Then the fiery virtue which is in the water, begins to act on our body, wasting and mortifying it, until at length the innate heat of the Sun is roused into activity. Our Stone is called a little world, because it contains within itself the active and the passive, the motor and the thing moved, the fixed and the volatile, the mature and the crude—which, being homogeneous, help and perfect each other. We have already shown that our object in adding matured Sulphur to crude Mercury (the same thing in different stages of development), is to shorten and accelerate the natural process. Gold is a hot and dry body; silver a frigid and humid one, Mercury the means of conveying tinctures. The body of the Sun is most highly digested, that of the Moon imperfect and immature, while Mercury is the bond by which these two contraries are united. Join the Moon to Mercury by means of proper heat, so that the two become one Mercury which retains its inward fire; then the Mercury will be freed from all dross and superfluities, and it will become transparent like the tears we shed, though not exactly perspicuous. If you then unite this purified Mercury to gold, in which is the Moon and fire, the hot and dry will love the cold and humid, and they will unite on the bed of the fire of friendship; the man will dissolve over the woman, and the woman be coagulated over the man, till the spirit and the body become one by commixtion. Continue the same operation (let the heaven descend to the earth) till the spirit puts on the body, and both are fixed together. Then our Stone will have obtained its royal virtue. For Mercury is the water of all metals, and they are digested in it. When vegetables are boiled in ordinary water, which is naturally frigid and humid, it partakes of their qualities, and is yet separable from them; so the pure Mercury, which is in all metals and minerals, is perfectly separable from the dross and foreign matter which has become mixed up with them; yet the different minerals and metals qualify the Mercury in the same way as the water is qualified by the vegetables cooked in it. There are these two differences between the Mercury and the water, that the water is not coagulated and fixed with the vegetables as our water is with the metals; and that, while the colour of common water is changed by anything boiled in it, Mercury retains its own colour and fluxibility, though its essence is qualified. Therefore the Mercury is effectual in the dissolution of the metal, and the metal in the coagulation of the Mercury; and as, in the dissolution, the form and colour of the metal is latent in the form and colour of the Mercury, so, in coagulation, the form and colour of the Mercury is hidden in the form and colour of the metal; neither do the qualities of the metal in dissolution prevent the fluxibility of the Mercury, nor the qualities of Mercury in coagulation the fixity of the metal. Do you not here observe a wonderful harmony between Mercury and the metals? For their love is like that of mother and son, sister and brother, male and female. Hence they are calculated mutually to perfect each other, the water imparting to the body a spiritual and volatile nature, while the body gives to the water a corporeal substance. The reason that the colour of Mercury is not changed in coction by the dissolved body, is this: the earth and water in the Mercury are homogeneous, and so well tempered that neither can be separated from the other, and they are so well mixed that the whole substance exhibits (together with great fluxibility) so great a consistency as entirely to conceal the colours—and only if a part of the Mercury is destroyed or marred by some deleterious chemical corrosive, are the colours seen. The relations of Mercury in respect of earth and water are these: in respect of water it is fluxible and liquid, in respect of earth it moistens nothing but what is of the same essence with it. These hints will enable you to detect any errors in your treatment of Mercury. Some obstruct or divide its homogeneity by unduly drying up its water; others corrupt the earth and render it diaphanous by disproportionate mixing. Mercury is the sperm of the metals; it contains in itself the Sulphur by which alone it is digested (through which Nature would in course of time have matured it into gold); nor would it be possible to convert Mercury into gold without it. This mature Sulphur, then, is radically mixed with the Mercury, and rapidly digests it, while itself is putrefied by the Mercury, and is revived again, not as common, but as spiritual, penetrative, and tinging gold, which has power to purify imperfect metals of all their dross, and to change them into its own nature. Thus you see that none of the Mercury should be destroyed, or violently dealt with; all you have to do is to add to it a mature body sprung from the same root, and mix the two in their smallest parts, by means of our cunning conjunction (which is performed, not by a manual, but by a purely natural process, of which the Artist does not even understand the cause). We must distinguish, however, between our transmutative conjunction, and a sort of conjunction practised by sophists which is merely a fusing together of the two substances, and leaves each exactly what it was before. In our operation the spirit of gold infuses itself into the spirit of Mercury, and their union becomes as inseparable as that of water mixed with water. The conjunction can take place only by means of the Moon or an imperfect body and fire; and this Moon is the sap of the water of life, which is hidden in Mercury, and is stirred up by fire; it is a spirit which enters the body, and compels it to retain its soul. We speak not of common Mercury (which lacks the spirit and fire), but of our Mercurial water—though common Mercury may be made like it by the addition of that which it lacks. Our conjunction is the grand secret of our Art; for earth is not inseparably united to water, but the union of water with water is indissoluble; hence our conjunction can take place only after dissolution, which dissolution takes place through the Moon and fire that are in the Mercury. For the Moon penetrates and whitens, and the fire mortifies and frets, while water combines both these properties, according to the philosophical dictum: "The fire which I show you, is water," and, "Unless the bodies are subtilized by fire and water, nothing can be done in our Magistery." Thus everything, from beginning to end, is accomplished, not by sophistical operations, but by our Mercury, which, unless it be violently impeded, is kept to the right road by the necessity of arriving at a certain goal.

Some Alchemists fail because they put (common) gold with Mercury in a phial over the fire, and thus sow good seed in barren earth. But gold is not the substance of our Stone in its whole essence, nor yet Mercury. What we want for our work of generation is the seed of gold which is profoundly hidden in our metal. This seed must be received into its own proper womb, and there mingle with the female seed, in order that, being kindly fostered with heat, and fed with its proper aliment, it may become that part of gold which is of abundant use in our work. It is not the whole of a man that generates the infant, but only his seed, which is rightly disposed in the proper womb; and so only the seed of gold (and not the whole metal) is useful for our metallic generation. Gold is the Father of our Stone, the substance of our Stone is in gold, but gold is not the substance of our Stone; yet there is that in gold (the sperm) which, by right manipulation, may become our Stone. We extract from gold, by a cunning process, that which is its most highly matured virtue, and this is called, not common, dead, but our living gold. The difference between common gold and our gold, is that which exists between a Father and his seed; common gold is dead and useless, as far as our work is concerned, until it emits its living seed. Take the body of gold, then, and gently extract from it its seed, and you will have the living male seed of our Stone, which we now no longer call gold, but ore, magnesia, lead, etc.—because it is no longer a body, like gold, but a chaos, or spirit, which cannot revert to its corporeal form. Aristotle says: "The first thing you should do is to sublime the Mercury, then you should put a pure body into the pure Mercury." The sublimation of the Mercury which is here referred to, is not an artificial, but a true and natural one. It is the "first preparation of the thin substance," by which the eclipse caused by the interposition of Earth is removed from the Moon, enabling her to receive the light of the Sun—which happens when the murky sphere of Saturn (that overshadowed the whole horizon) is removed, and Jupiter ascends the throne; then there rises upward a mist of dazzling whiteness, whence there is distilled upon the earth a pure, sweet, and fragrant dew, that softens it and stirs up great winds at its centre;

these winds bear our Stone upward, where it is endowed with heavenly virtue, and thence descending once more to its nurse, the earth, is clothed upon with a corporeal nature, and thus receives the strength both of things above and of things below. This living gold is "that which is, but does not appear till it pleases the Artist, and in the knowledge of which is the secret of all perfection." Mercury is our field, in which the Sun rises and sets; let the two be inseparably united on the bed of love, till from this (regenerate) Mercury there comes forth a quickening virtue, which is able to raise the dead. Then there will appear the royal child, whose father is the Sun, whose mother is the Moon. . . Besides these things, we need, of course, a furnace of clay, a vessel of glass, and a triple fire; but we do not call these three *our* vessel, *our* fire, or *our* furnace, because ordinary sophists employ these things as well as the Sages; when we speak of our vessel, our furnace, and our fire, the terms are to be interpreted in accordance with the explanation which we gave above. Of this fire a Sage might well say: "Behold, the fire, which I will show you, is water"; and again, "The vessel of the Sages is their water." Another Sage says, that all our operations take place in our humid fire, in our secret furnace, and our hidden vessel, and thereby clearly shows that there must be a fire, vessel, and furnace, other than those which ignorant Alchemists possess in greater perfection and abundance than we. Our appliances are part of our substance, and are described by Sendivogius, for instance, as the "vessel of Nature," and the "fire of Nature." This practice is followed by Flamellus, Artephius, Lullius, and all other Sages; and I tell you that these three appliances are, after all, only one; for the nature of our substance is one. Our fire is that which dissolves and heats bodies more effectually than ordinary fire; hence it is called ardent wine and a most strong fire, and the Sages bid us burn our ore with our most strong fire—words which are falsely interpreted of an ordinary coal fire. Of this fire John Mehungus writes: "No artificial fire can infuse so high a degree of heat as that which comes from heaven."

JOHN FREDERICK

HELVETIUS'

GOLDEN CALF,

WHICH THE WORLD WORSHIPS AND ADORES:

IN WHICH IS DISCUSSED

THE MOST RARE MIRACLE OF NATURE

IN THE TRANSMUTATION OF METALS,

VIZ.:

HOW AT THE HAGUE A MASS OF LEAD WAS IN
A MOMENT OF TIME CHANGED INTO GOLD
BY THE INFUSION OF A SMALL
PARTICLE OF OUR STONE.

JOB, xxvii., 5:—'Great things doeth God which we cannot comprehend."

SENECA, Epist. 77:—"We must learn, in our pursuit of wisdom, to listen with equanimity to
the reproaches of the foolish, and to despise contempt itself."

TO THE

MOST HONOURABLE AND EXCELLENT

DR. THEODORE KETJES,

*A great physician, and traveller in Turkey and other
foreign lands, now in practice at Amsterdam,
and my intimate friend;*

AND TO THE

MOST HONOURABLE AND PROFOUNDLY LEARNED

DR. JOHN CASPAR FAUSIUS,

*Councillor and Court Physician to the Count
Palatine of Heidelberg;*

AND

DR. CHRISTIAN MENTZELIUS,

Councillor and Court Physician to the Elector of Brandenburg,

MY HONOURED PATRONS, AND

BELOVED FRIENDS.

DEDICATORY EPISTLE
TO THE ABOVE-NAMED NOBLE AND HONOURABLE
FRIENDS AND MASTERS.

I neither can nor will withhold from my honoured and beloved friends the knowledge of this Spagyric Art, and of the most precious and miraculous Arcanum, which I have not only seen with my own eyes, but also executed with my own hands, by changing a mass of lead into solid gold, persistently resisting any test of fire, through the addition of a small particle of our transmutatory powder. It can no longer be pretended that our Art does not possess the power which it claims, or that the Mercury of the Sages is not the great and glorious fountain of all natural marvels. This wonderful secret has, through the grace of God, been revealed to me, and as it is unworthy of man, created in the image of God, to maintain silence in regard to God's miraculous works, like the brute beasts, I have determined to unveil this grand Arcanum to you, my beloved friends; and I will now gird myself to tell you all that I know and have heard of the sayings and doings of the Great Artist Elias. It was not, indeed, he who revealed to me the grand secret; yet his conversation was so instructive that I cannot refrain from reporting it to you word for word. It is my earnest wish, honoured friends and masters, that this Book may meet with a kindly reception at your hands, and that you may derive from it both enjoyment and profit. With this hope, I remain,

Your humble Servant,
JOHN FREDERICK HELVETIUS

CHAPTER I.

BEFORE I begin to write about the philosophical Pygmy vanquishing the Giants, my honoured friends and masters, you must permit me to transcribe a passage from the works of Helmontius (*Arbor Vitæ*, folio 630): "I cannot but believe that there is such a thing as a gold and silver making Stone. At the same time, I cannot shut my eyes to the fact that hundreds of painstaking Alchemists are daily being led astray by impostors or ignorant professors of the Spagyric Art." For this reason I shall not be astonished if—immediately upon perusing my book—multitudes of these deluded victims start up, and contradict the assertion which I have made in regard to the truth of this Art. One of these gentry denounces Alchemy as a work of the Devil; another describes it as sheer nonsense and humbug; a third admits the possibility of transmuting metals into gold, but maintains that the whole process costs more money than it is worth. But I do not wonder at these opinions. It is a hackneyed saying of human nature that we gape at those things whose purpose we do not understand, but we investigate things pleasurable to know. The Sages should therefore remember the words of Seneca (*De Moribus*): "You are not yet blessed, if the multitude does not laugh at you." But I do not care whether they believe or contradict my teaching about the transmutation of metals; I rest calmly satisfied in the knowledge that I have seen it with my own eyes, and performed it with my own hands. Even in our degenerate age these wonders are still possible; even now the Medicine is prepared which is worth twenty tons of gold, nay, more, for it has virtue to bestow that which all the gold of the world cannot buy, *viz.*, health. Blessed is that physician who knows our soothing medicinal Potion of Mercury, the great panacea of death and disease. But God does not reveal this glorious knowledge to all men indiscriminately; and some men are so obtuse (with a judicial blindness) that they wonder at the activity of the simplest forces of Nature, as, for instance, the attractive power which the magnet exercises upon the steel. But (whether they believe it or not) there is a corresponding magnetic force in gold which attracts Mercury, in silver which attracts copper, and so with all other metals, minerals, stones, herbs, plants, etc. . . . We must not be surprised at this persistent opposition to truth: the light of the sun pains the eyes of owls.

As a matter of fact, we human beings take too much upon ourselves in hastily and dogmatically judging of things which we do not understand. We deny the influence of the stars upon earthly things, and by that denial only exhibit our ignorance. And what do we know of the secret forces which slumber in plants. You may know nothing of the glory of the Angels, the brightness of the heavens, the transparency of the air, the limpidity of the water, the variety of colours in flowers, the hardness of stones and metals, the proportionate beauty of men and animals, the image of God in regenerate souls, the faith of believers, the rationality of the mind, &c.—for we may be blind and without feeling or understanding—and yet the beauty of all these things is not in the least affected by our ignorance.

If we bear these considerations in mind, they ought to stop our mouths when we feel tempted to deny the possibility of such wonderful transmutatory virtue being inherent in our Stone. Still, it must not be supposed that I wish to force this knowledge upon any one. God has reserved it for the worthy, and I know that it can never become known to the wicked, the irreligious, or the scornful. All I propose to do is to lay before the reader, for his diligent consideration, those conversations which have passed between the Artist Elias and myself, in regard to the nature of this Stone, the splendour of which (being more glorious than the dawn, more brilliant than a carbuncle, more bright than the sun or gold) has not yet faded from my mind. The contempt of the scornful, and the ignorance of the foolish I despise. Their ephemeral babble will soon be swept away by the river of forgetfulness; but our triumphant Art, which is established upon a foundation of adamant, upon the foundation' of God's own truth, will abide unshaken throughout all ages. For adepts according to ancient experience have given their word that this natural mystery is only to be found with JEHOVA Saturninely placed in the centre of the world. But those we call blessed, who can purge the Queen of the Sages of her impurity, who can circulate the Catholic Virgin Earth by means of our crystalline Physico-magical Art, and who have beheld the King, with his crown on his head, and his strength of inward fire, come forth from the chamber of his crystal grave, his bodily semblance glorified with all the most beautiful hues that the world affords, like a shining carbuncle, or like a transparent, compact, and diaphanous crystal—like a salamander that has spued forth all water, and washes away the leprosy of base metals with fire. Moreover, they shall behold the abyss of the Spagyric Art, where in the mineral kingdom, the same so royal art has, to a certain extent, for many years (in, as it were, the safest retreat of all) lain concealed. The Sages have seen the river in which Æneas was cleansed of his mortality—the river of Pactolus in Lydia which was changed into gold by King Midas bathing in it—the bath of Diana—the spring of Narcissus—the blood of Adonis trickling upon the snowy breast of Venus, whence was produced the anemone—the blood of Ajax, from which sprang the beautiful hyacinth flower— the blood of the Giants killed by Jupiter's thunderbolt—the tears which Althea shed when she doffed her golden robes—the magic water of Medea, out of which grass and flowers sprang forth—the Potion which Medea prepared from various herbs for the rejuvenescence of old Jason—the Medicine of Aesculapius—the magic juice, by the aid of which Jason obtained the Golden Fleece—the garden of the Hesperides, where the trees bear golden apples in rich abundance—Atalanta turned aside from the race by the three golden apples—Romulus transformed by Jupiter into a god—the transfiguration of the soul of Julius Cæsar into a Comet— Juno's serpent, Pytho, born of decomposed earth after Deucalion's flood—the fire at which Medea lit her seven torches—the Moon kindled by Phaëthon's conflagration—Arcadia, in which Jupiter was wont to walk abroad—the habitation of Pluto in whose vestibule lay the three-headed Cerberus—the Pile, on which Hercules burnt those limbs which he had received from his mother, with fire, till only the fixed and incombustible elements derived from his father were left, and he became a god—and the rustic cottage whose roof was made of pure gold. Blessed, yea, thrice blessed, is the man to whom Jehovah has revealed the method of preparing that Divine Salt by which the metallic or mineral body is corrupted, destroyed, and mortified, while its soul in the meantime is revived for the glorious resurrection of the philosophical body—blessed, I say, is he to whom the knowledge of our Art is vouchsafed in answer to prayer throughout all his work for the Holy Spirit! For it should be remembered that this is the only way in which our Art of Arts is vouchsafed to man, and if you would attain it, the service of God ought to be your chief business. By committing themselves to this sacred and practical path of piety, and to theosophical colloquies alone with Jehovah, all true students of this Art will in due course of time, behold the sight which will gladden their hearts. Blessed, also, is he to whom some adept graciously flings wide the gates of knowledge, and to whom the golden road of the King is thus manifested! . . I am afraid that the Preface will not please all my readers; nevertheless, I have a good hope that it will cheer and hearten the better part of them. Drink, my friends, from the fountain of truth, which wells forth in the Dialogue that I shall hereafter set down, and slake therewith the thirst of your souls, for my words shall be sweeter to you than nectar or ambrosia. For I bear in mind the saying of Julius Cæsar Scaliger that "the end of wisdom is its communication," and the teaching of Gregory of Nyssenus, who affirms "that the good delight to impart their knowledge to others, because it is the greatest joy to them to be useful."

CHAPTER II.

The truth of this Art is maintained by many illustrious writers, of whom the following are the most distinguished representatives of their class:

Paracelsus (*Rev. Natur.*, ix., fol. 358) has the following words: "The true sign by which the Tincture of the Physicists is known, is its power of transmuting all imperfect metals into silver (if it be white) or gold (if it be red), if but a small particle of it be injected into a mass of such metals liquefied in a crucible."

Again: "The invincible Star of the Metals vanquishes all things, and changes them into a nature similar to its own. This gold and silver are better than those found in mines for the preparation of arcane medicines from it."

Again: "I say that any Alchemist, who has the Star of Gold, can change all metals into that precious substance."

Again: "Our Tincture of Gold contains stars, is a substance of the greatest fixity, is unchangeable in multiplication, is a red powder (with almost a saffron tinge), liquid like resin, transparent like crystal, fragile like glass, is of a rubinate colour, and of great specific gravity."

Again, in Paracelsus' book called "The Heaven of the Sages," and in his seventh book on the "Transmutation of Natural Things," he bears witness to the same fact: "Transmutation is a great natural mystery, which is by no means—as fools suppose—contrary to the course of Nature, or the law of God. Without this Philosopher's Stone, the imperfect metals can be transmuted neither into gold nor silver."

Paracelsus, in his Manual concerning the Medicinal Philosopher's Stone, says: "Our Stone is the heavenly and super-perfect Medicine, because it washes away all the impurities of metals."

Henry Khunrath, in his "Amphitheatre of Eternal Wisdom" (fol. 147), has the following words: "I have visited many lands, and had speech of many learned men. I have seen the Green Catholic Lion, and the Blood of the Lion, *i.e.*, the Gold of the Sages, with my own eyes, have touched it with my hands, tasted it with my tongue, smelt it with my nose. By its means I have cured many whose life was despaired of."

Again (fol. 202): "That which I describe is not a myth: you shall handle it with your hands, see it with your eyes,—that Azoth, or Catholic Mercury of the Sages, which, together with inward and outward fire, in sympathic harmony, through an unavoidable necessity, physico-magically united, is alone sufficient for the preparation of our Stone."

Again: "You shall see the Philosopher's Stone, our King and Lord of Lords, go forth from the chamber of its crystal tomb into this world, with its glorified body, regenerate and transcendently perfect, a brilliant carbuncle, whose most subtle and fully purified parts, being harmoniously mixed, are bound inseparably into one, altogether smooth, translucid as crystal, compact and exceedingly weighty. It is easily fused in fire, as resin, and after the flight of artificial quicksilver, just as wax. Without smoke it enters and penetrates solid bodies as oil enters paper. It is soluble in any liquid, melting and commingling with the same, fragile as glass, in a powder saffron-coloured, but in a solid mass, red like the ruby. Its purple colour is the mark of perfect fixation and fixed perfection, for it remains fixed and incombustible, even when exposed to fire, corrosive waters, or burning sulphur, since it is, like the salamander, incapable of being consumed by fire."

Again: "When the White Tincture is added to metals as a ferment, it transmutes them into purest silver; when the Red Tincture is mixed with pure gold, it is, within three days, multiplied by the quantity of the gold."

Helmontius ("On Life Eternal," page 590) has the following words:—"I have seen the Stone, and touched it with my own hands. . . . . One-fourth of a grain of this powder, wrapped up in paper, I have cast upon eight ounces of boiling quicksilver in a crucible, and immediately the whole mixture was congealed into a mass like yellow wax; when the fusion was completed, the crucible contained eight ounces of purest gold (less eleven grains). So one grain of our powder had transmuted into purest gold 19,186 times its own weight of quicksilver,—and this process can be repeated indefinitely. The powder cleanses the metal from all impurity, and protects it from rust, decay, and fire, etc.

Again, the same Helmontius says, in his "Tree of Life" (page 630):—"I am compelled to believe that there is a Stone which produces gold and silver; for I have several times, with my own hands, projected one grain of powder upon one thousand grains of boiling quicksilver, which was thereby, in the presence of a great multitude of spectators, immediately transformed into precious gold. He who first gave me some of this transmutatory powder, had of it at least as much as would have sufficed for the production of 200,000 pounds of gold. He gave me about ½ grain of the powder, with which I transmuted 9¾ ounces of quicksilver.

Moreover, the most honourable and profoundly learned Dr. Theodore Ketjes, an eminent physician resident at Amsterdam, gave me a medal on which were the following inscriptions:

Nummi craſſities

DIVINA METAMORPHOSIS.

EXHIBITA PRAGÆ
XV IAN : A°. MDCXLVIII
IN PRÆ SENTIA
SAC : CÆS.MA
IEST: FERDINANDI
TERTII.

On the obverse of the medal there appeared the following words:

AS THIS ART IS RARE AMONG MEN,
SO IT IS RARELY EXHIBITED:
PRAISED BE GOD FOR EVER WHO
HAS COMMUNICATED PART OF
HIS INFINITE POWER TO US HIS MOST
ABJECT CREATURES.

It is also said that, in 1660, Alexander (a Scotch adept) effected a change of imperfect metals into gold, at Cologne, and at Hanover, etc.

There are also other instances on record of such transmutations having taken place.

The following is a genuine extract from a letter written by Dr. Kuffler:—

"First I found in my own laboratory, aquafortis, next in that of *Charles de Roy*, I poured it over calx of gold prepared in the ordinary way, and after the third cohobation, it sublimated with itself the tincture of gold in the neck of the retort, which I mingled with silver precipitated in the ordinary way, and I beheld that it had transmuted one ounce of sublimated tincture of gold in the crucible with the usual flux, and two ounces of precipitated silver, into an ounce-and-a-half of the best gold, while the third portion remained silver. The gold was white and fixed,

427

but the remaining two parts were the best silver, fixed under the test of any fire. This is my experience, and I need not say that it has made me a most enthusiastic believer in Alchemy."

I, Helvetius, have seen this gold, without the tincture, white.

Another proof of the genuineness of this Art was given at the Hague, in the year 1664, when a silversmith, of the name of Gril, in the presence of many witnesses, transformed one pound of lead, partly into gold, and partly into silver. Gril had obtained the Tincture from a certain weaver of the name of John Caspar Knöttner, with the injunction to use it for metals only Gril placed it with some lead in a glass cake dish, and after about a fortnight the above change was found to have taken place. I can testify to the genuineness of this case, as Gril was personally known to me, and I saw the transmuted lead, which exhibited on its surface a most beautiful silver crystal, in the form of a star, as though prepared by most ingenious artifice with a circle. The pity was that Gril, being obstinate and crafty, would not let Knöttner know whether it was his "Spirit of Salt" that had effected the change; and some time afterwards, when Gril's obstinacy had at length been overcome, Knöttner had forgotten which of his many chemical preparations he had given to him, and, before he was able to find out, he and his family were swept away by the plague, while Gril fell into the water and was drowned. Afterwards, not one of the many goldseekers was able to discover the secret which died with them. Nevertheless, it is a matter of never ceasing admiration that the Philosopher's Stone should have the power of transmuting, in so short a time, the dull and heavy nature of lead into the bright and brilliant nature of silver and gold; of this natural law, however, we have an illustration in the fact that steel, by contact with the magnet, acquires its magnetic power.

CHAPTER III.

Since promises are all the more acceptable, the more quickly they are fulfilled, I will now, without any further delay, address myself to the task which I have set myself to accomplish.

On the 27 December, 1666, in the forenoon, there came to my house a certain man, who was a complete stranger to me, but of an honest, grave countenance, and an authoritative mien, clothed in a simple garb like that of a Memnonite. He was of middle height, his face was long and slightly pock-marked, his hair was black and straight, his chin close shaven, his age about 43 or 44, and his native province, as far as I could make out, North Holland.

After we had exchanged salutations, he asked me whether he might have some conversation with me. He wished to say something to me about the Pyrotechnic Art, as he had read one of my Tracts (directed against the Sympathetic Powder of Dr. Digby), in which I hinted a suspicion whether the Grand Arcanum of the Sages was not after all a gigantic hoax. He, therefore, took that opportunity of asking me whether I could not believe that such a grand mystery might exist in the nature of things, by means of which a physician could restore any patient whose vitals were not irreparably destroyed. I answered: "Such a Medicine would be a most desirable acquisition for any physician; nor can any man tell how many secrets there may be hidden in Nature; yet, though I have read much about the truth of this Art, it has never been my good fortune to meet with a real Master of the

Alchemical Science." I also enquired whether he was a medical man, since he spoke so learnedly about the Universal Medicine. In reply, he modestly disclaimed my insinuation, and described himself as a brassfounder, who had always taken a great interest in the extraction of medicinal potions from metals by means of fire. After some further conversation; the Artist Elias (for it was he) thus addressed me: "Since you have read so much in the works of the Alchemists about this Stone, its substance, its colour, and its wonderful effects, may I be allowed the question, whether you have not yourself prepared it?" On my answering his question in the negative, he took out of his bag a cunningly-worked ivory box, in which there were three large pieces of a substance resembling glass, or pale sulphur, and informed me that here was enough of the Tincture for the production of 20 tons of gold. When I had held the precious treasure in my hand for a quarter of an hour (during which time I listened to a recital of its wonderful curative properties), I was compelled to restore it to its owner, which I could not help doing with a certain degree of reluctance. After thanking him for his kindness in showing it to me, I then asked how it was that his Stone did not display that ruby colour which I had been taught to regard as characteristic of the Philosopher's Stone. He replied that the colour made no difference, and that the substance was sufficiently mature for all practical purposes. My request that he would give me a piece of his Stone (though it were no larger than a coriander seed), he somewhat brusquely refused, adding, in a milder tone, that he could not give it me for all the wealth I possessed, and that not on account of its great preciousness, but for some other reason which it was not lawful for him to divulge; nay, if fire could be destroyed in that way, he would immediately throw it all into the fire. Then, after a moment's consideration, he enquired whether I could not shew him into a room at the back of the house, where we should be less liable to the observation of passers-by. On my conducting him into the state parlour (which he entered without wiping his dirty boots), he demanded of me a gold coin, and while I was looking for it, he produced from his breast pocket a green silk handkerchief, in which were folded up five medals, the gold of which was infinitely superior to that of my gold piece. On the medals appeared the following inscriptions:—

Holy, Holy, Holy
is the Lord our God;
the universe is full of
His Glory.
Lion. Balance.

Jehovah's
wonderful and miraculous
Wisdom
in the Catholic Book of
Nature.
———
I was made the
26 August, 1666.

☉ ☿ ☽
God, Nature, and
the Spagyric Art
make nothing
in vain.

Holy, Sacred Spirit !
Halleluia, Halleluia.
Avaunt, Satan.
Speak not of God
without Light.
Amen

To the Eternal,
Invisible, Triune, Thrice
Holy, and only wise God,
the Governor and
Preserver,
be praise now and
ever.

I was filled with admiration, and asked my visitor whence he had obtained that wonderful knowledge of the whole world? He replied that it was a gift freely bestowed on him by a friend who had stayed a few days at his house, who had also taught him to change common flints and crystals into stones more precious than rubies, chrysoliths, and sapphires; he also revealed to me the preparation of crocus of iron (an infallible cure for dysentery), of metallic liquid (an efficacious remedy for dropsy), and of many other infallible Medicines, to which, however, I paid no great heed, as I was impatiently anxious to have the chief secret of all revealed to me. The Artist told me that his Master had bidden him bring him a glass full of warm water, to which he had added a little white powder, and in which one ounce of silver had melted like ice in warm water. Of this draught he emptied one-half, and gave the rest to me. Its taste resembled that of fresh milk, and its effect was most exhilarating."

I asked my visitor whether the potion was a preparation of the Philosopher's Stone? But he answered: "You should not be so inquisitive."

Then he told me that, at the bidding of the Artist, he had taken down a piece of leaden water-pipe, and melted the lead in a pot, whereupon the Artist had taken some sulphureous powder out of a little box on the point of a knife, and cast it into the melted lead, and that after exposing the compound for a short time to a fierce fire, he had poured forth a great mass of molten gold upon the brick floor of the kitchen.

"The Master bade me take one-sixteenth of the gold for myself as a keepsake, and to distribute the rest amongst the poor; which I did by making over a large sum in trust to the Church of Sparrendam. At length, before bidding me farewell, my friend taught me this Divine Art."

When my strange visitor had concluded his narrative, I besought him to give me a proof of his assertion, by performing the transmutatory operation on some metals in my presence. He answered evasively, that he could not do so then, but that he would return in three weeks, and that, if he was then at liberty to do so, he would shew me something that would make me open my eyes. He appeared punctually to the promised day, and invited me to take a walk with him, in the course of which we discoursed profoundly on the secrets of Nature in fire, though I noticed that my companion was very chary in imparting information about the Grand Arcanum; he spoke very learnedly and gravely concerning the holiness of the Art (just as if he were a clergyman), and said that God had commanded the initiated to make the secret known only to the deserving. At last I asked him pointblank to show me the transmutation of metals. I besought him to come and dine with me, and to spend the night at my house; I entreated; I expostulated; but in vain. He remained firm. I reminded him of his promise. He retorted that his promise had been conditional upon his being permitted to reveal the secret to me. At last, however, I prevailed upon him to give me a piece of his precious Stone—a piece no larger than a grain of rape seed. He delivered it to me as if it were the most princely donation in the world. Upon my uttering a doubt whether it would be sufficient to tinge more than four grains of lead, he eagerly demanded it back. I complied, in the hope that he would exchange it for a larger piece; instead of which he divided it in two with his thumb, threw away one-half and gave me back the other, saying: "Even now it is sufficient for you." Then I was still more heavily disappointed, as I could not believe that anything could be done with so small a particle of the Medicine. He, however, bade me take two drachms, or half an-ounce of lead, or even a little more, and to melt it in the crucible; for the Medicine would certainly not tinge more of the base metal than it was sufficient for. I answered that I could not believe that so small a quantity of Tincture could transform so large a mass of lead. But I had to be satisfied with what he had given me, and my chief difficulty was about the application of the Tincture. I confessed that when I held his ivory box in my hand, I had managed to extract a few small crumbs of his Stone, but that they had changed my lead, not into gold, but only into glass. He laughed, and said that I was more expert at theft than at the application of the Tincture. "You should have protected your spoil with 'yellow wax,' then it would have been able to penetrate the lead and to transmute it into gold. As it was, your Medicine evaporated, by a sympathetic process, in the metallic smoke. For all metals, gold, silver, tin, and mercury, are corrupted by the fumes of lead, and degenerated into glass." I showed him the crucible, and there he discovered the yellow piece of Medicine still adhering to it. He promised to return at nine o'clock the next morning, and then he would shew me that my Medicine could well be used for transmuting lead into gold. With this promise I had to declare myself satisfied. Still I asked him to favour me with some information about the preparation of the Arcanum. He would not tell me anything about the cost and the time; "as to its substance," he continued, "it is prepared from two metals or minerals; the minerals are better because they contain a larger quantity of mature Sulphur. The solvent is a certain celestial Salt, by means of which the

Sages dissolve the earthy metallic body, and this process elicits the precious Elixir of the Sages. The work is performed from beginning to end in a crucible over an open fire; it is consummated in four days, and its cost is only about three florins. Neither the Mineral from the Egg nor the Solvent Salt are very expensive." I replied that his statement was contradicted by the sayings of the Sages, who assign seven or nine months as the duration of the Work. His only answer was that the sayings of the Sages were to be understood in a philosophical sense and no ignorant person could apprehend their true meaning. I besought him that, as a stranger had made known to him this precious mystery, so he would extend to me the same kindness, and give me at least some information which would remove all the most formidable obstacles out of my path; for if one knew one thing, other facts connected with it were more easily discovered. But the Artist replied: "It is not so in our Magistery; if you do not know the whole operation from beginning to end, you know nothing at all. I have told you all; yet you do not know how the crystal seal of Hermes is broken, and how the Sun colours it with the marvellous splendour of its metallic rays, or in what mirror the metals see with the eyes of Narcissus the possibility of their transmutation, or from what rays adepts collect the fire of perfect metallic fixation." With these words, and a promise to return at nine o'clock the next morning, he left me. But at the stated hour on the following day he did not make his appearance; in his stead, however, there came, a few hours later, a stranger, who told me that his friend the Artist was unavoidably detained, but that he would call at three o'clock in the afternoon. The afternoon came; I waited for him till half-past seven o'clock. He did not appear. Thereupon my wife came and tempted me to try the transmutation myself. I determined, however, to wait till the morrow, and in the meantime, ordered my son to light the fire, as I was now almost sure that he was an impostor. On the morrow, however, I thought that I might at least make an experiment with the piece of "Tincture" which I had received; if it turned out a failure, in spite of my following his directions closely, I might then be quite certain that my visitor had been a mere pretender to a knowledge of this Art. So I asked my wife to put the Tincture in wax, and I myself, in the meantime, prepared six drachms of lead; I then cast the Tincture, enveloped as it was in wax, on the lead; as soon as it was melted, there was a hissing sound and a slight effervescence, and after a quarter of an hour I found that the whole mass of lead had been turned into the finest gold. Before this transformation took place, the compound became intensely green, but as soon as I had poured it into the melting pot it assumed a hue like blood. When it cooled, it glittered and shone like gold. We immediately took it to the goldsmith, who at once declared it to be the finest gold he had ever seen, and offered to pay fifty florins an ounce for it.

The rumour, of course, spread at once like wildfire through the whole city; and in the afternoon, I had visits from many illustrious students of this Art; I also received a call from the Master of the Mint and some other gentlemen, who requested me to place at their disposal a small piece of the gold, in order that they might subject it to the usual tests. I consented, and we betook ourselves to the house of a certain silversmith, named Brechtil, who submitted a small piece of my gold to the test called "the fourth": three or four parts of silver are melted in the crucible with one part of gold, and then beaten out into thin plates, upon which some strong aquafortis is poured. The usual result of this experiment is that the silver is dissolved, while the gold sinks to the bottom in the shape of a black powder, and after the aquafortis has been poured off, and melted once more in the crucible, resumes its former shape. . . . When we now performed this experiment, we thought at first that one-half of the gold had evaporated; but afterwards we found that this was not the case, but that, on the contrary, two scruples of the silver had undergone a change into gold.

Then we tried another test, *viz.*, that which is performed by means of a septuple of Antimony; at first it seemed as if eight grains of the gold had been lost, but afterwards, not only had two scruples of the silver been converted into gold, but the silver itself was greatly improved both in quality and malleability. Thrice I performed this infallible test, discovering that every drachm of gold produced an increase of a scruple of gold, but the silver is excellent and extremely flexible. Thus I have unfolded to you the whole story from beginning to end. The gold I still retain in my possession, but I cannot tell you what has become of the Artist Elias. Before he left me, on that last day of our friendly intercourse, he told me that he was on the point of undertaking a journey to the Holy Land. May the Holy Angels of God watch over him wherever he is, and long preserve him as a source of blessing to Christendom! This is my earnest prayer on his and our behalf.

CHAPTER IV.

I will now proceed to give an account of the conversations which passed between the Artist Elias and myself (the Physician), on the occasion of his kindly visits to my house. The reader is to imagine the Artist entering my room, and introducing himself with the following words:

I salute you, Dr. Helvetius. I am one of the readers of the Tract you wrote against Dr. Digby, and his Sympathetic Pills, and I should like to have some conversation with you on 'his and kindred subjects. I am a close student of Nature's secrets, and delight in the company of those who have a kindred aim. And, certainly, I have found as the result even of my paltry investigations, that no natural marvels are to be rashly pronounced impossible.

PHYSICIAN.

Let me bid you a hearty welcome. Discourses on the secrets of Nature are the great delight of my heart, as they are of yours. Come with me, I pray you, into my study.

ARTIST ELIAS.

You do, indeed, possess a wonderfully well-equipped laboratory, and I make no doubt that, by its means, you have sounded all the secret depths of Alchemy. But why do you keep so many medicines? Do you not believe that there exists in the nature of things one or more remedies, fully capable of counteracting disease in all cases, where neither the heart, the liver, nor the lungs, are entirely destroyed, or the vital juices altogether consumed?

PHYSICIAN.

From what you say I conclude that you are either one of the profession, or else a Master of the Chemical Art. I do believe, as you say, that there exist in Nature other more excellent medicines than any that I possess. This view is both natural and reasonable, and it is supported by the authority of many celebrated writers. They tell us of a certain Universal Medicine, which, as they say, is known only to the elect, but it enables its possessors to heal all diseases (even those otherwise incurable), and to prolong their lives almost indefinitely. Yet is anyone able to conduct us to this miraculous fountain, whence this vitalizing water is drawn? I am afraid it is a hopeless aspiration.

ARTIST ELIAS.

I am not, as you suppose, a physician, but only a brass-founder. I have, however, from a very early age, taken an all-absorbing interest in the Art of Alchemy, and the secret qualities of metals. And as a result of my investigations (humble as they have been), I most decidedly incline to the belief that the discovery of the Medicine you mention will, even in our degenerate age, be vouchsafed to some earnest student, as a reward of prayer and work.

PHYSICIAN.

It is true that God grants His gifts to those who love Him ungrudgingly and without upbraiding. But I also find that in former ages, as in our own, there have lived hosts of chemists who have spent their lives, as the saying is, in scooping up water with a sieve. Moreover, it seems quite impossible to gain from the writings of the genuine Sages any intelligible information, either as to the substance or the mode of preparation of this Universal Philosopher's Stone. . . . In the meantime, it is the duty of a good physician to make the most of those appliances for the cure of disease, which are actually within his reach. If he refused to give any medicines until he had discovered the Universal Remedy, his patients would suffer through his folly and carelessness. Moreover, taking into consideration the great variety of human constitutions, I really do not see how one Medicine can possibly cure all diseases; the effect of morbid matter upon the glands and vital juices of different persons being well known to be utterly different. If you give a certain quantity of wine to Peter, it will make him quarrel-some, and even furious; its effect on Paul is to produce in him the mildness and timidity of a lamb; in Matthew it causes gaiety and laughter; while it makes Luke melancholy and tearful. In the same way, the morbid matter known as scorbutic poison becomes, in Peter's case, an acid, consuming the whole of the vital juices and organs, and breaking out on his hands and feet in the shape of bluish, discoloured boils. The same poison in the body of Paul is changed into a bitter aperient, which shows itself on the arms and feet in the form of subcutaneous red spots, with punctures like flea-bites, and, in times of plague, turns to anthrax. In the body of Matthew the poisonous fluid is of a sweetish taste, and produces on arms and legs watery tumours, like those seen in dropsical subjects; in times of plague, they turn to plague sores. In Luke's case, the humour is saltish and acrid; the swellings on his arms and legs are dry and inflammatory; and when there is infectious matter in the air, the sores become so red and malignant as to produce madness and death. It stands to reason, then, that these different symptoms require different treatment, and that no one herb or medicine could possibly suffice for such different cases. The volatile bitter salt of Cochlearia, which relieves Peter, makes Paul worse; a fixed acid salt only aggravates the symptoms of Luke, but it very often suffices to produce a complete cure in the case of Paul. In every instance we require a remedy which is different from the morbid matter already in the system, and therefore capable of counteracting it. In the face of this need of specific remedies for every particular form of disease, you must pardon a medical man if he does not quite see the possibility of an Universal Medicine.

ARTIST ELIAS.

I admit the truth of all that you say, as far as the Vegetable Kingdom is concerned, though very few physicians employ this method of cure. At the same time, I see no reason why there should not be in the Mineral Kingdom an Universal Medicine which combines all the virtues of the different vegetable remedies you have named. I acknowledge that this Gift of Grace is bestowed only on a few persons; but the truth of the Alchemistic Art is too strongly supported to admit of any doubt.

PHYSICIAN.

I have by no means exhausted the list of objections which may with reason be urged against the existence of this Universal Medicine. But how can the same remedy be equally suited to the case of a man or a woman, a delicate and a robust person, the initiatory or the final stage of a disease, a chronic or an acute affection?

ARTIST ELIAS.

Your arguments against the Universal Medicine are very learned and orthodox, and I am not disinclined to allow to them some importance. At the same time, you will admit that "many men many minds" is a saying of some weight, and those who know anything by experience, are the best qualified to speak about it. The sweetest music does not delight all hearers; the best story appears dull to some readers; some like one kind of food or wine and some another: and so there are as many different verdicts about this Universal Medicine as there are (self-constituted) judges. But only he who is acquainted with its properties has a right to deliver an authoritative opinion. Now, it is quite true that in your common, tinkering Medicinal Art, which seeks to counteract only the separate symptoms or manifestations of disease, there is no room for an Universal Medicine. But the true physician knows that all disease (whatever shape it may assume) is simply a depression of the vital spirits, and that whatever strengthens vitality, will cut off the possibility of disease at the very source, expelling the humours which each produce their own peculiar malady, and I maintain that our Universal Medicine is a remedy of this radical kind. It gently promotes and quickens the movement of the vital spirits, and thus, by renewing the source of life, renovates and quickens the whole frame, infusing new vitality and strength into every part. For this reason adepts call it the Great Mystery of Nature, and the preventive of old age and disease. By its aid any man may live the full term of days naturally allotted to him, and need have no fear of contagion, even when the plague, or some other malignant epidemic, is striking down hundreds of his neighbours.

PHYSICIAN.

If I take your meaning, this Remedy does not set itself merely to correct depraved humours, but directly restores the vital spirits themselves; and it cannot prolong existence beyond the span of life originally allotted to each man by the Creator, though it does prevent his being cut off prematurely by weakness or disease. All this sounds very reasonable. But there is another question I should like to ask. Does this Medicine change a man's temperament, so as to convert a phlegmatic person into one of a sanguine character, or a melancholy person into a gay and jovial boon companion?

ARTIST ELIAS.

Certainly not. It is impossible for any medicine of any kind to alter the nature of a man: just as wine does not produce a change in a man, but only brings out his true character. The effect of the Universal Medicine is of a corresponding kind. It is like the warmth of the Sun, which does not change or even modify the shapes, colours, and scents of the different flowers, but only fully develops all that is in them by means of its genial influence. . . . If our Universal Medicine possessed the property of prolonging the life of man beyond the term assigned to each individual by Divine foreknowledge, no doubt Sages like Hermes Trismegistus, Paracelsus, Raymond Lullius, Count Bernhard, and many other genuine possessors of this Great Mystery, would be still with us in the land of the living. It would be folly and madness to suppose that any medicine in the whole world can do more than protect a man against being cut off prematurely, *i.e.*, before his appointed time.

PHYSICIAN.

All that you have said about the operation of this Blessed Universal Medicine seems both reasonable and in harmony with Nature's general plan of working. The worst of it is that, though I now fully believe in the existence of the Medicine, all my efforts to find it have hitherto resembled the futile endeavours of a mariner who, attempting to put out to sea in a frail boat, is again and again driven back to the shore by the united force of wind and wave. Though many illustrious persons have written concerning the preparation, they have so cautiously veiled it, that the smallest possible number might become acquainted with the steps to be taken to arrive at their desire. The best thing one can do, I think, is to stay in one's laboratory, work and pray, and wait for God's blessing.

ARTIST ELIAS.

You reason well, my friend; yet you must not despair of learning the secret of the Alchemists' Art, especially if you can induce some adept to become your teacher. But we will now proceed to discuss the transmutatory virtues of our most precious Stone, which are still more wonderful than its medicinal properties.

PHYSICIAN.

Oh, I see! You wish to discuss the transmutation of metals. In the possibility of such transmutation, I certainly do feel constrained to believe, considering that I have heard and read of cases which admit of no manner of doubt, and in which such transmutation is attested by the most authentic and trustworthy witnesses (such as Dr. Kiffler, Helmont, Scotus, &c.), as having really taken place. I am especially thinking of that wonderful experiment of metallic transformation which was achieved at Prague, in the presence of the German Emperor Ferdinand III., when, by means of one grain of the Tincture, three pounds of Mercury were changed into the best gold; for that event was commemorated by a medal struck at the Imperial Mint. But though I firmly believe in the possibility of such a transmutatory Tincture, I have never in the whole course of my life come across any one who possessed it.

ARTIST ELIAS.

You are quite right in what you say, albeit your belief or unbelief could not make any difference to the truth of our Art, just as a magnet would go on attracting steel, and rendering it magnetic by such contact, even if you did not credit it. It is also true that hitherto our secret has been rather hidden than revealed by those who have written about it in the obscurest of language. But you can no longer feel disposed to doubt that which you see with your own eyes; and here in this box you behold a large quantity of the true substance of the Sages. There! Examine it.

PHYSICIAN.

Is this yellow, sulphureous, glassy substance really and truly the Philosopher's Stone? Did you prepare it yourself? Surely you are hoaxing me!

ARTIST ELIAS.

No, indeed; you now hold the most precious of mundane treasures in your hand; and I myself prepared it from beginning to end. If you can take me to a room where we shall be more secret, I will show you some gold obtained through its means (and having been ushered into the state parlour, he produced the five medals described above). These (said he) I keep in memory of my Master.

PHYSICIAN.

So you had a Master from whom you learned the glorious secret! How wonderful that I should at this moment be holding the true substance in my hands! Can you not give me a small piece of it, just enough to transmute four grains of lead into gold, so that I may be able to test the truth of your statement? Do give me a piece, at least as large as a grain of mustard seed, and let me make the trial! It would be a great kindness.

ARTIST ELIAS.

I admit that a certain stranger once instructed me both as to the possibility of this Art, and in its methods of procedure. But I cannot give you even a small fragment of my Tincture, though you offered me this room full of ducats; not because the substance is so precious in my eyes, but for another momentous reason which I may not reveal. Indeed, if fire could consume fire, I should at once throw the whole of this Tincture on the hearth. I will, however, return to you after the lapse of three weeks, and show you some beautiful experiments which will both surprise and delight you. If by that time I shall have obtained leave to do so, I will also satisfy your curiosity by performing in your presence a change of lead into gold. In the meantime, I bid you good-bye, and warn you not to invest too much of your substance in the pursuit of this Art, as it will all turn to ashes.

PHYSICIAN.

I am deeply obliged to you for your kindness in coming to me, and showing me this Stone; but you can hardly expect me to be satisfied with the mere sight of it. I am one of those whose souls are always athirst for knowledge; and I believe that if our first parent Adam, who lost Paradise by touching the forbidden fruit, were alive at the present day, he would once more risk the happiness of his life in order to become possessed of the "golden apples from the garden of Atlas." I thank you most heartily, however, for comforting me with the prospect of your return in three weeks. I will endeavour to spend the interval in strict obedience to your wise and kindly counsel; but you may easily suppose that the feeling uppermost in my mind will be one of eager hope and longing for the fulfilment of your promise. I also thank you for the proof of your confidence involved in making yourself known to me as an adept of this Art. If the secret which you have entrusted to my safe keeping, were, by any accident, to come to the ears of a tyrannical prince or noble, would you be terrified by his threats into betraying it?

ARTIST ELIAS.

I have never made this secret known to anyone except to. yourself and one good old man. Nor must any human being hear or see the like in future. But if any prince or king were to cast me into prison, or put me to the rack, he would not be able to extract a single syllable of direct or indirect information from me by the most cruel tortures which he could devise; not even death itself would make me shrink from the path of duty, or become disloyal to my trust.

PHYSICIAN.

Are there any Alchemistic writers that are more easily understood than the rest, or who can at least be warranted to possess a real knowledge of those things wherein they undertake to instruct others?

ARTIST.

I do not read many of these books; but of all the writers on Alchemy whose works I have studied, I have found Sendivogius, the Cosmopolitan, to be the most trustworthy; also Basilius, in his twelve Keys. Truth has chosen the obscure style of Sendivogius for her hiding-place, if you could only discover her—just as our Substance is really and truly hidden and concealed in the outward bodies of all metals and minerals.

PHYSICIAN.

Accept once more my warmest thanks for all your kindness and friendly counsel. I do indeed believe that, as you say, the essences of metals are hidden in their outward bodies, as the kernel is hidden in the nut. Every earthly body, whether animal, vegetable, or mineral, is the habitation and terrestrial abode of that celestial spirit, or influence, which is its principle of life and growth. The secret of Alchemy is the destruction of the body, which enables the Artist to get at, and utilize for his own purposes, the living soul. But what man is sufficient to search out this wonderful secret?

ARTIST ELIAS.

You have spoken truly, and judged rightly concerning the natural destruction of things; and if you find grace in the sight of God, He will commission either me or some other adept of our Art to unfold to you the right way of destroying the outward bodies of metals and seizing the inward, vital, life-giving soul. This gracious gift, I say, God may bestow on you sooner than you think, in answer to devout and earnest prayer. Once more, farewell, and rest assured that I will always remain your friend. I cherish a fond hope that I shall soon see you again, in a flourishing state of health.

With these words he departed; and I have already told you how after three weeks he came back and gave me a small piece of the transmutatory Tincture. But since our second parting I have neither set eyes on him, nor heard either of him or from him.

He has, however, left deeply seated in my heart the conviction that through metals and out of metals purified by highly refined and spiritualized metals there may be prepared the living gold and quicksilver of the Sages, which bring both metals and human bodies to perfection. If my friend had condescended to give me one or two practical hints as to the best method of proceeding in this Magistery, I might have discovered the grand secret of collecting the rays of the Sun and Moon in their own proper womb, whereby their power of metallic transmutation by magnetic sympathy might have been brought out. Thus I might have obtained the red seed which transmutes into gold, and the white seed which transmutes into silver. For the Artist Elias told me that the Chalybs of Sendivogius was that true Mercurial metallic humour which—without the aid of any corrosive—would suffice to separate the fixed rays of the Sun and Moon from their body, and to render them volatile and Mercurial for the dry philosophical Tincture which he showed me, and the efficacy of which I subsequently experienced. This is the same method by which metals are still being produced day by day in the bowels of the earth, and stones developed, in their different saline wombs, out of the spiritual tingent sulphureous seed. . . . . Metallic sulphur mixed with saltpetre, may be converted, by gentle heat, first into solid earth, then into air, then into limpid water, and then into glass of a most beautiful colour, and of a penetrativeness superior to that of fire—just as the chicken is developed out of the apparently lifeless egg by gentle heat. Between the different metals there exists a sympathy such as that between the magnet and steel, gold and quicksilver, silver and copper; and this sympathy is the *rationale* of the transmutation of metals. On the other hand, there are also metallic antipathies, such as that of lead to tin, of iron to gold, of lead to mercury—antipathies which have their counterpart in the animal and vegetable worlds. An accurate and comprehensive knowledge of these sympathies and antipathies is the one great qualification of every man who aspires to be a Master of this Art.

In making known to you all that I have seen and experienced, I am only following the maxim of Seneca, who said that he desired knowledge chiefly that he might impart it to others. If anyone doubts the truth of my statements, let him but live a pious and Christ-like life here below, and he will learn the truth of all things in the new Jerusalem above. That a share of this glory may be vouchsafed to you and him, is the prayer of

Your faithful and loving servant,
JOHN FREDERICK HELVETIUS, M.D.

439

THE

ALL-WISE DOORKEEPER,

OR

A FOURFOLD FIGURE,

EXHIBITING ANALYTICALLY TO ALL THAT ENTER THIS
MUSEUM THE MOSAICO-HERMETIC SCIENCE OF
THINGS ABOVE AND THINGS BELOW.

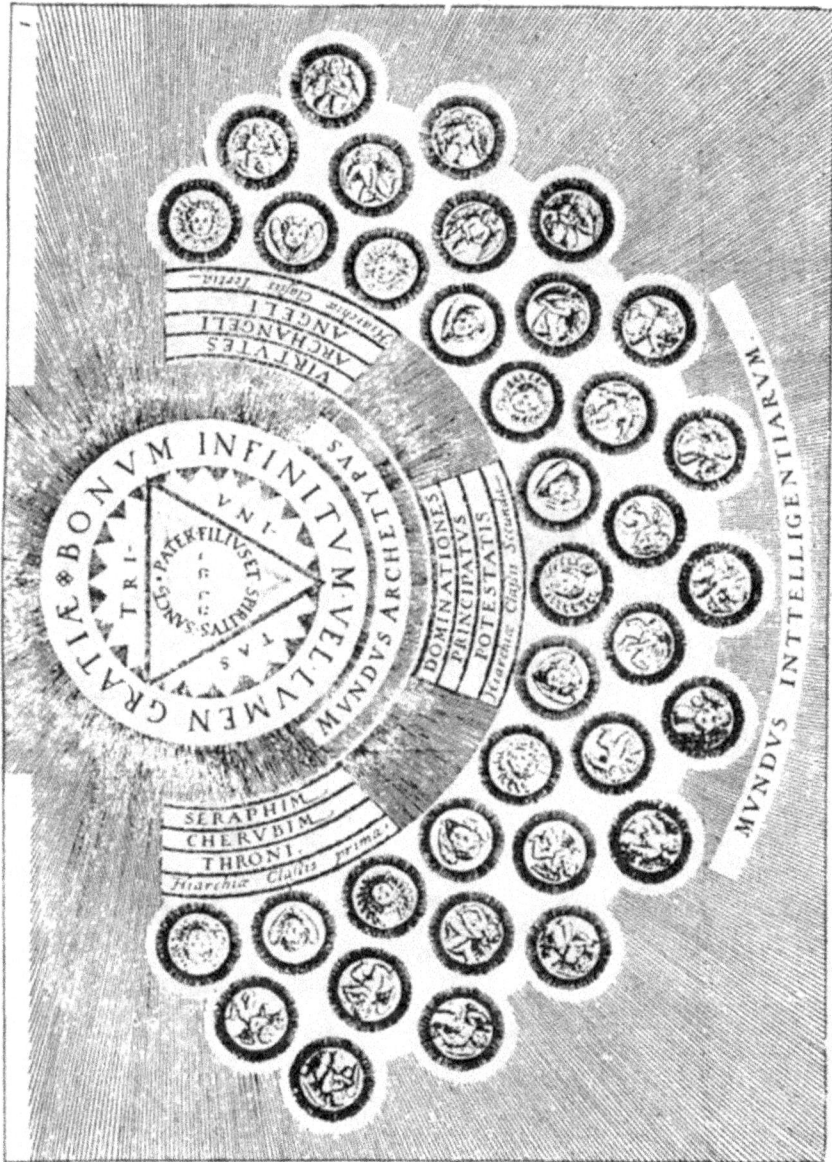

FIGURE 1.

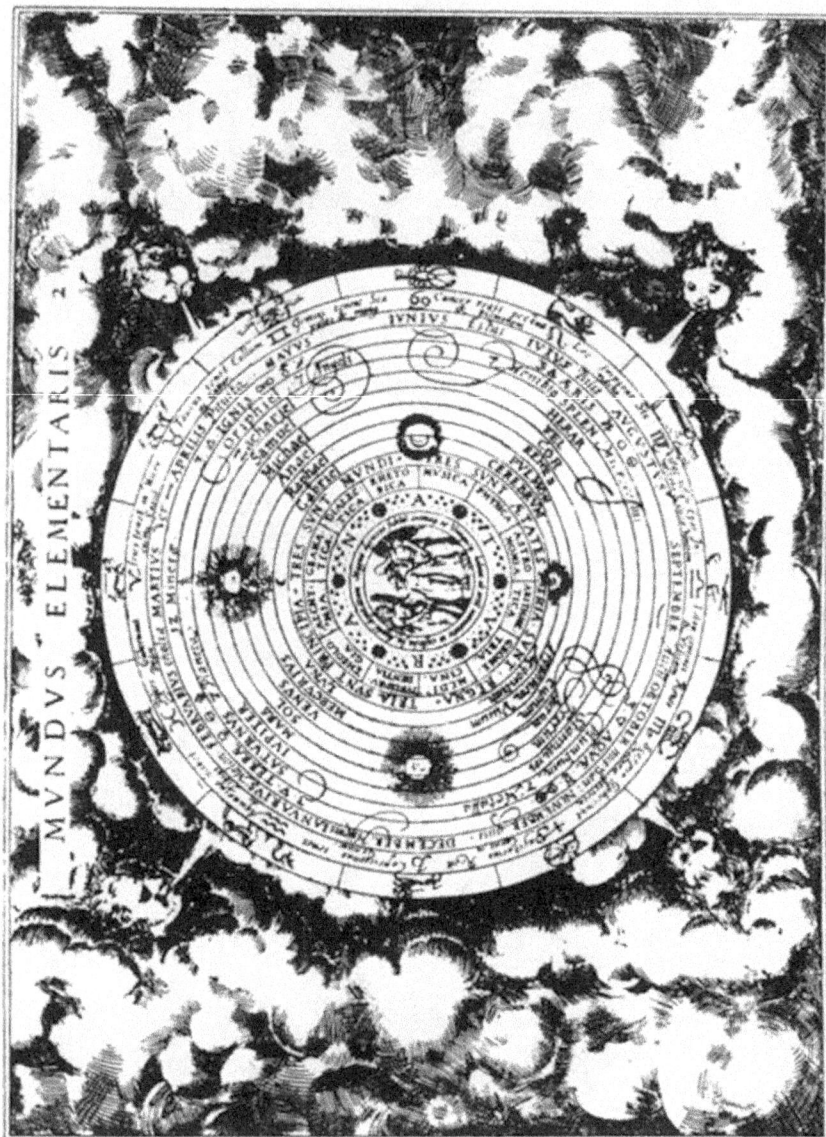

FIGURE II.

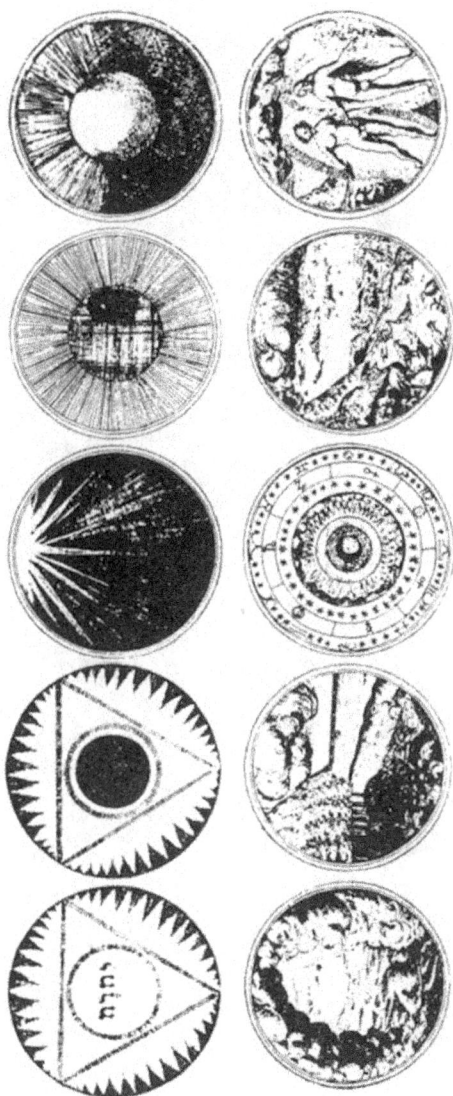

FIGURE III.

443

FIGURE IV.

THE ALL-WISE DOORKEEPER.

A KEY TO THE FOURFOLD FIGURE,

FIGURE I.

BONUM INFINITUM VEL LUMEN GRATIÆ = The Infinite Good or the Light of Grace. TRIUNITAS = Trinity in Unity. יהוה, = Jehovah. PATER, FILIUS, ET SPIRITUS SANCTUS = Father, Son, and Holy Spirit. MUNDUS ARCHETYPUS = The Archetypal World. SERAPHIM, CHERUBIM, THRONI = Seraphim, Cherubim, Thrones, *i.e.*, *Hierarchiæ, Classis Prima* = First Class of the Hierarchy. DOMINATIONES, PRINCIPATUS, POTESTATES = Rulers, Principalities, and Powers, *Hierarchiæ Classis Secunda* = Second Class of the Hierarchy. VIRTUTES, ARCHANGELI, ANGELI = Virtues, Archangels, Angels, *i.e.*, *Hierarchiæ Classis Tertia* = Third Class of the Hierarchy. MUNDUS INTELLIGENTIARUM = The World of Rational Beings.

HOLY, HOLY, HOLY, LORD GOD OF HOSTS;
ALL THE EARTH IS FULL OF HIS GLORY.

MARCELLIUS PALINGENIUS (in Zod. Vit., Book ix.): Great Father of Gods, Highest Power of the World, than whom Thought knows nothing greater; far from the bodily world, yet forming all Bodies, those which cannot change, and those which are destroyed by the lapse of time; Beginning without a beginning; Fountain from which all manner of good things flow forth; Ruler and Multiplier of Nature; Who comprehendest All Things, yet art comprehended of none; Infinite Majesty, Goodness, Wisdom, Life, Order, Beauty, Perfection, Mind, Truth,—Light, Way, Strength; dwelling nowhere, and yet dwelling everywhere; immovable, yet constantly moving all things: Of whom, To whom, and Through whom are all. things; always remaining the same, unchangeable through all time: Greatest of Causes, who, revolving according to a fixed law the starry heavens, dost govern the circle of human Destiny; King of Kings, waited on and worshipped by thousands of Angelic Hosts singing joyous Hymns in the Infinite Domain of Light, beyond the uttermost borders of the [lower] World, where is the fit abode of true Archetypal Things; Thee I worship, to Thee I pray, Thee I reverently adore. Deign to look on me with gracious eye, and hear my voice when I cry to Thee. Send to me the rays of Thy Light, dispel the darkness of my soul, weighed down by the grossness of a mortal body. Grant me to find the Right Way, lest hurtful error, vain credulity, and blind opinion drag me headlong to the ruinous domain of falsehood. For if without Thee a mortal mind or human strength strive to rise upward, their waxen wings are melted, and they fall headlong, like Icarus of old. Without Thee, I cannot see the hidden depths of Divine Truth, or the art and skill by which salvation is attained. Grant unto me, therefore, most gracious King of Kings, that I may know Thee and please Thee; then that I may know myself, what I am, the reason of my life on earth, whence I came, and whither I am going, what is my duty in this life, and what I must eschew—so that when Lachesis has finished the thread of my life, and the last hour has cast my weary body into the Tomb, Death may be unto me a grateful rest, and the haven of peace.

FIGURE II.

MUNDUS ELEMENTARIS = Elementary World.

The First Circle contains the Zodiacal Symbols.

SECOND CIRCLE.

Capricornus tenet Genua = Capricorn holds the knees.
Aquarius habet Tibias = Aquarius rules the thighs.
Pisces gubernant Pedes = The Fishes govern the feet.
Aries tenet in Microcosmo Caput = Aries holds the head of the microcosm.
Taurus tenet Collum et Guttur = Taurus holds the neck and the throat.
Gemini tenent Scapulas et Manus = Gemini hold the shoulders and the hands.
Cancer regit Pectus et Pulmonum = Cancer rules the breast and the lungs.
Leo imperat Stomacho = The Lion governs the stomach.
Virgo tenet Hepar, Intestina, et circa Ventrem = The Virgin holds the liver, the intestines, and the parts about the stomach.
Libra cantina Renes et Vesicam = The Balance contains the reins and the bladder.
Scorpio gubernat Naturæ Secreta = The Scorpion governs the secret parts of Nature.
Sagittarius regit Coxas = Sagittarius governs the thighs.

THIRD CIRCLE.

JANUARIUS, FEBRUARIUS, *Melancholia* = January, February, Melancholy.
MARTIUS, *Ver* = March—Spring.
APRILIS, *Pituita* = April—Phlegm.
MAYUS = May. JUNIUS, *Æstas* = June—Summer.
JULIUS, *Bilis* = July—Bile.
AUGUSTUS = August. SEPTEMBER, *Autumnus*= September—Autumn.
OCTOBER, NOVEMBER, *Sanguis* = Sanguine Temperament.
DECEMBER, *Hiems* = Winter.

FOURTH CIRCLE.

Mineræ = Minerals. IGNIS = Fire. ÆRIS = Air. AQUÆ = Waters. *Metalla* = Metals. TERRÆ = Earth.

FIFTH TO ELEVENTH CIRCLES.

The Seven Planets.	The Seven Angels.	The 7 Members of Microcosmus.	The Seven Metals.
SATURN.	*Oriphiel.*	SPLEEN.	*Lead.*
JUPITER.	*Zachariel.*	LIVER.	*Tin.*
MARS.	*Samuel.*	DIAPHRAGM.	*Iron.*

SUN.	*Michael.*	HEART.	*Gold.*
VENUS.	*Anael.*	REINS.	*Copper.*
MERCURY.	*Raphael.*	LUNGS.	*Quicksilver.*
MOON.	*Gabriel.*	BRAIN.	*Silver.*

TWELFTH CIRCLE.

TRIA SUNT PRINCIPIA, TRES SUNT MUNDI, TRES SUNT AETATES, TRIA SUNT REGNA = There are Three Principles, Three Worlds, Three Ages, and Three Kingdoms.

THEOLOGIA (Theology). ALCHYMIA (Alchemy).   GRAMMATICA (Grammar). DIALECTICA (Dialectics).   RHETORICA (Rhetoric). MUSICA (Music). PHYSICA (Physics). ASTRONOMIA (Astronomy). ARITHMETICA (Arithmetic). GEOMETRIA (Geometry). MEDICINA (Medicine).
JURISPRUDENTIA (Jurisprudence).
NATURA = NATURE.

INMOST CIRCLE.

Magna dignitas fidelium animarum ut unaquæquæ habeat, etc. = It is the great honour of faithful souls, that from their very birth an angel is appointed to preserve and keep each of them.

The Author of the "Handbook of Physical Science Restored" writes as follows:

§ 1. God is an Eternal Being, an Infinite Unity, the Radical Principle of all things. His Essence is Infinite Light. His Power—Omnipotence; His Will—Perfect Goodness; His Wish—Absolute Reality. As we strive to think of Him, we plunge into the Abyss of Silence, of infinite Glory. § 2. Many Sages have held that an Archetypal World existed long before the world of sense, when the Archetypal Light began to unfold Himself, and set forth in an Ideal World a counterpart of the Divine Mind. This belief is borne out by the words of Hermes Trismegistus, who says that when God changed His form, the universe was suddenly revealed and put forth in the Light of Actuality—this world being nothing but a visible Image of a Hidden God. This is what the Ancients meant when they said that Pallas leapt forth in divine perfection from the forehead of Jupiter, with the aid of Vulcan (or Divine Light). § 3. The Eternal Father of All Things, being not less wise in the ordering, than powerful in the creation, of the world, has made the whole Universe to cohere by means of secret influences and mutual subjection and obedience, things below being analagous to things above, and *vice versâ;* so that both ends of the world are nevertheless united by a real bond of natural cohesion. Thus Hermes tells us that things below are the same as things above, and that things above are analagous to things below. § 4. He who looks upon Nature as anything but the constant expression of God's Will, is an Atheist; every smallest part of the great universe is constantly vitalized and conserved by the Spirit of the Divine Master, and there is no life or existence apart from His consciously exerted Will. It was He that in the beginning moved upon the face of the waters, and brought forth the Actual out of the Chaos of Potentiality.

FIGURE III.

FIRST CIRCLE.

יהוה = Jehovah, *i.e.*, A Ω = Alpha and Omega

SECOND CIRCLE.

Genesis, i. 2.—The earth was empty and void, and darkness was upon the face of the deep.

THIRD CIRCLE.

Genesis, i. 2.—And the Spirit of God moved the face of the waters.

FOURTH CIRCLE.

Genesis, i. 3, 4.—And God said: Let there be light: and there was light. . . . And God saw the light that it was good.

FIFTH CIRCLE.

Genesis, i. 4, 5.—And He divided the light from the darkness. And He called the light day, and the darkness He called night. And the evening and the morning were the first day.

SIXTH CIRCLE.

Genesis, i. 6-8.—And God said, Let there be a firmament in the midst of the waters, and let it divide the waters from the waters.

And God made the firmament, and divided the waters which were under the firmament from the waters which were above the firmament: and it was so.

And God called the firmament Heaven, and the evening and the morning were the second day.

Psalm xxxiii. 6.—By the word of the Lord were the heavens made; and all the host of them by the breath of His mouth.

Psalm cxlviii. 4, 5.—Praise the Lord, ye heavens of heavens, and ye waters that be above the heavens. Let them praise the name of the Lord: for He commanded, and they were created.

Daniel, iii. S9, 60.—Praise the Lord, ye heavens; bless Him and magnify Him for ever. O ye waters that be above the firmament, praise ye the Lord: bless Him and magnify Him for ever.

SEVENTH CIRCLE.

Genesis, i. 9-13.—And God said: Let the waters under the heaven be gathered together unto one place, and let the dry land appear: and it was so.

And God called the dry land Earth; and the gathering together of the waters called He seas: and God saw that it was good.

And God said: Let the earth bring forth grass, the herb yielding seed, and the fruit tree yielding fruit after his kind, whose seed is in itself upon the earth: and it was so.

And the earth brought forth grass and herb yielding seed after his kind, and the tree yielding fruit whose seed was in itself, after his kind: and God saw that it was good.

And the morning and the evening were the third day.

Psalm, civ. 5, 14.—Who laid the foundations of the earth that it should not be removed for ever. He causeth the grass to grow for the cattle, and herb for the service of man; that he may bring forth food out of the earth: and wine that maketh glad the heart of man, and oil to make his face to shine, and bread which strengtheneth man's heart.

EIGHTH CIRCLE.

Genesis, i. 14-19.—And God said: Let there be lights in the firmament of heaven to divide the day from the night; and let them be for signs, and for seasons, and days and years.

And let them be for lights in the firmament of the heaven, to give light upon the earth: and it was so.

And God made two lights: the greater light to rule the day, and the lesser light to rule the night; He made the stars also.

And God set them in the firmament of the heaven to give light upon the earth,

And to rule over the day and over the night, and to divide the light from the darkness.

And the evening and the morning were the fourth day.

Sirach, xliii. 1.—He made the lofty firmament in its glory, and the stars, a vision of beauty. The eastern Sun announces the day. It is a wonder of the Most High. Great is God who created it, and bade it run its course Moreover, the Moon shines throughout the world, in due season, dividing months and years. It waxes and wanes in wonderful guise. The host of the stars shines gloriously in the firmament of heaven. God, the Most High, has commanded them to light up the world. By the word of the Lord they are fixed, and do not neglect their vigils.

NINTH CIRCLE.

Genesis, i. 20-23.—And God said: Let the waters bring forth abundantly the moving creature that hath life, and fowl that may fly above the earth in the open firmament of heaven.

And God created great whales, and every living creature that moveth, which the waters brought forth abundantly, after their kind, and every winged fowl after his kind: and God saw that it was good.

And God blessed them, saying: Be fruitful and multiply, and fill the waters in the seas, and let fowl multiply in the earth.

And the evening and the morning were the fifth day.

Psalm civ., 24.—O Lord, how manifold are Thy works: In wisdom hast Thou made them all: the earth is full of Thy riches. So is this great and wide sea, wherein are things creeping innumerable, both small and great beasts. There go the ships; there is that leviathan whom thou hast made to take his pastime therein. These all wait on Thee, that Thou mayest give them their meat in due season.

TENTH CIRCLE.

Genesis, i. 24-31—And God said: Let the earth bring forth the living creature after his kind, cattle and creeping thing and beast of the earth, after his kind: and it was so.

And God made the beast of the earth, after his kind, and cattle after their kind, and everything that creepeth upon the, earth, after his kind; and God saw that it was good.

And God said: Let us make man in our image, after our likeness; and let them have dominion over the fish of the sea, and over the fowl of the air, and over the cattle, and over all the earth, and over every creeping thing that creepeth upon the earth.

So God created man in His own image, in the image of God created He him: male and female created He them.

And God blessed them, and said unto them: Be fruitful and multiply and replenish the earth, and subdue it: and have dominion over the fish of the sea, and over the fowl of the air, and over every living thing that moveth upon the earth.

And God said: Behold I have given you every herb bearing seed which is upon the face of all the earth, and every tree in the which is the fruit of a tree yielding seed; to you it shall be for meat.

And to every beast of the earth, and to every fowl of the air, and to everything that creepeth upon the earth, wherein there is life, I have given every green herb for meat: and it was so.

And God saw everything that He had made, and behold it was very good. And the evening and the morning were the sixth day.

GEORGE RIPLEY, in the Prologue to his "Twelve Gates," says: O incomprehensible Light, glorious in Majesty, the brightness of whose rays obscures our lights: O Unity in the substance, and Trinity in the Godhead. Merciful purifier of souls, who dost exalt us from this troublesome vale of vanity to heaven. Infinite power and wisdom, unspeakable goodness, sustain and govern me day by day so that I may displease Thee in nothing. O Thou with whom are all treasures of wisdom and knowledge, out of whose infinite mind this universal frame sprang forth in a moment of time—when heaven and earth were made by Thy word, and all that is in them by the breath of Thy mouth—grant unto me grace to know Thy blessedness and Thy goodness. In no other way shall I come to the knowledge of the Blessed Stone. As Thou didst make all things out of *one* chaos, so let me be skilled to evolve our microcosm (little world) out of *one* substance in its three aspects of Magnesia, Sulphur, and Mercury!

FIGURE IV.

יהוה = Jehovah.

ANNUS SOLARIS =The Solar Year. ANNUS STELLATUS = The Year of the Stars. ANNUS VENTORUM = The Year of the Winds.
  Mercurius Philosophorum = Mercury of the Sages.
  Mercurius Corporeus = Corporeal Mercury.
  Mercurius Vulgaris = Common Mercury.
  Sulphur Combustibile = Combustible Sulphur.
  Sulphur Fixum = Fixed Sulphur.

Sulphur Æthereum = Volatile Sulphur.
Sal Terrenum = Earthy Salt.
Sal Elementorum = Elementary Salt.
Sal Centrale = Central Salt.
Ignes quatuor ad opus requiruntur = Four kinds of fire are requisite for the work.
Phœnix = Phœnix   *Aquila* = Eagle.

BY THE WORD OF THE LORD WERE THE HEAVENS ESTABLISHED, AND THEIR HOSTS BY THE BREATH OF HIS MOUTH. THE SPIRIT OF THE LORD HAS FILLED THE WORLD. ALL THINGS ARE SATISFIED WITH THY GOODNESS, O LORD. THOU TURNEST AWAY THY FACE, THEY ARE TROUBLED. THOU TAKEST AWAY THY SPIRIT, THEY DIE AND RETURN AGAIN TO THEIR DUST. THOU SENDEST FORTH THY SPIRIT AND THEY ARE CREATED, AND RE NEWEST THE FACE OF THE EARTH. THY GLORY IS FOR EVERLASTING.

THE EMERALD TABLE OF HERMES.

It is most true, it is without error, it is the sum of verity: That which is beneath is like that which is above, and that which is above is like that which is below, for the performance of the wonders of one thing. As all things were created from the Mind of One, so all things arose by modification of this One Thing. It is so with our Substance. Its father is the Sun, its mother the Moon. The Wind bore it in its belly. The earth is its nurse. The father of all, the Thelema of the whole world, is here. Its strength is undiminished if it is changed into earth. Separate the earth from the fire, the subtle from the gross, gently, but with great skill. It rises from earth to heaven, and again descends to the earth, and receives the strength of things above and of things below. Thus you have the GLORY OF THE WHOLE WORLD, and all darkness will flee away from you. This is the strength of every strong thing: it overcomes every subtle thing, and penetrates all solids. IN THIS WAY WAS THE WORLD CREATED. These are the wonderful modifycations, the manner of which I have described. Hence I am called Hermes Trismegistus, having the three parts of the wisdom of the whole world. I have now said all I have to say concerning the operation of the Sun.

ADDENDUM.

The verses which accompany the frontispiece to the first volume may be translated thus: The things that are in the realms above are also in the realms beneath; What heaven shows is oft found on earth. Fire and flowing water are contrary one to another; Happy thou, if thou canst unite them: let it suffice thee to know this!

The Cross on the title-page of "The Golden Tract" bears the following inscription: All Glory is a Birth in the Sand. The Stone unites in itself all blessings.

The Symbol at the end of the Preface contains, within the second circle, the names of the four elementary natures, Air, Fire, Earth, and Water, and in the central circle the words—Marvel of Nature.

The inscription on the Emblem which accompanies the title page of "The Golden Age Restored" should be read thus: There are three marvels—God and Man—Mother and Virgin—Three and One. The Centre in the Triangle of the Centre.

The Symbol which accompanies "The Book Alze" contains these words: Visit the interior parts of the earth: by rectifying thou shalt find the Hidden Stone.

The inscription on the Symbol of the Seventh Key of Basil Valentine signifies: The Seal of Hermes. Winter. Spring. Summer. Autumn. Water. The Salt of the Philosophers. That upon the Symbol of the Tenth Key: I am issued from Hermogenes. Hyperion elected me. Without Jamsuph I am compelled to perish.

In the second volume, the Diagram which accompanies "The Ordinal of Alchemy" may be explained as follows:

Mundus Archetypus = Archetypal World.

Deus Jehovah Bonum Infinitum = God Jehovah the Infinite Good.

ii. Angels.   iii. Ether.   iiii. Elements.

Bonum Finitum = finite Good.

Cælum = Heaven. *Angeli* = Angels. *Stellæ* = Stars.

Homo = Man. *Meteor* = Meteors. *Aves* = Birds.

Bestiæ = Beasts. *Pisces* = Fishes.

AER = Air. TERRA = Earth. AQUA = Water.

Planetæ = Planets. *Lapides* = Stones.

Metalla = Metals. *Sal* = Salt.

Infernalis = That which is under the earth.

Ignis = Fire. *Procellæ* = Winds. *Inane* = The Void.

Tenebræ = Darkness. *Abyssus* = Abyss.

CHAOS, MALUM, SATAN = Evil.

The inscription on the Medal in the text of "The Golden Calf" reads: The Divine Metamorphosis exhibited at Prague, Jan. 15, 1648, in the presence of his most sacred Majesty, Ferdinand III. *Nummi Crassities:* The thickness of the Medal.

FINIS.

www.ingramcontent.com/pod-product-compliance
Lightning Source LLC
Chambersburg PA
CBHW060322100426
42812CB00003B/848